RECONSIDERING BOCCACCIO

Medieval Contexts and Global Intertexts

Reconsidering Boccaccio

Medieval Contexts and Global Intertexts

EDITED BY OLIVIA HOLMES
AND DANA E. STEWART

UNIVERSITY OF TORONTO PRESS
Toronto Buffalo London

Toronto Buffalo London
utorontopress.com

ISBN 978-1-4875-0178-5

Toronto Italian Studies

Library and Archives Canada Cataloguing in Publication

Reconsidering Boccaccio : medieval contexts and global intertexts / edited by Olivia Holmes and Dana E. Stewart.

(Toronto Italian studies)
Includes bibliographical references and index.
ISBN 978-1-4875-0178-5 (cloth)

1. Boccaccio, Giovanni, 1313–1375 – Criticism and interpretation.
I. Holmes, Olivia, editor II. Stewart, Dana E., editor III. Series: Toronto Italian studies

PQ4286.R43 2018 853′.1 C2018-902150-0

University of Toronto Press acknowledges the financial assistance to its publishing program of the Canada Council for the Arts and the Ontario Arts Council, an agency of the Government of Ontario.

Canada Council for the Arts
Conseil des Arts du Canada

Funded by the Government of Canada
Financé par le gouvernement du Canada
Canada

Contents

Acknowledgments

This volume began with a series of backyard meetings under a canopy of leaves, sometimes with a glass of wine, among ourselves and our colleague Marilynn Desmond, with the purpose of organizing a conference at the Center for Medieval and Renaissance Studies (CEMERS) at Binghamton University for the then-upcoming Boccaccio centenary. We talked in those meetings about our hopes to build a conference and eventual publication that would reflect the interdisciplinary orientation and global perspectives of CEMERS. Since then, many have had a hand in this project, and we are indebted to all of them. Our deepest gratitude goes to Marilynn for all of her input and guidance. We also thank Deirdre Riley for reading the manuscript in its entirety, as well as Suzanne Rancourt at University of Toronto Press for her belief in the volume, and the Press's anonymous readers for their useful suggestions and rigorous critiques. In addition, we are grateful for the support of the Harpur College Dean's Office and the Aldo and Reta Bernardo Fund. Finally, we wish to recognize CEMERS for providing such a conducive environment for collaboration and innovation. We thank all of our CEMERS colleagues for ongoing conversations and collegiality, and we dedicate this volume to them.

Contributors

Filippo Andrei	California State University
Todd Boli	Independent Scholar
Katherine A. Brown	Dartmouth College
Kevin Brownlee	University of Pennsylvania
Mary Anne Case	University of Chicago Law School
Elizabeth Casteen	Binghamton University
K.P. Clarke	University of York
Rhiannon Daniels	University of Bristol
Grace Delmolino	Columbia University
Sara E. Díaz	Fairfield University
Olivia Holmes	Binghamton University
Jason Houston	Gonzaga University
Franklin Lewis	University of Chicago
Nora Martin Peterson	University of Nebraska–Lincoln
Alessia Ronchetti	University of Cambridge
Dana E. Stewart	Binghamton University
Lori J. Walters	Florida State University

RECONSIDERING BOCCACCIO

Medieval Contexts and Global Intertexts

Introduction

OLIVIA HOLMES AND DANA E. STEWART

The life and works of the great Florentine writer Giovanni Boccaccio (1313–1375) unfolded at the nexus of a large number of international trends that were coming to fruition in his time: the expansion of international trade in which Italian merchants played a central role, improvements in manufacturing and economic bookkeeping, the rise of cities and concurrent consolidation of larger political entities, geographical exploration, the humanists' enthusiasm for classical art and learning, innovations in contemporary artistic and literary practices, reforms in scribal practices and methods of book production, and so forth. Boccaccio came of age in Angevin Naples, a cosmopolitan port city through which all the goods and cultures of the Mediterranean passed, and later returned to his native Tuscany, where he was active not only as a creative writer but also as a Florentine ambassador, politician, scribe, glossator, mythographer, biographer, geographer, and priest. No literary figure better synthesizes the economic and artistic enterprises of his age or better exemplifies the cultural vitality of fourteenth-century Italy, both north and south. Recent scholarship has begun to highlight Boccaccio's remarkable achievements as a cultural mediator, his exceptional social, geographic, and intellectual range, and the way that his legacy illuminates the interconnectivity of numerous cultural networks.[1]

This collection comes out of the anniversary year of 2013, which produced a number of conferences and publications celebrating the seventh centennial of Boccaccio's birth. The essays in this volume arise from papers given at the conference "Boccaccio at 700: Medieval Contexts and Global Intertexts," sponsored by the Center for Medieval and Renaissance Studies of Binghamton University (SUNY) on 26–7 April 2013.[2] They advance several contemporary scholarly trends, such as an increased academic focus on interdisciplinarity and recent historical work that analyses the medieval period from the global perspective, depicting a pluralistic world composed of many centres and permeable boundaries, in which materials and ideas circulated along the same routes as long-distance travel and trade.[3] Indeed, for a number of decades historians have sought to see the world from a less top-down perspective, focusing more attention on the "non-elite" strata of the population and on social organization, as evidenced by such things as marriage patterns, administrative cultures, legal systems, and economic and technical developments. Literary studies have followed a similar trajectory. Boccaccio's "high cultural" antecedents in both classical and early Italian literature have been extensively – although not exhaustively – investigated, but scholars are now pushing in different directions. Recent work has come out looking at his texts' relations not only to the elite literary productions of his fellow Florentines Dante and Petrarch (which had long been a primary focus of Boccaccio studies) but also to ethical and legal frameworks, contemporary translations and vulgarizations, sermons and devotional writings, behavioural treatises, linguistic systems, innovations in scribal practices and book production, and even such things as sanitation infrastructure and wine consumption.[4]

The present volume continues to expand Boccaccio studies in new directions by bringing a variety of methodologies and critical approaches to his works, with essays by scholars not only of Italian but also of history, law, classics, book history, and Spanish, French, Persian, and comparative literature. The contributions are not restricted to the literary context, but address a range of topics relating to Boccaccio's biography and texts, as well as to his political, socio-cultural, and legal contexts. Together they show the productiveness of setting Boccaccio's body of works in relation to an assortment of places and periods, as well as to a number of different kinds of systems and traditions, and a variety of realms and levels of discourse.[5] This volume as a whole, then, participates in the current trend towards reading a "Global Middle Ages," a critical movement that has demonstrated the importance of thinking across both geopolitical and disciplinary boundaries when approaching texts, not merely to acknowledge the global interconnectedness that long preceded the globalism of the modern era, but also to be able to discern more fully the multifaceted and complex nature of both texts and their contexts. As Geraldine Heng recently wrote, a global approach "asks scholars to step outside their discipline and specialization to engage with … others to make sense of an interconnected past."[6] Indeed, given Boccaccio's position as someone who participated actively in so many sectors of society, such an approach to studying his texts is not only in line with current scholarly trends but also of particular importance if we are to obtain a more complete picture of this author and his works.

Boccaccio's method of composition has often been compared to the making of a mosaic; according to Giuseppe Velli, one can detect throughout the author's Latin and vernacular works his habit of incorporating "spezzoni," fragments or pieces, of differing dimensions and various provenances; among these sources, Velli specifies primarily literary ones: medieval and classical Latin poetry, the new Tuscan poetic tradition, and Dante.[7] For Lucia Battaglia Ricci, too, Boccaccio juxtaposes squares or chips of heterogeneous provenance, but she also uses the analogue of electronic broadcast signals, and speaks of Boccaccio's mixing of different elements as provoking "interferenze," which tend to blur or erase notions of authorial paternity or originality.[8] She significantly widens the spectrum of Boccaccio's influences as well, referring not only to his familiarity with prestigious fields such as literature, philosophy, and law, but also to his omnivorous poaching from such varied sources as geographical maps, merchant's manuals, papal decrees, glosses, and scientific treatises.[9] Tobias Foster Gittes has more recently doubted the pertinence of the mosaic metaphor, pointing out that "while the tessera does not evoke the marble slab, or the scrap of wood, the tree, the literary fragments used by Boccaccio do consistently call to mind the plots, themes, and characters of the works from which they are drawn," and that "Boccaccio's art does not consist in joining colours, shapes, forms, or scraps of metre, but meanings."[10] Yet while more learned and significant interpretive paradigms are surely at play, the brightly coloured bits of glass also remain visible: the map of the Mediterranean used in constructing Alatiel's journey in *Decameron* 2.7, the historically accurate description of the fourteenth-century customs system in Palermo at the opening of *Novella* 8.10, the scraps of popular metres in the prayers of Gianni Lotteringhi's wife (*Dec.* 7.1), and so forth.

Ultimately one of the best analogues for Boccaccio's recombinatory method (repetition with variation) may be neuroscientific models for the kind of playful hypothesis testing that is recognized as among the principal cognitive benefits of all literature and art – what Paul B. Armstrong describes as art's "paradoxical system of similarities constructed out of differences."[11] Armstrong is referring here to what he calls "harmonious art," but, as he points out, dissonance, too, "is based neurobiologically on the values and pleasures of making neuronal connections and breaking their grip to enable new modes of cortical organization"; "dissonant art," he writes, "defamiliarizes by violating a norm, and this requires the invocation of the norm, the structure that is laid bare by being transgressed, opposed, and overturned."[12] A common theme in Boccaccio studies has long been that his texts recall and parody a number of established genres, but as Gittes observes, "no genre passed through Boccaccio's fingers without undergoing some fundamental and enriching transformation."[13] Boccaccio's collected works can almost be seen as a catalogue of contemporary themes, manners, plots, and commonplaces, to which he applies a self-consciously experimental approach, intentionally playing with – arousing and then sometimes satisfying, sometimes frustrating – readers' expectations.

Regardless of the figure(s) we use to describe Boccaccio's writing, it is vital to recognize both the multilayered complexity of his approach, the number of different systems and domains from which he draws, and that Boccaccio's works themselves also take part in and contribute to a complex system of interconnected networks.[14] As Guyda Armstrong, Rhiannon Daniels, and Stephen J. Milner put it, the breadth of his experiences and interconnections makes of Boccaccio "a key nexus of mediation and exchange: a symbol for – and in fact a physical dealer in – literary and political transactions."[15] The essays in this collection also suggest how Boccaccio's extraordinary interconnectedness in numerous social and intellectual domains (his training in both banking and law in Naples and later activities as a communal office holder in Florence, for instance) put him in constant dialogue with the multiple voices and traditions – the mercantile, scholarly, clerical, legal, political, social, and popular cultures – that he inherited and in which he was immersed, making his work particularly suited to a global approach.[16]

It is important to extend our critical gaze not only to encompass a wider geographic scope but also forward in time, as Boccaccio's texts invited copious imitation and interpretation by later writers. The essays in this volume examine both the historical and intertextual networks that furnished sources for his works and the texts' own subsequent itineraries. Although numerous fields were touched by Boccaccio's legacy, one can scarcely exaggerate his specific impact on the evolution of Western literature. His influence on Chaucer, for instance, has been generally (although perhaps not sufficiently) recognized, but recent scholarship has also excavated his capillary influence on the chivalric epic, on Renaissance and later theatre, on the modern European novel, and even on film.[17]

The itinerary of a work of this scope must necessarily be selective, however. Among the intellectual threads that this volume particularly follows are the conclusions that can be drawn from the material evidence itself, the actual inscribed objects that convey the author's meanings (see the section "Material Contexts"). In recent decades, scholars of medieval and Renaissance literature have increasingly turned their attention away from the coherent, corrected text of the modern critical edition, preferring the singularity and instability of individual manuscripts and printed books.[18] Boccaccio's works have proven an extraordinarily rich scholarly vein. The manuscripts directly attributable to him, in all or in part, are exceptionally numerous, upwards of thirty.[19] He also exhibits an acute concern with the minutiae of the material production of books such as the visual disposition of the page, writing his own rubrics for his vernacular epic *Teseida delle nozze di Emilia* and for the *Decameron*'s stories (pre-empting what would typically be the later work of scribes or editors), for instance, and devising a system of illuminated capital letters for the *Decameron* to indicate different levels of structural organization. The opening two essays ground the volume in Boccaccio's own writings: that is, not just in their linguistic content, but in the very act of writing, as well as of drawing, and in the author's autograph copies of his own works. Both essays are concerned with Boccaccian paratexts – the material surrounding the main text in a published work. K.P. Clarke sets his scholarship outside the more usual literary-philological context, in that of contemporary codicological and art-historical developments in Boccaccio studies. Rhiannon Daniels's essay then moves beyond the author's own manuscripts to an itinerary oriented more towards the audience and the book trade, examining the different incarnations of his texts in later print editions; her piece thus encapsulates the movement we see in the entire volume from understanding Boccaccio as maker of an intricate, multilayered collage, which draws on the works of others, to seeing his works, in turn, as contributing to an infinitely complex matrix that reaches across time and space.

Among the many cultural domains in which Boccaccio must be situated are also those of societal organization: networks of friendship, patronage, and marriage, codified systems of laws and politics, of church rituals and sacraments, and so forth. The next essay group ("Social Contexts: Friendship") focuses on Boccaccio's biography and his immediate social context, as evidenced by his letters, especially addressing his conception of friendship. The pieces by Jason Houston and Todd Boli offer new interpretations of Boccaccio's interactions with friends and fellow authors, and explore how he drew upon both classical and medieval Tuscan ideals of *amicitia*. In addressing Boccaccio's personal relationships and the extent to which his cultural self-construction depended on whom he met and whom he mingled with, these essays also suggest the interconnectedness of different kinds of contemporary social contexts, including literary, political, economic, geographic, and symbolic ones.[20]

In the long tradition of Boccaccio scholarship, an even more debated area has been the author's treatment of gender issues – and the following section ("Social Contexts: Gender, Marriage, and the Law") shows that there is still a great deal to be said on the topic. The essays here address the larger framework of contemporary social conventions and legal concepts (one should not forget that Boccaccio was a trained canon lawyer), drawing on such diverse fields as the history of emotions, canon – or Church – law, and both legal and literary discussions of marriage, to shed new light on Boccaccio's contradictory, multifaceted approach to the status of women in medieval society. Alessia Ronchetti's piece places Boccaccio's female-voiced vernacular work, the *Elegia di Madonna Fiammetta*, in the context of philosophical and rhetorical definitions of compassion and its traditionally negative association with the feminine, whereas Grace Delmolino contextualizes *Decameron* 2.10 in that of the legal profession, examining the legal and economic theory of conjugal debt, which treated men and women equally. Sara E. Díaz then sets Boccaccio's later vernacular work, the *Trattatello in laude di Dante*, against the foil of the humanist movement's contempt both for the vernacular and for the kind of love-centred poetry that they saw as undermining the poet's masculine authority; she shows how Boccaccio adopts misogamous (or anti-matrimonial) discourse as a way of mitigating the dangers of Dante's linkage to femininity. The final essay of this section, by Mary Anne Case, directly addresses the legal and ontological status that Boccaccio accords to women, comparing his position on the topic to that of the later, explicitly philogynous French writer who reprises and recombines elements of his work, Christine de Pizan (1365–c. 1430).

The next cluster of essays, "Political and Authorial Contexts: On Famous Women," is pivotal in the volume's trajectory from seeing Boccaccio as a collage artist and constructor of matrixes to examining his works' subsequent itineraries in numerous interconnected networks, and highlights especially the importance of his Latin treatise *De mulieribus claris* for the later literary debate that came to be known as the "querelle des femmes." These essays also pivot from investigating fictionalized accounts of women's status to shedding light on the intersection between Boccaccio's work and the lives of historical women. In Elizabeth Casteen's essay, we see the active role that Boccaccio took in helping to shape the reputation of Queen Johanna of Naples, which established his voice as an important one in contemporary politics. Kevin Brownlee's and Lori Walters's essays then show how the pioneering vernacular author Christine de Pizan (surely among Boccaccio's best readers) harnessed, in her turn, many of Boccaccio's rhetorical and narrative devices to her own ends, to position herself in a place of authority both within and beyond her texts.

The essays of the final section, "Literary Contexts and Intertexts," offer new insights not only into Boccaccio's dialogue with – and destabilization of – his many source materials, but also into his legacy, both in terms of how he influenced his literary successors and of how his texts were themselves effectively transformed by successive interpretations of them. These essays further evidence the need to discuss Boccaccio through a prism that is not exclusively "high cultural" or exclusively Western. If we are to expand our vision to a global one, it is crucial to draw attention to the important role played by the enormous patrimony of Eastern and Islamicate narrative materials that penetrated Europe around time of the Crusades, and Franklin Lewis's piece constitutes a significant step in this direction.[21] Lewis looks both backward and forward in time, however, examining the relationship of *Decameron* 7.9 not only to earlier analogues in Persian and Arabic literature but also to the later one of Chaucer's *Merchant's Tale*. Like Lewis, Katherine A. Brown also explores the roots of Boccaccio's *novelle* in what may generally be referred to as the genre of the *fabliau* (a short, usually ribald story of trickery, especially popular from the twelfth to the fourteenth century), examining how a single French intertext plays out in two different *Decameron* tales. Filippo Andrei then investigates the extraordinary influence on fifteenth-century Spanish sentimental fiction, particularly on the play *La Celestina* by Fernando de Rojas (1465–1541), not of the *Decameron*, but rather of Boccaccio's *Fiammetta* (thus linking back to Ronchetti's essay). Finally, Nora Martin Peterson sets Boccaccio's story collection both in one of its many social and historical contexts – the yearly obligation to confess, following the Fourth

Lateran Council's establishment in 1215 of the individual Christian's sacramental obligations – and in the literary context of a later French rewriting of it, the *Heptaméron*, by Marguerite de Navarre (1492–1549).

In sum, this study focuses on an essential figure in the transition to social, political, and philosophical modernity and to modern narrative realism, approaching his work from many different disciplinary and methodological perspectives. A number of significant themes emerge: the text as material object and as work-in-progress, its interaction with historical contexts and contemporary cultural networks, the author's obsessive interest in and return to social questions such as those of sex and gender, his omnivorous collation and overlaying of diverse sources and genres, and the impact of narrative strategies such as literary framing devices. Boccaccio assembles a collage of different traditions, geographically diverse in origin and from both high and low cultures, in which old tales take on new meanings; and new tales, old ones. It is the radically cardinal nature of his innovations, poised as they are at the turning point from medieval to Renaissance, that helps set in motion the changes that ultimately lead (as the final two essays suggest) to the psychological novel and the confessional memoir. He not only excavates countless traditional structures and themes, combining and recombining them at will, but his legacy is then mined in turn by subsequent authors and thinkers – to an extent that is only now coming to be recognized – thus marking with his recognizable and indelible imprint the social thought, scholarly ideas, and imaginative creations of the modern world.

Chapter Summaries

Material Contexts

K.P. Clarke provides an apposite opening for this collection with his essay "Text and (Inter)Face: The Catchwords in Boccaccio's Autograph of the *Decameron.*" He focuses on the author-illuminations, tiny portrait busts of characters from the tales, that illustrate the catchwords – the first word or phrase from the next quire that is placed in the margin of a quire's final page, to ensure that the sections are ordered correctly when the book is bound – in the one surviving *Decameron* autograph (Hamilton 90). He interprets these images not as decorative and accessory, but as theatrical and intrinsic to the specific text of this particular manuscript. As he puts it, the images do not comment on or interact with the text of the catchwords; "rather, they *are* the text of their catchwords, emerging out of and embodying those words." Clarke considers Boccaccio's decision to attend to the *bas de page* of the final leaf of each quire as highly significant inasmuch as the drawings are cardinal in the word's etymological sense, serving as hinges in the book's structural language, and both rhetorically proleptic, representative of what is to come, and analeptic, looking back at what came before, to the book in its pre-bound state. Thus the collection embodied in this codex is marked by "a resistance to closure," as only one in a sequence of authorial rewritings, and as a work perpetually in progress, but always pointing to its ultimate realization in the finished book.

Rhiannon Daniels's "Reading Boccaccio's Paratexts: Dedications as Thresholds between Worlds" also brings to bear on Boccaccio's works a material and codicological perspective (grounded in narratology and reception history as well), and also focuses on one particular form of Boccaccian paratext – in her case, the dedications. She sets her analysis in the context of both structuralist and rhetorical approaches to the components of literary texts, analysing the dedications not only for content but for form and function as well. Like catchwords for Clarke, she sees dedications as performing a sort of cardinal or connective role, joining the world outside the narrative to the one inside it. Boccaccio emphasizes the transmissive and communicative nature of the text, its intermediate position between author and audience, by foregrounding the act of storytelling in the *Decameron* and creating a differentiated structure of multiple narrators, which he then subverts by blurring the boundaries between one level and another. As Daniels points out, Boccaccio dedicates different works to both historical and fictional figures, and, in the latter case, seems to use dedicatory epistles as a sort of parody of the historical paratext, linking public to private. After considering a number of authorial dedications, this essay concludes by looking also at the editorial dedications added to a number of print editions of the *Decameron* in the early sixteenth century. Daniels examines two Venetian editions in particular (a 1522 edition of the *Decameron* by Andrea Torresani and his two sons and a 1516 *Decameron* with an editorial preface by Nicolò Delfino) in which editors echo Boccaccio's own strategies for framing and defending his work. As Boccaccio's inscriptions play with the boundaries between history and fiction, so, too, these editorial paratexts blur any clear distinction between authorship and reception.

Social Contexts: Friendship

The next two pieces, Jason Houston's "Boccaccio on Friendship (Theory and Practice)" and Todd Boli's "Among Boccaccio's Friends: A Profile of Mainardo Cavalcanti," turn to Boccaccio's biography, and particularly to his relationships with friends and to the theme of friendship in his correspondence. Houston examines Boccaccio's rhetorical treatment of his friends Niccolò Acciaiuoli and Zanobi da Strada, members of the Tuscan cohort at the Neapolitan court, highlighting the stylistic dissonance in his rhetoric of friendship between that of abstract generalizations and that of personal observations. Houston concentrates on four of Boccaccio's epistles: an early Latin exercise haranguing a "bad" friend, a letter addressed to Acciaiuoli attempting to convert him from friend to patron, a letter to Zanobi lauding both his virtues and his poetic vocation, and a much later letter to another friend lamenting Acciaiuoli's slights of his erstwhile friend upon Boccaccio's return to Naples at his invitation. Houston observes that when Boccaccio writes theoretically about friendship, he relies on well-known classical authors, such as Virgil, Cicero, and Ovid, whereas when he addresses his own (largely disappointing) experiences with it, he has recourse to medieval Tuscan writers, such as Boncompagno da Signa and Brunetto Latini. The letters draw on a variety of literary sources and rhetorical modes, mingling fiction with personal experience. They also influenced subsequent literary-historical narrative; as Houston points out, Boccaccio's verdict on his friends' poetic talents helped to determine their place in – or, better, absence from – the Italian literary canon.

Boli's essay also draws from the epistolary and historical records to paint a much more flattering portrait of another of Boccaccio's associates, Mainardo Cavalcanti, and to explore Boccaccio's notions of the important role of friendship in literary culture. Boli reconstructs the reasons for the younger Florentine's presence in Naples, and the probable occasion of his first encounter with Boccaccio. After the misunderstandings and disappointments that seem to have characterized Boccaccio's dealings with contemporaries and elders, he apparently found solace in the admiration and company of younger patrons and acolytes. Cavalcanti was assiduous in his material and emotional support of the aging author, which Boccaccio recognizes by dedicating one of his most learned works, the *De casibus virorum illustrium*, to his relatively unlearned friend, explicitly rejecting more illustrious and conventional candidates as less worthy in terms of character (thus linking us back to the topic of dedications, explored by Daniels's essay in the previous section).

Social Contexts: Gender, Marriage, and the Law

Alessia Ronchetti's "Reading Like a Woman: Gendering Compassion in the *Elegia di Madonna Fiammetta*" asks how we should understand the gendered positioning of compassion in Boccaccio's *Fiammetta*. As Ronchetti reminds us, the text's female narrator (Fiammetta) opens the work with an address to female readers, in whom she means to awaken pity, specifically stating that she hopes male readers will stay away from her work, as she imagines it would arouse in them "jeering laughter … rather than compassionate tears." Ronchetti outlines the opposing critical interpretations of Fiammetta's stance. Some commentators have maintained that Boccaccio's female narrator is undermined in various ways throughout the text and ought therefore to be regarded as a negative example of someone who (like Dante's Francesca) abdicated reason in favour of the pursuit of sensual love. Others have set out to show that the compassion promoted by Fiammetta was a fundamental characteristic of Boccaccio's ethics and poetics. Turning her attention to a specific passage in which Fiammetta attempts to prevail upon her lover Panfilo's sense of *pietà* (which he says he feels for his father, but which Fiammetta argues he ought to feel for her), Ronchetti teases out the many implications and layers of meaning to make a convincing case that Boccaccio is inviting readers to understand compassion from multiple, intersubjective perspectives – male and female, ethical and aesthetic, public and private, and moral and emotional.

The context in which Grace Delmolino's essay "The Economics of Conjugal Debt from Gratian's *Decretum* to *Decameron* 2.10: Boccaccio, Canon Law, and the Loss of Interest in Sex" sets Boccaccio's tales is legal, rather than literary or philosophical. There has been little scholarly work on law in the *Decameron* until recently, although Boccaccio himself spent a number of his early years studying jurisprudence, and his legal erudition informs the detailed realism of his portrayals of the workings of justice.[22] Delmolino interprets *Decameron* 2.10 – the tale of a wealthy but foolish old judge who loses his beautiful young wife because of his failure to satisfy her sexually – as engaging Gratian's *Decretum*, a twelfth-century legal textbook. As Delmolino points out, many of the *Decretum*'s *causae* convey hypothetical cases that read like plots for *novelle*. *Causa* 33 treats the concept of "conjugal debt," the obligation that each spouse provide sex to the other, and outlines a scenario strikingly similar to 2.10, in which a husband is not able to render his debt because of a vow of continence, and the wife is corrupted by another man who meets her sexual needs. Delmolino's lucid exposition of Boccaccio's story associates the judge's impotence with his excessive reliance on an outdated calendar for sexual abstinence prescribed by the Church and with his failure to understand Gratian's more holistic and egalitarian treatment of marital relations. The wife's rhetorical ability to address the legal (and metaphorically fiscal) ramifications of their situation comes across as more up to date. In conclusion, Delmolino discusses the implications of her legal reading of the *novella* for the *brigata*'s decision at the end of Day Two to abstain from storytelling for several days of rest; she details how the judge's final *motto*, "Il mal furo non vuol festa [The wicked hole (*or* the bar, the legal profession) does not want a holiday]" (2.10.42), elaborately puns on Dante's definition of Gratian as the one who served "l'uno e l'altro foro [one and the other forum]" (*Paradiso* 10.104–5).

In "Authority and Misogamy in Boccaccio's *Trattatello in laude di Dante*," Sara E. Díaz considers the rhetorical functions of the anti-matrimonial diatribe found in that work. Noting that scholars have shown that Boccaccio painstakingly revised and copied the *Trattatello* over the years and that it was always placed in collections with the *Vita Nova*, Díaz emphasizes how the work reflects Boccaccio's investment in establishing an "authorizing frame" for both Dante's vernacular autobiography and Italian literature generally. As Díaz points out, Dante's status as literary authority was seen as compromised by his use of the vernacular and his emphasis on love, both of which were deemed overly feminine and therefore not befitting an *auctor*. She references how misogyny was used in vernacular French letters as a strategy to establish masculine authority; then, delineating the distinctions between misogyny and misogamy – while also noting that the two are related – Díaz demonstrates how Boccaccio used misogamous discourse to promote Dante's authorial prestige in the male-centric sphere of Latin humanistic letters.

Mary Anne Case's essay – "What Turns on Whether Women Are Human for Boccaccio and Christine de Pizan?" – returns us to the topic of law and to the larger philosophical question, much debated in the Middle Ages, as to whether women can be defined as and accorded the status of *homines* (human beings). Christine de Pizan explicitly argues in *Le livre de la cité des dames* that women are indeed human, and Case looks back to Christine's principal source-text, Boccaccio's *De mulieribus claris,* to determine whether he gives them the same status. In his dedication of the treatise to Andrea Acciaiuoli (a dedication that Daniels and Walters also discuss in their essays), Boccaccio conflates *andres,* the Greek word for "males," with *anthropoi,* the term for "human beings," thus – according to Case – excluding women from the latter category. In the *Decameron,* however, in the topic that Lauretta sets for Day Eight, "quelle beffe che tutto il giorno, o donna ad uomo, o uomo a donna, o l'uno uomo all'altro si fanno [the tricks that people in general, men and women alike, are forever playing on one another]," the "uomo" of the final clause does indeed seem to refer to both men and women.[23] Case delineates the subsequent historical battle, especially in France, to apply what English speakers frequently call "the Rights of Man" also fully to women, showing how political progress along these lines depended on a Latin maxim, which had migrated into medieval canon law, "What touches all must be approved by all." This is the principle that Madonna Filippa alludes to when she is taken in adultery and serves as her own lawyer, reasoning that in the creation of the law condemning adulterous women to death, no woman was ever consulted, and thus the law is illegitimate ("malvagia"; *Dec.* 6.7.14). Case argues that Madonna Filippa successfully demonstrates not only women's full humanity but also their Christlike nature, and that the integrated democratic society constructed by the frame-story's *brigata* is ultimately as egalitarian and utopian as Christine's City of Ladies.

Political and Authorial Contexts: On Famous Women

Elizabeth Casteen's essay, "On She-Wolves and Famous Women: Boccaccio, Politics, and the Neapolitan Court," examines the intertwining of literature, history, and politics in fourteenth-century Naples. Noting that the influence on Boccaccio of his stay in the Angevin court is well established, Casteen turns her attention to how the writer himself responded to and influenced political trends, focusing on his treatment of Queen Johanna I of Naples. Casteen traces and explicates the wildly divergent attitudes that Boccaccio displays towards Johanna over the course of his career. From joyful, innocent girl (in *Amorosa visione*) to a caricature of feminine vice and animalistic sexuality (in the eclogues), Johanna's image undergoes a final transformation in *De mulieribus claris,* where Boccaccio portrays her as a paragon of queenly virtue. Casteen shows that Boccaccio's varying treatment of Johanna reflects and reinforces wider views of the queen, who was both loved and hated at various points of her reign, and also participates in contemporary debates about queenship in general. She further demonstrates that Boccaccio's portrayals of Johanna not only served to help shape the queen's reputation for the future, but simultaneously helped to shape Boccaccio's own reputation as political commentator and as a political figure with his own stake in Neapolitan politics.

Kevin Brownlee's "Christine Transforms Boccaccio: Gendered Authorship in the *De mulieribus claris* and the *Cité des dames*" turns to Boccaccio's influence on Christine de Pizan. Through a careful examination of Christine's explicit citations of Boccaccio's name throughout her *Cité*, Brownlee elucidates the complexity of the French author's relation to her Italian model, demonstrating the ways in which Christine bolsters her own authority (and that of her vernacular text) through a combination of allusions to and subversions of Boccaccio as poet and author of *De mulieribus*. As Brownlee points out, Boccaccio "is revealed both as an authoritative model for Christine-author and as a male third-person master who must be placed into a female, first-person voice." Her work's incorporation and transformation of Boccaccio's text successfully sets his treatment of women in an overtly feminist context.

Lori J. Walters's essay "Reading Like a Frenchwoman: Christine de Pizan's Treatment of Boccaccio's Johanna I and Andrea Acciaiuoli" then intersects in compelling ways with both Casteen's and Brownlee's essays. Working from extensive codicological research, Walters explores how Christine fashioned her portrayals of France's Queen Ysabel de Bavière after Boccaccio's treatment of Queen Johanna in his *De mulieribus*. Walters further suggests that Christine modelled her own position as advisor to Queen Ysabel on Boccaccio's depiction of his dedicatee, Andrea Acciaiuoli, described as an esteemed, influential lady in Johanna's service. This modelling, Walters argues, allowed Christine to bolster both Ysabel's reputation, by comparing her to the renowned Queen Johanna, and her own, by establishing her authorial persona as a powerful combination of the male author and his female dedicatee. Like Casteen, Walters moves beyond the literary-critical perspective, to shed further light on the complex functioning of Christine's imitations of Boccaccio, inside and outside the text; and like Brownlee, she demonstrates Christine's masterful use of Boccaccio's own rhetoric and arguments to correct and surpass her predecessor and ethnic compatriot, as well as to defend and promote the female sex and the French monarchy.

Literary Contexts and Intertexts

Franklin Lewis's study, "A Persian in a Pear Tree: Middle Eastern Analogues for Pirro/Pyrrhus," returns us to the topic of Boccaccio's far-flung literary sources, finding medieval Islamicate parallels for the final trick of *Novella* 7.9. In this episode, Lidia, wife of Nicostrato, contrives to "solazzare [enjoy herself]" with her lover Pirro in her husband's presence by convincing Nicostrato that the sexual acts that he sees from his perch in a pear tree are visions caused by the tree's enchantment. Lewis traces the nucleus of this story back through its proximate source, the twelfth-century Latin poem *Comoedia Lydiae*, to its appearance in Book 4 of *Maṡnavī-yi ma'navī*, by the well-known thirteenth-century Persian poet Jalāl al-Dīn Rūmī, and then even further back to a lesser-known twelfth-century Arabic version, involving a date palm. Through Rumi's allegorical reading of the tale (as referring not to an actual pear tree, but to the Tree of Existence, atop which our ego deceives us and makes us see awry), Lewis also connects the tree motif here to the True tree mentioned in Qur'an 14.24 as having its branches in heaven, to the fruit of the Tree of Knowledge in Christian and Jewish tradition, to Hellenistic and Roman depictions of *Venus genetrix* as holding a fruit, and to Rabbinic material. He traces the motif forward as well to Chaucer's *Merchant's Tale*, in which (as also in a version in the *Novellino*, an Italian short story-collection from the century before Boccaccio) the love-making actually takes place *in* the tree, and the husband is blind. Earlier critics have distinguished two sub-categories, the "optical illusion caused by an enchanted tree" tale type, originating in the Middle East, and the "blind husband and the fruit tree" type, which occurs only in the West, but Lewis concludes that Chaucer incorporates components of both types, which cannot clearly be disentangled, and that seeds of the *fabliau* genre, characterized by a concern with epistemology and misperception, were scattered across the Mediterranean.

The next contribution, Katherine A. Brown's "Splitting Pants and Pigs: The *Fabliau* 'Barat et Haimet' and Narrative Strategies in *Decameron* 8.5 and 8.6," also focuses on the relation between Boccaccio's tales and an earlier (in this case, French) *fabliau*, as well as addressing the relation between the *Decameron* and its sources more generally. Boccaccio took the plots of the *Decameron*'s tales from anywhere and everywhere, and indeed explicitly denies in the epilogue that he was the stories' inventor, claiming that he was just a transcriber of tales told by others (*Concl. dell'Autore* 17). Brown applies a narratological approach to

Boccaccio's recombinatory method, whereby he combines elements of different source-stories in one *novella*, or reutilizes one basic plot in different *novelle*. She concentrates on Day Eight, dedicated to *beffe* or tricks, observing parallels between the trickster figure and the storyteller as creators of illusion. Like Daniels, Brown emphasizes the intermediate position of the text between writer and reader, interpreting the victims of *beffe* as an inscribed audience, and the dupes' passive acceptance of illusion as truth as a sort of negative exemplum for audiences to avoid. She suggests both that Boccaccio's method of splitting and recombining stories points to the instability of narrative meaning, and that the *beffe*, by rearranging the order of future and past, underline the relativity of even historical time.

In "The Tragicomedy of Lament: *La Celestina* and the Elegiac Legacy of Boccaccio's *Fiammetta*," Filippo Andrei makes a compelling case for the influence of Boccaccio's *Fiammetta* on fifteenth-century Spanish literature. First, Andrei outlines the critical controversies surrounding the question of *Fiammetta*'s role in the development of the *novela sentimental*, and then he turns his attention to Fernando de Rojas's *Celestina*. While critics have until now mostly focused on Petrarch's works – especially *De remediis utriusque fortunae* – as the most important sources for the *Celestina*, Andrei lays out the multiple ways in which Boccaccio's text is fundamental for Rojas's tragicomic masterpiece, which itself has sometimes been seen as part of the genre of Spanish sentimental fiction and at other times not. Engaging in a side-by-side analysis of various passages from the texts, Andrei demonstrates not only their many similarities (structural, thematic, and otherwise) but also the pervasive influence on Rojas's *Celestina* of the *Fiammetta*'s characteristic elegiac voice, consisting of inner struggles and constant weeping. Andrei concludes that Rojas's Boccaccian elegiac style serves as "an important bridge towards a modern vision of the interior world."

In the book's final essay, "Sins, Sex, and Secrets: The Legacy of Confession from the *Decameron* to the *Heptaméron*," Nora Martin Peterson considers the status of the rite of confession in the centuries following Lateran IV (1215), which was a turning point in the formalizing of confession as a required, yearly sacrament. Scholars have debated how widely confession was practised both before and after this date, despite its having been mandated at the Council. Through an analysis of the portrayals of confession in the *Decameron* and in Marguerite de Navarre's subsequent framed story-collection, the *Heptaméron*, Peterson offers compelling evidence that confession was indeed prevalent in Christian society during these centuries and of how it was carried out. Furthermore, she shows how Boccaccio and Marguerite use the trope of confession to explore the connections between storytelling and confession and contemporary attitudes towards religion and the clergy. Finally, Peterson sheds light on the shifting role of confession from a community-oriented ritual in the fourteenth century to an increasingly individual one in the sixteenth century.

NOTES

1 See especially the introductory essay, "Boccaccio as Cultural Mediator," in *The Cambridge Companion to Boccaccio*, ed. Guyda Armstrong, Rhiannon Daniels, and Stephen J. Milner (Cambridge: Cambridge University Press, 2015), 3–19. On Boccaccio's multicultural origins in Naples, see *Boccaccio angioino: Materiali per la storia culturale di Napoli nel Trecento*, ed. Giancarlo Alfano, Teresa d'Urso, and Alessandra Perriccioli Saggese (Brussels: Peter Lang, 2012); Roberta Morosini, "Napoli: *Spazi rappresentativi* della memoria," *Boccaccio geografico*, ed. R. Morosini (Florence: Mauro Pagliai, 2010), 179–204.

2 The plenary speeches from this conference appeared in a special issue of the journal *Mediaevalia* entitled "Boccaccio at 700: Tales and Afterlives" (vol. 34, 2013, co-edited by Olivia Holmes and Dana E. Stewart). See also esp. *Boccaccio autore e copista*, ed. Teresa De Robertis et al. (Florence: Mandragora, 2013); *Heliotropia 700/10: A Boccaccio Anniversary Volume*, ed. Michael Papio (Milan: LED, 2013); *Boccaccio: A Critical Guide to the Complete Works*, ed. Victoria Kirkham et al. (Chicago: University of Chicago Press, 2014); *Boccaccio 1313–2013*, ed. Francesco Ciabattoni et al. (Ravenna: Longo, 2015); *Boccace, entre Moyen âge et Renaissance: Les tensions d'un écrivain*, ed. Sabrina Ferrara et al. (Paris: Champion, 2015). For a survey of the conferences and publications that celebrated Boccaccio in 2013, see Christopher Kleinhenz and Elsa Filosa, "Rassegna critica dell'anno boccacciano," *Arnovit* 1 (2016): 266–88.

3 See Catherine Holmes and Naomi Standen, "Defining the Global Middle Ages," *Medieval Worlds* 1 (2015): 106–17.

4 See Filippo Andrei, "The Variants of *Honestum*: Practical Philosophy in the *Decameron*," in *Boccaccio in America*, ed. Elsa Filosa and Michael Papio (Ravenna: Longo, 2012), 157–71; Marilyn Migiel, *The Ethical Dimension of the "Decameron"* (Toronto: University of Toronto Press, 2015); Michael Sherberg, *The Governance of Friendship: Law and Gender in*

the "Decameron" (Columbus: Ohio State University Press, 2011); Carlo Delcorno, "Boccaccio and the Literature of the Friars," and Olivia Holmes, "Beyond Exemplarity: Women's Wiles from the *Disciplina Clericalis* to the *Decameron*," both in *Boccaccio 1313–2013*, 161–86 and 145–56; Judith Serafini-Sauli,"The Pleasures of Reading: Boccaccio's *Decameron* and Female Literacy," *MLN* 126 (2011): 29–46; Lucia Battaglia Ricci, *Scrivere un libro di novelle: Giovanni Boccaccio autore, lettore, editore* (Ravenna: Longo, 2013); Beatrice Arduini, "Boccaccio and His Desk," in *The Cambridge Companion to Boccaccio*, 20–35; Marco Cursi, *La scrittura e i libri di Giovanni Boccaccio* (Rome: Viella, 2013); Rhiannon Daniels, *Boccaccio and the Book* (London: Legenda, 2009); Charmaine Lee, "Boccaccio's Neapolitan Letter and Multilinguism in Angevin Naples," *Mediaevalia* 34 (2013): 7–21; and Maggie Fritz-Morkin, "Andreuccio at the Well: Sanitation Infrastructure and Civic Values in *Decameron* 2.5," and Giovanni Spani, "Il vino di Boccaccio: Usi e abusi in alcune novelle del *Decameron*," both in *Heliotropia 700/10*, 49–59 and 106–21.

5 As Boccaccio himself recognizes in the *Decameron*'s Proem (§14), the tales themselves are also, in fact, intentionally set in in both ancient and modern times, and in a wide variety of locales, from ancient Greece and the Middle East, to various places in Europe and the Mediterranean, to distant China. Janet Smarr has shown how, in tales involving non-Christians, "the foreigner serves as a vantage point from which to assess and criticize behavior in the West"; "Non-Christian People and Spaces in the *Decameron*," in *Approaches to Teaching Boccaccio's "Decameron,"* ed. James H. McGregor (New York: Modern Language Association, 2000), 35. See also the essays in *Boccaccio geografico*.

6 Geraldine Heng, "Early Globalities, and Its Questions, Objectives, and Methods: An Inquiry into the State of Theory and Critique," *Exemplaria: Medieval, Early Modern, Theory* 26, no. 2–3 (Summer/Fall 2014): 234–53; 236. See also Robert I. Moore, "A Global Middle Ages?" in *The Prospect of Global History*, ed. James Belich, John Darwin, Margret Freyz, and Chris Wickham (Oxford: Oxford University Press, 2016), 80–92, and Roberta Morosini and Cristina Perissinotto, eds., *Mediterrananoesis: Voci dal Medioevo e dal Rinascimento mediterraneo* (Rome: Salerno, 2007).

7 Giuseppe Velli, "Memoria," in *Lessico critico decameroniano*, ed. Renzo Brigantini and Pier Massimo Forni (Turin: Bollati Boringhieri, 1995), 224; see also his *Petrarca e Boccaccio* (Padua: Antenore, 1979), 112–21. Velli also compares Boccaccio's compositional technique to that of the *cento*, a poetic work wholly composed of verses or passages from other authors disposed in a new order.

8 Lucia Battaglia Ricci, "*Decameron*: Interferenze di modelli," in *Autori e lettori di Boccaccio*, ed. Michelangelo Picone (Florence: Cesati, 2002), 179–80.
9 Ibid., 180.
10 Tobias Foster Gittes, "Boccaccio and Humanism," in *The Cambridge Companion to Boccaccio*, 159.
11 Paul B. Armstrong, *How Literature Plays with the Brain* (Baltimore: Johns Hopkins University Press, 2013), 44. For Boccaccio's "ars combinatoria," see esp. Guido Almansi, *The Writer as Liar: Narrative Technique in the "Decameron"* (London: Routledge and Kegan Paul, 1975); Velli, *Petrarca e Boccaccio*, 112–21.
12 Armstrong, *How Literature Plays with the Brain*, 49–50. For Boccaccio's procedure of repeatedly creating and dissolving patterns, echoing past plots and anticipating future ones, while constantly reconfiguring how the different parts fit together, see also Olivia Holmes, "*Decameron* 8.8: Do unto Others, or 'Chi te la fa, fagliele,'" in *The "Decameron": Eighth Day in Perspective*, ed. W. Robins (Toronto: University of Toronto Press, forthcoming).
13 Tobias Foster Gittes, *Boccaccio's Naked Muse* (Toronto: University of Toronto Press, 2008), 7.
14 Simone Marchesi complicates the mosaic metaphor by introducing the dimension of depth into it and seeing the *Decameron*'s references to the literary culture of the past as functioning more like geological rock strata, through which different sectors of Boccaccio's audience are invited to move from one interpretive level to another; *Stratigrafie decameroniane* (Florence: Olschki, 2004), xiii.
15 "Boccaccio as Cultural Mediator," 4.
16 The Boccaccian corpus may thus also be seen as "dialogical" in the Bahktinian sense: multi-voiced, polyphonic, chaotic, destructive of previous pieties and intellectual hierarchies, and thereby allowing for the emergence of new harmonies; see M.M. Bakhtin, *The Dialogic Imagination*, trans. Caryl Emerson and Michael Holquist (Austin: University of Texas Press, 1981).
17 See Roberto Bigazzi, "Boccaccio, Ariosto, and the European Novel"; Janet Levarie Smarr, "Marriage or Politics? Dramatizing Griselda"; F. Regina Psaki, "'Alcuna paroletta piú liberale': Contemporary Women Authors Address the *Decameron*'s Obscenity"; and "Boccaccio and the Seventh Art: The Decameronian Films of Fellini, De Laurentiis, Pasolini, Woody Allen," all in *Mediaevalia* 34 (2013): 155–68, 221–39, 241–66, and 267–79; Igor Candido, "Boccaccio sulla via del romanzo," *Arnovit* 1 (2016): 8–28.
18 See, for instance, John Dagenais, *The Ethics of Reading in Manuscript Culture* (Princeton: Princeton University Press, 1994); Stephen G.

Nichols, "Why Material Philology?" *Zeitschrift für Deutsche Philologie* 116 supplement (1997): 10–30; William Robins, ed., *Textual Cultures of Medieval Italy* (Toronto: University of Toronto Press, 2011); Martin Eisner, *Boccaccio and the Invention of Italian Literature* (Cambridge: Cambridge University Press, 2013).

19 There is a list of Boccaccio's autograph manuscripts in the *Cambridge Companion to Boccaccio*, xviii–xxii. See also esp. *Boccaccio autore e copista*; Cursi, *La scrittura e i libri di Giovanni Boccaccio*, and "Authorial Strategies and Manuscript Tradition," *Mediaevalia* 34 (2013): 87–110. Another contribution to the present volume that focuses on materiality and manuscript culture is Lori Walters's essay on Christine de Pizan's treatment of Boccaccio (chapter 11 below).

20 For an essay that approaches friendship in terms of network theory, see Hannah Chapelle Wojciehowski, "Petrarch and His Friends," in the *Cambridge Companion to Petrarch*, ed. Albert R. Ascoli and Unn Falkeid (Cambridge: Cambridge University Press, 2015), 26–35.

21 Although a great deal of work was done in the late nineteenth and early twentieth centuries investigating this important set of sources for Boccaccio – see, for instance, Letterario Di Francia, "Alcune novelle del *Decameron* illustrate nelle fonti," *Giornale storico della letteratura italiana* 44 (1904): 1–103; Pietro Toldo, "Dall' *Alphabetum narrationum*: Gli ebrei e il falso nome," *Archiv für das Studium der neueren Sprachen und Literaturen* 11, no. 7 (1906): 287–303; and, for a compilation of previous scholarship, A.C. Lee, *The Decameron: Its Sources and Analogues* (New York: Haskell House, 1966) – scholars then went on largely to ignore these texts for many decades, in response to the perceived excesses of overly positivist criticism and perhaps also, at least in part, to a general lack of the relevant language skills. With the huge expansion in Middle Eastern studies in North America in recent years, however, the influence of Islamicate literature on medieval European story-collections is ripe for exploration. For more recent work, see Alessandra Toce, "Dalle novelle orientali al *Decameron*," *Levia gravia* 2 (2000): 165–80; and, for a reconsideration of previous orientalist scholarship, Costanzo Di Girolamo and Charmaine Lee, "Fonti," in *Lessico critico decameroniano*, 320–43.

22 For Boccaccio's juridical formation and its relation to the *Decameron*, see Battaglia Ricci, *Scrivere un libro di novelle*, 116–33; Justin Steinberg, "Mimesis on Trial: Legal and Literary Verisimilitude in Boccaccio's *Decameron*," *Representations* 139 (Summer 2017): 118–45.

23 Giovanni Boccaccio, *Decameron*, ed. Vittore Branca (Turin: Einaudi, 1980), 8.intro.1; translation from Boccaccio, *The Decameron*, 2nd ed., trans. G.H. McWilliam (London: Penguin, 1995), 551. Quotations of the *Decameron* are from Branca's edition and McWilliam's translation, and subsequent citations by day, story, and sentence number in this volume will be inserted parenthetically into the text of the essays.

PART ONE

Material Contexts

1 Text and (Inter)Face: The Catchwords in Boccaccio's Autograph of the *Decameron*

K.P. CLARKE

So kommandiert allein der abgeschriebene Text die Seele dessen, der mit ihm beschäftigt ist

[Only the copied text thus commands the soul of him who is occupied with it]
Walter Benjamin[1]

car copier, c'est ne rien *faire*; c'est *être* les livres qu'on copie

[Because to copy is *to do* nothing; it is *to be* the books being copied]
Michel Foucault[2]

An unusually large number of books survive that are in part or in whole autographs of Giovanni Boccaccio. The richness of this body of material has fuelled some of the most exciting of the various recent developments in Boccaccio criticism.[3] Among them is an increasingly acute awareness of Boccaccio's highly visual, iconographic attention to his books, and his deliberate articulation of a self-conscious relationship between book format and text.[4] The surviving autographs have made it possible to see Boccaccio deciding how he put his books together, that is, how he designed, copied, and organized them. Emanuele Casamassima – in a beautiful reflection on the autographs – has asserted that Boccaccio "is a tireless experimenter … not just of script but also the structural language of the book and the presentation of the page [è uno sperimentatore instancabile … non solo della scrittura ma anche della sintassi costruttiva del libro e della presentazione della pagina]."[5] The subject of this essay will be restricted to what art historians often call "secondary decoration," namely, the catchwords in the only surviving autograph of the *Decameron*.[6] I shall argue here that the experimentalism of Boccaccio is much in evidence in this autograph and that the *sintassi costruttiva* of the book must inflect the way we read its "secondary" decoration in the catchwords.[7] These catchwords, so frequently read as a vivid literary expression of the contents of the *Decameron*, are in fact wholly governed by the material construction of the book: rather than being characters drawn from the book, they represent the Book itself. Boccaccio emerges as an author in supreme control of the paratext, with an acute awareness of the material complexity of the reader's interpretative encounter with the page.[8]

The "corpus" of Boccaccio's drawings in his books grew rapidly from the early attributions in the late 1960s onwards. This work began in earnest with Bernhard Degenhart and Annegrit Schmitt's monumental *Corpus der italienischen Zeichnungen, 1300–1450*, and continued in a series of publications by a range of literary scholars, codicologists, and art historians, such as Vittore Branca, Filippo Di Benedetto, Maria Grazia Ciardi Dupré dal Poggetto, Giovanni Morello, and Marcello Ciccuto.[9] The corpus comprises marginal pointing hands, figures, heads, and little sketches, and has grown to include more elaborate, artistically sophisticated work such as the *bas de page* drawings in the Riccardiano copy of Dante's *Comedìa* (Florence, Biblioteca Riccardiana, MS 1035, *olim* O. II. 17) and the highly complex iconographic cycle in the Paris "Capponi" *Decameron* (Paris, Bibliothèque nationale, MS Ital. 482).[10] The full extent of these attributions can now be appreciated synoptically in the enormous catalogue edited by Vittore Branca entitled *Boccaccio visualizzato: narrare per parole e per immagini fra Medioevo e Rinascimento*, published in 1999 by Einaudi.[11] Recently there have been some important and necessary notes of caution sounded regarding the attributions of the more extensive cycles of drawings.[12] The attribution to Boccaccio of the *Decameron* catchwords, however, has never been seriously challenged.

The Berlin copy of the *Decameron* (Staatsbibliothek Preussicher Kulturbesitz, MS Hamilton 90) is undoubtedly one of the most famous and most studied of Boccaccio's autographs.[13] Definitively identified as an autograph by Vittore Branca and Pier Giorgio Ricci in a 1962 publication, this manuscript has been squarely at the centre of textual work on the *Centonovelle*, and is the basis for the standard modern critical edition, published by Branca in 1976.[14] Indeed, the manuscript was the subject of intense scrutiny in this period, with an abundance of highly specialized material being made widely available. Two years previously, in 1974, a diplomatic transcription appeared with Johns Hopkins University Press, described on the title-page – in Italian – as an "Edizione diplomatico-interpretativa dell'autografo Hamilton 90, a cura di Charles S. Singleton," complete with a preface by Singleton on the recognition of the autograph, as well as a valuable codicological description by Armando Petrucci, the criteria for the transcription by Franca Petrucci Nardelli, concluding with a short "Nota" on the text by Giancarlo Savino.[15] In 1975 a good-quality facsimile of the manuscript was published, with an introduction and codicological description by Branca, which would in turn appear a year later in the introduction to his Accademia della Crusca critical edition.[16] The authority of MS Ham. 90 remains of fundamental importance for all textual work on the hundred stories.

The manuscript is of parchment, of somewhat uneven quality, and measures 371 × 266 mm, with a text area of 263 × 184 mm. The text is ordered in two columns, and the script is a formal semigothic bookhand, with cursive tendencies characteristic of Boccaccio's late hand.[17] It comprises 112 folios, bound in fourteen quires of eight leaves. Three quires are now lost: the first preceded the current first quire, probably containing the summary rubrics, as well as the *Proemio* and up to *Decameron* intr.15; the second followed the current tenth quire, containing *Decameron* 7.1.16 to 7.9.32; and the third would have followed the current thirteenth quire, containing *Decameron* 9.10.12 to 10.8.50. The book is decorated with rubricated initials and summaries. The first folio has a space evidently intended to accommodate an illumination. The final folio of each quire has a catchword at the bottom of the page, centred between both columns of text, around which are drawn portrait busts. While it could be described as handsome, it is by no means a luxury book and is not of the quality one would associate with a presentation manuscript. It has been suggested that, given its large dimensions and parchment support, it was intended as a presentation book, but that at some stage it underwent a "downgrade" to working copy, which then remained on Boccaccio's desk until his death.[18] There are generous margins, which are mostly free of decoration or other marginal activity. The book could well be characterized as sober and understated.

The large dimensions of Ham. 90, its serious bookhand, its careful *ordinatio* and sober *mise-en-page* in two columns of text have all led Armando Petrucci to assert that it deliberately looked like those large, learned university books, which he defined as a "libro da banco" or "desk book."[19] Corrado Bologna, too, has seen Ham. 90 as clearly reflecting "l'abito intellettuale dello studioso educato nell'università gotica, in cui la didattica si fondava sulla lettura sul commento dei grandi trattati [the intellectual custom of the scholar educated in the medieval university, in which teaching was grounded upon the study of the commentaries on the great texts]." He goes on to assert that "la struttura del *tractatus* scientifico ... viene con esattezza trascritta nell'opera narrativa [the structure of the scientific treatise ... is precisely transcribed in the work of fiction]."[20] Manlio Pastore Stocchi went as far as to say that we might think differently about the *Decameron* were it copied more modestly, in a smaller paper book, and in a cursive script, while Lucia Battaglia Ricci, reflecting acutely on the way the format primed the audience, has wondered how this is compatible with the *Decameron*'s intended female readers.[21]

Critics have long admired Boccaccio's attention to the paratext, his attention to how the page filters and conditions the reader's encounter with the text. For example, pre-empting the common practice of a later editor or copyist adding rubrics, Boccaccio devises his own.[22] Indeed, his description of the rubric could be a word-perfect description of the catchwords in MS Ham. 90: "Elle per non ingannare alcuna persona tutte nella fronte portan segnato quello che esse dentro dalloro seno nascose tengono [so as not to deceive anyone, each bears the mark on its brow of what lies hidden in its bosom]" (citing from fol. 110vA [*Concl. dell'autore* 19]).[23] Scholars are becoming ever more sensitive to the material dimensions of Boccaccio's manuscript page. A good example of this is the way the prose is articulated with a system of carefully modulated capital letters. The most recently published new edition of the *Decameron*, with a critical text prepared by Maurizio Fiorilla, is particularly sensitive to Boccaccio's capitals.[24] As Battaglia Ricci has said, it is possible to see how Boccaccio wished to indicate various levels in the text, giving equal weight, for example, to the didactic opening and the story itself, expertly managing the reader's encounter with the text.[25] Teresa Nocita has identified five different kinds of capitals deployed on the page, and has argued for the system of capitals having a firm hermeneutic underpinning, speaking of the text's vocalization and *teatralizzazione*.[26] She wondered if this system of rendering the narrative visible, vocalized, and theatricalized might not offer a way of reading another aspect of Boccaccio's page: the catchwords.[27] Martina Mazzetti has suggested that MS Ham. 90 needs to be considered as a whole, and as such, the catchwords need to be thought of as "a certain kind of drawing, static and not invasive, which suited the specific text of the *Decameron* in the Berlin manuscript [che un certo tipo di *figura*, statica e non invasiva, si attagliasse allo specifico testo del *Decameron* contenuto nel manoscritto berlinese]." She goes on to assert that Boccaccio has the text and image merge in ever new and interesting ways ("Boccaccio fa sì che il testo e la figura vadano a compenetrarsi ogni volta in modo nuovo e sorprendente").[28] The rest of this chapter will take a cue from these various though interrelated strands and consider the catchwords further, especially in terms of Boccaccio's compelling *sintassi costruttiva*.

Critical attention was focused early on the decorated catchwords, especially their striking similarity to the hand responsible for the text.[29] Degenhart and Schmitt prounounced in 1968, "That Boccaccio invented these himself is self-evident [Daß Boccaccios selbst sie erfunden hat, erscheint]," and the attribution has been widely accepted.[30] The thirteen catchwords have long been admired for the liveliness and wit of their execution. Ciardi Dupré, for example, has spoken of their "notable expressive qualities [notevoli qualità espressive]," while Maria Cristina Castelli has asserted that the catchwords "comprise a truly psychological portrait of those characters who, whether protagonists or other figures, embody the spirit of the *novella* [costituiscono infatti un vero e proprio ritratto psicologico di quei personaggi che, protagonisti o figure trasversali, incarnano anche lo spirito della novella]"; Vittore Branca has said that the catchwords are distinguished by a "capacity for 'psycho-gestural' observation and a desire for characterization as far, even, as caricature [una capacità di osservazione psichico-gestuale e una volontà di caratterizzazione fino alla caricatura]."[31] Despite the acuteness of these observations, it is also true that many references to the catchwords see them in terms of secondariness, as "decorative." Branca himself referred to them as "modest and amateurish [modesti e dilettanteschi]," while Marco Cursi sees that they are "the result of an elegant distraction [il risultato di un elegante gioco]."[32] This sense of the catchwords being secondary, almost incidental, has discouraged readers from fully engaging with their uniqueness and their power.

It is worth briefly describing what Boccaccio drew in the *bas de page* of his book. The catchwords are each placed just below the space between the two columns of text. The script is that used in the main text, and each catchword has a small *punctus* on each side. The figures are executed with pen and wash. They represent the abbot (1.4.7, on fol. 8v, "mente"), bearded and wearing a hood, shown in profile; Landolfo Rufolo (2.4.13, on fol. 16v, "al suo"), in three-quarter profile, wearing a fashionable hat, coloured in ochre; Alatiel (2.7.80, on fol. 23v, "uiuere"), in profile, wearing a crown, and in a red dress with open neckline; Neifile (2.concl.8, on fol. 31v, "licentia") in three-quarter profile, wearing a garland on her head, in a brown dress, similar in style to that of Alatiel, and with a somewhat lugubrious expression; Tedaldo degli Elisei (3.7.4, on fol. 39v, "Tedaldo"), in three-quarter profile, wearing a forked beard and ochre garment with a brown collar;[33] Filippo Balducci (4.intr.17, on fol. 47v, "e Filippo"), in three-quarter profile, wearing a simple brown garment and a hat, similar to that worn by Landolfo; guard of the Signoria (4.6.32, on fol. 55v, "sia ardito"), in full profile, bearded, wearing a tight skullcap and holding a shield that directly faces the reader; armed man (5.3.13, fol. 63v, "et essendosi"), in three-quarter profile, wearing a pointed hat and a beard, and holding an axe in one hand and a shield in the other, which directly faces the reader; Pietro di Vinciolo (5.10.37, on fol. 71v, "che poco"), in full profile, wearing a hat and an ochre garment with a high collar; Gianni Lotteringhi (7.1.16, on fol. 79v, "pare"), in full profile, wearing a remarkable head covering that identifies him as belonging to the Laudesi, and depicted sticking his tongue out; the scholar Rinieri (8.7.29, on fol. 87v, "al suono"), in full profile, shown with his tonsured head uncovered, and wearing a red habit with a brown hood; the courtesan Jancofiore (8.10.47, on fol. 95v, "che uoi"), in full profile, wearing a red dress with an open neckline and dots running down her front, her hair elaborately tied up; and Donno Gianni (9.10.12, on fol. 103v, "tu di"), in full profile, wearing a brown habit and hood, with his head uncovered showing a tonsure. Noteworthy is Boccaccio's insistence upon representing the human figure in these catchwords, especially the focus on the face as locus of expressive individual personality.

Vittore Branca has offered the most extensive literary reading of the catchwords, returning to them often in his developing work on Boccaccio *visualizzato*.[34] After a detailed analysis of each figure, he concludes that in the iconographic choices for decorating the catchwords, Boccaccio was highlighting two main ideas. The first was the *Decameron*'s thematic frame of Fortune ["Fortuna"], Wit ["Ingegno"], and Love ["Amore"]. The theme of Fortune would be represented in Landolfo, Alatiel, and Neifile; Love in Tedaldo and Filippo, with Pietro di Vinciolo appearing in a somehow undefinable counter-melody ("controcanto") to this theme; Wit in Gianni Lotteringhi, Jancofiore, and donno Gianni. The abbot is representative of Boccaccio's desire to show "a new, realistic and humorous touch to the story [un nuovo tocco realistico e umoristico alla novella]," while the two soldiers are indicative of "a narrative taste … for feats of arms [un gusto narrativo … per le avventure d'armi]." The second motivation guiding the choice of catchwords is the desire to highlight the presence of the mercantile class, who were so important as readers of the *Decameron*.[35] Of the ten men represented, six are merchants. Indeed, the catchwords avoid any kind of scholastic or heavily symbolic representations: they are directed at simple interlocutors, "a bourgeois, even popular public [un pubblico borghese e anche popolaresco]."

The catchwords, according to this account, are programmatic, and may be identified thematically with the *Decameron*'s broad concerns. For Branca they are the result of a Boccaccio who is making artistic and literary choices. So most of the catchwords represent the protagonist of a *novella*, and the exceptions, such as the two armed men, are the result of Boccaccio's "desire to vary from the usual bourgeois men and woman [volontà di variare dai soliti uomini e donne borghesi]." The decision to represent Neifile, for example, who is the only member of the *brigata* to make it into a catchword, was made "probably because she is emblematic of the 'new love' … and also she who proclaims and defends the chastity of the *brigata* [probabilmente perché è la figura emblematica del 'nuovo amore' … e anche la proclamatrice e la difenditrice della castità della brigata]."[36]

Ciardi Dupré asserted that "Boccaccio ably exploited the coincidence of quires with the stories that create a kind of *comédie humaine* [il Boccaccio ha abilmente sfruttato la coincidenza dei fascicoli con le novelle relative per realizzare una sorta di *comédie humaine*]."[37] In the later version of this essay, published in *Boccaccio visualizzato,* Ciardi Dupré claimed that the presence of the catchwords "does not correspond with any precise project [non corrisponde a un progetto preciso]," before allowing for Branca's interpretation above.[38] Similiarly, Lucia Battaglia Ricci has recently pointed to the "occasional" nature of the catchwords, the result of a "sudden firing of the imagination of the editor [un'improvvisa accensione della fantasia dell'editore]," "occasional," too, in the sense that each catchword image is born at the suggestion of the what is on the page closing each quire ["disegni nati, ciascuno, su sollecitazione del contenuto della carta che si trova a chiudere il fascicolo"].[39]

But these suggestions of a lack of precision and occasionality are not quite correct. Each figure represented is carefully connected to the text of the catchword such that their iconography is intimately tied up with the structure of the book. That is, the range of choices available to Boccaccio is limited, dictated by the size of the page, number of ruled lines, and number of folios in the gathering. Had any of these technical choices been different, so too would the iconography of the catchwords. It is the book itself and its *sintassi costruttiva* that governs the catchwords. The text of seven of the thirteen catchwords is uttered by the tale's narrator, while one occurs within the *cornice* and is uttered by the reigning monarch.[40] The text of the remaining catchwords occurs in direct speech. Two portraits are of the character speaking the text in the catchword: Pietro (fol. 71v; 5.10.37) and Gianni (fol. 79v; 7.1.16); two represent the interlocutor: Andreuola speaks to the guards of the Signoria, warning them not to touch her (fol. 55v, 4.6.32: "ma niuno di voi // *sia ardito* di toccarmi"); Salabaetto is speaking to the courtesan Jancofiore (fol. 95v, 8.10.47); and finally, comar Gemmata is speaking to her husband, compar Pietro, about donno Gianni (fol. 103v, 9.10.12). The aleatory aspect is further emphasized in two of the portraits actually illustrating a catchword that is their own name (Tedaldo, on fol. 39v, and Filippo, on fol. 47v).

The kind of catchword Boccaccio devised for MS Ham. 90 is exceptionally difficult to find in other medieval manuscripts. Martina Mazzetti, for example, has alluded to this difficulty in relation to finding analogous catchwords in late fourteenth-century Tuscany.[41] The striking originality of the catchwords in MS Ham. 90, however, lies not just in their design and execution, but in the way they emerge out of the text on the page. This is not the kind of humorous punning that happens at the end of the page in some manuscripts, memorably discussed by Michael Camille in *Image on the Edge*.[42] Paul Gehl, too, has discussed the vivid catchwords in Chicago, University of Chicago Library, MS 99, and indeed makes a direct analogy with the catchwords in MS Ham. 90.[43] But the catchwords in the Berlin *Decameron* do not *do* anything with the texts of their catchwords and do not interact with them. Rather, they *are* the text of their catchwords, emerging out of and embodying those words.[44] Rather than being chosen from a wide iconographic range of possibilities, the figures in the catchwords *present themselves* for inclusion. What makes these catchwords so different is that they are a vivid and remarkable expression of the Book, fully engaged in the reality of the Book's material construction.

When compared with the kinds of catchwords Boccaccio inserts into his other books, those that appear in MS Ham. 90 also emerge as quite different in articulation. Catchwords clearly caught Boccaccio's attention, and his autographs contain numerous examples. In his copy of Terence's *Comedies* (Florence, Biblioteca Medicea Laurenziana, Plut. 38,

17, on fol. 8v), the catchword is decorated very simply, with a *punctus* placed around it at cardinal points.[45] In the Riccardiano Dante (MS Ricc. 1035), the catchwords are also treated very simply, sometimes with a *punctus* on each side (e.g., see fol. 8v).[46] This is how the catchwords are treated by Boccaccio in his copy of the work of Dante and Petrarch, Vatican City, Biblioteca Apostolica Vaticana, MS Chigi L V 176 (e.g., fol. 8v).[47] In his *Zibaldone*, in Florence, Biblioteca Medicea Laurenziana, MS Plut. 29, 8, for example, on fol. 5r, a bull or a cow is drawn around the catchword, while on fol. 4r the catchword is surrounded by a drawing of the sun and the moon.[48] In the autograph of the *Teseida* (Florence, Biblioteca Medicea Laurenziana, MS Acq. e Doni 325, on fol. 64v), the catchword is decorated with vines and above it is placed a crown.[49] In the rather late autograph of the *De mulieribus claris* (Florence, Biblioteca Medicea Laurenziana, MS Plut. 90 sup 98[1]), a humorously sketched face on fol. 24v looks straight out at the reader with the catchword placed in the figure's mouth.[50] All of the *Decameron* catchwords are in full or three-quarter profile, and all look back to the left side of the *bas de page*. In this respect, the catchwords in MS Ham. 90 resemble the frequent heads and faces Boccaccio draws in the margins of his other manuscripts, especially in their left-facing aspects, and the full profile or half profile formats.[51]

In an essay entitled "Frontal and Profile as Symbolic Forms," Meyer Schapiro suggested that the frontal and profile portrait were used to convey opposite meanings and values. He saw the profile as detached from the viewer, belonging with the body in action in a space shared with other profiles on the surface of the image; the image facing outward is credited with intentness, a latent or potential glance directed at the observer. He went on to assert that "while the full-face has an ideal closure and roundness – smooth, regular and symmetrical – the profile is indented and asymmetrical and shows a less complete but more sharply characterized face."[52] Schapiro makes a linguistic analogy, suggesting that the frontal aspect is similar to the figure saying "I am here," while the profile is akin to the statement "S/he is there." None of the catchwords in MS Ham. 90 is in a full frontal pose, none engages fully or directly with the viewer/reader. Instead, they all look out retrospectively to the blank space of the *bas de page*, under the text the reader has just encountered: they engage with the page and with the book.

The notion alluded to above that the figures in the catchwords *present themselves* for inclusion, that they are latent in the pages of MS Ham. 90, finds support in the way Boccaccio produced them. It would seem that the idea of drawing figures around the catchwords was not originally planned by Boccaccio, but rather occurred to him in the process of copying. During his minute analysis of the manuscript, in particular in his analysis of the layers of ink on the page, Cursi has argued that the catchwords were not produced consistently; the first two figures, he argues, were drawn around the catchword, whereas the rest were drawn first and had their catchword written over the figure.[53] Cursi hypothesizes that Boccaccio had added catchwords to the first two quires in a typical manner, but when he came to add the catchword at the end of the third quire decided it should be illustrated, adding the catchword afterwards. The process of the book's becoming occasions the appearance of the busts. As Walter Benjamin observed in *One-Way Street* [*Einbahnstraße*], in a section entitled "Chinese Curios" ["Chinawaren"], "the power of a text is different when it is read from when it is copied out [die Kraft eines Textes eine andere, ob einer ihn liest oder abschreibt]."[54]

Considered within the context of the economy of the manuscript page, Boccaccio's decision to attend to the space between text columns in the *bas de page* of the final leaf of each quire is highly significant. As a locus of interest, a catchword is in no sense neutral, but rather may be described as of *cardinal* importance (in its etymological sense), because its purpose is to aid in correctly binding the work, hinging together the book's constituent quires. The catchword occupies a *limen*, a space between two quires, a physical gap of separation. One gathering of leaves has finished, and lies without connection to the next. Liminality, as Victor and Edith Turner assert, "is not only *transition* but also *potentiality*, not only 'going to be' but also 'what may be.'"[55] The word in the catchword also participates in the liminal, in that it is a word not yet encountered, not yet read, but proleptically represents what is to come. The technical words we use to describe this device at the end of the quire are ripe with an anxious sense of bridging, of both forward and backward motion: the word "catches," and "recalls" (in Italian the term is *richiamo*; in German *Reklaman*; in French *réclame*).[56] The threat of loss is constant.

That these illustrated busts do not engage with the reader is perhaps not surprising when we consider that catchwords are not aimed at readers at all, but rather serve a much more mechanical purpose, functioning only as long as the book exists in its unbound state, and keeping its gatherings in order. Their audience is not that of the text, but that of the book, more precisely the person responsible for copying and binding. Catchwords have a vital but relatively short shelf life. Once the book is bound, the catchword becomes superfluous, and often ends up cropped. Its power to catch and recall is now a memory, the marginal remains of the book in its pre-bound state. At the limen of the page, they look back to its pre-book form.

MS Ham. 90, then, is marked by a resistance to closure. The text in MS Ham. 90, as Branca has shown, is one that has sustained numerous changes, and there are even moments when the margins accommodate a variant reading evidently left because Boccaccio could not or did not wish to make a final decision.[57] Bologna has suggested that rather than speaking of different and successive redactions, one might instead speak of "a *sequence of authorial rewritings* [una *sequenza di riscrizioni d'autore*]," and Alberto Asor Rosa has referred to the multiplicity of authorial versions as a "fascinating philological *work in progress* [un affascinante *work in progress* filologico]."[58] There has been an increasingly sharp sense among philologists and codicologists that Boccaccio worked and reworked his texts over an extended period. This has long been noted for the Latin works, but critics have been slower to recognize the same phenomenon in the vernacular works.

The catchwords emerge in particularly high relief when it is considered that Boccaccio worked from loose quires and leaves, especially throughout his later years. Giorgio Padoan, for example, has plausibly suggested that this would explain the loss of the three quires in MS Ham. 90.[59] Perhaps the production of MS Ham. 90 is best understood in the context of this late Boccaccio, an ailing Boccaccio, attempting to draw together and assess his own literary and ethical legacy with ever more urgency, perhaps recalling Dante at the end of the *Paradiso*, whose vision of the divine left him at a loss:

> Così la neve al sol si disigilla;
> così al vento ne le foglie levi
> si perdea la sentenza di Sibilla.
>
> [Thus the snow comes unsealed in the sun, thus in the wind, on the fluttering leaves, the Sibyl's meaning was lost]
>
> (*Par*. 33.64–6).

This scattering is answered in turn with Dante's reference to the book:

> Nel suo profondo vidi che s'interna,
> legato con amore in un volume,
> ciò che per l'universo si squaderna:

> [In its depths I saw internalized, bound with love in one volume, what through the universe becomes unsewn quires]
>
> (*Par.* 33.85–7)[60]

The binding of the book, then, is the ultimate aim.

The psychological power of the portrait busts is to be accounted for not just in the evident skill of Boccaccio's drawing but also in his unique appreciation for the book's *sintassi costruttiva* and the potential offered by the manuscript page. They remain compelling because of the unusual way in which they hinge together text and book, carefully placed at the edge of the page. They offer themselves as both instantly recognizable, almost having a mind of their own, and at the same time rooted in the specific imperative of the last word on the page. They are a vital component of the syntax of this book. If Boccaccio's Berlin autograph was indeed one of these unbound working copies, it helps account for the highly specialized kind of attention afforded the catchwords as he put together his book of a hundred stories, looking inexorably to the moment when it, with the help of those same catchwords, would be *legato con amore in un volume*.[61]

NOTES

1 Walter Benjamin, *Gesammelte Schriften*, ed. Rolf Tiedemann and Gerhard Schweppenhäuser, vol. 4 (Frankfurt am Main: Suhrkamp, 1991), i, 90; *Selected Writings*, ed. Marcus Paul Bullock, and Michael W. Jennings, vol. 1 (Cambridge, MA: Belknap, 1996), 448 (in the translation of Edmund Jephcott).

2 Michel Foucault, *Dits et écrits 1954–1988*, ed. Daniel Defert and François Ewald, vol. 1 (Paris: Éditions Gallimard, 1994), 312; "Afterword to *The Temptation of St. Anthony*," in *The Essential Works of Michel Foucault, 1954–1984*, ed. Paul Rabinow and James D. Faubion, trans. Robert Hurley et al., vol. 2 (London: Penguin, 1997–2001), 103–22; 121.

3 Of immense importance are Marco Cursi, *La scrittura e i libri di Giovanni Boccaccio* (Rome: Viella, 2013); *Boccaccio autore e copista*, ed. Teresa De Robertis et al. (Florence: Mandragora, 2013), the catalogue of the exhibition of manuscripts held at the Biblioteca Medicea Laurenziana (11 October 2013–11 January 2014); the *scheda* on Giovanni Boccaccio prepared by Marco Cursi and Maurizio Fiorilla in *Autografi dei letterati italiani. Le origini e il Trecento*, vol. 1, ed. Giuseppina Brunetti, Maurizio Fiorilla, and Marco

Petoletti (Rome: Salerno, 2013), 43–103; and Sandro Bertelli, "Codicologia d'autore. Il manoscritto in volgare secondo Giovanni Boccaccio," in *Dentro l'officina di Giovanni Boccaccio. Studi sugli autografi in volgare e su Boccaccio Dantista*, ed. Sandro Bertelli and Davide Cappi (Vatican City: Biblioteca Apostolica Vaticana, 2014), 1–80. See also Marco Cursi, "Authorial Strategies and Manuscript Tradition: Boccaccio and the *Decameron*'s Early Diffusion," *Mediaevalia* 34 (2013): 87–110, and Cursi, "Boccaccio architetto e artefice di libri: i manoscritti danteschi e petrarcheschi," *Critica del testo* 16, no. 3 (2013): 35–62.

4 Important contributions to this "material turn" are Rhiannon Daniels, *Boccaccio and the Book: Production and Reading in Italy 1340–1520* (Oxford: Legenda, 2009), and Martin Eisner, *Boccaccio and the Invention of Italian Literature: Dante, Petrarch, Cavalcanti, and the Authority of the Vernacular* (Cambridge: Cambridge University Press, 2013); and see Beatrice Arduini, "Boccaccio and His Desk," and Brian Richardson, "Editing Boccaccio," in *The Cambridge Companion to Boccaccio*, ed. Guyda Armstrong, Rhiannon Daniels, and Stephen J. Milner (Cambridge: Cambridge University Press, 2015), 20–35 and 187–202. See also Michelangelo Zaccarello, "Boccaccio as a Scribal Editor: Book Concept, Language Innovation, Cultural Intermediation," *Heliotropia* 11, no. 1–2 (2014): 65–72.

5 Emanuele Casamassima, "Dentro lo scrittoio del Boccaccio. I codici della tradizione," *Il Ponte* 24 (1978): 730–39, rpt. in Aldo Rossi, *Il Decameron: pratiche testuali e interpretative* (Bologna: Cappelli, 1982), 253–60; 259. The translations here are mine.

6 A catchword is (usually) placed in the lower margin of the final page of a quire, and comprises the first word or words of the next quire, ensuring the correct order of quires. For useful definitions, see Marilena Maniaci, *Terminologia del libro manoscritto* (Rome and Milan: Istituto centrale per la patologia del libro, Editrice Bibliografica, 1996), 172, and fig. 99; *The Oxford Companion to the Book*, 2 vols., ed. Michael F. Suarez and H.R. Woudhuysen (Oxford: Oxford University Press, 2010), 593 (entry signed by Margaret M. Smith); Raymond Clemens and Timothy Graham, *Introduction to Manuscript Studies* (Ithaca: Cornell University Press, 2007), 49–50. For this definition of "secondary decoration" see Kathleen L. Scott, *Later Gothic Manuscripts, 1390–1490*, vol. 2 (London: Harvey Miller, 1996), 376. In the following discussion the term "catchword," with reference to MS Ham. 90, will refer both to the image decorating the word and to the word itself.

7 Because the catchwords in MS Ham. 90 are so well known, they are not reproduced here; excellent images may be consulted in Vittore Branca, ed., *Boccaccio visualizzato: narrare per parole e per immagini fra Medioevo e*

Rinascimento, 3 vols. (Turin: G. Einaudi, 1999), vol. 1, 15–18, figs. 20–32; vol. 2, 63–5, figs. 21–33; excellent reproductions are also available in *Boccaccio autore e copista*, 51 (fig. 1), and 58 (fig. 14).

8 The term "paratext," now abundantly deployed in manuscript studies, is used here with reference to Gérard Genette, *Seuils* (Paris: Éditions du Seuil, 1987; *Paratexts: Thresholds of Interpretation*, trans. Jane E. Lewin [Cambridge: Cambridge University Press, 1997]).

9 Bernhard Degenhart and Annegrit Schmitt, *Corpus der italienischen Zeichnungen, 1300–1450* (Berlin: Mann, 1968–2010), esp. vol. 1 (1968) and the addenda in vol. 2 (1980); Filippo Di Benedetto, "Considerazioni sullo Zibaldone Laurenziano del Boccaccio e restauro testuale della prima redazione del 'Faunus,'" *Italia Medioevale e Umanistica* 14 (1971): 91–129; Vittore Branca, "Interpretazioni visuali del *Decameron*," *Studi sul Boccaccio* 15 (1985–6): 87–119; Maria Grazia Ciardi Dupré dal Poggetto, "Boccaccio 'visualizzato' dal Boccaccio: Corpus dei disegni e cod. Parigino It. 482," *Studi sul Boccaccio* 22 (1994): 197–225; Vittore Branca, *Boccaccio medievale e nuovi studi sul Decameron*, rev. ed. (Florence: Sansoni, 1996), esp. "Prime interpretazioni visuali del *Decameron*," 395–432; Vittore Branca, "Introduzione: Il narrar boccacciano per immagini dal tardo gotico al primo Rinascimento," in *Boccaccio visualizzato*, vol. 1, 3–37; Maria Grazia Ciardi Dupré dal Poggetto, "L'iconografia nei codici miniati boccacciani dell'Italia centrale e meridionale," in *Boccaccio visualizzato*, vol. 2, 3–52; Maurizio Fiorilla and Patrizia Rafti, "*Marginalia* figurati e postille di incerta attribuzione in due autografi del Boccaccio," *Studi sul Boccaccio* 29 (2001): 199–213; Maria Grazia Ciardi Dupré dal Poggetto, "Il rapporto testo e immagini all'origine della formazione artistica e letteraria di Giovanni Boccaccio," in *Medioevo: immagine e racconto. Atti del Convegno internazionale di studi: Parma, 27–30 settembre 2000*, ed. Arturo Carlo Quintavalle (Milan and Parma: Electa; Università di Parma, 2003), 456–73; Maurizio Fiorilla, *Marginalia figurati nei codici di Petrarca* (Florence: Olschki, 2005), esp. 75–81; Marcello Ciccuto, "Immagini per i testi di Boccaccio: percorsi e affinità dagli zibaldoni al *Decameron*," in *Gli zibaldoni di Boccaccio: memoria, scrittura, riscrittura. Atti del seminario internazionale di Firenze-Certaldo, 26–28 aprile 1996*, ed. Michelangelo Picone and Claude Cazalé-Bérard (Florence: Cesati, 1998), 141–60; Giovanni Morello, "Disegni marginali nei manoscritti di Giovanni Boccaccio," in ibid., 161–77.

10 On these manuscripts see, respectively, the *schede* by Sandro Bertelli and Marco Cursi in *Boccaccio autore e copista*, 268–70, and 142–4.

11 One should also note the very recent discovery of a drawing of the head of Homer on the final leaf Boccaccio's copy of the work of Dante (Toledo,

Biblioteca Capitular, MS 104, 6, fol. 267v), which has been attributed to Boccaccio; see the *scheda* by Sandro Bertelli, in *Boccaccio autore e copista*, 266–68; see also Sandro Bertelli and Marco Cursi, "Novità sull'autografo Toledano di Giovanni Boccaccio. Una data e un disegno sconosciuti," *Critica del testo* 15, no.1 (2012): 287–95; Sandro Bertelli, "L'immagine di Omero nel Dante Toledano," in *Boccaccio letterato. Atti del convegno internazionale: Firenze–Certaldo, 10–12 ottobre 2013*, ed. Michaelangiola Marchiaro and Stefano Zamponi (Florence: Accademia della Crusca, 2015), 171–6; Francesca Pasut, "Una recente scoperta e il rebus di Boccaccio disegnatore," in ibid., 177–88; and cf. Stefano Martinelli Tempesta and Marco Petoletti, "Il ritratto di Omero e la firma greca di Boccaccio," *Italia Medioevale e Umanistica* 54 (2013): 399–408.

12 In particular see Lucia Battaglia Ricci, "Edizioni d'autore, copie di lavoro, interventi di autoesegesi: testimonianze trecentesche," in *Di mano propria: gli autografi dei letterati italiani. Atti del convegno internazionale di Forlì, 24–27 novembre 2008*, ed. Guido Baldassarri et al. (Rome: Salerno, 2010), 123–57, now in her *Scrivere un libro di novelle: Giovanni Boccaccio autore, lettore, editore* (Ravenna: Longo Editore, 2013), 57–96. Francesca Pasut has similarly expressed doubts about some of the attributions: for a limpid overview see her essay "Boccaccio disegnatore," in *Boccaccio autore e copista*, 51–9 as well as her "Una recente scoperta." See too Victoria Kirkham, "A Visual Legacy (Boccaccio as Artist)," in *Boccaccio: A Critical Guide to the Complete Works*, ed. Victoria Kirkham, Michael Sherberg, and Janet Levarie Smarr (Chicago: University of Chicago Press, 2013), 321–40.

13 Important descriptions of the manuscript include that by Branca in *Decameron: edizione critica secondo l'autografo hamiltoniano*, ed. Vittore Branca (Florence: L'Accademia della Crusca, 1976), xvii–liii; Emanuele Casamassima, in *Mostra di manoscritti, documenti e edizioni. Firenze – Biblioteca Medicea Laurenziana, 22 maggio–31 agosto 1975*, vol. 1 (Certaldo: A cura del Comitato promotore, 1975), 47–50 (Cat. 29); and now Marco Cursi, *Il Decameron: Scritture, scriventi, lettori. Storia di un testo* (Rome: Viella, 2007), Cat. 1, 161–4. See also Cursi's *scheda* (Cat. 22) in *Boccaccio autore e copista*, 137–8. I should like to record formally here my gratitude to the Librarian of the Staatsbibliothek zu Berlin for graciously permitting me to consult MS Ham. 90. A digital copy is now available online, at: http://digital.staatsbibliothek-berlin.de/werkansicht/?PPN=PPN725545607.

14 Vittore Branca and Pier Giorgio Ricci, *Un autografo del Decameron (Codice hamiltoniano 90)* (Padua: Cedam, 1962); Giovanni Boccaccio, *Decameron: edizione critica secondo l'autografo hamiltoniano*, ed. Vittore Branca (Florence: L'Accademia della Crusca, 1976). This text was published the same year

as *Tutte le opere di Giovanni Boccaccio*, ed. Vittore Branca, vol. 4 (Milan: Mondadori, 1964–98).

15 Giovanni Boccaccio, *Decameron: Edizione diplomatico-interpretativa dell'autografo Hamilton 90*, ed. Charles S. Singleton (Baltimore: Johns Hopkins University Press, 1974): Singleton's "Preface," ix–xiii; Armando Petrucci, "Il MS. Berlinese Hamiltoniano 90. Note codicologiche e paleografiche," 647–61; Franca Petrucci Nardelli, "Criteri e norme della presente edizione diplomatico-interpretativa," 643–5; and Giancarlo Savino, "Nota sull'edizione del *Decameron* Hamiltoniano 90," 663–6. Singleton failed to cite Branca and Ricci's 1962 study of the manuscript. See Vittore Branca's damning review in *Studi sul Boccaccio* 8 (1974): 321–9. Petrucci's description of the manuscript had appeared in a previous version as "A proposito del MS Berlinese Hamiltoniano 90. (Nota descrittiva)," *MLN* 85 (1970): 1–12.

16 Giovanni Boccaccio, *Decameron: facsimile dell'autografo conservato nel Codice Hamilton 90 della Staatsbibliothek Preussischer Kulturbesitz di Berlino*, ed. Vittore Branca (Florence: Alinari, 1975); *Decameron: edizione critica*, xvii–liii; see also Vittore Branca, *Tradizione delle opere di Giovanni Boccaccio. II. Un secondo elenco di manoscritti e studi sul testo del 'Decameron' con due appendici* (Rome: Edizioni di storia e letteratura, 1991), 211–62.

17 Branca and Ricci, *Un autografo*, 51–61, 67 (rpt. subsequently in Pier Giorgio Ricci, *Studi sulla vita e le opere del Boccaccio* [Milan: R. Ricciardi, 1985], 286–96); A.C. de la Mare, *The Handwriting of Italian Humanists* (Oxford: Printed at the University Press for the Association Internationale de Bibliophilie, 1973), 17–29; Petrucci, in *Decameron: Edizione diplomatico-interpretativa*, 652–4; Cursi, *Il Decameron*, 162. On Boccaccio's script, see also Cursi, *La scrittura*, passim, and Teresa De Robertis, "Boccaccio copista," in *Boccaccio autore e copista*, 329–35, as well as her "Il posto di Boccaccio nella storia della scrittura," in *Boccaccio letterato*, 145–70.

18 For the suggestion of a downgrade, or *declassamento*, see the *scheda* prepared by Casamassima in *Mostra di manoscritti*, vol. 1, 49.

19 Armando Petrucci, "Il libro manoscritto," in *Letteratura italiana*, ed. Alberto Asor Rosa, vol. 2: *Produzione e consumo* (Turin: G. Einaudi, 1983), 499–524; 515; for a translation see *Writers and Readers in Medieval Italy: Studies in the History of Written Culture*, trans. Charles Radding (New Haven: Yale University Press, 1995), 169–235; 189.

20 Corrado Bologna, *Tradizione e fortuna dei classici italiani* (Turin: Einaudi, 1993), 344, orig. published as "Tradizione testuale e fortuna dei classici italiani," in *Letteratura italiana*, ed. Asor Rosa, vol. 6: *Teatro, musica, tradizione dei classici* (1986), 445–928; 653. Cf. "il fatto importante è che la

struttura del trattato scientifico, quasi d'obbligo per un repertorio come le *Genealogie*, sia stata tradotta nell'opera narrativa [the important thing is that the structure of the scientific text, almost obligatory for a reference work such as the *Genealogy*, has been translated into a work of fiction]" (Casamassima, "Dentro lo scrittoio," 259).

21 Manlio Pastore Stocchi, "Su alcuni autografi del Boccaccio," *Studi sul Boccaccio* 10 (1977–8): 123–43; 139n3; Lucia Battaglia Ricci, "Leggere e scrivere novelle tra '200 e '300," in *La novella italiana: Atti del convegno di Caprarola, 19–24 settembre 1988*, 2 vols. (Rome: Salerno Editrice, 1989), vol. 1, 629–55; Battaglia Ricci, *Boccaccio* (Rome: Salerno, 2000), 143–6; and see now her *Scrivere un libro di novelle*, 27–56 (esp. 41–4).

22 On the rubrics, see Jonathan Usher, "Le rubriche del *Decameron*," *Medioevo romanzo* 10 (1985): 391–418; Antonio D'Andrea, "Le rubriche del *Decameron*," *Yearbook of Italian Studies* 3 (1973): 41–67 (rpt. in his *Il nome della storia: studi e ricerche di storia e letteratura* [Napoli: Liguori, 1982], 98–119); and Angela Milanese, "Affinità e contraddizioni tra rubriche e novelle del *Decameron*," *Studi sul Boccaccio* 23 (1995): 89–111.

23 I should like to thank Tom Stillinger and Disa Gambera for making this most felicitous connection. Their generous and enthusiastic sharing of it with me characterized the spirit of the Binghamton conference. For the transcription, see *Decameron: Edizione diplomatico-interpretativa*, 640; the translation cited is that of G.H. McWilliam, *The Decameron*, 2nd ed. (London: Penguin, 1995).

24 *Decameron*, introduction and notes by Amedeo Quondam, text edited by Maurizio Fiorilla and introductory *schede* and bibliography by Giancarlo Alfano (Milan: BUR Rizzoli, 2013). This is in contrast to the previous major editions, where they were not indicated. A valuable contribution to the study of Boccaccio's system of punctuation in Ham. 90 has been Patrizia Rafti, "'*Lumina dictionum*': Interpunzione e prosa in Giovanni Boccaccio. IV," *Studi sul Boccaccio* 29 (2001): 3–66.

25 Battaglia Ricci, *Bocccaccio*, 144–5, and her *Scrivere un libro di novelle*, 27–30.

26 Teresa Nocita, "La redazione hamiltoniana di 'Decameron' I 5. Sceneggiatura di una novella," in *Il racconto nel medioevo romanzo. Atti del Convegno, Bologna 23–24 ottobre 2000. Con altri contributi di Filologia romanza* (Bologna: Pàtron Editore, 2002), 351–66, and her "Per una nuova paragrafatura del testo del 'Decameron'. Appunti sulle maiuscole del cod. Hamilton 90 (Berlin, Staatsbibliothek Preußischer Kulturbesitz)," *Critica del testo* 2/3 (1999): 925–34. See also Francesca Malagnini, "Mondo commentato e mondo narrato nel *Decameron*," *Studi sul Boccaccio* 30 (2002): 3–124; her "Il sistema delle maiuscole nell'autografo berlinese del

Decameron e la scansione del mondo commentato," *Studi sul Boccaccio* 31 (2003): 31–69; and her "Tra i gialli dell'autografo del *Decameron*: 'Fiammetta e dioneo' (cc. 3*r* e 4*r*)," in *Boccaccio letterato*, 255–95.

27 Nocita, "La redazione hamiltoniana," 360–1.

28 Martina Mazzetti, "Boccaccio disegnatore. Per un'idea di 'arte mobile'," *Letteratura & Arte* 10 (2012): 9–37; 33, 34, and 34n1 for some very apposite reference to Aldo Rossi's work. See too Martina Mazzetti, "Boccaccio e l'invenzione del libro illustrabile: dal *Teseida* al *Decameron*," *Per Leggere* 21 (2011): 135–61. On the linguistic "finish" of the text of the *Decameron* in MS Ham. 90, of fundamental importance is Maurizio Vitale and Vittore Branca, *Il capolavoro del Boccaccio e due diverse redazioni*, 2 vols. (Venice: Istituto Veneto di Scienze, Lettere ed Arti, 2002); see also Paola Manni, *La lingua di Boccaccio* (Bologna: Il Mulino, 2016), 87–111, 113–64.

29 An early, and accurate, description of the catchwords may be found in A. Tobler, "Die Berliner Handschrift des Decameron," *Sitzungsberichte der königlich preussichen Akadamie der Wissenschaften zu Berlin* 25 (1887): 375–405; 380.

30 Degenhart and Schmitt, *Corpus der italienischen Zeichnungen*, vol. 1, i, p. 138 (Kat. 67), Taf. 114c–k; see the description of Maria Cristina Castelli in *Boccaccio visualizzato*, vol. 2, Cat. 6, 62–6 and figs. 21–32. Her transcription of the text of the catchwords is problematic, with several misreadings. They are reproduced correctly below.

31 Ciardi Dupré, "L'iconografia nei codici miniati boccacciani," 10; Castelli in *Boccaccio visualizzato*, vol. 2, 63; Branca, "Introduzione: Il narrar boccacciano per immagini," 15.

32 Branca, "Interpretazioni visuali del *Decameron*," 95; Cursi, *Il Decameron*, 42.

33 On Paul Watson's observation that the second "fork" in Tedaldo's beard is a *pentimento*, see Kirkham, "A Visual Legacy," 327 and n23.

34 Branca, "Interpretazioni visuali del *Decameron*"; his *Boccaccio medievale e nuovi studi sul Decameron* (Florence: Sansoni, 1996), 395–432, esp. 401–6, and figs. 49–61; until eventually: "Introduzione: Il narrar boccacciano per immagini," 14–20.

35 Branca famously defined the *Decameron* as the epic of the merchants ("l'epopea dei mercatanti"); see his *Boccaccio medievale*, 134–64.

36 Boccaccio, "Introduzione: Il narrar boccacciano per immagini," 15, 16.

37 Ciardi Dupré, "Boccaccio 'visualizzato' dal Boccaccio," 202.

38 Ciardi Dupré, "L'iconografia nei codici miniati boccacciani," 10.

39 Battaglia Ricci, *Scrivere un libro di novelle*, 95.

40 These are fol. 8v, the abbot (1.4.7); fol. 16v, Landolfo (2.4.13); fol. 23v, Alatiel (2.7.80); fol. 39v, Tedaldo (3.7.4); fol. 63v, armed man (5.3.13); and

fol. 87v, Rinieri (8.7.29); on fol. 47v, Filippo is represented (4.intr.17), but the narrator is the author; and on fol. 31v, Neifile, newly elected as the following day's monarch, is speaking.

41 Mazzetti, "Boccaccio disegnatore," 32. Both she and Ciardi Dupré refer to the famous Missal of San Pier Maggiore, sumptuously decorated by one of the dominant figures in Florentine illumination in the second quarter of the fourteenth century, an artist known as the Master of the Dominican Effigies (Florence, Biblioteca e Archivio del Seminario Arcivescovile Maggiore, inv. 325); see: Degenhart and Schmitt, *Corpus*, vol. 1, i, Kat. 59, Taf. 102–3 a–d. On the Master of the Dominican Effigies, see Francesca Pasut, "Florentine Illuminations for Dante's *Divine Comedy*: A Critical Reassessment," in *Florence at the Dawn of the Renaissance: Painting and Illumination, 1300–1350*, ed. Christine Sciacca (Los Angeles: John Paul Getty Museum, 2012), 155–69, esp. 165–8. For further observations on this figure see now Francesca Pasut, "Nell'antica vulgata fiorentina. Due varianti miniate della *Commedia* dantesca," a contribution to an online exhibition catalogue for *Il collezionismo di Dante in casa Trivulzio*, Milan, Biblioteca Trivulziana, 4 August–18 October 2015, available online at: http://graficheincomune.comune.milano.it/GraficheInComune/attdbs/bachecaroot/danteincasatrivulzio/approfondimenti_ita/Pasut.pdf (accessed 25 November 2017). Cf. too Manchester, Chetham's Library, MS 6713, for some highly decorated catchwords, and Kathleen L. Scott, "The Remains of a Missal: Chetham's Library MS 6713," in *Tributes to Lucy Freeman Sandler: Studies in Manuscript Illumination*, ed. Kathryn A. Smith and Carol H. Krinsky (London: Harvey Miller, 2007), 299–314.

42 Michael Camille, *Image on the Edge* (London: Reaktion, 1992), 36–47; Camille considers the example of the word "iuuencularum," under which there is a man exposing his bottom, punning on *cul*.

43 Paul Gehl, "Texts and Textures: Dirty Pictures and Other Things in Medieval Manuscripts," *Corona* 3 (1983): 68–77. I owe this reference to Mary J. Carruthers, *The Book of Memory: A Study of Memory in Medieval Culture* (Cambridge: Cambridge University Press, 1990), 344n56 (the note, however, has undergone some revision in the second edition published in 2008, and the reference to Gehl's study is excised; see there, 450n65). For unusual decorated catchwords, Carruthers makes reference to Cambridge, Trinity College, MS O. 9. 1, a mid- to late fifteenth-century manuscript collection of texts including the Brut Chronicle. See, in particular, fols. 64v and 80v for faces in profile and looking out directly at the reader. For a description of this manuscript, see John Page, *The Siege of Rouen*, ed. Joanna Bellis (Heidelberg: Universitätsverlag C. Winter, 2015), lviii–lx

(and my thanks to Dr Bellis for sharing her research on this manuscript). For some wonderful marginal faces talking, in scrolls of text, to the reader, see the (English) fifteenth-century Closworth Missal, Oxford, Bodleian Library, MS Don. b. 6, fols. 31r, 34v, 47r, 48v, and 52v.

44 The way the figures "wear" the text of the catchword is reminiscent of the three usurers wearing their coats of arms on moneybags hanging around their necks (*Inf* 17.52–81), in Florence, Biblioteca Riccardiana MS Ricc 1035 (*olim* O. II. 17), fol. 29v. See Peter H. Brieger, Millard Meiss, and Charles Southward Singleton, *Illuminated Manuscripts of the Divine Comedy*, 2 vols. (London: Routledge and Kegan Paul, 1969), vol. 1, 249–50; vol. 2, 203 plate c. The manuscript has been digitized and can be consulted at http://www.danteonline.it. These drawings have been attributed by Ciardi Dupré to Boccaccio (see her "Boccaccio 'visualizzato' dal Boccaccio," 206); see note 9 above.

45 On this manuscript see the *scheda* by Michaelangiola Marchiaro and Silvia Finazzi, in *Boccaccio autore e copista*, 339–41; on Boccaccio's marginal glosses in this manuscript see Silvia Finazzi, "Le postille di Boccaccio a Terenzio," *Italia Medioevale e Umanistica* 44 (2013): 81–133.

46 See note 10 above; cf. BML, MS Plut. 54, 32, fol. 77v (illustrated in Morello, "Disegni marginali," 173, fig. 2); and see too the *scheda* by David Speranzi and Maurizio Fiorilla in *Boccaccio autore e copista*, 341–3 (with a plate of fol. 77v reproduced on p. 342).

47 A facsimile of this manuscript is available: *Il codice Chigiano L. V. 176*, ed. Domenico De Robertis (Rome; Florence: Archivi Edizioni; Fratelli Alinari, 1975); see also Sandro Bertelli's *scheda* in *Boccaccio autore e copista*, 270–2.

48 See the *scheda* by Stefano Zamponi, in *Boccaccio autore e copista*, 300–5.

49 On this manuscript, see the *scheda* by William E. Coleman in *Boccaccio autore e copista*, 94–5; see also Giovanni Boccaccio, *Teseida delle nozze d'Emilia*, ed. Edvige Agostinelli and William Coleman (Florence: Edizioni del Galluzzo per la Fondazione Ezio Franceschini, 2015).

50 Marcello Ciccuto has spoken here of "an explicit overlapping between the identity of the writer and the artist in parodic, self-referential terms [un'esplicita sovrapposizione fra identità dello scrittore e attività disegnativa in chiave di auto-riferimento parodico]." See his "Immagini per i testi di Boccaccio," 151. Another such figure, though, is found on fol. 56v; see Casamassima, *Mostra di manoscritti*, plate IV (Cat. 61, and description on p. 79). On the manuscript, see the *scheda* by Sandro Bertelli in *Boccaccio autore e copista*, 201–2, and on 201 a plate reproduces fol. 56v.

51 Examples include Florence, Bibl. Ricc, MS Ricc. 489, fol. 53r, and 53v (Degenhart and Schmitt, *Corpus*, vol. 2, ii, p. 334, Kat. 703, Taf. 166e);

Florence, Biblioteca Medicea Laurenziana, MS Plut. 66, 1, fol. 11v, and fol. 43 (Degenhart and Schmitt, *Corpus*, vol. 2, ii, pp. 336–7, Kat. 705, Taf. 166f–g); Paris, BnF, MS Lat. 8082 fol. 4v; BnF, MS 6802, fol. 220. See the round-up in Ciardi Dupré, "Boccaccio 'visualizzato' dal Boccaccio," 198–201.

52 Meyer Schapiro, *Words, Script, and Pictures: Semiotics of Visual Language* (New York: George Braziller, 1996 [1973]), 73, 87.

53 Cursi, *Il Decameron*, 41–2.

54 See above, note 1.

55 Victor Turner and Edith Turner, *Image and Pilgrimage in Christian Culture: Anthropological Perspectives* (New York: Columbia University Press, 1978), 3.

56 Jean Vezin, "Observations sur l'emploi des réclames dans les manuscrits latins," *Bibliothèque de l'école des chartes* 125 (1967): 5–33; 5n2.

57 See Branca's introduction to *Decameron: edizione critica*, xxxiii–xxxv. For efforts to engage with this open nature of the autograph, see now Maurizio Fiorilla, "Per il testo del *Decameron*," *L'Ellisse* 5 (2010): 9–38; his "Ancora per il testo del *Decameron*," *L'Ellisse* 8 (2013): 75–90; his "Sul testo del *Decameron*: per una nuova edizione critica," in *Boccaccio letterato*, 211–37; and his text for the new BUR Rizzoli *Decameron* (see note 24 above).

58 Bologna, *Tradizione*, 353 (= "Tradizione," 659); Alberto Asor Rosa, "*Decameron*," in *Letteratura italiana: Le opere*, ed. Alberto Asor Rosa, vol. 1 (Turin: G. Einaudi, 1992), 473–591; 491.

59 Giorgio Padoan, "'Habent sua fata libelli'. Dal Claricio al Mannelli al Boccaccio," *Studi sul Boccaccio* 25 (1997): 143–212; 202–6 and 208–9; "'Habent sua fata libelli'. II. Dal Gaetano al Boccaccio: il caso del 'Filocopo,'" *Studi sul Boccaccio* 27 (1999): 19–54; 48. These essays are now reprinted in Giorgio Padoan, *Ultimi studi di filologia dantesca e boccacciana*, ed. Aldo Maria Costantini (Ravenna: Longo, 2002). The position would seem to be endorsed by Marco Cursi; see e.g., *Il Decameron*, 38.

60 Dante Alighieri, *La Commedia secondo l'antica vulgata*, ed. Giorgio Petrocchi, 2nd rpt. ed., 4 vols. (Florence: Le Lettere, 1994), vol. 4, 549–50; Dante Alighieri, *The Divine Comedy of Dante Alighieri*, ed. and trans. Robert M. Durling, intro. and notes Ronald L. Martinez and Robert M. Durling, 3 vols. (New York: Oxford University Press, 1996–2011), vol. 3, 663, 665. On this passage, see the beautiful essay by John Ahern, "Binding the Book: Hermeneutics and Manuscript Production in *Paradiso* 33," *Publications of the Modern Language Association* 97 (1982): 800–9.

61 For its support towards this research, my gratitude is warmly extended to the Department of English and Related Literature, University of York, and the Danish National Research Foundation (DNRF102ID).

2 Reading Boccaccio's Paratexts: Dedications as Thresholds between Worlds

RHIANNON DANIELS

The final book of Boccaccio's *Comedia delle ninfe fiorentine* contains the following address:

> E tu, o solo amico, e di vera amistà veracissimo essemplo, o Niccolò di Bartolo del Buono di Firenze … prendi questa rosa, tra le spine della mia avversità nata … E questa non altramenti ricevi cha da Virgilio il buono Augusto o Erennio da Cicerone, o come da Orazio il suo Mecena, prendevano i cari versi, nella memoria riducendoti l'autorità di Catone dicente: "Quando il povero amico un picciolo dono ti presenta, piacevolmente il ricevi."[1]
>
> [And you, O singular friend, who are the most genuine example of true friendship, Niccolò di Bartolo del Buono of Florence … take this rose which was born amongst the thorns of my adversity … And accept it as Augustus received beloved verses from Virgil, or as Herennius did from Cicero, or Maecenas did from Horace, while adapting in your mind the authority of Cato, who said: "When a poor friend presents you with a small gift, receive it with pleasure."]

It is clear from the phrasing of the text that this extract acts as a dedication: Boccaccio addresses his friend, Niccolò di Bartolo del Buono, directly, and with the express aim of conferring upon him the gift of his completed text of the *Comedia delle ninfe*. It is less clear from the material disposition of the text-object, however, that this is a dedication. In other words, the extract is not part of the front matter of the text, marked off within a rubricated section labelled "Dedication," but instead is embedded within the main body of the text itself; indeed it occurs towards the end. It is, at one and the same time, both a declaration and confirmation of a private relationship between two friends, and a public statement located within a published work. The text functions both as a historical witness to a message transmitted from one friend to another and as an integral part of the fictional world, where an authorial persona addresses an ideal reader who is aligned with his intentions. It is a unique instance in which a specific author dedicates his text to a specific dedicatee, and yet it is also embedded within a history of literary dedications which are signalled in the reference to the authorized dedicatory pairings of Virgil-Augustus, Cicero-Herennius, and Horace-Maecenas.

The dedicatory address from an author to his audience is thus a complex site of ontological shifts between the text and paratext, public and private spheres, history and fiction, unique instance and universalizing tradition. The instability of these transmissive texts is exploited to the full by Boccaccio, who employs a range of different techniques to address his readers, from the dedicatory address embedded within the fictional framework, as in the case cited above, to the more traditional dedicatory letter, such as that addressed to Mainardo Cavalcanti, recipient of the second redaction of the *De casibus virorum illustrium*.[2] Within Boccaccio scholarship, these addresses are often read for *content* in order to help us interpret the work, but less attention is paid to the precise nature of their *form* and *function*.[3] Thus, there are various kinds of terminology in operation to refer to the same parts of the text: for example, the opening section of the *Decameron* is variously described as a dedication, proem, preface, or prologue.[4]

My aim is to explore the complexity of the reading process by studying the role and nature of the dedication derived from two different perspectives: first, from that of the author, via a selection of texts penned by Boccaccio, and the representation of his authorial personae who address both fictional characters and historical figures; and second, from the perspective of a select group of consumers of Boccaccio's works, via the editors of early sixteenth-century editions of the *Decameron*. This approach is rooted in the recognition that our understanding of the function of the dedication is historically situated and will inevitably be interpreted by different readers at different times and in different receiving contexts. Alongside a historical and historicizing perspective that is centred on Boccaccio, I will link this analysis of the function of the dedication to a broader and more theoretical discussion about the way in which we choose to define parts of the text and text-object in current literary criticism. As we have already glimpsed, by looking at the dedicatory portion of the *Comedia delle ninfe*, the dedication involves a linguistic transaction between the author and the reader, which can hover between the world of fiction (the dedication to Niccolò is embedded within a fictional text and voiced by the Narrator of that text) and the world outside it (Niccolò is a historical figure and friend of Boccaccio, a historical author). Is the dedication therefore a text or a paratext?

This question has specific resonances within Boccaccio studies: we have reached a period in the history of Boccaccio criticism where it has become common to question the idea that we can automatically overlay the historical author on to his fictional authorial personae,[5] but the lesson of the dedication to Niccolò has already suggested that these two apparently separate figures can operate within the same text. Therefore, in order to avoid an unproductive critical reaction that does not allow the historical author and his or her fictional voice ever to meet, it is timely to scrutinize the borders of the text with a careful eye. Since these questions and concerns involve both literary analysis and reception history, I will begin by arguing for a new, integrated approach to the study of dedications that combines two theoretical approaches – narratology and material culture – which are usually treated separately.[6] In this way I aim to draw on structuralist readings in order to describe the rules governing the way in which dedicatory texts operate, as well as taking into consideration the importance of the cultural and historical context in which texts are produced.

Dedicatory Texts and Contexts

The relationship between the world of the text and the world outside it has come into greater focus in recent decades within literary theory in general, which has seen a move from scrutiny of the author and his or her intentions towards a more recent concentration on the role of the reader and his or her response. This, in turn, has led to an increased flourishing of interest in charting the transmission process of the text as it moves between the author and the reader, as that process is figured both within the text and outside it.[7] Accordingly, within the world of fiction, literary scholars are no longer concerned to distinguish only between the historical author and the narratorial voices performing authorial roles, but also to plot the variety and richness of different types of audience members receiving the narrative act as it is performed. Thus, narrators and implied authors have come to be complemented by narratees and implied readers, and supplemented by a huge range of different terms used to describe fictional audiences, such as mock, invoked, intended, ideal, and inscribed.[8] Outside the world of the text, interest in authorial intention has been overlaid, on the one hand, with a concern to trace the production context of texts among a wide array of figures framing and disseminating the author's text, such as scribes, printers, editors, and publishers, and on the other hand, with the social and cultural status of those reading texts.

Of fundamental importance to my conception of the dedicatory text in its context is an understanding of the text as a form of communication. The principle by which a text is figured as a mediating form between author and reader, sender and receiver, producer and consumer, brings literary theories concerned with the world of fiction into contact with methods for reconstructing the history of the book, as both of these approaches emphasize the centrality of communication. Wayne Booth opens his now classic book on the rhetorical approach to formalism, *The Rhetoric of Fiction*, by framing narrative fiction as a communicative act between author and audience:

> My subject is the technique of non-didactic fiction, viewed as the art of communicating with readers – the rhetorical resources available to the writer of epic, novel, or short story as he tries, consciously or unconsciously, to impose his fictional world upon the reader.[9]

In a work of fiction like the *Decameron*, the communication process is easily visible and has been amply charted by formalist readings. Boccaccio's use of multiple narrators, from the Primary Narrator who says he is writing for the consolation of women in love, to the *brigata*, to the characters within the *novelle* who tell their own stories – each of whom addresses a particular audience – foregrounds the processes of telling stories and receiving them in the correct manner. The *Decameron* therefore mirrors in a fictional setting the external, historical processes of production and reception which must take place if this text is to be produced by its historical author and consumed by a reading public.[10] The importance of communicative processes has been similarly stressed within the field of material culture by scholars revising the traditional bibliographer's emphasis on describing the parts of the book in order to highlight the influence of producers and consumers upon the form of the books.[11] The communications circuit devised by Robert Darnton in order to study the circulation of books within society became an essential starting-point for historians of the book.[12] The fundamental dialectic between author and reader continues to be recognized in more recent studies. For example, in the context of his work on the printed paratext, Marco Santoro comments: "l'autore scrive testi che non sono opere fino al momento in cui non sono lette: scrive testi, in altre parole, che intanto divengono tali allorché trovano un destinatario [authors write texts which don't become works until the moment in which they are read: authors write texts, in other words, which only become such when they find a reader]."[13]

Within these systems that emphasize the role of communication, pairings of "author and reader," "production and reception," and "fictional and historical" risk becoming binaries which suggest that each component in the pair implicitly resists the other; in other words, an impression is created that these are two separate elements existing in their own spheres which cannot overlap. For example, diagrams drawn by narratologists which set out the roles of narrators and narratees encourage us to see them as entirely separate in a way that is not necessarily intended by the historical author.[14] Indeed, in the context of the *Decameron*, Boccaccio seems to delight in setting out a highly complex and differentiated structure of narrators and audience members seemingly confined within different layers of the narrative, which he then subverts by allowing the boundaries dividing them to be crossed. This happens when, for example, the Primary Narrator enters the diegesis and becomes a temporary member of the *brigata* who tells his own story at the beginning of Day Four, or when the *novellieri* reach beyond the diegesis and appear to address the "donne oziose [idle ladies]" of the *Proemio*.[15] As the boundaries within the world of the text can be crossed and re-crossed at will, so the boundary between the fictional and non-fictional world also appears less impermeable than first anticipated when we consider audiences within the *Decameron*. The Narrator interrupts the opening of Day Four to defend his work against criticisms levelled at him, and scholars are still divided over whether these criticisms are invented by the Narrator himself in order to demonstrate his own rhetorical prowess, highlighting their fictional origins, or whether this moment can be supported by material evidence for continuous publication and therefore read as evidence for the intrusion of a historical audience into the fictional text.[16]

In order to avoid seeing the relationship between author and reader, production and reception, and the world of the text and the world outside it as oppositional binaries, it seems more productive to emphasize the "blended" nature of the transmission process. Jack Selzer provides a useful summary of the ways in which the boundaries between authors and readers, fictional and non-fictional worlds, can blur and elide:

> In practice the concept of audience is dynamic: it is their experience with addressing real readers and reading real texts that tells writers what to include and how; it is in terms of the reader in the text and the author's intention that real audiences situate themselves (usually) during the act of reading; and it is with reference to real people and to accomplish authorial aims that texts create their fictional readers. Intention and understanding are two ends of the act of reading that meet in a text.[17]

What Selzer ignores in this otherwise valuable visualization of a dynamic audience function is the fundamental role played by the material form. Sandwiched between the fictional world of the text and the non-fictional, historical world lies the text-object. Selzer's "text" cannot be accessed by a real audience unless it is clothed within a container (whether that is made of the voice, vellum, paper, a screen, or other transmitter). There can be a meeting of "intention and understanding" at a textual level between the author and his or her intended or ideal audiences, and/or any fictional audiences, but the real reader as an agent in his or her own right can only come to the text via its physical medium. The fictional world also recognizes that it can only be successful (in other words, be consumed by historical readers) if it exists in material form. Boccaccio's narrators frequently comment on the process of writing and publishing, and the *congedo* metaphorically prefigures the transmission process.[18] In this context, the call to recognize materiality in current literary criticism is not a project of anachronistic back-projection. Boccaccio is supremely attuned to the material dimension, not only as an author but also as an experienced compiler and commentator, and as a scribe, rubricator, and illustrator of his own and others' works.[19]

Dedications as Unstable Locations within the Paratext

In the same way that reader-response criticism understands each reading act to be a unique experience created by the reader, so book historians read each physical copy of a text, anchored into its material container, as the function of its unique experience, shaped by the particular circumstances of those involved in its production and conservation and the specificity of its presentation, which includes the materials used to construct it, and the design and content of the paratexts which are chosen to enhance it. Gérard Genette published his seminal work on paratexts in 1987, which defined them as fundamentally liminal spaces where the worlds of fiction and non-fiction can collide (the original French title of his work on paratexts is *Seuils*, meaning thresholds or doorways): an "'undefined' zone between the inside and the outside, a zone without any hard and fast boundary on either the inward side (turned towards the text) or the outward side (turned towards the world's discourse about the text)." Genette goes on to describe the paratext's mediating function as a space that brings together author and reader, playing also on the pairing production/reception:

> Indeed, this fringe, always the conveyor of a commentary that is authorial or more or less legitimated by the author, constitutes a zone between text and off-text, a zone not only of transition but also of *transaction*: a privileged place of a pragmatics and a strategy, of an influence on the public, an influence that – whether well or poorly understood and achieved – is at the service of a better reception for the text and a more pertinent reading of it.[20]

The dedication is included within Genette's system of paratexts as a text that is on the borders of the world of the text, but nevertheless outside it, and he devotes a chapter to explaining its function. The study of paratexts has now become widespread enough to incorporate an increasing quantity of critical modifications to Genette's original definitions, particularly in the context of medieval and early modern studies, where the material under scrutiny is often very different from the nineteenth-century French fiction with which Genette was most familiar.[21] However, in the context of the dedication, Genette's distinction (inherent within the French noun "dédicace") between the practice of dedicating "the material reality of a single copy" of a work (the letter of transmission) and that of dedicating "the ideal reality of the work itself" (the dedicatory letter) remains a useful starting point.[22] Both of these dedicatory functions exist in manuscript and print culture, and involve the epistolary form addressed to an individual reader, although a broader, plural audience lurking behind the dedicatee is implicitly recognized, even if the letter of transmission is intended as a private piece of correspondence. This is true of dedications circulating within scribal culture, and confirmed within print culture where hundreds or even thousands of readers would potentially access dedicatory letters appended to each copy of an edition. Brian Richardson writes:

> dedications to individuals normally imply an unspoken second person plural: that is, what an author is saying directly to and about a dedicatee is also being communicated to others who are reading, as it were, over the author's shoulder. In looking at what these paratexts have to say, we must bear in mind that they were habitually used by authors to address single and multiple readers simultaneously, in a complex process of self-fashioning.[23]

The same work could also be copied again, or reprinted, and addressed to a different person. Multiple dedications addressed to different dedicatees could even accrue within the same edition.

The dedication arose from a practical need for authors to be remunerated for their work. The dedicatee would be expected to confer a gift on the author in return for the prestige of being named in a dedicatory letter. Thus, dedicatees are often wealthy and well connected, because alongside the material gift, the author might also hope to gain an increased social standing for him- or herself, and an increased level of authorization for the book. The contents of the dedicatory letter reflect its function, commonly employing hyperbolic praise of the dedicatee (and sometimes his or her family), and with the author contrasting his or her own efforts with an equally excessive degree of modesty and humility.

A preface or proem should be distinguished from a dedication because its main aim is to "explain the nature and purpose of the work and justify choices of subject-matter or language, thus dealing in advance with possible criticisms and directing the reader towards a certain way of approaching the work."[24] There can be a degree of overlap between dedications and prefaces, however, with some prefatory functions bleeding into the dedicatory letter. Thus, the "classic" structure of the printed dedication found in the sixteenth-century editions surveyed by Santoro includes spelling out the importance of the topic.[25]

How do these definitions of the dedication and preface apply to addresses to the reader authored by Boccaccio? One of Boccaccio's early biographers, Leonardo Bruni, noted that Boccaccio was disdainful of patronage: "Tenero fu di natura e disdegnoso, la qual cosa guastò molto i fatti suoi, perché né da sé aveva, né d'essere appresso a' príncipi e signori ebbe sofferenza [he was delicate by nature and disdainful, which damaged his affairs very much, because he did not have by him, and could not suffer to have near him, princes or noblemen]."[26] Bruni may well have developed this opinion after reading the passage in *Genealogia* 15.13.3 in which Boccaccio argues strenuously that he was commissioned to write the work, and has not simply taken it upon himself to dedicate it to a King in order to elevate his own position. In this context Boccaccio writes: "In hoc me superbum Confiteor, si superbia dicenda hec est; in talibus nisi Deo celi honorem seu titulum irrequisitus inferrem, et hoc etiam non omnibus requirentibus exhiberem [In this I confess I am by nature proud, if you can call this pride: in such cases [i.e., the dedication of books], I should uninvited offer the honour and title only to God; and nor would I give it to everyone that asked for it]."[27] He goes on to argue that dedications are of more benefit to the dedicatee desirous of glory than they are to the author:

> Non equidem magnorum ducum nomina claros scriptores faciunt, imo potius ipsi reges scriptorum opere cognoscuntur a posteris. Insuper si approbandum sit opus, quid illi adiectum regis nomen potest autoritatis afferre, aut bene merito autori glorie superaddere? Et, si improbandum sit, quo iure poterit prescriptio illa fecisse probabile, aut notam autori iniectam abstergere? Decus igitur et gloriam agenti approbatio virorum illustrium affert, non regii nominis ascriptio. Ego autem, ut iterum dixerim, adeo superbe obstinatus sum, ut nisi Deo glorie, cuius ascribenda sunt omnia, unius carminis tantum decus … nisi rogatus, aut si amicus esset, ascriberem. (15.13.8–9; vol. 7–8, pt. 2, 1578–80)

> [It is not the names of great leaders that make authors famous; rather, kings are known to posterity with the help of authors. Besides, if the work is really praiseworthy, what increase of authority can a king's name give it, or what reputation add to an author who rests on his own merits? And if it is undeserving, how can the dedication rightly make it otherwise, or purge the blot on the author's reputation? It is the approval of great men that brings honor and glory to the performer, not the inscription of a royal name. But, to repeat, I am too proud and obstinate to dedicate even one poem to anybody unrequested, except to God, to whose glory all works should be ascribed ... only a request, or friendship, would move me.][28]

These comments were made in the context of a work which Boccaccio is keen to stress he was commissioned to write by Hugo, King of Jerusalem and Cyprus. The *Genealogia* opens with an address to King Hugo that is often identified as a dedication, although it does not take the form of a letter. The work's most recent translator, Jon Solomon, writes: "Boccaccio begins with a general Preface (*Prohemium*) *dedicated* to King Hugo IV of Jerusalem and Cyprus" (my emphasis).[29] The opening rubric suggests a dedicatory formula ("Genealogia deorum gentilium ad Ugonem Inclitum Ierusalem et Cypri regem secundum Iohannem Boccaccium de Certaldo [Genealogy of the Pagan Gods for the Illustrious Hugo King of Jerusalem and Cyprus by Giovanni Boccaccio of Certaldo]"), and the King is praised both by the authorial voice and through the figure of his officer, Donnino, sent to persuade Boccaccio to take up the task of compiling the *Genealogia*. In many respects, however, this opening address only pays lip-service to the dedicatory function and in fact resembles a proem more closely, preparing the reader to understand the nature of the work he or she is about to read and the methodology used to assemble it.

Boccaccio's reluctance to dedicate his works to anyone unless requested, set out in the *Genealogia*, seems to be borne out in his wider practice as an author, as only five of his works contain addresses to historical figures. Most of these could be described as expressions of friendship, and only two addresses use the epistolary format.[30] The circumstances surrounding the decision to dedicate the *De mulieribus claris* to Andrea Acciaiuoli suggest that, of all the addresses penned by Boccaccio, this was the one most calculated to result in a tangible practical benefit for the author. Boccaccio had been invited to Naples by Andrea's brother, and was keen to curry favour with the Acciaiuoli family in order to secure a permanent residence in the city.[31] Virginia Brown writes:

> The greater part of the *Famous Women*, it will be remembered, was already written before the arrival of Niccolò Acciaiuoli's invitation [to Naples] and the likelihood is that Boccaccio was compelled by circumstances to present his hosts with the one original work he had available at the moment, whether or not it was completely suitable to his purposes.[32]

In other words, this appears to have been a dedication written for a specific purpose, which was not conceived as an integral part of the original fictional work. It was added after the work had begun, and remains distinct from the rest of the text in the autograph manuscript (which also includes a preface and authorial conclusion), marked out with a separate rubric and decorated initial.[33] The text of the address to

Andrea is clearly distinguished from the proem that follows, which is concerned with setting out the reasons behind the genesis of the work and defining the decisions made regarding the contents, and contains conventional tropes reflecting the dedicatory function, such as praise for the dedicatee contrasted with modesty on the part of the dedicator; for example: "precorque, inclita mulier, per sanctum pudicitie nomen, quo inter morales plurimum emines, grato animo munusculum scholastici hominis suscipias [illustrious lady, I beg you in the name of holy modesty, for which you are preeminent among mortals, accept with favor this small gift from a scholar]."[34] Critics keen to read the dedication as a pro-feminist text have commented that the praise accorded to Andrea is of a rather ambiguous nature, as she is the second choice after Queen Johanna of Naples, and women are clearly seen as secondary to men:[35]

> adverterem videremque quod sexui infirmiori natura detraxerit, id tuo pectori Deus sua liberalitate miris virtutibus superinfuserit atque suppleverit, et eo, quo insignita es nomine, designari voluerit – cum *andres* Greci quod latine dicimus *homines* nuncupent – te equiparandam probissimis quibuscunque, etiam vetustissimis, arbitratus sum.
>
> [as I saw that what nature has denied the weaker sex God has freely instilled in your breast and complemented with marvelous virtues, to the point where he willed you to be known by the name you bear (*andres* being in Greek the equivalent of the Latin word for "men") – considering all this, I felt that you deserved comparison with the most excellent women anywhere, even among the ancients.] (Dedication, 5, pp. 4–5)

However, in an analogous manner, more than half of the dedication to Mainardo Cavalcanti, which was appended to the second redaction of the *De casibus*, consists of listing the many possible dedicatees Boccaccio considered among pontiffs, caesars, kings, or princes, before finally arriving at Mainardo: "et quasi desperans ... in laudabile consilium incidi: nemini scilicet, quantumcunque eminenti atque prefulgido principi, posse quid fidentius quam amico commicti [and, almost desperate ... the laudable thought fell into my mind that to no one, even if he were an exalted and magnificent prince, could I recommend it more confidently than to a friend]."[36] The praise for Mainardo's intellect is similarly backhanded according to modern sensibilities: "Preterea is, esto plene phylosophicis eruditus non sit, amantissimus tamen studiorum est, et probatorum hominum precipuus cultor, atque eorum operum solertissimus indagator [What is more, even though he is not fully learned in philosophy, nevertheless he is a great lover of studies and an especial cultivator of experts and a zealous investigator of their works]" (Dedication, 15, p. 7). Comparing the two dedications to Andrea and Mainardo, we can therefore begin to discern Boccaccio's dedicatory style, which can then assist with the interpretation of their contents.

Although the dedication to Andrea was not conceived as part of the first draft of *De mulieribus*, after its composition during the fourth redactional stage,[37] it nevertheless must have become – from Boccaccio's perspective – consciously or not, a more deeply embedded part of the collection of biographies; it certainly seems to have been viewed as such within the subsequent manuscript and printed tradition, which reproduces it as part of the canonical text. The presentation of the text-object reveals how design choices can simultaneously separate and bring together the parts of the text. For example, in the first printed edition of *De mulieribus* (Ulm, 1473), the dedication is presented as a text that is distinct from the preface which follows it, with its own rubric and decorated initial marking the opening, and the rubric for the preface signalling the transition to another part of the text. The use of the same style and size of typeface, and woodcut initials of the same size and style, however, mark these two text-types – dedication and preface – as belonging to the same world. The rubric for the dedication is also listed at the beginning of the edition in the table of contents, together with the rubrics for each chapter.[38] As an authorial paratext (an additional text written by the author of the main text, rather than by a different figure such as an editor or printer), the dedication can become absorbed into the fictional space of the main text, and be considered part of the narrative "semantically." As H. Porter Abbott comments:

> the division between narrative and world is not quite so neat. Written narratives usually come packaged in additional words and sometimes even pictures – chapter headings, running heads, tables of contents, prefaces, afterwords, illustrations, book jackets (often with blurbs) ... All of this tangential material can inflect on our experience of the narrative, sometimes subtly, sometimes deeply. So in this sense all of this material *is* part of the narrative.[39]

The voicing of the dedication also binds it together with the preface that follows, since there is a first-person narrator in each text. The historical reader might interpret each of those narrating voices as the voice of the same historical author, or take the view that both voices must be separated from the historical author. In either case, the worlds of fiction and history blend into each other (albeit from different directions: history into fiction; fiction into history) and there seems to be less urgency to treat the dedication as a "historical" text that is separate from the world of fiction.

The dedication to Mainardo Cavalcanti, penned to accompany the second redaction of the *De casibus* in 1373, is the only other example of an address to a historical reader composed within the format of the dedicatory epistle.[40] It is clear from both the contents of the letter of transmission to Mainardo and its material presentation that it was intended by Boccaccio to function as a paratext, in other words, as separate from the text of the *De casibus*, and possibly for the eyes of Mainardo alone, as copies of the first redaction of the text of *De casibus* had circulated for several years before the dedication was composed.[41] Although it is fairly long, the letter does not stray into the realms of a proem or preface, because it does not introduce the contents of the text in any detail, but limits itself to explaining the process by which Mainardo was selected as the appropriate dedicatee. In material terms, it is clearly set apart from the proem, which is marked with its own rubric and includes the word "Prohemium" within a rubric addressing Mainardo.[42] However, some scribes and readers evidently considered the letter to be an important adjunct to the text, and included it in manuscripts copied from the first redaction, as well as circulating it widely in witnesses deriving from the second redaction.[43] In this manner, the dedication to Mainardo quickly became similar in status to an authorial paratext such as the "Prohemium," and began to edge towards the realms of the fictional text despite its non-fictional origins.

The addresses to historical readers found within the *Comedia delle ninfe* and *Buccolicum carmen* appear to be first and foremost expressions of disinterested friendship, made without expectation of material gain, beyond the strengthening of social and political networks. They do not follow the usual encomiastic formula of the dedicatory epistle, but are more restrained in tone, preferring to play down the greatness of the gift rather than heap praise on the recipient. Both of these addresses are embedded within the fictional world, and seem to have been intended to function as parts of the narrative, rather than being conceived as authorial paratexts. Eclogue 16 is a dialogue between two figures named "Appenninus" – whom Boccaccio identifies in his letter to Fra Martino da Signa as his friend, Donato degli Albanzani – and "Angelus," identified as the text itself. Angelus speaks on behalf of Cerretius, who is Boccaccio, named after Certaldo. Thus, both the dedicator and dedicatee of the *Buccolicum carmen* are veiled behind pseudonyms, unlike the *Comedia*, which blends the voice of historical author and fictional narrator but gives the dedicatee his historical name.

Other texts are dedicated to fictional characters but use the form of dedicatory epistles in a parody of the historical paratext. While Boccaccio may not have envisaged his dedicatory letter to Mainardo being absorbed into the fictional world of the *De casibus*, he seems to have enjoyed deliberately playing with notions of fiction and history in the *Teseida*. Here, the dedicatory address forms a discrete text distinguished from the opening sonnet and first book, like those letters addressed to Andrea and Mainardo, such that it is commonly described as a dedicatory letter.[44] In this case, however, the dedicatee is the fictional Fiammetta, and the voice of the dedicator that of the fictional poet-lover who narrates the whole work, so there can be no expectation of material gain within the historical world. Indeed, the contents of the dedication read more like a proem than a dedication, with the narrator's love for Fiammetta presented as part of the fictional context for the decision to write and for the choice of subject matter. The address includes a detailed description of the contents set out in the manner of the *ordo libri* that formed part of the academic prologue, thereby forming part of the method by which Boccaccio authorized his vernacular work.[45] However, the dedicatory function is unexpectedly underlined in the autograph manuscript of the *Teseida*, which includes a miniature visualizing the act of dedicating a work, with the author on his knees presenting his work to a lady. Since no other letter of transmission associated with this manuscript has survived, the miniature is usually interpreted as a visual illustration of the opening address, and therefore the lady is understood to be Fiammetta, investing an integral part of the fictional text with paratextual qualities.[46]

The same playful use of fictional and historical voicing takes place in the *Amorosa visione*, whose three acrostic sonnets contain a dedicatory inscription:

> Cara Fiamma, per cui 'l core ò caldo,
> que' che vi manda questa Visione
> Giovanni è di Boccaccio da Certaldo.

[Dear Flame, through whom my heart takes heat,
he who sends You this Vision
is John of Boccaccio from Certaldo.][47]

As in the *Teseida*, the fictional Fiammetta is being addressed, but whereas her name is concealed further within the fiction with only an allusion to her already fictive name ("Cara Fiamma"), this is the only place within his works where Boccaccio fully reveals himself as a historical author by explicitly naming himself (Giovanni è di Boccaccio da Certaldo),[48] once again deliberately blurring the boundaries between fiction and history.

I will finish this consideration of the dedicatory function in Boccaccio's works with a brief mention of the *Decameron*, as this work will be the focus of the final section of this article. The *Decameron* opens with a proemial text which is marked as a proem in the autograph manuscript,[49] and conforms to a proem in its contents, which set out the motivations and aims of the work. Its dedicatory inscription to the fictional audience of "donne oziose" for whom the narrator says he is composing the text means that it is often loosely referred to as a dedication.[50] However, despite some possible divergence over terminology, and – historically – some divergence over whether we hear in the Proem the voice of the historical author or that of the fictional narrator, criticism dating from the twentieth century, at least, is content to read the Proem as an integral part of the text known as the "*Decameron*." The idea of publishing an edition that excises the Proem and begins from the first day has, as far as I am aware, never received any support. It could be argued, however, that this position seems unimaginable, not necessarily because the text could not support the excision, but because of the nature of the interpretive community in which we read Boccaccio. In an interpretive community removed from ours by several centuries, Guyda Armstrong has shown how seventeenth-century English translators of Boccaccio were unclear about which elements of the *Decameron* constituted the source text, and therefore "after the first and second editions of Volume I [of the 1620 edition], the *Proemio* disappears, while the authorial conclusion is nowhere to be found,"[51] demonstrating that what readers view as belonging to the world of fiction or operating outside it in relation to authorial dedications depends on interpretive "habitus," or convention, as much as the contents or the physical signs marking out the text.

The process can also happen in reverse: authorial paratexts can disappear, while additional paratexts authored by persons other than the originating author get absorbed and recycled into the text-object. Thus Armstrong describes how the 1620 translation

> contains three additional texts: the Epistle Dedicatory, which introduces the text as a whole and precedes the translated text at the beginning of Volume I ... the translator's second Dedication, which forms part of the front-matter of the second volume ... and the printer's address "To the Reader" ... these (explicit) editorial paratexts are quickly adopted as a constituent part of the canonical text, and are reproduced in all the subsequent editions of the first translation.[52]

The authors of these additional dedicatory texts – the translator and printer – are clearly distinguishable from the fictional world, but dedications are accepted as a "normal" and even appealing part of the text-object, bestowing an element of prestige on the owner of the book as much as on the editor or printer who composed the dedication.

The Editor as Mediator

Thus far, I have focused on the function of the dedication written by Boccaccio, and some of the ways in which this paratext has been read. I would like to finish by looking in more detail at dedications written by others involved in the production process of the text-object: in this case, editors of *Decamerons* printed in Italy in the early sixteenth century. We have already seen how the dedication is a paratext on the borders of the text and off-text. The editor occupies a similarly slippery mediating role between author and reader: his or her role is to shape the container holding the text written by the author, and, in some cases, to add to it with additional [para]texts of his or her own. The way in which the editor chooses to present the author's text will naturally be influenced by a subtle blend of personal taste, the modes and conventions of the culture in which the editor is operating, and expectations of the cultural tastes of the type of reader for whom the editor is presenting the text. Overlaying these forces is the commercial drive to sell the commodity being produced. As well as acting on behalf of the author, therefore, the editor is first and foremost a reader, or "hyper-reader." Santoro writes:

> l'editore iperlettore, come qualsiasi altro lettore, è condizionato dai propri gusti, i quali lo spingono ora a valorizzare ora a sacrificare una serie di elementi. Le sue scelte quindi non solo non sono neutre ma altresì sono,

rispetto a quelle del lettore commune, più o meno vistosamente vincolanti, giacché possono incidere sia sull'autore con consigli e suggerimenti (talvolta direttive) di modifiche (non sempre condivise), sia sulla struttura del prodotto concluso.[53]

[the hyper-reader editor, like any other kind of reader, is conditioned by his own tastes, which drive him to appreciate a set of elements one moment and sacrifice them the next. His choices therefore are not only not neutral but likewise are (with respect to those of the general reader) more or less obviously binding, in as much as they can influence both the author with advice and suggestions for changes (which are sometimes obligatory but not always shared), and the structure of the finished product.]

The editor is thus a Janus-like figure: as a reader, he or she looks backwards towards the author as the originating source of the text; and as an editor, he or she must look forward towards the new set of readers who will be attracted to the new edition. As the creator of new [para] texts, the editor is both an author and a reader.

The earliest editions of the *Decameron*, produced from c. 1470 onwards, are relatively bare of paratextual material. Editorial time spent on producing an accurate and reliable text was kept to a minimum, with many printers probably dispensing with the need to employ an editor altogether and simply reprinting the text of a previous edition with minimal changes to presentation style.[54] The first editions that include an editorial preface appeared in 1516, and paved the way for all subsequent sixteenth-century editions of the *Decameron* printed in Italy to include an address to the reader authored by an editor or printer-publisher.[55] These vary in kind between dedications written as letters and addressed to single, named, historical individuals, prefaces written in the form of a letter but addressed to an unnamed reader or group of readers (e.g., the "gentili et valorose donne" addressed by Nicolò Delfino, and included in editions printed in 1516, 1525, and 1526), and much shorter notes to the (unspecified) reader (often addressed as "A gli lettori"). These latter have an unadorned practical function, such as explaining why particular spellings were chosen, how the word list included in the edition was constructed, and other brief notes describing the system of editing. Dedicatory letters and prefaces share the same concerns for authorizing the volume as would an author, and therefore adhere to the rhetorical conventions governing dedication writing, such as hyperbolic praise for the dedicatee. Notes to the reader, on the other hand, are the least personal and most perfunctory form of address. By the middle of the sixteenth century, editions of the *Decameron* were crammed full of all kinds of paratextual material, often including dedicatory letters to specific individuals alongside more general notes to the collective readership. Here, I will focus on only two editions, printed in 1522 and 1535, which provide valuable insights into the mediating functions of the editorial dedication.

The 1522 edition of the *Decameron* was printed in Venice by Aldo Manuzio's father-in-law, Andrea Torresani, and Andrea's two sons. One of these sons, who styles himself Francesco "Asolano," authors the dedication to Roberto Magio, an apostolic protonotary. Francesco follows the classic topos in dedication writing of the author who has to be persuaded to publish his work, making it very clear that it was the dedicatee himself who pushed Francesco to finish the editing work that Aldo had left unfinished at his death:

> Et certamente non era mio intendimento, tra che per la irrecuperabile perdita di lui anchora tutto stordito mi trovava, tra che per le molte altre occupationi mie mal agevole sentivami, di recare al disiderato fine questa sua principiata fatica, se voi ... non m'haveste punto.[56]

> [And, as I found myself still dazed by the irretrievable loss of him, and not feeling at ease with my many other jobs, it certainly would not have been my intention to bring this labour, which he had begun, to the desired end, if you ... had not compelled me to do it.]

The dedication continues with a justification of subject matter, both in terms of Boccaccio's use of the vernacular language and in terms of its contents, which the *Decameron*'s narrator had already recognized could be accused of being frivolous and lacking in moral weight. Francesco writes:

> Ne dovete sdegnare che da me sotto 'l nome vostro compiuta & a voi dirizzata sia, parendovi peraventura, per esser opera in volgar lingua iscritta; & che in se cose piacevoli & giocose anzi che no contiene, non molto al stato & professione vostra convenevole. (fol. a1v)

> [If by chance it seems to you not especially suitable for your status and profession, since this work is written in the vernacular language and contains within it things which are pleasing and playful, you should not

> scorn the fact that it is accomplished by me in your name and dedicated to you.]

The degree to which this passage reflects genuine anxiety about the status of the text is difficult to determine, but what comes to the fore, as Francesco's argument progresses, is the manner in which the editor has chosen to frame his dedication with authorial strategies used in the world of the *Decameron*, thereby blurring the distinction between text and paratext. Thus, in order to argue for the inherent flexibility of the vernacular, Francesco sets Boccaccio's work within an established and authoritative context of other vernacular authors:

> Percio che, dove la verita con giudicioso occhio riguardar vogliamo, non a minor loda veggiamo hoggi di arecarsi lo elegante & dottamente parlar volgare; che il latino, ne con minor dignita & leggiadria con esso potersi spiegare tutti e nostri concetti; che col latino si faccia, & cosi bene potersi con esso trattare tutti glialtri segreti, & profondi misteri & di Philosophia & di Theologia & d'ogni altra scienza, come in altra lingua che sia, far si possa: siccome veggiamo & lo autore istesso in molti luoghi havere fatto, et Dante, et Petrarcha, & dopo questi il Conte Giovanni Pico della Mirandola; nel comento sopra la Canzone d'amore di Girolamo Benivieni Fiorentino; secondo lo intendimento de Platonici; & molti altri assai. (fol. a1v)

> [Since, where we wish to consider the truth with a judicious eye, we see today the elegant and learned vernacular language bearing no little praise; as it is with Latin, so it is that the vernacular is capable of explaining all our concepts with no less dignity and gracefulness; as it is with Latin, so it is that the vernacular can treat all the other secrets and profound mysteries of both philosophy and theology and every other science in whatever other language they are expressed: as we can see that our author himself has done in many places, as well as Dante and Petrarch, and after these authors, the count Giovanni Pico della Mirandola in his commentary on the Florentine Girolamo Benivieni's *Song of Love*, according to the understanding of the Platonists; and very many others.]

The same strategy is used by the Narrator of the *Decameron*, who rebuts his critics in the Introduction to Day Four by pointing out that his practice of writing about women is continuing a tradition already established by reputable poets:

> E quegli che contro alla mia età parlando vanno, mostra mal che conoscano che, perché il porro abbia il capo bianco, che la coda sia verde: a' quali, lasciando il motteggiar da l'un de' lati, rispondo che io mai a me vergogna non reputerò infino nello stremo della mia vita di dover compiacere a quelle cose alle quali Guido Cavalcanti e Dante Alighieri già vecchi e messer Cino da Pistoia vecchissimo onor si tennero, e fu lor caro il piacer loro.[57]
>
> [As for those who keep harping on about my age, they are clearly unaware of the fact that although the leek's head is white, it has a green tail. But joking apart, all I would say to them is that even if I live to be a hundred, I shall never feel any compunction in striving to please the ones who were so greatly honoured, and whose beauty was so much admired, by Guido Cavalcanti and Dante Alighieri in their old age, and by Cino da Pistoia in his dotage.]

Francesco defends the status of Boccaccio's *novelle* by underlining their moral utility:

> Meno anchora da voi sprezzata esser dee, perche Novelle racconti, percio che, & per tai novelle, dove leggendole dirittamente a quelle l'arco dell'intelletto vogliamo tendere, & a che fine elle iscritte fussero riguardare, & che seguire; & che fuggire; & da che guardarci; & a che appigliarci in questa vita dobbiamo, come voi (tanto, & forse me ch'ognaltro) saper dovete, acconciamente apparare possiamo. (fol. a1v)
>
> [The fact that I am telling you tales should be scorned even less by you, since if you read these tales honestly we can learn from them very well: we want to stretch the bow of the intellect, and consider the aims for which they were written, and what to follow, and what to avoid, and what to guard against, and what we should seize hold of in this life, as you should know how to.]

The argument put forward that readers should not be led astray because the text teaches what to follow and what to avoid, what to guard against and what to grasp hold of, is in direct dialogue with the Narrator's comments in the *Decameron*, *Conclusione dell'autore*, 11–14, that readers are free to interpret the text as they wish; therefore, if they read expecting to find negative things, they will find them, but equally if they set out to look for useful things, they will be satisfied: "e chi utilità e frutto ne vorrà, elle nol negheranno, né sarà mai che altro che utile e oneste sien dette o tenute (*Conclusione*, 14) [And if anyone should study them for the usefulness and profit they may bring him, he will not be disappointed. Nor will they ever be thought of or described as anything but useful and seemly]." It is also a direct echo of the Narrator's statement in the Proem that the audience will know what to follow and what to avoid:

> Nelle quali novelle piacevoli e aspri casi d'amore e altri fortunati avvenimenti si vederanno cosí ne' moderni tempi avvenuti come negli antichi; delle quali le già dette donne, che queste leggeranno, parimente diletto delle sollazzevoli cose in quelle mostrate e utile consiglio potranno pigliare, in quanto potranno cognoscere quello che sia da fuggire e che sia similmente da seguitare: le quali cose senza passamento di noia non credo che possano intervenire. (Proem, 14)
>
> [In these tales will be found a variety of love adventures, bitter as well as pleasing, and other exciting incidents, which took place in both ancient and modern times. In reading them, the aforesaid ladies will be able to derive, not only pleasure from the entertaining matters therein set forth, but also some useful advice. For they will learn to recognize what should be avoided and likewise what should be pursued.]

This statement of the text's intent, and defence of the work's dual purpose, which Boccaccio had inserted into the Proem, becomes a key refrain in early prefaces and dedications as editors seek to authorize their own undertakings and appeal to both new and established audiences by eliding the worlds of text and paratext. In fact, the Narratorial Proem is referenced in the very first editorial preface to the *Decameron*, written by Nicolò Delfino and printed in May 1516.[58] Referring to his correction of the text, Delfino writes "della quale parimente non picciol diletto dalle varie cose in essa narrate, et utile consiglio pigliare potrete [from which you will be able to derive not only pleasure from the varied things told within it, but also some useful advice]." The choice of words seems deliberately and unmistakably Boccaccian. However, Delfino is keen to avoid his own framing of the *Decameron* being plagued with the same kind of accusations of immorality attached to earlier publications of the text, resulting from ambiguity about the type of "utilità" intended to be derived. Therefore, rather than embrace the tenets of reader-response theory and accept that different readers will approach the text in different ways, as the Narrator explains in *Conclusione*,

18–19, Delfino outlines the boundaries of his intended readership with extreme care. His preface spells out the qualities of this audience within the opening rubric, "Alle gentili et valorose donne [to the noble and excellent ladies]," and their select nature is underlined within the text itself: "Adunque, Amorose Donne (a voi dico, che non solamente per nobiltà di cuore, ma etiandio per eccellenza di leggiadri costumi dall'altre divise siete, perciò che a tutte questa opera non è iscritta) ... [And so, amorous ladies (I address you, since you are set apart from others not only by the nobility of your hearts but also by the excellence of your charming manners) ...]." Thus, Delfino's audience of female readers are not simply "amorose," like the women in Boccaccio's proem, but set apart from others by their particular qualities, which render them capable of reading in the correct manner, and therefore able to focus only on the good which is to be learned from the text and able to ignore anything negative. In fact, Delfino is keen to conclude that if these ladies read the text, they will *increase* their virtue and therefore their status among others: "hora con lieto volto leggete, et rileggete il vostro non mai bastevolmente lodato *Decamerone*; che percerto leggendolo, anchora quella virtù ... sentirete ne' vostri animi gentili destarsi talmente, che da molto più tenute, et più di loro dal mondo honorate sarete [now, with a happy mind, read and reread your *Decameron*, which can never receive enough praise; for certainly by reading it, you will feel that moral virtue spread through your noble souls such that you are more greatly esteemed and honoured by the world]." In this way, Delfino upcycles the authorial paratext into his editorial preface: using Boccaccio's text to authorize his own, whilst carefully reframing it in order to prove acceptable to a new audience.

The editor of the 1535 edition of the *Decameron*, Lucilio Minerbi, is also keen to emphasize that a profitable reading experience will ensue by using Boccaccio's own phrasing.[59] Minerbi writes: "io dico, che queste mie favole gioveranno a molti, & rimoverannogli da molti strani, & schiocchi pensieri, & di utilità non picciola saranno cagione (fol. a1v) [I tell you that these tales of mine will be beneficial to many people, and will help them avoid many strange and silly thoughts, and will be the cause of no small quantity of useful advice]." Once again, the emphasis is on the dual aims of pleasure and utility. In this context, the "utilità" described by Minerbi includes practical guidance in the art of writing which would be facilitated by a list of vocabulary drawn up by Minerbi and included for the first time with the text. However, the opening of the preface also suggests that Minerbi was concerned to defend the *Decameron* on moral grounds, using the Narrator's comments for guidance:

> Molti saranno generosi giovani, & amorevoli donne; li quali non da colorata ragione, ma da rabbiosa invidia mossi in detrimento della fatica mia sconciamente s'ingegneranno biasmarmi, parendogli sconvenevole molto; che io gia maturo d'età habbia posto l'animo mio à queste favole; le quai ad huomo pesato, & grave mal si convengono. Ma se con ragionevole occhio, & animo intiero riguarderanno qual sia della mia intentione il termine; assai agevolmente conosceranno me non di biasimo, ma di laude degno. (fol. a1v)
>
> [noble youths and amorous ladies, there will be many who will be moved to accuse me indecently, not out of good reason, but because they are moved, to the detriment of the undertaking, by violent envy; to them the work will appear very unseemly because I, when already at a mature age, have dedicated myself to these tales, which are not suitable for a man of weight and gravity. But if these will consider, with a reasoned eye and a wholesome soul, what the aims of my intentions are, they will understand very easily that I am worthy of praise rather than blame.]

This passage resounds with echoes from the *Decameron*. In the Introduction to Day Four, the Narrator describes his critics as being motivated by "invidia [envy]" and both the Narrator and Minerbi use the adjective "rabbioso [violent]." Minerbi's reference to the inappropriate conjunction of age and subject matter, while being a commonplace, must surely be a conscious channelling of the Narrator, as it not only reflects the Narrator's comments in the Introduction to Day Four quoted above but also uses exactly the same description of himself as "uomo pesato e grave [man of weight and gravity]" as that used by the Narrator in *Conclusione*, 22.

Conclusion

If we take these examples as evidence of anxiety about the moral contents of the *Decameron*, we can perhaps read them as a subtler antecedent of the later trend for prefacing each *novella* with moralizing rubrics. These rubrics, which were included for the first time in Gabriele Giolito's 1546 edition of the *Decameron* edited by Francesco Sansovino, also imitate the form of Boccaccio's work whilst deliberately overwriting his ambiguity with direct instruction.[60] The rubrics are likewise a softer antecedent of the expurgation carried out in the 1570s and 1580s, after the work was put on the Index of Prohibited Books. Similarly, the practice of recycling and manipulating the text of the *Decameron*, which we have explored here in relation to editorial dedications and prefaces, is a cousin of another strain of authorization which relies on resurrecting Boccaccio himself to speak on behalf of the book.[61] Sixteenth-century editors are thereby actively engaged in their mediating functions, both as readers involved in interpreting authorial intention with close readings of the authorial paratexts and as authors of their own texts, which employ these readings to attract and guide new audiences. As Boccaccio himself plays with the boundaries between the world of the text and the world outside, through his experimentation with different forms of dedicatory letters and inscriptions, so the intertextual echoes in the editorial paratexts blur the boundaries between author and editor, text and paratext. As Boccaccio's dedicatory letters become absorbed into the world of the text by readers unwilling or unable to make a distinction between text and paratext, so we should also consider that sixteenth-century paratexts may have become a canonical part of the text for early modern audiences.

The motivations behind editorial borrowings from Boccaccio's text are more difficult to define – we may never know whether they reflect genuine anxiety about the moral index of the text that printers and editors were marketing, or whether they form part of the formulaic structure of the dedication and nothing more. In a sense, however, the interpretative dilemma that this raises for us itself mirrors the interpretative ambiguity set out for us by the Narrator of the *Decameron*; in other words, the extent to which the Narrator's defence of his work in the Introduction to Day Four and final Conclusion reflects genuine anxiety about how his work will be received and how much of it is simply a rhetorical exercise. Even at this level, therefore, we have another example of the ways in which the world within the text overlaps and spills out onto the world outside it, blending the fields of authorship and reception.

NOTES

1 Giovanni Boccaccio, *Comedia delle ninfe fiorentino*, ed. Antonio Enzo Quaglio, in *Tutte le opere di Giovanni Boccaccio*, ed. Vittore Branca, 2nd ed., vol. 2 (Milan: Mondadori, 1964), 667–835, 50.3–5 (834–5). Translations of this and other works are my own, unless otherwise noted.

2 For the text of the letter and a translation into Italian, see Giovanni Boccaccio, *De casibus virorum illustrium*, ed. Pier Giorgio Ricci and Vittorio Zaccaria, in *Tutte le opere*, ed. Vittore Branca, vol. 9 (Milan: Mondadori, 1983), 2–7.

3 One of the few studies expressly considering openings and closures in Boccaccio's vernacular works is chapter 4 of Robert Hollander's *Boccaccio's Two Venuses* (New York: Columbia University Press, 1977): "The Book as Galeotto," 92–116.

4 For example, Victoria Kirkham alludes to the dedicatory function of the *Decameron*'s proem in her valuable study "Boccaccio's Dedication to Women in Love," in *The Sign of Reason in Boccaccio's Fiction*, ed. Victoria Kirkham (Florence: Olschki, 1993), 117–29; whereas Furio Brugnolo refers to Boccaccio as "il primo grande ideatore di prefazioni – e postfazioni – autoriali," in his "Testo e paratesto: la presentazione del testo fra medioevo e rinascimento," in *Intorno al testo: tipologie del corredo esegetico e soluzioni editoriali: atti del convegno di Urbino 1–3 ottobre 2001* (Rome: Salerno, 2003), 41–60; 51.

5 Early biographies of the author were largely constructed from comments made by Boccaccio's narrators, which were interpreted as autobiographical. See, for example, Girolamo Squarzafico, the first biographer to discuss Boccaccio's vernacular works in any detail, who writes: "[Boccaccio] fu molto dato alla libidine delle donne, et de diverse fu inamorato, e tra l'altre d'una fiorentina, la quale era dicta Lucia, dove lui Lya sempre l'apella. Ancora che non gli era già convenevole per la sua bassa condizione, se lassò spingere ad amare la figliola naturale del serenissimo re Roberto, la quale madonna Maria era chiamata … Et per amore de costei compose il *Filocolo* et la *Fiammetta* [Boccaccio was very given to lusting after women and fell in love with several of them, amongst whom was a Florentine named Lucia, although he always called her Lya. Even though it was not appropriate to his lowly circumstances, he let himself be driven to love the illegitimate daughter of His Serene Highness, King Robert, who was called Lady Maria … And through his love for her he composed the *Filocolo* and the *Fiammetta*]"; Angelo Solerti, ed., *Le vite di Dante, Petrarca e Boccaccio scritte fino al secolo decimosesto* (Milan: Vallardi, [1904–5]), 697. The practice of reading Boccaccio's fictions as autobiography reached its full heights in the late nineteenth century, but continued into twentieth-century lives of the author. See, for example, an introduction to a translation of the *Filostrato* published in 1928 which does not sound too dissimilar in tone to Squarzafico's biography: "Boccaccio's romances ... were the product of his ardent and impetuous

youth, being written while and soon after he was, as lover of Maria d'Aquino, experiencing in his own person all the raptures and torments of that passion of which he afterward gives us in the *Decameron* such impersonal and dispassionate representations"; see Nathaniel Edward Griffin and Arthur Beckwith Myrick, *The "Filostrato" of Giovanni Boccaccio: A Translation with Parallel Text*, intro. Nathanial Edward Griffin (New York: Biblio and Tannen, 1928), 3–4.

6 A criticism frequently levelled at narratology is that it does not consider the world outside the text. See, for example, Michael Kearns, *Rhetorical Narratology* (Lincoln: University of Nebraska Press, 1999), who argues similarly for the importance of bringing the audience function to bear on a text. Martin Eisner has also called for the utility of combining historicist and formalist modes in order to use the diachronic history of a work's survival to shed light on its fundamental structures: see his "The Return to Philology and the Future of Literary Criticism: Reading the Temporality of Literature in Auerbach, Benjamin, and Dante," *California Italian Studies* 2, no.1 (2011) http://escholarship.org/uc/item/4gq644zp (accessed 7 March 2014).

7 Interest in the transmission process both inside and outside the text can be subsumed under the label "audience-oriented criticism." Within this broad category, Susan R. Suleiman identifies six different "varieties" of criticism which cover both textual and historical concerns: rhetorical; semiotic or structuralist; phenomenological; subjective and psychoanalytic; sociological and historical; and hermeneutic. See her introduction to *The Reader in the Text: Essays on Audience and Interpretation*, ed. Susan R. Suleiman and Inge Crosman (Princeton: Princeton University Press, 1980), 3–45.

8 On voicing and receiving in the context of Boccaccio's works, see Rhiannon Daniels, "Boccaccio's Narrators and Audiences," in *The Cambridge Companion to Boccaccio*, ed. Guyda Armstrong, Rhiannon Daniels, and Stephen J. Milner (Cambridge: Cambridge University Press, 2015), 36–51.

9 Wayne C. Booth, *The Rhetoric of Fiction* (Chicago: Chicago University Press, 1961), Preface.

10 Interpretation of the *Decameron* as a meditation on the art of good storytelling has become a key trope within structuralist readings of the text. See, for example, Marga Cottino-Jones, *Order from Chaos: Social and Aesthetic Harmonies in Boccaccio's "Decameron"* (Washington, DC: University Press of America, 1982); Lucia Marino, *The "Decameron" "Cornice": Allusion, Allegory, and Iconology* (Ravenna: Longo, 1979); Guido Almansi, *The Writer*

as Liar: Narrative Technique in the "Decameron" (London: Routledge and Kegan Paul, 1975); Marcel Janssens, "The Internal Reception of the Stories within the *Decameron*," in *Boccaccio in Europe: Proceedings of the Boccaccio Conference*, ed. Gilbert Tournoy et al. (Louvain: Louvain University Press, 1977), 135–48.

11 See, for example, D.F. McKenzie, *Bibliography and the Sociology of Texts* (Cambridge: Cambridge University Press, 1999).

12 Robert Darnton, "What Is the History of Books?," in *The Book History Reader*, ed. David Finkelstein and Alistair McCleery (London: Routledge, 2002), 9–26. See also the reworking of the model in Thomas R. Adams and Nicolas Barker, "A New Model for the Study of the Book," in *A Potencie of Life: Books in Society, The Clark Lectures 1986–1987*, ed. Nicholas Barker (London: British Library, 1993), 5–43; and Robert Darnton, "'What Is the History of Books?' Revisited," *Modern Intellectual History* 4 (2007): 495–508.

13 Marco Santoro, "Appunti su caratteristiche e funzioni del paratesto nel libro antico," in his *Libri edizioni biblioteche tra cinque e seicento con un percorso bibliografico* (Rome: Vecchiarelli, 2002), 51–92; 51.

14 See, for example, Monica Fludernik, *An Introduction to Narratology*, trans. Patricia Häusler-Greenfield and Monika Fludernik (London: Routledge, 2009), 26, fig. 4.1.

15 See Franco Fido, "Architettura," in *Lessico critico decameroniano*, ed. Renzo Bragantini and Pier Massimo Forni (Turin: Bollati Boringhieri, 1995), 13–33.

16 On the rhetorical nature of the Introduction to Day Four, see, for example, Simone Marchesi, *Stratigrafie decameroniane* (Florence: Olschki, 2004), 31–66; for the debate over the likelihood that Days One to Three were published in separate instalments, see Giorgio Padoan, "Sulla genesi e la pubblicazione del *Decameron*," in *Il Boccaccio, le Muse, il Parnaso e l'Arno*, ed. Padoan (Florence: Olschki, 1978), 93–121; and Marco Cursi, *Il "Decameron": scritture, scriventi, lettori. Storia di un testo* (Rome: Viella, 2007), 57–9.

17 Jack Selzer, "More Meanings of *Audience*," in *A Rhetoric of Doing: Essays on Written Discourse in Honor of James L. Kinneavy*, ed. Stephen P. Witte, Neil Nakadate, and Roger D. Cherry (Carbondale: Southern Illinois University Press, 1992), 161–80; 172–3.

18 See, for example, Hollander, "The Narrator's Congedo and Eventual Hope" and "The Book in the Lady's Hands," in his *Boccaccio's Two Venuses*, 100–2. On Boccaccio's appreciation of the relationship between material form and content, see Rhiannon Daniels, *Boccaccio and the Book: Production and Reading in Italy 1340–1520* (London: Legenda, 2009), 16–17.

19 See K.P. Clarke's essay in this volume, which includes a comprehensive review of the relevant literature: "Text and (Inter)Face: The Catchwords in Boccaccio's Autograph of the *Decameron*"; other recent key works include Marco Cursi, *La scrittura e i libri di Giovanni Boccaccio* (Rome: Viella, 2013), and *Boccaccio: autore e copista*, ed. Teresa De Robertis et al. (Florence: Mandragora, 2013).

20 Gérard Genette, *Paratexts: Thresholds of Interpretation*, trans. Jane E. Lewin (Cambridge: Cambridge University Press, 1997), 2.

21 See, for example, *Renaissance Paratexts*, ed. Helen Smith and Louise Wilson (Cambridge: Cambridge University Press, 2011).

22 Genette, *Paratexts*, 117. On the relationship between the dedicatory letter and letters of transmission see also Brian Richardson, *Manuscript Culture in Renaissance Italy* (Cambridge: Cambridge University Press, 2009), 199–202.

23 Ibid., 203.

24 Ibid., 214.

25 In relation to dedications included in two sixteenth-century Neapolitan editions, Santoro comments: "si segue una struttura in qualche modo classica e collaudata, impostata su tre passaggi: primo, importanza dell'argomento (ed eventuale novità dell'approccio); secondo, accondiscendenza nei confronti delle pressioni di amici e studiosi volte a sollecitare la pubblicazione dell'opera; terzo, enfatico richiamo delle qualità e del prestigio del dedicatario [a structure is followed, which in some respects has become the classic tried and tested model, based on three points: the first is the importance of the argument (and the likely novelty of the approach used); second, compliance with pressure from friends and scholars who are set on pressing for publication of the work; third, emphasis on the qualities and prestige of the dedicatee]" ("Appunti su caratteristiche," 80).

26 Leonardo Bruni, "Notizia del Boccaccio," in *Le vite di Dante, Petrarca e Boccaccio*, ed. Solerti, 679.

27 Boccaccio, *Genealogie deorum gentilium*, ed. Vittorio Zaccaria, in *Tutte le opere*, ed. Vittore Branca, vol. 7–8, pt. 2 (Milan: Mondadori, 1998), 1574.

28 *Boccaccio on Poetry: Being the Preface and the Fourteenth and Fifteenth Books of Boccaccio's "Genealogia deorum gentilium,"* ed. and trans. Charles Osgood (Indianapolis: Bobbs-Merrill, 1956), 139–40. See also Epistle 18 to Niccolò Orsini, in which Boccaccio politely, but firmly, refuses what seems to have been an offer of patronage from Orsini, and in the process lists three previous offers which he has also refused: *Epistole e lettere*, ed. Ginetta Auzzas, in *Tutte le opere*, vol. 5, pt. 1 (Milan: Mondadori, 1992), 652–7.

29 Giovanni Boccaccio, *Genealogy of the Pagan Gods*, ed. and trans. Jon Solomon, vol. 1 (Cambridge, MA: Harvard University Press, 2011), xxi.

30 *De mulieribus claris* (Andrea Acciaiuoli); *De casibus* (Mainardo Cavalcanti); *Buccolicum carmen* (Donato degli Albanzani); *Genealogia* (Hugo, King of Cyprus); *Comedia delle ninfe fiorentine* (Niccolò di Bartolo del Buono).
31 On the invitation to Naples, see Giovanni Boccaccio, *Profilo biografico*, ed. Vittore Branca, new ed. (Florence: Sansoni, 1997), 129, as well as Jason Houston's essay in the present volume. Margaret Franklin also notes: "the timing and content of Boccaccio's dedication strongly suggest that Andrea Acciaiuoli, with her close Neapolitan connections, was a screen dedicatee through whom Boccaccio hoped to recommend himself to a substantially more powerful and illustrious personage: Queen Johanna of Naples"; see her *Boccaccio's Heroines: Power and Virtue in Renaissance Society* (Aldershot: Ashgate, 2006), 23. On this dedication, see also the essays by Mary Anne Case and Lori Walters in this volume.
32 Giovanni Boccaccio, *Famous Women*, ed. and trans. Virginia Brown (Cambridge, MA: Harvard University Press, 2001), xv.
33 An image of the opening leaf containing the dedication is reproduced in *Boccaccio: autore e copista*, 201.
34 *Famous Women*, Dedication, 7 (4–5).
35 See, for example, Stephen Kolsky, *The Genealogy of Women: Studies in Boccaccio's "De mulieribus claris"* (New York: Peter Lang, 2003), 114–15.
36 *De casibus*, Dedication, 10 (5).
37 See V. Zaccaria, "Le fasi redazionali del *De mulieribus claris*," *Studi sul Boccaccio* 1 (1963): 253–332.
38 A digital facsimile of the editions is available via the MDZ: Münchener Digitalisierungszentrum, http://daten.digitale-sammlungen.de/~db/0002/bsb00029099/images/index.html?id=00029099&groesser=&fip=xdsydeayaxdsydfsdryztssdasfsdreayasdasen&no=5&seite=1 (accessed 30 August 2013).
39 H. Porter Abbott, *The Cambridge Introduction to Narrative*, 2nd ed. (Cambridge: Cambridge University Press, 2009), 30.
40 Mainardo was a good friend, but also a patron, who sent Boccaccio several gifts. See Vittorio Zaccaria, *Boccaccio narratore, storico, moralista e mitografo* (Florence: Olschki, 2001), 38, as well as Todd Boli's essay in this volume.
41 For dating of the first redaction to the late 1350s, see Zaccaria, *Boccaccio narratore*, 35–36.
42 See *Boccaccio visualizzato: narrare per parole e per immagini fra medioevo e rinascimento*, vol. 2, ed. Vittore Branca (Turin: Einaudi, 1999), 146–8.
43 See Richardson, *Manuscript Culture*, 200.
44 See, for example, the description of the autograph manuscript in the centenary catalogue, *Mostra di manoscritti, documenti e edizioni: Firenze –*

Biblioteca Medicea Laurenziana, 22 maggio–31 agosto 1975, vol. 1 (Certaldo: A cura del Comitato Promotore, 1975), 33: "Il *Teseida delle nozze d'Emilia*, preceduto dalla lettera dedicatoria a Fiammetta [the *Teseida delle nozze d'Emilia*, preceded by the dedicatory letter to Fiammetta]."

45 On the form of academic prologues, see Alastair Minnis, *Medieval Theory of Authorship: Scholastic Literary Attitudes in the Later Middle Ages*, 2nd ed. (Philadelphia: University of Pennsylvania Press, 2010), 19–25. On authorizing the *Teseida* with a commentary, see Daniels, *Boccaccio and the Book*, 52–4.

46 See the description of the autograph manuscript in *Mostra di manoscritti*, vol. 1, 33. The *Filostrato* contains a similar opening address, which operates within the fictional realm of the text as a dedication from the narrator, named Filostrato, to his lady, Filomena. The overriding function of the text is as a proem; in this case there is no autograph manuscript to check whether a dedicatory miniature would have accompanied it in Boccaccio's copy.

47 *Amorosa visione*, in *Tutte le opere*, ed. Vittore Branca, vol. 3 (Milan: Mondadori, 1974), 1–272; 23; translation from Giovanni Boccaccio, *Amorosa visione*, trans. Robert Hollander, Timothy Hampton, and Margherita Frankel, with an introduction by Vittore Branca (Hanover: University Press of New England, 1986), 3.

48 Other figures interpreted as authorial alter egos, such as Caleone in the *Filocolo* or Cerretius in the *Buccolicum carmen*, are never explicitly linked to Boccaccio within the world of fiction.

49 The opening rubric on fol. 1r reads: "Comincia il libro chiamato Decameron, cogniominato principe Galeotto, nel quale si contengono cento novelle in diece dì dette da sette donne e da tre giovani huomini. Proemio. [Here begins the book known as the *Decameron*, subtitled Prince Galahalt, which contains one hundred stories told in ten days by seven women and three young men. Proem.]" For a full description of the autograph, see Cursi, *Il "Decameron,"* 161–4.

50 See, for example, Kirkham's article "Boccaccio's Dedication to Women in Love."

51 Guyda Armstrong, "Paratexts and Their Functions in Seventeenth-Century English *Decamerons*," *Modern Language Review* 102, no. 1 (2007): 40–57; 45.

52 Ibid., 52.

53 Santoro, "Appunti su caratteristiche," 53.

54 See Paolo Trovato, *Con ogni diligenza corretto: la stampa e le revisioni editoriali dei testi letterari italiani (1470–1550)* (Bologna: Il mulino, 1991); Brian Richardson, "Editing the *Decameron* in the Sixteenth Century," *Italian Studies* 45 (1990): 13–31.

55 Venice: Gregorio de Gregori, May 1516; Florence: Filippo Giunta, 29 July 1516. An exception is Agostino Zanni's edition of 1518, printed in Venice.

56 Giovanni Boccaccio, *Decameron* (Venice: case d'Aldo Romano & d'Andrea Asolano, 1522), fol. a1v.

57 Giovanni Boccaccio, *Decameron*, ed. Amedeo Quondam, Maurizio Fiorilla, and Giancarlo Alfano (Milan: BUR, 2013), 4.intro.33. All further quotations from the *Decameron* are taken from this edition. Positioning himself as part of a coterie of authors is a recurring strategy Boccaccio uses across both his vernacular and Latin works. See Jonathan Usher, "'Sesto fra cotanto senno' and *Appetentia primi loci*: Boccaccio, Petrarch, and Dante's Poetic Hierarchy," *Studi sul Boccaccio* 35 (2007): 157–98; Daniels, "Boccaccio's Narrators and Audiences," 42–4.

58 Venice: Gregorio de Gregori, May 1516. Delfino's text is defined as a preface rather than a dedication because it addresses a collective audience of women who are not named individually. For a transcription of the full text, see Daniels, *Boccaccio and the Book*, Appendix VI, 200.

59 Venice: Bernardino Vitali, 1535.

60 Venice: Gabriele Giolito, 1546. See Christina Roaf, "The Presentation of the *Decameron* in the First Half of the Sixteenth Century with Special Reference to the Work of Francesco Sansovino," in *The Languages of Literature in Renaissance Italy*, ed. Peter Hainsworth et al. (Oxford: Clarendon Press, 1988), 109–21.

61 See, for example, Giunta's Florentine edition of 1516, where the preface is apparently written in Boccaccio's own voice, signalled with the rubric "Messer Giovanni Bocchaccio al lectore," and also Giolito's 1546 dedication to the Dauphine of France, "Alla illustrissima et eccellentissima Signora la Delphina di Francia Gabriel Giolito de Ferrari."

PART TWO

Social Contexts: Friendship

3 Boccaccio on Friendship (Theory and Practice)

JASON HOUSTON

In the third decade of the fourteenth century, the Angevin King Robert the Wise ruled Naples. At court, three young Florentines found themselves studying together under the guidance of Tuscan masters. Their families had been drawn to Naples in the service of Florence's economic engine, the banking industry, and although they were frequent guests at the Angevin court, Tuscan culture remained strong among them. These young men, Niccolò Acciaiuoli, Giovanni Boccaccio, and Zanobi da Strada, comprised a Tuscan cohort at court, continuing an association that started in Florence where they began their studies with Zanobi's father, Giovanni.[1] In Naples, the Tuscan poet and jurist Cino da Pistoia taught the young Florentines about the greatness of Dante's vernacular masterpiece the *Commedia*, and about his Latin treatise *De vulgari eloquentia*, spurring Boccaccio to become a devoted *dantista*.[2] Cino must have lauded the new European prodigy Francesco Petrarch, whose poetry in Latin and Italian was the marvel of the literary world. It was in this elegant Neapolitan context that Acciaiuoli gave Boccaccio an ambiguous and lukewarm nickname, "Iohannem tranquillitatem [tranquil Giovanni]."[3]

Many years later, in 1363, the spirit of their friendship had been irrevocably broken. Zanobi died in 1361, and Boccaccio and Acciaiuoli were soon trading insults, not even sparing the reputation of their recently deceased friend Zanobi. A conflict of politics, money, and poetic accomplishment opened a rift between them, leading Acciaiuoli, through their mutual friend Francesco Nelli, to excoriate Boccaccio, going so far as to insult him with a new nickname, "uomo di vetro [man of glass]."[4] In this essay, I follow the epistolary record of the interconnected friendships among Boccaccio, Acciaiuoli, and Zanobi da Strada with the intention of considering Boccaccio's rhetoric of friendship and his rhetorical treatment of his friends. These relationships, formed among Florentines while living in Naples, will expand to become integral parts of Boccaccio's broad literary network; he, Acciaiuoli, and Zanobi will all move around the political and literary geography of the Mediterranean and Southern, Central, and Western Europe.[5] I repeat the term "rhetoric" to distinguish my approach from an ethical judgment or psychological evaluation of Boccaccio's character, which is far beyond my scope.[6] Instead, I contrast how Boccaccio writes about friendship, his theory of friendship, and how he treats his friends within the specific confines of his epistolary missives, understanding both of these modes to be rhetorical. In other words, how does Boccaccio describe friendship? Does Boccaccio behave as a friend under the terms of friendship that he sets forth in his letters? Within this limited view, however, I hope to point out some dissonance between Boccaccio's theory and practice of friendship, particularly in the difficult distinction between the offices of friend, patron, and poet.

In Florence and Naples, these young men studied and practised the *ars dictaminis*.[7] Boccaccio's earliest extant texts in Latin record his activity and practice in epistolary writing. His first four letters owe their survival exclusively to the fact that he copied them out in his notebook, the *Zibaldone laurenziano* (Biblioteca Medicea Laurenziana, MS Plut., 29.8). All four of the letters date to 1339, as indicated by the dates Boccaccio himself provides in the conclusions of three of the four letters; he copied them into the *Zibaldone laurenziano* at the time of composition or shortly thereafter, but, in any case, prior to his return to Florence from Naples in 1341.[8] The presence of these four letters in the *Zibaldone laurenziano* attests to Boccaccio's intent to preserve them, at least for his own reference. For scholars of Boccaccio, they offer a hazy portrait of the author *in cursu discendi* (in the course of learning); they record Boccaccio's earliest, often clumsy, attempts at finding his way among ancient and contemporary authorities. In all the letters, Boccaccio references directly and indirectly many classical and medieval sources to colour and validate his prose. Already in these earliest fragments of Boccaccio's writings, the theme of friendship emerges as central to his literary ethos: a topos that Boccaccio employed frequently throughout his voluminous corpus.

Scholars have already noted the importance of the theme of friendship in Boccaccio's writing. Ginetta Auzzas, the editor and translator of the standard edition of Boccaccio's letters, has summarized Boccaccio's continued concern with the theme of friendship throughout his letters.[9] Most scholars, unsurprisingly, have focused instead on Boccaccio's representation of friendship in the *Decameron*.[10] Indeed, recent scholarship has taken renewed interest in the subject. In only the last few years, scholars have added two new monograph studies to this subject.[11] As both Michel Sherberg and Franco Masciandaro note in their discussions, critical consensus is that Boccaccio relies, particularly in the *Decameron*, on the best-known sources on friendship: Books VIII and IX of Aristotle's *Ethics* through the mediation of Aquinas's commentary, and Cicero's *De amicitia*.[12] But as both Sherberg and Masciandaro show, Boccaccio's application of the theme of friendship in the *Decameron* does not simply mimic the usual authorities; instead, he adapts the conventions of friendship to resonate with his readership, which includes women. In the four letters under consideration in this essay, Boccaccio struggles with the application of friendship to a very specific audience: two friends from his youth.

Boccaccio's experimentations with the rhetoric of friendship began in the four letters he composed in Naples in 1339. Friendship stands out as a source of thematic unity in the letters, and the third of these letters consists entirely of a harangue of a bad friend. Boccaccio recounts how he invited a rustic friend to visit him, only to see him lose his way in the depraved diversions of the city, describing with exaggerated detail his participation in all of the vices. Boccaccio plays the role of the betrayed friend attempting to coerce his wayward friend back to virtue through his erudite counsel and moral teachings. What is interesting in this letter is not the content beyond the general theme of friendship; rather, the letter offers an early example of Boccaccio's rhetoric of friendship, both in terms of his sources and his literary style.

Boccaccio begins his letter with classical commonplaces about friendship, reciting the conventional description of it as a force stronger than nature, able to unify individual souls in a shared bond. He then goes on to list famous good friends (Pirithous, Nisus, and Damon) from classical sources.[13] Boccaccio faithfully follows his authorities, either mimicking Cicero directly or drawing upon the medieval compendia of authorities – nothing surprising from the young student. However, in this epistolary exercise, Boccaccio uses the trope of friendship to bring in more extravagant source material and language. In one spectacular passage, a youthful enthusiasm for his abilities comes out in his description of a friend gone astray:

> Sed in effectu contrarius, ritu aspidis surdi, farmaciis monitis aures obturabas, et sine castimonia babillusque, veluti agriofagite tuam baburram ac baccaniam prosequens cathafronitus, agapem contempsisti: et quem argutulum dicaculumque credebam, catamitum recongnovi, cytrosos querentem amiculos, loca famica farcinantem, necnon et sotiantem

satellites lenoninos, euntem una cum eis suppetiatum baccatum luxuriatumque multimode, et lasciviis aliis pluribus miserrime inmiscentem, inter hos etiam crumenam prodige denudantem, invirtuosis actibus te phylargrium turpissimum ostendentem.

[But in effect you were the opposite, like a mute asp, you blocked up your ears against therapeutic admonitions, unabashed and foolish, despicably pursuing your ignorance and madness just like the Agriophagi, you scorned charity: And the one I thought clever and talkative, I recognized as a Ganymede, looking for little friends who smell of citrus, stuffing your hungry places, sometimes even associating with companies of pimps, going along with them to assist in their various frenzied revelries, and mixing in with many other wanton acts, among them prodigiously plundering your wallet and revealing through your base actions that you are most foully avaricious.][14]

In addition to the hyperbolic rhetoric, Boccaccio privileges outlandish vocabulary in this letter. The Latinate-Hellenic vocabulary ("babillusque," "baburram ac baccaniam … cathafronitus, agapem" etc.) that dominates this passage, as it does much of the letter, derives from Boccaccio's reference to Uguccione da Pisa's *Derivationes*.[15] Boccaccio's harangue gives him the subject matter that permits him to show off his Greek, rudimentary as it is, and to test his literary skills. He also shows himself to be promiscuous with his sources, adding to his own account of *amicitia* a hodgepodge of sources, classical and medieval, found in Uguccione's lexicon. Boccaccio's arcane letter constitutes an example of the seldom-used epistolary *stilus obscurus*, a style by which an author aims to impress his readers with his erudition and uncommon vocabulary. Boccaccio uses the theme of friendship as a proving ground for his literary talents and for his employment of varied literary sources.

Only a few years later, Boccaccio composes a letter (Epist. 5, originally in Latin, but only extant in a fragment of a *volgarizzamento*) destined for one of his friends from Naples, Niccolò Acciaiuoli, who has risen in status and wealth in that kingdom.[16] Boccaccio assumes the role of lover to Acciaiuoli's epic hero; although not attempting to seduce the new magnate, he does flatter him:

Io vi giuro per la dolente anima mia che non altrimenti alla cartaginese Didone la partita del troiano Enea fu grave, che fosse a me la vostra … né similemente con tanto disidero la ritornata di Ulixe fu da Penelope aspettata quanto la vostra da me.

[I swear to you by my stricken heart that no differently was the departure of Aeneas sad to Carthiginian Dido than was yours to me: similarly the return of Ulysses was awaited with no greater desire by Penelope than yours by me.][17]

Boccaccio, having been recently forced back to Florence from Naples, welcomes Acciaiuoli as a conquering, if wandering, epic hero whose exploits in Greece have made him a rising star in the expanding kingdom of Naples. In this letter, Boccaccio undertakes the rather delicate task of converting Acciaiuoli from a friend to a patron, now that their political status and personal wealth have diverged. As Boccaccio frames the letter, Acciaiuoli could have served as Boccaccio's saviour: "come del pirrata Antigono la fortuna rea in buona trasmutò Allessandro, così da voi spero doversi la mia trasmutare [just as Alexander the Great transmuted the pirate Antigone's bad fortune into good, in this way I hope you can change mine]."[18] Even though the original Latin text is lost, we can take note of a rhetorical tactic; Boccaccio has changed his rhetorical approach from that of two years earlier, using a clear and lofty tone instead of artificial obscurity. With easily recognizable references, he seeks to flatter by identifying himself and his subject with familiar figures. Alexander and Ulysses are well known for their masculine virtues, but Boccaccio identifies himself with passive characters, first with the spurned lovers Dido and Penelope, and then with the pirate Antigono, either a conflation or confusion of two classical characters – one a teacher of Alexander, the other a pirate who impressed Alexander with his intelligence.[19] As far as we know, Boccaccio did not receive a reply from Acciaiuoli, and thus could not return to Naples under the protection of a new patron. With this letter, Boccaccio sought to flatter his friend to win support for his budding literary career – but without immediate success.

A few years after that, in the next letter (Epist. 6), Boccaccio stays with the theme of friendship when he writes to the third member of that triumvirate of friends, Zanobi da Strada. This letter is a mirror image of his third letter; although the subject remains friendship, here Boccaccio lauds Zanobi's virtues instead of castigating a bad friend:

Quam pium quam sanctum quam venerabile sit amicitie numen, quis posset verbis debitis explicare? Non ego, "si centum deus ora sonantia linguis ingeniumque capax totumque Elicona dedisset." Hoc Nature potentissime leges excedit ut plurimum; nam, etsi ipsa omnium parens egregia variis sanguineis nexibus mortalium corpora sepe iungit, celestes tamen spritus Promethei sagacissimo furto in luteis carceribus expirati, nisi hoc interveniat numen dulce, prisco corporum more nectere non valebit.

[How pious, how holy, how venerable is the spirit of friendship! Who could ever explain it in the proper words? Not I, "even if God had given me a hundred mouths sounding with tongues, a great genius, and all of Helicone." Frequently this friendship exceeds the laws of most powerful Nature; for although the highest mother of all things often joins together mortal bodies through blood relations, nevertheless the divine spirit of Prometheus, who died in a vile prison because of his most clever trick, will not prevail in binding them together in the ancient manner of bodies unless this sweet spirit intervenes.][20]

Boccaccio remains faithful to classical authorities much more than he did in the first letter; a direct citation from Ovid on friendship opens the letter, while Virgil, Cicero, Horace, and others add authority to it throughout by attesting to the erudition of the correspondents. The friendship between Boccaccio and Zanobi described in this letter closely adheres to classical rhetorical tropes of friendship among virtuous literary friends: mutually beneficial moral equanimity defines the bond, even stronger than what nature can forge. Boccaccio omits the obscure language and sources found in his earlier letter (Epist. 3); he puts his authorities to use here in appealing to an actual recipient, rather than in pursuit of a schoolboy exercise. He emphasizes one point not found in his classical sources: the material forged by the friendship between Zanobi and Boccaccio will be their shared obedience to the Muses:

Insuper tamen, per amicitiam nostram perque amicitie fidem obsecro, si qua vestra musa nova meum cecinit post discessum, ud videam faciatis. Valete.

[Moreover, I beseech you by our friendship and by the faith of friendship that if your muse sang any new songs after my departure, let me see them. Farewell.][21]

In what may be another attempt to adapt a Dantean concept, the subject of friendship occurs within a discourse on the shared vocation of the two poets.[22] Just as Dante did with his poetic friends Guido Cavalcanti, Guido Guinizelli, and Forese Donati, Boccaccio with his old friend Zanobi tracks his own development as a poet as the progress of his friendship with fellow poets. The *salutatio* of the letter calls for Zanobi to continue sharing his vocation with Boccaccio. In this conspicuously rhetorical description of the value of their friendship, Boccaccio aims to impress his friend with the quality of his Latin erudition. Boccaccio himself must have seen this letter as a related effort to the earlier letters, as he grouped it with Epistle 3 in his autograph *Zibaldone laurenziano.*

Moving ahead twenty years, and skipping over the exchange of letters between Boccaccio and Petrarch (which likewise centres on the two friends' shared poetic vocation), which I have discussed elsewhere,[23] Acciaiuoli, now the Grand Seneschal of the Kingdom of Naples, needs a new court poet. Zanobi da Strada filled that role until his death in 1361, and Acciaiuoli initially approached Petrarch through their mutual Florentine acquaintance Francesco Nelli, now Chancellor for Acciaiuoli in Naples. Petrarch refused this offer, as he had done before after similar solicitations, but suggested Boccaccio in his place. Boccaccio seemed an obvious choice, as he had previously sought out Acciaiuoli as a patron and was friends with Zanobi. So, more than twenty years after asking for Acciaiuoli's patronage in Naples, Boccaccio left Florence for a position at the Neapolitan court.

Whatever Boccaccio may have hoped for upon his return to Naples as Acciaiuoli's court poet in 1363, his disappointment could hardly have been more acute, judging from the venom of his response in a letter to Nelli (Epist. 13). The reader will recall that it is in this letter that Nelli calls Boccaccio a "man of glass," changing his earlier nickname, tranquil Giovanni. As Manlio Pastore Stocchi has shown, the term "man of glass" finds its origin in the category of "amicus vitreo" or "friend of glass" that the Tuscan Boncompagno da Signa delineated in his early thirteenth-century treatise on friendship.[24] The term finds its way to Boccaccio either directly or through Brunetto Latini's "Il Favolello," a short epistolary poem that treats the rhetorical terms of friendship. Boccaccio's thirteenth letter varies from the classical rhetoric of friendship, using medieval rhetorical texts (Boncompagno and Brunetto) to complicate the rhetorical treatment of his real friendships.

Boncompagno's text offers a different methodological lens through which to consider the categories of friendship. Instead of the philosophical extrapolation of friendship into categories (utility, pleasure, good) within a larger investigation of ethics, as found in Aristotle, Boncompagno, a teacher of grammar and rhetoric, reflects on friendship as a rhetorical construct, similarly to Cicero in *De amicitia,* but divorced from Cicero's language of virtue. Boncompagno stages his discussion as a dialogue between body and soul, in which the body dominates, expressing scepticism about the value of friendship. Body recites an encyclopedic list of the types of friends and their faults, whereby Boncompagno can unpack the meaning of each metaphorical usage. In Chapter 36 of his treatise, Boncompagno describes the "friend of glass" as not only metaphorically fragile but also dangerously transparent:

> Amicus vitreus habet conscientiam vitream, quia celare non valet cordis archana ... Sic namcque amicus vitreus frangible est, quia pro modica offensa, inmo pro suspitione sola, illum amittis. Per vitreum namcque amicum intellegerer debes invidum ... Est etiam invidia plurium curialis.
>
> [A friend of glass has a glass conscience, because he is not able to hide the secrets of his heart ... For this fact he is fragile, because for a modest offence, or even the suspicion of one, he breaks up a friendship. In fact, for glass you must understand this to mean envy ... and it is indeed mostly envy of courtly position.][25]

In Boncompagno's definition of a man of glass, envy threatens friendship. Specifically, the envy of courtly positions renders one fragile, and thus capable of shattering the bonds of friendship.

In his epistolary poem "Il Favollelo," Brunetto Latini pithily describes the characteristics of good and bad friends. The poem likely relates to Brunetto's *Tesoretto*, as it shares not only its form (*settenari* in rhyming couplets) but also its didactic purpose, giving simple vernacular definitions of the rhetorical tropes, indebted, as in Boncompagno, to Cicero. However, Latini's poem also translates Boncompagno's Latin treatise into vernacular poetic form, maintaining the definition of the "amico di vetro" as a fragile person, quick to abandon his friendships:

> E l'amico di vetro
> L'amor getta di dietro
> Per poco afendimento,
> E pur per pensamento
> Si parte e rompe tutto
> Come lo vetro rotto.
>
> [And the friend of glass
> throws love away
> for little offence,

and even if just supposed
he departs and shatters all
just like broken glass.][26]

Both Brunetto and Boncompagno incorporate Ciceronian concepts of friendship into their particular Tuscan – whether Latin or vernacular – rhetorical culture. Cicero's emphasis on the equanimity and virtue of friendship certainly found a place in thirteenth-century Florentine didactic tracts; these works also emphasize the rhetorical language and figures of speech used to describe friends, particularly defective friends. Both Boncompagno and Brunetto explain rhetorical categories, rather than debate philosophical truths. Boccaccio and his given nickname "man of glass" will find the courtly context described by Boncompagno, as well as the fragility of friendship sung by Brunetto, in the Naples of Acciaiuoli.

Like the previously discussed fifth letter addressed to Acciaiuoli, the thirteenth letter exists today only in a *volgarizzamento* of its original Latin. The profound differences between these two letters mark the rupture in Boccaccio's friendship with, and the potential patronage from, Acciaiuoli. The earlier letter addressed to Acciaiuoli employed readily familiar classical tropes; this letter, addressed to Boccaccio's fellow humanist Francesco Nelli, engages in a sophisticated classical satire like that found in Petronius's *Satyricon*.[27] Moreover, where the earlier letter is brief, this letter expands to nearly fifteen thousand words. In the letter to Nelli, Boccaccio describes Acciaiuoli's court in Naples, from which he had recently returned, as a false and illusory Arcadia, or better yet, as a *locus inamoenus*: a once-pleasant place defiled by the rule of a deficient lord. The length of this letter does not allow for a full exploration of Boccaccio's satirical vengeance in the present discussion, but one extraordinary passage will serve as an example of his vitriol at the perceived slights of his erstwhile friend. Instead of dining upstairs with Acciaiuoli and his well-to-do courtiers, Boccaccio finds himself downstairs consorting with lesser sorts. He offers unflattering caricatures of his dining companions:

> Dico ghiottoni e manicatori, lusinghieri, mulattieri e ragazzi, cuochi e guatteri, ed usando altro vocabolo, cani della corte e topi dimestichi, ottimi roditori di rilievi. Ora di qua ed ora di là discorrendo, con discordevole mugliare di buoi riempievano tutta la casa; e, quello che m'era gravissimo al vedere ed all'odorato, mentre che le mezzine ed i vasi da

vino spesse ... rompessono, il rotto suolo immollando, e la polvere ed il vino co'piedi in fango convertissono, di fetido odore riempievano l'aria del luogo. Ohimè! quante volte non in fastidio solamente, ma in vomito fu provocato lo stomaco!

[I call them gluttons and gobblers, playboys, muleteers and field hands, cooks and dishwashers, in other words, dogs of the courts and domestic mice, the greatest consumers of leftovers. Now here, now there they run about, filling the house with the grating mooing of cows ... and that which was the most difficult for my sight and smell, they would often break the pitchers and vases of wine, softening the dirt below, so that their feet mixed the wine and dirt creating a mud that filled the air of that place with a fetid odour. Alas, how many times was my stomach not only irritated but also forced to vomit!][28]

In the course of the letter, Boccaccio never names Acciaiuoli explicitly, but refers to him as either the Seneschal or, more commonly, Maecenas, as well as by the more generic title of Lord. The reference to Maecenas is, of course, a parody of Gaius Maecenas, the famous patron of Horace and Cicero.[29]

Boccaccio counters his complaints with moments of reasoned humility as he reminds Nelli, and Acciaiuoli by proxy, of his previous nickname, Giovanni the tranquil. He then defends himself from the charge of being a "friend of glass" by saying that he did not expect much, just a clean room, simple food, and a place for his books:

Ma arei io voluto quello che spessissimamente domandai, cioè una caselina rimossa da'romori de'ruffiani garritori, una tavola coperta di netti ed onesti mantili, cibi popolareschi ma nettamente parati; e, con queste cose così temperate, vini vulgari ed in netto vaso e dalla diligenzia del celleraio conservati; un letticello secondo la qualità della mia condizione, posto in una camera netta.

[I would have wanted that which I very often asked for: namely a little house away from the racket of the fighting ruffians, a table covered with a tidy and clean little tablecloth, simple food but cleanly prepared. And, together with these simple things, a table wine in a clean pitcher stored carefully by the winemaker, and a little bed fitting the condition of my station, in a tidy room.][30]

Boccaccio craftily understates his Neapolitan ambitions and his expectations of life at court so that the subsequent hyperbolic description of his inadequate reception might ring true. He puts himself in a position of apparent humility, while also claiming rights according to "la qualità della mia condizione." The hierarchical distinction of status between Boccaccio and Acciaiuoli, through Boccaccio's use of Acciaiuoli's acquired noble titles of Seneschal and Lord, signals Boccaccio's discomfort with the shift from using the rhetoric of friendship to that of patronage.

Boccaccio's disappointment at his poor treatment at the hands of the man he once called a friend, and had hoped to call his patron, culminates when he writes of Acciaiuoli's literary pretensions. Boccaccio, who came to Naples to serve as Acciaiuoli's court poet, could not stomach the thought of Acciaiuoli claiming excellence in his field, and he subsequently derides Acciaiuoli's pretensions to literary ability:

> ... lui spesse volte veggiamo intra' più sommi sedere, e parlare e recitare storiuzze note alle femminelle, ed alcuna volta mandare fuori alcune parole che sanno un poco di gramatica, libri palesemente trassinare e leggere alcuni versicciuoli ... queste cose, per non dire l'altre, non arò io in orrore di scrivere in sua loda con mio migliore stile? ed il nimico delle Muse, dirollo io amico? Tolga Dio dalla mia sottile penna questa vergogna, la quale se io temo, tu, che se' uomo litterato, maravigliare non ti déi.

> [... we often see him sit among the most important men speaking and reciting little stories that all the ladies already know, and sometimes he spits out some words that that sound like he knows Latin, and he makes a show of his books and reads his bad poetry ... For these things, not to mention the others, should I not be horrified to use my best style to praise him? And the enemy of the Muses, will I say he is my friend? May God forbid that this shame come to my quill, and I should not fear that you, who are a literate man, should be surprised at this.][31]

In this passage, Boccaccio's overheated rhetoric camouflages a literary ploy. He wants to prove to Acciaiuoli and Nelli how skilled and erudite an author he can be, how able to marshal literary faculties – the very talents that Acciaiuoli spurned in his mistreatment of Boccaccio. Furthermore, Boccaccio's renunciation of this friendship coincides with his declaration of Acciaiuoli's status as a "nimico" (enemy) of the Muses.

Boccaccio had earlier declared his friendship with Zanobi as formed under the protection of the Muses; here, in stark contrast, he proclaims the death of this friendship as a product of Acciaiuoli's abuse of them. Acciaiuoli's elevated political status renders him suitable for the role of patron, but Boccaccio cannot even feign to share his poetic vocation with such a man. In ridiculing Acciaiuoli, Boccaccio compromises himself, basing his rejection of his friend on his composition and performance of degraded literature, his "recitare storiuzze note alle femminelle." In his condemnation of Acciaiuoli's literary abilities, Boccaccio seems to disregard his lifelong promotion of vernacular literature, whether his own or that of his fellow Tuscan poets Dante and Petrarch.

Let us return to the third friend of the group of young Florentines in Naples in the 1330s, Zanobi da Strada. Boccaccio's final mention of Zanobi in his letters comes nearly ten years after his death, and, as in the relation to Acciaiuoli just described, Boccaccio compromises his friendship with Zanobi by dismissing his literary ability. Although Boccaccio ultimately received offers of patronage in the 1370s, he was too old and ill to return to Naples to take these positions. Instead, he spent the rest of his days between Florence and the little village of Certaldo, but his old age and chronic ailments did not muzzle his criticism of another friend who enjoyed more satisfying relationships with important patrons. In Epistle 19, written to the young Sicilian nobleman Jacopo Pizzinga, he encourages the study of Tuscan authors, proposing three poetic models; the first two are, naturally, Dante and Petrarch, and the third is Zanobi da Strada. However, after mentioning Zanobi among the other two *Corone*, Boccaccio adds a pointed critique:

> Avidulus glorie, nescio utrum in satis meritos evolavit honores, et veteri omni parvipenso ritu, boemi Cesaris manu non romanam lauream sed pisanam capiti impressit suo, et unico tantum homini paucis carminibus placuisse contentus, quasi eum decoris assumpti peniteret, tractus auri cupidine in Babilonem occiduam abiit et obmututit, quam ab rem, cum laboris modicum et fere nil glorie sacro nomini attulerit, omittendum censui.
>
> [Desirous of glory, he [Zanobi] flew to honours that I am not sure he merited, and bringing down an ancient rite, he took on his brow the Pisan, not Roman, laurel from a Bohemian Caesar. Content to be pleasing to one man for a few poems, he came to regret having taken this honour. Attracted by the desire for gold, he moved to Western Babylon and fell silent.][32]

Boccaccio accuses Zanobi of profiting too much from too little literary merit, or at least too little production. Boccaccio strongly critiques Zanobi for accepting a laurel crown as poet laureate from Charles V in 1355, at Acciaiuoli's recommendation, in Pisa instead of Rome. The laurel crown, the ultimate reward for those who serve the Muses, escaped Dante's grasp only to find Petrarch's brow, much to Boccaccio's joy. Boccaccio mentions Zanobi among the other two, only to then rudely dismiss him. Boccaccio never mentioned Zanobi again in his letters in defence of the Tuscan poets, and indeed, Zanobi's writings have been almost entirely ignored by scholars of Italian literature.[33]

In sum, these letters and what they reveal about Boccaccio's rhetoric of friendship in theory and practice both modify and enrich our understanding of Boccaccio. When Boccaccio writes "theoretically" about friendship, he most often utilizes a conventional rhetoric of friendship, favouring Cicero, Virgil, and Ovid; when he writes about his personal disappointment in his friends, he finds recourse in other sources, whether the arcane vocabulary of Uguccione of Pisa or the rhetorical categories of his Tuscan contemporaries. This mixing of rhetorical modes, from classical to medieval, philosophical to satirical, marks Boccaccio's literary style.

Despite the deployment of conventional rhetorical language that I have detailed, Boccaccio's letters trace the course of relationships that developed, and even dissolved, over his life. These letters reveal moments of intense introspection and self-revelation to a small group of friends. In this way, Boccaccio's epistolary style differs from that of his two models, Dante and Petrarch, both of whom wrote and promulgated their letters as public and political statements. It is this guarded fragility apparent in the letters that led Nelli to call Boccaccio a "man of glass." Boccaccio maintains one consistent theme in his treatment of friendship and of his friends that is particular to him: they must share his poetics. I contend that the history among these three men offers more than just rich biographical detail; it helps to explain a moment in Italian literary history. Boccaccio was a friend both to Dante, even if only to his legacy, and to Petrarch, often serving, in his letters and elsewhere, as a promoter of their writings. Conversely, his sharp attacks on the literary production of his Neapolitan friends helped determine their meagre literary afterlives. In the cases of Acciaiuoli and Zanobi, their works remain not only unread but also unedited, to some extent because of their old friend, Giovanni Boccaccio.

NOTES

1 Vittore Branca describes Boccaccio's time in Naples in *Giovanni Boccaccio: Profilo biografico* (Florence: Sansoni, 1977), 13–39. *Boccaccio angioino: Materiali per la storia culturale di Naploli nel Trecento*, ed. Giancarlo Alfano, Teresa D'Urso, and Alessandra Perriccioli Saggese (Brussels: Peter Lang, 2012), offers a number of essays pertaining to Boccaccio's experience in Naples; in particular see Roberta Morosini's reflective esssay, "La 'bona sonoritas' di Calliopo: Boccaccio a Napoli, la polifonia di Partenope e i silenzi dell'Acciaiuoli," 69–88. See also the essay by Elizabeth Casteen in this volume.

2 Vittore Branca, "L'incontro napoletano con Cino," *Studi sul Boccaccio* 5 (1971): 28–75.

3 Boccaccio himself mentions this nickname in a letter to Zanobi da Strada in 1353; Giovanni Boccaccio, Epist. 9.1–2. All citations of Boccaccio's letters are from Giovanni Boccaccio, *Epistole e lettere*, ed. Ginetta Auzzas, in *Tutte le opere di Giovanni Boccaccio*, ed. Vittore Branca, vol. 5, pt. 1 (Milan: Mondadori, 1992), Epist. 13.2. All translations of Boccaccio's letters are from Giovanni Boccaccio, *Shorter Latin Works*, ed. and trans. Jason Houston and Sam Huskey, in *I Tatti Renaissance Library Series*, vol. 90 (Cambridge, MA: Harvard University Press, forthcoming).

4 Here again, Boccaccio informs us of this new nickname in a letter, this time addressed to Francesco Nelli, Epist. 13.1–2.

5 On literary friendships and network theory in the "Global Middle Ages," see Hannah Chapelle Wojciehowski, "Petrarch and His friends," in *The Cambridge Companion to Petrarch*, ed. Albert Russell Ascoli and Unn Falkeid (Cambridge: Cambridge University Press, 2015), 26–38.

6 The French scholar Michel-Henry Bailet has used the tag "uomo di vetro" as point of entry for a psychoanalytical reading of Boccaccio, particularly the *Decameron*, in *L'Homme de Verre: Essai d'interprétation thematique de l'échec et de la maîtrise dans le "Decameron"* (Nice: L'Imprimerie Universelle, 1972).

7 On the *ars dictaminis* in the Middle Ages and specifically among the early Italian humanists such as Boccaccio and his friends in Naples, see Ronald G. Witt, "The Arts of Letter-Writing," in *The Cambridge History of Literary Criticism: The Middle Ages*, ed. Alastair J. Minnis and Ian Johnson (Cambridge: Cambridge University Press, 2005), 68–83.

8 On the transmission history of Boccaccio's epistolary writings in general, see Marco Petoletti, "Epistole," in *Boccaccio autore e copista*, ed. Teresa De Robertis et al. (Florence: Mandragora, 2013), 223–41. On these letters in

the *Zibaldoni* see also Petoletti, "Gli zibaldoni di Boccaccio," in *Boccaccio autore e copista*, 291–326, and Stefano Zamponi, Martina Pantarotto, and Antonella Tomiello, "Stratigrafia dello Zibaldone e della Miscellanea Laurenziano," in *Gli zibaldoni di Boccaccio: Memoria, scrittura, riscrittura. Atti del Seminario Internazionale di Firenze-Certaldo*, ed. Michelangelo Picone and Claude Cazalé Bérard (Florence: Franco Cesati, 1998), 181–258. See also Jason Houston, "A Portrait of a Young Humanist," in *Boccaccio: A Critical Guide* (Chicago: University of Chicago Press, 2013), 69–77.

9 Ginetta Auzzas, "'Quid Amicitia Dulcius?'" in *Boccaccio e dintorni: Miscellanea di Studi in Onore di V. Branca*, ed. Vittore Branca (Florence: Olschki, 1983), 181–206; 182. Petoletti notes the importance of the theme of friendship especially in his letters to Zanobi da Strada ("Epistole," 234).

10 Giuseppe Mazzotta discusses friendship in his *The World at Play in Boccaccio's "Decameron"* (Princeton: Princeton University Press, 1986), 152–3, 254–5. Victoria Kirkham focuses on one story in "The Classic Bond of Friendship in Boccaccio's Tito and Gisippo (*Decameron*, 10.8)," in *The Classics in the Middle Ages*, Papers of the Twentieth Annual Conference of the Center for Medieval and Early Renaissance Studies, ed. Aldo S. Bernardo and Saul Levin (Binghamton: Medieval and Renaissance Texts and Studies, 1990), 223–35.

11 Michel Sherberg, *The Governance of Friendship: Law and Gender in the "Decameron"* (Columbus: Ohio State University Press, 2011), and Franco Masciandaro, *The Stranger as Friend: The Poetics of Friendship in Homer, Dante, and Boccaccio* (Florence: Firenze University Press, 2013).

12 Sherberg, *The Governance of Friendship*, 1–8; Masciandaro, *The Stranger as Friend*, 117–45, esp. 128.

13 Boccaccio, *Epistole e lettere*, 3, 2–3. "amicitie scilicet maiestatem; cuius sacratissime vires id faciunt, quod et ipsa Natura non potest suis viribus adinplere, sed decreto sanctissimo vetuit inter vivos. Ipsa quidem voluntates unit varias et diversas, extraneas animas iungit equat et sotiat … [the majesty of friendship, whose most holy powers accomplish that which Nature herself cannot complete with her powers, but with a most holy decree forbids it to the living. This friendship brings together diverse and distant wills; it joins together, makes equal, and unites unfamiliar souls …]." See Cicero's *De amicitia*, par. 19–21; for a parallel passage, see Cicero, *De senectute, De amicitia, De divinatione*, trans. W.A. Falconer (Cambridge, MA: Harvard University Press, 1971).

14 Boccaccio, *Epistole e lettere* 3.8.

15 In Auzzas's notes in her critical edition, she often cites Uguccione da Pisa as Boccaccio's source for his arcane vocabulary. Uguccione da Pisa,

Derivationes, ed. Enza Cecchini et al. (Florence: SISMEL, Edizioni del Galuzzo, 2004).

16 Petoletti confirms the current critical consensus that this letter was originally composed in Latin ("Epistole" 237–8). On Acciaiuoli, see F.P. Tocco, *Niccolò Acciaiuoli: vita e politic in Italia alla metà del VIV secolo* (Rome: Istituto storico italiano per il medio evo, 2001); and C.U. della Berardenga, *Gli Acciaiuoli di Firenze nella luce dei loro tempi*, 2 vols. (Florence: Olschki, 1962).

17 Boccaccio, *Epistole e lettere* 5.1.

18 Ibid., 5.6.

19 Boccaccio has mistaken Antigono for Dionides from John of Salisbury's *Policraticus* (3.14). Antigonus was a teacher of Alexander; Dionides was the pirate who challenged Alexander. On this mistake see also Morosini, "La 'bona sonoritas,'" 77–8.

20 Boccaccio, *Epistole e lettere* 6.1–2.

21 Ibid., 6.11.

22 Filippa Modesto's study shows how Dante incorporates literary affinity into his concept of friendship. See *Dante's Idea of Friendship: The Transformation of a Classical Concept* (Toronto: University of Toronto Press, 2015), especially chapter 5, "The *Vita Nuova*: Dante's Friendship with Guido Cavalcanti and Others," 75–92.

23 Jason Houston, "Boccaccio at Play in Petrarca's Pastoral World," *Modern Language Notes* 127, no. 1 (2012): S47–S53.

24 M.P. Stocchi, "Note e chiose interpretative," *Studi sul Boccaccio* 2 (1964): 235–52. Auzzas, following Stocchi, also attests to Boccaccio's citation of Boncompagno's treatise on friendship in her article on Boccaccio's letters "Quid Amicitia Dulcius." On Epistle 13, also see the next essay in this volume by Todd Boli.

25 Boncompagno da Signa, *De amicitia*, ed. S. Nathan, vol. 3 in *Miscellanea di letteratura del medio evo* (1909), 46–88, ch. 36. Translation mine.

26 Brunetto Latini, "Il Favolello, 105–10," in *Poeti de Duecento*, vol. 1, ed. Gianfranco Contini (Milan: Riccardo Ricciardi, 1995), pt. 1. Translation mine.

27 In a recent study, Ginetta Auzzas has argued that this letter can be characterized as a "*pamphlet*" imitating the invective style as rejuvenated by Petrarch a few years earlier in his *Invective contra medicum*: "Sull'epistola a Francesco Nelli," in *Boccaccio Letterato* (Florence: Accademia della Crusca, 2015), 339–50.

28 Boccaccio, *Epistole e lettere* 13, 21–3.

29 Boccaccio's other uses of Maecenas figure him as the good patron, in reference to his importance for Horace. In the *Ameto*, Boccaccio writes,

"E questa non altrimenti ricevi che da Virgilio il buono Augusto o Erennio da Cicerone, o come da Orazio il suo Mecena, prendevano i cari versi" (50.3–4). Here Maecenas is another Niccolò, Niccolò del Buono. Boccaccio refers to Maecenas again in his *Esposizioni sopra la Comedia di Dante*: "Fu, oltre a ciò, fatto maestro della scena, e singularmente usò l'amistà di Mecenate, nobilissimo uomo di Roma, ed in poesia ottimamente ammaestrò" (*Esp. litt.* 4). He also mentions Maecenas as a positive figure in his nineteenth letter, par. 16, where Maecenas the patron is also a friend and poet. On the figure of Maecenas, see S. Byrne, *Maecenas in Seneca and Other Post-Augustan Poets,* in *Veritatis amicitiaeque causa: Essays in Honor of Annay Lydia Motto and John R. Clark,* ed. S. Byrne and E. Cueva (Wauconda: Bolchazy-Carducci Publishers, 1999), 21–41.

30 Boccaccio, *Epistole e lettere* 13.36.

31 Ibid., 13.166, 175–7.

32 Ibid. 19.30.

33 On Zanobi da Strada, see Paola Guidotti, "Un amico del Petrarca e del Boccaccio: Zanobi da Strada, poeta laureate," *Archivio Storico Italiano* 88 (1930): 249–93.

4 Among Boccaccio's Friends: A Profile of Mainardo Cavalcanti

TODD BOLI

Boccaccio's Epistle 13 of June 1363 to Francesco Nelli relates how, in late 1362 when Boccaccio had travelled to Naples only to be consigned by his Florentine host, Niccolò Acciaiuoli, to unsuitable accommodations, Mainardo de' Cavalcanti, another Florentine in Naples and Acciaiuoli's kinsman, rescued Boccaccio by receiving him into his own home, where Boccaccio could enjoy Cavalcanti's far more agreeable "tavola ed albergo [table and lodgings]."[1] This is the earliest event involving both Cavalcanti and Boccaccio for which there is direct evidence. Whether they had any previous contacts is open to conjecture.

When was Mainardo Cavalcanti born? Boccaccio himself mentions their considerable difference in age. In Epistle 13 he refers to Cavalcanti as a "nobile giovane cittadino nostro [noble young citizen of ours],"[2] and nine years later in Epistle 22 he acknowledges a gift that he, "senex [an old man]," has received from Cavalcanti, "a iuvene [from a young man]."[3] Just how much younger was Cavalcanti? The earliest known mention of Cavalcanti is as Captain General of the Duchy of Amalfi, a post in which he served the Kingdom of Naples from 1358 to 1359.[4] Such assignments could come when the recipient was still young. Acciaiuoli's son had already served in high Neapolitan administrative and military positions when he died at the age of twenty-four,[5] and Acciaiuoli himself had received a knighthood[6] and become chief adviser to the king's sister-in-law by the time he was twenty-five.[7] Cavalcanti's being in his early twenties when he served as Amalfi's Captain General would not be inconsistent with what Ginetta Auzzas has characterized as a "rapida e brillante [rapid and brilliant]" career.[8] Cavalcanti did not marry until 1372.[9] A Captain General in his early twenties would not be too young for Cavalcanti's service in Amalfi in 1358, a bridegroom in his late thirties would not be too old for Cavalcanti's marriage in 1372, and both would suggest that Mainardo Cavalcanti was born around 1335 and so was about twenty-two years younger than Boccaccio.

Cavalcanti probably did not leave Florence for Naples until after the turbulence following the assassination of Queen Johanna's first husband and the invasion of the kingdom by King Louis I of Hungary had subsided in 1352. It was principally through Acciaiuoli's exertions that the Queen retained her throne, and when Acciaiuoli's relatives and associates began pouring into the kingdom, it seems certain that Mainardo Cavalcanti, then around seventeen years old, was among them.[10] Significant contact between Boccaccio and Cavalcanti before this date seems unlikely, especially because, once Mainardo was in his teens, Boccaccio's presence in Florence was sporadic.

An opportunity for an encounter between Boccaccio and Cavalcanti is offered by the 1355 trip that took Boccaccio into the Neapolitan kingdom. Cavalcanti was in the kingdom as an associate and relative of Acciaiuoli's (Cavalcanti's cousin had married an Acciaiuoli), and it was at Acciaiuoli's invitation that Boccaccio found himself in the realm. Boccaccio, of course, was soon disappointed by not receiving the position that Acciaiuoli's invitation had seemed to promise, but Cavalcanti was not Acciaiuoli, and it would be natural for Boccaccio and Cavalcanti, who would later be good friends, to have met on this occasion. Had there been such a meeting, though, Boccaccio would surely not have failed to mention it when he acknowledged Cavalcanti's generous intervention on the occasion of Boccaccio's subsequent visit to Naples in 1362. The reason that Boccaccio and Cavalcanti failed to meet in 1355 cannot have been that Boccaccio's journey, as is often suggested, did not actually take him to Naples itself. Although Boccaccio's silence with regard to Neapolitan experiences in his 1355 metrical epistle to Zanobi da Strada has been taken to indicate that he never reached the capital, Giuseppe Velli has removed that suggestion by redating the epistle to a time preceding Boccaccio's trip.[11] More likely it was Cavalcanti who was outside the city. Boccaccio gives a hint of the royal deputy's busy comings and goings when he mentions in his letter to Nelli how, during his 1362–3 visit, he returned to the city where he had been staying with Cavalcanti and "il mio Mainardo al servigio della reina obligato trovai essere andato a Sant'Eramo [found that my Mainardo, obliged by his service to the queen, had gone to Sant'Eramo]."[12]

In December of 1359, however, Boccaccio's and Cavalcanti's paths may indeed have crossed. Acciaiuoli, who was seeking support for his campaign against the brigands molesting the Papal States, returned to his native Florence, where, entertaining lavishly, according to Matteo

Villani, "da' parenti e dagli amici, e dagli altri cittadini discreti e da bene, a grande onore fu ricevuto [he was by his relatives, friends, and other discreet and well regarded citizens received with great honour]."[13] In view of the connections Mainardo Cavalcanti enjoyed with Florence and especially with Acciaiuoli's relatives, he was an ideal recruit for Acciaiuoli's entourage. At the same time, Boccaccio, given his standing in Florentine affairs, was likely to be someone whom Acciaiuoli, sincerely or not, wanted to entertain. Would it not have been precisely because Boccaccio and Cavalcanti already were friends in 1362–3 that the poet, as he says in his letter to Nelli, was able "tornare alla liberalità [to fall back on the generosity]"[14] of the young Mainardo when Acciaiuoli so grievously defaulted on his promise of hospitality? If someone were not already Boccaccio's friend, would he be "consapevole [aware]" of Boccaccio's straits and "spessissimamente [again and again]" be entreating the poet to accept his hospitality?[15] When Boccaccio later dedicates the *De casibus virorum illustrium* to his friend, he says that Cavalcanti has "iam diu [now for a long time]" enjoyed Boccaccio's high regard.[16] Is the "long time" only the years that have passed since Cavalcanti rescued Boccaccio with his hospitality in Naples, or is it the even longer time that Boccaccio says the completed *De casibus* has lain unpublished, a span of years that just reaches, as chance would have it, back to the Florentine visit of Acciaiuoli's entourage?

Boccaccio's 1362–3 trip to Naples put an end to his hope of ever returning to live in the beloved city of his youth. Never again would he turn to Acciaiuoli for help, and it was Cavalcanti who now would prove a source of the support and affection that Boccaccio had so often failed to find in others. Cavalcanti, however, was not the only person who relieved Boccaccio's misery. When Boccaccio was obliged to leave Cavalcanti's roof in Naples to join Acciaiuoli and the royal household on holiday at the baths near Pozzuoli, he was apparently unwilling to let his precious library out of his sight, and he brought all his books with him. Again his lodgings proved indecent, and he says he was embarrassed to have "coloro che venivano, tratti dalla fama de' libri [those who came, attracted by the fame of my books]"[17] see his shabby cot – until, that is, an unnamed "giovane napolitano di sangue assai chiaro [young Neapolitan of distinguished birth]"[18] brought him a more suitable bed. It is tempting to think that Boccaccio's amenable manner was as attractive to his visitors as his books were and that the unnamed bringer of the fresh bed was not the only youth among them. One imagines something of a coterie of enthusiastic acolytes, among whom

Cavalcanti perhaps stood preeminent. When Boccaccio's letter relates that "seperato con l'ottimo giovane un pochetto mi ristorassi [alone with the excellent young man I would somewhat restore myself]," it seems clear that his refreshment owed as much to Cavalcanti's regardful companionship as it did to the material comforts he provided.[19]

Some three years later, Boccaccio writes to his colleague Pietro da Moglio about two young scholar-protégés whom he asks Pietro to help. One is Giovanni da Siena, a teacher who is looking for students to tutor, and the other is Agnolo Giandonati, the young prior of Boccaccio's parish, who is more partial to hunting than to learning and would profit from the older scholar's guidance. Boccaccio's asking Pietro to take on Agnolo "non solum in scolarem, sed in filium tuum [not only as your student but as your son]" suggests the affection Boccaccio felt for these young men.[20] Boccaccio's efforts on their behalf bore fruit when Giovanni da Siena became Pietro da Moglio's assistant, and the sporting Agnolo Giandonati matured into the sober cleric who, nine years later, was entrusted with the construction of Boccaccio's tomb.[21] Boccaccio seemed determined that the misunderstanding and disappointment that so often beset his dealings with contemporaries and elders – with Acciaiuoli, with Zanobi, with Petrarch, with his own half-brother, Francesco, with his father, Boccaccino – should be banished from his friendships with younger people.[22]

In 1371, Boccaccio made his last journey south, apparently drawn by the suggestion of an old friend that Boccaccio might join him in the monastery where he lived in the country near Catanzaro. The friend greeted Boccaccio warmly when he arrived in Naples, but soon, as the offended Boccaccio wrote to him after the event, "Tu me, more furis atque deceptoris, nedum consulto, verum nec salutato, per noctem in Calabros discessurus conscendisti lembum [like a thief and a con man, without consulting me or even saying good-bye, you boarded the boat one night and returned to Calabria]."[23] Again it was from younger people that Boccaccio gained solace. From a previously unknown admirer, Matteo d'Ambrasio, Boccaccio received a letter to which he replied encouragingly, addressing Matteo as "michi dilectissime iuvens [my most highly esteemed young man]."[24] It is not known whether Matteo d'Ambrasio and Boccaccio ever met, but Matteo did go on to serve as chancellor of the court of Naples and even achieve some standing as a poet.[25] And, of course, Boccaccio was also looked after by Mainardo Cavalcanti, whose attention to the poet on this occasion Vittore Branca called "ancora una volta filiale [once again filial]."[26] On Boccaccio's return to Florence, he corresponded with another aspiring poet, Iacopo

Pizzinga, of whose poetic productions little remains, but whose service as chancellor to the young Sicilian king, Frederick the Simple, would bring him renown.[27] In Boccaccio's later life, there was no dearth of young poets, from Coluccio Salutati to Franco Sacchetti, who benefited from Boccaccio's encouragement and friendship.

If, as Luisa Miglio has suggested, Boccaccio's and Cavalcanti's friendship was "maturatasi [brought to maturity]" during Boccaccio's Neapolitan sojourn of 1362–3,[28] it was during Cavalcanti's visit to Florence in 1372–3 that their friendship bore its richest fruit. Cavalcanti came to Florence to marry Andrea Acciaiuoli. Andrea was Cavalcanti's third cousin, and Cavalcanti was anxious lest their consanguinity, however slight, should threaten the validity of their marriage and cast doubt on their offspring's legitimacy. Because Boccaccio was learned in canon law and was well regarded by the bishop of Florence, Mainardo asked him for professional advice. Boccaccio advised Cavalcanti to proceed with the wedding and ask for dispensation when Cavalcanti could present Church authorities with a *fait accompli*. Boccaccio then fell ill, was unable to attend Cavalcanti's nuptials, and for four months heard no more from his younger friend. When Boccaccio had somewhat recovered and decided to contact Cavalcanti, his letter, Epistle 21, was tinged with that complaint and resentment which in the past had often served only to worsen Boccaccio's dealings with his friends. Cavalcanti, however, in acknowledgment of Boccaccio's help and out of sincere affection for his admired friend, instantly responded with a sumptuous remittance and what seems to have been a letter of heartfelt apology. While Boccaccio composed a thankful reply, he unexpectedly received from Cavalcanti a second sum doubling the amount, whereby, Boccaccio writes, "non expectatis precibus, quibus grandi precio emuntur obsequia, prevenisti ... necessitudinem pauperis amici [without waiting for entreaties, with which favours are so dearly bought, you have anticipated your poor friend's need]."[29]

The same letter suggests that Boccaccio may have invited Mainardo to read some of his lighter works, and it is not impossible that Boccaccio may even have given him copies of the works that he had made himself – the only gifts, perhaps, that were in his power to give. Cavalcanti had apparently still not read these works when Boccaccio's complaining letter reached him, and, indeed, embarrassment for this delinquency may be the reason Cavalcanti did not contact Boccaccio sooner. Now comforted by Cavalcanti's attention and generous gift, it was with good humour and condescension that the older Boccaccio sought to reassure his generous patron by saying, "Te libellos meos non legisse, quod quasi magnum fateris crimen ... non miror ... [I do not wonder that you have not read my trifling books, which you confess as though it were some great crime]." Boccaccio assures Cavalcanti that his works "non ... tanti sunt ut, aliis pretermissis, magna cum solertia legi debeant [are not of such weight that, with everything else set aside, they must be read with great application]." Indeed, Boccaccio says, the responsibilities of Cavalcanti's new household "nedum novum et iuvenem militem, sed etate provectum, canum et scolasticum hominem a sacris etiam studiis et amovisse potuissent et excusatum redderent [could distract, let us say not even a fresh young knight, but an old white-haired scholar from his sacred studies and excuse him]."[30] It would appear, however, that at this point Boccaccio is not altogether without qualms in excusing Cavalcanti's deferral of his pursuit of learning. Boccaccio has already expressed uneasiness about writing a "tumultuariam epistolam [confused letter],"[31] and, in closing, as though uncertain as to what he has suggested about the value of reading, he begs Cavalcanti not to show others the letter, "quas tibi familiariter scribo et forte fidenter nimis [which I write you in a familiar and perhaps too confidential manner]."[32]

More than merely serving to alleviate Boccaccio's need, Cavalcanti's generosity was a token of his sincerity, a sincerity that must have touched Boccaccio in that characteristic humanity of his and persuaded him that Cavalcanti's admiration for his learning, even coming as it did from someone whose learning was so limited, was nevertheless something of worth. That the admiration of learning by the less-than-learned is indispensable to the support and advancement of learning is a proposition that Boccaccio would finally confront directly when he decided to dedicate his perhaps most learned work, the *De casibus virorum illustrium*, to his relatively unlearned friend. None of the conventional candidates he reviewed would do. Popes have given themselves over to warfare, the emperor declines to come to Italy and enforce his authority, one king is persuaded the pursuit of philosophy is "turpissimum [filthy],"[33] another is "bilinguis [double-tongued]," and another is "mollis et effeminatus [soft and effete]."[34] It is not their learning that Boccaccio assesses, but their character. It is not surprising, then, that when he thinks he might better dedicate the book to a friend, he thinks of Mainardo, "cuius fidem cuius dilectionem cuius munificentium [whose faith, whose affection, whose munificence]," Boccaccio tells himself, "sepe expertus es [you have so often experienced]."[35]

Not long after securing the dispensation Boccaccio had advised, Cavalcanti and his bride had a son, and Cavalcanti asked Boccaccio to be the child's godfather. Faith and affection indeed. "Nonne ... huic [are you not to him]," Boccaccio asks himself in the dedication of the *De casibus*, "sacra affinitate iunctus es? Secum, si meminit, unici filii eius communis pater es [bound to him by sacred tie? With him, if I rightly recall, you are in common the father of his only child]."[36] "Preterea [moreover]," says Boccaccio's dedication, "is, esto plene phylosophicis eruditus non sit, amantissimus tamen studiorum est, et probatorum hominum precipuus cultor, atque eorum operum solertissimus indagator [though he may not be fully erudite in philosophy, he is nevertheless a great lover of learning and a most especial cultivator of those who are accomplished and a most diligent follower of their works]."[37] Boccaccio may ask Petrarch, as he does in the work's conclusion, to serve as its censor, but it is to Mainardo that he entrusts the book's publication: "Suscipe ergo illud liberali animo; et si quid sanctum amicitie nomen, iam diu inter te et me equis firmatum animis, meretur, queso susceptum ... legas ... et dum videbitur ... inter amicos comunes et postremo tuo [numine?] emictas in publicum ... [Receive it, therefore, with a generous spirit, and if the sacred name of friendship, now long cemented between you and me with equal minds, means anything, I beg you ... to read it ... and when it seems right, pass it among our common friends, and finally release it under your auspices to the public ...]."[38]

Boccaccio's search for literary relationships based on faith and affection led him to understand that learning cannot thrive in isolation, but must be both shared and supported, ideally not by the powerful so much as by the appreciative. Cavalcanti, with his sensitivity to the strengths and needs of genius, as well as his patient spirit, gave Boccaccio the necessary opportunity to give his concept of literary friendship its highest expression. Boccaccio makes his dedication of the *De casibus* the ideal counterpart to Mainardo's patronage of friendship, which Boccaccio had received from him as "homo ... ab homine, pauper a divite, obscurus a splendido, senex a iuvene [a man from a man, a poor man from a rich one, an obscure man from an eminent one, an old man from a young one]."[39] Boccaccio's dedication recasts the equation so that the poet and the admirer, the master and the novice, the older generation and the younger, the artist and the patron affirm Boccaccio's view of learning and letters "with equal minds," and in so doing reflect the humane and democratic impulse of Boccaccio's better self.[40]

NOTES

1 Giovanni Boccaccio, *Epistole e lettere*, ed. and trans. Ginetta Auzzas with an appendix ed. Augusto Campana, in *Tutte le opere di Giovanni Boccaccio*, ed. Vittore Branca, vol. 5, pt. 1 (Milan: Mondadori,

1992), 493–878, Epist. 13.42. Only a few lines from the end of Epistle 13 survive from its Latin original; the epistle survives in its entirety only in a vernacular translation dating from the early fifteenth century. On this letter and Boccaccio's visit to Naples in 1362–3, see also the previous essay in this volume by Jason Houston. All English translations are mine.

2 Epist. 13.42.

3 Epist. 22.32.

4 Luisa Miglio, "Cavalcanti (de Cavalcantibus) Mainardo (Maghinardo)," *Dizionario Biografico degli Italiani*, vol. 22, 1979.

5 Auzzas, in *Epistole e lettere*, 787n11.

6 Nino Cortese, "Acciaiuoli, Niccolò," *Enciclopedia Italiana*, 1929.

7 E.G. Léonard, "Acciaiuoli, Niccolò," *Dizionario Biografico degli Italiani*, vol. 1, 1960.

8 Auzzas, in *Epistole e lettere*, 832n1.

9 For Cavalcanti's marrying in mid-1372, see Boccaccio's Epist. 21, written in August of that year, esp. sections 15 and 29.

10 For "i trapianti di interi nuclei di suoi [dell'Acciaiuoli] familiari e seguaci [the relocation of whole groups of his [Acciaiuoli's] relatives and followers]," including Mainardo Cavalcanti, into the Neapolitan kingdom, see Francesco Sabatini, *Napoli angioina: Cultura e società* (Naples: Edizioni scientifiche italiane, 1975), 86–7. On the assassination of Queen Johanna's first husband and the invasion of Naples by King Louis I of Hungary, see Elizabeth Casteen's essay in this volume.

11 For Velli's discussion of the date of *Carmen* 7, see introduction, *Carmina*, ed. and trans. Giuseppe Velli, in *Tutte le opere*, ed. Vittore Branca, vol. 5, pt. 1 (Milan: Mondadori, 1992), 375–492.

12 Epist. 13.60.

13 *Croniche di Giovanni, Matteo e Filippo Villani secondo le migliori stampe e corredate di note filologiche e storiche*, ed. A. Racheli, vol. 2 (Trieste: Sezione letterario-artistica del Lloyd austriaco, 1858), 337.

14 Epist. 13.42.

15 Ibid.

16 Boccaccio, *De casibus virorum illustrium*, ed. and trans. Pier Giorgio Ricci and Vittorio Zaccaria, in *Tutte le opere*, ed. Vittore Branca, vol. 9 (Milan: Mondadori, 1983), dedication.13. On Boccaccio's dedications, see the essay by Rhiannon Daniels in this volume.

17 Epist. 13.51.

18 Epist. 13.52.

19 Epist. 13.45.

20 Epist. 14.10.

21 For the young scholars' subsequent activities, see Auzzas, in *Epistole e lettere*, 815nn4, 6.

22 See Houston's essay in this volume for an account of how the souring of relations with Acciaiuoli and Zanobi was accompanied by Boccaccio's attacking the former as a "'nimico' of the Muses" and belittling the latter "by dismissing his literary ability."

23 Epist. 16.10.

24 Epist. 17.1.

25 For the young admirer's later achievements, see Auzzas, in *Epistole e lettere*, 820n1.

26 Vittore Branca, *Giovanni Boccaccio: Profilo biografico* (Florence: Sansoni, 1977), 169.

27 See Epist. 19 and Auzzas, in *Epistole e lettere*, 823n1.

28 Miglio, "Cavalcanti (de Cavalcantibus) Mainardo (Maghinardo)."

29 Epist. 22.29.

30 Epist. 22.17. For what works are referred to in this epistle and Boccaccio's motives for minimizing their importance, see Todd Boli, "Personality and Conflict (*Epistole, Lettere*)," in *Boccaccio: A Critical Guide to the Complete Works*, ed. Victoria Kirkham, Michael Sherberg, and Janet Levarie Smarr (Chicago: University of Chicago Press, 2013), 295–306, and Rhiannon Daniels, "Rethinking the Critical History of the *Decameron*: Boccaccio's Epistle XXII to Mainardo Cavalcanti," *Modern Language Review* 106, no. 2 (2011): 423–47.

31 Epist. 22.2.

32 Epist. 22.44.

33 *De casibus* dedication.8.

34 *De casibus* dedication.9.

35 *De casibus* dedication.13.

36 Ibid.

37 *De casibus* dedication.15.

38 *De casibus* dedication.19.

39 Epist. 22.32.

40 For how another writer of Boccaccio's time and milieu – indeed, an intimate of Boccaccio's – relied on a far-flung network of friends for both moral support and the affirmation of literary values, see Hannah Chapelle Wojciehowski, "Petrarch and His friends," in *The Cambridge Companion to Petrarch*, ed. Albert Russell Ascoli and Unn Falkeid (Cambridge: Cambridge University Press, 2015), 26–35.

PART THREE

Social Contexts: Gender, Marriage, and the Law

5 Reading Like a Woman: Gendering Compassion in the *Elegia di Madonna Fiammetta*

ALESSIA RONCHETTI

Critics have repeatedly stressed the novelty and significance of the feminization of the authorial voice in the *Elegia di Madonna Fiammetta*, and they have acknowledged the emphasis given to compassion as an authorizing device for this gendered authorial voice.[1] In relation to these two aspects, it is interesting to reflect further on the persisting lack of consensus regarding the final, "true meaning" that readers should extract from the text. This problem concerning interpretation is strictly linked to the difficulty of defining the *intentio auctoris*, because more than one name can be associated with the function of authorship here: one is Boccaccio; another is Madonna Fiammetta, the first-person narrator.[2]

One of the factors accounting for readers' divergent opinions is the question of whether the hermeneutic key provided by compassion should ultimately be retained or discarded. As I will discuss, what needs to be evaluated by the interpreter is, in fact, a specific mode of reading that can be defined as "reading like a woman." I will reflect on the hermeneutic risks as well as on the liberating potential associated with this mode of reading.[3] In order to do so, I will look at how previous scholarly research on the *Elegia* has dealt with this issue, but I will also reconsider Fiammetta's discourse against the background of some of the classical and medieval texts forming Boccaccio's encyclopedia. Classical and medieval *auctores* reflected on the notions of pity and compassion from different perspectives, and this essay will highlight how the *Elegia* presents at various points and *on different levels* a complex and often ironic interplay between various approaches found in tradition. My analysis of the *Elegia* will take into account those passages in which the author Fiammetta uses the category of pity to define the terms of the pact between herself and her readers. Furthermore, it will reconsider the metanarrative value of a particular section of Fiammetta's diegesis, that is, the "bed scene" in Chapter 2. In this episode, readers can witness what could be considered a "staged dramatization" of the encounter and the clash between two different hermeneutic schemes centred on the pity motif. It is in the narrative development that follows this episode, and the consequent open-ended structure of the *Elegia*, that some answers to the general question of the function of compassion in textual production can possibly be found.

Let us begin by looking at Fiammetta's authorial prologue in the *Elegia*, in which the mode of reading "like a woman" is strongly promoted:

> Suole a' miseri crescere di dolersi vaghezza, quando di sé discernono o sentono compassione in alcuno. Adunque, acciò che in me, volonterosa più che altra a dolermi, di ciò per lunga usanza non menomi la cagione, ma s'avanzi, mi piace, o nobili donne, ne' cuori delle quali amore più che nel mio forse felicemente dimora, narrando i miei casi, di farvi, s'io posso, pietose. Né m'è cura perché il mio parlare agli uomini non pervenga; anzi, in quanto io posso, del tutto il niego loro, però che sì miseramente in me l'acerbità d'alcuno si discopre, che gli altri simili imaginando, più tosto schernevole riso che pietosa lagrima ne vedrei. Voi sole, le quali io per me medesima conosco pieghevoli e agl'infortunii pie, priego che leggiate. (*Elegia di Madonna Fiammetta, Prologo*, 1–3)[4]
>
> [Unhappy people customarily take greater pleasure in lamenting their lot when they see or hear that someone else feels compassion for them. Therefore, since I am more eager to complain than any other woman, to make certain that the cause of my grief will not grow weaker through habit but stronger, I wish to recount my story to you, noble ladies, and if possible to awaken pity in you, in whose hearts love perhaps dwells more happily than in mine. And I do not care if my speech does not reach the ears of men; in fact if I could, I would entirely keep it away from them, for the harshness of one of them is still so alive in me that I imagine that others to be like him, and I would expect jeering laughter from them rather than compassionate tears. I pray that you alone, in whom I recognize my own open-mindedness and inclination for misfortunes, may be my readers.][5]

In Fiammetta's authorizing strategy, the binary opposition of compassion/cruelty becomes a gendered opposition. The legitimacy of her text depends entirely on the recognition that she hopes to obtain from a readership composed of sympathetic women – a public that she herself intends to shape for this purpose. Male, unsympathetic readers are, at least at first, explicitly excluded from the communication.[6] The association between women and pity is underlined throughout the book. In the several addresses to the ladies that, as Cesare Segre noted, function as connectives between the different parts of the text,[7] the epithet *pietose* (piteous) or its superlative *pietosissime* is predominant, occurring twelve times in total (*pietose*, referring to *donne*, occurs seven times,[8] and the styleme *pietosissime donne* occurs five times).[9]

There is no doubt regarding Fiammetta's view of how her ideal public should respond to her text. However, some modern readers have repeatedly claimed that her desire for a compassionate reading would hardly be shared by Giovanni Boccaccio, Fiammetta's creator. In light of this problem regarding the *intentio auctoris*, let us now briefly reflect on the arguments formulated in the past decades for and against the adoption of compassion. I begin the survey with the words of an illustrious scholar: "Boccaccio is not interested in psychology per se. He does not want us to empathize with Fiammetta; he wants us to see in her steadily worsening condition a demonstration of the effect of sin."[10] At the basis of Janet Smarr's claim is the assumption that Fiammetta's perspective on the world and on love could not coincide with Boccaccio's. Smarr's hypothesis is supported by both intratextual and intertextual evidence. To begin with, there is the legitimate suspicion of Fiammetta's inadequacy in performing the role of protagonist of a tragic love story that she, as an author, has assigned to herself. This inadequacy is repeatedly underlined through the unintentionally comic effects resulting from some of her statements and behaviour. Writing a few years before Smarr, Robert Hollander arrived at the point of stating that "not to see the many caustic elements that perforate Fiammetta's pretensions to amorous nobility is to miss one of the better pleasures of modern fiction – for the *Elegia* is 'the first psychological novel' written in the middle ages … and it is … *a very funny one.*"[11]

Fiammetta's inability to fulfil the role of tragic heroine seems to stem from an originary mistake made by Fiammetta the author: that is, her attempt to project the facts of her life onto a mythical level, constantly comparing her own vicissitudes to those of famous *relictae* such as Dido, Medea, Ariadne, and others. This tendency is given free rein in Chapter 8, where Fiammetta recalls a long catalogue of ancient women in order to present herself as the lover who has endured the greatest suffering of all. Her rhetoric has thus been seen as an indicator of a fundamentally ingenuous, delusional, and/or manipulative use of language and of classical tradition.[12] It also reveals the woman's inability to come to terms with an essential trait pertaining to her condition, namely her being a "modern" woman, a woman of Boccaccio's time. She cannot possibly share the same mythical horizon with the ancient women by analogy with whom she defines herself. For in the transition that has occurred, and that Fiammetta seems to ignore, from the pagan past to the Christian present, the necessity of fate has long been replaced by the possibility of choice.

In this regard, Smarr connects the character of Fiammetta to the negative exemplum *par excellence* on the matter, Dante's Francesca. The validity of this comparison is confirmed by the presence of several references to *Inferno* 5 in the *Elegia*. Unable or unwilling to see the difference between life and literature, Fiammetta, like Francesca, "la ragion sommett[e] al talento [submits reason to appetite]," first by embarking on an adulterous relationship with Panfilo, and subsequently by refusing to change her attitude towards this sinful love. As a consequence of her moral blindness, Fiammetta too, like Francesca, is frozen in a hellish condition of permanent wretchedness.[13]

According to this reading, then, the *Elegia di Madonna Fiammetta* provides an interesting case of an author without authority. Boccaccio, the true *auctor*, is here allegedly offering his readers a well-known lesson that finds its cultural origin in Aristotle and medieval Aristotelianism, as well as in the Augustinian model, which had recently played a crucial role in informing the plan of Dante's *Commedia*: the lesson that abdicating reason for the unregulated pursuit of one's own sensual appetites is morally wrong, and that literary tradition cannot be used to justify this.

Smarr's reading also finds support in documented medieval hermeneutic practices. For our purposes, it suffices to briefly consider the Ovidian commentary tradition (Vincenzo Crescini pointed to Ovid's *Heroides* as the *Elegia*'s main hypotext long ago).[14] In the late Middle Ages, the *Heroides* and more generally the Ovidian *corpus* were consistently acknowledged as useful readings because of their moral and didactic value. Ovid's *intentio* in writing the *epistolae mulierum* was claimed to be that of providing examples of licit and illicit love, praising the former and condemning the latter. The moral lesson that could be drawn was precisely what legitimated the text itself and its fruition – at least in the official context of school teaching.[15]

Hence, Fiammetta would be nothing but another negative example of illicit or, more precisely, foolish love – Fiammetta as another Francesca, then, or rather, an even more pernicious version of Francesca. Not merely "un'intellettuale di provincia [a provincial intellectual]" (to use Contini's famous definition) who has misread tradition and lost her earthly and spiritual life because of it, but rather someone who has also dared to pick up the pen in order to *make* tradition,[16] with the risk of causing even greater damage if her readers believe her words. Should her public therefore feel pity for her, a foolish lover, an unrepentant sinner, an unreliable author? Hollander and Smarr suggest that readers should indeed resist Fiammetta's appeal, because this appeal is just part of a strategy of seduction. Were readers not able to do so, it would mean that they had not learned the lesson resulting from Dante's life-threatening swoon at his hearing Francesca's words.

Having considered what I believe to be the strongest arguments *contra compassionem*, by which critics aim at discouraging readers from employing the hermeneutic tool of compassion to legitimate Fiammetta's text, let us now look at some in favour of its adoption. Previous studies have already highlighted how Boccaccio's exploitation of this theme may be considered an original response to the dominant cultural schemes of his time.[17] This response can be best appreciated once we are reminded of the ambiguous position that compassion is granted, for instance, in the Aristotelian and Scholastic discussions on human emotions and virtues.[18]

Aristotle classified compassion (*eleos*, in Latin translations consistently indicated as *misericordia*) as an emotion, and as such intrinsically neither good nor bad, because emotions (*passiones*) are mere physiological phenomena pertaining to the sensitive soul:

> Dico autem passiones quidem, concupiscentiam, iram, timorem, audaciam, invidiam, gaudium, amicitiam, odium, desiderium, zelum, misericordiam et universaliter quibus sequitur delectatio vel tristitia …
>
> Passiones quidem igitur non sunt neque virtutes neque malitiae. Quoniam neque dicimur secundum passiones studiosi vel pravi. Secundum autem virtutem vel malitiam dicimur. Et quoniam secundum passiones quidem neque laudamur neque vituperamur. Non enim laudatur qui timet neque qui irascitur. Neque vituperatur, qui simpliciter irascitur, sed qui qualiter. (*Ethica ad Nicomachum* 2.4, 182 and 185–6, p. 83)[19]

> [By emotions I mean appetite, anger, fear, boldness, envy, joy, friendly feeling, hatred, longing, jealousy, pity, and in general all passions that are followed by pleasure or pain …

> Emotions are neither virtues nor vices, for we are not to be defined as good or bad because of our passions, but because of our virtues and vices. And we are neither praised nor blamed for our passions. We do not praise the person who is frightened or who is angry, nor do we blame the angry person simply for being angry, but because he is angry in a certain way.]

According to Aristotle, it is not the emotion itself (*simpliciter*) that is subject to praise or condemnation, but rather the moral choices that are made in relation to that emotion (*qualiter*).

Already in late antiquity, however, the lexeme *misericordia* came to designate not only the *emotion* of pity but also the *virtue* of mercy. In accounting for the ambiguity of this signifier, Christian authors such as Augustine and Thomas Aquinas tried to establish some clear conceptual distinctions. They affirmed that *misericordia* should be intended as a virtue in those cases in which the emotion of pity is mastered, directed, sometimes even summoned, by reason.[20] And *misericordia* understood as a virtue, a *habitus* in Aristotelian terms, was considered the *maxima virtus* in God, whilst among men it was second only to charity (*caritas*), from which it derived.[21]

In the transition from Latin to vernacular, the same semantic overlapping invests the term *pietà*, to the point that Dante in the *Convivio* feels the need to establish a lexical distinction between *pietà* (which designates the virtue) and *misericordia* (which designates the emotion):

> E non è pietade quella che crede la volgar gente, cioè dolersi de l'altrui male, anzi è questo uno suo speziale effetto, che si chiama misericordia ed è passione; ma pietade non è passione, anzi è una nobile disposizione d'animo, apparecchiata di ricevere amore, misericordia e altre caritative passioni. (*Convivio* 2.10.6)[22]

> [And *pietade* is not what is commonly believed, that is, feeling sorry for the suffering of others: the latter is actually a passion called *misericordia*, which is a specific effect of it [scil. *pietade*]. But *pietade* is not a passion, on the contrary, it is a noble disposition of the soul ready to receive love, pity and other passions connected to charity.]

Dante himself did not retain this rigorous separation of signifiers in the *Commedia*, however, and Boccaccio correctly described the lexeme *pietà* occurring in *Inferno* 5.72 and 140 as a synonym of *compassione*, an emotion.[23]

As Michael Papio has observed, the regular use of the vernacular term *compassione* as synonym of *pietà* seems to have been Boccaccio's own innovation.[24] In this regard, it is interesting to note that the use of the Latin word *compassio* as synonym of *misericordia* (the emotion) is repeatedly found in Thomas Aquinas's *Summa theologiae*, specifically in *Quaestio 30 de misericordia*. The interchangeability of these two terms is probably the result of the influence of Augustine's definition, quoted by Aquinas, of *misericordia* as "compassion felt in our heart for another person's wretchedness, for which we feel urged to come to the aid of the sufferer, if this is in our power."[25]

Aquinas's discussion of *misericordia* also includes a detailed analysis of the phenomenology of this passion. Here again the main *auctoritas* is Aristotle. In order to feel compassion, the subject must establish a connection with the sufferer, either through love or more frequently through a process of self-mirroring; for instance, by recognizing the possibility that s/he may feel the same pain in the future, or by remembering a similar past experience.[26]

This second type of empathetic bond, based on seeing one's own weaknesses and misfortunes reflected in those of a suffering other, had been the object of detailed discussion in the rhetorical tradition. One aspect that should be considered carefully is that Aristotle had explicitly acknowledged the *hermeneutic importance of pity and of emotions in general*: "the emotions," he stated in the *Rhetoric*, "are all those feelings that so change men as to affect their judgements."[27] That is, emotions make us look at the world in a certain way; they play a fundamental role in cognition.[28] This means that within emotions lies an immensely creative power. Emotions, including compassion, make certain worlds possible. Therefore, because manipulating the perception that people have of the world is among the primary tasks of the rhetorician, treatises on rhetoric offered readers lists of commonplaces that could be used to favour empathetic identification and thus win the public's benevolence.[29]

This type of compassion, however, had also been criticized severely for its moral flaws, which were exacerbated if the process of self-identification was achieved through fictional artifices. Augustine's position in this regard is well known. What Augustine found morally wrong in empathetic identification stimulated through fiction was that such identification was also accompanied by a dose of self-complacency, that is, a feeling of *delectatio*, of pleasure. How could it be right to feel pleasure as a result of joining the sufferer in his/her suffering? In contrast to this morally dubious type of *misericordia*, Augustine pointed to an ideal model analogous to God's mercy towards his creatures – a sort of emotionless *misericordia*, free from sorrow, let alone the narcissistic enjoyment derived from seeing the other's miseries as a reflection of one's own.[30]

All these discourses on compassion leave their traces in Boccaccio's works. But was he interested in compassion mainly in itself, that is, as morally neutral? Or did he grant so much attention to this emotion mostly because of its association with a moral *habitus*? To go back to the general problem highlighted at the beginning of my essay, what is the *intentio auctoris* behind Boccaccio's recurrent employment of the pity motif in his texts and specifically in the *Elegia di Madonna Fiammetta*?

The two most important studies on Boccaccio's hermeneutics of compassion, both published in 2000, have provided some interesting answers to these questions. The author of the first study, Michael Papio, mentioned above, considers compassion a fundamental component of Boccaccio's "ethical poetics."[31] His analysis reconstructs the discourses on compassion and pity available in Boccaccio's time, retracing the various theorizations in Patristic and Scholastic writers, as well as in the rhetorical tradition, from Aristotle to Cicero to late medieval authors such as Brunetto Latini. For Papio, Boccaccio's treatment of compassion embraces all these traditions and in so doing transcends their respective limitations of scope. For instance, if Boccaccio shows his authorial ability in making his characters employ those topoi that a good orator is expected to use in order to summon compassion in his audience, he also seems to subordinate the display of this rhetorical expertise to some well-defined ethical purposes.[32]

But what are these ethical purposes? According to Papio, Boccaccio evidently does not adhere to the Augustinian condemnation of compassion when this emotion is aroused through fictional literature. For Boccaccio, this type of "artificial" compassion too can be morally good if summoned for therapeutic and cathartic ends, because the shared suffering that compassion makes possible helps the sufferer to establish a healthy distance from those very emotions that caused his/her wretchedness. Papio's conclusion is that "[i]n Boccaccio's view, it is not enough to cause others to feel compassion; they must share in the suffering for the right reasons. When suffering is part of convalescent compassion, even a 'fictionally' inspired emotion is virtuous."[33]

The second study, which presents a very different (although in some respects complementary) approach, is that of Luigi Surdich. Surdich considers especially the socio-cultural and anthropological function of empathetic identification in the formation of collective memory. Relying mostly on contemporary studies on the philosophy of emotions, Surdich emphasizes the importance of compassion in the transition from the immediacy of passions, experienced by the individual, to intersubjective communication, through which these passions assume the forms that constitute shared knowledge. Because of the key role played by literature in this process (for literature is inextricably linked to the shaping of individual and collective memories), Surdich sees in literature itself the place that makes compassion possible, that is, its constitutive locus: "è la scrittura, è il libro, è la letteratura, insomma, il luogo di fondazione della compassione, della sua trasmissibilità e della sua ricezione [writing, the book, in sum, literature, is the foundational locus of compassion, of its transmissibility and of its reception]."[34]

This theoretical framework is the basis for Surdich's analysis of Boccaccio's re-semanticization of compassion after Dante. For Surdich, the difference between the two authors lies in the fact that, whereas in Dante's model compassion must ultimately be transcended in favour of higher values (equity, justice, rectitude), in Boccaccio's poetics passions cannot be transcended: hence the necessity to maintain compassion as a primary hermeneutic tool. Without the mediation of compassion, Surdich seems to imply, this type of literature would not be "authorized" to enter the communication circuit.[35]

Although Surdich's discussion of the social and cognitive importance of compassion relies mostly on contemporary philosophical and psychoanalytic research, it nevertheless presents a view that is in some respects consonant with discourses on pity found in the medieval canon. An author such as Lactantius, for instance, explicitly indicates in compassion (which he calls *miserationis affectus*) the most distinctive trait of *humanitas*. Compassion is what determines the capacity of humans to bond with other humans; that is, it is the precondition for their life as social animals.[36] In a similar vein, Isidore of Seville explains the meaning of the lexeme *humanus*, integrating Lactantius's definition with the addition of love as another essential component of human nature: "Humanus, quod habeat circa homines amorem et miserationis affectum. Unde et humanitas dicta, qua nos invicem tuemur [*Humane*, in that one has love and compassion for humans. Hence *humanity*, by which we protect one another]."[37]

When Boccaccio begins the *Decameron*'s *Proemio* with the proverbial sentence "Umana cosa è avere compassione degli afflitti [To take pity on people in distress is a human quality],"[38] he is in fact connecting his text to a well-established and authoritative discourse that sees in compassion the defining quality of being human. In moral terms, Boccaccio's statement is, however, more ambiguous than it seems at first glance. On the basis of the distinctions outlined above, the emotion of compassion itself is not sufficient to guarantee the moral value of the book-as-*Galeotto*. This morality will therefore have to be subsequently evaluated, judging not the emotion itself but rather the authorial choices that followed, which involve not only the selection of the narrative material but also the type of practical response that a book with given formal qualities elicits from its addressees. And readers of the *Decameron* know that confronting the difficulty of this process of evaluation is part of the literary game set out by the text.

In his earlier works, before arriving at the complex equilibrium of the *Decameron*, Boccaccio seems to be progressively testing the possibilities offered by the literary device of compassion by considering it from different perspectives. Among these, we can notice how the appeal to compassion found in the *Elegia di Madonna Fiammetta* produces interesting results in relation to the *pre-moral* domain that was implicitly individuated in Aristotle's *Rhetoric*: in other words, compassion can function as a hermeneutic tool that allows the intersubjective exchange of alternative representations of the world.

Hans Robert Jauss rightly underlined the growing importance in the late Middle Ages of what, in our post-Kantian era, we would call the aesthetic function of compassion. Jauss saw in "the striking development of the pity motif" in visions of the other world, culminating in Dante's *Commedia*, a marker of a transgression, with reference to traditional exegesis, that had the effect of undermining the dogmatic contents of these texts without openly challenging them.[39]

My claim is that the semantic instability generated by the lexicon of pity allows Boccaccio just this type of controlled transgression, although the traditional readings challenged are in his case those pertaining to the this-worldly dimension. Boccaccio seems to be profoundly aware of how compassion can regulate social interactions by conditioning the processes of attribution of meaning and value. At the same time, he shows how the alternative – and even subversive – representations of the world that a hermeneutics of compassion makes possible are often considered acceptable precisely because they are voiced by subjects whose authority is constructed as "weak." Among these "weak" subjects, women are granted the highest degree of visibility.

Boccaccio seems to have understood the literary possibilities connected to the traditional association between the feminine and pity. This association was certainly a fundamental feature of courtly love ideology, but if we look further back in time we can find that Aristotle already sees compassion as an emotion to which women are particularly prone.[40] In stating this, Aristotle is far from praising women: in fact, his claim is consonant with his views on nature, on the human soul, on society, and on the relationship between the sexes. According to Aristotle, women are less able than men to use their reason to exercise control over the *motus animae*, that is, the mutations and alterations that affect the *anima sensitiva*. Women's natural passivity makes them more easily affected by the impressions and emotions that are produced in their encounter with the outside world; the consequence of this is that they are constitutively incapable of valid, authoritative deliberations over their lives and those of others.[41]

A rhetoric/hermeneutic of compassion used as a device to empower the feminine voice – precisely the rhetoric used by Fiammetta – thus rests on a paradox: its main weapon derives from what tradition indicates as the cause of women's natural and social inferiority, namely what Thomas Aquinas, in glossing Aristotle, indicates as the *mollities naturae* that characterizes the female sex, and that makes it opportune, if not necessary, for those women who aspire to be virtuous to entrust themselves to the guidance of men.[42]

It is this paradox that Boccaccio highlights through Fiammetta's appeal to her female or feminized readers. Within an Aristotelian and Scholastic framework, that is, within the sphere of official discourse, neither the narrator of the *Elegia* nor her public can ever be considered authoritative. In support of this, we can observe that what Fiammetta seems to be invoking is precisely the sort of compassionate response condemned by Augustine as immoral for its indissoluble connection with narcissistic pleasure. In fact, the circuit of complicity established by Fiammetta and her ideal audience sustains this pleasure: the pleasure of the narrator, who thus fulfils her wish to prolong her lament indefinitely; and the pleasure of readers, for Fiammetta is one of them, a *donna innamorata* occupying a position within a fictional narrative in which they can easily imagine themselves, but in relation to which they are temporarily free from the burden of having to make their own moral choices.[43]

Even if discredited as an author, Fiammetta still provides a different vision of the world for those who wish simply to consider it. Perhaps Boccaccio's purpose in doing so is not only to offer readers the opportunity to reflect on the moral dangers of such representation but also to create the conditions in which this view is possible, that is, narratable. In other words, before (and without excluding) any ethical concern, there may be an aesthetic one that should equally be taken into account.

The clash between this feminine, "scandalous" hermeneutics and a much more potent, authoritative mode of reading is not only evoked by Fiammetta the author in her initial and concluding addresses to her public. It is also powerfully dramatized in the diegesis. Let us now look at the "bed scene" in Chapter 2, more specifically at the conversation that takes place between Fiammetta and her lover, Panfilo. When Fiammetta notices that Panfilo is crying, she exhorts him to reveal the reason for his distress. Panfilo confesses that he cannot refrain from crying because he sees that *he cannot split himself in two*:

> – di me due fare non posso, com'io vorrei, acciò che ad Amore e alla debita pietà ad una ora satisfare potessi, qui dimorando e là, dove necessità strettissima mi tira per forza, andando. Dunque non potendosi, in afflizione gravissima il mio cuore misero ne dimora, sì come colui che, da una parte traendo pietà, è fuori delle tue braccia tirato, e dall'altra in quelle con somma forza da Amore ritenuto – . (*Elegia di Madonna Fiammetta* 2.3.1–2)
>
> [I cannot divide myself into two as I would like to do, so as to satisfy at once the demands of Love by staying here and proper compassion by going where a compelling need forces me to go. Since this is impossible, my deeply afflicted heart aches, as does the heart of one who on the one hand is pulled and dragged out of your arms by compassion, and, on the other, is held in them with the greatest force by Love.]

As Panfilo subsequently explains, his old father is requesting his presence in Florence. The "debita pietà filiale [due filial pity/piety]" that Panfilo feels is required in these circumstances prompts him to comply with his father's last wish. On the other hand, if his devotion to his father drives him towards his hometown, Love leads him in the opposite direction, that is, it urges him to stay in Naples with Fiammetta. In her attempt to persuade Panfilo to stay, Fiammetta opposes to his "debita pietà" the "pietà" that he should feel for her as his lover:

> – Dunque, la *pietà del vecchio padre* preposta, a quella che di me dèi avere, mi sarà di morte cagione, e tu non amadore, ma nemico, se così fai. Deh,

vorrai tu, o potrail fare, pure che io il consenta, i pochi anni al vecchio padre serbati ai molti, che ancora a me ragionevolmente si debbono, antiporre? Oimè, *che iniqua pietà sarà questa*? È egli tua credenza, o Panfilo, che niuna persona, sia di te quantunque egli vuole o puote per parentado di sangue o per amistà congiunta, t'ami sì come io t'amo? Male credi, se di sì credi: veramente niuno t'ama così come io. Dunque, se io più t'amo, più pietà merito, e perciò degnamente antiponmi, e *di me essendo pietoso, d'ogni altra pietà ti dispoglia ch'offenda questa*, e sanza te lascia riposare il tuo padre, e così come, tu non con lui, lungamente è vivuto, se li piace, per inanzi si viva; e se no, muoiasi. Egli è fuggito molti anni al mortal colpo, s'io odo il vero, e più c'è vivuto che non si conviene; e s'egli con fatica vive, come i vecchi fanno, *sarà vie maggiore pietà di te verso lui il lasciarlo morire, che più in lui con la tua presenza prolungare la fatichevole vita* … – . (*Elegia di Madonna Fiammetta* 2.6.9–12; my emphasis)

[Therefore, it is your pity for your old father, placed before that pity you should feel for me, which will be the cause of my death, and if you do this, you will be an enemy instead of a lover. Alas, would you or could you, even if I allowed it, really put the few years of life still left to your father to live ahead of the many years I most likely have coming to me? Alas, what wicked pity would this be? Do you believe, Panfilo, that anyone, however closely he wants to be or can be joined in kinship or by ties of friendship, can love you as much as I do? If you believe that, you are wrong, because no one can indeed love you as much as I do. So if I love you more, I deserve more compassion; therefore, let me properly be your first choice, and by feeling sorry for me you may forget any other pity that may detract from this, and let your father remain without you; since he has lived without you for so long, let him continue to do so if it pleases him, and if not, let him die. If I understand correctly, he has escaped the mortal blow for many years and has lived longer than he should; and if he is weary of living, as old people are, it would be much more compassionate of you to let him die than to prolong his weary life through your presence.]

Here we have an example of the humour that Hollander noted in the *Elegia*. In a typically Boccaccian fashion, however, this comical passage makes acceptable what is in fact a challenge to the hermeneutic power of well-established moral schemes. The lexeme *pietà* occurs fifty-five times in the *Elegia*; more than a third of these occurrences (twenty) are concentrated in this dialogue between the two lovers. Clearly the signifier *pietà* becomes here the centre of an intense "semantic conflict" between Panfilo and Fiammetta. For what does the term *pietà* mean here? Which system of values, that is, which model(s) of the world and of society, should be framing this signifier?

The numerous references to Dantean, Virgilian, and Ovidian sources, already detected by scholars, help us answer these questions.[44] "Pietà del vecchio padre" is derived from *Inferno* 26.94–5. As in Dante's text, *pietà* recalls the concept indicated with the Latin term *pietas*. In *Inferno* 26, Ulysses mentions this virtue only to underline his guilty dismissal of it in favour of that insatiable appetite for knowledge that led him to his death. This way, Dante famously constructs the Greek hero as an anti-Aeneas. For *pietas* is the sacred devotion to the fathers and the fatherland that represents the most defining quality of the Virgilian hero.[45] It is to honour his commitment to the will of the gods, to his father's memory, and to his son's future that Aeneas rejects his erotic passion for Dido, leaving the woman to her tragic destiny.

The relationship between Panfilo and Fiammetta is thus modelled analogically on that of Aeneas and Dido. To consider Fiammetta's vicissitudes those of a modern Dido is, after all, a reading suggested by the author herself, who in Chapter 8 indicates the Queen of Carthage as the figure of *relicta* with whom she feels the greatest proximity.[46] This overt connection between the dyad Aeneas-Dido and that of Panfilo-Fiammetta is interesting for more than one reason. In a way, it supports those moralizing readings of the *Elegia* that suggest that one should resist Fiammetta's appeal to compassion. In the previously mentioned commentaries on Ovid's *Heroides*, Dido's epistle to Aeneas was traditionally indicated as an example of discourse typically uttered by the *stultus amans*.[47] More generally, in Boccaccio's time, the practice – already present *in nuce* in authors such as Servius and Augustine – of reading Aeneas's journey allegorically, as an ideal biographical model representing a man's moral development, had long been consolidated.[48] In this model, Dido, symbolizing lust, erotic love, or more generally the power of the passions, functioned as an obstacle that had to be overcome in the transition from youth to maturity.[49] A compelling example in this regard is that offered by Augustine. Arguing that emotions should not weaken the capacity for rational judgment in the wise man, Augustine recalls a line from *Aeneid* 4.449 ("mens immota manet; lacrimae volvuntur inanes [the soul remains unmoved; tears fall in vain]"), which describes Aeneas's firm refusal to show compassion for Dido, who has been pleading with him, through her sister, to at least delay his departure from Carthage.[50] In this way, Augustine also establishes a distance between his present self and his past self, relinquishing the deep empathetic bond that he had felt in his youth for the abandoned Queen.[51]

Yet this moral type of reading is not the only one available. Fiammetta's (and Boccaccio's) decision to represent the story of her love by adopting the scheme of the Ovidian elegy allows her to take advantage of a fundamental characteristic of this genre: the fact that it provides an established form through which voices which are potentially subversive of the symbolic order affirmed in master narratives can nevertheless be heard.[52]

The pivot of Fiammetta's counter-reading of Panfilo's "text" is precisely the recontextualization of *pietà* within elegiac discourse: not *pietas*, but rather compassion; that is, the feeling of *misericordia* that the abandoned lover, the subject of elegy, invokes for herself.[53] In this emphasis on compassion as a tool that can potentially destabilize official value systems, Boccaccio shows his originality with respect to his sources. Neither in Virgil nor in Ovid does Dido appeal to Aeneas's *misericordia* as often as Fiammetta does with Panfilo. If the Virgilian and Ovidian heroine is *misera*, the exhortative *miserere* addressed to Aeneas occurs only once (l. 318) in *Aeneid* 4, and never in Dido's epistle.

In Boccaccio's heightened interest in the theme of pity we might also detect the mediation of early fourteenth-century *volgarizzamenti* of the *Heroides*. One of these *volgarizzamenti*, which Boccaccio is likely to have known, is that by Filippo Ceffi (c. 1325).[54] Ceffi's case is particularly interesting because of the great attention and precision with which he translates from the original. There are, however, a few slight departures from the Ovidian text. Below are two examples that are relevant to our discussion, in which we can compare Ovid's lines with Ceffi's translation. In both cases we can see some significant interpolations:

> Nec mihi tu curae; puero parcatur Iulo.
> Te satis est titulum mortis habere meae. (*Heroides* 7.75–6)[55]

> E se *tanta tenera pietade* e dubbiosa paura non ti muove, perdona al giovanissimo figliuolo Giulio e bastisi che tu abbi della mia morte il titolo. (Ceffi 7 §73; my emphasis)[56]

> vix tibi continget terra petita seni.
> Hos potius populos in dotem, ambage remissa
> accipe … (*Heroides* 7.148–50)[57]

> et a pena giugnerai al tuo desiderato aquisto, che tu non sii imprima vecchio. *Ora dunque abbi pietade di Dido* e prendi questi popoli in dote e lascia la tua dubbiosa impresa … (Ceffi 7 §147; my emphasis)

The example of Ceffi may be taken as indicative of a cultural tendency to emphasize the pathetic elements that are traditionally associated with specific discursive forms. In this context, Boccaccio's attention to the theme of compassion may be explained also, although in my view not exclusively, in the light of his being "a man of his time."

Elsewhere, I have reflected on the possible autobiographical concerns that could have led Boccaccio to select the model of Ovidian elegy to represent the relationship between Panfilo and Fiammetta. I consider both Panfilo and Fiammetta as embodiments of Boccaccio's self, but I also suggest that it is in the dynamic interaction between these two gendered authorial polarities that this self may be expressing his desire for unity.[58] This could partly explain, on a deeper level, why Boccaccio's Panfilo could never match the figure of Virgil's Aeneas, despite Fiammetta's attempt to construct Panfilo as a classical hero. Among the various differences between the two, one is especially pertinent to my analysis: whereas Aeneas sternly rejects Dido's appeal to stay, denying any validity to her discourse on the world and on their relationship (*Aeneid* 4.33–61), Panfilo seems initially to authorize Fiammetta's reading of his present situation:

> – Pensare dèi e essere certa che, bene che la pietà del vecchio padre mi stringa assai, e debitamente, non meno, ma molto più quella di noi medesimi mi costrigne; la quale, se lecita fosse a discoprire, scusato mi parrebbe essere, presummendo che, non che da mio padre solo, ma ancora da qualunque altro fosse giudicato quel che dicesti, e lascerei il vecchio padre, sanza vedermi, morire. Ma *convenendo questa pietà essere occulta*, sanza quella palese adempiere, non veggo come sanza gravissima riprensione e infamia fare lo potessi … – . (*Elegia di Madonna Fiammetta* 2.7, 3–4; my emphasis)

> [You must believe and be certain that while I am duly and strongly pressed by the compassion I feel for my aged father, I am not less but much more strongly compelled by the pity I feel for ourselves which, if it were possible to reveal, I would seem to be justified (supposing that what you said were to be judged not just by my old father alone, but by everyone else) and because of which I could let my father die without his seeing

> me again. But since this kind of devotion must be kept hidden, I fail to see how I could fall short of fulfilling the demands of the kind that is visible, except with extreme criticism and shame …]

What is Panfilo saying to Fiammetta? He is saying that yes, *pietà* may have the meaning that she suggests. In the privacy of their relationship, Panfilo agrees to talk about the world using the same "grammar" as his lover. The problem is that Fiammetta's text cannot be accepted if its author demands its validation within the sphere of official discourse. Panfilo knows this, and for this reason he leaves the woman, having chosen to belong to the world ruled according to the symbolic order centred on *pietas*.

Through Panfilo's departure Fiammetta has thus painfully experienced her limits as the author of her own text. At this point, we can fully appreciate the importance of defining a public of female readers for her *piccolo libretto*. In order to preserve Fiammetta's voice, in order to protect her words and her world from the threat of being silenced and erased, another mode of reading is needed, an alternative to the official, masculine gloss to which Panfilo has ultimately decided to conform. Unlike Panfilo, the "donne pietose" – or those who wish to assume that reader position – will be able to grant Fiammetta the pity she asked for. I am far from claiming that this latter mode of reading is the only valid one; after all, we must not forget that Boccaccio is *both* Panfilo and Fiammetta in this story. Where Panfilo fails to split himself into two, Boccaccio succeeds. And could this not be considered also a model for readers? That is, being able not only to read "as a man," in accordance with what a powerful tradition has defined as "reason," but also "as a woman": through a deep emotional involvement that *precedes* any moral judgment, and that is justified by the pleasure of discovering, now as then, that awareness of and respect for human suffering is often the only instrument that allows the sharing of texts.[59]

NOTES

1 On the function of compassion in the *Elegia di Madonna Fiammetta* and more generally in Boccaccio's poetics, see Cesare Segre, "Strutture e registri nella *Fiammetta*," in *Le strutture e il tempo* (Turin: Einaudi, 1974), 87–115; Michael Papio, "*Non meno di compassion piena che dilettevole*: Notes on Compassion in Boccaccio," *Italian Quarterly* 37 (2000): 107–25; Luigi

Surdich, "Tra Dante e Boccaccio: qualche appunto sulla *compassione*," in *Le passioni tra astensione e riserbo*, ed. Romana Rutelli and Luisa Villa (Pisa: ETS, 2000), 35–50. These and other views will be discussed in the course of this essay.

2 I have discussed this aspect in greater depth in a recent article, written for the purpose of investigating the *Elegia di Madonna Fiammetta* as a text signalling a new stage in Boccaccio's autobiographism in the years immediately following his return to Florence. See Alessia Ronchetti, "Boccaccio between Naples and Florence, or the Desire to Become Two: Gendering the Author's Past in the *Elegia di Madonna Fiammetta*," *Italian Studies* 72 (2017): 203–15. The present essay differs in its scope from my previous study; however, particularly in the last section, it overlaps with and integrates the analysis that I developed there.

3 In the last decades, important scholarly works on Boccaccio's treatment of gender and of female authority have been published, which have contributed to shaping the analytical approach presented in this study. See in particular Joy Hambuechen Potter, "Woman in the *Decameron*," in *Studies in the Italian Renaissance: Essays in Memory of Arnolfo B. Ferruolo*, ed. G.P. Biasin, A.N. Mancini, and N.J. Perella (Naples: Società Editrice Napoletana, 1985), 87–103; Claude Cazalé Bérard, "Filoginia/misoginia," in *Lessico critico decameroniano*, ed. Renzo Bragantini and Pier Massimo Forni (Turin: Bollati Boringhieri, 1995), 116–41; Regina Psaki, "Women in the *Decameron*," in *Approaches to Teaching Boccaccio's Decameron*, ed. James McGregor (New York: Modern Language Association of America, 2000), 79–86; Psaki, "Voicing Gender in the *Decameron*," in *Cambridge Companion to Boccaccio*, ed. Guyda Armstrong, Rhiannon Daniels, and Stephen J. Milner (Cambridge: Cambridge University Press, 2015), 101–18; the introduction and essays by various authors contained in the volume *Boccaccio and Feminist Criticism*, ed. Regina Psaki and Thomas C. Stillinger (Chapel Hill: Annali d'Italianistica, 2006); Marilyn Migiel, *A Rhetoric of the Decameron* (Toronto: University of Toronto Press, 2003); Migiel, "Boccaccio and Women," in *Cambridge Companion to Boccaccio*, 171–84; Kristina Olson, "The Language of Women as Written by Men: Boccaccio, Dante and Gendered Histories of the Vernacular," *Heliotropia* 8–9 (2011–12): 51–78.

4 All references to the *Elegia di Madonna Fiammetta* follow Carlo Delcorno's edition, in *Tutte le opere di Giovanni Boccaccio*, ed. Vittore Branca, vol. 5, pt. 2 (Milan: Mondadori, 1994), 1–412.

5 All translations of passages from Boccaccio's *Elegia di Madonna Fiammetta* cited in this article are from *The Elegy of Lady Fiammetta*, ed. Mariangela

Causa-Steindler and Tomas Mauch (Chicago: University of Chicago Press, 1990). Translations from other authors are mine.

6 In Chapter 9, Fiammetta considers the possibility that Panfilo himself might read the book "con umana mente [with a humane mind]" (9.1.16) and consequently return to her. This, however, is introduced only as a remote possibility.

7 Segre, "Strutture e registri nella *Fiammetta*," 93–4.

8 Boccaccio, *Elegia di Madonna Fiammetta, Prol.* 1; 1.9, 1 and 1.18, 1; 3.9, 1; 4.1, 1; 5.1, 1 and 4.

9 Ibid., 1.8, 1 and 23, 9; 5.18, 1; 6.1, 1; 8.1, 1.

10 Janet Levarie Smarr, *Boccaccio and Fiammetta: The Narrator as Lover* (Urbana: University of Illinois Press, 1986), 132.

11 Robert Hollander, *Boccaccio's Two Venuses* (New York: Columbia University Press, 1977), 41–2; my emphasis.

12 See Marina Brownlee, "Voyeuristic Betrayal: *Elegia di Madonna Fiammetta,*" in *The Severed Word: Ovid's "Heroides" and the "Novela Sentimental"* (Princeton: Princeton University Press, 1990), 58–69: "deluded" (59); Hollander, *Boccaccio's Two Venuses*: "self-deceiver" (46); Smarr, *Boccaccio and Fiammetta*: "Rhetoric for her is the means to deceive herself" (146); Michael Calabrese, "Feminism and the Packaging of Boccaccio's *Fiammetta,*" *Italica* 74 (1997): 20–42: "deluded," "self-indulgent" (23). See also, more recently, Giuseppe Chiecchi, "*Elegia di Madonna Fiammetta*: in margine alla mitologia del personaggio," *Studi sul Boccaccio* 43 (2015): 77–122: "predisposizione a ingannare e a ingannarsi [predisposition to deceive and to deceive oneself]" (84).

13 Smarr, *Boccaccio and Fiammetta*, esp. 129–30. See also Vittore Branca, *Giovanni Boccaccio. Profilo biografico* (Florence: Sansoni, 1997; first published in 1977), 67; Hollander, *Boccaccio's Two Venuses*, 40–9, esp. 48.

14 Vincenzo Crescini, *Contributo agli studi sul Boccaccio con documenti inediti* (Turin: Loescher, 1887), 156–62.

15 On the medieval reception of the *Heroides*, see *Accessus ad auctores*, Collection Latomus 15, ed. R.B.C. Huygens (Brussels: Berchem, 1954), 24–8; Ralph J. Hexter, *Ovid and Medieval Schooling: Studies in Medieval School Commentaries on Ovid's "Ars Amatoria," "Epistulae ex Ponto," and "Epistulae Heroidum"* (Munich: Arbeo-Gesellschaft, 1997), 137–218; Suzanne Hagedorn, *Abandoned Women: Rewriting the Classics in Dante, Boccaccio, and Chaucer* (Ann Arbor: University of Michigan Press, 2004), 27ff.

16 In this regard, Fiammetta's project is highly ambitious, as her self-image, her autobiographical narrative, and her stylistic register are fashioned against the background of classical and Dantean texts. For a recent survey

of Fiammetta's rereading, as well as misreading, of many of these texts, see Chiecchi, "*Elegia di Madonna Fiammetta*."

17 See especially Papio, "*Non meno di compassion piena*," and Surdich, "Tra Dante e Boccaccio," both discussed below.

18 For a recently updated list of existing studies on the influence of Aristotle and Thomas Aquinas on Boccaccio, see Alessia Ronchetti, "Between *Filocolo* and *Filostrato*: Boccaccio's Authorial Doubles and the Question of *amore per diletto*," *Italianist* 35 (2015): 318–33; 329–30n10.

19 All subsequent references to this work will follow the numeration of R.M. Spiazzi's edition, *Ethica ad Nicomachum*, in *Sancti Thomae Aquinatis in decem libros Ethicorum Aristotelis ad Nicomachum expositio* (Turin: Marietti, 1964), which contains the Latin translation by William of Moerbeke, accompanied by Thomas Aquinas's commentary.

20 Thomas Aquinas, *Summa theologiae* 2a–2ae, 59, 1 r. 3: "*misericordia* dicitur esset virtus, id est, virtutis actus, secundum quod motus ille animi rationi servit … Si tamen misericordia dicatur aliquis habitus quo homo perficitur ad rationabiliter miserendum, nihil prohibet misericordiam sic dictam esse virtutem. Et eadem est ratio de similibus passionibus [*misericordia* is said to be a virtue, that is, an act of virtue, when that movement of the soul serves reason … If *misericordia* is defined as a habit by which man perfects himself in feeling compassion in accordance with reason, nothing prevents *misericordia* from being defined a virtue. And the same applies to similar passions]." All references to this work follow the Blackfriars edition (London: Blackfriars, 1964).

21 Aquinas, *Summa theologiae* 2a–2ae, 30, 4.

22 I am following here Giorgio Inglese's edition of Dante's *Convivio* (Milan: Rizzoli, 1993).

23 Boccaccio, *Esposizioni sopra la Comedia* V (1), 138–40 and 185.

24 Papio, "*Non meno di compassion piena*," 122.

25 Augustine, *De civitate Dei* 9.5: "Quid est autem *misericordia*, nisi alienae miseriae quaedam in nostro corde compassio, qua utique, si possumus, subvenire compellimur?" (All references to this text follow J.P. Migne's edition, *Sancti Aurelii Augustini Hipponensis Episcopi De Civitate Dei Libri XXII*, in *Patrologia Latina* 41 (1841). See also Aquinas, *Summa theologiae* 2a–2ae, 30, 1.

26 Aquinas, *Summa theologiae* 2a–2ae, 30, 2 r: "semper defectus est ratio miserendi: vel inquantum aliquis defectum alicuius reputat suum, propter unionem amoris, vel propter possibilitate similia patiendi [what causes compassion is always some lack: someone considers a lack in another as his own, either because they are bound together by love, or because of the possibility of suffering in a similar way]."

27 Aristotle, *Rhetorica*, in *Aristoteles Latinus*, ed. B. Schneider (Leiden: Brill, 1978), 2.1 (1378a 21–3), 221: "Sunt autem passiones propter quascumque commoti differunt ad iudicia ad quas sequitur tristitia et delectatio, puta ira misericordia timor et quecumque alia talia, et hiis contraria [The emotions are all those feelings that so change men as to affect their judgments and that are followed by pain or pleasure, such as anger, pity, fear and the like, as well as their opposites]." On the influence of the second book of the *Rhetoric* in the *Decameron*'s *Proemio*, see Simone Marchesi, *Stratigrafie decameroniane* (Florence: Olschki, 2004), 6–16.

28 On this aspect, see especially Stephen R. Leighton, "Aristotle and the Emotions," *Phronesis* 27 (1982): 144–74; Martha Nussbaum, "Compassion: The Basic Social Emotion," *Social Philosophy and Policy* 13 (1996): 27–58.

29 Aristotle, *Rhetorica* 2.8; Cicero, *Rhetorici libri duo qui vocantur De inventione*, in *Marci Tulli Ciceroni scripta quae manserunt omnia*, vol. 2, ed. E. Stroebel (Stuttgart: B.G. Teubner, 1977; first published in Leipzig in 1915), 1.106–9; *Cornifici Rhetorica ad C. Herennium*, ed. Gualtiero Calboli (Bologna: Pàtron, 1969), 2.31, 50. See also Papio, "*Non meno di compassion piena*," 123n59.

30 *Sancti Aurelii Augustini Hipponensis Episcopi Confessionum Libri XIII*, in *Patrologia Latina* 32, ed. J.P. Migne (1845), 3.2, 3, 684: "Haec certe verior misericordia; sed non in ea delectat dolor. Nam etsi approbatur officio charitatis qui dolet miserum; mallet tamen utique non esse quod doleret, qui germanitus misericors est [This is real compassion; but in it pain is not a source of pleasure. Although those who suffer for the wretched should be praised because they comply with the precepts of charity, those who feel brotherly compassion would prefer that the cause of their suffering did not exist at all]."

31 Papio, "*Non meno di compassion piena*," 107.

32 Ibid., 117–18.

33 Ibid., 109

34 Surdich, "Tra Dante e Boccaccio," 51.

35 Some other useful remarks on the social dimension of compassion in Boccaccio's texts are in Eugenio Giusti, *Dall'amore cortese alla comprensione. Il viaggio ideologico di Giovanni Boccaccio dalla "Caccia di Diana" al "Decameron"* (Milan: LED, 1999), 123–74, and Teodolinda Barolini, "The Wheel of the *Decameron*," *Romance Philology* 36 (1983): 521–39, esp. 522 and 527.

36 *Lactantii Divinarum Institutionum Libri Septem*, in *Patrologia Latina* 6, ed. J.P. Migne (1844), 3.23, 423–4: "Cum enim natura hominis imbecillior sit quam caeterum animalium, quae vel ad perferendam vim temporum, vel ad incursiones ad suis corporis arcendas, naturalibus munimentis providentia

coelestis armavit: homini autem quia nihil istorum datum est, accepit pro istis omnibus miserationis affectum, qui plane vocatur humanitas, qua nosmet invicem tueremur [For the nature of man is more feeble than that of other animals, which celestial providence has armed with natural means of protection, either in order to endure the harshness of the weather or to defend their bodies from the attacks of others; because none of these things is given to man, he was given, instead of all of them, the feeling of pity, which is plainly called humanity, by which we can protect one another]."

37 *S. Isidori Hispalensis Episcopi Etymologyarum Libri XX*, in *Patrologia Latina* 82, ed. J.P. Migne (1850), 10.117.

38 Giovanni Boccaccio, *Decameron*, ed. Vittore Branca (Turin: Einaudi, 1980); translation is from G.H. McWilliam, *The Decameron*, 2nd ed. (New York: Penguin, 1995).

39 Hans Robert Jauss, "The Alterity and Modernity of Medieval Literature," *New Literary History* 10 (1979): 181–229; 197.

40 Aristotle, *Historia animalium* 608b8–11. This Aristotelian statement soon acquired the status of *sententia*, as witnessed by an excerpt found in Bede's *Sententiae philosophicae*: "Mulier majoris est pietatis et compassionis quam vir; sed est majoris invidiae, contentionis et litis, et malitiosior est viro et de facili decipitur (IX libr. de Historiis animalium) [Woman feels pity more strongly than man; but she is also more envious, more querulous, more quarrelsome, more malicious than man, and more easily misled]" (Book 9 of the History of Animals). See *Venerabilis Bedae Sententiae, Sive Axiomata Philosophica*, in *Patrologia Latina* 90, ed. J.P. Migne (1850), 1016A.

41 Aristotle, *Libri Politicorum*, in *Sancti Thomae Aquinatis in octo libros Politicorum Aristotelis expositio*, ed. R.M. Spiazzi (Turin: Marietti, 1966), 1.107, p. 47.

42 *Sancti Thomae Aquinatis in octo libros Politicorum Aristotelis expositio*, 1.159, p. 49: "Sed femina cum sit libera, habet potestatem consiliandi, sed consilium eis est invalidum. Cuius ratio est, quia propter mollitiem naturae ratio eius infirmiter inhaeret consiliatis, sed cito ab eis removetur, propter passiones aliquas, puta concupiscientiae, vel irae, vel timoris vel alicuius huiusmodi [But because woman is free, she has the power to deliberate, yet her deliberation is not valid. The reason is that, because of her soft nature, she does not remain firm in her decisions; instead she often changes her mind because of passions such as appetite, anger, fear, or the like]."

43 In many respects, the relationship that Fiammetta establishes with her readers presents the characteristics that Aristotle considers typical of female or effeminate friendship. According to Aristotle, whereas virile

men tend to avoid complaining about their own misfortunes, because they do not find pleasure in such activity and because they do not wish to make their friends sad, women, or those who behave like women, find great pleasure in sharing their suffering with others. Aristotle concludes that in this, as in all things, it is appropriate to follow the best example: "viriles quidem secundum naturam reverentur contristari amicos ipsis. Et si non supertendat in tristitia, eam, quae illi fit, tristitiam non sustinet totaliter. Neque in complorantibus complacet, propter neque ipsos esse plorativos. Muliebriter autem, et tales viri coangustiatis gaudent, et amant, ut amicos, et condolentes. Imitari autem in omnibus oportet, videlicet meliorem" (*Ethica ad Nicomachum* 9.9, 1399–1400, p. 504).

44 See Carlo Delcorno's notes to his edition of the *Elegia*: 2.6, n3 (265), 2.7, n5 (268), and 2.8, nn15, 17, 23 (269).

45 To repeat Cicero's words, "pietas est per quam sanguine junctis, patriaeque benevolis officium et diligens tribuitur cultus [*pietas* is that by which kind offices and loving services are offered to one's kin and country]" (cf. *De inventione* 2.53). This Ciceronian definition must have been quite popular in the Middle Ages. We find it quoted by Thomas Aquinas in his *Quaestio de pietate* (*Summa theologiae* 2a–2ae, 101, 1).

46 Boccaccio, *Elegia di Madonna Fiammetta* 8.5, 1–4.

47 Hexter, *Ovid and Medieval Schooling*, 256.

48 On this topic, see Domenico Comparetti, *Virgilio nel Medio Evo*, ed. Giorgio Pasquali, 2 vols. (Florence: La Nuova Italia, 1937; first published in 1872), 69–71 and 128–46.

49 See for instance Dante, *Convivio* 4.26.5–15.

50 Augustine, *De civitate Dei* 9.4.

51 See Augustine, *Confessiones* 3.2.

52 In her study of the popularity of the Ovidian figure of the *relicta* among medieval authors, Suzanne Hagedorn follows Lipking in noting how, "by their very nature, abandoned women are subversive figures, for they call into question not only the integrity of individual heroes, but their necessity for heroic action – and even action – itself … The sense of pain and loss that abandoned women pour out in their laments offers a challenge to traditional social structures, values, and even poetic genres that enshrine and celebrate male dominance and male exploits" (*Abandoned Women*, 9).

53 Note that the confusion between the two Latin terms *pietas* and *misericordia* must have occurred already in late antiquity. The tendency to replace *misericordia* with *pietas* in everyday speech is recorded by Augustine (*De Civitate Dei* 10.1), later quoted by Thomas Aquinas (*Summa theologiae* 2a–2ae, 101, 1 r. o. 2).

54 Evidence of Boccaccio's knowledge of this *volgarizzamento* has been provided by Stefania Trotta, "*L'Elegia di Madonna Fiammetta* di Giovanni Boccaccio e un volgarizzamento delle *Epistulae Heroidum* di Ovidio attribuito a Filippo Ceffi," *Italia medioevale e umanistica* 38 (1995): 217–61, and by Massimo Zaggia in his edition with commentary of Ceffi's work, *Heroides. Volgarizzamento fiorentino trecentesco di Filippo Ceffi* (Florence: Sismel, Edizioni del Galluzzo, 2009). See also Stefano Carrai, "Boccaccio, i volgarizzamenti e l'invenzione dell'elegia volgare," in *Gli antichi e i moderni. Studi in onore di Roberto Cardini*, vol. 1, ed. L. Bertolini and D. Coppini (Florence: Edizioni Polistampa, 2010), 293–309.

55 "I am not concerned about you; but spare Iulus. It suffices that you are remembered for my death." Extracts from the *Heroides* are taken from the following edition: *Ovidio. Opere*, ed. Luigi Galasso, intr. Alessandro Perutelli, and trans. Guido Paduano, 2 vols. (Turin: Einaudi, 2000).

56 All extracts from Ceffi are taken from Zaggia's edition. *Heroides* 7.75 is a difficult line to interpret. It seems in fact a contradiction that at this point in the letter Dido declares that she is not concerned about Aeneas. Ceffi might have read in the copy that he used for his translation one of the several variants of this line found in the manuscript tradition, or his interpolation might at least partly have been motivated by the desire to reduce the obscurity of this passage.

57 "You will be old by the time you succeed in reaching the desired land. Therefore, renounce your uncertain wanderings and accept these peoples as dowry ..."

58 Ronchetti, "Boccaccio between Naples and Florence."

59 I would like to thank the Modern Humanities Research Association for their financial support during the final stage of composition of this essay.

6 The Economics of Conjugal Debt from Gratian's *Decretum* to *Decameron* 2.10: Boccaccio, Canon Law, and the Loss of Interest in Sex

GRACE DELMOLINO

Boccaccio levels a vicious attack against lawyers in the third book of the *De casibus*, decrying their "feigned *gravitas*, tongues of honey, teeth of iron, and insatiable hunger for gold" (3.10.8).[1] The young Boccaccio studied canon law for approximately six years – roughly the amount of time necessary for a doctorate, though he left his studies unfinished – and an obvious strain of vitriol against lawyers, judges, and other legal professionals runs throughout his work. Less well documented are the ways in which his legal erudition informs his depiction of those officials who administer the law.[2] In the *Decameron*, both the legal profession and legal professionals are portrayed in a very negative light: consider the greedy inquisitor who profits by abusing his power as a judge of others' faith (1.6), or the biased judge in 2.1 who is eager to hang Martellino because he is a Florentine.[3] When Dioneo tells the story of Riccardo di Chinzica, the enfeebled judge of *Decameron* 2.10 who invents a calendar of religious holidays to excuse himself from the marital bed, we find one of the most memorable characters in a series of lawyers who are woefully ill equipped to adjudicate the lives of others.

Riccardo di Chinzica is the personification of all that is wrong with the legal profession, according to Boccaccio, for he is both extremely rich and extremely foolish. Nor does his skill in the courtroom, by which he has earned so much money, help him in the slightest to win back his unsatisfied wife, Bartolomea, when a virile pirate abducts her. Riccardo is revealed to be a naive old man, ignorant of the laws of nature, whose authority is rejected by Bartolomea even as he plies her with legalistic rhetoric, begging her to return to him.[4] When tested against a historical text of medieval law, Riccardo's arguments prove sophistic, characterized by a myopic distortion of the law rather than a balanced interpretation that takes into account both legal precepts and human realities. *Decameron* 2.10 engages particularly with *Causa* 33 of Gratian's *Decretum*, and a reading of the Boccaccian *novella* in dialogue with this text will show that Boccaccio both echoes and edits the principles of law laid out by Gratian.[5]

To begin, it is useful to have some background on Gratian's *Decretum* and the development of canon law in the two centuries before Boccaccio. The *Decretum* is usually seen to mark a new era in the history of the Church, a veritable legal renaissance, for the twelfth century saw the beginning of systematic legal study and the birth of "canon law" as a profession distinct from both theology and pastoral care. Gratian's text, probably written over a period from the 1120s to the 1140s, constituted a major systematic collection of a scattered, redundant, and contradictory body of law: thence its full title, *Concordia discordantium canonum* (A Harmony of Discordant Canons). Gratian's *Decretum* is far from the first organized collection of canons – for example, the *Decretum* of Burchard of Worms dates to the early 1000s – but the later text gained lasting fame and popularity for the efficacy of its dialectic approach to categorizing the law.[6] The texts cited in the *Decretum* are discussed, linked, and sometimes challenged by *dicta*, or commentary in the voice of Gratian, that surround them. For the sake of convenience, I refer to the authorial persona in the *Decretum* as "Gratian," but in fact almost nothing is known about the author, other than that he is called Gratian and he wrote the *Decretum*, and even these facts have been called into question by modern scholarship.[7] The name "Gratian" has become all but synonymous with the *Decretum* itself, which was and remains one of the most important texts in Church history, forming the first part of the *Corpus iuris canonici* (where it retained legal validity until 1917) and constituting an essential textbook for any medieval student of canon law. Although by the fourteenth century other canonical collections such as the *Decretals* of Gregory IX (*Liber extra*) and Boniface VIII's *Liber sextus* had taken their places in legal curricula alongside the *Decretum*, it is inconceivable that Boccaccio would not have become familiar with the text during his six years of study.

My particular focus within the *Decretum*, for a reading of *Decameron* 2.10, is on *Causa* 33, which deals (among other subjects) with conjugal debt, or the obligation of each spouse to provide sex to the other.[8] Like every *causa*, 33 presents a hypothetical scenario which is used to elicit several inquiries into finer points of the law (*quaestiones*); the answers to these questions, in the form of collected canons interspersed with *dicta*, make up the bulk of each *causa*. The *causae* are not intended to reflect a realistic legal environment, but to serve as examples that highlight precisely the legal conundrums Gratian intends to resolve. This is the strategy of a teacher in his lecture hall, not a lawyer in the courtroom, and has led many scholars to conclude that Gratian must have taught canon law at some point in his career.[9] The *Decretum*'s didactic strategy often results in a highly improbable (but decidedly memorable) confluence of scandalous events, such that many of the *causae* – particularly those in the *Tractatus de matrimonio* – read like outlines for *novelle* that could have been told in the *Decameron*. The situation of *Causa* 33 is as follows:

> Quidam uir maleficiis inpeditus uxori suae debitum reddere non poterat. Alius interim clanculo eam corrupit; a uiro suo separata corruptori suo publice nubit; crimen, quod admiserat, corde tantum Deo confitetur; redditur huic facultas cognoscendi eam: repetit uxorem suam; qua recepta, ut expedicius uacaret orationi, et ad carnes agni purus accederet, continentiam se seruaturum promisit; uxor uero consensum non adhibuit.[10]

> [A certain man, having been impeded by witchcraft, had not been able to render the debt ["debitum reddere"] to his wife. Meanwhile, another man secretly seduced her. Having been separated from her husband, the woman publicly married her seducer. The man confessed a sin, which he had committed, only in his heart to God.[11] The faculty of carnally knowing her is restored to the man: he seeks to have his wife back, and upon receiving her, in order that he might more devotedly take time off ["vacaret"] for prayer, and be pure when approaching the flesh of the Lamb, he promised that he would be continent; but the wife did not give her consent to this.]

An attentive reader may already begin to see thematic parallels with *Decameron* 2.10. To recapitulate, the elderly Riccardo has married the lovely Bartolomea,[12] barely managed to consummate the marriage, and imposed on her an extremely restrictive calendar of holidays, explaining that on days of religious devotion, intercourse is prohibited. His actions parallel those of Gratian's hypothetical husband, who takes a vow of continence and refuses to have sex with his wife, citing devotion to God as his justification. The wife, in both cases, is tempted by a man who is able to meet her sexual needs, and each woman leaves her husband for that man, taking her husband's sexual inadequacies as grounds to live publicly with her lover as if he were legitimately her husband. Though the plot of *Causa* 33 does not unfold in the same order as *Decameron* 2.10, the *novella*'s backbone is present, resulting in *quaestiones* that can be used as a framework to "try" the various legal issues that occur in Boccaccio's *novella*.

These legal issues occur as a result of Riccardo's failure to understand the applications and limitations of the law, or, more precisely, the limitations on his knowledge of it. The entire story is set against the backdrop of Riccardo's twisted relationship to his legal studies:

> Fu adunque in Pisa un giudice, piú che di corporal forza dotato d'ingegno, il cui nome fu messer Riccardo da Chinzica; il quale, forse credendosi con quelle medesime opere sodisfare alla moglie che egli faceva agli studii, essendo molto ricco, con non piccola sollecitudine cercò d'avere e bella e giovane donna per moglie, dove e l'uno e l'altro, se cosí avesse saputo consigliar sé come altrui faceva, doveva fuggire. (2.10.5)
>
> [There once lived, in Pisa, a very wealthy judge called Messer Riccardo di Chinzica, who had rather more brain than brawn, and who, thinking perhaps he could satisfy a wife with those same talents that he brought to his studies, went to a great deal of trouble to find himself a wife who was both young and beautiful; whereas, had he been capable of giving himself such good advice as he gave to others, he should have avoided marrying anyone with either of the attributes in question.]

Riccardo is so beguiled by the prospect of having a young and beautiful wife that he ignores his better judgment (which ought to be acute, for he is literally a judge) and finds a match in Bartolomea Gualandi, a young and beautiful lady. Although Riccardo makes a great show of marrying her, it turns out that he is, unfortunately for Bartolomea, unable to capitalize on the assets she brings to the marriage, those qualities of youth and beauty he so desired: "la quale il giudice menata con grandissima festa a casa sua, e fatte le nozze belle e magnifiche, pur per la prima notte incappò una volta per consumare il matrimonio a toccarla [the judge brought her home with an air of great festivity, and although the wedding was celebrated in truly magnificent style, on the first night he only managed to come at her once in order to consummate the marriage]" (2.10.7). The buildup of modifiers around the verb in the final clause ("pur per la prima notte," "una volta," "per consumare il matrimonio") ends in the disappointingly simple infinitive "toccarla." Dioneo encourages his listeners to laugh at the judge's disproportionate exhaustion, contrasting the meagre action of touching one's wife with the elaborate meal of "vernaccia e confetti ristorativi" by which Riccardo brings himself back to the world of the living afterwards.

Amid the humour of this interrupted crescendo – an elaborate, beautiful wedding; a lacklustre wedding night; an elaborate array of fancy wines and sweetmeats – a crucial legal detail is tucked away in the phrase "consumare il matrimonio." Riccardo cannot accurately be deemed an impotent husband, as some critics like to call him, because Dioneo specifies that he successfully consummates the marriage. According to the *Decretum*, a wife could be allowed to separate from her impotent husband only if consummation had never taken place. More simply put, what is decided by consent alone may also be dissolved by consent alone; what is reified by consummation may not be sundered. The first of the marriage *causae* inquires whether a woman may renounce the man to whom she was betrothed and marry someone else, and this question results in a useful definition of marriage that stresses the importance of consent, but also locates the formation of the marriage in the act of consummation:

> Coitus sine uoluntate contrahendi matrimonium, et defloratio uirginitatis sine pactione coniugali non facit matrimonium, sed precedens uoluntas contrahendi matrimonium, et coniugalis pactio facit, ut mulier in defloratione suae uirginitatis uel in coitu dicatur nubere uiro, uel nuptias celebrare.[13]
>
> [Intercourse without consent to enter into matrimony, and the deflowering of virginity without the marriage agreement do not make a marriage, but the preceding consent to enter into marriage and the conjugal pact make a marriage, so that a woman, in the deflowering of her virginity or during intercourse, may be said to marry a man, or rather celebrate her nuptials.]

In *Causa* 33, Gratian applies the same principle to conclude that impotence may only dissolve a marriage if it was never consummated, that is, if it never truly became a marriage at all:

> Coniugium confirmatur offitio, ut supra probatum est; postquam uero offitio confirmatum fuerit, nisi causa fornicationis non licet uiro uxorem dimittere, uel uxori a uiro discedere. Verum ante, quam confirmetur, inpossibilitas offitii soluit uinculum coniugi.[14]
>
> [Marriage is confirmed by this duty, as proved above; after it has been confirmed by this duty, a husband may not dismiss his wife except on account of adultery, nor may a wife leave her husband. However, before the union is confirmed, the inability to perform the duty dissolves the bond of matrimony.]

Gratian's insistence on consummation was not necessarily representative of other theorists of marriage law, either before or after the *Decretum*. The "Italian model" of Gratian stood in contrast to the "French model" as put forth by Peter Lombard, where consent alone created a marriage, even in the absence of consummation.[15] Though Gratian's view on consummation per se does not alter the verdict in Bartolomea and Riccardo's case (they are well and truly married according to either view), the emphasis on the physical realization of a marriage will be crucial for *Decameron* 2.10. Gratian's description of the marital bond acknowledges the importance of sex for both the initial formation of the marriage and the continued health of the union. It soon becomes clear that Riccardo does not fulfil his duty on the latter count.

After his wedding night, the judge proceeds to teach his wife a certain sort of calendar, according to which:

> niun dí era che non solamente una festa ma molte non ne fossero, a reverenza delle quali per diverse cagioni mostrava l'uomo e la donna doversi abstenere da cosí fatti congiugnimenti, sopra questi aggiungendo digiuni e quatro tempora e vigilie d'apostoli e di mille altri santi e venerdí e sabati e la domenica del Signore e la quaresima tutta, e certi punti della luna e altre eccezion molte, avvisandosi forse che cosí feria far si convenisse con le donne nel letto, come egli faceva talvolta piatendo alle civili. (2.10.9)

> [there was not a single day that was not the feast of one or more Saints, out of reverence for whom, as he would demonstrate by devious arguments, man and woman should abstain from sexual union. To the foregoing, he added holidays of obligation, the four Ember weeks, the eves of the Apostles and a numerous array of subsidiary Saints, Fridays and Saturdays, the Sabbath, the whole of Lent, certain phases of the moon, and various special occasions, possibly because he was under the impression that one had to take vacations from bedding a woman, in the same way that he sometimes took vacations from summing up in the law-courts.]

To a modern reader, Riccardo's litany of sexual loopholes seems ridiculous, and Dioneo's presentation makes it clear that the medieval audience should find it ridiculous too. The juxtaposition of such delicate legalistic language as "abstenere da cosí fatti congiugnimenti" with the frank depiction of "le donne nel letto" verges on the absurd. Yet Riccardo's calendar has a legal precedent. His restrictions mirror those found in the penitentials: books intended as manuals for confessors which detail various sins for which a person might need to atone, generally presented in a list along with the appropriate penance. Some of these manuals were incorporated into officially recognized collections of canon law, though the genre originated in the sixth century, long before "canon law" existed as such.[16] By far the most treated topic in the penitentials was sex, and by the time penitentials began to fall out of fashion in the twelfth century, there had accumulated such an immense body of literature that nearly every act was prohibited and nearly every occasion on which a couple might have sex became for various reasons unsuitable.

Many of the prohibitions in the penitentials can be traced back to the Bible. For instance, the wife (because, of course, sex was only permissible within the bonds of matrimony) could not be pregnant, menstruating, or recently postpartum, nor was it advisable to have sex too soon after being married. Wednesdays, Fridays, and Saturdays were typical days of rest, as were all religious holidays such as Lent, Ember Days, days of feasting, days of fasting, and even minor saints' days.[17] James Brundage comments that "any couple who paid close attention to the rules outlined in the penitentials would have found the process of deciding whether or not they could in good conscience have intercourse at any given moment a complex, perhaps even frightening, process."[18] Whether couples at any point in history have faithfully observed the labyrinthine restrictions of the penitentials is a matter for debate, though according to the model developed by Jean-Louis Flandrin, even strict obedience to the penitentials might allow up to five instances of intercourse per month, which is still rather more than Riccardo's calendar seems to permit.[19] At any rate, one can say with certainty that couples in the *Decameron*, with the singular exception of Riccardo and Bartolomea, obey no such proscriptions.

Riccardo's system more than compensates for the lack of calendric devotion among the rest of the *Decameron*'s sexually active characters. Though his work is described as "piatendo alle civili" (2.10.9), suggesting that he is a civil lawyer, his facility with the restrictions on sexual intercourse rivals that of any aspiring legal author attempting to compile texts on fast days, times of prayer, and other religious holidays. Because he restricts himself to the kind of argument found in the penitentials – many of which lacked an overarching narrative that would even begin to provide a conceptual framework for the individual prohibitions – Riccardo's knowledge comes across as antiquated and obsolete, much like the man himself. Bartolomea laments in this vein that he seems to be a "banditor di sagre e di feste [a town crier of feasts and festivals]" rather than a judge (2.10.32). Following the model of the early penitentials, Riccardo seems determined to remain ignorant of even contemporary penitential literature, which tended to more closely resemble *summae* that had a unifying narrative rather than a simple and sometimes arbitrary-seeming list of prohibitions.

Restrictions on sexual intercourse hardly disappeared from canonical collections in later centuries, but Gratian's *Decretum*, in contrast to the penitentials, presents a holistic view of marital relations that depends on the concept of *debitum*, or conjugal debt. Both the idea and the economic metaphor come from Paul:

> Uxori vir debitum reddat similiter autem et uxor viro. Mulier sui corporis potestatem non habet sed vir similiter autem et vir sui corporis potestatem non habet sed mulier. Nolite fraudare invicem nisi forte ex consensu ad tempus ut vacetis orationi et iterum revertimini in id ipsum ne temptet vos Satanas propter incontinentiam vestram.[20]
>
> [Let the husband render the debt to his wife and likewise the wife to her husband. A wife does not have power over her body, but her husband does; likewise a husband does not have power over his body, but his wife does. Do not defraud each other except perhaps by mutual consent, for a time, so that you might take time off for prayer, and then return to each other again lest Satan tempt you on account of your incontinence.]

The reciprocal nature of this debt receives a great deal of attention in Gratian. Gendered language in the *Decretum* is not always reversed to suggest that principles apply equally to men and women; in discussions of adultery, the man and woman tend to remain on unequal sides of the situation.[21] In treatments of conjugal debt, by contrast, the language emphasizes that both the husband and the wife have the right to demand the debt from their spouse, making this mutually owed *debitum* a site of remarkable equality between the sexes. Elsewhere in the *Decretum*, Gratian insists that the wife should be subservient to her husband, but where the exchange of sex is concerned, primacy is given to each spouse's equal right to the body of their partner.[22]

Sexual equality is a crucial principle in *Decameron* 2.10. The affirmation of sexual equality found in Dioneo's *novella* serves to adapt and edit the rhetoric found in canon law, which often is rooted in misogynist stereotypes of women's carnal insatiability.[23] Teodolinda Barolini has already argued that Dioneo "does not arrive at female inconstancy by way of female inferiority; rather he seems to insist on women's right to sexuality as a way of instituting some parity between the sexes."[24] Boccaccio, through Dioneo, takes the theoretical principle of equality underlying the concept of a mutual *debitum*, as found in canon law, and puts that theory into practice within the fictional world of *Decameron* 2.10. Of course, the idea of conjugal debt can never be fully isolated from its context within a largely misogynistic tradition of writings on women's sexuality, nor from the context of a patriarchal society, and one should not overstate the degree of sexual freedom that medieval women would historically have enjoyed in their marriages. Nevertheless, *Decameron* 2.10 presents a legalistic theory of sexual equality that draws on canonical views of conjugal debt, while also adapting and altering those same canons.

The main legal problem in *Decameron* 2.10 is Riccardo's calendar and the validity of the reasoning behind his exemptions. According to Gratian, if spouses are equally obligated to render the debt when asked, neither spouse may take a vow of continence that requires him or her to cease rendering the debt, unless one spouse agrees that the other may take time off from their marital duties:

> Si dicat uir: continere iam uolo; nolo iam uxorem; non potest. [*Editio Romana: "Si dicat vir, continere iam volo, nolo autem, uxor; non potest."*] Quod enim tu uis illa non uult. Numquid per tuam continentiam debet illa fieri fornicaria? si alii nupserit te uiuo, adultera erit. Non uult tali lucro Deus tale dampnum conpensari. Redde debitum, et, si non exigis, redde. Pro sanctificatione perfecta Deus tibi conputabit, si non quod tibi debetur exigis, sed reddis quod uxori debetur.[25]

> [If a man should say, "I now wish to be continent, I do not now want a wife," he is not allowed. [*Editio Romana: "If a man should say, 'I now wish to be continent,' and his wife, 'I do not want that,' he is not allowed."*][26] For you want what she does not want. Surely she should not have to be made a fornicator for the sake of your continence? If she married another man while you were alive, she'd be an adulteress. God does not wish for such a loss to become compensation for such a gain. Render the debt, and even if you do not ask for it, render it. God will calculate it towards your salvation if you do not ask for what is owed to you, but render what is owed to your wife.]

Riccardo's "una volta il mese e appena [once a month at the most]" (2.10.10) does not fulfil his obligations as a husband, for he has effectively taken a vow of continence for the remainder of the month without his wife's consent. As with monetary debts, it is possible to make regular payments that are nevertheless insufficient to the total amount, and that is exactly what the judge does.

Riccardo seems to lack any understanding of *debitum* as put forth in the *Decretum*, which by the 1300s is hardly a new text itself, though it is recent compared to the centuries-old tradition of the penitentials on which Riccardo so heavily relies. The *Decretum*, when it deals with restrictions on sexual intercourse, presents these restrictions not as an isolated series, but rather woven into a discourse on conjugal debt and each spouse's duty to render it. *Quaestio* 4 of *Causa* 33 inquires whether a spouse may "take a holiday" (Latin *vacare*) from marital duties for the sake of prayer; this *quaestio* does indeed contain some of the same prohibitions found in older penitentials.[27] However, Gratian's list of restrictions is brief when compared to either Riccardo's elaborate calendar or the broader discussion of spousal sexual obligation in the *Decretum*. Moreover, *quaestio* 4 ends with a reiterated emphasis on mutual consent:

> Nisi ex consensu communi orationi coniuges uacare non possunt. Apostolus nec ad tempus, ut uacent orationi, nisi ex consensu uoluit coniuges inuicem carnali fraudari debito.[28]
>
> [Spouses cannot take time off (from their marital duties) for the sake of prayer, except by mutual consent. The Apostle did not want spouses to mutually defraud each other of their carnal debt, unless they did so by mutual consent, in order to devote themselves to prayer for a time.]

Though Gratian acknowledges the importance of abstinence during certain times of the year and at points in woman's menstrual cycle – restrictions that have been present throughout the history of Christianity – he ultimately considers it more important to fulfil one's marital obligation than to observe every "day of rest" prescribed by Church law.[29]

Because of the "grave malinconia" resulting from her husband's ostensibly devotional vow of chastity, Bartolomea is easily convinced to commit adultery when Paganino abducts her. Her period of devastation lasts approximately half a sentence, and she goes from "forte [piangendo]" to "[vivendo] più lietamente del mondo" [from weeping bitterly to living a joyous life] in barely a paragraph (2.10.15–16). Paganino too is so happy to have her that, as Dioneo tells us, he "onoratamente come sua moglie la tenea [treated her with all the respect due to a wife]" (2.10.16), creating a situation much like that of the hypothetical wife in *Causa* 33, who publicly marries another man while her husband is still living. Because Bartolomea's marriage to Riccardo was consummated, there is no legal way to spin this second marriage to Paganino as anything but adultery.

Quaestio 2 of *Causa* 33 asks whether a woman might marry the man with whom she has committed adultery. The answer comes unequivocally in the negative, at least so long as the woman's original husband still lives.[30] The *Decretum* therefore does not condone Bartolomea's decision to "live in sin" with Paganino, but nor can Riccardo be excused for his behaviour, as adultery is precisely the sort of sin that he ought to have prevented by rendering the conjugal debt, as Gratian explains in *quaestio* 5. The first canon of this *quaestio* challenges husbands who yearn for chastity: "Numquid per tuam continentiam debet illa fieri fornicaria? si alii nupserit te uiuo, adultera erit [Surely she should not have to be made a fornicator for the sake of your continence? If she married another while you lived, she would become an adulteress]."[31] This canon neatly encapsulates what all of the merchants in *Decameron* 2.9, with the exception of Bernabò, acknowledge: that women who are sexually neglected by their husbands – whether for business reasons or spiritual ones – do not simply "[tenere] le mani a cintola [twiddle their thumbs]" while their men are gone (2.10.3).[32] This reality does not make Bartolomea's adultery any less of a crime, yet neither is it entirely her fault in the eyes of the law.

Riccardo's main argument to justify why Bartolomea should return to him rests on the illegitimacy of her "public marriage" to Paganino. He is technically correct, but Bartolomea scoffs at this line of argument, telling Riccardo she would rather be a whore with Paganino than a wife with him, because that is not how it feels to her: "qui mi pare esser moglie di Paganino e a Pisa mi pareva esser vostra bagascia [I feel as though I am Paganino's wife here and it was in Pisa that I felt like a whore]" (2.10.37). Bartolomea further argues for Riccardo's own culpability in her decision to leave him, telling him that "se egli v'era piú a grado lo studio delle leggi che la moglie, voi non dovavate pigliarla [if you were more interested in studying the law than in keeping a wife, you should never have married in the first place]" (2.10.32). In fact, had Riccardo spent more time on his "studio delle leggi," he might not have needed Bartolomea to tell him this, for the *Decretum* contains canons to the same effect. For example:

> Quisquis igitur conpatiens infirmitati uxoris reddit, non exigit debitum, aut si propter propriam infirmitatem ducit uxorem, plangens potius, quia sine uxore esse non potuit, quam gaudens, quia duxit.[33]

> [Whoever therefore renders the debt because he has compassion for his wife's infirmity [i.e., sexual incontinence] does not ask for the debt. But if he took a wife on account of his own infirmity, he should rather be weeping because he could not be without a wife, than rejoicing because he took one.]

Riccardo might well have been *gaudens* that he did not require a wife to make his *infirmitas* licit, because in fact he does not suffer from the "illness" of incontinence. Instead, he is wrongfully "gaudens, quia duxit" and yet can scarcely bring himself to render the debt he thereby incurs to his wife. As a judge, he should have known this from the beginning, yet he ignores what would have been solid legal counsel and takes a wife for a reason not specifically encouraged by the law (viz., to increase his social standing) while simultaneously refusing to pursue the reason that canon law does sanction: sex for the purpose of procreation. According to Bartolomea, Gratian, and Paul, Riccardo's best course of action would have been to never take a wife in the first place.

The first canon of *quaestio* 5 cautions husbands who might wish to be chaste without their wives' consent, thereby tempting them into adultery: "Non uult tali lucro Deus tale dampnum conpensari. Redde debitum, et, si non exigis, redde [God does not wish for such a loss [i.e., her adultery] to be compensation for such a gain [i.e., your continence]. Render the debt, and even if you do not ask for it, render it]."[34] The words *lucrum* and *damnum* merit further consideration. Though one might understand them to mean, for Gratian, "(moral) gain, salvation" and "(spiritual) loss, damnation," these nouns possess the technical economic meanings of loss and gain as well. Both Gratian's canons and Boccaccio's *novella* belong to a discourse on the exchange of sex within marriage – cast in the language of *debitum*, a word that refers to fiscal debt – and Bartolomea uses economic vocabulary when she confronts Riccardo, claiming that "con mio grandissimo danno e interesse vi stetti una volta: per che in altra parte cercherei mia civanza [life with you was an enormous loss with interest added, as far as I was concerned, so I'd rather seek my livelihood somewhere else]" (2.10.40). In this passage, the terms "grandissimo danno e interesse [enormous loss and interest]" allude to the medieval economic principles that permitted lenders to charge interest on loans without committing usury.

In the Middle Ages, usury was defined as "any excess whatsoever above the principal of a *mutuum*, or loan, exacted by reason of the loan itself, either according to contract or without previous agreement."[35] This definition is important, because it means that in order to justify the charging of interest, lenders had to find reasons demonstrably external to the loan itself. Of these so-called "extrinsic titles," two of the most-cited are *damnum emergens* and *lucrum cessans*, literally "loss occurring" and "profit ceasing."[36] *Damnum emergens* is defined as any actual loss incurred by the lender as a result of having lent his money. For instance, the lender might be forced to borrow money at usury because the borrower has failed to repay him, leaving the lender financially worse off than if he had never made the loan in the first place. *Lucrum cessans* is the lender's lost ability to make a profit on the money he has lent; the concept is very similar to what modern economists call opportunity cost. When a lender chooses one of several investment options for his money, the potential profit from all of the alternative choices is lost. Therefore, a lender might justify charging interest on the basis of *lucrum cessans*, because during the period of the loan, the lender could have invested that money elsewhere and made a profit, so it is fair for him to be compensated accordingly. Making a loan at no interest would effectively be a loss to the lender, if it is assumed that a different investment of that money would have yielded profit. Both economic principles apply in *Decameron* 2.10.[37]

Bartolomea has incurred *damnum emergens*, "grandissimo danno," insofar as Riccardo's failure to pay his debt has forced her into adultery, which occasions the loss of social standing as a legitimate wife as well as the spiritual *damnum* of adultery. She is also subject to *lucrum cessans*, which corresponds to the "interesse" in her speech: in addition to her actual loss, she is effectively paying interest on that loss in the form of further lost profits. The loan she made to Riccardo when she married him – thereby generating the conjugal debt – prevents her from using that capital to make a profit elsewhere, by marrying a more age-appropriate man and receiving full payments on her *debitum*. After all, by Gratian's definition, a married woman must have lost her virginity, which is not so much a loan as it is a non-refundable deposit that can never be repaid in kind. Thus Boccaccio defines loss of virginity in the *Esposizioni*: "viziare alcuna vergine [è] gravissimo peccato, per ciò che le si toglie quello che mai rendere non le si può, di che ella riceve *grandissimo danno* [to violate a virgin is a grievous sin, because one takes from her that which can never be returned to her, as a result of which she sustains *enormous loss*]" (5.all.67).[38] The "grandissimo danno" of the *Esposizioni* echoes Bartolomea's more explicitly economic "grandissimo danno e interesse." Then, in the final story of the *Decameron*, Griselda will take the metaphor to its logical conclusion as she begs Gualtieri, "ma io vi priego, in *premio* della mia virginità che io ci recai e non ne la porto, che almeno una sola camiscia sopra *la dota mia* vi piaccia che io portar ne possa [but I beg you, in *recompense* for my virginity, which I brought to you and cannot retrieve, that you at least allow me, in addition to *my dowry*, to take one shift away with me]" (10.10.45). Here the economic metaphor becomes fully literalized, for Griselda's virginity *is* the dowry that she brings to her marriage with Gualtieri. Bartolomea, by contrast, has sustained her loss at a more abstract level. As Barolini notes, Bartolomea's loss is ultimately the loss of children, so unlikely does it seem that she will ever have them with Riccardo.[39] This loss increases the longer she stays with him, as the passage of time steadily decreases the likelihood she will have a chance to make a profit. Interest can compensate for the time it takes to pay back a monetary debt, but the repayment of a woman's conjugal debt is on a fixed schedule, which is the schedule of her biological clock.

In *Causa* 33 of the *Decretum,* the economics of sex and the economics of childbearing are explicitly linked:

> Tunc saluabitur mulier, si illos genuerit filios, qui uirgines permansuri sunt; si quod ipsa *perdidit acquirat* in liberis, et *dampnum* radicis et cariem flore *conpenset* et pomis.[40]
>
> [The woman will be saved, if she has children who will remain virgins; if she *gains*, through her children, what she *lost*, and the *loss* and decay of her root is *compensated* with flowers and fruit.]

The *damnum* a wife sustains when she engages in sexual activity with her husband receives its recompense in the form of children, making a woman's right to sex within marriage conceptually equivalent to her right to children. Riccardo's infrequent relations with his wife do not constitute adequate payment of his debt to Bartolomea, because he does not give her children: this is a profit granted to her by canon law. In light of the judge's failure to make good on his debt, it is no wonder that Bartolomea pretends not to recognize him when he comes to Monaco, offering to *pay* Paganino to get her back. Riccardo is willing to spend any amount of money so that the pirate might render Bartolomea to him, but he could not even manage adequate monthly payments on the debt he owed to Bartolomea herself.

The charade of non-recognition that takes place in Monaco constitutes an extended pun on the verb *conoscere*, which is of course the root of *riconoscere*, to recognize and to know again. When Bartolomea finally lifts the façade, she upbraids Riccardo for his ignorance:

> Ben sapete che io non sono sí smimorata, che io non *conosca* che voi siete messer Riccardo di Chinzica mio marito; ma voi, mentre che io fui con voi, *mostraste assai male di conoscer me*, per ciò che se voi eravate savio o sete, come volete esser tenuto, dovavate bene avere *tanto conoscimento*, che voi dovavate vedere che io era giovane e fresca e gagliarda, e per conseguente *conoscere* quello che alle giovani donne, oltre al vestire e al mangiare, benché elle per vergogna nol dicano, si richiede: il che come voi il faciavate, voi il vi sapete. (2.10.31)

> [You are well aware that I possess a sufficiently good memory *to know* that you are my husband, Messer Ricciardo di Chinzica. But you showed very little sign *of knowing me*, when I was living with you, because if, either then or now, you were as wise as you wish to pretend, you should certainly have had *enough knowledge* to realize that I was a fresh and vigorous young woman, and *you should have known* that young women need something more than food and clothes, even if modesty forbids them to say so. And you know how little of that you provided.]

Given the placement of this passage within a discourse on sex, Bartolomea's emphasis on forms of the verb *conoscere* cannot help but recall the biblical sense of the word: to have *carnal* knowledge, to know another person sexually.[41] Even if Riccardo did not know better, intellectually speaking, than to take a young wife, once he had gone ahead and taken a young wife anyway, he ought to have known *her* better. Bartolomea's feigned lack of recognition and her subsequent speech could even be interpreted as a rewriting of part of *Causa* 33, which states that in a dispute over whether a marriage was consummated, "in ueritate uiri consistat, si mulier negat se cognitam ab eo [let it be settled in the truth of the husband('s word), if the wife denies herself to have been known by him]."[42]

Boccaccio expands the principle of sexual equality in the bedroom to equality in the courtroom, or at least in the chamber where Bartolomea and Riccardo present their cases, allowing Bartolomea's female voice a claim to truth that the law would have denied her. Bartolomea explains in detail how her husband failed to know her, and how well Paganino has succeeded.[43] After hearing her arguments, Riccardo is rendered truly impotent, both physically and rhetorically: after Bartolomea gets the last word in their conversation, Riccardo says "parole assai a Paganino le quali non montavano un frullo [many words to Paganino that made no difference whatever]," then makes his way back to Pisa and soon dies (2.10.42). With Riccardo dead, Paganino is able to marry Bartolomea: "Il che Paganin sentendo e conoscendo l'amore che la donna gli portava, per sua legittima moglie la sposò [when the news reached Paganino, knowing how deeply the lady loved him, he made her his legitimate wife]" (2.10.42–3). Paganino has known Bartolomea and her love all along, and she him. Riccardo's death is the missing piece that finally allows them a union recognized by the Church, rendering valid what Bartolomea already felt was a legitimate marriage.[44]

Thus *Decameron* 2.10 concludes with a happy ending for Bartolomea and Paganino, a rousing defence of a woman's right to sex within marriage, and an indictment of a judge who is feeble in both body and mind.[45] As so often happens in the *Decameron*, however, the story complicates and is complicated by the text that surrounds it, so that a legal reading of *Decameron* 2.10 has direct implications for the Conclusion of Day Two. In the Conclusion of Day Two, the *brigata* makes two important decisions: to change location before the third day, and to observe several days of rest in accordance with the Church calendar. In light of the extended metaphor in 2.10 of the *festa* – a religious holiday, as opposed to those days on which the work of sex is done – the *brigata*'s days of rest take on another layer of meaning.[46] Neifile, once crowned queen of the third day, addresses the *brigata* as follows:

> Come voi sapete, domane è venerdí e il seguente dí sabato, giorni, per le vivande le quali s'usano in quegli, alquanto tediosi alle piú genti; senza che il venerdí, avendo riguardo che in esso Colui che per la nostra vita morí sostenne passione, è degno di reverenza, per che giusta cosa e molto onesta reputerei che, a onor di Dio, piú tosto a orazioni che a novelle vacassimo. (2.concl.5–6)
>
> [As you know, tomorrow is Friday and the next day is Saturday, both of which, because of the food we normally eat on those two days, are generally thought of as being rather tedious. Moreover, Friday is worthy of special reverence because that was the day of the Passion of Our Lord, who died that we might live, and I would therefore regard it as perfectly right and proper that we should all do honor to God by devoting that day to prayer rather than storytelling.]

In this passage, Neifile imposes the same restrictions on storytelling that Riccardo imposed on sex; he, too, encouraged the observance of "digiuni ... e venerdì e sabati e la domenica del Signore [fasts and Fridays and Saturdays and the Sabbath]" (2.10.9). Moreover, Neifile uses language barely translated from Latin to describe these days of reverence, suggesting that "a onor di Dio, piú tosto a orazioni che a novelle vacassimo [we should all do honor to God by devoting that day to prayer rather than storytelling]." The verb *vacare*, which in Latin generally means "to be absent from or lacking (something)" or "to be idle,"[47] appears in previously quoted passages of the *Decretum* and 1 Corinthians to describe the particular type of *vacatio* that a person may take for the purpose of prayer: e.g., "nisi ex consensu communi *orationi* coniuges *vacare* non possunt [spouses may not *take time off for prayer* except by mutual consent]."[48] "Vacare orationi" is a set phrase that indicates a period of time set aside for the purpose of prayer, as in the aphorism "orationi vacare non desinas [do not cease to take time off for prayer]" from the *De modo studendi*.[49] Neifile's "a orazioni vacassimo" could not be a more literal translation of the Latin construction. Likewise, the authorial voice describes the *brigata* as "*a quelle cose vacando* che prima la reina avea ragionate [taking time off for those matters about which the queen had spoken earlier]" (2.concl.16). These are the only two instances of the verb "vacare" in the entire *Decameron* and it is no coincidence that this language follows a *novella* about a character who relies on devotional days of rest as an excuse to get out of sex.

The metaphoric language of 2.10 turns literal in the Conclusion to Day Two, as the *brigata*'s decision to *vacare orationi* is drawn into the *contaminatio* to which Bartolomea, in the voice of Dioneo in the voice of Boccaccio, has subjected the vocabulary of rest and work. Neifile's strictures qualify and circumscribe the unequivocal defence of sexuality offered by Bartolomea: she may never observe a *festa* or *digiuno*, but the *brigata* certainly will. At the same time, the act of limiting the *brigata*'s language proves the power of that language, for Neifile has drawn an implicit connection between abstinence from sex and abstinence from storytelling, suggesting that the *brigata*'s words truly can become deeds.[50] Another charged reference to days of rest comes at the end of Day Seven, when Lauretta announces, "volendo il buono essemplo datone da Neifile seguitare, e estimo che onesta cosa sia, che domane e l'altro dí, come i passati giorni facemmo, *dal nostro dilettevole novellare ci astegniamo*, quello a memoria riducendoci che in cosí fatti giorni per la salute delle nostre anime addivenne [being desirous to follow the good example which Neifile has set us, I feel that for the next two days it would be seemly for us to abstain from our pleasant storytelling, as we did last week, and meditate upon the things that were done on those two days for the salvation of our souls]" (7.concl.17). The verb "astegniamo" again echoes *Decameron* 2.10: Riccardo's calendar shows that on certain days, men and women should "*abstenere* da così fatti congiugnimenti" (2.10.9), and likewise the *brigata* will abstain from storytelling.

However, the *brigata*'s observance of these days of rest does not cancel out the very real work done in their storytelling. In the conclusions to both Day Two and Day Seven, the call to *vacare orationi* comes on the heels of stories that examine the nature of marital obligation. Indeed, the entire theme of Day Seven – women who trick their husbands – evolves out of the principle articulated by Dioneo in 2.10: when husbands fail to perform their spousal obligations, women are entitled to seek relief on their debt elsewhere.[51] But the time for *feste* proposed by Neifile and Lauretta is fundamentally different from Riccardo's attempt to shirk his marital duties. The *brigata* makes these decisions out of mutual consent, and their days of rest are for a small, set period of time: when the *feste* are over, they will return to work and to telling stories, many of which will continue to deal with sexual themes.

While Riccardo's devotions are nothing more than a screen behind which to conceal his paucity of vigour, the *brigata* observes ritual days of rest as a socially conditioned time to attend to "la salute delle nostre anime," and their observance is compatible with the duties of storytelling imposed on them by their own law.[52] The word "salute," which may be understood in both its senses of health and salvation, recalls the constitution of the *brigata* in the Introduction to Day One: Pampinea asks her companions in Santa Maria Novella, "perché piú pigre e lente alla nostra salute che tutto il rimanente de' cittadini siamo? [why do we lag so far behind all the rest of the citizens in providing for our safety/ health/salvation?]" (1.intro.63). The very health of society – not to mention the physical health of the *brigata* – is at stake when the seven women and three men set out from the city, for the total dissolution of laws has resulted in devastation, as the Introduction to Day One describes: "era la reverenda autorità delle leggi, cosí divine come umane, quasi caduta e dissoluta tutta per li ministri e essecutori di quelle, li quali, sí come gli altri uomini, erano tutti o morti o infermi o sí di famiglie rimasi stremi, che uficio alcuno non potean fare [in the face of so much affliction and misery, all the laws of God and man had virtually broken down and been extinguished in our city. For like everybody else, those ministers and executors of the laws who were not either dead or ill were left with so few subordinates that they were unable to discharge any of their duties]" (1.intro.23).

To replace the crumbled society of plague-ridden Florence, the men and women of the *brigata* establish their own rules, guided by the principle of *misura*, and the microcosm of their new society reflects but also modifies the principles of the Florentine society it leaves behind, just as *Decameron* 2.10 reflects but also modifies principles of canon law. The *brigata* remains subject to a socio-legal code that maintains order and requires the observance of *feste*, as mandated by both canon law and contemporary social norms.[53] Riccardo obsesses over the law as a force to micromanage and stifle every aspect of his married life, and is shown to be misguided in doing so. Bartolomea's determination to live "senza mai guardar festa o vigilia o far quaresima [without paying any heed to holy days or vigils or observing Lent]" is, if anything, perhaps too expansive and unconstrained for the *brigata* (2.10.43). The *brigata*'s observance of holidays is not the manipulative piety of Riccardo, but rather a form of law (much like the laws that govern the topics and structure of each Day) that balances out – but does not cancel out – the remarkable liberty, creative and otherwise, conceded to the *brigata* during their sojourn away from Florence.

The balancing act of the entire *Decameron* is achieved by means of a programmatic *ars combinatoria*, whereby the arrangement and juxtaposition of differing elements generate complementary, contradictory, and constantly shifting meanings. The *Decretum* and the *Decameron* are similar in this respect. With so many components vying for attention, it can be difficult to gather the disparate parts in a harmony; even a text that claims to create "harmony from dissonance" can still be confusing and difficult to interpret.[54] Though the *Decretum*'s longer title, *Concordia discordantium canonum*, styles it as a harmony of discordant canons, its dialectic approach often fails to satisfactorily reconcile conflicting opinions, even in the *dicta* that discuss and interpret the canons. Gratian can be difficult to pin down on one or the other side of a question, much like Boccaccio himself. In both the *Decretum* and the *Decameron*, abstract categories – law, literature, harmony, synthesis – are mediated through the particular interpretation of an individual reader, who is forced to pick and choose parts from the whole in order to construct an interpretation. A *Concordia* may retain notes of dissonance, and a neatly structured text of one hundred *novelle* may remain impossibly slippery, but it is a human impulse to attempt to reconcile the contradictions.[55] In fact, the first word of the *Decretum*, like the first word of the *Decameron*, is *human*: "Humanum genus duobus regitur, naturali uidelicet iure et moribus [the human species is ruled by two things, as one can clearly see: by natural law and by customs]."[56]

The human impulse towards order recalls Dante's words on the *magister* himself in the Heaven of the Sun: "Grazian, che l'uno e l'altro foro / aiutò sì che piace in paradiso [Gratian, who served one and the other forum such that it pleases in paradise]" (*Par.* 10.104–5). The phrase "l'uno e l'altro foro" alludes to the idea of balance while at the same time retaining a certain irreconcilable ambiguity, namely the ambiguity surrounding the interpretation of the two forums. Many modern commentators of Dante understand these to be civil and ecclesiastical, whereas scholars of canon law interpret them as the judicial and penitential forums within the Church.[57] One might even interpret the *fora* more generally as the forum of law in the abstract and the forum of human practice, or as human justice in contrast with the ultimate justice of God. From the perspective of a canonist, the judicial/penitential interpretation seems most plausible, but in the end Dante's text does not elaborate enough to give a definitive answer either way, and in this multiplicity of meanings lies the beauty of the phrase.

Boccaccio, too, plays on the ambiguity of the word *foro* in the phrase that Riccardo di Chinzica, demented and despairing in his old age, repeats at the end of *Decameron* 2.10: "il mal furo non vuol festa [the wicked *furo* does not want a holiday]" (2.10.42). *Furo,* taken as *foro* rendered in Riccardo's Pisan dialect, encapsulates the sexual and legal registers of this *novella* within a single word.[58] In addition to the more obscene reading of "hole," whose sexual connotations are obvious, *foro* retains the meaning of "forum," the arena in which Riccardo would have exercised that "studio delle leggi" he held so dear. According to both readings of *foro,* Riccardo is correct: not only does Bartolomea refuse to take a holiday from the work she does with Paganino, but even the law, as represented in the *Decretum,* would have refused Riccardo his right to indulge in endless *feste.* If the confrontation in Monaco was the trial in which both parties presented their arguments, then Riccardo's *motto* is the verdict, and it is clear that Bartolomea has won the case. Unlike the judge, who can do little more than ineffectually repeat that the woman's forum is evil, Bartolomea is able to build complex arguments about the institution of marriage based on a legal and economic theory of conjugal debt. Her forum is therefore both *l'uno e l'altro foro* at once: the space of sex, but also the space of law and legal rhetoric, a space where words can turn into deeds, a judge can be found guilty, and a medieval woman can become a lawyer.

NOTES

1 "Ficta gravitas, lingua melliflua, dentes ferrei, et breviter auri insatiabilis appetitus"; in Giovanni Boccaccio, *De casibus virorum illustrium*, ed. Pier Giorgio Ricci and Vittorio Zaccaria, in *Tutte le opere di Giovanni Boccaccio*, ed. Vittore Branca, vol. 9 (Milan: Mondadori, 1964–92). All translations from Italian and Latin in this essay, except those of the *Decameron*, are my own. Citations of the *Decameron* are from Vittore Branca's edition (Turin: Einaudi, 1980, rev. 1992). Translations are from G.H. McWilliam's *The Decameron*, 2nd ed. (New York: Penguin, 1995). I have made minor modifications to McWilliam's text in order to preserve the literal meanings of words and the flow of my own prose.

2 Boccaccio critiques the legal profession in Books 14 and 15 of the *Genealogie deorum gentilium*, discussing lawyers' greed as well as the law's (inferior) relationship to poetry. Yet it is evident from Boccaccio's personal correspondence that he used his legal training well into later life. In a letter to Mainardo Cavalcanti of 1373, Boccaccio refers to advice given to his friend, who at the time of the letter had just married a distant relative. Consanguinity was a serious impediment to marriage according to canon law, but on Boccaccio's counsel, Mainardo married quickly and secretly, receiving a papal dispensation to sanction the marriage only after it had taken place. See Todd Boli's essay in this volume, as well as his "Personality and Conflict (*Epistole, Lettere*)," in *Boccaccio: A Critical Guide to the Complete Works*, ed. Victoria Kirkham, Michael Sherberg, and Janet Levarie Smarr (Chicago: University of Chicago Press, 2013), 303. On the known facts of Boccaccio's legal career, see two useful pieces in the series of "Notizie e documenti per la biografia del Boccaccio": Vittore Branca, "L'incontro napoletano con Cino da Pistoia," *Studi sul Boccaccio* 5 (1969): 1–12, and Pier Giorgio Ricci, "Dominus Johannes Boccaccius," *Studi sul Boccaccio* 6 (1971): 1–10. Historical context for Boccaccio's study of canon law can be found in James A. Brundage, "The Teaching and Study of Canon Law in the Law Schools," in *The History of Medieval Canon Law in the Classical Period*, ed. Wilfried Hartmann and Kenneth Pennington (Washington, DC: Catholic University of America Press, 2008), 98–120. Brundage notes, writing generally about legal education in the medieval period, that it was fairly common for students not to finish their degrees, since a short period of academic study proved sufficient for the realities of a legal occupation, and few students possessed the financial resources to finish an entire doctorate in canon law.

3 Branca notes certain "negative and accusatory tones" in Boccaccio's treatment of lawyers; see the "Chiave di lettura" to his edition of the *Decameron* (xxvii).

4 Giuseppe Mazzotta has discussed Boccaccio's treatment of the law in *Decameron* 2.10 within the context of *lex naturae*, arguing that "what to the judge is the pirate's lawlessness turns out to be the woman's law"; *The World at Play in Boccaccio's "Decameron"* (Princeton: Princeton University Press, 1986), 226. In fact, Bartolomea's laws will prove to be more valid than the judge's when considered from both a natural *and* a legal perspective. See also Aldo Scaglione, *Nature and Love in the Late Middle Ages* (Berkeley: University of California Press, 1963).

5 Relatively little work has been done on law in the *Decameron*, with the recent exception of Michael Sherberg, *The Governance of Friendship: Law and Gender in the "Decameron"* (Columbus: Ohio State University Press, 2011). An article by Kenneth Pennington shows Boccaccio's use of the legal maxim *quod omnes tangit* in *Decameron* 6.7, and several *Boccaccisti* have subsequently discussed the legal resonances of that story, largely following Pennington's argument; Kenneth Pennington, "A Note to *Decameron* 6.7: The Wit of Madonna Filippa," *Speculum* 52, no. 4 (1977): 902–5; Sherberg, *The Governance of Friendship*, 92–9; Mazzotta, *The World at Play in Boccaccio's "Decameron,"* 229–32. Sara Russell's unpublished doctoral dissertation, which treats Boccaccio, Bandello, and Gratian, uses Gratian's definition of consent to argue for a critique of forced marriage in *Decameron* 2.10; Sara Elizabeth Christina Russell, "Courtship, Violence, and the Formation of Marriage in the Early Modern Italian Novella Tradition" (PhD dissertation, University of California, Berkeley, 2010), 65–9, ProQuest Dissertation Publishing [3413474]. Finally, Lucia Battaglia Ricci has previously noted that *Decameron* 2.10 bears a similarity to *Causa* 33 of Gratian's *Decretum*, although she does not linger on the implications of this connection; "*Decameron*: interferenze di modelli," in *Autori e lettori di Boccaccio*, ed. Michelangelo Picone (Firenze: F. Cesati, 2002), 179–94.

6 On Burchard's *Decretum* and its value as a systematic collection and theory of law, see Greta Austin, *Shaping Church Law around the Year 1000: The "Decretum" of Burchard of Worms* (Burlington: Ashgate, 2009).

7 For a discussion of the extant biographical accounts of Gratian – all of which, when carefully examined, are revealed to be either hearsay or unfounded speculation – see the classic study of John T. Noonan, "Gratian Slept Here: The Changing Identity of the Father of the Systematic Study of Canon Law," *Traditio* 35 (1979): 145–72. A more recent book by Anders Winroth argues that the received (vulgate) text of the *Decretum* is actually

the second recension of an originally much shorter work; see *The Making of Gratian's "Decretum"* (Cambridge: Cambridge University Press, 2000). Winroth hypothesizes, basing his conjecture on the near-absence of Roman law in the first recension and its substantial presence in the second, that the two *Decreta* may have been written by two different authors (or two different teams of authors).

8 A general idea of the *Decretum*'s structure will help to place *Causa* 33 in context. The *Decretum* is divided into three sections. The first contains 101 *distinctiones*, dealing with general principles of law, ecclesiastical hierarchy, offices, and discipline. The third section contains 5 *distinctiones* dealing with sacraments; it is generally called the "De consecratione" to avoid confusion with the first section, as both contain *distinctiones*. The second section contains 36 *causae* dealing with a wide array of topics, including simony, heresy, monastic orders, and marriage; the *causae* that deal with marriage law (the *Tractatus de matrimonio*) are CC. 27–36. Each *causa* is divided into between 2 and 11 *quaestiones*. Each *quaestio* contains both canons (*canones*) and Gratian's own commentary introducing or discussing the canons (*dicta*). When citing from the second section of the *Decretum*, it is standard to refer to *Causa, questio*, and *canon/dictum*. *Dicta* are cited as either d.a.c (*dictum ante canonem*, a dictum preceding the canon) or d.p.c. (*dictum post canonem*, a dictum following the canon). For example, "C. 33 q. 2 d.p.c. 3" would refer to Gratian's commentary after the third canon in *quaestio* 2 of *Causa* 33, whereas "C. 33 q. 2 c. 3" would refer to the third canon itself.

9 Brundage poetically describes the pedagogical feel of the *Decretum*, which "evokes the smell of ink, of warm bodies wrapped in damp gowns, the chill of classrooms on winter mornings, the tattoo of dialogue between student and teacher" ("The Teaching and Study of Canon Law in the Law Schools," 99).

10 *Decretum* C. 33. The *Decretum* has a complicated textual history. In 1578, Gregory XIII appointed a committee (known as the *Correctores Romani*) to set about the task of editing the *Decretum*, and in 1582 the *Editio Romana* was produced. However, the *Correctores* were less concerned with reproducing the *Decretum* as Gratian wrote it than with writing the *Decretum* as Gratian "should have" written it; this resulted in an authoritative text which, however, did not always match the *Decretum* as it had circulated in the Middle Ages. The only critical edition of the *Decretum* is that of Emil Friedberg, first published in Leipzig in 1879 and reprinted in 1959 (Graz: Akademische Druck- und Verlagsanstalt). Friedberg's edition falls short of modern critical standards: his limited

manuscript base results in an edition that is fully accurate neither to any medieval manuscript tradition of the *Decretum* nor to the *Editio Romana*. Furthermore, his edition lacks the ordinary gloss, which would have accompanied any edition of the *Decretum* from the 1200s onward. However, since Friedberg's edition is the closest thing to a critical edition available, it is the version from which I cite. Friedberg's edition is available online at the *Digitale Bibliothek* of the Münchener DigitalisierungsZentrum (http://geschichte.digitale-sammlungen.de/decretum-gratiani/online/angebot). The 1582 *Editio Romana* has been digitized and is available from UCLA's Digital Collections (http://digital.library.ucla.edu/canonlaw/index.html). For further discussion of the philological problems surrounding the *Decretum*, see Winroth, *The Making of Gratian's "Decretum"*; Mary E. Sommar, *The Correctores Romani: Gratian's "Decretum" and the Counter-Reformation Humanists* (Berlin: Lit Verlag, 2009).

11 I follow Atria Larson's translation in making the husband the subject of "admiserat," although the subject of this clause is ambiguous in the Latin, given that the subject of the previous clause is the wife: "a uiro suo separata corruptori suo publice nubit; *crimen, quod admiserat, corde tantum Deo confitetur*; redditur huic facultas cognoscendi eam." See Atria Larson, *Master of Penance: Gratian and the Development of Penitential Thought and Law in the Twelfth Century* (Washington, DC: Catholic University of America Press, 2014), 14.

12 Even the name "Bartolomea" may, very faintly, evoke the *Decretum* by way of its ordinary gloss, which was revised in 1245 by a jurist named Bartholomaeus Brixiensis. On the *glossa ordinaria*, see Rudolf Weigand, "The Development of the *Glossa Ordinaria* to Gratian's *Decretum*," in *The History of Medieval Canon Law in the Classical Period, 1140–1234: From Gratian to the Decretals of Pope Gregory IX*, ed. Wilfried Hartmann and Kenneth Pennington (Washington, DC: Catholic University of America Press, 2008), 55–97.

13 *Decretum* C. 27. q. 2 d.p.c. 45.

14 *Decretum* C. 33 q. 1 d.a.c. 1.

15 James A. Brundage, *Law, Sex, and Christian Society in Medieval Europe* (Chicago: University of Chicago Press, 1987), 235–9.

16 The beginning of canon law as an academic discipline is dated contemporaneously with the emergence of the *Decretum*, but even in that text the distinctions between law and theology are far from clear, making it difficult to speak of "canon law" as a monolith. For example, the *Tractatus de penitentia* (the disproportionately long *quaestio* 3 of *Causa* 33)

is an extended treatise in the *Decretum* that deals predominantly with theological rather than legal issues: what is the nature of penance and how does it work? (It should be noted that Gratian's theological and theoretical treatment of penance is far removed from the mechanical punishments listed in the penitentials, though both are nominally concerned with "penance.") The seemingly random placement of the *De penitentia* in a *causa* that otherwise deals with an unrelated topic, marriage, has caused a great deal of perplexity and even led some to speculate that the *De penitentia* was a later insertion in Gratian's text. However, the presence of the *De penitentia* even in early manuscripts of the *Decretum* suggests that it is indeed Gratian's. Though the *De penitentia* appears in *Causa* 33, it functions as an independent treatise, much like the *De consecratione* that constitutes the final part of the *Decretum*. For a full treatment of the *De penitentia* and its reception after Gratian, see Larson, *Master of Penance*.

17 A study of penitential literature that emphasizes the treatment of sexual behaviour in these manuals can be found in Pierre J. Payer, *Sex and the Penitentials: The Development of a Sexual Code, 550–1150* (Toronto: University of Toronto Press, 1984). Critical editions and translations of penitentials are scarce, but see John T. McNeill and Helena M. Gamer, *Medieval Handbooks of Penance: A Translation of the Principal "Libri Poenitentiales" and Selections from Related Documents*, Records of Western Civilization 29 (New York: Columbia University Press, 1938).

18 Brundage, *Law, Sex, and Christian Society in Medieval Europe*, 161. Brundage's tome on sex and the law also includes, on the following page, his infamous flowchart detailing the sexual decision-making process according to the penitentials.

19 Flandrin suggests that, although married men and women of the Middle Ages did not easily accept restrictions on their sex lives, the penitentials reflected a way of conceiving the "propriety of time" that would have generated a great deal of guilt in couples who pursued sexual activity even at the proper time; Jean-Louis Flandrin, *Un temps pour embrasser: aux origines de la morale sexuelle occidentale (VIe–XIe siècle)* (Paris: Editions du Seuil, 1983), 159–61. The second chapter of Flandrin's book attempts to reconstruct medieval sex lives according to the penitentials, basing his models on complex calculations of female fertility; see in particular pages 44–5, 48–9, 61–3. The experience of reading Flandrin's elaborate charts may recall the anguish of Bartolomea at Riccardo's obsession with "punti di luna e isquadri di geometria [the moon's phases and all those geometrical calculations]" (2.10.38).

20 1 Corinthians 7.3–5.

21 See *Decretum* C. 32 q. 6, which discusses whether a husband who has committed adultery may dismiss his adulterous wife. He may not, because it would be hypocritical for him to punish his wife for a crime he is guilty of; this is a promising start, but the *quaestio* concludes (cc. 4–5) that adultery is in fact a worse sin for the man than the woman, since men are the heads of women and should set a better example. This is almost precisely the same argument presented by Ambruogiuolo in *Decameron* 2.9: "avendo [l'uomo] piú di perfezione, senza alcun fallo dee avere piú di fermezza e cosí ha, per ciò che universalmente le femine sono piú mobili [man is generally considered more perfect, and being more perfect, it inevitably follows that he has a stronger will, and this too is confirmed by the fact that women are invariably more fickle]" (2.9.15).

22 If there should be a dispute over whether a marriage was consummated, "et ipsa femina dicit, quod numquam coisset cum ea, et ille uir dicit, quod sic fecit, in ueritate uiri consistat, quia uir est caput mulieris [and the woman says that the man never joined with her, and the man says that he did, let the man's word be considered the truth, because man is the head of woman]" (C. 33 q. 1 c. 3). But compare this to both earlier and later language on the conjugal debt, e.g., "ex premissis apparet, quod continentiae uota nec mulier sine uiri consensu, nec uir sine mulieris consensu Deo reddere potest [from these premises it is apparent that neither the wife without the husband's consent, nor the husband without his wife's consent, may render a vow of continence to God]" (C. 33 q. 5 d.p.c. 11). Gratian even stipulates that an agreement reached through coercion is not valid (C. 33 q. 5 c. 2), though practically speaking, in a society where women have virtually no power over men, it is difficult to legislate against the many subtle means through which a man might extort consent.

23 Marilyn Migiel argues that Bartolomea is a character who, along with other female characters in Day 2, exists "for the express purpose of satisfying male protagonists and their own carnal needs"; *A Rhetoric of the "Decameron"* (Toronto: University of Toronto Press, 2003), 68. But Bartolomea is not portrayed as sexually insatiable, for she reaches a state of satisfaction as Paganino's "legittima moglie [legitimate wife]" at the end of the story (2.10.43). Nor can we read her as a passive receptacle of Paganino's desire, because in the climactic speech of the tale, she articulates her own will, makes a clearly active choice to stay with Paganino, and even uses principles of canon law to undergird her argument.

24 Teodolinda Barolini, "*Le parole son femmine e i fatti son maschi*: Toward a Sexual Poetics of the *Decameron* (*Decameron* 2.9, 2.10, 5.10)," 1993; rpt. in Barolini, *Dante and the Origins of Italian Literary Culture* (New

York: Fordham University Press, 2006), 289. Migiel follows Barolini in summarizing Dioneo's argument that "women can, at least metaphorically, enter the world of male deeds when they participate in the 'work' of sex," but then rejects this argument as "sophistic," though she does not identify a specific fallacy or suggest an alternate reading (Migiel, *A Rhetoric of the "Decameron,"* 68; 179n12).

25 *Decretum* C. 33 q. 5 c. 1. Canons in the *Decretum* are not properly "Gratian's" (this one can technically be traced back to Augustine's commentary on Psalm 149), but one notes when reading the *Decretum* that similar phrases, words, and concepts appear and reappear, sometimes attributed to another source and sometimes not, generating a tangle of recycled language to the point that the idea of "citation" as it exists today becomes completely anachronistic. Because it was such a common practice in canon law collections to reuse the work of previous authors, it is important to keep in mind the distinction between *fontes materiales* and *fontes formales*. Material sources are original texts (the Bible, a papal letter, a notarial register, etc.), whereas formal sources are the collections that include sections of material sources, isolated from their original context and placed instead within the narrative of the law. Most of these collections, including Gratian's *Decretum*, are collections of other *fontes formales* rather than direct compilations of *fontes materiales*. On the sources of canon law see Robert Somerville and Bruce Clark Brasington, *Prefaces to Canon Law Books in Latin Christianity: Selected Translations, 500–1245* (New Haven: Yale University Press, 1998), 3–15.

26 I include the variant from the *Editio Romana* because it seems to more correctly illustrate the idea expressed in this canon: when a wife voices her disagreement with her husband's desire to take a vow of chastity (her "nolo" as opposed to his "volo"), the disagreement is settled by the terms of their marriage, which require that he continue to render the conjugal debt.

27 *Decretum* C. 33 q. 4 c. 8–c. 11.

28 *Decretum* C. 33 q. 4 c. 12.

29 Brundage, *Law, Sex, and Christian Society in Medieval Europe*, 235–42.

30 See *Decretum* C. 34.

31 *Decretum* C. 33 q. 5 c. 1.

32 This idea has vast implications for the *Decameron*'s sexual poetics, as well as its sexual economics: the idea that women will respond to their husbands' inadequacies by taking a lover forms the core of many Decameronian plots, including those of 2.9, 2.10, 5.10, and most of the stories in Day Seven; see Barolini, *"Le parole son femmine."*

33 *Decretum* C. 33 q. 5 c. 5.
34 *Decretum* C. 33 q. 5 c. 1.
35 Raymond De Roover, "The Scholastics, Usury, and Foreign Exchange," *Business History Review* 41, no. 3 (1967): 258.
36 John T. Noonan, *The Scholastic Analysis of Usury* (Cambridge, MA: Harvard University Press, 1957), 115.
37 Of course, the legitimacy of these titles was not a constant throughout the history of writings on usury, and the arguments on *lucrum cessans* and *damnum emergens* are far more complex than can be fully treated here. For a more detailed explanation of the titles' usage and their varying stages of acceptance within the usury doctrine, see Noonan, *The Scholastic Analysis of Usury*, 115–28. On the development of the usury doctrine, see, in addition to Noonan's volume, De Roover, "The Scholastics, Usury, and Foreign Exchange"; Joel Kaye, "Changing Definitions of Money, Nature, and Equality c. 1140–1270, Reflected in Thomas Aquinas' Questions on Usury," in *Credito e usura fra teologia, diritto e amministrazione: linguaggi a confronto (sec. XII–XVI)*, ed. Diego Quaglioni, Gian Maria Varanini, and Giacomo Todeschini (Rome: École française de Rome, 2005); Odd Langholm, *The Aristotelian Analysis of Usury* (Bergen: Universitetsforlaget, 1984); Giacomo Todeschini, *Ricchezza francescana: dalla povertà volontaria alla società di mercato* (Bologna: Il Mulino, 2004).
38 Boccaccio, *Esposizioni sopra la Comedìa di Dante*, ed. Giorgio Padoan, in *Tutte le opere*, ed. Vittore Branca, vol. 6; my emphasis in this and the following quotations. On Boccaccio's discussions of marriage and marital obligations in the *Esposizioni* and the *Trattatello in laude di Dante*, see Sara E. Díaz's essay in this volume.
39 Barolini, "*Le parole son femmine*," 295–7. Branca also cites the Italian version of these economic principles, "lucro cessante e danno emergente," though he does not connect them to the specifics of Bartolomea's case (*Decameron* 2.10.40n6).
40 *Decretum*, C. 33 q. 5 c. 7, my emphasis. This passage mixes naturalistic metaphors with economic ones, and it should be noted that both systems are sexualized: in medieval Latin as in modern English, the loss of a woman's virginity was often called her "deflowering" (Latin *defloratio*).
41 E.g., Luke 1:34: "Quomodo fiet istud, quoniam virum non cognosco? [How can this be, since I do not know a man?]" Fascinatingly, the English phrase "carnal knowledge" is a *legal* term that to this day appears in the law codes of several US states. Alessandro Duranti briefly observes, in his essay on Dioneo's stories, that this "commedia del non riconoscimento … di conoscenza biblica ovviamente si metaforeggia"; "Le novelle di Dioneo,"

in *Studi di filologia e critica offerti dagli allievi a Lanfranco Caretti* (Roma: Salerno editrice, 1985), 14–15.

42 *Decretum* C. 33 q. 1 d.a.c. 3.

43 Michael Calabrese notes that the name Paganino is a play on the adjective *pagano*, or precisely the sort of person who would not celebrate Christian religious festivals. See "Male Piety and Sexuality in Boccaccio's *Decameron*," *Philological Quarterly* 82, no. 3 (2003): 266.

44 See *Decretum* C. 34 on remarriage after the death of one's spouse.

45 So Emma Grimaldi frames the story, writing that "l'eros, e l'eros femminile in particolare – in quanto entità che la novella precedente rimuoveva con aprioristica ostinazione – diventa così valore trionfante, mezzo di rivalsa contro ogni soperchieria intellettuale [eros, and female eros in particular – a quality that the preceding *novella* dismissed *a priori* – becomes [in 2.10] the triumphant value, a means of revenge against intellectual arrogance]"; *Il privilegio di Dioneo: l'eccezione e la regola nel sistema "Decameron"* (Naples: Edizioni scientifiche italiane, 1987), 41.

46 Playing on the sexual metaphors of work and rest, Bartolomea tells Riccardo, "E dicovi che se voi aveste tante feste fatte fare a' lavoratori che le vostre possession lavorano, quante faciavate fare a colui che il mio piccol campicello aveva a lavorare, voi non avreste mai ricolto granel di grano [And I can tell you this, that if you had given as many holidays to the workers on your estates as you gave to the one whose job it was to tend my little field, you would never have harvested a single ear of corn]" (2.10.32). Bartolomea is being ironic, but the idea is not actually so unrealistic: the economist and historian Carlo Cipolla notes that, in Renaissance Lombardy, "religious festivities and climatic and seasonal conditions had a marked effect on the amount of labor actually put into productive activities," observing that the Reformation "noticeably reduced" the number of work days lost to religious celebrations; *Before the Industrial Revolution: European Society and Economy, 1000–1700*, 3rd ed. (New York: Norton, 1994), 75.

47 This is the root of the word "vacation," i.e., the time during which a person is *vacando.* The thing *from which* one is absent is generally expressed with an ablative of separation, e.g., "Nulla enim vitae pars … vacare officio potest [No part of your life may be absent from your duty]" (Cicero, *De officiis* 1.4, cited under "vaco" in Lewis and Short's *Latin Dictionary* [Oxford: Clarendon Press, 1879]). The thing *for which* one takes time off (from something else) is expressed with a dative of purpose (as in *vacare orationi* [to take time off for prayer]), though this use is less common in classical Latin.

48 *Decretum* C. 33 q. 4 d.p.c. 12. Cf. 1 Corinthians 7.5: "nolite fraudare invicem nisi forte ex consensu ad tempus *ut vacetis orationi*."

49 Unknown author, *De modo studendi* (Textum Taurini, 1954), Corpus Thomisticum (http://www.corpusthomisticum.org).

50 Barolini writes that the sexual-metaphoric language of the *Decameron* is "a verbal mechanism ... for effecting the translation – the literal translation, since 'metaphor' is the Greek for trans-latio, or carrying over – of words into deeds" ("*Le parole son femmine*," 300).

51 In *Decameron* 6.7, Madonna Filippa will invert this argument, suggesting that full payment of her debt to her husband entitles her to distribute the rest of her capital elsewhere: "se [mio marito] ha sempre di me preso quello che gli è bisognato e piaciuto, io che doveva fare o debbo di quel che gli avanza? debbolo io gittare a' cani? [if he has always taken as much of me as he needed and as much as he chose to take, I ask you, Messer Podestà, what am I to do with the surplus? Throw it to the dogs?]" (6.7.17). The legal and economic resonances of her argument are evident; the verb "avanza" is economic, and the insistence on forms of the verb *dovere* (Latin *debere*) may well be a linguistic nod to *debitum*. Filippa understands the sexual economics inherent in the metaphor of conjugal debt, though of course her argument distorts the principle somewhat: a "conjugal debt" is a debt generated by marriage and owed only within that marriage, not to any third party who might wish to take out a line of credit.

52 On the *brigata*'s ritualistic exercise of piety, see Joy Hambuechen Potter, *Five Frames for the "Decameron": Communication and Social Systems in the Cornice* (Princeton: Princeton University Press, 1982), 55; Sherberg, *The Governance of Friendship*, 63.

53 On these social norms and the "sociology of the *brigata*" see Teodolinda Barolini, "Sociology of the *Brigata*: Gendered Groups in Dante, Forese, Folgore, Boccaccio – From 'Guido, i' vorrei' to Griselda," *Italian Studies* 67, no. 1 (2012): 4–22.

54 The phrase "harmony from dissonance" is Stephan Kuttner's take on Gratian's *Concordia discordantium canonum*, a title which "sums up the signal achievement of the medieval mind in organizing the law of the Church into a harmonious system out of an infinite variety of diverse, even contradictory, elements." See *Harmony from Dissonance: An Interpretation of Medieval Canon Law*, Wimmer Lecture 10 (Latrobe: Archabbey Press, 1960), 10.

55 As Boccaccio encourages his readers to do, telling them in the *Proemio* that they are responsible for recognizing "quello che sia da fuggire e che

sia similmente da seguitare [what should be avoided and likewise what should be pursued]" among the hundred *novelle* (*Proemio* 14).

56 *Decretum* D.1. *Distinctiones* 1–20 in the first part of the *Decretum* constitute what is known as the *Tractatus de legibus*, or the treatise on laws, in which Gratian lays out the general principles of natural, divine, civil, and ecclesiastical laws. This treatise has been translated into English: Gratian, *The Treatise on Laws*, trans. Augustine Thompson and James Gordley (Washington, DC: Catholic University of America Press, 1993). On the category of "human" as one that, in a legal sense, may or may not include women, see Mary Anne Case's essay in this volume.

57 Anders Winroth cites Dante's *terzina* on the very first page of *The Making of Gratian's "Decretum,"* giving the interpretation of the two forums as "the exterior, public court of justice and the interior, sacramental court of the confessional" (1). Joseph Goering also references these verses in his essay "The Internal Forum and the Literature of Penance and Confession," in *The History of Medieval Canon Law in the Classical Period*, ed. W. Hartmann and K. Pennington (Washington, DC: Catholic University of America Press, 2008), 379–428. Goering explains that "the allusion to two 'courts' (*'fora'*) would have puzzled Gratian," since this way of talking about the Church's authority did not develop until several decades after the *Decretum*, "but to both Thomas and Dante it would have been a clear reference to the two broad arenas in which the Church's canon law was operative: the external forum of ecclesiastical courts and the internal forum of conscience and of penance" (379).

58 Francesco Bruni discusses *Decameron* 2.10 in the context of the *ars dictaminis*, citing a letter of Guido Faba to illustrate that writers in the tradition would often draft, among their various "parascholastic" compositions, letters revolving around the *contaminatio* of jurisprudential and sexual matters; see *Boccaccio: L'invenzione della letteratura mezzana* (Bologna: Il Mulino, 1990), 363–4. Branca notes that, in addition to the two meanings of *foro*, "furo" could also be the Latin *fur*, thief (2.10.42n2).

7 Authority and Misogamy in Boccaccio's *Trattatello in laude di Dante*

SARA E. DÍAZ

Thus seistow, lorel, whan thow goost to bedde;
And that no wys man nedeth for to wedde,
Ne no man that entendeth un-to hevene.
With wilde thunder-dint and firy levene
Mote thy welken nekke be to-broke!

Chaucer, *The Wife of Bath's Tale*, 273–7

"*Oh fatica inestimabile* ... Oh immeasurable toil, to have to live, converse, and ultimately grow old or die with such a suspicious animal!"[1] So cries out Boccaccio at the height of a tirade against marriage that abruptly interrupts his *Trattatello in laude di Dante* (*Treatise in Praise of Dante*). Following an embellished account of Dante's ancestry, his early years of study, and his first encounter with the daughter of Folco Portinari, Boccaccio manufactures a connection between Beatrice's death and the promise of consolation offered by taking a wife. It was Dante's concerned friends and relatives, alleges Boccaccio, who convinced the grieving poet to get over the loss of one woman by acquiring another.[2] This ill-advised union – in no way supported by what we know to be the actual circumstances surrounding Dante's engagement to Gemma Donati – serves as the pretext for the anti-matrimonial invective that follows.[3] Boccaccio cites a litany of *molestiae nuptiarum*, or pains of matrimony, drawn from classical, patristic, and medieval sources. He complains of the expenses, vanities, and vulgar trivialities that come with supporting a wife. Tailoring the list of torments to suit his illustrious subject, he rails against the feminine distractions that he imagines kept a beleaguered Dante from his sacred studies. The pleasant conversations with kings and emperors, the virile disputations with philosophers and poets, and the male camaraderie that somewhat mitigated Dante's initial anguish, all these are drowned out by the incessant prattle of female speech. Boccaccio's anti-uxorial digression ends with one final admonition: let lords, labourers, and rich fools marry flesh-and-blood women, but leave philosophers free to enjoy the solitary pleasures of philosophy.[4] Wives, he insists, are not to be suffered by wise men.

We might ask what, specifically, prompted Boccaccio to insert this anti-matrimonial diatribe into the biography of a man who never so much as mentioned his wife Gemma in any of his works, much less inveighed against the burdens of sharing a life with her?[5] Why interrupt a narrative of love and loss to introduce a completely extraneous polemic against wives? In the pages that follow I argue that Boccaccio's digression against matrimony forms part of a larger program designed to alleviate gendered anxieties over the form and content of Dante's works. The Dante of Boccaccio's making heroically wrestles with his passions, obligations, exile, and intolerable poverty, but it is his involvement with the feminine that most tellingly defines, or threatens, his masculine *auctoritas*. Taking a page from Gretchen Angelo's study of misogyny in medieval French literature, I look at how the *Trattatello*'s invective against wives serves to offset Boccaccio's own ambivalence over what he would later call Dante's "volgare delle femine" [women's vernacular].[6] I maintain that Boccaccio's use of misogamy, namely the rhetorical dissuasion against marriage, is part of a concerted effort to advance Dante's fame as the poet-lover of Beatrice, while bringing him closer in line to the androcentric world of Latin humanism. If read as part of a larger defensive strategy, it becomes apparent that Boccaccio's misogamous digression rhetorically sacrifices one class of woman to build the authorial prestige of a specific type of man.

The *Trattatello in laude di Dante* was at its inception materially and conceptually linked to Dante's non-Latin production. Boccaccio's sustained effort to establish a vernacular canon anchored in Dante's poetry is in fact manifest in the *Trattatello*'s earliest manuscript editions.[7] The first and longest version of the *Trattatello* survives in an autograph copy (Toledo 104.6) bearing Boccaccio's original Latin title: *De origine vita, studiis et moribus viri clarissimi Dantis Aligerii Florentini, poete illustris, et de operibus compositis ab eodem* (*Concerning the origins, life, studies, and habits of that most great man and illustrious poet Dante Alighieri, and the works composed by him*).[8] Written sometime in the early 1350s, the Toledano codex places the *Trattatello* before a collection of Dante's vernacular work copied in Boccaccio's own hand: the *Vita Nova,* the *Commedia,* and fifteen of Dante's so-called *canzoni distese.* A second autograph redaction of the biography (Chigi L. V. 176) was begun as early as 1359 and then repeatedly edited over the next six to seven years. Commonly referred to as the *Vita di Dante,* this shorter version again precedes Dante's *Vita Nova* and *canzoni distese,* but here instead of the *Commedia* we find Guido Cavalcanti's *Donna me prega* and Dino del Garbo's commentary, Petrarch's *Fragmentorum liber,* and a Latin *carmen* by Boccaccio dedicated to Petrarch entitled *Ytalie iam certus honos.*[9] As recent codicological analysis of the Toledano and Chigi redactions demonstrates, the *Trattatello*'s physical proximity to the *Vita Nova* in both autographs reflects Boccaccio's desire for the two to be read in tandem, constituting what Jelena Todorovic calls a micro-unit within Boccaccio's larger project of promoting Dante as a literary authority.[10] Painstakingly copied and revised over the course of two decades but always yoked to the *Vita Nova,* the *Trattatello* speaks to Boccaccio's perceived need to provide an authorizing frame for Dante's vernacular autobiography.

Boccaccio reimagines Dante's life for the *Trattatello* by combining established rhetorical models with pure fantasy. The result is a patchwork of different biographical genres: it is part Latin *accessus ad auctores* chronicling the development of an exemplary *auctoritas,* part Occitan *vida* historicizing the erotic subject of the poet's lyrics, and part hagiography venerating its persecuted hero.[11] Its Dante-protagonist bears more than a passing resemblance to a number of other authors, including Cicero, Saint Thomas, and, as we shall see, Petrarch.[12] From his mother's prophetic dream foretelling his poetic glory to his son's discovery of the missing *canti* of the *Paradiso* hidden within a wall, the poet's life and death are graced with miracles not unlike those found in medieval biographies of Virgil.[13] Naturally, Boccaccio also draws material from his subject's autobiographical corpus: the *Trattatello*'s account of Dante's youthful sighs and tears for Beatrice is culled directly from the *Vita Nova,* while its political digressions against Florence are reminiscent of those penned by the exiled poet of the *Commedia.* Furthermore, Boccaccio's reliance on the language of Dante's source-texts is clearly advertised in the opening pages of the *Trattatello.* Assuming a self-deprecating, even apologetic tone, Boccaccio explains that his decision to tell Dante's story using the humble Florentine vernacular was motivated by a desire to harmonize their works.[14] Boccaccio's act of heuristic imitation thus further binds the *Trattatello* to its subject, while cautiously deflecting criticism of its language back onto Dante.

Boccaccio did have good reason to fear that a biography penned in the Florentine idiom would not be taken seriously. As Todd Boli has shown in his work on the subject, the *Trattatello*'s many digressions form part of a consistent defensive strategy designed to combat the anti-vernacular bias of the early humanists.[15] The close association between the vernacular and secular, erotic themes was treated with contempt by those who preferred to read their philosophy and theology in the sober Latin of the ancients. In his own life, Dante responded to his detractors in several of his works: in the *Convivio*, he addressed those who would criticize his passionate lyrics and vernacular commentary, and in the *Eclogues* he sparred with Giovanni del Virgilio over treating weighty subjects in a mercantile and far-too-accessible language.[16] Naturally, any given page of the *De vulgari eloquentia* speaks to the controversial nature of his vernacular agenda. After his death, a new generation took Dante to task for his politics, unorthodoxy, and excessive devotion to women. Francesco Stabili, for example, crudely objected that Dante's exaggerated love for Beatrice showed a slavish devotion to the wanton female gender.[17] Stabili's concerns were not exceptional, for, as Alistair Minnis muses, late medieval audiences wondered, "how could a poet who wrote about love, and/or expressed his own (limiting and probably demeaning) emotional experiences, be trusted as a fount of wisdom, accepted as a figure worthy of belief?"[18] And while the dominating erotic current of Dante's work remained a stumbling block for some, it was Dante's correlated use of the vernacular that consistently proved to be most problematic for his learned readers. Within this context, the *Trattatello*'s portrait of its *auctor amans* must be understood as a revisionist one, designed to protect its subject from his degrading contact with the *volgare*.[19] Charged with the self-appointed task of canonizing an author whose literary corpus revolved around a love expressed overwhelmingly in the vernacular, Boccaccio accordingly adopted a number of strategies to grant his subject an air of Latin gravitas.

The Toledano and Chigi autographs display many of the possible ways by which literary authority might be conferred upon a vernacular poet. Commenting on the Chigi manuscript, Martin Eisner observes that Boccaccio attempted to legitimize the amorous verse showcased in his anthology by including erudite commentary (Dino del Garbo's gloss on Cavalcanti's *Donna me prega*) and selectively reassembling lyrics into a cohesive poetic form (Petrarch's *Fragmentorum liber* and Dante's *canzoni distese*).[20] And as discussed above, the *Trattatello* is coupled to the *Vita Nova* in both manuscript redactions, in effect imposing a paratextual biography upon a lyrical autobiography already held together by Dante's own authorizing prose frame.[21] As if these external defences were not enough to shield his poet from criticism, Boccaccio punctuates his heroic narrative with a rhetorical digression purposefully designed to create some distance between Dante and the female sex. As we shall now see, Boccaccio's anti-uxorial excursus anticipates misogynist contempt for the kind of love-centred literature which, for someone like Stabili, undermined Dante's virile authority.

Angelo's work on misogynous strategies in vernacular French letters illustrates how antifeminism could be used to establish a textual voice of masculine authority. As she argues, misogyny allowed "male authors to place themselves in an illustrious line of scholarship. It simultaneously weakened the association of vernacular literature with the feminine by creating a masculine textual community and a masculine vernacular."[22] Using Jean de Meun's *Roman de la rose*, Eustache Deschamp's *Miroir de mariage*, and Christine de Pizan's *Rose* debate as models, Angelo demonstrates how misogynist topoi helped orient texts gendered as female towards male audiences.[23] Learned readers might enjoy stumbling upon a familiar catalogue of female defects in a vernacular piece and gain respect for the author's mastery of his Latin sources, even when reading works penned in a characteristically feminine and therefore humbler language. Misogyny could also help define the implied subject of these texts, namely the author himself, as a scholar at odds with the comic frivolities, and distractions, of women. And while Angelo's study helps explain how *Trattatello*'s anti-uxorial digression might mitigate Boccaccio's anxieties over a gendered vernacular, as we move forward it is important to differentiate between misogyny and misogamy. For while Boccaccio certainly does pack a considerable amount of misogynist vitriol into his *Trattatello*, it is misogamy that most properly defines his poet-subject as a philosopher saddled with the unbearable burden of caring for a wife.

Though often conflated as one, misogyny and misogamy constitute two separate albeit closely interrelated categories. In its broadest sense, misogyny was, and is, a sexual prejudice marked by a visceral aversion to women as an undifferentiated class.[24] It is the ritual denunciation of the female, symbolically exchanged between men from antiquity to the Middle Ages and beyond, and as such is one of the most enduring discourses in Western thought. In medieval literature, rhetorical misogyny is a "citational mode" that displaces "its own source away from anything that might be construed as personal and confessional and toward sacred authorities."[25] Antifeminist material from patristic writers including Paul, Tertullian, and Jerome, for instance, could be uncritically copied with little regard for their original celibate agendas. As Katharina M. Wilson and Elizabeth M. Makowski note in their seminal work on medieval anti-matrimonial literature, because "woman was commonly associated in medieval theology and law with gross corporeality, sexual temptation, and lust, it is logical to assume that any polemic against carnal union necessarily included, or assumed, rejection of the gender that symbolized the lower appetites; [and] that a caution against marriage ... necessarily involved a hatred or a distrust of women."[26] Strictly speaking, however, misogamy rejects marriage and the institutional obligations of matrimony, though not necessarily women en masse.[27] A misogamous dissuasion might draw "evidence" against women from Juvenal's *Sixth Satire*, for example, yet still keep the main thrust of the argument focused on marriage and its incumbent responsibilities. No less "citational" than literary misogyny, rhetorical misogamy recites the defects of women to dramatize the masculine burdens of the conjugal state.

Within medieval misogamy, two distinct sub-categories emerge: general or unlimited misogamy cautioning all men against marriage, and limited misogamy cautioning only wise men against marriage. General misogamy was addressed to a varied, often vernacular public, and piled hyperbolic levels of abuse upon wives, often to ironic and farcical effect.[28] The latter vein, limited or philosophic misogamy, was elitist by design. Addressed to an exclusive audience of professional male scholars, philosophic misogamy urged its readers to avoid the shackles of matrimony and its related domestic charges for the good of their studies. It engaged in discourses about women, to the complete exclusion of women, to create a textual community composed by and for men. The preferred language for erudite misogamy, Latin, further distanced its assumed reader from the unlearned laity of men and women. If read through a gendered lens, it becomes apparent that the mechanism of textual recognition that encouraged male audiences to self-identify with the wise philosopher in these tracts served as a medium for the construction of elite masculinity. Citing a variety of antifeminist authorities, misogamous writers built up the masculine prestige of the scholarly vocation by placing it in opposition to burdensome women and unschooled men.

An interesting example of Boccaccio's strategic use of this citational mode of misogamy can be found in his *Esposizioni sopra la "Comedia."*

Boccaccio produced detailed literal and allegorical commentaries on the *Commedia* for his public lectures on Dante at the church of Santo Stefano in Badia (1373–4). Shortly before abandoning his ambitious project midway through the *Inferno*, Boccaccio lifted an anti-matrimonial excerpt from his earlier *Zibaldone laurenziano* to help explain the relationship between Iacopo Rusticucci and his "fiera moglie" [fierce wife] (*Inf.* 16.45).[29] Translating two of the most influential misogamous tracts into the Florentine vernacular – the so-called Book of Theophrastus preserved in Jerome's *Adversus Jovinianum*, and Walter Map's *Dissuasiones Valerii ad Rufinum* – Boccaccio launches into a lengthy harangue over the ills of taking a wife. Wives are presented as quarrelsome, vain, fickle, jealous, and demanding. They require constant validation, reassurance, supervision, and fatuous praise. A husband must also supply them with expensive jewels, fine garments, and a costly retinue of servants and vendors. But most importantly, Boccaccio, like Jerome before him, begins his invective by questioning whether a philosopher should marry – an issue of no apparent relevance for an understanding of the Guelph politician Rusticucci.[30] Boccaccio's answer is a resounding "no."

Boccaccio's gloss on Rusticucci is notable for several reasons. First and foremost, Boccaccio recopies the anti-uxorious diatribe from the *Zibaldone* into his *Trattatello*, *Corbaccio*, and *Esposizioni* almost verbatim. Second, he uses a misogamous discourse to defend a sodomite, and not, as one might expect, to condemn the adulterous wives of *Inferno* 5. His defence is in fact twofold: it touts Rusticucci as a wealthy, courteous, and magnanimous knight, while conversely presenting his wife as being so perverse as to cause him to renounce women altogether.[31] Boccaccio builds him up by tearing her down, using misogyny to obliquely excuse Rusticucci's sodomy. The second part of Boccaccio's argument seems almost disconnected from the first, forcing a philosophical dissuasion against marriage onto a civic figure far removed from the life of speculative thought. The stock woes of matrimony are cited as a matter of convenience to explain the toll this "fiera moglie" took on her husband, illustrating Boccaccio's repeated use of misogamy to defend a vulnerable masculine type.

These rhetorical invectives against matrimony and its associated burdens tell us more about the male subjects they defend than about the generic class of women they defame. In the *Trattatello* and *Esposizioni*, misogamy diverts criticism away from a fallible male onto a scapegoated female. Furthermore, it confers an air of masculine prestige by aligning its subject with the archetypal wise man. Admittedly, it would be a gross oversimplification to read the persistence of misogamy in Boccaccio's works as a true indication of his hatred of marriage. For it could be argued, as Thomas Greene has, that the *Decameron* bears witness to Boccaccio's faith in marriage as an instrument of social order.[32] Indeed, female adultery is treated comically in the *Decameron*, and youthful sexual licence is happily resolved in the sanctioning marriages of the *novelle*. It must be noted, however, that the *Decameron* contains a multiplicity of discourses about women and marriage, making it near impossible to reduce the author's views into a singular and consistent gender ideology.[33] For while Boccaccio explicitly makes allowances for certain classes of men to marry in the *Trattatello* (viz. the lords, labourers, and rich fools), in the *Decameron* even these types can be seen to betray some discomfort with the institutional pressures of matrimony (*Tratt.* I, 59).

The conjugal burdens alluded to in the *Trattatello* and *Esposizioni*, though derivative, would have resonated with audiences that placed great stock in the performance of patriarchal masculinity within marriage. Marrying men, generally speaking, were expected to materially provide for their families, sexually perform for their wives, and produce demonstrable proof of these efforts in the form of children, though the import placed on these duties varied according to a man's age, profession, and station.[34] In the *Decameron*'s tale of Masetto da Lamporecchio, however, Boccaccio playfully indulges in a fantasy of hyper-masculine performance that circumvents some of the more cumbersome obligations of matrimony. In the first tale of the third *giornata*, Filostrato tells the story of a young gardener who, feigning to be a deaf-mute, finds himself in the difficult position of having to satisfy a convent of sexually demanding nuns. Masetto proves to be an energetic husbandman for his cloistered harem, and is rewarded for his toil with prestige, wealth, and a litter of children, or little "monachin." When Masetto finally retires from his life of service, he is a "vecchio, padre e ricco, senza aver fatica di nutricare i figliuoli o spesa di quegli [elderly and prosperous father who was spared the bother of feeding his children and the expense of their upbringing]" (3.1.43).[35] Never having married any of his brides of Christ, he is able to partake in the physical joys of wedlock without shouldering the burdens. His children, as Marilyn Migiel observes, are "'trophy offspring,' testimony to Masetto's virility."[36] His riches, on the other hand, are the happy earnings of a man unencumbered by any financial responsibility to his family. Within this fantasy of sex, money, and masculine prowess, much of Masetto's enviable success lies in his ability to slip out of the bonds of matrimony.

A very different picture of the masculine obligations of matrimony emerges from the final *novella* of the *Decameron*, where conjugal and dynastic responsibilities coincide. Boccaccio's ambiguous commentary on patriarchal authority in the tale of Griselda has long engaged readers, including Petrarch and Christine de Pizan, who both felt compelled to rewrite the story to provide less equivocal pictures of gendered exemplarity.[37] But a gendered reading of Boccaccio's text also unmasks masculine anxieties, and fantasies, about the weight of patriarchal responsibility. As the narrative begins, the young marquis of Saluzzo, Gualtieri, happily enjoys a carefree bachelorhood engaged in manly pastimes. For this, remarks Boccaccio, Gualtieri should have been considered "molto savio" [very wise]:

> Già è gran tempo, fu tra' marchesi di Sanluzzo il maggior della casa un giovane chiamato Gualtieri, il quale, essendo senza moglie e senza figliuoli, in niuna altra cosa il suo tempo spendeva che in uccellare e in cacciare, né di prender moglie né d'aver figliuoli alcun pensiero avea; *di che egli era da reputar molto savio.* (10.10.4; my emphasis)

> [A very long time ago, there succeeded to the marquisate of Saluzzo a young man called Gualtieri, who, having neither wife nor children, spent the whole of his time hunting and hawking, and never even thought about marrying or raising a family, *which says a great deal for his intelligence*].

Caving to the demands of his vassals to produce an heir for his people, Gualtieri submits to the conjugal yoke to achieve a political end. He is reluctant, since, according to him, the value of a woman can never truly be known from the qualities of her parents, and mothers conceal impenetrable secrets that might be passed down to their daughters. Arguing in terms that vaguely echo the misogamy of Jerome's Theophrastus or Boccaccio's *Zibaldone*, Gualtieri objects that a life spent with a poorly matched woman would be a grievous cross to bear (10.10.6–7). He finally consents, only to then test his wife's mettle through an intolerably harsh probation lasting years, systematically denying her those very goods – clothes, affection, even children – which were commonly presented as burdensome in anti-matrimonial tracts. Gualtieri justifies his actions by explaining that it was his desire to teach Griselda how to be a proper wife, and his subjects how to keep such a woman, which drove him to these cruel lengths.[38] He also freely admits to have tormented Griselda in order to selfishly guard the peace and quiet ["perpetua quiete"] he feared his wife would destroy. In the end, as Teodolinda Barolini notes, the marquis "has taught the lesson of how to be married while keeping oneself at the *status quo ante,* how to deprive marriage – and any other social contract – of its power to effect change."[39] Gualtieri thus seems to achieve the impossible, enjoying both an exemplary wife *and* the quiet repose that was so emphatically denied to the wise men addressed in misogamous literature. Not unlike the story of Masetto da Lamporecchio, *Decameron* 10.10 gives voice to an androcentric fantasy of marriage-less marriage – a personally and socially rewarding union with few of the responsibilities, or inconveniences, of reciprocally binding matrimony.

The masculine paradigms and accompanying duties alluded to in these two *novelle* are only distantly related to the ones in Boccaccio's *Trattatello*. Dante, to be sure, was neither a humble labourer like Masetto nor a draconian marquis like Gualtieri. He was a scholar, a *theologus-poeta*, but saddled nonetheless with familial encumbrances which, as Boccaccio stresses in his second redaction of the *Trattatello*, forced him to set aside his "eccelse meditazioni":

> Tirò appresso di sé lo stimolo della moglie al nostro poeta un'altra quasi inevitabil gravezza, e questa fu la sollecitudine d'allevare i figliuoli, perciò che in brieve tempo padre di famiglia divenne; e, strigendolo la domestica cura, quel tempo, che alle eccelse meditazioni, soluto, soleva prestare, costretto da necessità, conveniva che egli concedesse a' pensieri donde dovessero i salari delle nutrici venire, i vestimenti de' figliuoli, e l'altre cose opportune a chi piú secondo la opinion del vulgo che secondo la filosofica verità convien che viva. (*Tratt.* II, 46)

> [Along with the desire for a wife, another almost inevitable burden weighed down our poet, and this was the concern for the care for his children, since in little time he had fathered a family. And being bound by domestic responsibilities, and constrained by necessity, it behooved him to cede the solitary time he used to dedicate to lofty meditations to thinking about where to find salaries for nursemaids, clothes for the children, and other suitable things which, according to the opinion of the common people more than to the philosophical truth, one needs to live.]

Clothing and sheltering children cost money, and it fell upon Dante to provide for these decidedly mundane matters. Now admittedly, Boccaccio's insistence on the incompatibility of a life of study and the care for a wife and family is at least partially in keeping with Dante's own words. For as Dante himself concedes in the opening passages of his *Convivio*, "la cura familiare e civile [domestic and civil responsibilities]" bar the greater number of men from a life of speculative thought (*Conv.* 1.1.4). However, Dante's admission never devolves into misogamy. He attempts to compensate for these domestic impediments by offering his readers an inclusive feast of vernacular learning; Boccaccio, on the other hand, appends his complaint to the end of a protracted misogamous digression.

The Dante that emerges from the Certaldan's biography is a philosopher, a scholar, a man of letters. As such, he bears an uncanny resemblance to other Boccaccian literati, men whose literary professions, perhaps not coincidentally, are couched in narratives of misogynist and misogamous rage. The vengeful *scolare* Rinieri of *Decameron* 8.7, for example, is repeatedly said to have studied in Paris.[40] His pursuit of knowledge stemmed from an interest in learning the "reasons and causes of things," with no regard for base profits:

> Avvenne in questi tempi che un giovane chiamato Rinieri, nobile uomo della nostra città, *avendo lungamente studiato a Parigi*, non per vender poi la sua scienzia a minuto, come molti fanno, ma *per sapere la ragion delle cose e la cagion d'esse*, il che ottimamente sta in gentile uomo, *tornò da Parigi a Firenze;* e quivi onorato molto sí per la sua nobiltà e sí per la sua scienza cittadinescamente viveasi. (*Dec.* 8.7.5; my emphasis)

> [Now it happened around that time, a young nobleman of our city called Rinieri, *having spent some years studying in Paris with the purpose,* not of selling his knowledge for gain as many people do, but *of learning the reasons and causes of things* (a most fitting pursuit for any gentleman), *returned from Paris to Florence.* There he was held in high esteem for his nobility and his learning, and he led the life of a gentleman.]

In the *Trattatello*, Boccaccio makes similar claims about Dante's engagement with the Parisian intelligentsia, despite the absence of any such reference in Dante's own works (*Tratt.* I, 123). Boccaccio also asserts that Dante enjoyed speculating about first causes – that is, until his wife put an end to such contemplative pursuits:

> Egli, costumato, quante volte la volgar turba gli rincresceva, di ritrarsi in alcuna solitaria parte e, quivi speculando, vedere quale spirito muove il

cielo, onde venga la vita agli animali che sono in terra, quali sieno *le cagioni delle cose*, o premeditare alcune invenzioni peregrine o alcune cose comporre, le quali appo li futuri facessero lui morto viver per fama; ora non solamente dalle contemplazioni dolci è tolto quante volte voglia ne viene alla nuova donna, ma gli conviene essere accompagnato di compagnia male a così fatte cose disposta. (*Tratt.* I, 51; my emphasis)

[Whenever he used to grow weary of the vulgar herd, he would withdraw to some solitary place and, while speculating there, observe which spirit moves the sky, where life comes to the animals that are on earth, *what are the causes of things*, or consider some unusual theories or compose some works which, because of his fame, in death would give him life among future generations. Now, not only is he taken away from these sweet contemplations whenever a whim seizes his new lady, but he must be accompanied by company ill-disposed to these sorts of things.]

Also much like Rinieri, Dante is commended for his youthful dedication to the liberal arts, particularly poetry, while eschewing the lucrative yet transitory rewards that might have attracted lesser men.[41] As scholars, Boccaccio's Rinieri and Dante appear to have been cut from the same cloth.

No study of misogamy and Boccaccio would be complete without a few words on the *Corbaccio*. Unquestionably the most overtly misogynous of his literary endeavours, the *Corbaccio* proudly draws from stockpiles of misogamous literature to create a comprehensive "*summa* of the anti-feminist tradition."[42] It is vulgar, hyperbolic, and farcical, and presents itself as a cautionary tale for a mixed vernacular audience. It paints a grotesque picture of the female body and counsels all men not to marry, and as such falls under the rubric of general misogamy.[43] And whether the *Corbaccio* should be read as an act of generic experimentation, a send-up of misogynous discourse, or, less likely, the sincere confession of a bitter old man, the fact remains that couched within his antifeminist narrative lies a damning critique of the philosopher-type. Like Rinieri, the dreamer of the *Corbaccio* is a scholar of sorts. As the ghost of the widow's husband points out, the jilted lover often boasted to anyone who would listen about his disdain for commerce and the manual trades.[44] From an early age he dedicated himself to sacred philosophy and, somewhat unsuccessfully, to poetry. His studies, chides the spirit-guide, should have distinguished him from the common throng of men, the "meccanica turba [vulgar herd]."[45] But rather than teach him the nature of love, woman, man, and his duties, the dreamer's uninspired attempts at courtly poetry predisposed him to the debasing effects of erotic desire.[46] The result is a comic foil to the kind of philosopher-ideal which Dante also imperfectly embodies in the *Trattatello.*

Taken together, these passages reinforce the idea that there is something unseemly about a scholar in love. The *savio* Rinieri, humiliated and emasculated on that cold night in the widow's courtyard, regains his dignity only after exacting his cruel revenge upon the wanton widow. The excoriating misogyny of the *Corbaccio*, on the other hand, might be read as a curative measure designed to restore the lovesick narrator to his senses. Turning back to the *Trattatello*, Boccaccio is forced to admit that despite Dante's otherwise solemn and commendable character, the glorious poet suffered from a lifelong propensity for passionate love:

> Tra cotanta virtù, tra cotanta scienzia, quanta dimostrato è di sopra essere stata in questo mirifico poeta, trovò ampissimo luogo la lussuria, e non solamente ne' giovani anni, ma ancora ne' maturi. Il quale vizio, come che naturale e comune e quasi necessario sia, nel vero non che commendare, ma scusare non si può degnamente. Ma chi sarà tra' mortali giusto giudice a condennarlo? Non io. (*Tratt.* I, 172)

> [Amid all the virtue, amid all the knowledge that has been amply shown above to have belonged to this marvellous poet, lust found most ample place, and not only in his youth, but also in his maturity. This vice, though it may be natural and common and almost necessary, in truth cannot be commended for it cannot be properly excused. But who among us mortals shall be a righteous judge to condemn it? Not I.]

Dante was prone to the shameful effects of lust, not only as a young man but, worse still, well past his prime. Boccaccio declares himself incapable of fully condemning Dante for this common fault, and then proceeds to draw parallels between Dante's amorous failings and those of Jove, Hercules, and Paris, and then Adam, David, and Solomon (*Tratt.* I, 172). Dante, it would seem, was in good company. And while it was typical for medieval biographers to chastise the subject of their *vita auctoris* only to see them develop into a moral exemplum, Boccaccio makes it clear that Dante's affinity for women continued unabated throughout his life.[47] This tepid censure of the poet, perhaps a mixture of false shame and admiration, is even more notable when we consider the second redaction's claim that an elderly Dante pined away for a certain Pargoletta, and later even fell for an Alpine woman with a goitre (*Tratt.* II, 35). Dante's relationship to women, including Beatrice, is further problematized once it is linked to his linguistic choices.

Boccaccio recounts how it was Dante's love for a woman that first moved him to "divenir dicitore in volgare," and even boasts that it was this linguistic choice that eventually brought him glory and a host of imitators.[48] Further on in the *Trattatello*, Boccaccio has a mature Dante disavow the *Vita Nova*, dismissing it as a shameful little volume, irrespective of its beauty and broad appeal among the unlettered, or "volgari."[49] This contradictory stance on the feminine-inspired vernacular, and the vast unlearned public it addressed, finds confirmation in the biographical *accessus* of the *Esposizioni*. Writing in the early 1370s and no doubt swayed by Petrarch's vocal preference for Latin letters, Boccaccio struggles to defend what he increasingly defines as a "volgare delle femine," or "feminette."[50] It is a discomfort with the maternal tongue that naturally extends to Boccaccio's own works. But setting aside his reservations about his own vernacular production, a subject which has already received some attention in feminist criticism, it is fair to conclude along with Alison Cornish that "Boccaccio's attitude towards vernacular letters was notoriously ambivalent," to say the least.[51]

Further confirmation of Boccaccio's conflicting attitude towards the form and content of Dante's early works can be found in Boccaccio's *Vita Petracchi* – a biography entirely free from the kind of gendered anxiety I have been tracing up until now.[52] Written approximately ten years prior to the *Trattatello* and based largely on Petrarch's own *Coronation Oration* (*Collatio laureationis*, 1341), the *Vita Petracchi* has a protagonist who nevertheless bears many generic resemblances to the Dante of the *Trattatello*.[53] Like Dante, Petrarch is said to have been a lover of music, a moderate eater, a singular genius, and, in his youth, a prodigious student of philosophy and theology. And like Dante, Petrarch is said to have suffered from only one vice: *libidine*. It is here, however, that the biographies of the two *corone* diverge. Unlike Dante, Petrarch is said to have been only slightly troubled ("molestatus") by lust. Though he may have succumbed to its effects from time to time, Boccaccio tells us that Petrarch ultimately knew how to put an end to his unchaste urges. Boccaccio then whitewashes the products of this desire, Petrarch's vernacular *rime* for Laura, with a few lines explaining the allegorical connection between *Laurettam* and the laurel crown. The focus thus remains squarely on Petrarch's Latin production and classical influences. Written in Latin for an erudite public, tracing a predominantly Latinate output, and in close conformity with Petrarch's emphasis on his own Latinity, Boccaccio's *Vita Petracchi* safely relegates the language of erotic desire to a younger version of the poet. Petrarch's *vita* is that of exemplary author, truly the solitary wise man unencumbered by wifely distractions or feminine threats to his *auctoritas*, and thus has no need for rhetorical misogamy.

Boccaccio had to adopt a different strategy for Dante. Just as the sober Latinist of the *Vita Petracchi* resembled the subject of Petrarch's coronation speech, Boccaccio's decision to cast Dante as the too-amorous poet was no doubt rooted in Dante's own erotic self-fashioning. Dante built his textual identity in the *Vita Nova* and *Commedia* around his amorous devotion to Beatrice, and as we have seen, Boccaccio intended his *Trattatello* to be read as a companion piece to these works. Dante's love for women, even if for just one woman, was inescapable, as was his tumultuous life of civic engagement. Misogamy was thus called to the defence. It created a masculine contextual community that recognized itself within an anti-matrimonial discourse. It granted an air of Latinate authority to an erotic narrative. It mitigated the tarnishing association between feminine ignorance and vernacular letters by stressing a gendered difference. And it glorified the figure of the solitary philosopher in bitter conflict with that enemy of philosophical study – his wife. The misogynist current running through the early humanist critique of Dante's love for Beatrice was redirected at a large and indiscriminate group of wives – a chatty, vain, and corruptible class of women with a long and documented record of disrupting the quiet idyll needed for serious scholarship. In short, philosophic misogamy both constructed Dante in variance with the feminine and in line with elite Latin masculinity. The burdens of matrimony that Boccaccio heaped on Dante's back, heroically shouldered by the *Trattatello*'s anti-uxorious protagonist, ultimately served to build up Dante's masculine *auctoritas*.

NOTES

1 "Oh fatica inestimabile, avere con così sospettoso animale a vivere, a conversare, e ultimamente ad invecchiare o a morire!" Giovanni Boccaccio, *Trattatello in laude di Dante* I, 52. All citations from the *Trattatello* and its subsequent redactions come from Pier Giorgio Ricci's edition in *Tutte le*

opere di Giovanni Boccaccio, ed. Vittore Branca, vol. 3 (Milan: Mondadori, 1974). I will be referring to the first version of Boccaccio's biography based on the Toledano autograph (Toledo, Archivo y Biblioteca Capitulares, Zelada 104.6) as the *Trattatello in laude di Dante*, or *Trattatello* (*Tratt.* I in citations). A later Chigi autograph (Vatican City, Biblioteca Apostolica Vaticana, Chigi L.V. 176) contains the second redaction of the *Trattatello*, often referred to as the *Vita di Dante*. A third version of the *Trattatello* survives, or rather a modified version of the second redaction, but not in autograph copies. Following Ricci's critical edition of the so-called *Redazioni compendiose*, I will refer to the second redaction (based on the Chigi manuscript) as *Trattatello* II. See Pier Giorgio Ricci, "Le tre redazioni del *Trattatello in laude di Dante*," *Studi sul Boccaccio* 8 (1987): 197–214; or the notes to his edition in *Tutte le opere*, 848–56. Unless otherwise indicated, translations are mine.

2 "i suoi parenti ... ragionarono insieme di volergli dar moglie; acciò che, come la perduta donna gli era stata di tristizia cagione, così di letizia gli fosse la nuovamente acquistata [his relatives … decided together that they wanted to find him a wife because, since the loss of a woman had been the cause of his sorrow, the acquisition of a new one might be cause for joy]" (*Tratt.* I, 45).

3 Victoria Kirkham points out that Dante's engagement to Gemma Donati took place on 9 February 1277, long before Beatrice's death and Dante's ensuing period of mourning. See "The Parallel Lives of Dante and Virgil," *Dante Studies* 110 (1992): 248.

4 "Lascino i filosofanti lo sposarsi a' ricchi stolti, a' signori e a' lavoratori, e essi con la filosofia si dilettino, molto migliore sposa che alcuna altra [Let philosophers leave the marrying to wealthy fools, to lords, and to labourers, and let them enjoy philosophy, who is by far a better bride than any other]" (*Tratt.* I, 59).

5 Boccaccio confesses that he does not actually know what went on behind closed doors in the Alighieri home, yet nonetheless interprets the fact that Dante never reunited with his wife following his exile as a sign of their unhappy marriage (*Tratt.* I, 58).

6 Gretchen V. Angelo, "Creating a Masculine Vernacular: The Strategy of Misogyny in Late Medieval French Texts," in *The Vulgar Tongue, Medieval and Postmedieval Vernacularity*, ed. Fiona Somerset and Nicholas Watson (University Park: Pennsylvania State University Press, 2003), 85–98. As I will discuss in greater detail below, Boccaccio refers to Dante's Florentine as both the "volgare delle femine" and "feminette" in the *Accessus* to his *Esposizioni*, 19.

7 A number of recent studies explore Boccaccio's material engagement as the scribe, compiler, commentator, and transmitter of Dante's oeuvre. See Guyda Armstrong, "Boccaccio and Dante," in *The Cambridge Companion to Boccaccio*, ed. Guyda Armstrong, Rhiannon Daniels, and Stephen J. Milner (Cambridge: Cambridge University Press, 2015), 121–38; Marco Cursi, *La scrittura e i libri di Giovanni Boccaccio* (Rome: Viella, 2013), especially 83–128; Martin Eisner, *Boccaccio and the Invention of Italian Literature: Dante, Petrarch, Cavalcanti, and the Authority of the Vernacular* (New York: Cambridge University Press, 2013); Edoardo Fumagalli, "Boccaccio e Dante," in *Boccaccio autore e copista*, ed. Teresa De Robertis et al. (Florence: Mandragora, 2013), 25–31; and Jelena Todorovic, "Nota sulla *Vita Nova* di Giovanni Boccaccio," in *Proceedings of the 2010 International Boccaccio Conference at The University of Massachusetts Amherst*, ed. Elsa Filosa and Michael Papio (Ravenna: Longo, 2012), 108. Beatrice Arduini provides fascinating insights into Boccaccio's scribal practices in her "Boccaccio and His Desk," in *The Cambridge Companion to Boccaccio*, 20–35, especially 29.

8 For the full titles and translations of Boccaccio's works, see the *Cambridge Companion to Boccaccio*'s "List of Editions and Translations," xxviv–xxviii.

9 Dante's *Commedia* originally formed part of this edition as well, but the codex was soon divided in two, thus separating the *Commedia* and Boccaccio's accompanying verse summaries and rubrics into their own discrete manuscript (Chigi L. VI. 213). See Armstrong, "Boccaccio and Dante," 127; and Giancarlo Breschi, "Boccaccio editore della *Commedia*," in *Boccaccio autore e copista*, 247.

10 Todorovic notes that one blank page separates the *Trattatello* and the *Vita Nova* in the Toledano manuscript, but that Boccaccio copied the *incipit* of the *Vita Nova* directly onto the same page containing the *explicit* of the *Trattatello* in the Chigi codex, making the two materially inseparable ("Nota sulla *Vita Nova*," 108). See also Eisner's exhaustive work on the Chigi manuscript, where he calculates that it would have taken Boccaccio more than six months to transcribe Dante's works each time – a figure that speaks to Boccaccio's dedication to his larger cultural project of canonizing Dante's vernacular works (*Boccaccio and the Invention of Italian Literature*, 27).

11 Jason Houston offers a detailed discussion of the *Trattatello*'s generic resemblance to other forms of medieval biography in *Building a Monument to Dante: Boccaccio as Dantista* (Toronto: University of Toronto Press, 2010), 56–89. Alistair Minnis concludes his work on literary authority by considering the many ways ancient and modern literary models influenced Boccaccio's biography of Dante in his *Medieval Theory of Authorship: Scholastic Literary Attitudes in the Later Middle Ages*

(Philadelphia: University of Pennsylvania Press, 1988), especially 214–17. For more on Boccaccio and hagiography, see Giuseppe Billanovich, "La leggenda dantesca del Boccaccio: Dalla lettera di Ilaro al *Trattatello in laude di Dante*," *Studi Danteschi* 28 (1949): 45–144; Susanna Barsella, "Boccaccio, Petrarch, and Peter Damian: Two Models of the Humanist Intellectual," *Modern Language Notes* 121, no. 1 (2006): 16–48; and Elsa Filosa, "To Praise Dante, to Please Petrarch (*Trattatello in laude di Dante*)," in *Boccaccio: A Critical Guide to the Complete Works*, ed. Victoria Kirkham, Michael Sherberg, and Janet Smarr (Chicago: University of Chicago Press, 2013), 216–17.

12 See Karen Elizabeth Gross, "Scholar Saints and Boccaccio's *Trattatello in laude di Dante*," *Modern Language Notes* 124, no. 1 (2009): 66–85.

13 Kirkham explores the similarities between Boccaccio's *Trattatello* and biographies of classical authors, including the *Vita Virgiliana*, in "The Parallel Lives of Dante and Virgil."

14 "E scriverò in istilo assai umile e leggiero ... e nel nostro fiorentino idioma, acciò che da quello, che egli usò nella maggior parte delle sue opere, non discordi [And I shall write in a very humble and light style … and in our Florentine language, so that it does not depart from what he used in the greater part of his works]" (*Tratt.* I, 9).

15 Todd Boli, "Boccaccio's *Trattatello in laude di Dante*, Or Dante Resartus," *Renaissance Quarterly* 41, no. 3 (1988): 389–412.

16 *Convivio* 1.2.16 and 1.5.1–15. Giovanni del Virgilio famously chastises Dante for making the *Commedia* accessible to the *vulgo* by using their lowly vernacular, thus casting pearls before swine (*Eclogues* 1.1).

17 In his overview of Trecento objections to the language and content of Dante's works by authors including Antonio Beccari, Giovanni del Virgilio, and Petrarch, Boli cites the misogynist passage from Stabili's *Acerba* criticizing Dante's excessive love for a mere woman: "lussuriosa, maligna, molle e vaga, / conduce l'uomo a frusto ed a capello; / gloria vana ed insanabil piaga [wanton, evil, soft, and restless, / woman leads man to the whip and the noose; / an empty glory and an unhealing sore]" (*L'acerba* 4412–13, as quoted and translated by Boli, "Boccaccio's *Trattatello in laude di Dante*," 393n10).

18 Alistair Minnis, *Fallible Authors: Chaucer's Pardoner and Wife of Bath* (Philadelphia: University of Pennsylvania Press, 2011), 7.

19 Todd Boli, "Boccaccio's Biography, Dante's Biography, and How They Intersected," in *Boccaccio in America: Proceedings of the 2010 International Boccaccio Conference at the University of Massachusetts Amherst*, ed. Elsa Filosa and Michael Papio (Ravenna: Longo, 2012), 115.

20 Eisner, *Boccaccio and the Invention of Italian Literature*, 8.

21 For more on the *Vita Nova*'s prosimetrum structure and Boccaccio's editorial hand in the subsequent transmission of the *libello*, see Armstrong, "Boccaccio and Dante," 125–6; and Jelena Todorovic, *Dante and the Dynamics of Textual Exchange: Authorship, Manuscript Culture, and the Making of the "Vita Nova"* (New York: Fordham University Press, 2016).

22 Angelo, "Creating a Masculine Vernacular," 85.

23 Angelo notes that allegorical love quests, debates on marriage and love, and advice literature addressed to women would typically be considered feminine genres (ibid., 86).

24 See David Gilmore's eye-opening cross-cultural anthropology of misogyny: *Misogyny, the Male Malady* (Philadelphia: University of Pennsylvania Press, 2001), 9.

25 Howard Bloch, "Medieval Misogyny," *Representations* 20 (1987): 6; and again in *Medieval Misogyny and the Invention of Romantic Love* (Chicago: University of Chicago Press, 1991).

26 Katharina M. Wilson and Elizabeth M. Makowski, *Wykked Wyves and the Woes of Marriage: Misogamous Literature from Juvenal to Chaucer* (Albany: State University of New York Press, 1990), 1. My ensuing remarks on medieval misogamy are based largely on their indispensable work.

27 Wilson and Makowski note that dualistic heresies or proponents of clerical celibacy might reject marriage as an institution while still extolling the female gender (ibid., 1).

28 Ibid., 5.

29 *Zibaldone Laurenziano* (Florence, Biblioteca Medicea Laurenziana, 29.8). Though copied in several phases over the years, the folios containing the pseudo-Theophrastus excerpt from Jerome's *Contra Jovinianum* (fol. 52v) and Walter Map's *Dissuasiones Valerii ad Rufinum* (fols. 53r–54r) are datable between 1338 and 1348. See Claude Cazalé Bérard, "Boccaccio's Working Notebooks," in *Boccaccio: a Critical Guide to the Complete Works*, 311. For more on Boccaccio's misogynist sources, see Silvana Vecchio's "*De uxore non ducenda*. La polemica antimatrimoniale fra XIII e XIV secolo," in *Gli zibaldoni di Boccaccio: Memoria, scrittura, riscrittura*, ed. Michelangelo Picone and Claude Cazalé Bérard (Florence: Cesati, 1998), 53–64.

30 "Non deono adunque gli uomini esser molto correnti a prender moglie, anzi deono con molto avedimento a ciò venire, per ciò che, dove elle si deono prendere per aver figliuoli e consolazione e riposo in casa, assai spesso avviene che, per lo strabocchevolmente gittarsi a prender qualunque femina, l'uomo si reca in casa fuoco inestinguibile e battaglia senza triegua. Recita santo Ieronimo in un libro, il quale egli compose

Contro a Gioviniano eretico, che Teofrasto, il quale fu solenne filosofo e uditore d'Aristotile, compose un libro il quale si chiama *De nuptiis*, e in parte di quello domanda se il savio uomo debba prender moglie; e avvegna che egli, a se medesimo rispondendo, dicesse, dove ella sia bella, ben costumata e nata d'onesti parenti, e se esso fosse sano e ricco, il savio alcuna volta poterla prendere, incontanente aggiunse che queste cose rade volte intervengono tutte nelle noze, e però il savio non dover prender moglie, per ciò che essa, inanzi all'altre cose, impedisce lo studio della filosofia, né è alcun che possa a' libri e alla moglie servire [Men should not, then, be so quick to take a wife; indeed, they must approach marriage with great care because, whereas one is obliged to marry in order to have children, a helpmeet, and tranquility at home, it very frequently happens that, on account of a headlong rush to have any woman at all, what a man brings into his house is an inextinguishable fire and a battle without truce. St Jerome writes in one of his books called *Against Jovinianus the Heretic* that Theophrastus, who was a venerable philosopher and a student of Aristotle, composed a book that is called *de nuptiis*. In a part of that work, he questions whether a wise man should take a wife. It so happens that he, as he answers himself, first states that a wise man may sometimes take a wife (if she is beautiful, well mannered, and of decent parentage, and if he is healthy and rich), but then he straightaway adds that all these conditions are seldom to be seen in marriage. Thus, a wise man should not take a wife because, first of all, she impedes the study of philosophy; nor is there any man alive who can serve both his books and his wife]" (*Esposizione litterale, Inf.* 16.43–5). Citations from the *Esposizioni* come from *Esposizioni sopra la "Comedia" di Dante*, ed. Giorgio Padoan, in *Tutte le opere*, ed. Vittore Branca, vol. 6 (Milan: Mondadori, 1965). Translations are from *Boccaccio's Expositions on Dante's "Comedy,"* ed. and trans. Michael Papio, The Lorenzo Da Ponte Italian Library (Toronto: University of Toronto Press, 2009).

31 "Dicono alcuni che costui ebbe per moglie una donna tanto ritrosa e tanto perversa e di sì nuovi costumi e maniere, come assai spesso ne veggiamo, che in alcuno atto con lei non si poteva né stare né vivere; per la qual cosa il detto messer Iacopo partitosi da lei e stimolandolo l'appetito carnale, egli si diede alla miseria di questo vizio [Some people say that he had for a wife a woman who was so backwards and so bizarre and of such odd ways and manners (as we quite often see nowadays) that he could in no way stay or live with her. Consequently, the said Jacopo left her and, being stimulated by carnal appetite, gave in to the misery of this vice]" (ibid., 43).

32 Thomas M. Greene, "Forms of Accommodation in the *Decameron*," *Italica* 45 (1968): 297–313.
33 Marilyn Migiel makes this point in her "The Untidy Business of Gender Studies: Or, Why It's Almost Useless to Ask If the *Decameron* Is Feminist," in *Boccaccio and Feminist Criticism*, ed. Thomas Stillinger and Regina Psaki (Chapel Hill: *Annali d'italianistica*, 2006), 220; and more recently in her chapter "Boccaccio and Women," in *The Cambridge Companion to Boccaccio*, ed. Guyda Armstrong, Rhiannon Daniels, and Stephen J. Milner (Cambridge: Cambridge University Press, 2015), 171–86. See also Claude Cazalé Bérard, "Filoginia/misoginia," in *Lessico critico decameroniano*, ed. Renzo Bragantini and Pier Massimo Forni (Turin: Bollati Boringhieri, 1995), 116–41; and Kristina M. Olson, "The Language of Women As Written by Men: Boccaccio, Dante and Gendered Histories of the Vernacular," *Heliotropia* 8–9 (2011–12).
34 Several studies on the multiplicity of masculine paradigms current in Dante and Boccaccio's day can be found in *Conflicted Identities and Multiple Masculinities: Men in the Medieval West*, ed. Jacqueline Murray (New York: Garland, 1999); and *Medieval Masculinities: Regarding Men in the Middle Ages*, ed. Clare E. Lees, Thelma Fenster, and Jo Ann McNamara (Minneapolis: University of Minnesota Press, 1994), especially Verne Bullough's "On Being a Male in the Middle Ages," 31–46. On a related note, Grace Delmolino's essay in this volume demonstrates how legalistic rhetoric couched in *Decameron* 2.10 ironically serves to indict a negligent husband who refuses to adequately honour his wife's conjugal rights.
35 All citations from the *Decameron* come from Vittore Branca's edition (Torino: Einaudi, 1980, rev. 1992). English translations are by G.H. McWilliam, *Decameron*, 2nd ed. (New York: Penguin, 1995).
36 Marilyn Migiel, *The Rhetoric of the Decameron* (Toronto: University of Toronto Press, 2003), 73.
37 In Christine de Pizan's retelling of the Griselda story in *The City of Ladies*, Griselda is given a voice and eloquently defends the virtue of her sex. Petrarch's Latin translation of the *Decameron*'s closing tale in his *Seniles* 17, 3 and 4 has received much attention over the years, particularly from feminist criticism interested in the correspondence between the Griselda story and Petrarch's efforts to strip the narrative of its vernacular form. For more on Petrarch's and Chaucer's reformulations of Boccaccio's Griselda, see David Wallace, "Letters of Old Age. Love between Men, Griselda, and Farewell to Letters. *Rerum senilium libri*," in *Petrarch: A Critical Guide to the Complete Works*, ed. Victoria Kirkham and Armando Maggi (Chicago:

University of Chicago Press, 2009), 321–30; and Amy Goodwin, "The Griselda Game," *Chaucer Review* 39, no. 1 (2004): 41–69.

38 "volendoti insegnar d'esser moglie e a loro di saperla tenere, e a me partorire perpetua quiete mentre teco a vivere avessi: il che, quando venni a prender moglie, gran paura ebbi che non m'intervenisse, e per ciò, per prova pigliarne, in quanti modi tu sai ti punsi e trafissi [I wished to show you how to be a wife, to teach these people how to choose and keep a wife, and to guarantee my own peace and quiet for as long as we were living beneath the same roof. When I came to take a wife, I was greatly afraid that this peace would be denied me, and in order to prove otherwise I tormented and provoked you in the ways you have seen]" (*Dec.* 10.10.61).

39 Teodolinda Barolini, "The Marquis of Saluzzo, or the Griselda Story Before It Was Hijacked: Calculating Matrimonial Odds in *Decameron* 10.10," *Mediaevalia* 34 (2013): 42.

40 Millicent Marcus discusses Rinieri's Parisian pretensions in "Misogyny as Misreading: A Gloss on *Decameron* VIII.7," in *Boccaccio and Feminist Criticism*, 132.

41 "E crescendo insieme con gli anni l'animo e lo 'ngegno, non a' lucrativi studi, alli quali generalmente oggi corre ciascuno, si dispose, ma da una laudevole vaghezza di perpetua fama [tratto], sprezzando le transitorie ricchezze, liberamente si diede a volere avere piena notizia delle fizioni poetiche e dello artificioso dimostramento di quelle [And as his spirit and mind grew together with the years, he disposed himself not to those lucrative studies to which everyone commonly runs these days, but compelled by a laudable desire for perpetual fame, he scorned transitory riches and freely gave himself over to the desire to learn everything about poetic fictions and their artistry]" (*Tratt.* I, 22).

42 Guyda Armstrong, "Boccaccio and the Infernal Body: The Widow as Wilderness," in *Boccaccio and Feminist Criticism*, 85.

43 Wilson and Makowski, *Wykked Wives*, 5.

44 "Tu, se io già bene intesi, mentre vivea, e ora così essere il vero apertamente conosco, mai alcuna manuale arte non imparasti e sempre l'essere mercatante avesti in odio; di che più volte ti se' con altrui e teco medesimo gloriato, avendo riguardo al tuo ingegno [If I understood correctly before, while I was alive (and now I know it plainly to be the truth), you never learned any manual trade and always hated commerce; of this you have boasted many times to yourself and others, crediting your intellect" (*Corbaccio* 125).

All citations from the *Corbaccio* come from Giorgio Padoan's edition in *Tutte le opere*, ed. Vittore Branca, vol. 5, pt. 2 (Milan: Mondadori, 1994),

413–614. Translations are from Anthony K. Cassell's *The "Corbaccio" or "The Labyrinth of Love"* (Binghamton: Medieval and Renaissance Texts and Studies, 1993).

45 "Nobilissima cosa adunque è l'uomo il quale dal suo fattore fu creato poco minore che gli angeli. E, se il minore uomo non è tanto, da quando dovrà essere colui la cui virtù ha fatto ch'egli dagli altri ad alcuna eccellenzia sia elevato? Da quanto dovrà essere colui il quale i sacri studi, la filosofia ha dalla meccanica turba separato? Del numero della quale tu per tuo ingegno e per tuo studio, aiutandoti la grazie di Dio, la quale a niuno che se ne faccia degno, domandandola, è negata, se' uscito e tra' maggiori divenuto degno di mescolarti. Come non ti conosci tu? Come così t'avvilisci? Come t'hai tu così poco caro che tu ad una femina iniqua, insensatamente di lei credendo quello che mai non le piacque, ti vada a sottomettere? [A most noble thing, therefore, is man, who was made by his Creator a little lower than the angels. And if the least man is of so great account, of what worth must he be whose virtue has raised him above the others to some excellence? Of what worth must he be whom sacred studies, philosophy, have removed from the vulgar herd? From their number you have taken yourself by your intellect and studies, and, aided by the grace of God (which, when requested, is denied to no one who is deserving), have become worthy to mingle among the greatest. Why do you not know yourself? Why do you debase yourself in this way? How can you consider yourself of so little worth that you go and subject yourself to a wicked woman, foolishly believing about her something which never pleased her?]" (*Corb.* 194).

46 "Gli studi adunque alla sacra filosofia pertinenti, infino dalla tua puerizia, più assai che il tuo padre non avrebbe volute, ti piacquero; e massimamente in quella parte che a poesia appartiene; la quale per avventura tu hai con più fervor d'animo che con altezza d'ingegno seguita. Questa, non menoma tra l'altre scienzie, ti dovea parimenti mostrare che cosa è amore e che cosa le femine sono, e chi tu medesimo sii e quel che a te s'appartiene [Far more than your father would have wished, right from your childhood you liked studies pertaining to sacred philosophy, and especially that part dealing with poetry, which perhaps you have pursued with more fervor of spirit than with heights of genius. This, not the least among the disciplines, must also have shown you what love is, what women are, and who you are yourself and what your duties are]" (*Corb.* 127).

47 Houston, *Building a Monument to Dante*, 56.

48 "Quanto ferventemente esso fosse ad amor sottoposto, assai chiaro è già mostrato. Questo amore è ferma credenza di tutti che fosse movitore del suo ingegno a dovere, prima imitando, divenir dicitore in volgare; poi, per vaghezza di più solennemente mostrare le sue passioni, e di gloria, sollecitamente esercitandosi in quella, non solamente passò ciascuno suo contemporaneo, ma intanto la dilucidò e fece bella, che molti allora e poi di dietro a sé n'ha fatti e farà vaghi d'essere esperti [It has already been clearly demonstrated how fervently he was subject to love. It is firmly believed by all that this love moved his genius, first by imitating, to have to become a vernacular poet. Then because of a desire to set forth his passions most solemnly, and for glory, he diligently practised it, not only excelling over all of his contemporaries, but at the same time clarifying and beautifying the vernacular, so much so that he made, and shall make, many past and future desirous to follow him and become experts]" (*Tratt.* I, 119).

49 "Egli primieramente, duranti ancora le lagrime della morte della sua Beatrice, quasi nel suo ventesimosesto anno compose in un volumetto, il quale egli intitolò *Vita nova*, certe operette, sì come sonetti e canzoni, in diversi tempi davanti in rima fatte da lui, maravigliosamente belle … E come che egli d'avere questo libretto fatto, negli anni più maturi si vergognasse molto, nondimeno, considerata la sua età, è egli assai bello e piacevole, e massimamente a' volgari [First, while still in tears over the death of his Beatrice, almost in his twenty-sixth year, he assembled together in a little volume, which he called the *Vita Nova*, certain little rhymed works (such as sonnets and *canzoni*) which he had made earlier at different times, marvellously beautiful … And although in his more mature years he was much ashamed of himself for having written this little book, nevertheless, taking into account his age, it is very lovely and pleasing, especially for the common folk]" (*Tratt.* I, 175).

Compare this to Dante's own pronouncement on the subject in the *Convivio*: "E se nella presente opera, la quale è *Convivio* nominata e vo' che sia, più virilmente si trattasse che nella *Vita Nova*, non intendo però a quella in parte alcuna derogare, ma maggiormente giovare per questa quella; veggendo sì come ragionevolemente quella fervida e passionata, questa temperata e virile essere conviene [If in the present work, which is called *The Banquet*, as I wish it to be, the subject is treated more maturely than in the *Vita Nuova*, I do not intend by this in any way to disparage that book but rather more greatly to support it with this one, seeing that it understandably suits that one to be fervid and passionate, and this one tempered and mature]." *Convivio*, ed. Franca Brambilla Ageno (Florence: Le Lettere, 1995), 1.1.16. Translation by Richard Lansing, *Dante's "Il Convivio"* (New York: Garland, 1990).

50 "Oltre a questo, lo stilo comico è umile e rimesso, acciò che alla materia sia conforme; quello che della presente opera dire non si può, per ciò che, quantunque in volgare scritto sia, nel quale pare che comunichino le *feminette*, egli è nondimeno ornato e leggiadro e sublime, delle quali cose nulla sente il *volgare delle femine*. Non dico però che, *se in versi latini fosse, non mutato il peso delle parole volgari, ch'egli non fosse più artificioso e più sublime molto, per ciò che molto più d'arte e di gravità ha nel parlare latino che nel materno* [What is more, the comic style is humble and unassuming, in conformity with its material. Such a thing, though, cannot be said of the present work (despite its being written in the vernacular, the *language girls use for chatting*) because its style is beautiful, graceful, and sublime (characteristics that have nothing in common with *the chatter of girls*). I do not mean by this, however, that *had it been written in Latin verse, without changing the impact of the vernacular terms, it would not have been even more beautiful and much more sublime, for there is much greater artfulness and gravity in Latin than in our maternal tongue*]" (*Esposizioni, Accessus*, 19; my emphasis). For more on Boccaccio's gendering of language in the *Esposizioni*, see Olson's "The Language of Women."

51 Alison Cornish, *Vernacular Translation in Dante's Italy: Illiterate Literature* (New York: Cambridge University Press, 2011), 36.

52 For a modern critical edition and translation into Italian of Boccaccio's biography of Petrarch, or *De vita et moribus domini Francisci Petracchi de Florentia* (*On the Life and Mores of Francesco Petrarca of Florence*), see *Vite del Petrarca, Pier Damiani e Livio*, ed. Renata Fabbri, in *Tutte le opere*, ed. Vittore Branca, vol. 5, pt. 1 (Milan: Mondadori, 1992), 879–962.

53 According to Giuliano Tanturli and Stefano Zamponi's "Biografia e cronologia delle opere," the *Vita Petracchi* is datable to sometime between 1348 and 1350 (*Boccaccio autore e copista*, 63).

8 What Turns on Whether Women Are Human for Boccaccio and Christine de Pizan?

MARY ANNE CASE

When Christine de Pizan asserts, "Et n'est mie doubte que les femmes sont aussi bien au nombre du peuple de Dieu et de creature humaine que sont les hommes, et non mie d'une autre espece[1] [There is not the slightest doubt that women belong to the people of God and the human race as much as men, and are not another species]," [2] she is guilty of some rhetorical overstatement. This essay will examine Christine's explicit treatment of women as human in her *Livre de la cité des dames*, and also consider her principal source-text, Boccaccio's *De mulieribus claris*, and other works of Boccaccio, to determine whether these texts accord them the status of humans as well. The question of whether women were human was, in fact, hotly debated from the time of the Church Fathers onward. Even as late as the French Revolution,[3] debates about women's participation in public life made reference to a vote allegedly taken in 585 CE by the Council of Mâcon as to whether women could properly be called *homines* (human beings). According to the standard version of the apocryphal story,[4] after much discussion, the Council decided in the affirmative by the very narrow margin of a single vote.[5]

In the twelfth century, Hildegard von Bingen unproblematically referred to herself as a human being. Her *Scivias* begins with a heavenly voice who addresses her as "O homo fragilis, et cinis cineris, et putredo putredinis [O fragile human being, ash of ashes and putrefied putrefaction]." [6] The context makes very clear that this human is Hildegard herself and that she is in fact female: the addressee, for example, is called "timida … ad loquendum … et indocta ad scribendum [a woman fearful of speaking and untutored in writing]." [7]

But, by the time of Boccaccio, women were once again in danger, linguistically and conceptually, of being read out of the category of the human. In his Preface to *De mulieribus claris*, Boccaccio justifies his enterprise as follows:

> Et si extollendi sunt homines dum, concesso sibi robore, magna perfecerint, quanto amplius mulieres, quibus fere omnibus a natura rerum mollities insita et corpus debile ac tardum ingenium datum est, si in virilem evaserint animum et ingenio celebri atque virtute conspicua audeant atque perficiant etiam difficillima viris extollende sunt?[8]

> [If we grant that men deserve praise whenever they perform great deeds with the strength bestowed upon them, how much more should women be extolled – almost all of whom are endowed by nature with soft, frail bodies and sluggish minds – when they take on a manly spirit, show remarkable intelligence and bravery, and dare execute deeds that would be extremely difficult even for men?][9]

It is possible to read this passage as consistent with women's humanity, if we interpret it to mean that all human beings (*homines*) deserve praise for the deeds they perform with such strength as they are given, but women (*mulieres*) are particularly worthy of such praise when, given the comparative natural weakness of their sex, they nevertheless perform deeds difficult even for males (*viris*).

Yet there is the very real possibility that when Boccaccio speaks here of *homines*, he is not including women.[10] This is reinforced by the language he uses in justifying his dedication of *De mulieribus claris* to Andrea Acciaiuoli:

> cum his animi tui generositatem et ingenii vires, quibus longe femineas excedis, adverterem videremque quod sexui [in]firmiori natura detraxerit, id tuo pectori Deus sua liberalitate miris virtutibus superinfuserit atque suppleverit, et eo, quo insignata es nomine, designari voluerit – cum *andres* Greci quod latine dicimus *homines* nuncupent – te equiparandam probissimis quibuscunque, etiam vetustissimis, arbitratus sum.[11]

> [as I noted your generosity of soul and your powers of intellect far surpassing the endowments of womankind, as I saw what nature had denied the weaker sex God has freely installed in your breast and complemented with marvelous virtues, to the point that he willed that you be known by the name you bear (*andres* being in Greek the equivalent of the Latin word

for *men*) – considering all this I felt you deserved comparison with the most excellent women anywhere, even among the ancients.][12]

Boccaccio here asserts that Andrea is worthy because she possesses virile qualities of the mind and soul, and it is interestingly ambiguous to what sex[es] of excellent ancients Boccaccio announces himself here willing to compare Andrea. Virginia Brown's translation above assumes that he felt she "deserved comparison with the most excellent women anywhere, even among the ancients." By contrast, Pamela Joseph Benson translates the passage as saying that he felt she "should be set equal to the worthiest of men, even among the ancients."[13] Each reading can be supported by the context. After all, on the one hand, Boccaccio goes on to urge Andrea to be spurred by "reading" his account of "a pagan woman" displaying a "worthy quality" such as "probity, chastity or resolution [to] summon up the powers of your already strong character and do not allow yourself to be outdone but strive to outdo all women in noble virtues."[14] But on the other hand, Boccaccio describes Andrea as possessing qualities of mind and spirit that "nature had denied the weaker sex," qualities "far exceed[ing] those of women," suggesting the appropriate comparison is to men. Thus, "probissimis quibuscunque, etiam vetustissimis" can refer to excellent ancients of either or of both of the sexes.[15]

An expansive reading of the human is undercut, however, when Boccaccio declares that Andrea's virile qualities make her worthy of his dedication and the name she bears, *andres* being, according to Boccaccio, "the term in Greek for what in Latin are called *homines*." Of course, etymologically, *andres* is no such thing. *Andres*, the Greek word for males, has its Latin equivalent in *viri*, whereas "the term in Greek for what in Latin are called *homines*" is *anthropoi* (human beings). The effect of Boccaccio's mistake is to read women out of the category of the human. This is partly a linguistic problem, intensified in both medieval and modern Italian and French, which have no commonly used etymological descendant of *vir* and instead use *uomo* or *homme*, derived from the Latin *homo*, to refer at once to both males in particular and human beings in general.

Christine de Pizan, though, does her best to fight this conflation even on a linguistic level. In lamenting, for example, that God had not caused her to be "naistre au monde en masculin sexe, a celle fin … que je … fuesse de si grand perfeccion comme homme masle ce dit estre[16] [born into the world in the masculine sex so that … I might … have been as perfect as male human beings are said to be],"[17] Christine reminds the reader that *homme masle* is just one particular type of *homme* and that members of the female sex also belong to the category *homme*.

Subsequent events would show that this linguistic battle was an important one for Christine and other feminists to fight. To this day, what the Germans term "Menschenrechte" the French still tend to call "Droits de l'homme," while the English speak of "the Rights of Man" and not always of "Human Rights." When these rights were first inscribed in French law in the *Déclaration des Droits de L'homme et du Citoyen* (1789), there was serious question as to the extent to which women were included. In the French Revolution, women lost the rights of political participation that they had held, as discussed below, since before Christine's time and would not regain until the mid-twentieth century. Indeed, the recent inclusion of the principle of sexual *parité* in the French constitutional order confirms that women are still seen as an uncomfortable fit into the universal category of rights-bearing human beings.

The preface to the *Decameron*, whose very first word is "human" ("umana"), seems more readily than that of *De mulieribus claris* to include women among those capable of exhibiting a "human quality" ("umana cosa"), perhaps because the quality in question, "che a ciascuna persona stea bene [which every person should possess],"[18] is not a traditionally masculine one, but instead "compassione degli afflitti [compassion for people in distress]." Yet in Boccaccio's Italian as well as his Latin there remains a potentially significant linguistic ambiguity between the human universal and the sexed particular. The topic Lauretta sets for Day Eight of the *Decameron* is, for example, "di quelle beffe che tutto il giorno, o donna ad uomo, o uomo a donna, o l'uno uomo all'altro si fanno (7.concl.4) [the tricks that people in general, men and women alike, are forever playing on one another]." Given that the past day's topic, set by Dioneo and executed in the Valley of the Ladies, was the tricks that women played on their husbands, Lauretta prefaces her choice of topic by saying that, because she does not want to be thought one of "di schiatta di can botolo che incontanente si vuol vendicare (7.concl.3) [that breed of snapping curs who immediately turn round and retaliate]," she will not merely reverse the topic in a battle of the sexes, but rather universalize it to encompass tricks played by all sorts of people on one another. But there are interesting divergences from parallelism in her formulation of her topic. *Uomo* here, when paired with *donna*, means *man* as male; however, unless we are to think women playing tricks on other women either never occurs or is not to be discussed by the *brigata*,[19] *uomo* in the latter half of the topic description does indeed refer to "people in general, men and women alike." Moreover, *uomo* as male is paired here with *donna* (lady) and not with *femina* (woman) as it is elsewhere in the *Decameron*, notably in Pampinea's enumeration of women's weaknesses and their corresponding need for male guidance in the Introduction[20] and in the villain Ambrogiuolo's boastful and disproven claim of male superiority: "Io ho sempre inteso l'uomo essere il piú nobile animale che tra' mortali fosse creato da Dio, e appresso la femina (2.9.15) [I have always been told that man is the most noble of God's mortal creatures and that woman comes second]." In Boccaccio's Italian vernacular, the nobility of humanity centres more often on the man (*l'uomo*), while women's attempt to claim the noble title of "ladies" (*donne*) does not go unchallenged. Thus, when the narrator of *Il corbaccio* seeks to examine "what women are [che cose le femine sono]," he begins by observing that "a great many call themselves and have themselves called 'ladies,' although very few are found among them [delle quali grandissima parte si chiamono e fanno chiamare donne, e pochissime se ne truovano]."[21]

Christine de Pizan effects a more general ennobling of the female sex in constructing what she calls the City of *Ladies* (not the City of Women), explicitly designed to be a refuge for all good (and hence noble) women, those of low, middle, and high estate. The inclusiveness of the *Cité des dames* is confirmed by Christine's follow-up book of advice, *Le tresor de la cité des dames de degré en degré*. In this text, the same three allegorical figures who helped her construct the city offer advice to all the ranks and varieties of potential future inhabitants, ranging from princesses to prostitutes and the wives of poor labourers.[22]

On more than a linguistic level, Boccaccio calls into question, and Christine reaffirms, women's essential humanity. Whereas for Ambrogiuolo man is the most noble animal, for the narrator of *Il corbaccio*, "la femina è animale imperfetto[23] [woman is an imperfect animal],"[24] filthy as a pig, and "che le tigre, i leoni, i serpenti hanno più d'umanità, adirati[25] [less human than tigers, lions, or serpents when angry]."[26] To be sure, neither Ambrogiuolo nor the narrator of *Il corbaccio* can be said to express Boccaccio's own views, but to Christine, who sees the harms even fictionalized accounts of women's less than human status can do to real women, this does not sufficiently diminish the risk in a text denying to women a humanity equal to that of men. Responding to the dehumanization of women accepted by the defenders of the *Roman de la Rose*, she asks, "Qui sont fames? Qui sont elles? Sont ce serpens, loups, lyons, dragons, guievres ou bestes ravissables devourans et ennemies a nature humainne … Et, par Dieu! si sont elles vos meres, vos suers, vos filles, vos femmes, et vos amies; elles sont vous mesmes et vous mesmes elles [Who are women? Who are they? Are they serpents, wolves, lions, dragons, vipers, or raging devouring beasts, and enemies of human nature? … And by God if they are your mothers, your sisters, your daughters, your wives and your girlfriends, they are yourselves and you yourselves are they]."[27]

Not all comparisons of women to non-human animals deny that women possess a human nature just as men do, however. Consider one of the few stories the narrator of the *Decameron* tells in his own voice, that in the Introduction to Day Four concerning the sheltered young man who encounters for the first time "una brigata di belle giovani donne e ornate (4.intr.20) [a party of elegantly dressed and beautiful young ladies]," and asks his father what they are called:

> Il padre, per non destare nel concupiscilibe appetito del giovane alcuno inchinevole disiderio men che utile, non le volle nominare per lo proprio nome, cioé femine, ma disse: "Elle si chiamano papere." (4.intr.2)

> [Not wishing to arouse any idle longings in the young man's breast, his father avoided calling them by their real name, and instead of telling him they were women, he said: "They are called goslings."]

Any suggestion that this puts women on a sub-human footing as compared with men is mitigated when the Narrator describes the young man himself as "more of a wild beast than a human being [anzi a uno animal salvatico]" (4.intr.32). One of the morals of this story is that human men and women are attracted to one another precisely because they are on the same level:[28] just as the young man declares he finds the "goslings" more attractive than "the painted angels [his father] has taken him to see so often [che gli agnoli dipinti che voi m'avete piú volte mostrati]" (4.intr.28), so the narrator insists he finds human women both more inspiring and easier to live with than the Muses, as is only natural (4.intr.35–6).

There remains, however, a tension between Boccaccio's and Christine's views of women's nature, or the "meurs [d'une] femme naturelle[29] [behavior of a natural woman]."[30] Boccaccio asserts that God freely installed in Andrea's breast what nature had denied the weaker sex; whereas for Christine, nothing a woman does should be seen as surpassing the endowments of womankind, to use Boccaccio's phrase.[31] To Christine there is a world of difference between Boccaccio's *mulieris fere omnibus*[32] and women *tout court*. As I have previously argued, Christine, like other feminists, does not see an exceptional woman as "monstre en nature[33] [a monstrosity in nature]"[34] but as exemplary of what is within the capacity of a *femme naturelle*.[35] Judith Butler's work is very much on point here,[36] for another way of saying that gender is performative, as Butler does, is to say that, in philosophical terms, gender is an accident, not an essence, as I have argued Christine does.

The extent to which gender is an accident is more ambiguous in Boccaccio's texts. Teodolinda Barolini has rung the changes on essence, accident, and gender in the *Decameron* and *Il corbaccio*.[37] I will here examine some of the various approaches to this issue in *De mulieribus claris*. The dedication of *De mulieribus claris* sets up a seeming paradox that examples in the text itself reinforce – though Andrea is said to exhibit qualities beyond the reach of women, she remains a woman, not a freak of nature. Like other Christian women, Andrea may owe her exceptional masculine abilities to divine intervention, since, according to Boccaccio, "Hebrew and Christian women commonly steeled themselves for the sake of true and everlasting glory to an endurance often at odds with human nature[38] [he quippe ob eternam et veram gloriam sese fere in adversam persepe humanitati tolerantiam coegere]."[39] *De mulieribus claris* therefore focuses instead on pagan women because they "reached their goal, admittedly with remarkable strength of character, either through some natural gift or instinct[40] [seu quodam nature munere vel instinctu ... non absque tamen acri mentis robore]"[41] or desire for glory. Among Boccaccio's famous women are numerous examples of the virago – a woman who behaves as males ideally and typically do, without thereby ceasing to be female.[42] Although in *De mulieribus claris* he repeatedly entertains the possibility that viragos, who pair a "virile" spirit with a female body, are the result of an error or mismatch in nature,[43] Boccaccio is finally forced to conclude that God does not make mistakes, so that "we all receive perfect souls[44] [perfectas omnes arbitrandum est]";[45] what we do with them is up to us. Viragos are repeatedly favourably contrasted with men who behave like women,[46] confirming that gender is an accident, but also that to be gendered masculine is more admirable in both sexes.[47]

To the extent *De mulieribus claris* has a moral, it may be that both men and women would do well to exhibit more masculine virtues. Like Christine,[48] the Boccaccio of *De mulieribus claris* seems to think this is possible, as he declares "if women are willing to apply themselves, they share with men the ability to do everything that makes men famous[49] [cum omnia que gloriosos homines faciunt, si studiis insudare velint, habeant cum eis communia]."[50] And perhaps even more than Christine, the Boccaccio of *De mulieribus claris* seems to suggest this is desirable. In the *Cité des dames*, Reason explains to Christine that so long as there are already enough men to do so, women should not take on masculine tasks like arguing in court,[51] but should stick to their traditional tasks. This is indeed the approach taken by the women who of necessity take on masculine tasks such as defending themselves in court in the tales told in the *Decameron*. After successfully acting as her own advocate in court, for example, Madonna Filippa ends her story precisely by "returning to her house in triumph [alla sua casa se ne tornò gloriosa]" (6.7.19), as does Zinevra after successfully making her case to the Sultan and her husband. Zinevra, the clearest example in the *Decameron* of one who possesses "all the qualities of the ideal woman, but … also many of the accomplishments found in a knight or squire [tutte quelle virtú che donna o ancora cavaliere in gran parte o donzello]" (2.9.8) or merchant, manages to keep these gendered accomplishments in balance, with no suggestion that her "skill at horse-riding, falconry, reading, writing, and bookkeeping [cavalcare un cavallo, tenere uno uccello, leggere e scrivere e fare una ragione]" (2.9.10) is in any tension with her excellence at "womanly pursuits such as silk embroidery [alcuna cosa … che a donna appartenesse, sí come di lavorare lavorii di seta]" (2.9.8). But the Boccaccio of *De mulieribus claris* seems to see "womanish concerns" such as "the distaff" as lesser and to be scorned by women who can achieve higher things. "O femineum decus neglexisse muliebra[52] [How glorious it is for a woman to scorn womanish concerns]," he insists, praising Cornificia for "not wast[ing] the powers nature had given her [and] by means of talent and hard work … rising above her sex … acquiring for herself fame that is perpetual and rare precisely because it stands for an excellence few men have equalled[53] [Potuit hec nature non abiectis viribus, ingenio et vigiliis femineum superasse sexum, et sibi honesto labore perpetuum queisse nomen nec quippe gregarium, sed quod estat paucis etiam viris rarissimum et excellens]."[54] More generally, he chastises women for being so slothful and lacking in self-confidence as to think they are "useful only for the embraces of men, for giving birth and for raising children[55] [sibi ipse suadent se, nisi ad amplexus hominum et filios concipemdos alendosque utiles esse]."[56]

Moving from consideration of the human qualities of individual women to those of women in general, a question to be considered is whether one of the things women – and not just exceptional women but typical ones – should be viewed as good at and suited for is participation in civic life. How women fit into the human political order is also a measure of women's humanity. The remainder of this chapter will consider the ways in which Christine de Pizan and Boccaccio approach this question in respectively the *City of Ladies* and the *Decameron*, with consideration of the *Decameron* focusing on the frame and on one of the stories most directly concerned with political decision making, that of Madonna Filippa on Day Six.

At the outset, let me note a few respects in which the two authors contrast with one another, in ways that, in each case, form a counterpoint to the ways in which the societies in which they lived also differed. While Christine builds an ideal city, Boccaccio reconfigures existing ones: both the Florence from which the *brigata* retreats into their own idyllic society and the Prato in which Madonna Filippa defends herself are secular earthly communes. Christine, writing in an actual monarchy where Salic law was just beginning to exclude women from the possibility of ruling in their own right, but where women, as discussed below, did have some democratic participation in the very limited estates general, sets up a heavenly monarchy with the Virgin as queen in a thoroughly non-democratic setting – Christine follows the orders of a triumvirate of allegorical figures in building a city whose inhabitants cooperate in self-defence, but not in government. Her interest is more in intellectual than in political authority.[57]

Boccaccio's *brigata,* coming from more democratic Florence, itself appoints kings and queens, but only for a day, and only after a democratic agreement to do so in which each member of the *brigata* has an equal voice. Although in general Boccaccio's Italy was more democratic than the France of Christine's day, by contrast with France, women in Italy could reign (as did the shadow dedicatee of *De mulieribus claris,* Johanna, Queen of Naples), but they could not vote. This makes even more interesting Boccaccio's emphasis, in both the *Decameron* as a whole and in the story of Madonna Filippa, on the application of the maxim of canon law *quod omnes tangit*, short for either "Quod omnes tangit, ab omnibus approbetur," or alternatively "Quod omnes tangit omnibus tractari et approbari debet," meaning, "What touches all must be [debated and] approved by all."[58] Among the earliest prescriptions for democratic lawmaking, this Latin maxim, with origins in the Roman law of guardianship, migrated into the canon law, and then expanded into political theory in the Middle Ages. Some see this maxim behind the French king's invocation of the Estates General, which did include women in each of the three estates from the fourteenth century on, as discussed below. As a student of canon law, Boccaccio might well have been provided during his studies an occasion to entertain, at least for the sake of argument, the possibility that women should be considered as part of *omnes* in the framing of the law and in the constitution of a general council, as Ockham's Magister repeatedly suggests to his dismissive pupil in the *Dialogus*.[59]

Like her predecessor Novella, daughter of the Bolognese canonist Giovanni D'Andreae, Christine's view is that "femme est a l'omme pareille"[60] with "pareille" indicating that women are both equal to men and the same as men. Paradoxically, in the French legal and constitutional order, recognition of the parity of men and women suffered a setback just at the time that the French Revolution first recognized the parity of all men. In Christine's time in France, women of all classes already had a history of active participation in political life. Historians have claimed that for the Estates General convened by Philip the Fair in 1302, women of the first two estates had the same rights as in 1789 (i.e., noble women who owned fiefs and communities of religious women each had the right to name proxies to represent them). For the Estates of Tour of 1308, women in certain communes voted in their own names for communal representatives.[61] The right of non-noble female heads of households and property owners to participate in elections on the local level seems to have been generally recognized and widely exercised in the twelfth century. By Christine's time, women's rights of citizenship and participation in government may have been on the decline, however; "not only were women excluded from positions granting formal political authority in late medieval northern cities, they were deprived of independent access to citizenship and were rendered truly passive citizens once citizenship implied access to such positions."[62]

In 1789, all French women lost the right to vote in national elections, a right they would not regain until 1945. But the mere extension of a right to vote did not, according to many French women activists and theorists at the end of the twentieth century, guarantee women's full inclusion in citizenship and political power. Although subsequent proponents were to speak instead in terms of the irreducibility of sexual difference, the first generation of advocates of the *parité* later enshrined in French law stressed that legally guaranteed *parité* was a necessary precondition for true universalism, as argued by philosopher Françoise Collin, "to make apparent and to recognize that women are representative of the universal in the same way men are … It is paradoxical, but interesting to argue that it was universalism that best maintained the sexualization of power and that *parité*, by contrast, attempts to desexualize power by extending it to both sexes. *Parité* would thus be the real universalism."[63]

Using this early notion of *parité* as the means of achieving true universalism in a world that has called into question women's inclusion in the category of the abstract universal human, one can see the *Cité des dames* as a form of *parité* for Augustine's *De civitate dei*. When Christine says, "Gloriosa dicta sunt de te, civitas Dei[64] [glorious things of thee are spoken, of thee, city of God]," [65] she is making clear that the City of Ladies can itself be a City of God – not just an adjunct, supplement, or ghetto neighbourhood, but a microcosm, complete unto itself, containing women of all estates and classes, who among themselves fill all positions in the City.[66] As with *parité*, it is the failure to include women fully in the existing order, and the questioning of whether they are fully human, that has led to the necessity of creating a separate set of institutions for them.

Rejecting the claim that previous authors have acted for the common good in warning men about the dangers of women, Christine also has Rectitude argue in favour of true universalism, paraphrasing and explicitly including women in the definition of the *res publica* (commonwealth) that Scipio sets forth in *De civitate dei*, from which the line "Gloriosa dicta sunt de te, civitas Dei"[67] is taken:

> Autres chose n'est bien commun ou publique un une cité ou pays ou communité de peuple fors prouffit et bien general, ouquel chacun, tant femmes comme hommes, particippent ou ont part. Mais la chose qui seroit faicte en cuidant proffitter aux uns et non aux autres, seroit appellé bien privé ou propre, et non mie publique. Et ancore moins le seroit le bien que on touldroit aux uns pour donner aux autres et tele chose doit estre appellee non mie seulement bien propre ou privé mais droicte extorcion faite a autrui en faveur de partie et a son grief pour soustenir l'autre. Car ilz ne parlent point aux femmes en elles avisant que elles se gardent des agais des homes … Et n'est mie doubte que les femmes sont aussi bien au nombre du peuple de Dieu et de creature humaine que sont les hommes,

> et non mie une autre espece, ne de dessemblable genercion, par quoy elles doyent estre forcloses des enseignements moraulx. Doncques, je conclus que se pour le bien commun le feissent, c'est assavoir des .ij. parties, ilz eussent aussi bien parlé aux femmes.[68]

> [The common good of a city or land or any community of people is nothing other than the profit or general good in which all members, women as well as men, participate and take part. But whatever is done with the intention of benefiting some and not others is a matter of private and not public welfare. Even less so is an activity in which one takes from some and gives to others, and such an activity is perpetrated for the sake of private gain, and at the same time it constitutes, quite simply, a crime committed for the benefit of one person and to the disadvantage of the other. For they never address women nor warn them against men's traps even though it is certain that men frequently deceive women with their fast tricks and duplicity. There is not the slightest doubt that women belong to the people of God and the human race as much as men, and are not another species or dissimilar race, for which they should be excluded from moral teachings. Therefore, I conclude that if these men had acted in the public good – that is, for both parties – they should also have addressed themselves to women.][69]

In works of art from Christine's time, when women were represented withdrawing behind battlements to defend themselves from male assault, it was typically not in a city, but a castle, such as those in the "Siege of the Castle of Love" feebly defended by ladies armed with flowers. It was also often difficult to tell male protectors from attackers: the knight "as protector of [his lady's] body was also its penetrator."[70] Importantly, no male defender or "champion des dames" is necessary for the *Cité des dames*. In the words made famous by singer Aretha Franklin, "Sisters are doin' it for themselves." The work of intellectual defence can be done by Christine with the help of Reason, Rectitude, and Justice; the work of physical defence by women warriors, such as Semiramis and the Amazons who form the first row of "pierre au fondément de nostre Cité[71] [stone in the foundation of our city];"[72] and last, but not least, the Virgin Queen of Heaven, ruler of the city, will take her place among its inhabitants "comme leur deffenderresse, protectarresse et garde contre tous assaulx d'ennemis et du monde[73] [as their defender, protector, and guard against all assaults of enemies and of the world]."[74] The Virgin declares that she will not only rule over the city, but live in it as a citizen: "[T]res voulentiers je abiteray et demoureray entre mes seurs et amies, les femmes, et avecques elles, car Raison, Droitture, toy, et aussi Nature m'i encline … Si suis et seray a tousjours chief du sexe femenin[75] [I will live and abide most happily among my sisters and friends, for Reason, Rectitude, and you [Justice], as well as Nature, urge me to do so … I am and will always be the head of the feminine sex]."[76]

Several things are worthy of note in the Virgin's declaration. First, the fact that Nature is among those inclining the Virgin to dwell in the City is in itself an answer to *Il corbaccio*'s narrator, who says of women:

> E, oltre a questo, assai sovente molto meno consideratamente si gloriano, dicendo che Colei … con alquante altre (non molte però, della cui virtù spezial menzione e solennità fa la Chiesa di Dio) furono così femine come loro; e per questo immaginano dovere essere riguardate, argomentando niuna cosa contr'a loro potersi dire della loro viltà, che contro a Quella, che santissima cosa fu, non si dica; e quasi vogliono che lo scudo della loro difensione nelle braccia di Quella rimanga: che in niuna cosa la somigliano, se non in una. Ma questo non è da dovere consentire; per ciò che quella unica Sposa dello Spirito Santo fu una cosa tanto pura, tanto virtuosa … a rispetto dell'altre, quasi non dell'elementar composizione, ma d'una essenzia quinta fu formata.[77]
>
> [They often boast far more thoughtlessly, saying that [the Virgin Mary] … was a woman like them, along with a few others – not many, however – of whose virtue the Church of God makes special mention … For this women imagine they must be respected, arguing that nothing can be said against them about their baseness, which cannot be said against these others who were most saintly beings, as if they want the shield of their defense to remain in the arms of the latter, who resembled them in nothing but one thing. This however, must not be granted, since that only Bride of the Holy Spirit was such an undefiled, virtuous being … that in respect to the others, it is as if She were not composed of natural elements.][78]

Not so, Christine de Pizan has the Virgin say. For the Virgin is not only the head of the feminine sex, she is also a member of the sex,[79] a "femme naturelle."[80]

Second, with the Virgin as its head, Christine's *Cité* need not answer to any human male authority. Even those convents of women theoretically exempt from episcopal control were under the supervision of the pope and depended on "a bishop's sacramental Powers to regularize their members and validate their leaders."[81] And, like women in urban settings, "professed women [found that] by the thirteenth century, their gender was becoming the rationale for restricting their participation in public ceremonies."[82] By contrast, the City of Ladies is truly self-governing. When the *res publica* is theirs, women's humanity can finally be fully realized.

Like the inhabitants of the City of Ladies, the *brigata* of the *Decameron* also separate themselves in self-defence, but to escape not man-made hierarchical oppression but a plague of nature, which levels all social distinctions. Their place of refuge is not a fortified town, but a landed estate. Like Christine, they begin by justifying their right to self-defence:

> Donne mie care, voi potete, cosí come io, molte volte avere udito che a niuna persona fa ingiuria chi onestamente usa la sua ragione. Natural ragione é, di ciascuno che ci nasce, la sua vita quanto può aiutare e conservare e difendere. (1.intr.53)

> [Dear ladies, you will often have heard it affirmed, as I have, that no man does injury to another in exercising his lawful rights. Every person born into this world has a natural right to sustain, preserve, and defend his own life to the best of his ability.]

Yet, far from separating themselves from men, the women of the *brigata* deliberately seek out men to counteract and control their feminine weaknesses, because "it is certainly true that the man is the head of the woman, and that without a man to guide us it rarely happens that any enterprise of ours is brought to a worthy conclusion [Veramente gli uomini sono delle femine capo e senza l'ordine loro rade volte riesce alcuna nostra opera a laudevole fine]" (1.intr.76). The list of such weaknesses as enumerated by Filomena[83] in her objections to Pampinea's initial proposal of an all-female retreat could have been taken straight out of *Il corbaccio* or the works of the misogynists Christine de Pizan sets out to refute, and, put in the mouth of a woman who claims to know her own sex from personal experience, may seem to have more credibility:

> Ricordivi che noi siamo tutti femine e non ce n'ha niuna sí fanciulla che non possa ben conoscere come le femine sien ragionate insieme e senza la provedenza d'alcuno uomo si sappiano regolare.[84]

> [You must remember that we are all women, and every one of us is sufficiently adult to acknowledge that women, when left to themselves, are not the most rational of creatures and that without the supervision of some man or other their capacity for getting things done is somewhat restricted.]

The women want men to join them, not as patriarchal overlords, but as "guides and servants [guida e servidor]" (1.intr.80). In the society they create, men and women have an equal voice in determining what is to be done and who shall lead them, and women leaders take their turn in rotation[85] with authority equal to the men. As many commentators have noted, such an integrated egalitarian society did not and could not exist anywhere near Boccaccio's Florence.[86] It is in its own way as utopian as Christine's City of Ladies. The society is established as a monarchy, with the first monarch elected Pampinea, the woman whose idea the whole enterprise was, who also sketched out its system of government, and who by her own example disproves the proposition that women need male supervision to accomplish anything. Yet neither Pampinea as first ruler nor any of her successors exercises anything like absolute power. Instead, the rule of *quod omnes tangit* is frequently applied, with the group free by consensus to accept or reject the leader's suggestions, a form of proceeding Queen Pampinea herself puts into effect when she insists, "if the idea appeals to you, carry this proposal of mine into effect. But I am willing to follow your own wishes in this matter [e per ciò, quando questo che io dico vi piaccia, ché disposto sono in ciò di seguire il piacer vostro, faccianlo]" (1.intr.112).

The most explicit invocation of *quod omnes tangit* is, however, not in the *Decameron*'s frame, but in the story of Madonna Filippa, with which I will conclude this chapter because it illustrates the many different ways women can be human and what turns on them. The day on which her story is set begins with a dispute between a man and a woman, both servants of the *brigata*, in which, as in Madonna Filippa's story, women's sexual capacity is at issue, a woman has the principal speaking part, and an appointed male judge decides in the woman's favour.[87] Notably, as between the servants, the woman claims both the right to speak first, the superior point of view on account of age, and an insider's superior knowledge of women. The end of the day brings a temporary rebellion by the female members of the *brigata* to king Dioneo's proposed topic for the next day – he, like Madonna Filippa, has to persuade them that the subject of women playing tricks on their husbands need not be an unseemly one. Thereafter, the Valley of the

Ladies is entered seriatim first by the ladies alone, who go outdoors exploring and engage in activities previously explicitly coded male, like fishing, while the men stay behind indoors, and then by the men alone, before, finally, the group together, reunited in dancing that evening, go to the valley together the next day. According to Teodolinda Barolini, this progress through the sixth to the seventh day shows how "[w]ords can be liberating, words can lead to deeds, or, in the logic of the proverb ['words are feminine, deeds masculine'] women can become men."[88]

Madonna Filippa's story is set in Prato, a town whose long history as a free commune began when a siege by the troops of a woman, Mathilda of Canossa, drove out the ruling Alberti, and which, during the Plague year of 1348 in which the *Decameron* is set, was ruled by another woman, Johanna of Naples, to whom Boccaccio later contemplated dedicating *De mulieriebus claris*[89] and who would sell Prato to the Republic of Florence in 1351, before the *Decameron* was completed.

Much is unrealistic about Madonna Filippa's story, even beyond the outsized role it gives to women's arguments and their decision-making power. For example, Prato never did seek to impose the death penalty for adultery. And, although *quod omnes tangit* "was a familiar maxim of medieval law,"[90] even in the Italian city-states of Boccaccio's day, it was not generally extended to require the participation and consent of the governed as a condition for the legitimacy of criminal legislation. Nor, in a world where legal rights varied by class as well as sex, was there much content to the notion that all men, let alone women, should be equal before the law.

Nevertheless, it is precisely with a claim for procedural and substantive equality between the sexes that Madonna Filippa, acting as her own advocate, begins to make her case. Confessing that she has indeed committed adultery, she adds:

> [C]ome io son certa che voi sapete, le leggi deono esser comuni e fatte con consentimento di coloro a cui toccano. Le quali cose di questa non avvengono, ché essa solamente le donne tapinelle costrigne, le quali molto meglio che gli uomini potrebbero a molti sodisfare; e oltre a questo, non che alcuna donna, quando fatta fu, ci prestasse consentimento, ma niuna ce ne fu mai chiamata: per le quali cose meritamente malvagia si può chiamare. (6.7.13–14)

> [As I am sure you will know, every man and woman should be equal before the law, and laws must have the consent of those who are affected by them. These conditions are not fulfilled in the present instance, because this law only applies to us poor women, who are much better able than men to bestow our favors liberally. Moreover, when this law was made, no woman gave her consent to it, nor was any woman even so much as consulted. It can therefore justly be described as a very bad law.]

Although G.H. McWilliam translates "le leggi deono esser comuni" as "every man and woman should be equal before the law," in so doing he is assuming what is at issue, to wit, whether women are part of "omnes," whether, as Christine was to argue, "the common good of … of any community of people" is one in "which all members, women as well as men, participate and take part." Madonna Filippa is echoing Christine's notion that the common good should take account of women's interests in a way that it had not hitherto.

There was real world authority for Madonna Filippa's claim for substantive equality between the sexes in the contemporary canon law of marriage,[91] which ordinarily dealt with claims of adultery and which imposed reciprocal and equal rights and obligations on husband and wife, from the need to obtain spousal consent to the obligation to pay the marital debt to the obligation of marital fidelity. As Boccaccio would have known, the canon law of marriage would never do what she alleges the law of Prato does, to wit only constrain the wife and not the husband ("ché essa solamente le donne tapinelle costrigne").[92]

As for her claim of procedural equality, it is spectacularly vindicated in the world of the story. In the real world of fourteenth-century Italy, women might not even have been able to attend, let alone participate in, a trial like Madonna Filippa's or the lawmaking that accompanied it. Historian Carol Lansing's study of the civic courts of fourteenth-century Orvieto, for example, documents laws which increasingly "defined the sites of public administration as an exclusively masculine place":

> The most striking of these laws is a provision of Sept. 13, 1310 … which … denied women access to the town hall and its broad exterior stairs, where legal business was often transacted: "no woman may ascend to the Palazzo of the Popolo or that of the Orvietan commune or their stairs for any cause or reason. Women who must be questioned concerning accusations, inquests, testimony or any other necessity shall be examined at the foot of the stairs"… Officials who ignored the law [and] disobedient

> women were to be fined. In effect, women were not allowed in the places where government and justice took place.[93]

In the Prato of the story, however, Madonna Filippa is accompanied to court by "a numerous throng of men and women, all encouraging her to protest her innocence [assai bene accompagnata di donne e d'uomini, da tutti confortata al negare],"[94] and by the time she finishes her defence she "had brought almost all the citizens of Prato flocking to the court ... as with a single voice they all exclaimed that the lady was right ... And at the podesta's suggestion, before they left the court, they amended the harsh statute [quasi tutti i pratesi concorsi, li quali ... quasi a una voce tutti gridarono la donna aver ragione ... e prima che di quivi si partissono, a ciò confortandogli il podestà, modificarano il crudele statuto]" (6.7.18). This is the direct democracy of *quod omnes tangit* at work – what touches all is debated and approved by all, men and women alike.[95]

Of the numerous objections Madonna Filippa raises to Prato's harsh law on adultery, most work to establish the common and equal humanity of the sexes. But a crucial component of her winning argument is women's difference from men, a difference which, unusually, is one of superiority, contrary to *Il corbaccio*'s insistence that men are in all respects better – "women," Madonna Filippa claims, "are much better able than men to bestow [their] favors liberally [le quali molto meglio che gli uomini potrebbero a molti sodisfare]." She has already demonstrated her own superiority as an individual to her husband – while he is too cowardly to kill her *in flagrante* (6.7.6–7) and too ungenerous to forgive her, she is made fearless by her love and determines to confess rather than flee, impressing all with "the fortitude of spirit to which her words bear witness [secondo che le sue parole testimoniavano, di grande animo]" (6.7.11). In this respect she is like the Minyan wives of *De mulieribus claris* 31[96] who "showed themselves to be tried and true men and their husbands women[97] [verso certosque fuisse viros, Meniasque iuvenes ... feminas extitisse]." Now she turns what misogynists like the narrator of *Il corbaccio* claim is a defect in women, their sexual insatiability, into a categorical advantage. When her husband is forced to admit before the court that he "had always taken as much of me as he needed and as much as he chose to take [ha sempre di me preso quello che gli bisognato e piaciuto]," she asks, "What am I to do with the surplus, throw it to the dogs? [io che doveva fare o debbo di quell che gli avanza? debbolo io gittare a' cani?]" (6.7.17). There are biblical resonances to this question, not, as a misogynist might suspect, to the wicked Jezebel being thrown to the dogs,[98] but instead to the Christ. Matthew 7.6 forbids giving "that which is holy to the dogs [Nolite dare sanctum canibus]," and Keith Pennington points out that *sacrum* was sometimes a euphemism for a woman's body.[99] But an even more salient biblical verse is Mark 7.26–8:[100] "Suffer first the children to be filled: for it is not good to take the bread of the children, and cast it to the dogs," Jesus says to the "Greek woman of Syrophoenician origin" who "kept asking Jesus to drive the demon out of her daughter." Given the strength of the nuptial metaphor for the relationship between God and the people Israel, for a Gentile woman to ask this of Jesus is akin to soliciting marital infidelity of a committed spouse. But the Gentile woman's response is akin to that of Madonna Filippa – if the children have eaten their fill, others should be able to be nourished by the crumbs that remain. Jesus, granting her request that the demon be cast out, says to the woman what the podesta says to Madonna Filippa, "Because of this answer, you may go."

Beginning by arguing for and demonstrating women's full humanity, Madonna Filippa ends her defence by showing that women are in fact more than merely human, they are Christlike. Like Christ, they have the capacity to nourish the multitudes, and it behooves them to be generous. In her path-breaking examination of medieval women's gender strategies, Barbara Newman described two strategies available to women who wanted to escape "misogynist taboos and patriarchal strictures." The first, that of "a unisex ideal of the equality of souls before God or, in a secular framework, of rights before the law," she dubbed the model of the *femina virilis* or virago. The second, "diversely and sporadically theorized, [is] the possibility that women, qua women, could practice some form of the *imitatio Christi* with specifically feminine inflections."[101] In the end, Madonna Filippa, who self-consciously exhibits and articulates the characteristics of both the Virile Woman and the Woman-Christ, makes not only her own case but Boccaccio's case for Christine's proposition that, indeed, "women belong to the people of God and the human race as much as men."

NOTES

1 Christine de Pizan, *Le livre de la cité des dames* 2.54.1, in *La città delle dame*, ed. Earl Jeffrey Richards, trans. Patricia Caraffi (Milan: Luni Editrice, 1997).

2 Christine de Pizan, *The Book of the City of Ladies*, trans. Earl Jeffrey Richards (New York: Persea, 1982), 187.

3 For example, even the anticlerical Cordeliers justified Théroigne de Méricourt's admission before them as a petitioner (though her bid for membership, it must be noted, was simultaneously denied) with the observation that "since a canon of the Council of Mâcon has formally acknowledged that women have reason and a soul like men, they cannot be prevented from making good use of these faculties … in proposing that which they think advantageous to the country"; Camille Desmoulins, "Révolution de France et de Brabant" (March 1790), quoted in Frank Hamel, *Woman of the Revolution* (New York: Brentano, 1911), 150.

4 It may be that the following passage from Gregory of Tours is the source of this legend: "Extetit enim in hac synodo quidam ex episcopis, qui dicebat, mulierem hominem non posse vocitare. Sed tamen ab episcopis ratione accepta quievit, eo quod sacer Veteris Testamenti liber edoceat, quod in principio, Deo hominem creante, ait: Masculum et feminam creavit eos, vocavitque nomen eorum Adam, quod est homo terrenus, sic utique vocans mulierem ceu virum; utrumque enim hominem dixit … Multisque et aliis testimoniis haec causa convicta quievit (Gregory of Tours, *Histories* 8.20.3, *The Latin Library*, Web) [There came forward at this Council a certain bishop who maintained that woman could not be included in the term *man*. However, he accepted the reasoning of the other bishops and did not press his case; for the holy book of the Old Testament tells us that in the beginning, when God created man: Male and female he created them, and called their name Adam, which means earthly man; even so, he called the woman Eve yet of both he used the word *man* … They supported their argument with many other references, and he said no more]." Gregory of Tours, *The History of the Franks*, trans. Lewis Thorpe (London: Penguin, 1974), 452.

5 The early modern *locus classicus* of the debate on women's humanity was the 1595 exchange between the anonymous author of the *Disputatio nova contra mulieres qua probator eas homines non esse* (New disputation against women which attempts to prove they are not human beings) and German cleric Simon Gedik, who entitled his response *Defensio sexus muliebris, opposita futilissimae disputationi recens editae, qua suppresso authoris et typographi nomine blasphemé contenditur mulieres homines non esse* (Defence of the Female Sex, in opposition to the most futile disputation recently anonymously published in which it is blasphemously contended that women are not human beings). See *Disputatio perjucunda, qua anonymus probare nititur, mulieres homines non esse: Cui opposita est Simonis Gedicci, Defensio sexus muliebris, qua singula anonymi argumenta, distinctis thesibus proposita, viriliter enervantur* (Humorous disputation, in which anonymous

tries to prove that women are not human beings to which is opposed Simon Gedik's Defence of the female sex, by which the singular arguments of anonymous, with separate theses proposed, are weakened manfully) (Hagae Comitis: Burchhornius, 1644), reprinting verbatim both the *Disputatio* 3–63, and the *Defensio* 67–191. While there is substantial internal evidence that the anonymous treatise, often attributed to Valens Acidalius, was intended as a joke whose only purpose was to mock the excesses of Anabaptist biblical interpretation, it was taken very seriously by Gedik in his refutation and by the many who reprinted, translated, and imitated it.

6 Hildegard von Bingen, *Scivias Sive Visionum Ac Revelationum*, Book 1: Preface, in *Corpus Christianorum: Continuatio Mediaevalis*, vol. 43 (Turnholt: Brepols, 1978). The English translation is my own.

7 Ibid.

8 Giovanni Boccaccio, *De mulieribus claris*, Introduction 4, in *Tutte le opere di Giovanni Boccaccio*, ed. Vittore Branca (Milan: Mondadori, 1976).

9 Giovanni Boccaccio, *Famous Women*, ed. and trans. Virginia Brown (Cambridge, MA: Harvard University Press, 2001), 9.

10 A number of other passages in *De mulieribus claris* also can be read to draw a contrast between *homines* on the one hand and *femina[e]* or *muliere[es]* on the other. See, e.g., *De mulieribus claris* 32.7/*Famous Women* 131: marvelling that Penthesiliea and women (*mulieres*) like her dare to fight against men (*viros*) and become "more manly in arms than those born male who have been changed into women [quo hec et huiusmodo longe magis in armis homines facte sunt quam sint quos sexu masculos natura fecit ... vertit in feminas]"; and *De mulieribus claris* 93.7; 397, contrasting the bravery of the *femina* Epicharis with the weakness of the "eiusdem coniurationis egregiorum hominum [eminent men who were involved in the same conspiracy]."

11 *De mulieribus claris*, Dedication 5. On this dedication, see also the essays by Rhiannon Daniels and Lori Walters in this volume.

12 *Famous Women*, 1–2.

13 Pamela Joseph Benson, *The Invention of the Renaissance Woman: The Challenge of Female Independence in the Literature and Thought of Italy and England* (University Park: Pennsylvania State University Press, 1992), 13.

14 *Famous Women*, 7. This is Brown's translation of "in gentili mulieri quid dignum ... legeris ... honestate aut pudicitia vel virtute supereris ab extera et, provocato in vires ingenio, quo plurimum vales, non solum ne supereris patiare, sed ut superes quascunque egregia virtute coneris" (*De mulieribus claris*, Dedication 9).

15 See above, notes 10 and 11.

16 *Cité des dames* 1.1.2.
17 *City of Ladies*, 5.
18 Or, as G.H. McWilliam translates it, "a human quality which every man or woman should possess"; *The Decameron*, 2nd ed. (New York: Penguin, 1995), 1. Italian citations of the *Decameron* are from Vittore Branca's edition (Torino: Einaudi, 1980, rev. 1992); further English translations, from McWilliam.
19 In fact, none of the stories of the eighth day features a woman playing a trick on another woman, though in them men both fool and are fooled by women and by each other. See Valerio C. Ferme, "Ingegno and Morality in the New Social Order: The Role of the Beffa in Boccaccio's *Decameron*," *RLA* 4 (1992): 248–53: "The problem with this topic, from a feminist perspective, lies with the absence of opportunities for *l'una donna all'altra si fa*, creating an imbalance in the roles assumed by men and women in human relationships" (252).
20 *Dec.* 1.intr. See discussion below.
21 Giovanni Boccaccio, *Il corbaccio* §132, in *Tutte le opere*; Giovanni Boccaccio, *The Corbaccio*, trans. Anthony K. Cassell (Urbana: University of Illinois Press, 1975), 24.
22 Christine de Pizan, *Le livre des trois vertus*, ed. Charity Cannon Willard and Eric Hicks (Paris: Honoré Champion, 1989), 1.7, 3.10, and 3.12, respectively. By contrast, when a Boccaccian text bestows the title of "lady" on a woman of the lower classes, it is done somewhat mockingly, as when Dioneo refers to the servant whose bawdy dispute begins the sixth day as "donna Liscia" in crediting her with the inspiration for the seventh day's theme, having just disparaged his own nobility as king for a day (*Dec.* 6.concl.3–6).
23 *Il corbaccio* §133.
24 *The Corbaccio*, 24.
25 *Il corbaccio* §158.
26 *The Corbaccio*, 29.
27 *Débat sur le roman de la rose*, ed. and trans. Eric Hicks (Paris: Honoré Champion, 1977), 139.
28 According to Shirley S. Allen, "the whole message of the *Decameron*" can be summed up as Boccaccio's assertion "that women are neither angels nor devils but human beings, like men"; "The Griselda Tale and the Portrayal of Women in the *Decameron*," *Philological Quarterly* 56 (1977): 1, 6.
29 *Cité des dames* 1.1.1.
30 *City of Ladies*, 4.

31 See above, notes 10 and 11.
32 See above, notes 8 and 9.
33 *Cité des dames* 1.1.1.
34 *City of Ladies*, 5.
35 See Mary Anne C. Case, "Christine and the Authority of Experience," in *Christine De Pizan and the Categories of Difference*, ed. Marilynn Desmond (Minneapolis: University of Minnesota Press, 1997), 71–88; 79.
36 See Judith Butler, *Gender Trouble* (New York: Routledge, 1990).
37 Teodolinda Barolini, "The Essential Boccaccio, or an Accidental Ethics," afterword to *The Decameron*, trans. M. Musa and P. Bondanella, rev. ed. (New York: Signet, 2010), 809–21.
38 *Famous Women*, 13.
39 *De mulieribus claris*, Proemio 10. Christine makes a similar point in her 1429 *Ditié de Jehanne d'Arc*.
40 *Famous Women*, 13
41 *De mulieribus claris*, Proemio 10.
42 See Julia Smith Holderness, "Feminism and the Fall: Boccaccio, Christine de Pizan, and Louise Labé," *Essays in Medieval Studies* 21 (2004): 97–108; for a discussion of how Boccaccio, by contrast with Christine, stresses the gendered aspects of Semiramis's behaviour, from her "feminine cunning [astu muliebri]" to her "manly spirit [virili animo]," see 98–100.
43 See *De mulieribus claris* 57.21/*Famous Women*, 241–3 ("Sed quid, Artemesie acta spectantes, arbitrari possumus, nisi nature laborantis errore factum ut corpori, cui Deus virilem et magnificam infuderat animam, sexus femineus datus sit [As we admire the deeds of Artemesia, what can we think except that the workings of nature erred in bestowing a female sex on a body which God had endowed with a virile and lofty spirit]." Similarly, see *De mulieribus claris* 93.8/*Famous Women*, 399.
44 *Famous Women*, 399.
45 *De mulieribus claris* 93.8.
46 See, e.g., *De mulieribus claris* 31 (suggesting that, when the Minyan wives changed clothes with their husbands in order to save them, the wives showed themselves to be tried and true men and their husbands women).
47 As Stephen D. Kolsky puts it, in his analysis of the process through which one of the famous women, Tamyris, "take[s] on male defined qualities and casts off 'feminine' ones … such a procedure negates the specificity of the feminine and sets up maleness as the desirable goal for both sexes." See *The Genealogy of Women: Studies in Boccaccio's "De mulieribus claris"* (New York: Peter Lang, 2003), 89. As I have previously discussed, Christine

de Pizan, by contrast, values feminine qualities and commends them as well as masculine ones to men as well as women. See "Christine and the Authority of Experience," 78.

48 See *Cité des dames* 1.27.1: "[S]e coustume estoit de mettre les petites filles a l'escole et que suivamment on les feist apprendre les sciences, comme on fait au filz, qu'elles appren / droient aussi parfaictement et entendroient les soubtilletez de toutes les ars et sciences comme ilz font [If it were customary to send little girls to school like boys, and if they were then taught the sciences, they would learn as thoroughly and understand the subtleties of all the arts and sciences as well as boys]."

49 *Famous Women*, 355. Note that the word Brown translates here as "famous" is not *claris* (well known) as in the book's title, but *gloriosos*, which has a more unequivocally positive connotation.

50 *De mulieribus claris* 86.3.

51 *Cité des dames* 1.11.

52 *De mulieribus claris* 86.3.

53 *On Famous Women*, 355. Kevin Brownlee's chapter in this volume analyses how Christine de Pizan quotes and expands on precisely this description of Cornificia, as she then goes on to provide further "proof of the equality between men's and women's minds."

54 *De mulieribus claris* 86.3.

55 *On Famous Women*, 355. It is worth highlighting that this passage denies precisely what the old woman of *Dec.* 5.10 affirms, to wit that by contrast with men who "are born with a thousand other talents ... women exist for no other purpose than to [have sex] and bear children [essi nascono buoni a mille cose ... ma le femine a niuna altra cosa che a fare questo e figliuoli ci nascono]" (5.10.18).

56 *De mulieribus claris* 86.3.

57 Although Christine does sees the relationship between the two, when she observes the effect that slanders in books about women have on the way women are treated by their husbands and by society.

58 Gaines Post, "A Romano-Canonical Maxim, *Quod omnes tangit*, in Bracton and in Early Parliaments," in *Studies in Medieval Legal Thought: Public Law and the State, 1100–1322*, ed. Post (Princeton: Princeton University Press, 1964), 163–238.

59 Although Kenneth Pennington, in "A Note to *Decameron* 6.7: The Wit of Madonna Filippa," *Speculum* 52, no. 4 (1977): 902–5, asserts first that the maxim's "logic was never extended to women in the Middle Ages," he then goes on to acknowledge that Ockham's "magister declares that women should not be excluded from a general council, especially in

matters of faith 'quae omnes tangit,'" but notes that "the student responds that he cannot take such an irrational argument seriously" and concludes that "Ockham meant to amuse his readers with the irony of this passage" (904).

60 Jehan Le Fèvre, "Le Livre de Leesce," *Les Lamentations de Matheolus*, ed. A.G. Van Hamel (Paris: É Bouillon, 1905), vol. 2, line 1151.

61 See Alfred Dessens, *Les Revendications des Droits de la Femme* (Toulouse: Impr. C. Marques, 1905), 25, citing Edgard Boutaric, *La France Sous Phillipe-le-Bel* (Paris: Académie des Inscriptions et Belles-Lettres, 1861). See also Marcel Garuad, *La Révolution et l'égalité civile* (Paris: Librarie du Recueil Sire, 1953), 173.

62 Martha C. Howells, "Citizenship and Gender: Women's Political Status in Northern Medieval Cities," in *Women and Power in the Middle Ages*, ed. Mary Erler and Maryanne Kowaleski (Athens: University of Georgia Press, 1988), 37–60; 48.

63 Françoise Collin, translated and quoted in Joan Wallach Scott, *Parité! Sexual Equality and the Crisis of French Universalism* (Chicago: University of Chicago Press, 2005), 60–1. In making use of the concept of *parité* in interpreting the work of Christine de Pizan, I am not endorsing the current French law of *parité*, let alone choosing between a universalist and differentialist vision of what *parité* in current French law signifies. In my own view as a legal theorist, there is much to be said for the objections of critics of the law of *parité* such as Elisabeth Badinter, "La parité est une régression," in *Le piège de la parité*, ed. Micheline Amar (Paris: Hachette Littératures, 1999), 40–8. While it is true that the French legal and constitutional order from 1789 on has done a terrible job of including women among the fungible abstract individuals who make up the nation, concretizing or abandoning the abstract universal may not be the best solution to the problem.

64 *Cité des dames* 3.18.9.

65 *City of Ladies*, 254.

66 As Barbara Newman observed, "Though restricted to one gender, her city is otherwise remarkably inclusive … This universality makes a theological as well as a historical point: the female no less than the male could stand as a synecdoche for the human." See Barbara Newman, *God and the Goddesses: Vision, Poetry, and Belief in the Middle Ages* (Philadelphia: University of Pennsylvania Press 2003), 23–4.

67 On discussing the need for and nature of justice in a commonwealth, see Augustine, *De civitate dei* 2.22, *The Latin Library*, Web.

68 *Cité des dames* 2.54.1.

69 *City of Ladies*, 187.
70 Michael Camille, *The Medieval Art of Love: Objects and Subjects of Desire* (New York: Harry Abrams, 1998), 89.
71 *Cité des dames* 1.15.2.
72 *City of Ladies*, 40.
73 *Cité des dames* 3.1.2.
74 *City of Ladies*, 218.
75 *Cité des dames* 3.1.3.
76 *City of Ladies*, 218.
77 *Il corbaccio* §176–7.
78 *The Corbaccio*, 32.
79 That Mary was a member of the female sex was one of the standard catalogue of arguments in favour of female superiority in the *querelle des femmes* tradition. As the best of women, Mary was better than all men but Jesus, but since she was fully human and he was also divine, he could not properly be counted on the male side of the ledger. Moreover, Judas, the worst of all men, was worse than any woman.
80 I am grateful to Lori Walters for drawing to my attention to the fact that Augustine insists that "Non est autem uitium sexus femineus, sed natura [the sex of a woman is not a vice, but nature]"; *De civitate dei* 22.17; Walters's translation, 245, in Lori A. Walters,"Magnifying the Lord: Prophetic Voice in *La Cité des Dames*," *CRM* 13 (2006): 239–53.
81 Penelope D. Johnson, *Equal in Monastic Profession: Religious Women in Medieval France* (Chicago: University of Chicago Press, 1993), 63.
82 Ibid., 67.
83 "Noi siamo mobili, riottose, sospettose, pusillamine, e paurose (*Dec.* 1.intr.75) [We are fickle, quarrelsome, suspicious, cowardly, and easily frightened]."
84 *Dec.* 1.intr.74–5. The narrator describes Pampinea here as *discretissima* (more prudent than the others) but her claim to speak from the authoritative experience of being a woman should not be compared with Christine's, for, of course, in the end, she remains the creation of a male author.
85 According to Joy Hambuechen Potter, "the Florentine insistence on the rotation of high office clearly comes into play here"; *Five Frames for the Decameron: Communication and Social System in the Cornice* (Princeton: Princeton University Press, 1982), 20.
86 According to Teodolinda Barolini, even the frame meeting in Santa Maria Novella of "a group of unmarried men and women [who then] leave the

city together," let alone the rest of the "mixed gender *brigata*'s" activities, would have been "a veritable impossibility" in the fourteenth-century Florence described by historians. See "Sociology of the Brigata: Gendered Groups in Dante, Forese, Folgore, Boccaccio – From 'Guido, i' vorrei,'" *Italian Studies* 67, no. 1 (2012): 4–22; 5. See also Potter, *Five Frames for the Decameron*, 23 (observing that while "males and females are completely equal in the life of the cornice" this would not have been "the case in 'secular' life").

87 In contrast to the frame dispute, which raises only questions of fact – do most women come to their bridal night as virgins and do they deceive their husbands – Madonna Filippa's case turns purely on a question of law. She freely and bravely admits to the fact of adultery, despite being advised to deny it; the only question for the judge in her case is what, if any, legitimate punishment may be imposed.

88 Teodolinda Barolini, "Le parole son femmine e i fatti sono maschi: Toward a Sexual Poetics of the Decameron (Decameron 2.9, 2.10, 5.10)" in *Dante and the Origins of Italian Literary Culture* (New York: Fordham University Press, 2006), 281–303; 285. On the women's swimming excursion at the end of Day Six, see also Thomas C. Stillinger, "The Language of Gardens: Boccaccio's 'Valle delle Donne,'" *Boccaccio and Feminist Criticism*, ed. T. Stillinger and F. Regina Psaki, *Annali d'Italianistica: Studi e Testi* 8 (2006): 105–27.

89 *De claris mulieribus*, Dedication 2; *Famous Women*, 3.

90 Gaines Post, "A Roman Legal Theory of Consent *Quod Omnes Tangit* in Medieval Representation," *Wisconsin Law Review* (1950): 68.

91 See Grace Delmolino's chapter in this volume for a further discussion of the canon law, in particular of marital debt.

92 Indeed, the canon law made reciprocal and equal what the Gospels had formulated asymmetrically and unequally. Thus, although Jesus, in line with Jewish law, had spoken only of a husband's ability to put away his wife for adultery (see, e.g., Matthew 19.9), the canon law insisted that what was good for the gander was equally good for the goose.

93 Carol Lansing, "Gender and Civic Authority: Sexual Control in a Medieval Italian Town," *Journal of Social History* 31, no. 1 (1997): 33–59; 40. Lansing sees these laws as part of an effort "to exclude irrational concupiscence from public life." She stresses that the laws "made no attempt to alter the legal privileges and obligations of female citizens and female residents; women could still lodge accusations, serve as witnesses, and so forth," so long as they did so away from public governmental spaces.

94 *Dec.* 6.7.10. The fact that the people of Prato are described as "rocking with mirth" as they declare Madonna Filippa to be right should not be seen as undercutting the persuasive power attributed to her speech. For further discussion, see Mary Anne Case, "From the Mirror of Reason to the Measure of Justice," 5 *Yale Journal of Law and the Humanities* 115 (1993): 115–35 (detailing the long history of feminist arguments which started out as jokes coming to be taken seriously). After all, when the men are first approached to join the ladies at the beginning of the *Decameron*, they, too, first think it is a joke, but when they realize Pampinea is speaking in earnest, gladly agree. On Filippa's status as a legal subject in this tale, see also Marilyn Miguel, *A Rhetoric of the "Decameron"* (Toronto: University of Toronto Press, 2003), 119–22.

95 It is not clear whether the law this democratic process produces treats the sexes equally – all that is specified by way of amendment is that henceforth penalties will only be imposed on wives who take money for cheating on their husbands.

96 *De mulieribus claris* 31.13.

97 *Famous Women*, 129.

98 2 Kings 9.10.

99 Pennington, "A Note to *Decameron* 6.7: The Wit of Madonna Filippa," *Speculum* 52, no. 4 (1977): 905.

100 To similar effect, Matthew 15.22–8.

101 Barbara Newman, *From Virile Woman to Woman-Christ: Studies in Medieval Religion and Literature* (Philadelphia: University of Pennsylvania Press, 1995), 2–3.

PART FOUR

Political and Authorial Contexts: On Famous Women

9 On She-Wolves and Famous Women: Boccaccio, Politics, and the Neapolitan Court

ELIZABETH CASTEEN

Naples formed a vital feature of Giovanni Boccaccio's imaginative landscape. Raised in Tuscany but educated in Naples – where, as an adolescent, he joined his banker father in 1327 – Boccaccio took shape as a poet at the fringes of the Neapolitan court, which left an indelible imprint on his consciousness.[1] While never at the centre of court circles, Boccaccio remained in the royal orbit, into which he was first introduced by his father, who became a counsellor to Naples's king, Robert of Anjou, in 1328. Boccaccio may have been in Naples to be trained as a banker, but his education there led him to his literary vocation.[2] He was part of a group of Florentines that included not only Naples's bankers but also much of its intelligentsia, including the poet Zanobi da Strada and Niccolò Acciaiuoli, who would ultimately become Naples's Grand Seneschal.[3] He forged lasting friendships as well with Neapolitan-born officials and intellectuals, such as Giovanni Barilli and Barbato da Sulmona, friends to both Boccaccio and Francesco Petrarch and important figures in the administrations of Robert "the Wise" (r. 1309–43) and his granddaughter, Johanna I (r. 1343–82). Perhaps most importantly, Boccaccio had access to the royal library, frequented the homes of leading members of the Neapolitan aristocracy, imbibed the romances popular at court, and developed a literary bond to Naples's most famous native poet, Virgil.[4] His poetic identity was, as a result, in significant ways both Neapolitan and Florentine.

As Victoria Kirkham points out, Boccaccio's early works "are all Neapolitan by setting, either in the fiction … or in the frame that explains how the fiction came to be … or both."[5] Beginning with the first canto of his first work, *Caccia di Diana*, probably written in 1334, Boccaccio's literary persona often frequented a fictive version of the Angevin court, which – both in culture and in setting – helped to inspire early works like the *Filocolo* (1336–8) and *Elegia di Madonna Fiammetta* (c. 1343–4). Court figures move through such early works, which speak fondly of members of the royal family – particularly the young Johanna and her sister, Maria – and lavish praise on the celebrated Robert the Wise.[6] Boccaccio's vision of the court was never strictly historical, and it began as – and remained – a court predominantly of women, one whose members formed Diana's cortège in *Caccia di Diana*, enacted the drama of the *Buccolicum carmen* (1342–67), danced through the stanzas of the *Amorosa visione* (c. 1342), and swelled the ranks of the famous who peopled *De mulieribus claris* (c. 1362–3) and *De casibus virorum illustrium* (c. 1355–60). Even in works with a Florentine backdrop, such as the *Decameron* (c. 1353) and *Il corbaccio* (c. 1355), Naples and the Angevins intrude.

Among the most famous of Boccaccio's famous Neapolitan women – and for Boccaccio, the most troubling – was Johanna I, whose reign as Naples's sovereign queen began after Boccaccio's reluctant return to Tuscany following a reversal of Bardi fortunes in late 1340 or early 1341. Johanna's long, often tumultuous reign extended from 1343 to 1382 and fascinated observers across Europe; these observers weighed in on the problems of regnant queenship, on Johanna's character, and on the major events of her reign.[7] Boccaccio, older by a generation than Johanna, became one of the most regular commentators as he grappled with her cultural significance and took a lively, deliberate part in shaping her reputation. Johanna and Naples both loom large in Boccaccio's work, allowing him to act as cultural commentator and recorder of history, reconstructing and refracting Neapolitan events in order to give them coherence and meaning. In so doing, he remained, even at a geographic remove, an active participant and vital voice in Neapolitan affairs. Indeed, Naples's centrality in his work helped to ensure Boccaccio a Neapolitan readership and thus to maintain his ties to the city and culture of his youth.[8] As Kirkham has argued, Boccaccio's "constant allegiance to Naples and its court" was both literary and political.[9] In incorporating Johanna and Neapolitan events into his literary work, Boccaccio took part in a burgeoning culture of political commentary by Florentines invested in Neapolitan history and politics, asserting his poetic authority to pass judgment on and interpret events that transpired in Naples after his unwilling exile to the north.[10]

Johanna first appears in Canto 42 of the *Amorosa visione* – written in 1342, the year before her succession to the throne – as a joyful, graceful girl who flits in and out of the scene in just under three short lines.[11] The following year, Johanna succeeded her grandfather as Naples's sovereign, despite the competing claims of eight male cousins, including two from the senior Hungarian branch of the Angevin family.[12] Queenship transformed Johanna's literary persona. No longer an innocent girl, she became in Boccaccio's subsequent work an ambivalent figure through whom he critiqued unjust political power, illegitimate succession, and the unfolding of Neapolitan history. Boccaccio's Johanna is unstable; she vacillates between monstrosity (in the eclogues) and near-saintly perfection (in *De mulieribus claris*). She is contradictory and problematic, a literary cipher whose evolution reveals Boccaccio's own complex, evolving, partisan stake in Neapolitan politics, as in the conceptual and political problems of regnant queenship.

Johanna was likely born in 1326, the elder of the two daughters of Robert's only surviving son, Charles, Duke of Calabria (1298–1328). Charles's death left Robert without an heir, and the Johanna whom Boccaccio knew and observed as a girl was destined and groomed for Naples's throne. In the contemporary political climate – Johanna became Naples's heiress in the same year that her maternal uncle, Philip of Valois, became France's king on the strength of the so-called Salic Law principle that women cannot inherit or transmit thrones – Johanna's succession in Naples was deeply controversial and stimulated lively debate. During the four decades of her rule, she was subject to near constant scrutiny. They were eventful, crisis-filled years, and it is for crisis that Johanna's reign is best remembered. She married four times; her first husband was murdered, her second considered a tyrant, and her third said to be mad. Her reign witnessed civil war, mercenary marauding, the Black Death, and the opening years of the Great Schism of the Western Church, in which Johanna herself was implicated because she was the first monarch to recognize Clement VII (r. 1378–94) as pope. She died childless – reportedly murdered by her Urbanist cousin and deposer, Charles III of Durazzo – in 1382, with her Provençal and Neapolitan lands divided and at war.

For Johanna's contemporaries, however, scandal and crisis did not wholly characterize her reign. She worked closely with the papacy, whose wars in northern Italy she supported militarily and financially. She was an active participant in the ultimately successful efforts to return the papal court to Rome from Avignon. She was a friend to Birgitta of Sweden, Catherine of Siena, and Birgitta's daughter, Katherine of Vadstena, and in the latter half of her reign, she came to be celebrated as a wise, pious queen who ruled ably and well. As a result, her reputation was complex and multifaceted, mulled over and given shape by committed apologists as well as detractors.[13]

A keen observer of Neapolitan events, Boccaccio provides us a lens through which to track Johanna's career and evolving public persona that is both partisan and personal. His first prolonged poetic treatment of her comes in the Latin eclogues of the *Buccolicum carmen*, written in the aftermath of and in direct response to the murder of Andrew of Hungary, Johanna's cousin and first husband. In mid-September of 1345, on the eve of his coronation – which Johanna, protective of her rights as a regnant queen, had struggled to prevent – the seventeen-year-old Andrew was attacked by a group of assailants at a hunting retreat in Aversa, a short distance from Naples. Under cover of darkness, they beat, suffocated, and strangled him before throwing his mutilated body from the castle walls to the garden below.[14] Commentators across Europe expressed shock and outrage, both at the crime's stunning brutality and at a perceived failure to punish the guilty. Andrew was a prince, one many people believed was Naples's rightful ruler, but his death was more suited to a criminal than to what Petrarch called "a consecrated prince made in God's image [principis sacrosanctam effigiem ad imaginem Dei factam]." Petrarch, a frequent guest in Naples, decried the "abominable and insidious savagery [tam nefarias et tam truces insidias]" with which Andrew was slain and wished that "he had been killed by a sword or through some other form of manly death so that he would appear to have been killed at the hands of men, not mangled by the teeth and claws of beasts."[15] Contemporary reports echo Petrarch's horror, and they advance a range of theories as to the identities of the inhuman perpetrators, although no literary or legal consensus was ever reached. A group of Neapolitan nobles – comprised substantially of Johanna's inner circle – was tried and publicly executed in a gruesome judicial spectacle staged by two of Johanna's cousins. Yet chronicles and letters from the period reveal a widespread suspicion that the spectacle served only to obscure either Johanna's guilt or that of others who stood to gain by eliminating Andrew and isolating Johanna. The Hungarian royals were likewise unsatisfied. Andrew's brother, King Louis of Hungary, continued to demand Johanna's deposition (and replacement by Louis himself) for several years, ultimately necessitating that a papal commission investigate the crime in Avignon in the early 1350s.

Contemporary commentators – including Boccaccio – offer multiple and conflicting accounts of the murder. Johanna was most often blamed, almost always in highly gendered, sexualized terms that indict her for a gross inversion of natural order through her insistence on her sovereignty. She protested her innocence, as did Pope Clement VI. The Hungarian royal family, however, excoriated Johanna both as an adulteress – playing on widespread rumours that intensified after the murder – and murderer, repeatedly referring to her as *Johanna viricida* in demanding her deposition.[16] Commentators who supported her, particularly those with papal sympathies, attempted to deflect guilt from her, often by portraying her as feminine, weak, and vulnerable. The Swiss Franciscan chronicler John of Winterthur, for instance, argued that, while Johanna was present when Andrew was murdered, she had only escaped sharing his fate through flight.[17] The Franciscan prophet John of Rupescissa defended her from prison in Avignon, describing Andrew's death as a great and ominous evil while attesting to Johanna's innocence and arguing that she had been falsely implicated.[18] And Giovanni da Bazzano contended in his *Chronicon Mutinense* that it was not the queen but the family of her second husband, Louis of Taranto (another cousin who gained both Johanna and the kingdom through the murder), who were responsible for Andrew's gruesome fate.[19]

On the other side of the debate were commentators who took up and elaborated Hungarian charges. They argued that Johanna ruled Naples only through an inversion of the natural order that should have made Andrew king, and that her throne should be forfeit. Most often, they built their claims that Johanna violated gender norms through her insistence on ruling over and in place of her husband around the charge that Johanna was flagrantly sexually licentious. Giovanni Villani blamed the murder on Johanna's disordered lust.[20] A glossator of Gentile of Foligno's commentary on the Joachite eschatological prophecy *Ve mundo in centum annis* linked Andrew's death to the prophesied strangulation of a king and attributed the murder to his queen's "abominable wantonness [abhominabiles lasscivias]," anticipating the characterization of Johanna as a murderous "harlot queen [regina meretrix]" by the stridently pro-Hungarian *Chronicon Estense*.[21] Such depictions of Johanna represent regnant queenship as a perversion of right order, and they effectively argue that Johanna, sexual criminal and murderer, should cede her throne to Louis of Hungary – the eldest son of the senior Angevin line – who might restore justice and balance to Naples.

At least initially, Boccaccio aligned himself with those who defamed Johanna as an adulteress and murderer. The eclogues reveal his sorrow and horror, both at the murder of Andrew – a young boy being raised at court during Boccaccio's time in Naples – and at its consequences for Naples. With his patron, Francesco degli Ordelaffi, lord of Forlí, Boccaccio may have joined forces besieging Naples in 1348 in the first of two vendetta-invasions led by Louis of Hungary. Writing to Zanobi da Strada that year, Boccaccio wrote of Francesco's preparations to take up "most just arms [arma iustissima]" in southern Italy alongside "the illustrious king of Hungary."[22] That conflict and its grim antecedent in Andrew's death provided the material for the third, fourth, fifth, and sixth of Boccaccio's eclogues.

Recalling Petrarch's lament that Andrew was mangled by beasts, in Boccaccio's third eclogue, *Faunus* (the name Boccaccio assigned Francesco degli Ordelaffi), a rabid, pregnant she-wolf – Johanna, pregnant at the time of Andrew's death – murders Andrew's poetic double, Alexis, the rightful heir to Robert (Argus) and the true king of Naples (the woods):[23]

> The mountains wept for Argus, satyrs wept,
> and nimble fauns, and even Apollo mourned.
> He had bequeathed the woods to young Alexis,
> who, careless as he led flocks through the fields,
> proceeding without light into the forest,
> encountered there by chance a pregnant wolf
> swollen with rage; this savage beast sprang up
> and plunged her teeth into his throat, nor could she
> be pulled away until his life expired
> upon that hidden path. That's what they say.
> But many claim this forest shelters lions
> and the ferocious beasts that killed Adonis,
> as fierce himself when he was hunting them.[24]

Faunus thus tells an allegorical tale of Andrew's murder. Boccaccio, poet and historian, acknowledges that some contemporaries suspected Johanna's courtiers – the lions and beasts – of Andrew's death, but suggests that it was Johanna herself, the enraged, gravid wolf, who was to blame, sinking her jaws into her husband's throat and draining his life's blood.

Boccaccio's portrait of Johanna in *Faunus*, which plays on an established trope of disordered queenship, equates her infamous sexuality with bestial irrationality, drawing on the Thomistic teaching that submission to bodily desire renders humans animal-like (*Summa* 1–2.73.5

ad 3).[25] Ovid, one of Boccaccio's poetic models, satirically describes female sexuality as "rabid" – a characterization repeated in *Faunus* – and unbounded, outstripping that of men in "keenness and frenzy."[26] Albert the Great provided the medieval natural philosophical corollary to this argument when he represented female sexual desire as subhuman, something that "deviates from the ideal course of nature" in its deep and irrational hunger.[27] Boccaccio amplifies this – his Johanna is not merely rabid, she is an animal, a wild beast of the forest whose savagery places her beyond the bounds of civilization. Her reign is unjust, a deviation from Robert's true intentions; her Naples is no longer Virgil's Parthenope but a wilderness dominated by brute beasts – a clear textual echo of the *selva oscura* and *lupa* of the opening canto of Dante's *Inferno*. She embodies sex and violence, her characterization as a prostitute (Latin: *lupa*) tied to her violent bestial nature in a metaphor that Edward Muir argues Italian chroniclers often used to "explain human violence by showing how [perpetrators] had crossed the line into bestiality."[28] Boccaccio thus strips Johanna of her humanity, discursively making her both a wolf and a prostitute, and links her to a long line of disordered queens, from the Roman Empress Messalina to *The Golden Legend*'s Lupa, antagonist of James the Greater.[29]

Boccaccio's maddened she-wolf functions as a scathing critique of both regnant queenship and Johanna herself. Yet, if Boccaccio's *lupa* epitomizes feminine evil, the Johanna of *De mulieribus claris*, written about fifteen years later, is an advertisement for the latent potential of powerful women. In *De casibus virorum illustrium* (begun c. 1355, completed 1360, revised 1373),[30] Boccaccio's narrator, in conversation with the Frankish queen Brunhildis, argues that crowns do not transform a woman's sex ("si sexum corona mutasset, non crederem") and questions whether queens, as women, can be trusted.[31] Boccaccio's Brunhildis – widowed, allegedly adulterous, subject to envy and rumour – shares much with Johanna, including Boccaccio's charge that she had her husband killed while he was on a hunting trip. Indeed, Brunhildis's placement in the text comes at the beginning of the ninth book of *De casibus*, which ponders the fates of figures closely associated with the Angevin court, such as Johanna's ancestor, Charles I of Anjou (19), who founded Naples's Angevin dynasty, and her contemporaries Walter of Brienne (24) and Filippa Catanese (25 and 26); Boccaccio's readers may well have recognized Johanna in Brunhildis.[32] While Boccaccio the narrator openly doubts Brunhildis's defence of herself, Boccaccio the author nonetheless records it, calling into question the seriousness of his assertion that crowns do not transform women. *De mulieribus claris* resumes that discussion, and it takes the position that Johanna, as a regnant queen, overcame the limitations of femininity.

The she-wolf and the glorious queen of *De mulieribus claris* are diametrically opposed, representing conflicting conceptions of femininity and of queenship born out of Boccaccio's and Naples's changing circumstances. The shift in Boccaccio's literary representation of Johanna may reflect practical exigency: hopeful of Neapolitan court patronage, Boccaccio flattered both Johanna and Andrea Acciaiuoli (the sister of Naples's Grand Seneschal, Boccaccio's old friend Niccolò), to whom he dedicated *De mulieribus claris*. Yet, Boccaccio's changed attitude towards Johanna also reflects his evolving understanding of the central players in the drama of the Neapolitan court, which led him to alter his stance both on Johanna and on the acceptability of regnant queenship.

Behind Boccaccio's new stance regarding Johanna was anger with Louis of Hungary, with whom he quickly became disillusioned. Early in the struggle between Naples and Hungary, Louis seemed to Boccaccio to pursue a vendetta that was both just and necessary, an impression shared by many of his contemporaries, who advocated Johanna's ouster and replacement by Louis. In Eclogue 3, *Faunus*, Louis is the avenger of his brother's death. Louis's poetic counterpart, Tityrus – named for the shepherd of Virgil's eclogues – rushes in a righteous rage from the Danube, gathering forces to "catch the wolf and tawny lions, / to punish those who merit it."[33] Like his brother, Alexis, Tityrus is a shepherd, but in *Faunus*, he is a shepherd turned hunter by necessity, one who represents civilization, as well as the promise that the right order and humanity might be restored to "the vile forest [infandam silvam]" if only the animals who render it perilous can be captured. Boccaccio is clear that Louis's fury was terrible, but it was also warranted, and he evokes the widespread support Louis's vendetta – framed as a classic revenge narrative – garnered, as he asks, "Do you recall / not long ago having seen him raging, / carrying the sharp iron hunting spear, / and many men behind him carrying nets / upon their shoulders as, trembling with fury, he crossed this way through the entire forest?"[34]

Louis's first incursion into Naples – launched in November 1347 – was a resounding Hungarian success. Johanna and her second husband, Louis of Taranto, fled Naples for the papal court in Avignon. Louis of Hungary briefly took the throne, ceded to him on 20 January 1348 by the remaining Angevin princes, the five sons of Robert of Anjou's younger brothers. Louis of Hungary left Naples in May, when the Black Death reached the kingdom, but his forces held Naples until Johanna and Louis of Taranto, with papal backing and the support of much of the Neapolitan nobility, returned in August. On their return, Johanna and Louis of Taranto inaugurated a war to reclaim their territory that would rage intermittently until 1352, when Johanna was formally exculpated of guilt in Andrew's death. Contemporary chroniclers describe Louis of Hungary's initial victory as nearly bloodless, greeted by Neapolitan subjects delighted by the restoration of order he seemed to promise. His effortless conquest and the apparent joy of his new subjects gave proof, in sympathetic accounts, to the righteousness of his cause.[35]

Boccaccio came, however, to view Louis of Hungary's conquest with deep ambivalence. As the consequences of Louis's rule became apparent, Boccaccio's eclogues, in the words of Vittore Branca, passed "from invective ... to the palinode, to the elegy, to the paean" when he described both Johanna and Louis of Taranto, whom he increasingly represented as Naples's rightful rulers.[36] Boccaccio's ambivalence stemmed, at least in part, from the harsh realities of the Hungarian invasion. Although Louis of Hungary's vendetta had appeared righteous as it began, its conclusion gave Boccaccio little to celebrate. Multiple contemporary accounts describe Louis's rule in Naples as both harsh and arbitrary. He imprisoned four of the Angevin princes who remained in Naples and summarily executed one, Charles of Durazzo. He likewise tortured and executed members of the Neapolitan nobility believed to be loyal to Johanna. The Florentine chronicler Matteo Villani reports that Louis was widely perceived as cruel, while Giovanni da Bazzano accuses him of behaving "fraudulently and unjustly."[37] Branca argues that Boccaccio, too, ultimately found himself unable to praise a "harsh and violent military occupation" marked by brutal reprisals against Naples's people and autocratic behaviour on Louis's part.[38]

Louis of Hungary's barbarity transformed him in Boccaccio's poetry. In the fourth eclogue, *Dorus*, Louis, no longer Tityrus, has become Polyphemus, who "tears apart the guilty" but also persecutes the innocent.[39] Although his cause remains just in Boccaccio's eyes, Louis himself has become "that ruthless man." Indeed, as a Cyclops, he has become a subhuman monster. Significantly, Boccaccio uses the word *rabie* – previously used to characterize the maddened she-wolf of Eclogue 3 – to describe Louis's wrath.[40] Louis has come to share Johanna's madness, and like her, he has descended into inhuman irrationality. In the process, the Kingdom of Naples is transformed from an uncivilized forest into a settled, pastoral land. Boccaccio calls Louis/Polyphemus "more vicious than a snake [truculentior angue]" and describes him devastating orchards and killing livestock, so that Naples's streams run with blood.[41]

Boccaccio's fifth eclogue, *The Falling Forest* (*Silva Cadens*), describes his grief at Naples's destruction. No longer a bucolic paradise, Naples is now a burning, demolished forest: "oaks have crashed, the mighty cypress fallen, / the Italian oak is burning with set fires / in every part, no pine remains."[42] His beloved Naples was irreparably altered, so that "[a]ll beauty here has perished, / but grief and care remain."[43] Although he was unprepared to forgive Johanna and Louis of Taranto – whose poetic counterparts, Liquoris and Alcestus, "departed full of fear," "left the wood in doubt / and sailed away," abandoning Naples – Boccaccio nonetheless condemns Louis of Hungary's savagery.[44]

That savagery and the suffering it inflicted on Naples shaped Louis of Hungary's persona in Boccaccio's work, which comes to reflect his lingering anger and disgust. Over time, Boccaccio's eclogues shift their attention from the Hungarian vendetta's abstract morality to the very real destruction it entailed. By the time he wrote his sixth eclogue, probably completed around the time of Louis of Taranto's death in 1362, Boccaccio's attitudes towards the two kings Louis had wholly changed. Louis of Hungary had been transformed into a barbarian, while Louis of Taranto and, ultimately, Johanna became, as his opponents, Naples's saviours. Louis of Hungary, "savage Polyphemus," was replaced as Naples's king by Louis of Taranto, whose poetic alter ego, Alcestus, Eclogue 6 celebrates.[45] Alcestus's restoration brings an end to grief, because "the wandering shepherds and their straying flocks / are all come back to us just as before; / with joy the woods grow green and valleys echo."[46] Louis of Hungary's mission of vengeance thus becomes, in the eclogues, not a justified vendetta but a barbaric invasion overcome by Louis of Taranto, who is transformed into a righteous and ultimately victorious king, one with whose reign Johanna was associated. Indeed, evidence that Boccaccio's opinion of Johanna was changing can be found in his biography of her nurse, Filippa Catanese, in *De casibus*, where he blames Filippa, rather than Johanna, for Andrew's death.[47] Yet the Johanna of *De casibus*, like that of *Faunus*, still rules illegitimately, having usurped Andrew's throne, and still bears a distinct resemblance to the *lupa*, in her sexual voracity if not in her thirst for blood.[48] In the first redaction of *De casibus* (c. 1355–60), Johanna is reduced to a common prostitute, one for whom Filippa acted as procuress: Boccaccio tells us, "it was said that the pandering of

Filippa was responsible for putting Johanna into [Filippa's grandson] Robert's embraces."[49]

In the introduction to *De mulieribus claris*, written in 1362, Boccaccio says that he initially planned to dedicate the work to Johanna, "that radiant splendor of Italy, that unique glory not only of women but of rulers," although he ultimately dedicated it instead to Andrea Acciaiuoli.[50] Elaborating on his first choice, Boccaccio explains that it seemed appropriate to dedicate a book about women to a woman; Johanna was the best candidate because of "the brilliance of her celebrated family and forebears as well as the more recent praises her own brave spirit had newly won."[51] The act of dedicating the book to Andrea Acciaiuoli came well into the text's development and coincided with Boccaccio's renewed quest for Angevin patronage in late 1362 – a quest that may have helped inspire him to devote the final chapter (CVI), composed in 1363, to Johanna, thus framing his *opusculum* with praise of her.[52] Boccaccio extols Johanna's wisdom, strength of character, and fortitude, praising her capacity to withstand trials that were "the fault of others [alieno crimine]" and that led to her undeserved infamy [sinistram nec meritam famam]. Her successes, he writes, "would have been magnificent accomplishments for a vigorous and mighty king, much less for a woman."[53] No longer a caricature of feminine evil or sexuality, in *De mulieribus claris* Johanna has become a paragon of feminine virtue, one who very nearly, Boccaccio suggests, has transcended her femininity to become kingly. Her crown has all but transformed her sex.

Paired with the *lupa* of *Faunus* and whore of *De casibus*, this new Johanna appears incongruous. The change in attitude regarding Neapolitan affairs discernible in the eclogues at least partially explains the metamorphosis of the rabid she-wolf into a radiant queen, as does Boccaccio's hope for court patronage. More important, however, was Boccaccio's response to a shift in the balance of power at the Neapolitan court, as in Johanna's own reputation. Louis of Taranto proved a singular disappointment to observers hopeful that he would restore Naples's fortunes. Early in his reign, Petrarch, like Boccaccio an avid observer of Neapolitan events, had been cautiously optimistic. He wrote to Niccolò Acciaiuoli – now Naples's Grand Seneschal – in February 1352 that, when Hungarian forces finally left Naples, "the worst side ha[d] been conquered … and the best side ha[d] triumphed."[54] Flattering Acciaiuoli, Petrarch hoped that, as Louis's adviser, he would restore "desired tranquility to the ravished kingdom and to the people."[55] Petrarch was destined to be disappointed. Louis was an unpopular and ineffective king, particularly when faced with the depredations of mercenary bands that marauded through the kingdom with near impunity. Thus, the exchange of one Louis for another did nothing to end Naples's misery. In April 1352, Petrarch lamented to Stefano Colonna that Naples "within and without its boundaries … is shaken and belabored."[56]

Growing disappointment with Louis led Petrarch and many of his contemporaries to revise their opinions of Johanna, marginalized and (gossip whispered) abused by Louis. Both commentators previously hostile to Johanna and those who supported her describe her as humiliated and slighted by her second husband. As far away as Avignon, where he was incarcerated, Rupescissa heard rumours of the estrangement between the royal couple, noting that Louis's hardness "wearied" Johanna, who avoided his bed.[57] It is likely that Rupescissa was responding to alarm at the papal court, where Clement VI, who charged Louis in a letter of September 1349 with treating Johanna more like a servant than like a wife, began to fear for Johanna's safety.[58] In late 1349, Clement and Johanna unsuccessfully attempted to remove Louis from power, only to be thwarted by Louis and Acciaiuoli, who forced Johanna to accept the secondary role of queen consort until Louis's death twelve years later. In the meantime, as Naples battled unrest and economic hardship, contemporaries began to hope for Johanna's return to power. Matteo Villani reports that the Neapolitans rioted in 1355, shouting, "Long live the queen, and death to her council!" in an indictment of Louis and his supporters for their de facto imprisonment of the queen.[59] Commentators bemoaned Louis's shortcomings, which included indolence and lasciviousness. Petrarch lamented Louis's tarnished reputation to Acciaiuoli shortly after the king's death in 1362, while Villani described him as "fickle, timid and cowardly [mobile fu, timido e pauroso]" and given to dissipating himself with wine and women.[60] The destruction of Louis's reputation contributed to the rehabilitation of Johanna's. In the early 1360s, Petrarch wrote to Count Hugo of San Severino, praising Johanna for her "generous, noble, and beneficent mind" and saying that he was "sorry for her … and … for Italy." Disillusioned with Louis, Petrarch pledged his support for Johanna as Robert's blood descendant ["sanguine ortum erit"] – a pledge that spoke to a new conviction that it was Johanna and not Louis who was the rightful ruler of Naples.[61]

Boccaccio's estimation of Louis and consequent re-estimation of Johanna followed a similar parabolic trajectory to that of Petrarch.

He portrayed Louis as Alcestus, which he claimed derived from *alce*, meaning "virtue," and *estus*, meaning "fervour."[62] In his sixth eclogue, *Alcestus*, Louis, even at the end of a chequered career, is represented as Naples's champion. Yet, not long after he extolled Louis's virtue – perhaps in order to flatter Acciaiuoli – Boccaccio criticized him in *De mulieribus claris*. He praises Johanna, among other things, for withstanding "the grim ways of her husbands [coniugum austeros mores]," who, along with "flight, exile, and papal threats" [fugam exiliumque ... pontificum minas], are listed among the burdens she has borne.[63] Given that *coniugum* is plural, this must refer to Andrew and to Louis, both of whom Boccaccio had earlier praised. Here, Boccaccio turns the tables, portraying Johanna as the victim and eventual victor in struggles against her husbands.

Scholars generally interpret Boccaccio's treatment of Johanna in *De mulieribus claris*, added at an intermediate stage in the text's development, as a bid for Angevin court patronage.[64] Certainly, the discrepancies between Boccaccio's textual Johannas may be linked to the decisive break between Boccaccio and Acciaiuoli, which occurred in 1362 when Boccaccio, finally invited back to Naples, felt slighted and mistreated while a guest in Acciaiuoli's home.[65] It may also represent Boccaccio's efforts to secure Johanna's favour after Louis's death. Yet Johanna's evolution within Boccaccio's work reflects more than a desire for court patronage, as it also mirrors a change in her public persona and the political realities of the time when she resumed independent rule. Boccaccio's disappointment with Louis of Hungary had tempered his disapproval of Johanna; disappointment with Louis of Taranto utterly transformed her. Immediately after Andrew's brutal death, no one would have praised Johanna for having tolerated him, but by 1363, Boccaccio plausibly could list both Andrew and Louis among her burdens. Their conflicts with her form a background of martyrdom and forbearance that facilitates her metamorphosis into the magnificent queen of *De mulieribus claris*, who stands in stark opposition to the monstrous caricature of femininity Boccaccio describes in Eclogue 3.

Boccaccio's transformative description hinges on a sense of Johanna as both victim and survivor. Her virtue in *De mulieribus claris* lies primarily in having overcome the assaults of adverse fortune ["fortune sevientis insultus"]; her virtue is the feminine virtue of endurance and patience.[66] Boccaccio's characterization of Johanna echoes common contemporary understandings of her relationship to Louis of Taranto.

Matteo Villani, earlier among Johanna's most impassioned detractors,[67] described Johanna with sympathy in ruminating on Louis's death:

> He was a lord of little weight and less authority ... To the queen he gave little honour ... As though she were a common woman and in great insult to the crown, he beat her often, and in that which was her own, he did not let her do either for herself or for others what honour required.[68]

Significantly, Villani elides Johanna and the Neapolitan crown, anticipating contemporary reconsideration of Johanna as a sovereign queen. Johanna's marginalization thus transformed her, prompting Florentine commentators such as Petrarch and Villani, like Boccaccio, to identify her as Naples's true ruler, one who now embodied the virtues of femininity and queenship instead of their evils.

For Boccaccio, Johanna had become a living Griselda, an abused wife whose marginalization and vulnerability paradoxically rendered her reign more palatable. Temporal distance from Andrew of Hungary's death and comparison of Johanna to unpopular opponents had served to amend her reputation. Boccaccio entered the renewed conversation about Johanna's queenship and character after Louis of Taranto's death, as she resumed independent rule of Naples, and immortalized her in *De mulieribus claris* not as an adulteress and viricide but as a virtuous queen whose misfortunes had been of others' making and whose "lofty and indomitable spirit [erecto invictoque ... animo]" made her the equal of any king.[69] Boccaccio describes her trials in the face of war and civil strife, and he exonerates her of all responsibility for them, depicting her as the epitome of queenly perfection. The restoration of kingship had failed, but Johanna – her claims by blood to the throne now recognized – emerges as a new saviour, her resilience demonstrating her right to rule.

As in the eclogues, Boccaccio's consideration of Johanna in *De mulieribus claris* revolves around her femininity – indeed, she is given pride of place precisely because she *is* a woman. In contrast to the *lupa* of the eclogues, however, the queen of *De mulieribus claris* embodies all of the virtues possible for a woman – although Boccaccio admittedly praises her most of all for the ways in which she has managed to surpass her femininity. Naples, Boccaccio reminds us, "is a mighty realm of the sort not usually ruled by women [quod cum permaximum sit dominium nec id sit a mulieribus possideri consuetum]," and it is remarkable that Johanna's "spirit is equal to its government [sufficit illi ad imperium animus]."[70] Not only is she equal to it – it is her birthright. While, in the eclogues and in *De casibus*, Boccaccio argued that Andrew was Naples's rightful ruler, he argues in *De mulieribus claris* that Johanna was Robert's designated heir and that Robert's choice was wise, because Johanna inherited her ancestors' shining character ["pelucidam adhuc avorum indolem servat"]. Johanna's regal character and spirit make her an ideal queen. Whereas the *lupa* was marked by her sexual hunger, the queen of *De mulieribus claris* "has ... curbed the leading men and princes of the kingdom and reformed their dissolute ways [insignes viros Regnique proceres tanta frenavit modestia et eorum mores solutos retraxit in melius]," earning even more respect than that formerly shown to kings – an implicit comment on the dissolution of Louis of Taranto's court.[71] The catalogue of virtues ascribed to Johanna as glorious regnant queen comes directly from the Mirror for Princes tradition: she is wise, generous, patient, and grateful for loyal service. Yet, perhaps most importantly, she also demonstrates the cardinal feminine virtue of suffering patiently and valiantly. Thus, she is living proof of the feasibility of regnant queenship.

Boccaccio was a skilled rhetorician, and it would be dangerous to interpret his revised portrayal of Johanna as merely an uncomplicated manifestation of a change of heart. His reevaluation of her may be indicative of his quest for patronage in a transformed political climate, but it also reflects a change in the terms of the discussion of both Johanna and regnant queenship. His manipulation of Johanna's image was part and parcel of his participation in contemporary discussion of Naples and of queenship, a vital component in a conversation in which he, Matteo Villani, and Petrarch all took part. Nonetheless, his voice was a significant one, and his portrayal of Johanna as a majestic queen and legitimate sovereign was important for her reputation, which he and his contemporaries – particularly fellow Florentines – helped to create. Boccaccio felt it appropriate to celebrate Johanna and to celebrate her as a woman, and his statements about her unjustified ill repute mirror broader trends. At the same time, his incorporation of her into the frame of *De mulieribus claris* as an exemplar of feminine and queenly virtue represents a decisive intervention in politics that reinforces Boccaccio's ties to the Angevin court and Naples itself.

Boccaccio's textual reevaluation of Johanna was lasting, surviving his decision in 1371 to decline a position at the Angevin court. Determining how Boccaccio ultimately judged Johanna is tricky. In his autograph manuscript of *De mulieribus claris*, which dates to between 1370 and 1373, Boccaccio preserves his praise of Johanna and dedication to Andrea Acciaiuoli, despite having declined Johanna's invitation to court.[72] Significantly, around the same time, in the revision of *De casibus* that he dedicated to his friend Mainardo Cavalcanti in 1373, Boccaccio excised the characterization of Johanna as a whore for whom Filippa Catanese pandered.[73] Yet his second redaction of *De casibus* preserves the account of Andrew's murder that describes Andrew as Naples's rightful king and describes Louis of Hungary's outrage with Johanna and her accomplices ["Ludovicus Hungarie rex egre ferens Andream fratrem suum adeo inigne a Iohanna et complicibus suis tractari"].[74] That Boccaccio simultaneously preserved and codified two different assessments of Johanna – so that he portrayed her both as Robert's true heir and as the usurper of Andrew's sovereignty – is perplexing. Vittorio Zaccaria has suggested that Boccaccio's 1373/4 redaction of *De casibus* omitted gossipy, salacious discussion of Johanna while preserving his real impression of the events around Andrew's death because Boccaccio no longer needed his work to be accepted at the Neapolitan court.[75] There is, however, compelling evidence that Johanna or someone close to her owned a manuscript of the 1373/4 redaction of *De casibus* (Vatican City, BAV, Ottoboniano Lat. 2145), suggesting that Boccaccio's discussion of Andrew's murder and Filippa's part in it were not as controversial at court as one might expect.[76] Boccaccio had certainly committed to a revised assessment of Johanna as a legitimate and virtuous queen, which must have endeared him to Johanna and her supporters. Andrew might once have been intended for Naples's throne, but after his death, Johanna had become the rightful sovereign of Boccaccio's Naples.

The vicissitudes of Boccaccio's treatments of Johanna present the reader with ambiguity and confusion. Charting Johanna's textual development in Boccaccio's work reveals his evolving sense of Neapolitan politics. It also reveals the extent to which Boccaccio's own identity as political commentator evolved and underwent constant renegotiation. In his guise as poet-cum-political pundit, he constructed and reconstructed Johanna to respond to shifting political exigencies, cultural developments, and his interpretation of history. Boccaccio's Johanna was never simply a portrait of a flesh-and-blood woman. She mirrors his own shifts in allegiance. She represents the debate about Naples's fate and about regnant queenship, and she represents the complexities of fourteenth-century Italian political culture. She is Boccaccio's link to Naples and the Angevin court. In shaping her reputation, Boccaccio inserted himself into political dialogue and exercised one of the greatest powers that he, as poet, could claim – that of determining and defining the legacy of those in power, including Johanna. Boccaccio's Johanna was, as a result, first and foremost a reactive construction, given literary form in response to his understanding of her larger cultural role and symbolism. Yet the textual Johanna that Boccaccio created also took an active part in a larger late medieval conversation about the abilities and nature of women, inspiring Christine de Pizan's *Book of the City of Ladies*, and helping to define how history has remembered the historical Johanna.

NOTES

1 Naples's Angevin monarchy relied heavily on Florentine banks, and Florentines dominated Naples's professional class. Boccaccio's father, Boccaccino di Chellino, worked for the Bardi in Naples and brought Boccaccio to the city to be trained in his profession. Florence's substantial investment in Naples and political ties kept the two cities closely linked throughout Boccaccio's life. On the influence of Florentine culture in Naples, see Charmaine Lee, "Boccaccio's Neapolitan Letter and Multilingualism in Angevin Naples," *Mediaevalia* 34 (2013): 7–21. On the economic ties between Florence and Naples, see David Abulafia, "Southern Italy and the Florentine Economy, 1267–1370," *Economic History Review* 34 (1981): 377–88, and Vittore Branca, *Boccaccio: The Man and His Works*, trans. Richard Monges (New York: New York University Press, 1976), esp. 19–55. On Boccaccio's time in Naples and its impact on his work – particularly his engagement with Neapolitan culture and his exposure to the French romances favoured by the Angevin court – see (most recently) *Boccaccio angioino. Materiali per la storia culturale di Napoli nel Trecento*, ed. Giancarlo Alfano, Teresa d'Urso, and Alessandra Perricciolі Saggese (Brussels: Peter Lang, 2012).

2 Indeed, as Virginia Brown has demonstrated, one of Boccaccio's surviving autographs, and one that reveals vital information about his early literary formation, was written over a Beneventan liturgical text that Brown argues "contains a gradual that may be the oldest mass book of Neapolitan origin presently known" – providing palpable evidence of the importance of his Neapolitan sojourn to Boccaccio's development. See "Boccaccio in Naples: The Beneventan Liturgical Palimpsest of the Laurentian Autographs (MSS. 29.8 and 33.31)," *Italia medioevale e umanistica* 34 (1991): 41–126; 43.

3 On Boccaccio's literary education and his friendships with fellow Florentines, see Jason Houston's chapter in this volume. The best recent

work on Acciaiuoli's career, including his fraught relationship with Boccaccio, is Francesco Paolo Tocco, *Niccolò Acciaiuoli: vita e politica in Italia alla metà del XIV secolo* (Rome: Nella Sede Dell'Istituto Palazzo Borromini, 2001), esp. 13–25. See also Branca, *Boccaccio: The Man and His Works*, 19–35.

4 Medieval Neapolitans claimed Virgil as their own; a tomb in the Piedigrotta district said to belong to Virgil was an important attraction during Boccaccio's time in the city.

5 Victoria Kirkham, *Fabulous Vernacular: Boccaccio's "Filocolo" and the Art of Medieval Fiction* (Ann Arbor: University of Michigan Press, 2001), 68.

6 See *Amorosa visione* 49 et passim, as well as multiple passages in *De Casibus*, *Filocolo*, *Genealogia*, *Fiammetta*, and *Buccolicum carmen*. Cf. Branca, *Boccaccio: The Man and His Works*, 25.

7 Johanna appears in most of the major chronicles of the period, as well as in the works of authors as diverse in their interests and allegiances as Francesco Petrarch, Birgitta of Sweden, Catherine of Siena, Christine de Pizan, and Francesc Eiximenis, among others.

8 This has been most recently noted and argued by Giancarlo Alfano, "In forma di libro: Boccaccio e la politica degli autori," in *Boccaccio angioino*, 15–29; 17.

9 Kirkham, *Fabulous Vernacular*, 68

10 Boccaccio's return to Florence apparently caused him great sorrow, leading him to write to Niccolò Acciaiuoli in late August 1341 about his "dolente anima" for being in Florence "contra piacere," in the hope that his increasingly influential friend could secure him an invitation to return to Naples. See Epistle 5 in *Epistole e Lettere*, ed. and trans. Ginetta Auzzas, in *Tutte le Opere di Giovanni Boccaccio*, ed. Vittore Branca, vol. 5, pt. 1 (Milan: Mondadori, 1992), 542–3. Boccaccio would continue to seek Acciaiuoli's favour and patronage as a means to return to Naples into the early 1360s, when their friendship suffered an irreparable rupture. Johanna herself subsequently offered him a place at court in 1371, which he declined. Cf. Branca, *Boccaccio: The Man and His Works*, 56–8, 169, as well as the chapters by Houston and Todd Boli in this volume.

11 *Amorosa visione* 42.13–42.15, in *Tutte le opere*, ed. Vittore Branca, vol. 3 (Milan: Mondadori, 1974), 126: "una giovinetta / dell' alto nome di Calavra ornata, / di Carlo figlia gaia e leggiadretta."

12 Johanna was the elder daughter of Robert's son and heir, Charles of Calabria, who died suddenly in 1328. Charles's death left Robert without a direct male descendant and made Johanna his heir. Her rights to the throne were contested almost immediately, despite Robert's determination to have them recognized. Many contemporary commentators argued that the

throne should revert to the line of Robert's eldest brother, Charles Martel (1271–1295), who had predeceased their father, Charles II. Charles Martel's son, Charles Robert or Carobert (1288–1342), had inherited the Hungarian throne via his mother, while Robert had inherited that of Naples. Charles of Calabria's death prompted the Hungarian royals to press the claims of Carobert's oldest son, the future King Louis of Hungary (1326–1382), arguing that he, the eldest male of the senior branch of the family, should succeed Robert (whose own succession the Hungarians viewed as illegitimate). In an effort to soothe Hungarian anger and keep the peace, Robert, with the support of Pope John XXII, negotiated a marriage alliance between the two kingdoms, marrying Johanna to Louis's younger brother, Andrew of Hungary (1328–1345) while promising Johanna's sister, Maria, to Louis himself (a marriage that never took place). Many people – including the Hungarian royal family – interpreted the marriage between Johanna and Andrew as intended to elevate Andrew to the Neapolitan throne, thus restoring just succession. To complicate matters even further, Robert's younger brothers, Philip, Prince of Taranto (1278–1331) and John of Gravina, Duke of Durazzo (1294–1336), each had three sons, all of whom were resident in Naples. Robert's brothers, particularly Philip, strenuously protested Johanna's designation as Robert's heir. On the struggle between Robert and his brothers over Johanna's right to the throne, see Émile G. Léonard, *Histoire de Jeanne 1re, Reine de Naples, Comtesse de Provence (1343–1382)*, 3 vols. (Monaco: Imprimerie de Monaco, 1932–6), esp. vol. 2, *La Jeunesse de la Reine Jeanne, Comtesse de Provence* (1932), 62–6.

13 On Johanna's reputation, see Elizabeth Casteen, "Sex and Politics in Naples: The Regnant Queenship of Johanna I, 1343–1382," *Journal of the Historical Society* 11 (2011): 183–210, and *From She-Wolf to Martyr: The Reign and Disputed Reputation of Johanna I of Naples* (Ithaca: Cornell University Press, 2015).

14 On Andrew's murder, see Léonard, *Histoire de Jeanne 1re*, vol. 1, esp. 464–73, and Casteen, *From She-Wolf to Martyr*, ch. 1. The closest thing to an official account of the murder can be found in letters sent by Johanna to Florence and Siena on 22 September and a papal pronouncement against the perpetrators published in February 1346; numerous and differing reports of the crime appear in letters and chronicles from the period. Johanna and Andrew struggled for power between the time of Robert's death and Andrew's murder, while factionalism divided the Neapolitan court. Johanna, who asserted her rights as Robert's sole heir, refused to allow Andrew to be crowned and given the title of king. Meanwhile, Andrew

and his supporters, both in Naples and in Avignon, asserted his right, as Johanna's husband and as a male of the senior Angevin line, to rule in her stead. The factionalism was intensified by the competition between the sons of Robert of Anjou's two younger brothers for power and influence. Clement VI, Naples's papal suzerain, initially supported Johanna's claims to power against Andrew's. Over time, however, he grew increasingly sympathetic to Andrew and determined to see him given the regal title and a limited, proscribed role in government. By February of 1344, Clement began to press for Andrew to be crowned in a joint coronation with Johanna, although he stated that only Johanna should swear the official oath of fealty to the papacy. See Reg. Vat. 137, nos. DCLSSII, DCSSIII–DCLXXV, DCLXXVI, fol. 185r in *Clement VI (1342–1352): Lettres closes, patentes et curiales publiees ou analysees d'après les registres du Vatican*, ed. Eugène Déprez (Paris: E. de Boccard, 1958), fasc., p. 317, items 643, 644, 645. That March, Clement began to extend Andrew public recognition as Johanna's titular equal, and by April, he began to seek to involve Andrew more directly in administrative affairs. Throughout, however, Clement continued to insist on Johanna's sole right to be Naples's sovereign. Relations between the queen and pontiff began to decline precipitously in early 1345, as Johanna alienated Neapolitan territory through gifts to her supporters. By 10 June 1345, when he wrote a letter to Johanna demanding that Andrew be crowned, anointed, and given an administrative role, Clement determined that Andrew's kingship should be more than symbolic (Reg. Vat. 139, fol. 31v, no. 94, in *Clement VI*, fasc. 3, p. 9, item 1774). That September, Clement sent a papal legate to Naples to perform a double coronation, although he continued to argue that Andrew should only be given an active but limited role in government as Johanna's consort.

15 Petrarch, *Fam.* 6.5: "aut virili morte alia, ut hominum manibus interfectus, non ferarum dentibus atque unguibus laceratus videretur." Francesco Petrarca, *Le Familiari*, critical edition, ed. Vittorio Rossi (Florence: Sansoni, 1968). Translation from Francesco Petrarch, *Rerum familiarium libri, I–VIII*, trans. Aldo S. Bernardo (Albany: State University of New York Press), 320.

16 Letters from the dowager queen Elisabeth of Poland and King Louis of Hungary to Clement VI insisting on Johanna's guilt are reproduced in Léonard, *Histoire de Jeanne 1re*, vol. 2, docs. XXV, XXVI, XXIX, XXX, XXXIX, and XL, 426–45. Writing to Elisabeth of Poland on 17 August 1346, Clement protested against the charge that Johanna was complicit in Andrew's death and begged Elisabeth to leave matters of justice to the

Holy See. See Ex Reg. orig. An. V. secr. ep. 255, Item MLXXXIII, in *Vetera Monumenta Historica Hungariam Sacram Illustrantia maximam partem nondum edita ex tabulariis Vaticanis deprompta collecta ac serie chronologica disposita. t. 1, ab Honorio PP. III. usque ad Clementem PP. VI*, ed. August Theiner (Rome: Typis Vaticanis, 1859), 716–17.

17 John of Winterthur, *Die Chronik Johanns von Winterthur*, ed. Friedrich Baethgen, *Monumenta Germaniae Historica, Scriptores rerum germanicarum*, new series, vol. 3 (Berlin: Weidmann, 1924), 260.

18 Rupescissa discusses Andrew's murder in his *Liber secretorum eventuum* (1349), *De oneribus orbis* (1354), and *Liber ostensor* (1356). See John of Rupescissa, *Liber secretorum eventuum, Edition critique, traduction et introduction historique*, ed. Robert E. Lerner and Christine Morerod-Fattebert (Fribourg: Éditions Fribourg-Suisse, 1994) and *Liber ostensor quod adesse festinant tempora*, ed. André Vauchez et al. (Rome: École Française de Rome, 2005). Léonard, *Histoire de Jeanne 1re*, 478, cites Rupescissa's *De oneribus orbis*, Tours MS 520. Mark Dupuy comments on Rupescissa's exoneration of Johanna in his article "The Unwilling Prophet and the New Maccabees: John de Roquetaillade and the Valois in the Fourteenth Century," *Florilegium* 17 (2000): 229–50; 246n33.

19 Giovanni da Bazzano, *Chronicon Mutinense* [AA. 1188–1363]; *Racolta degli Storici Italiani del cinquecento al millecinquecento, ordinata da L.A. Muratori. Rerum Italicarum Scriptores*, ed. Tommaso Casini, new ed., vol. 15, pt. 4 (Bologna: N. Zanichelli, 1917–19), 142.

20 Giovanni Villani, *Cronica di Giovanni Villani a miglior lezione ridotta*, vol. 4, ed. Gherardi Dragomanni (Florence: S. Coen, 1845), 87.

21 "Gentile of Foligno Interprets the Prophecy 'Woe to the World,' with an Edition and English Translation," ed. Matthias Kaup and Robert E. Lerner, in *Traditio – Studies in Ancient and Medieval History, Thought, and Religion*, vol. 56 (New York, 2001), 202–3; 203n20; Guilio Bertoni and Emilio Paolo Vicini, eds., *Chronicon Estense, cum additamentis usque ad annum 1478*, ed. L.A. Muratori, in *Raccolta degli Storici Italiani del cinquecento al millecinquecento. Rerum Italicarum Scriptores*, new ed., vol. 15, pt. 3 (Città di Castello: S. Lapi, 1908), 131 et passim.

22 See Epistle 6 in *Epistole*, 544–9, at 546. On Boccaccio's short-lived support for the Hungarian vendetta, see also Giovanni Boccaccio, *Eclogues*, trans. and ed. Janet Levarie Smarr (New York: Garland, 1987), Smarr's notes at n21, and Cornelia C. Coulter, "Boccaccio and the Cassinese Manuscripts of the Laurentian Library," *Classical Philology* 43 (October 1948), 217–30; 219, as well as Branca, *Boccaccio: The Man and His Works*, 73–4, and David Lummus, "The Changing Landscape of the Self," in *Boccaccio: A Critical Guide to the*

Complete Works, ed. Victoria Kirkham, Michael Sherberg, and Janet Levarie Smarr (Chicago: University of Chicago Press, 2014), 155–72; 157.

23 See Boccaccio's *Faunus*, line 84: "gravidam tum forte lupam rabieque" (Boccaccio, *Eclogues*, 27). Some scholars have argued that the pregnant she-wolf may not be Johanna at all, but rather Sancia de' Cabanni, the daughter of Johanna's nurse, Filippa Catanese, and a member of the queen's inner circle. Sancia was rumoured to have been Andrew's mistress and was one of several alleged conspirators tortured and executed in 1347 for his murder. Some chronicle accounts describe Sancia as the maker of a silken sash that was used to strangle her former lover. While this explanation is plausible, Boccaccio's support of the Hungarian cause, his insinuation that Johanna was a whore in *De casibus* (see below), and his reference to other reports implicating "lions" and "ferocious beasts" (lines 89–90) suggest that he was thinking of the queen and not of another member of her court. See *Eclogues*, 212, note on line 84, and Léonard, *Histoire de Jeanne 1re*, vol. 1, 472.

24 *Faunus*, in *Eclogues*, 27, lines 80–91: "Fleverunt montes Argum, flevere dolentes / et satyri faunique leves, et flevit Apollo. / Ast moriens silvas iuveni commisit Alexi, / qui cautus modicum dum armamenta per arva trahebat, / in gravidam tum forte lupam rabieque tremendam / incidit impavidus nullo cum lumine lustrum / ingrediens; cuius surgens sevissima guctur / dentibus invasit, potuit neque ab inde revelli / donec et occulto spirasset tramite vita. / Hoc fertur. Plerique volunt quod silva leones / nutriat hec dirasque feras, quibus ipse severus / occurrens venans mortem suscepit Adonis."

25 On Thomas Aquinas's treatment of sexual sin, humanity, and bestiality, see Mark D. Jorday, "Homosexuality, *Luxuria*, and Textual Abuse," in *Constructing Medieval Sexuality*, ed. Karma Lochrie, Peggy McCracken, and James A. Schultz (Minneapolis: University of Minnesota Press, 1997), 24–39; 30.

26 Ovid, "Libido," from *The Art of Love* 1.269–343.

27 Joan Cadden, *Meanings of Sex Difference in the Middle Ages: Medicine, Science, and Culture* (Cambridge: Cambridge University Press, 1993), 149.

28 Edward Muir, *Mad Blood Stirring: Vendetta in Renaissance Italy* (Baltimore: Johns Hopkins University Press, 1998), 149.

29 On Messalina's characterization as a *lupa*, see Juvenal's *Satire* 6, lines 114–35, and Pliny the Elder's discussion of her engagement in prostitution (*Natural History*, Chapter 83). The *Golden Legend*'s Spanish queen Lupa is not explicitly described as a prostitute, but she is an evil queen who stubbornly, irrationally opposes the Apostle James. Possibly, Johanna's characterization as a *lupa* is also an evocation of the papacy's protection

of her. As Cristina Mazzoni notes, the sculpted *lupa* today known as the Capitoline she-wolf was not understood as metonymic for the city of Rome in the Middle Ages. It was housed not on the Capitoline but in a niche at the Lateran Palace and was commonly deployed as a symbol of papal justice. See *She-Wolf: The Story of a Roman Icon* (Cambridge: Cambridge University Press, 2010), 46–9. I doubt whether this is Boccaccio's referent, however; the papacy had been resident not at the Lateran but in Avignon during his entire lifetime, and it is far more likely that his *lupa* recalls the she-wolf of Dante's *Inferno* and plays on the dual valence of *lupa* qua prostitute and *lupa* qua wild animal that would have been readily comprehensible to a medieval audience.

30 On the dating and composition of *De casibus*, see Vittorio Zaccaria, "Introduzione" and "Nota al Testo," in Giovanni Boccaccio, *De casibus virorum illustrium*, ed. Pier Giorgio Ricci and Vittorio Zaccaria, *Tutte le opere*, ed. Vittore Branca, vol. 9 (Milan: Mondadori, 1983), xv–lii, esp. xix–xx, and 875–904. See also Vittorio Zaccaria, "Le due redazioni del '*De casibus*,'" *Studi sul Boccaccio* 10 (1977–8): 1–26.

31 *De casibus* 9.1, "De Brunichilde, Francorum regina," in *De casibus*, ed. Ricci and Zaccaria, 748–60; 750.

32 Walter of Brienne, the so-called Duke of Athens, was Robert of Anjou's nephew. Filippa Catanese was the wife of Raimondo de' Cabanni, Naples's seneschal, and Johanna's nurse. She was also among the alleged conspirators executed for Andrew's murder; Boccaccio describes her gruesome death in *De casibus*.

33 Giovanni Boccaccio, *Eclogues*, Eclogue 3.27–8, lines 101–2: "lupam captare petit flavosque leones / ut penas tribuat meritis."

34 *Faunus*, lines 103–7, in *Eclogues*, 28: "Nunquid vidisse furentem / stat menti ferro nuper venabula acuto / gestantem manibus, multos et retia post hunc / portantes humeris, ira rabieque fermentes, / hac olim transire via silvaque per omnem?"

35 Among those who described Louis's easy victory and the "exultant spirits" (to quote Domenica da Gravina) of the Neapolitans were the Neapolitan chronicler Domenico da Gravina, the author of the *Chronicon Estense*, and Marco Battagli of Rimini. See Domenico da Gravina, *Chronicon de Rebus in Apulia Gestis*, ed. L.A. Muratori, in *Rerum Italicarum Scriptores, Raccolta degli Storici Italiani dal cinquecento al millecinquecento*, new ed., vol. 12, pt. 3 (Città di Castello: S. Lapi, 1903), 36; *Chronicon Estense*, 157, and Marco Battagli da Rimini, *Marcha di Marco Battagli da Rimini* [AA. 1212–1354], ed. Aldo Francesco Massèra, in *Rerum Italicarum Scriptores*, new ed., vol. 16, pt. 3 (Città di Castello: S. Lapi, 1912), 53.

36 Branca, *Boccaccio: The Man and His Works*, 74–5.

37 Matteo Villani, *Cronica a miglior lezione ridotta, coll'aiuto de' testi a penna*, 6 vols. (Rome: Multigrafica, 1980), 1.10–11; Giovanni da Bazzano, *Chronicon Mutinense*, 145.

38 Ibid., 76.

39 Eclogue 4. *Dorus*, lines 65–75, in *Eclogues*, 35: "iusta rabie succensus et ira, / irruit ut torrens qui hybernis imbribus auctus / monte cadit celso et rumoribus omnia complens / hec arbusta rapit, quatit hec, ruit atque superbus / in rupes et saxa trahens ingentia volvit. / Nec sevo lacerasse prius sub vindice sontes, / nec post innocui Paphi fedasse cruore / sydereos vultus, truncum et iecisse cadaver, / aut vinclis gratos nyphis onerasse puellos, / immitis potuere gravem minuisse fuorem." On Boccaccio's renaming of Louis of Hungary, see *Eclogues*, 216n62.

40 His ascription of innocence to the Neapolitan princes already represents a marked change in Boccaccio's perception of events in Naples. Presumably, the princes were the "tawny lions" of Eclogue 3, to whose capture by Tityrus the poem looks forward as the execution of justice. Apparently, between writing his third and fourth eclogues, Boccaccio became convinced that they were not responsible for Andrew's death.

41 Eclogue 4. *Dorus*, in *Eclogues*, lines 76–83.

42 Eclogue 5. "Silva Cadens," in *Eclogues*, 46–7, lines 78–80: "Delapse quercus, grandes cecidere cupressus, / Esculus exarsit summissis undique flammis, / Pinus nulla sedet ..."

43 Ibid., 48, line 115: "Omne decus periit, luctusque laborque supersunt."

44 Ibid., lines 113–14: "Alcestus trepidans abiit, tremebunda Liquoris / in dubium liquit silvas evecta per altum."

45 Smarr translates Boccaccio's introduction to the poem in her notes on p. 219. He explains that the king is called Alcestus because "near the end of his life" he adopted the manners of "an excellent and virtuous king."

46 Eclogue 6. *Alcestus*, lines 12–15 in *Eclogues*, 52, 53: "Parcendum lacrimis, nam trux Poliphemus abivit. / Alcestus rediit nobis, rediere vagantes / Pastores oviumque greges, rediere priores, / Letitiaque virent silve vallesque resultant ..."

47 Boccaccio, *De casibus virorum illustrium* 9.26.

48 Ibid. Boccaccio argues in his biography of Filippa that Robert designated Andrew his heir.

49 Boccaccio, *De casibus virorum illustrium*, ed. Louis Brewer Hall (Gainesville: Scholars' Facsimiles & Reprints, 1962), 238: "diceret lenocinio Philippae Ioannam in amplexus devenisse Roberti." Cf. *De casibus*, ed. Ricci and Zaccaria, "Appendici," 1107. Translation from

Giovanni Boccaccio, *The Fates of Illustrious Men*, trans. Louis Brewer Hall (New York: Ungar, 1965), 238. If one accepts the traditional dating of *Il corbaccio* to c. 1355, the characterization of Johanna in the original redaction of *De casibus* amplifies Boccaccio's comment that Florentine gossips speculate about whether Johanna recently slept with her husband. See Giovanni Boccaccio, *The corbaccio, or the Labyrinth of Love*, ed. and trans. Anthony K. Cassell (Binghamton: State University of New York Press, 1993), 51. Michaela Paasche Grudin argues that *Il corbaccio* should be seen in the context of Florence's 1375–8 war with the papacy and, thus, dated to the mid-1370s. See her "Making War on the Widow: Boccaccio's *Il corbaccio* and Florentine Liberty," *Viator* 38 (2007): 127–57. Grudin's argument is intriguing, but it begs the question of why Boccaccio should resexualize Johanna at a period during which he praised her virtue and suppressed his earlier characterization of her as sexually licentious. See below.

50 Giovanni Boccaccio, *De mulieribus claris* [Famous Women], ed. and trans. Virginia Brown (Cambridge, MA: Harvard University Press, 2001), 3: "ytalicum iubar illud prefulgidum ac singularis, non tantum feminarum, sed regum glorie, Iohanna, serenissima Ierusalem et Sicilie regina" (2).

51 Ibid.: "tam inclite prosapie et avorum fulgoribus, quam novis a se forti pectore quesitis laudibus."

52 On Boccaccio's dedications, see Rhiannon Daniels's essay in this collection. On his efforts to secure Angevin patronage in 1362, see the essays by Houston and Boli. On Boccaccio's appeal to Andrea and Johanna and its significance for Christine de Pizan, see Lori Walters's essay in this collection. On the stages of the redaction of *De mulieribus claris*, see Vittorio Zaccaria, "Le fasi redazionali de '*De mulieribus claris*,'" *Studi sul Boccaccio* 1 (1963): 253–332, esp. 293, 323–4.

53 *De mulieribus claris* 106, in *On Famous Women*, 472/3: "edepol grandia, nedum mulieri, sed robusto ac prevalido regi."

54 Petrarch, *Fam.* 12.2 in *Rerum familiarium libri*, vol. 2, 132; *Le Familiari*, vol. 3, 6: "in presenti certamine victa parte deterrima … optima pars triumphat."

55 Ibid.; *Le Familiari*, vol. 3, 6: "gloriossimus Siculi Regis vertex negatos honores invito livore suscipiet; ereptam restituens regno pacem, tranquillitatem populis exoptatam."

56 *Fam.* 15.7 in *Rerum familiarium libri*, vol. 3, 268; *Le Familiari*, vol. 3, 150: "totque regno Sicilie … intus enim atque extra concutitur ac laborat."

57 John of Rupescissa, *Liber ostensor* 150, §IV.28.

58 Reg. Vat. 143, fol. 68v, reproduced in *Clement VI*, vol. 3, item 4245, 20–2; 21: "restrinxisti ut non uxor, sed velut ancilla."

59 Matteo Villani, *Cronica* V.88: "tutti di concordia presono l'arme, e feciono armare tutti i forestieri mercatanti e artefici ch'erano nella città, e levarono il romore, gridando: Viva la reina, e muoia il suo consiglio."

60 *Fam.* 23.18 in *Le Familiari*, vol. 4, p. 203; Matteo Villani, *Cronica* 10.100, 10.16.

61 *Fam.* 23.17 in *Rerum familiarium libri*, vol. 4, 296; *Le Familiari*, vol. 4, 200: "illustrem ... reginam ... generosum illum serenumque ac benificum animum ... Doleo propter ipsam ... denique propter Italiam." The date and provenance of *Fam.* XXIII, 17 are unknown; cf. Ernest H. Wilkins, *Petrarch's Correspondence* (Padua, 1960), 87. In most collections, it comes immediately before a letter to Niccolò Acciaiuoli that discusses Louis's death as a recent event. The letter deals mostly with "the court dogs" and references Johanna's struggles within the court. This discussion and Petrarch's statement of sympathy and support for Johanna make most sense if one assumes Louis still to be living.

62 *Eclogues*, 219.

63 *De mulieribus claris* 471/2.

64 See, for instance, Zaccaria, "Le fasi redazionali di *De mulieribus claris*," esp. 293, and, more recently, Margaret Ann Franklin, *Boccaccio's Heroines: Power and Virtue in Renaissance Society* (Aldershot: Ashgate, 2006), 23–30.

65 Boccaccio's grievances against Acciaiuoli, whom he would attack as Midas in Eclogue 8, are described in his long letter to Francesco Nelli. See Epistle 13 in *Epistole*, 596–629. See also Houston's chapter in this collection on the end of Boccaccio's friendship with Acciaiuoli.

66 *De mulieribus claris* 470/2.

67 Villani initially saw Johanna as an inept and illegitimate sovereign, and he attributed the chaos in Naples and the evil of Andrew's death to her succession, writing that both were due to the fact that Johanna was "both master and lady of her Baron, who, as her husband, should have been her lord. And in this was Solomon's dictum verified, which says that if the wife has primacy she becomes contrary to her husband. Johanna, finding herself with dominion, and having immature, vain counsel, showed little honour to her husband and ruled and governed all of the Regno with great wantonness [e maestra, e donna del suo Barone, il quale come marito dovea essere suo signore. E cosi verificando la parola di Salomone: il quale disse, sela moglie haurà il primato diventerà contraria al suo marito. La detta Giovanna vedendosi nel dominio, havendo giovanile, e vano consiglio, rendeva poco honore al suo marito, e reggeva, e governava tutto il Regno con piu lasciva]." Translation mine. See Matteo Villani, *Cronica* 1.9.

68 Matteo Villani, *Cronica* 10.100: "Signore fu di poca gravezza e meno d'autorità … Alla reina facea poco onore … molte volte come una vil femina in grande vituperio della corona la battea, e di quello ch'ero suo non le lasciava fare nè a sè nè ad altrui il debito onore." Translation mine.

69 *De mulieribus claris* 472/3: "erecto invictoque … animo" (472).

70 Ibid.

71 Ibid.

72 See Zaccaria, "Le fasi redazionali de *De mulieribus claris*," 24. I am grateful to Lori Walters for drawing my attention to Boccaccio's reaffirmation of Johanna's virtuous queenship in the autograph manuscript.

73 Zaccaria, "Le due redazioni del '*De casibus*,'" 6, 17–18.

74 *De casibus* 9.26. Cf. Zaccaria, "Le due redazioni del '*De casibus*,'" 18.

75 Ibid.

76 Francesco Sabatini, *Napoli Angioina. Cultura e Società* (Naples: Edizioni Scientifici Italiane, 1975), 114. See also Guyda Armstrong, *The English Boccaccio: A History in Books* (Toronto: University of Toronto Press, 2013), 31, 44, and Guyda Armstrong, Rhiannon Daniels, and Stephen J. Milner, "Boccaccio as Cultural Mediator," in *The Cambridge Companion to Boccaccio*, ed. Guyda Armstrong, Rhiannon Daniels, and Stephen J. Milner (Cambridge: Cambridge University Press, 2015), 17. The manuscript, known conventionally as Manuscript "Vo," is richly illuminated and decorated. The argument that it belonged to Johanna or someone close to her rests on visual evidence in its decorative program: the French fleur-de-lys appears often in the borders, while two folios (10r and 82v) include the motto "Viva Madama" in their border decoration.

10 Christine Transforms Boccaccio: Gendered Authorship in the *De mulieribus claris* and the *Cité des dames*

KEVIN BROWNLEE

Giovanni Boccaccio is one of the master figures cited consistently by the French writer Christine de Pizan in her key works, in a systematic plan by which she legitimizes herself as a woman author.[1] The fact that both are Italian by origin makes their relationship especially important in this connection, and Boccaccio is the only forbear Christine uses both for his Latin and his vernacular work. It is in the *Cité des dames*[2] of 1405 that both of these processes reach their culmination. The citation of Boccaccio by name in the *Cité* is thus a key feature of the work, where it appears twenty-eight times in nineteen different chapters, more than that of any other author cited in the text. An overwhelming majority of these instances, twenty-four cases in sixteen chapters of the *Cité*, involve Boccaccio's Latin *De mulieribus claris* (1361–2),[3] which is thus explicitly presented as the essential source behind both Part 1 and Part 2 of Christine's tripartite text.[4] In this essay, I propose to examine how Christine de Pizan explicitly cites Boccaccio as *auctor* and thus the ways in which she rewrites the Boccaccian Latin text in terms of her own vernacular work in praise of women.[5] At issue is the creation of an authorial program involving Boccaccio by Christine-Author in the *Cité*.[6]

It is only at an important structural moment in the *Cité* (that does not exist as such in the *De mulieribus*) that Boccaccio is cited for the first time, by Raison. At the end of 1.26, Raison declares, "At this point the foundations of our City are complete: we must now build the high wall to surround it (62) [Mais dés or sont achevez les fondemens de nostre Cité. Or nous convient lever sus la haulte muraille tout a l'environ]." The key architectural metaphor (building a city is like writing a book) of Christine-Author's book is thus made into an important part of her use of Boccaccio's text.[7] In the very next chapter (1.27), Raison explains (in answer to Christine-Protagonist's questions) that the examples of female learning that she is about to give will demonstrate in more general terms that women's minds are equal to men's minds. Again, a key ideological feature of Christine's work (but not of Boccaccio's) is to be illustrated.

In the three chapters that immediately follow in the *Cité* we find the first explicit citations of Boccaccio in Christine's work. Each of these three chapters contains three repetitions of the Italian author's name, the only time that this occurs in the entire first two parts of the *Cité*. In addition, this naming is linked both to text of the *De mulieribus claris* and to the status of the three learned women being presented in the *Cité*. These latter thus function together as a coherent group in the *Cité* but not in the *De mulieribus*, as the recasting of the order from Boccaccio's text demonstrates. Christine gives us the set of Cornificia, Proba, and Sappho, thus combining contiguously in the *Cité*, as 1.28, 1.29, and 1.30, Chapters 86, 97, and 47 of the *De mulieribus claris*. Again, a key difference between the structure of the two texts functions to emphasize the very different status that each of them has: the first written in the third person by a man for a male audience in Latin, the second written in the first person by a woman for a female audience in the vernacular.

In *Cité* 1.28, Cornificia is presented as a "souveraine poete" whose works were prized by "Saint Gregoire."[8] The very first mention of Boccaccio's name immediately follows, as he is initially identified by his national origin (shared by Christine) and by his poetic calling (shared both by Cornificia the example and by Christine the author). At the same time, the *De mulieribus claris* is clearly identified by the word "book" ("livre"), the same term used for the works of Cornificia, who composed "tres nottables livres (154) [very famous books (64)]" that lived long after her, which is of course what Christine-Author is also doing. Here is the first citation of Boccaccio by name, as he is presented as affirming Cornifica's long-lived poetic production: "de laquelle chose Bocace l'Ytalien, qui fu grant poete, en louant ceste femme, dist en son livre (154) [Boccaccio the Italian, who was a great poet, discusses this fact in praising this woman in his book]" (64). As if to make sure that we get the point about the identity of the book by Boccaccio, a direct quotation of the *De mulieribus claris* (the first of a number of these, here from Chapter 86.3) immediately follows: "O tres grant honneur a femme qui a laissié toute œuvre feminine et a appliquié et donné son engin aux estudes des tres haulx clercs [O most great honour for a woman who abandoned all feminine activities and applied and devoted her mind to the study of the greatest scholars]" (65).[9] Boccaccio's name is mentioned again (for the second time) immediately after this as a guarantee of the truth of what Raison is telling Christine-Protagonist: Raison's words are presented as true because they are written in the *De mulieribus claris*: "Dist oultre cellui Bocace certiffiant le propos que je te disoie (154) [This Boccaccio goes on to certify what I have been telling you]" (65). We get an expanded version of what the *De mulierbus* says immediately thereafter, concerning women who are not like Cornificia, given as a proof of the equality between men's and women's minds, in such a way as to make Christine-Protagonist's earlier renunciation of her female identity (in 1.1.2) appear to be seriously misconceived. Again, a key issue is raised that is simply missing from the Boccaccian third-person text, which is visibly based on reading rather than on "experience" (as is the case for the *Cité*).

The third mention of the Italian author's name in this chapter comes in the final sentence: "Fille chiere, peus veoir comment cellui aucteur Bocace tesmongne ce que je t'ay dit et comment il loe et appreuve science en femme (156) [My dear daughter, you can see how this author Boccaccio testifies to what I have told you and how he praises and approves learning in women]" (65). The truth of the discourse of the *De mulieribus* is again definitively attested to, while the prestigious title "author" is added to that (earlier used) of "poet." Finally, Raison claims knowledge of the (here, unproblematic) intentionality of Boccaccio (in the *De mulierbus*), in a way that strengthens the feminist calling of both Christine-Protagonist and Christine-Author.

The very next chapter, *Cité* 1.29, treats Proba (from *De mulieribus* 97) as a female Christian Virgil figure, who used the latter's poetic works to make a complete Virgilian Bible, thus fusing pagan and Christian learning. Boccaccio is again given the title of "author" and the *De mulieribus claris* is presented as a source of truth, tied to a direct quotation: "Laquelle chose, pour certain, ce dit l'aucteur Bocace, n'est pas sanz admiracion que si haulte consideracion peust entrer en cervel de femme; mais moult fu chose plus merveilleuse, ce dist il, de mettre a execucion (156) [Which in itself, as the author Boccaccio noted, is not just admirable, that such a noble idea should come into a woman's brain, but it is even more marvellous, as he says, that she could actually execute it]" (65–6.)[10]

When Boccaccio's name is mentioned a second time in *Cité* 1.29, the *De mulieribus claris* (Ch. 97) is again referred to as a source of truth in such a way as to present Proba's knowledge of the Bible in extremely positive terms: "Pour lesquelles choses, ce dit meismes Bocace, grant recommendacion et louange affiert a ceste femme (158) [For these reasons, as Boccaccio himself states, this woman merits great recognition and praise]" (66); cf. *De mulieribus* 97.6). The third and final citation of Boccaccio's name here comes in the last sentence, setting up a key parallel with the preceding chapter (which of course does not exist in the Latin/French "original"). At the same time, it affirms the truth-value of Christine de Pizan's presentation of the *De mulieribus claris*. In addition, this final citation presupposes Raison's knowledge of the Italian author's intentionality in a way that overlaps with the requirements of the internal audience composed of Christine-Protagonist and the external audience composed of women in general: "De laquelle femme et de ses choses, ce dit Bocace, doivent ester en grant plaisir d'ouyr aux femmes (158) [Boccaccio observes that it should be a great pleasure for women to hear about her [Proba] and about her accomplishments]" (66–7).

The final chapter in the initial set of three that introduce Christine's explicit use of Boccaccio's name in the *Cité* (1.30) functions as an important culmination. It is devoted to Sappho, described in the rubric as "la tres soubtille femme, poete et philosophe" and presented as the author of numerous "livres et dictiez (158) [books and poems]" (67), and thus as a direct ancestor of Christine-Author. There are, once again, three instances of the citation of Boccaccio's name in this chapter. First, he is explicitly presented (for the second time) as a "poet" who describes Sappho directly (in *De mulieribus* 48): "de laquelle dit le poete Bocace par douceur de poetique lengage [in] ces belles paroles (158) [Concerning her, Boccaccio the poet has offered these fair words couched in the sweetness of poetic language]" (67). What follows is (yet again) a direct quotation of a passage from the *De mulieribus claris*,[11] making a total of three times that this happens, in each of the first of three instances of Boccaccio's name being used in each of these three key chapters of the *Cité*. The quoted passage here affirms Sappho's link with Mount Parnassus, the Muses, Apollo, and the Castelian spring, as well as explaining these in allegorical terms. Second, Boccaccio's treatment of Sappho in the *De mulieribus claris* is both adduced as definitive evidence and interpreted allegorically, especially in terms of the survival of her works to the present moment: "par ces choses que Bocace dist d'elle, doit estre entendu la profondeur de son entendement et les livres qu'elle fist de si profondes sciences que les sentences en sont fortes a savoir et entendre meismes aux hommes de grant engin et estude, selon le tesmoing des anciens et jusques aujourd'huy (160) [By these things that Boccaccio says of her it should be inferred that the profundity of both her understanding and her learned books can only be known and understood by men of great perception and learning, according to the testimony of the ancients, right up to the present time]" (67). Finally we get the third mention of Boccaccio's name in the last sentence devoted to Sappho in *Cité* 1.30, which thus forms an important parallel with Christine-Author's treatment of Cornificia and Proba in the preceding two chapters, suggesting that these three contiguous chapters of the *Cité* (1.28, 29, 30; unlike their sources in the *De mulieribus*, 86, 97, 47) form a single structural unit. Here, it is Boccaccio's authority with regard to the high value of the poet's reward that is stressed: "desquieulx, ce dit Bocace, les honneurs des dyademes et des couronnes des roys et les mitres des evesques ne sont point greigneurs (160) [than which, Boccaccio says, the honours of the diadems and the crowns of kings and the mitres of bishops are not greater]" (68).[12]

There are four additional uses of Boccaccio's name as author of the *De mulieribus claris* in Part 1 of the *Cité*, which serve (collectively) to nuance Christine's reading of her Italian model text.

In 1.34, Raison treats Minerva, and cites Boccaccio's work (*De mulieribus* 6) to valorize the euhemeristic explanation of this great inventor's divine origin: "car de tant que moins [the foolish people of that time] congnoisçoient sa venue, si que dit Bocace, de tant leur fu plus merveillable le grant savoir d'elle sur toutes femmes en son temps (170) [for the less they [the foolish people of that time] knew about her ancestry, as Boccaccio says, the more marvellous her great knowledge seemed to them]" (73).

In 1.37, Raison answers Christine-Protagonist's question about male ingratitude by praising woman's creative mind (supported by God's favour) as demonstrated by the invention of the Latin alphabet by Carmenta, which she has first explained in *Cité* 1.33. These two treatments of Carmenta's invention are presented as true by virtue of being guaranteed by the words of *De mulieribus* 27: "Et que on ne die que ycestes choses te die par faveur: ce sont les propres paroles de Bocace, desquelles la verité est nottoire et magnifeste (180) [And let no one say that I am telling you these things just to be pleasant: they are Boccaccio's own words, and their truth is well known and evident]" (78). Thus, Raison here uses Boccaccio's text to guarantee the truth of two different but related passages in the *Cité*, 1.37 and 1.33. The earlier chapter is a simple rewriting of *De mulieribus claris* 27, while the later one serves as a key part of the progressive, advancing dialogue between Christine-Protagonist and Raison.

In 1.39, the relation between the *Cité* and the *De mulieribus* becomes even more nuanced, more complicated. Patricia Phillippy sees Christine de Pizan as here marking her "ideological independence" from Boccaccio.[13] I certainly agree, but at the same time, I see a more intricate process at work: part of a program. The character Raison begins this chapter by praising the inventions of Arachne, which led to advances in human civilization. Then Raison engages in a negative consideration of the simple pleasures of the lost Golden Age, which leads her to a critical reading of Boccaccio's text: "Nonobstant que aucuns auteurs et mesmement cellui poete Bocace, qui raconte ces dites choses, ont dit que le siecle valoit mieulx quant la gent ne vivoient fors de cenelles et de glans, et ne vestoient ne mais les piaulx des bestes que il n'a fait depuis que les choses a plus delicativement vivre leur ont esté enseignees (186) [Nevertheless, several authors, and even the poet Boccaccio who relates those things, have argued that this world was better off when people lived only from haws and acorns and wore nothing more than animal skins than it is now that they have been taught to live in greater refinement]" (82). Raison ends by citing God and Jesus Christ himself against Boccaccio's stated belief in the Golden Age expressed in the Ceres chapter, *De mulieribus* 5. The earlier Ceres chapter of *Cité* (1.35) thus shows that Raison does not simply accept what Boccaccio states, but rather advances her own pro-female perspective in which Ceres is portrayed as an inventive woman who leads the human world along the pathway of progress. In 1.38, Ceres, Isis, and Minerva are all praised by Raison in this context, and Christine-Protagonist moves to advance her own opposition to both clerkly and chivalric criticism of women, while praising Carmenta's enlightened teaching. In 1.39, Raison presents Arachne as a positive female example, thus implicitly criticizing Boccaccio's negative portrayal of her in *De mulieribus* 18. What ultimately emerges from Raison's "disagreement" with Boccaccio in *Cité* 1.41 thus makes explicit what has already been demonstrated implicitly in the *Cité* by its changing of both the content and the order of Boccaccio's individual stories. Thus, the differences between the overall perspective of the *Cité* and the *De mulieribus* are explicitly stressed. At the same time, of course, Christine-Author requires Boccaccio to be established in her work as an *aucteur*, a key predecessor, and she uses him as such.

The last instance of the explicit naming of Boccaccio in Book 1 of the *Cité* is a particularly striking example of this key Boccaccian doubleness, building on everything that has gone before. In 1.41, Raison announces that she will list to Christine-Protagonist the names of women who learned both the speculative sciences and the manual arts, focusing on painting. The opening example is Thamaris "just as it is written ... who possessed such great subtlety in the art and science of painting that during her lifetime she was the most supreme painter known. As Boccaccio says she was the daughter of Mycon (84) [si qu'il est escript ... qui fu de si grant soubtiveté en l'art et science de painterie qu'elle en estoit a son vivant la souveraine qu'on sceust. Ceste, ce dist Bocace, fu fille de Nicon]" (188–90). The reference is to *De mulieribus* 56, which serves to valorize Raison's version of the story as being taken from this written, Boccaccian source. There then follows in the same chapter Raison's presentation of the Greek painter Irene and the Roman painter Marcia, coming from *De mulieribus* 59 and 66. Finally, Christine-Protagonist completes the *translatio* movement here by citing the key female example of Anastasia, the manuscript miniaturist from contemporary Paris who illustrated the works of Christine-Author. Her first-person authority (overlapping with that of Christine the writer) is explicitly based on experience, which is thus (within a single chapter of the *Cité*) combined with the written authority of Boccaccio's text evoked by Raison.[14]

In Part 2 of the *Cité*, it is Droitture who articulates Boccaccio's name (and reads his text), taking over from Raison the role of speaker to (and interlocutor with) Christine-Protagonist. The program begins in *Cité* 2.2, with the detailed introduction of the sibyl Erythrea, and is devoted to that woman, picking up on *De mulieribus* 21. Here the *translatio* used to describe her prophecy moves from Greek to Roman to Christian truth, with this latter being presented in the greatest detail from the Incarnation to the Last Judgment, so that Erythrea "semble avoir dit et composé en brief les misters de la foy crestienne ... [C]e dit Bocace – et tous autres sages aucteurs qui d'elle ont escript le tiennent – est a croire qu'elle fu tres amee de Dieu et qu'elle soit a honnourer plus que autre femme après les saintes crestiennes de Paradis (224) [seemed to have expressed and composed in brief the mysteries of the Christian faith ... As Boccaccio says – and all the other wise authors who have written about her concur – it is believed that she was much beloved of God and that, after the holy Christian women of Paradise, she ought to be honoured more than any other woman]" (102).

Several key features of this explicitly identified quotation from Boccaccio's text at the beginning of Part 2 of the *Cité* need to be emphasized here. First, there is Boccaccio's essential importance to Christine-Author as a written model. In writing the *Cité*, she will become what he is, because of his works, namely a poet and an author. At the same time, he is particularly important to her as an Italian writer. In addition, Boccaccio as an "aucteur" is grouped with other writers who are "wise" in praising Erythrea. Second, the key differences with the Boccaccian text in question are established: Christine's new order and her new perspective establish a new meaning for all of the Boccaccian examples of "famous women" that are used in the *Cité* – one which will be relevant for the first-person female figure of Christine-Author herself. Third, in this context Erythrea's Christian dimension assumes an even more important status: not only are her Christian prophecies treated more elaborately in Christine's text, but she is not explicitly identified there as a pagan. We are already in the realm of the *Cité*'s key inclusion (unlike the *De mulieribus*) of Christian women, especially in the all-important Part 3. Fourthly, Erythrea, in Chapter 2.2 of the *Cité*, initiates a series of exemplary tales of women prophets that extends through Chapter 2.6.

The next sequence in which Boccaccio's name figures explicitly in *Cité* Part 2 involves Chapters 14 through 19. By way of introduction, it is in Chapter 12 that Droitture announces that it is time to people the houses of the City, which are now completely constructed. The first category of inhabitants (announced at the conclusion of 2.13) involves the exemplary wives who have shown love and loyalty towards their husbands, beginning with Hypsicratea, wife of King Mithridates. She is treated in *Cité* 2.14, which tells how her devotion to her husband in his war with the Romans led her to be transformed from a soft, courtly lady into a vigorous, armed knight. This treatment is characterized by a quotation from Chapter 78 of the *De mulieribus* that follows the explicit naming of its author: "O!, ce dit Bocace, qui ceste histoire racompte, que est ce que amours ne face faire quant celle qui avoit accoustumé a vivre tant delicativement, coucher souef et toutes choses avoir a son aise est maintenant demenee par sa franche voulenté comme se fust homme dur et fort par montaignes et par valees nuit et jour gisant es desers et es forés, souventesfois sur la terre en paour des ennemis, avironnee de toutes pars de bestes et de serpens (258) [Boccaccio, who tells this story, could only wonder, 'What can love not achieve if such a woman, accustomed to living so delicately and to sleeping in soft beds, and to having everything at her ease, can drive herself by sheer force of will, as though she were a tough and strong man, through mountains and valleys, day and night, sleeping in deserts and forests, often on the ground, afraid of enemies, and surrounded on all side by wild animals and snakes?']" (121–2).

In the following chapter, *Cité* 2.15, the Roman Empress Triaria is presented as equally devoted to her spouse, as an explicit quotation in the final sentence makes clear: "Si demonstra bien, ce dit Bocace, la grant amour qu'elle avoit a son mari, en approuvant le lien de mariage que autres veulent tant reprocher (260) [Thus she demonstrated well the great love which she had for her husband, as Boccaccio notes, approving the marriage bond which others want to attack]" (123). The written text of *De mulieribus* 96 is made to serve as a guarantee of the truth of what is told in the *Cité*.

In *Cité* 2.16, the same kind of uxorial love characterizes Artemisia, who built for her husband, King Mausolus, a tomb so magnificent that since that moment all royal tombs have been called "Mausoleums," as Boccaccio in *De mulieribus* 57 testifies ["ce dit Bocace," 264].

A kind of culmination of this evocation of the text of the *De mulierbus* through its author's name occurs in *Cité* 2.17, which treats the love of Argia for her husband, Polynices of Thebes. This the only time in Part 2 of the *Cité* that Boccaccio is cited by name not once, but three times. A long direct quotation that purports to be from *De mulierbus* 29 portrays Argia's search for the cadaver of her beloved husband after he has been killed and left on the battlefield, beginning with the following words: "Et de ce qu'elle fist dist Bocace en ceste maniere (264) [Boccaccio tells of what she did in the following manner]" (125). The direct quotation is interrupted by a second citation of the author's name: "Et qui est chose plus merveilleuse, ce dit Bocace, ne doubta point le edit et commandement du roy Creonce (266) ['What is even more marvellous,' says Boccaccio, 'is that she did not fear the edict or the commandment of King Creon']" (125). Her discovery of her dead but beloved husband ends her search, and provokes a third mention of Boccaccio's name, linked to a direct quotation which duplicates the exact words of the French translation of *De mulierbus* 29: "O!, ce dit Bocace, merveilleuse amour et tres ardent desir et affection de femme!" (266)[15] ['Oh,' says Boccaccio, 'what marvellous love and most ardent desire and affection in a woman']" (126).

In *Cité* 2.19, we see the young and nubile Julia (daughter of Julius Caesar), who is described as married to and loving in a very serious way a husband who is much older than she is: "Ceste dame fu femme de Pompee le grant conquereur, lequel, ce dit Bocace, en vainquant les roys ... estoit ja enviellis et debrisez (270) [This lady was the wife of

Pompey, the great conqueror, who, according to Boccaccio, while he conquered kings … was already aged and in decline]" (128). It is the text of *De mulierbus* 81 that is referenced here.

After the onomostic Boccaccian citations in *Cité* 2.14–19 (in which we see wives who show exemplary love for their husbands), a rather different use of Christine's model Italian author is at issue in 2.36, the next time that her text explicitly cites Boccaccio by name.

In 2.36, Droitture responds to the questions of Christine-Protagonist by citing a series of examples of women who profited from learning the knowledge held by their fathers. The first of these is Hortensia, daughter of the Roman rhetorician and orator Quintus Hortensius, who "lui fist apprendre letres et estudier en la dicte science de rhetorique, dont elle tant en apprist que [elle ressemble] … ce dit Bocace, a son pere Ortencius par engine et vive memoire (314) [had her learn letters and study the science of rhetoric, which she mastered so thoroughly that she resembled, as Boccaccio says, her father Hortensius … in wit and lively memory]" (153). It is important to note that in this chapter we move immediately from Hortensia in ancient Rome to Bologna in modern Italy with the example of Novella (who learns from her professor father), then to Christine herself as a young girl, who learns from her father in Paris. From the Boccaccian example, we have moved to Christine herself as an intellectual (even as a writer).[16]

Beginning with the next chapter of the *Cité* (2.37), Droitture presents to Christine-Protagonist a series of exemplary biblical and Greek women who are chaste, and in 2.43 we are shown Antonia (the widow of Drusus Tiberius), a Roman pagan woman who is both chaste and beautiful, while remaining a virtuous widow. "Si fist de ceste chose plus a louer, ce dist Bocace, que en telle continence estoit demourant a court entre les jouvenceaulx bien parez et assesmez, jolis et amoureux, vivans oysivement (326) [What makes her continence all the more praiseworthy, as Boccaccio says, was that she resided in a court with many smart and gracious young men, handsome and eager for love, and living in leisure]" (159–60). Significantly, this the only time in Part 2 of the *Cité* that Boccaccio (the writer of *De mulieribus* 89, on which this chapter in Christine's book is based) is also referred to as "author": "laquelle chose, dit l'aucteur, est digne d'estre eslevee en louange (326) [Such a deed, says our author, is worthy of being highly praised]" (160). At this point, Antonia as a chaste widow resembles the historical Christine de Pizan, while Boccaccio as an authorial presence resembles the writing Christine de Pizan, author of the present book.[17]

The last explicit reference to Boccaccio in the *Cité* occurs as Part 2 is nearing its close, as Christine-Protagonist is increasingly visible and Christine-Author is ready to speak in her own voice in the final chapter, 2.69. In the opening sentence of Chapter 63 of Part 2, the authority of Boccaccio (in *De mulieribus* 77) is doubled by that of Valerius Maximus:[18] "Bocace raconte, et pareillement le dit Valere, que Claudine, qui fu noble dame de Romme, moult se delictoit en beaulx vestemens et curieux et en joliz atours (410) [Boccaccio tells, and Valerius reports the same thing, that Claudia Quinta, a noble lady of Rome, took great pleasure in vain and beautiful clothing and in pretty ornaments]" (205). The story proves simply that Claudia's chastity is more important than her being pretty and dressing in elegant clothes. At the same time, Droitture differentiates between the lies of paganism and the truth of Christianity, looking forward to Part 3 of the *Cité*, which treats Christian women as its culmination, unlike the *De mulieribus*.

This final citation of Boccaccio's *De mulieribus claris* thus works in tandem with the four preceding citations of Boccaccio's *Decameron*[19] to present the Italian author as simultaneously Latin and vernacular. As such he is revealed both as an authoritative model for Christine-author and as a male third-person master who must be placed into a female, first-person voice.[20] We can thus see that Christine de Pizan's strategic use of the programmatic citation of Boccaccio by name in the *Cité des dames* is strikingly successful. At the same time, her work's visible transformation and "incorporation" of the subject matter of the *De mulieribus claris* functions in a powerful, new feminist context.

NOTES

1 The other authors utilized in this context are Ovid, Boethius, Jean de Meun, Dante, and Christine herself. See Kevin Brownlee, "Le projet 'autobiographique' de Christine de Pizan: Histoires et fables du moi," in *Au Champ des escriptures*, ed. Eric Hicks et al. (Paris: Champion, 2000), 5–24.

2 For the French text of the *Cité des dames*, I use E. Jeffrey Richards in *Christine de Pizan. La Città delle Dame*, ed. Patrizia Caraffi (Milan: Luni, 1997), which includes an excellent Italian translation by Caraffi. The English translation (variously modified) is that of Richards (New York: Persea, 1982). Also quite useful for me is Maureen Cheney Curnow's thesis, "The Livre de la Cité des dames of Christine de Pisan: A Critical Edition," 2 vols. (Vanderbilt University, 1975).

3 For the Latin text I employ the definitive edition of Vittorio Zaccaria (including an Italian translation) in *Tutte le opere di Giovanni Boccaccio*, ed. Vittore Branca, vol. 10 (Milan: Mondadori, 1967; 2nd ed. 1970). The English translation is that of Virginia Brown in her dual-language *Famous Women* (Cambridge: I Tatti, 2001), which uses Zaccaria for the Latin. Both Zaccaria and Brown employ the manuscript copied in c. 1371, Florence, Biblioteca Medicea Laurenziana 90 sup. 98 (Gaddi 593), which represents the final stage of the text and is written in Boccaccio's own hand. It is important here to stress that Christine also used the French translation of the *De mulieribus claris*, the anonymous *Des Cleres et Nobles Femmes* done in 1401 (sometimes attributed to Laurent de Premierfait). Thus, in my opinion, both the Latin and the French texts of Boccaccio's work must be consulted in this connection. Curnow, for her part, argues ("The Livre de la Cité des dames of Christine de Pisan," 141–7) that Christine in the *Cité* uses the French translation to the exclusion of Boccaccio's Latin, and takes as her base MS Musée Condé 856 (done in the third quarter of the fifteenth century). I use BN f.fr. 12420 (completed at the end of 1402 and most likely in the possession of Philippe le Hardi, Duke of Burgundy, by the beginning of 1403), which is the basis of the partial edition (Chapters 1–52) of Jeanne Baroin and Josiane Haffen, *Boccace. "Des Cleres et Nobles Femmes"* (Paris: Les Belles Lettres, 1993).

4 For Part 3 of the *Cité* as an aggressive and positive response to Boccaccio's *De mulieribus*, see Kevin Brownlee, "Martyrdom and the Female Voice: Saint Christine in the *Cité des dames*," in *Images of Sainthood in Medieval Europe*, ed. Renate Blumenfeld-Kosinski and Timea Szell (Ithaca: Cornell University Press, 1991), 115–35; and Maureen Quilligan, *The Allegory of Female Authority: Christine de Pizan's "Cité des dames"* (Ithaca: Cornell University Press, 1991), esp. 192–6.

5 For the relationship between the two works, see in particular Giovanna Angeli, "Encore sur Boccace et Christine de Pizan: remarques sur le *De Mulieribus claris* et le *Livre de la cite des dames* ('Plourer, parler, filer mist Dieu en femme' 1.10)," *Le Moyen Français* 50 (2002): 115–25; Dulce Maria González Doreste and Francisca Del Mar Plaza Picón, "A propos de la compilation: Du *De claris mulieribus* de Boccace à *Le Livre de la Cité des dames* de Christine de Pisan," *Le Moyen Français* 51–3 (2002–3): 327–37; A. Jeanroy, "Boccace et Christine de Pisan: le *De claris mulieribus principale* source du *Livre de la cité des dames*," *Romania* 43 (1922): 93–105; Patricia Phillippy, "Establishing Authority: Boccaccio's *De Claris Mulieribus* and Christine de Pizan's *Le Livre de la Cité des dames*," *Romanic Review* 77 (1986): 167–93; and Maureen Quilligan, "Translating Dismemberment: Boccaccio and Christine," *Studi sul Boccaccio* 20 (1991–2): 253–66.

6 In this context, it is important to note Christine's overall program of the creation of a genealogy of key authorial models in Latin, French, and Italian with herself as the culmination, investigated in the article cited in note 1.

7 For the *Cité*'s architectural metaphor, see Patrizia Caraffi, "Il Libro e la Città: metafore architettoniche e costruzione di una genealogia femminile," in *Christine de Pizan. Una città per sé*, ed. Patrizia Caraffi (Rome: Carocci, 2003) 19–31; and Bernard Ribémont, "De l'architecture à l'écriture: Christine de Pizan et la *Cité des dames*," in *La Ville: du réel à l'imaginaire*, ed. J.-M. Pastré (Rouen: Publications de l'Université de Rouen, 1991), 27–35.

8 Both the Latin and the French give "Saint Jerome" rather than Saint Gregory, as Curnow remarks ("The Livre de la Cité des dames of Christine de Pisan," 1068).

9 See Zaccaria in Brown, *Famous Women*, 86, 354–5: "O femineum decus neglexisse muliebria et studiis maximorum vatum applicuisse ingenium! [How glorious it is for a woman to scorn womanish concerns and to turn her mind to the study of the great poets!]."

10 See Zaccaria in Brown, *Famous Women*, 412–13: "Non equidem admiratione caret tam sublimem considerationem muliebre subintrasse cerebrum, sed longe mirabile fuit executioni mandasse [Certainly it is no small wonder that such a lofty design made its way into a woman's mind, but more wondrous still is the fact of its fulfillment]."

11 Curnow correctly identifies the passage as coming from the French translation, *Des Cleres et Nobles Femmes*, rather than from Boccaccio's Latin original (see "The Livre de la Cité des dames of Christine de Pisan," 1069, as well as 145–6). See also *Boccace. "Des Cleres et Nobles Femmes*," ed. Baroin and Haffen, 156. The explicit allegorical "decoding" is particularly important in this respect. Christine de Pizan in the *Cité* thus treats the French translation and the Latin original as if they both constituted Boccaccio's "original" text (on which her visibly "corrective" transformation is based).

12 It is important to note here that Christine has Raison (without mentioning Boccaccio by name) add a short paragraph on Leontium to the end of this chapter, which presents her as a "femme de grant science" and a "philosopher" who challenged Theophrastus. With this greatly abbreviated and carefully selective presentation of *De mulieribus* 60, an alternative reading of the Boccaccian work is explicitly suggested here. Christine-Author simply eliminates Boccaccio's detailed presentation of the Greek woman as also an unseemly whore. See also Curnow, "The Livre de la Cité des dames of Christine de Pisan," 1069.

13 See Phillippy, "Establishing Authority," 168. See also Rosalind Brown-Grant, "Décadence ou progrès? Christine de Pizan, Boccace et la question de 'l'âge d'or,'" *Revue des langues romans* 92 (1988): 295–306.

14 "Et ce scay je par experience, car pour moy mesmes a ouvré d'aucunes choses qui sont tenues singulieres entre les vignetes des autres grans ouvriers (192) [And I know this from experience, for she has executed several things for me, which stand out among the ornamental borders of the great masters]" (85).

15 See *"De Cleres et Nobles Femmes,"* ed. Baroin and Haffen, 92, lines 71–2; and also note 11 above.

16 Cf. the astute analysis of Didier Lechat in *"Dire par fiction": Métamorphoses du "je" chez Guillaume de Machaut, Jean Froissart et Christine de Pizan* (Paris: Champion, 2006), 433–5.

17 It is important to note in this context that 2.43 ends with an explicit reference to Valerius Maximus (which reinforces that of Boccaccio), in reference to the story of Sulpitia, which figures both in the *Facta et Dicta Memorabilia* (Book 2, Chapter 15) and in the *De mulieribus* (Chapter 67). See Curnow, "The Livre de la Cité des dames of Christine de Pisan," 1099. There thus seems to be an anticipation of the final reference to Boccaccio in *Cité* 2.63.

18 See Curnow ("The Livre de la Cité des dames of Christine de Pisan," 1110 and 147) for her convincing argument that Christine's source is here the French translation rather than Boccaccio's Latin text. Note 11 is relevant in this case.

19 For the significance of the *Cité*'s explicit citations of the vernacular *Decameron*, see Kevin Brownlee, "Il *Decameron* de Boccaccio e la *Cité des dames* di Christine de Pizan: Modelli e contro-modelli," *Studi sul Boccaccio* 20 (1991–2): 233–51.

20 In the words of Lechat, Christine wants at once to write "sous l'autorité de Boccace, mais aussi d'écrire *contre* Boccace" (*"Dire par fiction,"* 398).

11 Reading Like a Frenchwoman: Christine de Pizan's Treatment of Boccaccio's Johanna I and Andrea Acciaiuoli

LORI J. WALTERS

Overview

This chapter[1] focuses on the way Christine de Pizan (1365–c. 1430) modelled her promotion of France's Queen Ysabel de Bavière on Boccaccio's endorsement of Johanna I in his *De mulieribus claris*.[2] Queen Johanna (1326–1382) ruled the kingdom of Naples from 1343 to 1382 as a sovereign queen; Queen Ysabel (1370–1435) reigned alongside King Charles VI from her coronation in 1389 until his death in 1422.[3] This essay has a second focus: to determine how and why Christine takes Boccaccio's dedicatee, Andrea Acciaiuoli,[4] the Countess of Altavilla, a distinguished and apparently learned lady in Johanna's service, as a model for her own role as the queen's advisor. I argue here that one of the ways Christine actively tries to establish Queen Ysabel's permanent reputation is to create for herself an authorial persona that both conflates and surpasses the combined roles of the male poet Boccaccio and his female dedicatee, Andrea, whom he had portrayed as an influential member of the Neapolitan queen's court.

Christine symbolically puts a new, female face on her renowned Italian compatriot. She adopts the persona of an Italian-born woman who takes Boccaccio's endorsement of women further than he had, first, by speaking about gender issues in her own female voice; second, by adopting France, rather than her native Italy, as her homeland because of her belief in the superiority of its distinctive sort of monarchy. In so doing, she follows the logic of the *Monarchia* (Monarchy), the treatise on ideal world governance penned by Dante, whom she takes along as her guide on her French-styled "path of long study" to become a credible royal advisor. Christine accordingly adopts the characterization of Boccaccio as Dante's interpreter and disciple, a characterization that Boccaccio had fostered as early as the early 1350s, and which others acknowledged during his own lifetime (1313–1375) and shortly afterwards.[5]

Responding to Boccaccio's explicit invitation to his readers to correct his text,[6] Christine reworks his *De mulieribus* in accordance with its stated goal to make the names of "illustrious women glorious on the lips of humankind" (*FW*, 7). This includes making more of Boccaccio's fostering of female rule.[7] In Christine's eyes, the most logical place to find contemporary examples of Boccaccio's category of illustrious women is in France, a country whose centralizing monarchy has the greatest potential to realize Dante's monarchical ideals.

I. A Misogynistic Boccaccio?

As preface to my analysis, we have to consider Christine's extensive and largely positive use of Boccaccio, despite the condescending attitudes he frequently expresses towards women.[8] The interpretation I offer here agrees with a nuanced reading of his attitudes towards the female sex.[9] It has been long recognized that the major source for her *Livre de la cité des dames* (Book of the City of Ladies) of 1404–5 was the *De mulieribus*, Boccaccio's compendium of one hundred and six women who had made names for themselves, whether for good or for ill.[10] Composed between 1362 and 1374, it was available to her in the 1401 French translation[11] as well as in Boccaccio's original Latin.[12] Earl Jeffrey Richards, editor and English translator of the *Cité des dames*, notes: "The amazing feature of Christine's debt to Boccaccio is the extent of her borrowing and the thoroughgoing reorganization of this same material" (xlv).[13] Christine recasts the *De mulieribus* by using Boccaccio's examples, now shorn of any details unflattering to women, to argue specific points in her defence of the female sex.[14] And Christine constructs her persona as women's erudite and articulate defender by adapting many of Boccaccio's portraits of studious and virtuous women, such as Erythrea, Almathea, Carmenta, Proba, Cassandra, Cornificia, and Sappho.

What has not been duly appreciated, however, is Christine's largely positive use of Boccaccio. For example, the canonical article by Patricia A. Phillippy fails to explain why the poet makes so many explicit and respectful references to him.[15] Christine does not hesitate to cite Boccaccio by name, which was an accepted way for authors of the time to designate their esteemed forbears. Is it not extraordinary that within the space of this one single text Christine names Boccaccio twenty-eight times, a full twenty-four times in reference to the *De mulieribus*, four times in reference to the *Decameron*?[16] She does not cite another author with as much frequency, in this text or in any other. As point of comparison, in her *Livre du chemin de long estude* (Book of the Path of Long Study) of 1402–3, which was the first French recasting of the *Commedia*, Christine only twice cites the name of Dante, her foremost Italian model.[17] On the face of it, Boccaccio holds a privileged status in her eyes, a privileged status that I seek to elucidate.

Christine's only explicit criticism of the *De mulieribus* is when she takes exception to Boccaccio's praise for the time when humans lived off the land and wore nothing but animal skins. Countering him with the comment that Christ himself liked to wear brightly coloured robes (*City* 1.39.3), Christine adds that priests and royalty now routinely wear such vestments (1.40.1).[18] This, her only explicit correction of the *De mulieribus*, has nothing to do with Boccaccio's thoughts about women. When Christine cites Boccaccio's examples (1.28.1) in Dame Raison's list of women whose behaviour argues against misogyny,[19] it is by and large to show "how he praises and approves learning in women" (R65). It follows, then, that Christine's aim was not to pillory Boccaccio as a misogynist. Instead, as I shall show, she enlists her recast version of him, now purged of his backhanded compliments and condescending asides, in order to promote Queen Ysabel and herself as her advisor.

In her *Cité des dames* Christine resituates the *De mulieribus* within an early fifteenth-century Parisian milieu that was heavily influenced by the *Grandes chroniques de France* (Great Chronicles of France). In this official French history, whose adaptation from Latin sources was sponsored and most likely commissioned by Louis IX, the future Saint Louis (1214–1270, canonized in 1294), the original chronicler, a monk of Saint Denis named Primat, devotes considerable space to the contribution of queens to establishing France as the world's "most Christian" monarchy.[20] Primat refers to France as the "Church's daughter" because of her relentless and determined defence of the Christian faith and doctrine.[21] In Primat's words: "like a loyal daughter France defends her mother [Holy Church] in her every need."[22] Primat describes France using yet a second personification. She is "a lady renowned over other nations because she did not suffer at length the servitude of idolatry and incorrect belief."[23] It is because the faith is "more fervently and correctly observed" in France than elsewhere that "by his grace Our Lord gave France a prerogative and an advantage over all other lands and nations."[24] Through his use of two female personifications, Primat implies that throughout history, women, through their ardent defence of the faith, have spearheaded France's efforts to be recognized as the leader of the Christian world. If all of Primat's readers were supposed to read as France's loyal subjects, women were to do so more particularly, because of his claim that the country's standing was reflected in the queen's good name. The *dame* whose renown surpasses all others was the Virgin Mary, "notre Dame." The most visible symbol of her majesty and power was Notre Dame cathedral, located in the heart of Paris on the *île de la cité*.

The *Grandes chroniques* were well known to both Christine and Queen Ysabel. Philippe le Hardi, the powerful Duke of Burgundy, whom Christine credits with placing Ysabel on the throne,[25] had lent a copy to the queen around 1398 in order to instruct her in her royal duties.[26] That same Philippe brought these chronicles to Christine's attention when in 1404 he commissioned from her the biography (hereafter *Charles V*) of his long-deceased brother, King Charles V (1338–1380).[27] The *Grandes chroniques* were the source for all her portraits of French queens, which she combines with Boccaccio's exempla in Parts 1 and 2 of her *Cité des dames*.

Christine's striking departure from Boccaccio was to devote the entire Part 3 of her *Cité des dames* to female saints. Boccaccio had expressly excluded such women from his collection because they had been treated extensively elsewhere and because their aspirations differed from those of the classical figures that were his focus (*FW*, 13). In *City* 3.9.4 Christine identifies the source of her hagiographic exempla as the *Miroir historial*, Jean de Vignay's translation of the *Speculum historial*.[28] Louis IX had commissioned the Latin original from Vincent de Beauvais, his chaplain and close friend. By directing her advice to the reigning queen of France in her *Cité des dames*, Christine implicitly appeals to her to emulate earlier French queens, such as the wife of Philippe VI de Valois, Jeanne de Bourgogne (c. 1293–1349), who continued her sainted grandfather's tradition by commissioning the translation from Jean de Vignay.

Christine more implicitly encourages Queen Ysabel to enhance the illustrious heritage of her Valois progeny by emulating Johanna I. Boccaccio points out that Johanna was a Valois on her mother's side. Endowed with outstanding Gallic maternal bloodlines, the "self-consciously French" Angevin queen[29] provided Christine with a natural choice of royal model for Ysabel. Johanna had ruled Naples for almost four decades, no mean accomplishment for any ruler, much less for a sovereign queen reigning in those misogynistic times. Johanna's attendant Andrea, whom Boccaccio commends for having increased the Angevin character of her line through her two marriages,[30] was a fitting dynastic model for both Ysabel and Christine.

Christine seeks to improve on Boccaccio in two ways. First, she bases herself on his own examples of daughters who outdid their fathers' accomplishments. Second, she responds to Boccaccio's explicit invitation to his followers to correct his text, which she does essentially by erasing traces of his unflattering attitudes towards women. What is more, in her *Cité des dames* Christine treats Boccaccio as a valued authority. By using his examples positively, in order to reinforce points in her arguments against misogyny, Christine enlists Boccaccio, a member of Italy's prestigious "triple crown,"[31] as her ally in promoting Queen Ysabel and her female court. Christine, moreover, suggests that Ysabel, daughter of Taddea Visconti, whose first cousin and brother-in-law Gian Galeazzo Visconti had invited Christine to join his court in 1401,[32] should model herself on Johanna's reputation for Gallic-oriented Neapolitan civic virtue.

II. Queen Johanna I as a Model for the French Queen, Ysabel de Bavière

Although not a sovereign queen like Johanna, Ysabel, living in a country governed by the Salic Laws, nonetheless assumed a more active role than was usual for the times. Beginning in 1392 with the onset of the mental illness that until his death in 1422 would intermittently incapacitate her husband, King Charles VI, Ysabel had to take over the dauphin's education and guidance, as well as assume some of the king's official duties such as presiding over the royal council. These were heavy responsibilities for the inexperienced mother of twelve children, who had arrived in France at age fifteen not knowing a word of French. Ysabel and Johanna were both in the public eye more than was usual for queens at the time. Their positions of prominence elicited similar attacks on their reputation and their ability to govern. These attacks were motivated and strengthened, in large part, by the misogyny attendant upon patriarchal lineage. Ysabel and Johanna continue to be subjects of controversy. Contemporary scholars attempt to separate historical fact about them from propaganda for and against them.[33] I concentrate instead on how Christine bases her promotion of Queen Ysabel on Boccaccio's positive portrait of Johanna, arguing that she aims to make Ysabel's regency as successful as the Neapolitan sovereign's reign, as portrayed by Boccaccio in his *De mulieribus*. I base myself in large measure on Elizabeth Casteen's work on the active role Boccaccio assumed in shaping Queen Johanna's reputation.[34]

As Casteen explains, Boccaccio's unconditional praise of Johanna in his *De mulieribus* represents a change from the attitude he had expressed towards her in his third Eclogue (c. 1347–8), where his opinion conformed to the prevailing view of Johanna as the "Harlot Queen." When Johanna's second husband, Louis of Taranto, became unpopular, Boccaccio shifted blame from her to him. After she had been, in Casteen's words, "cleansed of her past reputation by suffering,"[35] she became more likeable. In his *De mulieribus* Boccaccio circumvents earlier criticism of Johanna, including his own, and in its place issues what amounts to an advertisement for a powerful woman. Christine may have found Boccaccio to be an acceptable model because he had corrected his negative evaluation of Johanna. Thus, at least on the surface, in the image she projected, which was reinforced by supporters like Boccaccio, Johanna combined the same qualities of wisdom, intelligence, and piety that Christine would later hold up as her ideal for queens as well as for kings.

Christine's keen interest in the Neapolitan queen is evident in the three direct references she makes to her in texts she composed in 1403 and 1404, the years immediately preceding her *Cité des dames*: the *Livre de la mutacion de Fortune* (Book of Fortune's Transformation, vv. 23393–418), the *Chemin de long estude* (Path of Long Study, vv. 3657–74), and *Charles V* (2, xi). Christine's description of Johanna in the *Mutacion*[36] shows her high regard for the Queen of Naples. She portrays her as being in great estate at the court of Lady Fortune, where throughout the entire world no lady was more celebrated and loved. For a long time the queen remained at the top of Fortune's Wheel. But Johanna's fortunes took a swift downswing when her long-time rival, Charles of Durazzo (1345–1386), pursued her until he took her and had her killed. In her *Chemin*, Christine, after supplying the grisly detail that Charles had Johanna smothered between two pillows (v. 3660), triumphantly proclaims that he was punished for his injustice by being mortally wounded in the chest (vv. 3662–3). She sums up Johanna's life in the following way: "ainssy fu celle trebuchiee, / Qui si haut tot esté juchiee! [thus she who had been set so high, stumbled and fell]" (vv. 23409–10).[37]

When Christine portrays Johanna as an admirable ruler who ended her days as Fortune's victim, she closely follows Boccaccio's evaluation of her leadership, as we see in his words:

> She is so patient and steadfast that she cannot be easily deflected from her righteous path. This was clearly demonstrated some time ago by the blows of hostile fortune which often struck and buffeted her fiercely from every direction. Indeed, Joanna has endured internal struggles between princes of the royal family as well as foreign wars which at time raged within the heart of her kingdom. Through the fault of others, she has had to endure flight, exile, the grim ways of her husbands. (*FW*, 471)

In her assessment of Johanna, Christine imitates the way Boccaccio in this passage subtly shifts blame from the Neapolitan queen to "the blows of hostile fortune" and "the fault of others."

An important question is why Christine would endorse and develop Boccaccio's positive evaluation of Johanna. The first reason is that the Neapolitan queen strengthened France's position in Christendom. Christine praises Johanna for adopting Louis d'Anjou, King Charles V's next oldest brother, as her heir. She does so first in *Chemin*, vv. 3665–71, which I paraphrase in English prose:

> This queen, who had not given birth to a male heir, wanted to choose as her adopted son, without any other reason than his nobility and his glorious lineage, the illustrious Duke of Anjou, called the Wise. She thus chose him and made him her heir.[38]

It is noteworthy that she refers to Louis d'Anjou as "the Wise," thus likening him to his brother, the "Wise King" Charles V, and to Johanna's grandfather, Robert the Wise.

Christine then expands on this story in the chapter she devotes to Louis d'Anjou in *Charles V* 2.11. Acting upon his brother King Charles V's dream of extending France's empire in Italy by acquiring Arles and Provence, Louis undertook a fierce war against the Queen of Naples. The two finally made peace. On 29 June 1380, Queen Johanna took the momentous step of adopting Louis as heir to her kingdom of Naples and Puglia (2.138). Louis then had to return to France to administer the regency of the underage Charles VI after Charles V's death. When Louis returned to Naples two years later, Louis and Johanna met the resistance of Charles of Durazzo, who imprisoned Johanna and had her ignominiously assassinated.

On 30 May 1382, Louis received the investiture of the kingdom of Naples from Clement VII, taking the title of king. Christine recounts that, after being crowned, Louis d'Anjou would have gone on to conquer "the Roman empire"[39] except for another inopportune turn of Fortune's wheel. He died, leaving behind him his son, King Louis II. Christine appreciates Johanna as a sovereign queen who furthered French interests by helping Charles V and Louis d'Anjou extend French control over the southern part of the Italian peninsula. Johanna gave a major boost to French imperial ambitions by designating as her heir Louis d'Anjou, Charles V's brother and uncle to Ysabel's husband, King Charles VI.

That Christine considers Ysabel to be a key facilitator of French imperial ambitions is suggested when in her presentation manuscript, London, British Library, MS Harley 4431, she addresses the queen as "lofty lady of the line of emperors of worthy memory."[40] The alliance between France and Italy formed by King Charles VI (b. 3 December 1368) and his next younger brother (by a little more than three years), Louis d'Orléans (b. 13 March 1372), repeated the efforts in this regard made by King Charles V (b. 21 January 1338) and *his* younger brother by a year and a half, another Louis, Louis d'Anjou (b. 23 July 1339). Christine hints at this analogy by following her portrait of Louis d'Anjou in the *Chemin* with that of Louis d'Orléans (vv. 3675ff), who had designs on the imperial crown.[41] Her hope is that Ysabel's biological heritage and her wise guidance of her sons will help prepare the advent of a future emperor who can take Jerusalem back from the Saracens.[42]

Christine entertains the possibility of just such a saviour in her last and final poem, her *Ditié de Jehanne d'Arc* (Poem of Joan of Arc), which she composed to celebrate Joan's role in helping Ysabel's only surviving son be crowned as King Charles VII on 17 July 1429.[43] The poet prophesies that Charles will become emperor ("in the end he will be emperor [et en fin doit estre empereur]," v. 128), and that together with Joan he will conquer the Holy Land, v. 338).[44] Johanna's adoption of her cousin Louis d'Anjou,[45] whose dream, in Christine's words, was to conquer "the Roman Empire," had prepared Ysabel's pivotal position in France's marital strategy designed to strengthen France's position in the larger Christian arena. Ysabel would symbolically continue Johanna's role as Queen of Jerusalem, a hereditary title purchased in 1277 by the founder of the French Angevin dynasty, Charles d'Anjou (1226–1285), brother to the quintessential crusader king, Saint Louis. We note that Boccaccio always cites Jerusalem before Sicily in highlighting the family's title, as was customary.[46] Johanna's title as Jerusalem's queen proclaimed her to be a crusader queen positioned, in Casteen's words, "at the apex of Christendom's secular aristocracy."[47] Johanna had in fact anticipated the idea of a woman leading a crusade. Under Pope Gregory XI she had proposed to embark on one herself, in cooperation with Catherine of Siena.[48] Christine returns to the idea of women heading a crusade in her support of Joan of Arc.

The second reason why Christine would continue Boccaccio's positive evaluation of Johanna is that the queen's endorsement of the Avignon papacy coincided with Charles V's. Both of them supported the papacy of Clement VII over that of Urban V, and did so for similar reasons. Trouble arose when the election of the new pope, Urban VI (r. 1378–89), was declared invalid, and Clement VII was elected in his stead. Johanna first declared her obedience to Clement, then momentarily moved back to support Urban, before declaring her final obedience to Clement. Her support of the Avignon pope, Clement VII, led to her downfall and assassination. Urban retaliated by excommunicating her and replacing her as ruler by crowning her cousin and rival, Charles of Durazzo, who, as we have seen, had her imprisoned and killed in 1382. In a letter (addressed, interestingly, to Ysabel's father, Duke Stephen III), Johanna explained that once Urban's election was declared invalid and the cardinals had unanimously elected Clement, she had no choice but to transfer her obedience to him.[49]

This is the same stance taken by Charles V, who, together with his brother Louis d'Anjou, was Clement's most ardent supporter.[50] In *Charles V* 3.56 Christine specifies that Charles V had been entirely justified in recognizing the legality of Clement VII's election. She drives home her assertion with a well-crafted accumulation of terms, affirming that the cardinals had elected him "legally, canonically, and unanimously as pope, without any debate, difficulty, or dispute."[51] Christine adds that Charles V "consented to the aforesaid election, as did the queen of Naples and all the lords of the country."[52] Casteen notes that Johanna was the first monarch to declare her obedience to Clement, "and her decision proved pivotal."[53] Charles V followed suit. Christine recounts that Charles V then convened his own counsellors to ratify the decision that he and Johanna had reached.

Christine's citation of the agreement of Charles V and Johanna on this controversial point, which one could think she would prefer to pass over,[54] may have a hitherto unnoticed political motivation, besides the obvious one of exonerating the king for his unfortunate decision that led to the Schism (1378–1417). Charles V had a strong political rationale for allying himself with Johanna in backing Clement VII, the pope who in 1382 had invested Louis d'Anjou with the kingdom of Naples. Simply put, to question his papacy risked invalidating France's claims to Naples. Those claims would become uppermost when, in the late fifteenth century, King Louis XII traced his rights to the kingdom of Naples to Johanna.[55]

We can understand, then, why Christine would not have joined Johanna's critics in proclaiming that the queen's endorsement of Clement VII had compromised her rule. According to Casteen, Boccaccio composed his glowing portrait of Johanna in a conscious effort to promote her image. If, in Margaret Franklin's words, the queen has "been seen variously as bringing about a golden age of learning and prosperity to Naples and as presiding over a degenerate and amoral court,"[56] Christine follows the Latin and French renditions of the *De mulieribus* in viewing Johanna as a ruler to be admired.

Another indication of the strong political and ideological ties linking Johanna and her cousin Charles V was her construction of the church of Santa Maria dell'Incoronata.[57] The queen's purpose was to house several thorns from the crown of thorns, then in the Sainte Chapelle in Paris. Johanna requested the relics as a gift from the French king, who is depicted in the church's portal. Addressing Charles in her Latin letter as "most excellent prince, reverend and honoured brother," she explains the reasoning behind her choice of the name "Incoronata": "This chapel should be named for the saving Crown of our Redeemer following the example of that venerable chapel in the royal palace in Paris."

Johanna's enshrining of the thorns was an act of personal devotion designed to increase her subjects' devotion to her rule.[58] With this act, she proclaimed to the Neapolitan people her legitimate sovereignty over her kingdom,[59] by linking it to the sacredness of Christ, in the person of Saint Louis, the monarch who had constructed the Sainte Chapelle. Johanna's letter to Charles V reveals how she very consciously fashioned her public image on French models.

The French, for their part, took care to indicate Angevin dependency on Gallic models. The renowned theologian Jean Gerson, Christine's ally in the Debate on the *Romance of the Rose* of 1401–3,[60] did so in his sermon of 25 August 1401, "Considerate lilia agri." He delivered this meditation on Matthew 6.28 to the Collège de Navarre on the anniversary of Saint Louis's birth. It cannot be pure coincidence that, of the two sermons preached on Saint Louis's sacred royalty by Robert d'Anjou, Johanna's grandfather and benefactor, one also took as its theme the same biblical passage, which was "an allusion to the fleur-de-lys that graced both Capetian and Angevin heraldry."[61] The lines of influence appear even stronger when we realize that Gerson's sermon reiterates the position put forth by the author of a Dominican office commissioned during Saint Louis's reign, most likely by the king himself, to celebrate the preservation of the crown of thorns in the Sainte Chapelle. In a novel twist on traditional representations of the Second Coming, the office imagined Christ knocking at the door of the royal palace to retrieve the crown of thorns, which French kings had lovingly preserved for him.[62] The propagandist message conveyed by this office, whose theme was "Stat inter spinas lilium," was that the possession of the crown of thorns proclaimed France's superior standing among Christian nations. In requesting several thorns from the crown, Johanna tacitly acknowledged her deference to the French monarchy's preeminent spiritual authority.

Together with the *Grandes chroniques*, the office envisions doctrinally knowledgeable mothers as the Church's handmaidens in the home.[63] In it Saint Ambrose – the same saint whom Christine cites as supportive of Saint Augustine's mother in her *City of Ladies* 1.10 – praises the influence exercised on Saint Louis by "the vigilance of his religious mother Blanche [religiose matris sue Blance vigilantiam]."[64] With its unmistakable echoes of Robert d'Anjou's sermon, Gerson's discourse on the "lilies of the field" implicitly asserts that the Neapolitan line of sacred inheritance had its source in France's *beata stirps*, enshrined and preserved by a royal court backed by Paris's faculty of theology. Gerson's sermon also strongly asserts the importance of women's contribution to assuring the line's sacred quality. In it, he, rather strangely (at least to a modern mind), informs the professors assembled before him that their duty was to "address their students with the same words of maternal piety" pronounced by Blanche de Castille when she told her son that she would rather see him dead than commit a mortal sin.[65] Queen Ysabel bought into this ideology when in 1398 she commissioned a Passion text emphasizing the harmony uniting the Virgin and Christ, even in his greatest sufferings.[66] Like Johanna, Ysabel knew how to cultivate a self-image reflective of the French monarchy's "most Christian" status.

Stephen Kolsky points out that Boccaccio emphasizes Johanna's royal origins, in particular her French ones, more than is common in other historical biographies.[67] The Italian author places the queen's lineage first among her qualities:

> Joanna ... is more renowned than any other woman of our time for lineage, power, and character ... She was the eldest daughter of the Most Serene Prince Charles, the eminent Duke of Calabria, and first-born son of Robert of illustrious memory, king of Jerusalem and Sicily. (*FW*, 467, 469)

Boccaccio then lauds Johanna's maternal line, citing the fact that her mother was Marie de Valois (1309–1332), sister of France's King Philippe VI. Johanna was thus an offshoot of the Valois dynasty, which ruled France during Christine's lifetime. Boccaccio then explains how Johanna continues her paternal intellectual heritage:

> Joanna was still a small child when her father met a premature death. Since her grandfather Robert had no other male children, through his directive she became, as the only survivor, the legitimate heir to the kingdom at his death. (*FW*, 469)

Robert had the prescience to recognize his granddaughter's intelligence and educate her. Believing that the divinity itself, in its infinite wisdom, had favoured their royal line above all others (*beata stirps*), the French asserted spiritual and intellectual inheritance over strictly biological lineage. Robert reaffirmed this principle in designating his granddaughter Johanna over several of his nephews. And although none of her three children lived long enough to rule, Johanna continued the paternal line by designating Louis d'Anjou as her heir, through what the French would have considered to be the workings of her superlative wisdom, which she had inherited from Robert d'Anjou. This line of intelligent decisions led back to Robert's uncle, Saint Louis.

Boccaccio's portrait of Johanna in the *De mulieribus* reflects the exemplary qualities Casteen ascribes to her, a keen intelligence combined with the devotion to the Catholic faith that she developed during the last years of her reign.[68] These qualities enabled her to enforce justice in her realm, which was a ruler's highest function, as Christine acknowledges by giving Dame Justice dominion over the highest reaches of the

Cité des dames. After explaining that Johanna cleared her realm of outlaws, Boccaccio says, "No previous king had been willing or able to do this" (*FW*, 471). He accords Johanna his highest form of praise, which was that she ruled as well as any man, going so far as to state the idea a full five times in the space of one chapter. His praise of her is especially noteworthy in this passage:

> Joanna has besides a wonderfully charming appearance. She is soft-spoken, and her eloquence pleases everyone. When the occasion demands it, she has a regal and unyielding majesty; equally she can be affable, compassionate, gentle, and kind, so that one would describe her as her people's ally rather than as their queen. What greater qualities would one seek in the wisest king? (*FW*, 473)[69]

Boccaccio concludes his portrait of Johanna by saying: "I think that she is not only remarkable and striking for her splendid fame, but a singular glory of Italy such as has never before been seen by any nation" (*FW*, 473).[70] It is clear that the Italian poet sees Johanna an illustrious queen whose example should encourage emulation by other women.

Christine suggests that Ysabel should imitate Johanna by echoing Boccaccio's tribute to Johanna in her praise of the French queen:

> the noble queen of France, Isabella of Bavaria … reigning now by the grace of God, and in whom there is not a trace of cruelty, extortion, or any other evil vice, but only great love and good will toward her subjects. (*City* 2.68.1, R212)

Boccaccio and Christine both acknowledge that queens are as important to hereditary dynasties as kings, for their intelligence as well as for the children they bear. Boccaccio praises Johanna's lineage:

> If we trace her parents' ancestors to the beginning of the dynasty, we will not stop until we have made our way through many kings to Dardanus, founder of Troy and (according to the ancients) son of Jupiter. From this old and distinguished family have been born so many famous princes on both sides that every Christian king is related to it by blood or by marriage. No dynasty has shone more nobly throughout the world in our own time or our fathers' time. (*FW*, 469)

By birth and by marriage, Queen Ysabel likewise belonged to the illustrious royal dynasty described by Boccaccio. Her birth relations included her paternal grandmother, Elizabeth of Sicily (1310–1349), wife of Stephen II, Duke of Bavaria, son of Holy Roman Emperor Louis IV. Elizabeth and Stephen's first-born son was Duke Stephen III (1337–1413), Ysabel's father. By her marriage to King Charles VI, Ysabel united the Valois line with that of the illustrious house of Wittelsbach, which counted a recent Holy Roman Emperor among its number. Ysabel's brood of twelve children and their descendants would solder French-Angevin relations even more closely than had Johanna, and would additionally help foster French ambitions to be recognized as the head of the Christian world.

Queen Ysabel resembled Johanna in fostering French interests within Christendom. The French queen was at the heart of the alliance that Louis d'Anjou had forged with Milan's Bernabò Visconti, Ysabel's maternal grandfather. This is especially significant since in 1359 Boccaccio had been chosen as ambassador to Bernabò's court, when the latter was imperial vicar (although it does not appear that Boccaccio actually ever made the mission).[71] Along with Savoy's Amadeus VI, Bernabò had supported Louis d'Anjou's expedition to regain control of Naples for Clement VII after Johanna's death. Boccaccio, notably, also must have known Ysabel's paternal great-grandfather, Holy Roman Emperor Louis IV of Bavaria, given that in 1351 he had served as Louis's ambassador from the city-state of Florence.[72] As with her featuring of Dante, Christine's enthusiastic use of Boccaccio could very well have been motivated by the poet/diplomat's connections to Queen Ysabel's famous relatives. After all, by addressing the queen as "lofty lady of the line of emperors of worthy memory," as quoted above, Christine celebrates Ysabel's position in an illustrious line that included two key figures, one a Holy Roman emperor, another that emperor's imperial vicar, both having close ties to Boccaccio.

Although the French queen, unlike Johanna, was never a sovereign queen, Ysabel encountered problems similar to hers. The paragraph, quoted above, in which Boccaccio describes Johanna as buffeted about by hostile fortune, circumstances that did not deflect her from her "righteous path," could well serve as encouragement to the often similarly beleaguered Ysabel. In establishing Ysabel's portrait on that of the Angevin Queen Johanna praised by Boccaccio, Christine encouraged the French queen to accomplish what had been done by her predecessor, despite similarly dire circumstances. Ysabel was called upon to help guide a country divided internally and threatened by English invasion; her husband, the king, was subject to insane rages; she had to endure "undeserved ill-repute"; the stability of France, like Johanna's Angevin kingdom, was threatened by the continuing Schism of the Western Church. Like Boccaccio promoting the earlier disputed reign of a sovereign queen, Christine lent support to the difficult rule of a regent whose guidance was crucial to the functioning of the early fifteenth-century French monarchy.

III. Andrea Acciaiuoli, Countess of Altavilla, a Model for Christine's Sibyl de Monthault, Dame de la Tour

Christine brings about a fundamental transformation of the *De mulieribus* by casting herself as an ideal, virtuous, Italian-born female reader, a new, improved avatar of both Boccaccio and his dedicatee. Although Christine never mentions Andrea's name, given the many references she makes to Johanna, the queen she served, it is easy to believe that Andrea was never far from her thoughts. There are many reasons why Christine would adopt Boccaccio's dedicatee as a model for her own role as the French queen's counsellor. Andrea was a woman in Johanna's court whose functions in many ways resembled Christine's. She was one of the few available contemporary models of a queen's secular female advisor; she was, moreover, Italian-born like Christine.

Christine may suggest her dependency on Boccaccio's dedicatee by the name and function that she gives to one of her characters, Sibyl de Monthault, Dame de la Tour, who is generally considered to be Christine's chief alter ego. Lady Sibyl appears in Christine's cautionary tale, the *Duc des vrays amans* (Duke of True Lovers) of 1403, as a royal lady's high-minded advisor. Christine subsequently inserts Lady Sibyl's long letter of advice to her lady into her exclusively prose instructional manual for women, the *Trois Vertus* (Three Virtues) of 1405. Christine suggests her borrowing from Boccaccio by the name she gives to her alter ego. "Monthault" ("high mountain") recalls Andrea's title of Countess of "Altavilla" ("high villa").[73] Both terms evoke the exalted quality of the royal lady's mental and moral physiognomy. Christine additionally designates Sibyl de Monthault as "Lady of the Tower," a tower being another high place suggesting contemplation and moral transcendence. This title recalls the turrets and towers of the City of Ladies, in which reside the female saints, the highest models for Ysabel and her court ladies. Christine correspondingly substitutes herself for Boccaccio as clerkly poet, which she does by developing the similarities he had brought out between himself and Andrea.

In her role as royal advisor, Christine brings together the functions taken on by Andrea at Johanna's court and those that Boccaccio assumed vis-à-vis highly placed political figures, among whose number figured Ysabel's prominent relatives and their associates. It is not an exaggeration to say that Christine intimately linked France's future to Dante and Boccaccio through the woman who had been carefully chosen by Philippe le Hardi, Duke of Burgundy, to be Charles VI's queen. It would thus be logical for Christine to fashion Ysabel's persona on Queen Johanna's chief female advisor, and to do so along the lines of Boccaccio's portrayal of Andrea in the *De mulieribus*.[74]

In the following passage Boccaccio tells Andrea his reasons for believing her to be a better choice as his dedicatee than Queen Johanna:

> For as I reflected on your character, both gentle and renowned; your outstanding probity, women's greatest ornament; and your elegance of speech; and as I noted your generosity of soul and your powers of intellect far surpassing the endowments of womankind; as I saw that what nature has denied the weaker sex God has freely installed in your breast and complemented with marvelous virtues, to the point where he willed you to be known by the name you bear (*andres* being in Greek the equivalent of the Latin word for "men") – considering all this, I felt that you deserved comparison with the most excellent women anywhere, even among the ancients. (*FW*, 3, 5)

He then asks Andrea to accept this "humble and pious work [humilem devotumque]" (*FW*, 2–3) in the "holy name of modesty," for which she is "preeminent among mortals," and to accept with favour "this small gift from a scholar" (*FW*, 5). Her modesty complements his own; he sees himself reflected in her, a woman who must be learned, since she would have to know Latin well enough to read not only his dedication but also the rest of his book, which his words indicate that he wants her to do.

What is implicit but nonetheless striking here is that Boccaccio compares his moral physiognomy to Andrea's. When he cites her probity, elegant speech, generosity of soul, and powers of intellect, he likens these character traits to his own.[75] He metaphorically "mirrors" himself in his dedicatee when he claims that Andrea has risen above the common lot of women, most of whom, as he says later on, are "endowed by nature with soft, frail bodies and sluggish minds" (*FW*, 9), because she has taken on "a manly spirit or soul [virilem animum]," and shows "remarkable intelligence and bravery [ingeno celebri atque virtute]" (*FW*, 8–9).[76] God, so says Boccaccio, has willed Andrea to be known by the name she bears ("quo insignita es nomine," *FW*, 4), whereupon he glosses it (incorrectly) as *andres*, the Greek equivalent of the Latin word for "men."[77] Although Boccaccio points out the failings of innumerable other women, he singles out for praise Andrea's "virile spirit."

Gerson praises Christine in similar terms. His characterization of Christine as a "virilis femina" and a "virago" in the *Rose* Debate letter that he addressed to Pierre Col in winter 1402–3 (Hicks, 168) echoes Boccaccio's praise of Andrea's "manly spirit or soul [virilem animum]." As the chancellor of the University of Paris and chief canon of Notre Dame cathedral, Gerson acted as the supreme arbiter of Church doctrine.[78] He insists upon this point in the *Rose* Debate. "My profession," Gerson writes to one of Christine's opponents, Pierre Col, "requires me to struggle as vigorously as can be against errors and vices."[79] His official duties included pronouncing upon doctrinal matters treated by members of the university community. One reason for Gerson's approval of Christine's arguments was that they were exempt from heresy. In comparison to Pierre, whose university education should have prepared him to avoid repeating what amounts to the Pelagian heresy,[80] the secular woman Christine had shown a keener grasp of the basics of Christian doctrine. She argued her points correctly; whereas Pierre did not.

When Christine depicts herself as having a mind and heart able to cross gender lines, as she does most famously when she metaphorically becomes a man in *Mutacion* 1.12, vv. 1321–94 (*SW* 106–7), she forcefully brings to mind Boccaccio's earlier portrayal of Andrea's "virile or manly spirit." In using the terms "virilis femina" and "virago," which Barbara Newman singles out as staples of the female saint's life,[81] Gerson, the foremost theologian in France, identified Christine as a woman with a superlative, even, one could say, a divinely inspired intelligence. Gerson's support of Christine also certified that the advice she offered to the queen was doctrinally correct, a point vitally important to Primat. Women like Christine who gave advice in line with official Church doctrine helped France live up to its idea of itself as the "Church's most loyal daughter." Gerson's words of praise, which are reminiscent of those used to describe Johanna by Boccaccio, suggest the type of influence Christine hoped to have on Ysabel. Could this queen of France live up to the capacity for spiritually informed (and Gallic-oriented) leadership shown by her predecessor and blood relative Johanna?

Christine would additionally have been encouraged to model herself on Boccaccio's appreciative portrait of Andrea by the emphasis placed on the frame praising Johanna and Andrea in the illuminated copies of the French translation, which she undoubtedly knew well. The two *Cleres femmes* copies, Paris, Bibliothèque nationale de France, fr. 12420 and Paris, Bibliothèque nationale de France, fr. 598, were presented to her major patrons, Philippe le Hardi (the same Duke of Burgundy who had arranged Ysabel's marriage to King Charles VI) and Jean, the Duke of Berry, in January 1403, and February 1404, respectively.[82] As a book producer, and one known to supervise the production of her books' iconographic cycles as well as their text,[83] Christine would have been particularly influenced by the physical appearance of these *Cleres femmes* copies. I cannot overstate how much these diverge from copies of the Latin originals that can be securely dated to the period prior to 1403–4. Whereas the latter are by and large without illumination, the Burgundy copy has 109 miniatures, the Berry copy, 107. Most importantly, both generously illustrated copies foreground the frame constituted by the portrait of Andrea placed at the book's opening and the portrait of Johanna positioned at its conclusion. These copies conveyed powerfully to Christine (and to Queen Ysabel) the centrality of Queen Johanna and her counsellor Andrea to the catalogue of "cleres femmes" included within their covers.

A consideration of the way dedications can be interpreted within different physical contexts, as explained by Rhiannon Daniels in her contribution to this volume,[84] is essential for my analysis. Each *Cleres femmes* copy has a "double frontispiece"[85] consisting of an author portrait and a dedication scene; each of them ends with a similar miniature in which courtiers offer other gifts to a crowned Johanna.[86] In the earlier Burgundy copy (fr. 12420, fol. 3r), the first miniature depicts Boccaccio seated before a book wheel, reading to his audience.[87] In the second miniature (fol. 4v), Boccaccio presents his book to Andrea, who is crowned and accompanied by two court ladies. The double frontispiece of the Berry copy (fr. 598) observes the reverse order: there the book presentation scene precedes the author portrait.

The Berry copy makes explicit Boccaccio's modelling of himself on Andrea and his deep devotion to her, which we observed in the dedication paragraph quoted above. In the first miniature (fol. 3r), the poet is represented kneeling to the side of Andrea, who dominates the focal middle ground of the composition. All eyes are literally on her. Instead of presenting the book to his dedicatee, as is usual in such scenes, Boccaccio holds the book open before Andrea, as if he were reading her his dedication. The comparative size of figures typically indicates their status, and Andrea is noticeably larger than Boccaccio. For the Berry illuminator, Boccaccio's dedication to Andrea, which we have considered in detail above, is a key to understanding his entire compendium. The presentation miniature implies, and quite strongly, that Boccaccio considers Andrea to be his superior. The Berry *Cleres femmes* (fr. 598) projects an image of Boccaccio as a staunch supporter of women, and above all, of Queen Johanna and her attendant Andrea. The physical appearance of the two *Cleres femmes* copies would moreover have encouraged Christine to interpret Boccaccio as reinforcing the functions she had already begun to assume at Queen Ysabel's court. Christine's role as Ysabel's book producer became apparent in 1399 when she began preparing the first large compilation that she presented to the queen.[88]

Christine assumes the task of book distribution that Boccaccio had requested of Andrea at the conclusion of his dedication to her:

> If you judge it worthy, most excellent lady, give this book the boldness to appear in public. Under your auspices it will go forth, I believe, safe from malicious criticism, and it will make your name and the names of other illustrious women glorious on the lips of humankind. As you cannot be physically present everywhere, my book will make you and your merits known to those now alive and will preserve you forever for posterity. (*FW*, 7)

Boccaccio counts on Andrea to disseminate his book widely among women. He ascribes a high status to the *De mulieribus*: he describes the book as the physical substitute for Andrea and as a vehicle to publish her merits far and wide. Andrea's service to Queen Johanna is a key part of the goal he sets for his book, which is to place the names of illustrious women into a permanent archive of human memory.

Christine connects the campaign she engages against misogyny in the *Cité des dames* to her promotion of female courts through the dissemination of books. At the conclusion of the *Cité*'s sequel and companion piece, her *Trois vertus*, Christine proclaims herself to be the "servant" of all women and that she aims to improve their virtue and honour by distributing her work throughout the world.[89] She says:

> Therefore, I thought I would multiply this work throughout the world in various copies, whatever the cost may be, and present it in particular places to queens, princesses, and noble ladies. Through their efforts, it will be the more honored and praised, as is fitting, and better circulated among other women. I already have started this process; so that this book will be examined, read, and published in all countries, although it is written in the French language. Since French is a more common and universal language

> than any other, this work will not remain unknown and useless but will endure in its many copies throughout the world. (224)[90]

Like Boccaccio, Christine insists on the public utility of her book. She here emphasizes that she views the courts of queens, princesses, and other noble ladies as the place to promote the image of virtuous women. Taking her cues from Boccaccio's endorsement of Andrea as a powerful queen's attendant, Christine takes up, in the language of France, according to her the most universal of all vernaculars,[91] what she could interpret as being Boccaccio's aim to defend women's cause. Although we tend to think of Christine as an author, what she does in the above passage is to insist upon her role as book producer and distributor, and specifically as one who works for a female court. We know that Christine produced books, all devoted exclusively to her own French texts, for Queen Ysabel and her court.[92] Christine implies that one aim of female courts was to champion women's good name. The members of those courts could do so in two ways: by circulating books in defence of women, and by exhibiting the virtuous and wise behaviour that the books hold up as an ideal for women.

Many are the studies that deal with Christine's establishment of her own authority,[93] which is paramount in the analysis I advance here. But what has been frequently overlooked is the way Christine employs her own authority to legitimate the authority of Queen Ysabel and future French queens. In her *Cité des dames* Christine incorporates the examples she draws from Boccaccio into a list of women beginning and ending with queens, all drawn from the *Grandes chroniques*, a list culminating in Christine's high praise of Ysabel and her female court. The poet traces a progression from *City* 1.12 and the biblical queen Nicaula (whom Boccaccio had identified as the Queen of Sheba, *FW*, 183), to the reigning queen of France, Queen Ysabel, in 2.68. She introduces her line of queens with the rubric of 1.12.1: "Here she tells of Nicaula, Empress of Ethiopia, and afterwards about several queens and princesses of France." Christine's next chapter, 1.13.1, is about "a queen of France, named Fredegund," whom she couples with Blanche de Castille (1.13.2) as regents who supported their sons' interests during their minority. In 1.13.3–7 she names five other French aristocratic women who when widowed maintained the rule of law and safeguarded their husbands' lands and powers.[94] Christine returns to Fredegund in 1.23.1, this time to emphasize the Frankish ruler's cleverness in battle.

Christine then proceeds to intersperse Boccaccio's examples of exemplary ladies with those of other past French queens. Here is the list of French queens treated by Christine: Basine (2.5, "More Concerning Nicostrata, Cassandra, and Queen Basine"); Clothilda (2.35, "Here she speaks of Clothilda, Queen of France, who converted her husband, King Clovis, to the Faith"). Christine closely follows 2.63, devoted to Claudia Quinta, the last chapter in which she cites Boccaccio by name, with 2.65.1: "Here she speaks of Queen Blanche, the mother of Saint Louis, and of other good and wise ladies loved for their virtue." From Blanche it is not far to 2.68: "She speaks here of the princesses and ladies of France," where Christine introduces nine ladies of present-day France, beginning with Queen Ysabel. She caps Part 2 with Chapter 2.69. Bearing the rubric "Christine addresses herself to all princesses and to all women," this chapter urges princesses to set the standard for all women who "have loved and do love and will love virtue and morality" (R214). The framework into which Christine places Boccaccio's examples in Parts 1 and 2 is that of past queens, examples that lead up to the present-day French queen, Ysabel. In citing Boccaccio by name twenty-eight times in Parts 1 and 2 of her *Cité des dames*, always in ways respectful of his authority, Christine enlists this highly esteemed author as her ally in her campaign against misogyny. The immediate historical aim of her arguments was to persuade Queen Ysabel to improve her moral profile and thereby increase France's symbolic capital.

The concluding words of *City* 3.19, the chapter that caps Christine's catalogue of female saints that makes up the *City*'s Part 3, is introduced by the rubric: "The end of the Book: Christine addresses the ladies." Here the poet speaks directly to her female readers to explain how the City of Ladies can be the refuge of all virtuous women as well as their "defense and guard" against "enemies and assailants," those men who test women's virtue with their poisoned rhetoric. The advice Christine's proffers to women in the *Cité des dames* recalls the advice she gives them throughout her verse and prose texts. It sums up the message that she as royal counsellor offers to women in her entire *oeuvre*, which she delivers frequently to them under the guise of her mouthpiece, Sibyl of the High Mountain, Lady of the Tower.

It is likely that the representations of Boccaccio humbling himself before his virtuous dedicatee, which we observed him doing in his *De mulieribus* and which received emphasis in the *Cleres femmes* miniatures, inspired Christine to portray herself as a new, feminine version of the

Italian poet, one that she conflates with his dedicatee, Andrea. As we have seen in the *De mulieribus* dedication passage cited above, Boccaccio, like Christine after him, subscribes to the idea that the female mind can reflect the wisdom of the divine mind just as well as can the male mind. He recognized this principle in describing Andrea. But then he denigrated women whose intelligence is not as exceptional as hers; in other words, most women. Basing herself, I believe, on three things – first, Boccaccio's own suggestion that Andrea, and the queen she served, were his superiors; second, the invitation he extends to poets to improve his texts for the public good; third, the further emphasis that the *Cleres femmes* copies places on the first two things – Christine casts herself as a new French female Boccaccio who refutes the earlier poet's occasional denigration of women. She presents herself as a woman who outthinks her Italian precursor, specifically by combining superior intelligence with the piety that according to her is the defining characteristic of the "devout sex of women" (*City* 3.1.2; R218).

Christine was not alone in her belief that women were superior to men because of their capacity to be pious. In his 1402 sermon on Saint Bernard, Gerson, repeating the point about Blanche de Castille he had made in his 1401 sermon on Saint Louis, attributes much of the saint's success to his mother's upbringing.[95] By extolling women because "the feminine sex is said to be devout" (*EW*, 147), the university chancellor implicitly legitimizes Christine's arguments for the essential worth of the entire female sex,[96] arguments she was making during the period 1401–3. The support she received from Gerson was essential to Christine's success as women's public defender. Most importantly for my argument, Gerson's enthusiastic backing lent legitimacy to her self-representation as a French female Boccaccio, a poet who had cast himself and was cast by others as Dante's disciple and supporter.

IV. Christine as a French Female Boccaccio

Christine could represent herself as Boccaccio's follower because at the conclusion of the *De mulieribus* he authorizes later writers to correct his text in the interests of the common good. After replying first to those who criticize his omission of certain outstanding women, he adds:

> To my other critics, I say that it is possible (and I can easily believe it happened) that some things were improperly included. Certainly, an author is often deceived both by ignorance of events and by an excessive

> attachment to his own work. If this is the case, I am sorry, and I ask on behalf of the venerable dignity of honorable studies that my readers tolerate with a wise and kindly spirit what has not been skillfully executed. If they are charitably inclined, let them correct and emend the inappropriate passages by addition or deletion: in this way, the work will live for someone's benefit rather than perish, mangled by the teeth of envy, of service to no one. (*FW*, 475)

These lines constitute an outright invitation to later authors to amend his work, which he justifies as furthering the "venerable dignity of honorable studies." Christine correspondingly concludes her *Trois vertus* by asking her readers to add to the *Pater Nosters* said on her behalf a prayer to God to grant her "such light of knowledge and true wisdom" that she may continue to employ them in the "noble labor of study, in behalf of the praise and promotion of virtue through good example in every human being" (224).[97] The way that Christine's phrase, the "noble labor of study," echoes Boccaccio's reference to the "venerable dignity of honorable studies" indicates a commonality of purpose on the part of the two authors. Boccaccio's concluding lines in the *De mulieribus* are outstanding for the author's wish that his text serve the common good, for his idea that women are worthy of praise, and for his belief that the furthering of the common good is an ongoing project to which he invites others to contribute.[98]

Instead of rejecting Boccaccio for his misogynistic attitudes, Christine corrects them, basing herself on his own invitation to his readers to revise his work in the interests of the common good and on his humility, a characteristic associated with the Virgin.[99] His humility had also been apparent when he, a revered male author, had the perspicacity and humbleness to correct his own earlier demeaning evaluation of Johanna. Christine takes further Boccaccio's "mirroring" of himself in Andrea by developing the Italian poet's role as producer of presentation copies of his *De mulieribus*.[100] Christine's extensive work as author and book producer illustrates what women can actually achieve.[101] She presents herself as a virtuous, hardworking, and determined woman in order to spur on other women to reach similar heights.

Christine's recasting of Boccaccio involves resolving a contradiction in his stance.[102] Although he excludes the Christian saints from his catalogue of women, he evaluates some of his subjects according to Christian criteria. Boccaccio tells Andrea that Christian women should be able to surpass antique models because, as he says to her:

> Whenever you, who profess the Christian religion, read that a pagan woman has some worthy quality which you feel you lack, blush and reproach yourself that, although marked with the baptism of Christ, you have let yourself be surpassed by a pagan in probity or chastity or resolution. (*FW*, 5)

He then urges her to increase the distinction of her sex "through integrity, holiness, and the finest actions," so that she "will stand out among famous women in this earthly life," and, after casting off her mortal form, she "will be received into eternal light by the Giver of all blessings" (*FW*, 7). This is not a passing aside, because he comes back to it in Chapter 42, where he says that Christian women should surpass models like Dido because the former are marked "with the emblem of Christ [Christi insignite caractere]" (*FW*, 174–5). These words reveal a Christian orientation in Boccaccio's text, but one which he fails to develop.[103]

Furthermore, in his dedication Boccaccio employs the metaphor of a literary garden to tell Andrea to reject the "thorns" of readings that will offend her Christian sensibilities:

> You will find, at times, that an appropriate recital of the facts has compelled me to mix the impure with the pure. Do not skip over these parts and do not shy away from them, but persevere in your reading. As on entering a garden you extend your ivory hands towards the flowers, leaving aside the thorns, so in this case relegate to one side offensive matters and gather what is praiseworthy. (*FW*, 5)

From his comments here we see that Boccaccio expected Andrea to read his compendium of famous and infamous women critically, modelling her moral physiognomy on those of the famous ones, and especially on the way many such ladies prefigured Christian values. In these two passages there is no mistaking Boccaccio's traditional Christian address to his dedicatee. When Boccaccio belatedly added the dedication to Andrea to his original compilation (*FW*, xiii), he introduced into it a Christian interpretative framework that clashed with the classical one he had originally favoured. Christine resolved this contradiction by accentuating the Christian character of the compendium she had inherited from Boccaccio with the addition of her compendium of female saints. She did so to authorize the public voices of doctrinally savvy French women, chief among them herself and Queen Ysabel.[104]

By supplying her compendium of female saints' lives in Part 3 of her *City*, Christine resolves contradictions in the *De mulieribus*. In his conclusion Boccaccio comments upon the limited potential of women of his time and place to achieve true greatness:

> As is apparent, I have now come to the women of our own time. But so small is the number of those who are outstanding that I think it more honorable to end here rather than continue with the women of today ... (*FW*, 473)

Christine's exemplary royal ladies are superior to Boccaccio's because hers combine intelligence, skill, and Christian doctrine, as French women are supposed to do. She goes beyond Boccaccio's examples of daughters whose achievements surpassed those of their fathers by supplying more Christianized avatars of those examples.

Take Boccaccio's Hortensia, the subject of *City* 2.36.2.[105] She was a forerunner of Christine as master debater, the role that initially gave authority to the poet's public voice. Quintus Hortensius, the great Roman orator and rhetorician, recognized his daughter's intelligence and educated her himself, so that Hortensia eventually resembled her father in intelligence, memory, and eloquence. Christine adds that "in fact, he surpassed her in nothing" (R154), her use of litotes suggesting that Hortensia actually surpassed her father. She implies that the Roman maiden was braver than Quintus because she took up a cause that her father was unwilling to defend. With her example Christine foregrounds both her own courage in arguing her case for women against the opposition of Latin-trained, university-educated male clerics and her own success in bettering them, as attested by Gerson.

Christine presents Saint Catherine of Alexandria as the highest avatar of the female master debater:

> As a well lettered woman versed in the various branches of knowledge, she proceeded to prove on the basis of philosophical arguments that there is but one God, Creator of all things, and He alone should be worshipped and no other. (*City* 3.3.2; R220).

Arguing her case against fifty renowned philosophers, Catherine did so well that she not only won the debate but also converted many observers to her cause.[106] Catherine was a saint held in special regard by French royalty, including King Charles V (*Charles V* 1.33) and Jean de Berry and his wife Jeanne de Bourgogne,[107] the latter of whom Christine celebrates immediately after Queen Ysabel in *City* 2.68.2 (R212). Within the poet's own Parisian context, Catherine, a saint especially beloved of Christine's patrons, surpasses Boccaccio's Hortensia as master debater, as does Christine, Gerson's "virago" who debates with the force of a saint.

That Christine applies these examples to herself is abundantly clear when in her chapter on Hortensia she brings up the education given to her by her own scientist and philosopher father, Tommaso di Benvenuto da Pizzano, to whom the Parisians gave the name Thomas de Pizan. She supplements Boccaccio's story of Hortensia with two details that have to do with her family's physical displacement from Italy to France. Although Tommaso had at one time been a professor at the University of Bologna, he left his Italian university post to take up a position at King Charles V's court. When in *Charles V* 1.33 Christine mentions that Thomas was brought in to pronounce on the authenticity of a vial of the holy blood, she in actuality testifies to her father's sterling theological credentials and legitimizes her own position as theologically informed royal counsellor. In refusing offers to leave France to join the Italian court of Gian Galeazzo Visconti or the English court of Henry IV, as noted above, Christine asserted the intellectual superiority of France over other Christian monarchies, as had her father when he decided to move to Paris on King Charles V's invitation instead of accepting a similar position at the Hungarian court.

Christine amplifies her theme of women's outdistancing of their fathers or mentors in *City* 1.41.1–4, where she brings together three female artists whom Boccaccio had treated in separate chapters, Tamaris, Irene, and Marcia. In each case, Christine builds upon his claim that the artist surpassed her master, who in two cases was the artist's father. According to Boccaccio, Tamaris's reputation outclassed that of her father, the painter Micon. In fact, so little is known of him that Boccaccio finds it hard to say if Tamaris is the daughter of Micon the Younger or Micon the Older (*FW*, 230–3). As for Irene, she "surpassed her master [her father Cratinus] in art and in fame. Her name is still respected by many, while her father is hardly known except on her account" (*FW*, 249, 251). Marcia "surpassed Sopolis and Dionysius, the most famous painters of her day" (*FW*, 275).

But unlike Boccaccio, who accords the female artists only grudging praise, Christine gives them her unconditional admiration. Whereas Boccaccio's Tamaris and Marcia scorned the womanly tasks of spinning and weaving, Christine in *City* 1.10.3 refutes the misogynistic Latin saw that women were made to "speak, weep, and sew" (R27), to which Boccaccio had given voice. He had summed up his portrait of Irene with these condescending words:

> I thought that these achievements merited some praise because the art of painting is mostly alien to the feminine mind and cannot be attained without that great intellectual concentration which women, as a rule, are very slow to acquire. (*FW*, 251)

It is such an attack on women's capabilities that Christine's chapter 1.41 is meant to disprove. If intelligent women do not achieve as much as men, it is, she reasons, because they do not traditionally receive the same education or training. Christine praises all three of these female classical artists who, as she says of Irene, "marvelously surpassed and exceeded" their masters (R84).

Christine follows the *Cleres femmes* illuminators in giving these artists a Christianized interpretation. Stephen Perkinson points out that the Christian gloss found in the *Cleres femmes* miniatures of the three female artists is completely absent from the translation or its source, the *De mulieribus*.[108] In the Burgundy copy (fr. 12420, fol. 92v), Irene paints a statuette of a standing Virgin and Child, while an image of Christ's Holy Face stands behind it on her workbench. In the Berry copy (fr. 598, fol. 92), Irene paints an image of the Holy Face on one panel of a diptych, while the other panel remains blank. In both the Burgundy and Berry copies (each found on their respective fols 86), Tamaris paints an image of the Virgin and Child. This image, moreover, recalls the similar vision that the Sibyl indicates to Emperor Augustus on fol. 141r of Christine's *Epistre Othea* in MS Harley 4431,[109] where the Sibyl, like Saint Catherine of Alexandria, teaches that the Creator alone should be worshipped. The three classical artists in the *Cleres femmes* copies "prefigure" the period's ideal of skilful Christian artists, in particular the Parisian artists who illustrated the *Cleres femmes* copies and Christine's own texts.[110]

Of the three female artists, Christine envisions Marcia as the most pertinent prefiguration of her own achievement. This is because the classical artist had perfected the art of the self-portrait. Marcia, "who excelled all men" in the art of painting (R85), creates her own self-portrait with the aid of a mirror on fol. 101v of fr. 12420 and on fol. 100v of fr. 598. Christine evidently sees herself in Marcia. At the opening of the *Mutacion de Fortune* in Paris, Bibliothèque nationale de France, fr. 603, fol. 81v,[111] she has the Master of the *Cité des dames* portray her characteristically working alone in her cell-like study, but this time she has him add a mirror to her workbench.[112] This depiction of Christine appears to be a borrowing from the pictures of Marcia portrayed with a mirror in fr. 12420 and fr. 598, the closest resemblance being with the image in the Duke of Berry's manuscript.[113]

Christine builds on the idea that women artists/poets/scholars could surpass their fathers and masters, while omitting Boccaccio's grudging praise of these women.[114] In her *Mutacion* Christine had presented herself as an artist/poet/scholar who combines her father's intelligence and her mother's piety. In *Mutacion* 1.6 (*SW*, 94), she says: "I fully resembled my father in all things, only excepting my gender: in manner, body, face, we so resembled each other that you would have thought we had them in common." In *Mutacion* 1.8 (*SW*, 96), Christine describes how she inherited her mother's natural piety, which endowed her with a metaphorical crown of virtues. She inherited her exceptional intelligence from her father, while at the same time benefiting from her mother's natural piety, the same piety that she and Gerson claimed to be a woman's natural inclination.

Although Christine's combination of qualities makes her into the type of woman Boccaccio depicts in Andrea, he had refused to give Christian piety its full due anywhere but in his dedication to her. Christine and Gerson, on the other hand, emphasize that piety is a woman's highest quality; Primat, as we have seen, implicitly maintains that French daughters exhibit that quality to a greater extent than do women anywhere else. Even more than their intelligence, French women's piety reinforces the virtue of their line. The French term *vertu*, significantly derived from the Latin *vir*, or "man," conserved its classical sense of strength and vigour as well as the Christian sense of moral rectitude. One of the surest guarantees of France's claim to be the superlative example of a "holy" Roman empire was the virtue of French *dames*, which they manifested in their great piety. The two meanings of *vertu* come together in the symbolism inherent in Notre Dame, the cathedral dedicated to the Virgin, which dominated fifteenth-century Paris and the nation-state being formed from its spiritual and intellectual core. For Johanna, Boccaccio's "singular glory of Italy [singular decus ytalicum]" (*FW*, 472–3), Christine substitutes Ysabel, a queen of France related to Johanna by blood and even more closely by ideology. Under her guidance, the guidance of a woman whose singularity had been acknowledged not only by Gerson but also by the esteemed court poet

Eustache Deschamps,[115] she did her best to assist the French queen into becoming a singular glory of France.

In conclusion, by touting the superiority of her adopted homeland over her native Italy, according to the reasoning set forth in the *Grandes chroniques*, Christine tacitly made herself into a new French female Boccaccio, the latter author having already acquired a certain celebrity in her adopted *patria*. She was inspired to continue Boccaccio's tradition in France because his Latin book had been brought to Paris from Italy and subsequently translated into French, in conformity with the translation program initiated by Saint Louis and continued by Charles V.[116] Further accentuating the emphasis placed on Queen Johanna and Andrea Acciaiuoli in the two *Cleres femmes* copies, Christine symbolically brought the Neapolitan Angevin dynasty back into the French orbit from which it took its origins, its ideology, and its imperial ambitions.

NOTES

1 My title is inspired by the work of my colleague at Florida State University, Anne D. Coldiron, "Taking Advice from a Frenchwoman: Caxton, Pynson, and Christine de Pizan's *Prouerbes moraulx*," in *Caxton's Trace: Studies in the History of English Printing*, ed. William Kuskin (Notre Dame: University of Notre Dame Press, 2005), 127–66. Note also the similarity to the title and themes treated by Alessia Ronchetti in her chapter in this volume, "Reading Like a Woman: Gendering Compassion in the *Elegia di Madonna Fiammetta*."

2 All references to the *De mulieribus claris* are to the Latin edition and its English translation by Virginia Brown, published as *Famous Women* (Cambridge, MA: Harvard University Press, 2001). Page references will be given within parentheses in the body of my text as *FW*, followed by the page number. According to Brown, Boccaccio's autograph "was the basis of Vittorio Zaccaria's authoritative edition of 1967, and it serves as well as the basis of the present edition and translation" (*FW*, xiii). She introduces "occasional departures" from Zaccaria's edition (*FW*, 478). Throughout this essay, when there exists an authoritative English translation, I will reproduce citations from it, limiting my references to the original Latin or French when they are necessary to make my argument. I follow Boccaccio's usage in the *De mulieribus* and write Giovanna I's name as "Johanna," as does Elizabeth Casteen in "On She-Wolves and Famous Women, Boccaccio, Politics, and the Neapolitan Court," included in this volume, and in *From*

She-Wolf to Martyr: The Reign and Disputed Reputation of Johanna I of Naples (Ithaca: Cornell University Press, 2015). Note, however, that the queen's name appears as Joanna in quotations I take from Brown.

3 I will henceforth refer to the French queen as "Ysabel de Bavière," which is the way Christine invariably writes her name in the all of the presentation copies of her texts. (Presentation copies were manuscripts that she turned out in the scriptorium she headed.) For a detailed study of each of Christine's presentation copies, see *Album Christine de Pizan*, ed. Gilbert Ouy et al. (Turnhout: Brepols, 2012), hereafter *Album*. Jean Verdon, *Isabeau de Bavière, La mal aimée* (1981; Paris: Tallandier, 2001), affirms that the queen signed her name "Ysabel" (21); that her name was written this way on her official seal (213); and that the name "Isabeau" may have been used with malicious intent.

4 Her name is also written as Acciaioli or Acciajuoli, b. 10 September 1310. Very little is known about Andrea. Besides her two marriages, which I shall discuss below, she was the sister of Niccolò, Naples's Chief Seneschal, and of Lapa, who had close connections to Catherine of Siena and Birgitta of Sweden. In light of Boccaccio's promotion of Andrea over Johanna, and of Casteen's discussion of Niccolò as advisor to, and publicist of, Johanna's second husband, Louis of Taranto (*From She-Wolf to Martyr*, 68–100), it may well be that Niccolò enlisted his sister's help with advising Johanna and rehabilitating her reputation.

5 Robert Hollander, "Boccaccio's Dante," *Italica* 63, no. 3 (1986): 278–89: "Simply put, for Boccaccio, Dante was *the* writer worthy of emulation" (279). See also Jason M. Houston, *Building a Monument to Dante: Boccaccio as Dantista* (Toronto: University of Toronto Press, 2010). Boccaccio's position as the reigning expert on Dante explains why the Florentine elders selected him to deliver a series of sixty public lectures on the *Commedia*; see Michael Papio, *Boccaccio's Expositions on Dante's "Comedy"* (Toronto: University of Toronto Press, 2009).

6 I will discuss this passage further on in the essay.

7 Christine's reworking includes taking over and developing Boccaccio's role not only as author but also as editor, scribe, and publisher of the *De mulieribus*. I explore Christine's role as book producer in my current project, which bears the provisional title "Female Creators: The Books of Christine de Pizan in Their French and English Context."

8 Brown gives a succinct list of Boccaccio's misogynistic attitudes in *FW*, xviii–xix.

9 See the articles in *Boccaccio and Feminist Criticism*, ed. F. Regina Psaki and Thomas C. Stillinger (Chapel Hill: Annali d'Italianistica, 2006).

10 Maureen Cheney Curnow, ed., "The *Livre de la Cité des dames* of Christine de Pisan: A Critical Edition," 2 vols. (diss., Vanderbilt University, 1975), documents Christine's debt to Boccaccio, 2:138–67. Curnow (2:142–7) concludes that Christine borrowed extensively from the French translation of the *De mulieribus, Des cleres et nobles femmes,* henceforth *Cleres femmes.*

11 Patrick M. de Winter, *La bibliothèque de Philippe le Hardi, duc de Bourgogne (1364–1404): Etude sur les manuscrits à peintures d'une collection princière a l'époque du "style gothique international"* (Paris: CNRS, 1985), 206–7, says that Paris, Bibliothèque nationale fr. 12420 (henceforth fr. 12420) was the first known example of the anonymous French translation of the text. It was completed on 12 September 1401, as stated in the colophon on fol. 167v, where the translator is not named. The book is described in rubrics as "un livre en françois de pluseurs histoires de femmes de bonne renommee" (206).

12 Kevin Brownlee, "Christine de Pizan's Canonical Authors: The Special Case of Boccaccio," *Comparative Literature Studies* 32, no. 2 (1995): 244–61, states his belief that Christine knew both the Latin text and the French translation (257n3). My study reinforces this opinion, given that the translation and its illumination were done in circles associated with two of Christine's major patrons.

13 All English translations are taken from Earl Jeffrey Richards, *The Book of the City of Ladies* (New York: Persea, 1992; 1998) and indicated in the body of my text as R, followed by the page number. All references to Christine's Middle French text will be taken from Richards's edition, *La Città delle dame* (Milan: Luni Editrice, 1998), which contains an Italian translation by Patrizia Caraffi; these references will appear as Caraffi and Richards, followed by the page number. In this essay I cite only the English translations of Christine's texts, unless I find that the original Middle French is necessary to make my argument.

14 Curnow, "The Livre de la *Cité des dames,*" 1:152, estimates that Christine draws seventy-four of her examples from the *De mulieribus.* In *City* 1.39.3, which I discuss below, Christine echoes a passage in the French translation lacking in the original.

15 Patricia A. Phillippy. "Establishing Authority: Boccaccio's *De Claris Mulieribus* and Christine de Pizan's *Le Livre de la Cité des Dames," Romanic Review* 57 (1986): 167–94, rpt. *The Selected Writings of Christine de Pizan*, ed. and trans. Renate Blumenfeld-Kosinski and ed. Kevin Brownlee (New York: Norton, 1997), 329–61. Hereafter I will indicate, within parentheses in the body of my text, references to articles and texts present in this widely circulated volume by *SW*, followed by the page number(s).

16 Brownlee, "Christine de Pizan's Canonical Authors," lists all of Christine's citations of the *De mulieribus*, as well as of the *Decameron* (258n7). He analyses those references in his chapter in this volume. The references can also be found in the Concordance on the website devoted to Christine's masterpiece, her compilation of thirty of her own texts, London, British Library, Harley MS 4431, http://www.pizan.lib.ed.ac.uk/conc.html.

17 Christine de Pizan, *Le chemin de longue étude*, ed. and trans. Andrea Tarnowski (Paris: Livre de poche, 2000), v. 1128, v. 1141. All references to the *Chemin* will be taken from Tarnowski and placed within the body of my text. On the *Chemin* as a recasting of the *Commedia*, see Kevin Brownlee, "Literary Genealogy and the Problem of the Father: Christine de Pizan and Dante," *Journal of Medieval and Renaissance Studies* 23 (1993): 365–87.

18 Brigitte Buettner, *Boccaccio's "Des cleres et nobles femmes": Systems of Signification in an Illuminated Manuscript* (Seattle: College Art Association with the University of Washington Press, 1996), 21–2, argues that Christine here pays a compliment to the Luccan merchant of luxury cloth and books, Jacques Raponde (Rappondi), who both Buettner and de Winter believe directed the production of the translation and its illustration.

19 Dame Raison's list begins in 1.12 and extends until 1.48.

20 Anne D. Hedeman, *The Royal Image: Illustrations of the "Grandes Chroniques de France" 1274–1422* (Berkeley: University of California Press, 1991). Christine's "writings in particular focus on themes that became important in copies of the *Grandes Chroniques* produced during the second half of Charles VI's reign" (Hedeman, 139).

21 I use feminine pronouns in function of the feminine gender of "France."

22 "France comme loiaus fille secourt sa mere en touz besoinz" (Viard, 1:5). All quotations will be taken from *Les Grandes Chroniques de France*, ed. Jacques Viard, 10 vols. (Paris: Société de l'Histoire de France, 1920–53).

23 "Si ne fu pas sanz raison dame renommée seur autres nations, car ele ne souffri pas longuement la servitude d'idolatrie et de mescreandise" (Viard, 1:4).

24 "Si li a Nostre Sires doné par sa grace une prerogative et une avantage seur toutes autres terres et seur toutes autres nations … ne fu que la foi n'i fust plus fervemment et plus droitment tenue que en nule autre terre" (Viard, 1:5).

25 The reference is found in Christine's lyric lament on Philippe's death: "Plourez, roÿne, et ayés le cuer noir / Pour cil par qui fustes oû trosne offerte." *Autres balades*, London, British Library, MS Harley 4431, fols 45d–46a.

26 See Lori J. Walters, "Christine de Pizan, Jean Gerson, et un exemplaire des *Grandes Chroniques* prêté par Philippe le Hardi à la Reine de France (Paris, Bibliothèque de l'Arsenal MS 5223)," in *Christine de Pizan et son époque*, special issue of *Revue médiévales* 53 (2012): 220–5.

27 Christine de Pizan, *Le Livre des fais et bonnes meurs du sage roy Charles V*, 2 vols., ed. Suzanne Solente (Paris: Champion, 1936, 1940). Hereafter I cite the text as *Charles V*, followed by the book and chapter number(s).

28 Curnow documents Christine's debt to the *Grandes Chroniques* in "The *Livre de la Cité des dames*," 2:180–2; and to the *Miroir historial* in ibid., 2:183–93.

29 Elizabeth Casteen, "Sex and Politics in Naples: The Regnant Queenship of Johanna I," *Journal of the Historical Society* 11, no. 2 (2011): 183–210, outlines the history of the French Angevin dynasty (184n3). Ronald G. Musto, in *Medieval Naples: A Documentary History 400–1400* (New York: Italica, 2013), does this in greater detail (145–302).

30 "The book, I believe, will do as much to keep your name bright for posterity as (with Fortune's help) the county of Monteodorisio did formerly and the county of Altavilla does now" (*FW*, 5). Carlo d'Arto, Count of Monteodorisio, Andrea's first husband, died in 1346 (*FW*, 480). Francesco Paolo Tocco, *Niccolò Acciaiuoli: vita e politica in Italia alla metà del XIV secolo* (Rome: Istituto storico italiano per il Medio Evo, 2001), mentions that Andrea played a key role in the inclusion of the family in the ranks of the Angevin nobility (286).

31 Vittore Branca, *Boccaccio: The Man and His Works*, trans. Richard Monges (New York: New York University Press, 1976), notes that the tributes Boccaccio received at his death from figures including Coluccio Salutati raised Boccaccio "to a position equal to that of Dante and Petrarch" (191), two poets with whom he had allied himself during his lifetime. Salutati was well known in the circles surrounding Christine. See the references to him in André Combes, *Jean de Montreuil et le chancelier Gerson. Contribution à l'histoire des rapports de l'humanisme et de la théologie en France au début du XVe siècle* (Paris: Vrin, 1942).

32 Charity Cannon Willard, *Christine de Pizan: Her Life and Works* (New York: Persea, 1984), 165.

33 See Tracy Adams, *The Life and Afterlife of Isabeau of Bavaria* (Baltimore: Johns Hopkins University Press, 2010), for a recent reevaluation of the French queen. As for Johanna, Casteen, disclaiming "access to Johanna's interiority," instead focuses on her reputation (*From She-Wolf to Martyr*, 26).

34 Casteen, "Sex and Politics in Naples."

35 Casteen, *From She-Wolf to Martyr*, 114.

36 Christine de Pizan, *Le Livre de la mutacion de Fortune*, 4 vols., ed. Suzanne Solente (Paris: Picard, 1959; 1964; 1966). I shall cite this text by verse numbers, placing them in the body of my text within parentheses.

37 It is noteworthy that Christine often represents herself as a victim of Fortune.

38 This is essentially the image of Louis d'Anjou conveyed by the *Grandes chroniques*; see Casteen, *From She-Wolf to Martyr*, 214.

39 "il n'eust point failli à subjuguer ses anemis et après à conquerir l'empire de Romme, auquel avoit grant affection et esperance [he would not have failed to subjugate his enemies and afterwards conquer the Roman empire, which he greatly desired and hoped to do]," (2.139; my translation).

40 "Haulte dame d'atractïon / D'empereurs de digne memoire" (Prologue, 86–7, London, British Library, Harley 4431). See Lori J. Walters, "Christine de Pizan's *Prologue adreçant a la royne*: Translations into Modern French and English," 2013. http://www.pizan.lib.ed.ac.uk/TranslationsofPrologue.rtf. These translations can also be found in the Editions section of the Harley 4431 website at http://www.pizan.lib.ed.ac.uk/edit.html.

41 Gilbert Ouy and Christine M. Reno, "Ou mène le *Chemin de long estude*? Christine de Pizan, Ambrogio Migli, et les ambitions impériales de Louis d'Orléans (A propos du ms. BNF fr. 1643)," in *Christine 2000: Studies Offered to Angus Kennedy*, ed. Nadia Margolis and John Campbell (Amsterdam: Rodopi, 2000), 177–95.

42 Christine suggests that she sees Johanna as Ysabel's precursor by her depiction of the sovereign in the dedication miniature (fol. 1) of Brussels, BR 10982, a presentation copy of the *Chemin*. The sovereign, whom we would expect to be King Charles VI, instead here closely resembles Queen Johanna as she is portrayed on fol. 165 of fr. 12420, Philippe le Hardi's copy of the *Cleres femmes*.

43 See Kevin Brownlee, "Structures of Authority in Christine de Pizan's *Ditié de Jehanne d'Arc*," in *Discourses of Authority in Medieval and Renaissance Literature*, ed. Kevin Brownlee and Walter Stephens (Dartmouth: University Press of New England, 1989); rpt. *SW* 371–90.

44 Christine de Pizan, *Ditié de Jehanne d'Arc*, ed. and trans. Angus J. Kennedy and Kenneth Varty (Oxford: Medium Aevum Monographs, 1977). Here are the quotations in full: Stanza 16, 43: "For there will be a King of France called Charles, son of Charles, who will be supreme ruler over all Kings. Prophecies have given him the name of 'The Flying Stag', and many a deed will be accomplished by this conqueror (God has called him to the task) and in the end he will be emperor." Stanza 43, 47: "She will destroy the Saracens, by conquering the Holy Land. She will lead Charles there,

whom God preserve! Before he dies he will make such a journey. He is the one who is to conquer it. It is there that she will end her days and that both of them are to win glory. It is there that the whole enterprise will be brought to completion." Christine also refers to the Second Charlemagne prophecy in *Charles V* 2.15.

45 See the genealogical tables in Casteen, *From She-Wolf to Martyr*, xii–xiii.

46 See "The Testament of Robert, king of Sicily, 16 January 1343" in Musto, *Medieval Naples* (238–54), where Jerusalem always precedes Sicily in the titles of King Robert and Queen Sancia. As titular kings and queens of Jerusalem, the Angevin rulers were doubly important to the French. In the English translations included in this essay I restore the order that is invariably observed in the Latin and French texts, but which the translator inverts.

47 Casteen, *From She-Wolf to Martyr*, 146.

48 Gregory replied by requesting that she instead free Constantinople from Turkish threat (Casteen "Sex and Politics in Naples," 202–3; *From She-Wolf to Martyr*, 191).

49 Casteen, "Sex and Politics in Naples," 207n66.

50 Casteen, *From She-Wolf to Martyr*, 203.

51 "justement, canoniquement et concordablement en pape, sanz debat, difficulté ou contradiction aucune" (*Charles V* 2.146).

52 "se consenti à la ditte election, et aussi fist la royne de Naples et tous les seigneurs du pais" (*Charles V* 2.146). In note 2, Solente gives one possible reason for Johanna's shift in support from Urban to Clement VII: "peut-être que l'exemple et les conseils de Charles V agirent sur elle [perhaps the example and the advice of Charles V had an effect on her]," which could be taken to imply that she and Charles were in contact with one another.

53 Casteen, "On She-Wolves and Famous Women," 000.

54 French support of Clement VII is the subject of *Charles V* 3.51; 3.53; 3.54; 3.55; 3.56; 3.57; 3.58; 3.60; 3.61; 3.62.

55 To further his claim, Louis XII had a written summary of Johanna's reign prepared for him (Casteen, *From She-Wolf to Martyr*, 30, 31).

56 Margaret Franklin, *Boccaccio's Heroines: Power and Virtue in Renaissance Society* (Aldershot: Ashgate, 2006), 24n3.

57 See Casteen, *From She-Wolf to Martyr*, 158–9.

58 Musto translates this Latin document, which he dates between 19 May 1364 and 1367 (*Medieval Naples*, 289–91). For the dating and description of Santa Maria Incoronata, see Paola Vitolo, *La chiesa della Regina* (Roma: Viella, 2008). I am grateful to Professor Musto for his help on these issues.

59 See Casteen, *From She-Wolf to Martyr*, 158–9.

60 *Le Débat sur le "Roman de la Rose,"* ed. Eric Hicks (Geneva: Slatkine, 1996), 162. Hereafter the references to this edition will be given in the body of my text as Hicks, followed by the page number(s).
61 Samantha Kelly, *The New Solomon: Robert of Naples (1309–1343) and Fourteenth-Century Kingship* (Leiden: Brill, 2003), 125. See also Marianne Cecilia Gaposchkin, *The Making of Saint Louis: Kingship, Sanctity, and Crusade in the Later Middle Ages* (Ithaca: Cornell University Press, 2008), 85–6.
62 Chiara Mercuri, "*Stat inter spinas lilium*: Le Lys de France et la couronne d'épines," *Le Moyen Age* 110 (2004): 497–512.
63 Gerson will also do so in his sermon on Saint Bernard; see below.
64 Paris, Bibliothèque nationale de France, MS Lat. 1028, fol. 285v. Quoted by Mercuri, "*Stat inter spinas lilium*," 503.
65 *The Debate of the "Romance of the Rose,"* ed. and trans. David Hult (Chicago; University of Chicago Press, 2010). All future references to Hult will be taken from this edition/translation and indicated as Hult, followed by the page number(s). This quotation is found on 88; the selections from the sermon extend from 84 to 92.
66 In her review of Edelgard E. DuBruck's edition of *La Passion Isabeau. Une edition du manuscrit Fr. 966 de la Bibliothèque Nationale de Paris avec une introduction et des notes* (New York: Lang, 1990), which appeared in the *Revue de Linguistique Romane* 56 (1992): 312–21, Geneviève Hasenohr corrects her previous position (313), now claiming that this *Passion of 1398* (her revised title) had in fact been commissioned by the queen. I add that the text could also be referred to as the *Passion Ysabel*, based on the way the anonymous author writes the queen's name in the dedication.
67 Stephen Kolsky, *The Genealogy of Women: Studies in Boccaccio's "De mulieribus claris"* (New York: Lang, 2003), 167.
68 Casteen elaborates on this point in *From She-Wolf to Martyr*, 118–95.
69 Here are the other references: "If we examine her domain closely, our amazement will equal its fame, for it is a mighty realm of the sort not usually ruled by women" (*FW*, 471); "She is generous in the manner of a king rather than of a woman" (*FW*, 471); "Truly these would have been magnificent accomplishments for a vigorous and mighty king, much less for a woman (*FW*, 473).
70 Boccaccio's ending echoes the praise of Johanna he made in the opening lines of the *De mulieribus*. Casting around for a worthy recipient of his book, his choice first falls on Johanna: "the first woman who came to mind was that radiant splendor of Italy, that unique glory not only of women but of rulers: Joanna, Most Serene Queen of Jerusalem and Sicily" (*FW*, 3).

71 Branca, *Boccaccio*, 115.

72 Ibid., 90.

73 This becomes "Hauteville" in the French translation.

74 Andrea's importance is minimized by Franklin: "the timing and content of Boccaccio's dedication strongly suggest that Andrea Acciaiuoli, with her close Neapolitan connections, was a screen dedicatee through whom Boccaccio hoped to recommend himself to a substantially more powerful and illustrious personage: Queen Joanna of Naples" (*Boccaccio's Heroines*, 23), the idea being that Boccaccio was using Andrea to secure himself a place at Johanna's court. He did not find a place there in the 1360s, for reasons that remain unclear but may be related to his falling out with Andrea's brother Niccolò, Johanna's Grand Seneschal. However, during his last visit to Naples, c. 1371, Johanna did offer him a post. Branca, translating from original Latin sources, says: "Joanna caused Ugo to offer him a quiet post"; "When he was on the point of returning to Tuscany, once again the queen made a great effort to hold him, invoking the direct intervention of her husband, King James of Majorca" (*Boccaccio*, 169). Branca then explains that Boccaccio refused Johanna's offers out of his "jealous love of independence" and his "desire for meditative and productive solitude" (170). Most importantly for my discussion here, Boccaccio did not delete his praise of Andrea (or, for that matter, of Johanna) in the autograph edition he carefully prepared prior to his death in 1375. From this it is reasonable to infer that Boccaccio's interest in Andrea (and Johanna) extended well beyond a practical desire for employment and monetary reward. I leave open the question of whether the French were interpreting Boccaccio as he would have wanted to be seen, or were merely using him for their own ends, if the two explanations can indeed be separated or established with certainty.

75 Branca, *Boccaccio*, 111. If we consider the exact title of Boccaccio's *Trattatello in laude di Dante – De origine vita studiis et moribus viri clarissimi Dante Aligerii Florentini poete illustris et de operibus compositis ab eodem* – we see that Boccaccio perceives some of the same stellar qualities in Andrea that he sees not only in himself but also in Dante. All three were studious and illustrious (*claris*).

76 See Ronchetti, "Reading Like a Woman," in this volume, on how Boccaccio "splits himself" between the male quality of reason and the female quality of compassion.

77 The emphasis he places on the significance of Andrea's name would have attracted Christine's attention. On the care Christine takes to write her

name in MS Harley 4431, see Lori J. Walters, "Signatures and Anagrams in the Queen's Manuscript (London, British Library, Harley MS 4431)," 2012. http://www.pizan.lib.ed.ac.uk/waltersanagrams.html.

78 The chancellery of the Church of Paris or of Notre-Dame was "une charge d'essence doctrinale [qui] donne à son titulaire le droit de conférer la licence d'enseigner et l'obligation de surveiller la doctrine de tout ce qui se dit ou s'écrit dans le monde universitaire." Combes, *Jean de Montreuil et le chancelier Gerson*, 285–86, as quoted in *Le Débat sur le "Roman de la Rose,"* ed. Virginie Greene (Paris: Champion, 2002), 161n1.

79 "tum denique professio mea debens erroribus et viciis quantum valet obniti." See *Le Débat sur le "Roman de la Rose,"* ed. Hicks, 162.

80 Gerson points out to Pierre, "Hec est heresis Pelagii" (Hicks, 164). In this same letter Gerson informs Pierre that he has misunderstood a crucial passage from Augustine's *De doctrina christiana* (Hicks, 174).

81 Barbara Newman, *From Virile Woman to Woman Christ: Studies in Medieval Religion and Literature* (Philadelphia: University of Pennsylvania Press, 1995), 5.

82 Boccaccio, *Des cleres et nobles femmes (Ms. Bibl. Nat. 12420)*, 2 vols., ed. Jeanne Baroin and Josiane Haffen (Paris: Annales littéraires de l'Université de Besançon, 1993). All future references will be given as Baroin and Haffen, followed by the volume number, a colon and the page number(s). The dedication ("Proesme") in the table of contents, reads: "Cy commence la premiere rubriche, ouquel est le proheme de l'acteur, qui parle comment il envoya son livre a tresnoble et excellent dame Jehanne, la tresnoble royne de Jherusalem et de Secile" (Baroin and Haffen, 1:3). On fr. 12420, see Buettner, *Boccaccio's "Des cleres et nobles femmes."*

83 Christine refers twice to her supervision of the production of the manuscript's illuminations in the prologue she composed for MS Harley 4431. See Walters, "Christine de Pizan's *Prologue adreçant a la royne*," at http://www.pizan.lib.ed.ac.uk/TranslationsofPrologue.rtf and http://www.pizan.lib.ed.ac.uk/edit.html.

84 Rhiannon Daniels, "Reading Boccaccio's Paratexts: Dedications as Thresholds between Worlds." Note that Daniels draws her examples about the *De mulieribus* from printed rather than from manuscript copies.

85 The term is used by James Laidlaw to refer to Christine's use of a two-part frontispiece in the Harley manuscript, which has special parallels with the Berry copy, as I discuss below. For the Laidlaw reference, see the MS Harley 4431, at http://www.pizan.lib.ed.ac.uk/.

86 The *Cleres femmes* miniatures cited here can be viewed in colour online at http://mandragore.bnf.fr.

87 Interestingly, a similar rendition of the motif reappears on fol. 2r of Chantilly, Bibl. Du Château, 492 (reproduced in *Album*, 186), the first of the two collections Christine presented to Queen Ysabel, the previously discussed MS Harley 4431 of 1414, and Chantilly, Bibl. Du Château, 492–3. According to the latter's table of contents, the first volume, compiled between 1399 and 1402, contains twenty-four texts; the second volume, which Christine added to the first from 1403 to c. 1405, contains three texts. Unlike MS Harley 4431, this earlier collection does not open with a miniature of Christine presenting her book to the queen. However, a presentation miniature and prologue may have been originally present; see Christine Reno, "La mémoire de Christine de Pizan dans ses manuscrits," *Le Moyen Français* 75 (2014): 73.

88 Dante's coupling of Beatrice and the Virgin, a model that I shall treat in detail elsewhere, does not apply as closely as does Boccaccio's coupling of Johanna and Andrea to an actual, historical collaboration between a queen and her female advisor. Note that Christine may well have been advising the queen and/or composing poetry for her at an earlier date, perhaps as early as 1394, when it is believed she began to compose lyric poems. Unless I indicate otherwise, I base my information on Christine's life on Willard, *Christine de Pizan: Her Life and Works*.

89 We recall that she inserts Dame Sibyl's letter into the *Trois vertus*.

90 All references to the *Trois vertus* are made to the translation by Charity Cannon Willard, *A Medieval Woman's Mirror of Honor: The Treasury of the City of Ladies*, ed. Madeleine Pelner Cosman (New York: Persea, 1989).

91 Christine takes one of Dante's own political notions to its logical conclusion. In *De vulgari eloquentia* (On Eloquence in the Vernacular) 1.18, as well as in his *Monarchia*, Dante laments the absence of a monarchy to confer political and linguistic unity on Italy. It is precisely by connecting her work to the furthering of the French monarchy that Christine implicitly posits the superiority of French over Italian. Christine at once captures all of the force of Dante's "illustrious vernacular" while showing why France's vernacular is even more suited to be deemed "illustrious" than Italy's. See Lori Walters, "The Royal Vernacular: Poet and Patron in Christine de Pizan's *Sept Psaumes allégorisés* and *Charles V*," in *The Vernacular Spirit: Essays on Medieval Religious Literature*, ed. Renate Blumenfeld-Kosinski, Duncan Robertson, and Nancy Warren (New York: Palgrave, 2002), 145–82.

92 That court included Marguerite de Guyenne, the wife of Ysabel's son, the dauphin Louis de Guyenne. Marguerite was the woman slated to

become the next queen of France (her hopes were dashed when Louis died unexpectedly on 18 December 1415). Three copies of the *Trois Vertus* open with a dedication to Marguerite. See *Le livre des trois vertus*, ed. Charity Cannon Willard and Eric Hicks (Paris: Champion, 1989).

93 Maureen Quilligan, *The Allegory of Female Authority: Christine de Pizan's "Cité des Dames"* (Ithaca: Cornell University Press, 1991).

94 According to Curnow, "The *Livre de la Cité des Dames*," 2:1055–7, these are Jeanne d'Evreux (d. 1371), the third wife of King Charles IV; Jeanne's daughter, Blanche d'Orléans (1327–1392); Blanche de Navarre (d. 1398), the second wife of Philippe VI; Marie d'Anjou; Catherine de Bourbon, who ruled after the death of her husband, Jean de Bourbon, in 1393 until her own death in 1411, making her the only one in the group still alive at the time Christine composed the *Cité des dames*. All these women played an essential role in the maintenance of royal succession and primogeniture. Let us note that the lady Christine praises most highly is Louis d'Anjou's wife, Marie, to whom she devotes a long, enthusiastic encomium (R34–5), and that her praise of Marie d'Anjou resembles her praise of Queen Ysabel, both of them regents working on behalf of their underage children.

95 Gerson delivered this sermon to the Cistercian College in Paris on 20 August 1402. He assumed the persona of the saint, captivating his audience by saying: "For a little while then, turn your attention from me and imagine that it is Bernard himself who speaks and not I" (*EW*, 130). The entire sermon has a strong Augustinian subtext. Gerson cites Augustine by name twice (*EW*, 129), and emphasizes that Bernard had a mother whose upbringing prepared him for his role as churchman (*EW*, 146–8). His version of Bernard's story is similar to Christine's 1405 telling of the story of Augustine's mother's determinant effect on her son's sanctity in *City* 1.10.4. *Jean Gerson, Early Works*, ed. and trans. Brian Patrick McGuire (Mahwah: Paulist Press, 1998). I insert references to translations done by McGuire directly into my text, designating them by "*EW*" followed by the page number(s).

96 With his references to Zion and Jerusalem (*EW*, 128), Gerson casts himself as Bernard's latter-day spokesperson at the University of Paris. Gerson's words convey an implicit political message. They strengthen French claims to national superiority because Bernard had been designated by the pope to preach the Second Crusade. In Vezelay, France, he directed a famous sermon to the French king and queen, Louis VII and Aliénor d'Aquitaine (more popularly known today as Eleanor of Aquitaine, wife of England's Henry II Plantagenet).

97 The *Pater Noster* speaks of instituting God's realm "on earth as it is in heaven," thus establishing the heavenly court as the model of the earthly court. Christine's invocation of the universal prayer, the *Pater Noster*, in the final lines of her *Trois vertus* suggests her desire, linked to that of the French monarchy through texts such as the *Grandes chroniques*, to create a human society reflective of the divine society constituted by the Trinity, the Virgin, and the saints. Christine takes over much of Boccaccio's mission of improving society through the perpetuation of women's good name, but she does so in France rather than in their native Italy. One reason is that France is where Johanna's legacy is most apparent, evidenced by her bequeathing her kingdom to Louis d'Anjou. In so doing, Johanna had it revert to the French Angevins who had founded it many years before in the person of Charles d'Anjou, Saint Louis's brother.

98 We note that Boccaccio's original Latin passage is similar in the French translation, save for one telling detail. The French translator adds that it is up to "les plus sages [the wiser people]" (Baroin and Haffen, 2:194) to correct Boccaccio's recast text.

99 Christine lauds the Virgin's "humility, which surpasses all others" (*City* 3.1.1, R217).

100 See Rhiannon Daniels, *Boccaccio and the Book, Production and Reading in Italy 1340–1520* (Oxford: Legenda, 2009), 138–40 and Appendix 8, 204, for a useful summary of the redactional phases of the *De mulieribus* and the features of the extant manuscripts.

101 Her production amounts to forty-two texts and fifty-four manuscripts. Note that the *Album* bases its list of fifty-four manuscripts upon modern shelf marks, whereas Christine would have counted forty-nine presentation copies. See Lori J. Walters, "The Book as Gift of Wisdom: *Le Chemin de lonc estude* in the Queen's Manuscript," *Digital Philology: A Journal of Medieval Cultures* 5 (2016): 228–46; 238n3.

102 Kolsky cites Boccaccio's "impossible attempt to reconcile the extraordinary deeds performed by the pagan women of antiquity with the *mores* of Christian morality." This is one way that the text "represents the difficult fusion of two types of exemplary writing. The first is the narrative account in which the reader is left to draw conclusions with only the implicit guidance of authorial intervention (or, at most, brief comments), and the second is the direct moral imperative to draw a constructive lesson from the given *exempla*" (*The Genealogy of Women*, 166).

103 Despite Boccaccio's pronouncements that he will not include any female saints because they have been amply represented elsewhere, the fact

that he begins his collection with Eve reveals an underlying Christian orientation that clashes with his favouring of antique models. Boccaccio represents Eve as faced with the choice between good and evil, a choice that would influence all her "children." That choice remained a pertinent one for women in Boccaccio's time. He asks Andrea to distinguish between the positive and negative qualities of the women in his portraits and model her actions on their examples of virtue instead of vice. Boccaccio's highest female exemplar, implied rather than stated by him, is the Virgin, Eve's traditional counter model. Boccaccio's Christianizing dedication to Andrea may have been influenced by his religious vocation.

104 Dolly Weber, "Reading through the Text: Lives of Saint Catherine of Alexandria by Christine de Pizan and Pietro Aretino," in *Accessus ad Auctores: Studies in Honor of Chris Kleinhenz*, ed. Fabian Alfie and Andrea Dini (Arizona: ACMRS, 2011), judiciously points out that "The saint's life, and particularly the martyr's life, provides one of the very few medieval fora in which women engaged in an openly political and public discourse" (387).

105 Richards omits Boccaccio's name on R153, but rectifies his error in Caraffi and Richards, 314.

106 These included the emperor's wife, who was converted to Christianity through Catherine's example. Her conversion perhaps provides a model for the effect Christine desires to have on Ysabel, to whom she sends the dossier of her *Rose* Debate Epistles in order to enlist the queen's aid in stamping out misogyny. Hult gives an English translation of the cover letter Christine sent to Queen Ysabel on 1 February 1402 (Hult, 98–9).

107 The first of seven picture book cycles in the Duke of Berry's *Belles Heures* is devoted to Saint Catherine.

108 Stephen Perkinson gives detailed treatment of the representation of the three female artists in the *Cleres femmes* copies in *The Likeness of the King: A Prehistory of Portraiture in Late Medieval France* (Chicago: University of Chicago Press, 2009), 180–6, where he reproduces all the images. They can be viewed in colour at http://mandragore.bnf.fr, along with all the other miniatures in the *Cleres femmes* copies.

109 This image can be seen in the picture gallery at www.pizan.lib.ed.ac.uk/.

110 Millard Meiss, *French Painting in the Time of Jean de Berry*, vol. 3: *The Limbourgs and Their Contemporaries* (New York: Braziller, 1974) attributes the majority of the miniatures to the Master of the Duke of Berry's *Cleres femmes*, but adds: "In fr. 12420 an assistant of the *Cité des Dames* Master painted two miniatures on folios 46 and 46v. Certain other folios,

for instance 42v and 43, are by a weak artist influenced by both the Coronation and *Cité des Dames* styles" (287).

111 This comes at the beginning of the *Mutacion* in fr. 603. See *Album*, 294–306, for a description of this manuscript; for a colour reproduction of the image, see figure 22, p. 781.

112 This is the one instance, in all of her presentation copies, in which she is portrayed sitting before a mirror. See "Christine de Pizan mise en scène," table iconographique, *Album*, 749.

113 These can be viewed in colour online at mandragore.bnf.fr.

114 Christine appears to be the first writer to employ the term *artiste* to refer to artisans; it had previously been used to refer to scholars. Perkinson (*The Likeness of the King*, 187) cites Sandra Hindman, *Christine de Pizan's "Epistre Othéa": Painting and Politics at the Court of Charles VI* (Toronto: Pontifical Institute of Mediaeval Studies, 1986), 73.

115 Eustache Deschamps responded to a letter that Christine had addressed to him on 10 February 1404 (*SW*, 109–11) with a poem whose refrain was "Your achievements stand alone in the French realm." He also says to her: "you received knowledge from God, no one else" (4); "God gave you the gift of Solomon, / your heart is given to teaching" (11–12; *SW*, 112–13). These statements reinforce Gerson's implicit claim that Christine's teachings were divinely inspired.

116 *Charles V* 3.12. See Lori Walters, "Constructing Reputations: *Fama* and Memory in *Charles V* and *L'Advision-Cristine*," in *Fama: The Politics of Talk and Reputation in Medieval Europe*, ed. Thelma Fenster and Daniel Lord Smail (Ithaca: Cornell University Press, 2003), 118–42. On the early reception of Boccaccio in France, see Anne D. Hedeman, "Illuminating Boccaccio: Visual Translation in Early Fifteenth-Century France," *Mediaevalia* 34 (2013): 111–53; Hedeman, *Translating the Past: Laurent de Premierfait and Boccaccio's "De Casibus"* (Los Angeles: Getty, 2008); Buettner, *Boccaccio's "Des cleres et nobles femmes."*

PART FIVE

Literary Contexts and Intertexts

12 A Persian in a Pear Tree: Middle Eastern Analogues for Pirro/Pyrrhus

FRANKLIN LEWIS

European scholarship on sources and analogues for Boccaccio, and especially for Chaucer, has produced an impressive bibliography, some of which treats the question of "oriental" sources.[1] Other works have delved into the folklore traditions of the Middle East, especially the Arabic and Persian traditions.[2] Documenting the sources and analogues of medieval works of literature, including the Islamicate literatures, has thus made considerable progress, though there remains much to recover for a more solid understanding of the circulation of such materials.

Efforts, including motif and folklore indices, to trace earlier iterations of the pear tree episode in Chaucer's *Merchant's Tale* or Boccaccio's *Decameron* beyond any immediate European sources familiar to Chaucer or Boccaccio tend to place the tale's origins in that quaintly designated area to the east known as the Orient, though without any decisive findings about the chronology of the "oriental" versions, largely because there is a vast corpus of such materials in Arabic, Persian, and Turkish texts, which remains to be fully identified, explored, and indexed.[3] However, some significant headway has lately been made in this regard.[4] The present essay aims to clarify the discussion about the earlier Islamicate enchanted fruit tree tales; establish the analogic relationship of several earlier Arabic and Persian tales to their European counterparts; and explore the possibility of common sources for, or cross-fertilization of, these two tale types in their various European and Middle Eastern renditions. Furthermore, by recovering the earlier history of a particular tale and considering the moral that is derived from it or the point it is used to drive home – in other words, the relationship of example to principle in previous tellings – one can arrive at a greater appreciation of the purpose of an author in choosing particular tales from the vast repertoire of what has been called "the sea of stories." By knowing the full contours of a given tale and the moral attributed to it by earlier authors, we can better understand what intentional transformations Boccaccio, or other authors, have introduced to received or migrating literary/folkloric narratives, bringing us to a fuller appreciation of the interpretative turns each author employs in creatively reworking exempla and bending them to a particular purpose. An awareness of this process will help refine our theories of the principles motivating Boccaccio's narrative art.

Boccaccio embeds his telling of the pear tree episode in a longer narrative concerning the cuckolding of Nicostrato by Lidia and Pirro in the *Decameron*, seventh day, ninth *novella*.[5] In this tale, the only one in the *Decameron* to feature pears (pere) or a pear tree (pero), Lidia becomes infatuated with Pirro, the servant of her elderly husband, Nicostrato. Pirro rejects Lidia's love declaration (conveyed to him through the intermediary of Lidia's lady-in-waiting, Lusca), figuring it may be a trick to test his loyalty to Nicostrato. When Lidia persists, he demands she demonstrate her sincerity by performing three tasks: killing Nicostrato's favourite sparrowhawk in front of him, plucking a tuft of Nicostrato's beard hairs, and pulling one of his best teeth and giving them to Pirro. While this seems a most difficult assignment indeed to Lidia, she promises Pirro that not only will she perform these three tasks, but she will even contrive to cuckold Nicostrato right in front of him and make him disbelieve his own eyes. After fulfilling the first three demands, she feigns illness and gets Nicostrato and Pirro to carry her outside, to sit under a pear tree in the garden. She soon asks Pirro, whom she has briefed about her plan, to climb the tree and fetch her some pears. While perched up in the tree, Pirro claims to see Nicostrato and Lidia making vigorous love on the ground, and reproaches them for being so indiscreet, suggesting that they had better use the rooms in the house than satisfy their urge in full view of Pirro. When Pirro continues to insist on having seen them *in flagrante delicto*, Nicostrato decides to climb the pear tree to find out whether it is enchanted, or produces some kind of marvel. Lidia and Pirro quickly get down to business, and upon seeing them engaged in the act, Nicostrato accuses his wife of harlotry. But Lidia and Pirro return to their places before Nicostrato gets back down from the tree, and when he does, Pirro apologizes for his earlier mistake, now agreeing that earlier he himself must have been seeing an illusion, since Nicostrato has also seen a similar incredible thing. And surely a reputable lady like Lidia, even if she did wish to stain

Nicostrato's honour, would not do so in plain view of her husband. Lidia feigns indignation at the aspersions Nicostrato has made against her honour, and only after Pirro chops down the pear tree does her anger subside to the point where she can "forgive" Nicostrato.

A similar cuckolding of January, by May and Damyan, occurs in the *Merchant's Tale* of Chaucer, who was certainly aware of Boccaccio's telling.[6] But for this episode at the pear tree, there are at least two important earlier analogues from Islamicate literatures; a Persian analogue of the pear tree episode was already identified as such over a century ago, though its chronological position among Islamicate versions was not properly understood, and its significance was therefore not properly apprehended or addressed. Anterior to the Persian is an Arabic analogue from the twelfth century that has, as far as I am aware, not been well recognized by Western scholarship, and which may well be the source of the Persian.

This essay therefore attempts to set the Persian and the Arabic narratives in dialogue with Latin, Italian, and English versions of the pear tree tale. The two Islamicate versions do not agree on the kind of fruit tree in question, and unlike the *Decameron* or the *Canterbury Tales*, they do not situate the fruit tree of deception in a larger narrative, or take any interest in the character or psychology of the wife's paramour, who is never named. We thus have no developed character of Pirro/Pyrrhus, as in Boccaccio, or of Damyan, as in Chaucer, yet we do have a short *fabliau* narrative that involves a wife using her wiles to deceive a cuckolded husband in his presence with an unnamed paramour which is, in its particulars, close enough to discount polygenesis.[7]

The Persian Pear Tree of Deception

We will consider the two Islamicate versions of this tale in reverse chronological order, beginning with the much better known version, from the *Maṡnavī-yi ma'navī* (Couplets of True Meaning) of Jalāl al-Dīn Rūmī, a poem of about 25,500 lines that is perhaps one of the two or three most widely read poems in the Islamicate world from Bosnia to Bengal, everywhere that Persian was once a prestige language. The text was composed over a period of several years, with interruptions, beginning in about 660 AH/1262, continuing after a hiatus in 662 AH/1263–4,[8] and concluding perhaps in 1269 or 1270, some years before the poet's death in December 1273. The *Maṡnavī* is infamously desultory, embedding story within story, interrupting itself frequently to tell a different story, and without any fixed scheme, journey, or frame-tale to guide the unfolding sequence. The pear tree tale occurs in Book 4; we may guess that, if sequentially composed, Book 4 of the *Maṡnavī* dates originally to about 1266–7. But Rumi alludes to the pear tree story and its moral already in Book 1, which comments upon a Bedouin's boast over his own voluntary poverty and his total avoidance of covetousness or concupiscence ("ṭamaʿ"). This Bedouin's story entails no ribald scenes of adultery, though it does concern marital conflict with his wife, the context which no doubt triggers Rumi's mention of the tale. The narrator exhorts us (*Maṡnavī* 1.2361–2):

bar sar-i amrūd-bun bīnī chunān
z-ān furūd ā tā namānad ān gumān
chūn tu bar gardī u sar gashta shawī
khāna rā gardanda bīnī v-ān tu'ī [tuwī][9]

On the top of the wild pear tree you see such things
come down from it so that your suppositions will not remain.
When you turn around and make yourself all dizzy,
you'll see the room spin around, but that is you (who spins).

Rumi presents most of the *fabliaux* and ribald or obscene tales of the *Maṡnavī* in Books 4 and 5, so this allusion seems somewhat out of place chronologically and tonally. It may reflect a later stage of authorial revision as a final corrected presentation copy of the text was being prepared. It is likely, on the other hand, that the tale was already known to the author and his circle of disciples from before the composition of Book 1 got under way (c. 1262). Either way, it would seem that this tale had some enduring didactic value for Rumi, enough so that he recounts it at one place and refers to it again at another junction.

Rumi composes his pear tree *fabliau* in Konya, the Seljuk capital of Anatolia, in an ethnically and religiously diverse society of Turks, Greeks, Arabs, and Persians, where a staunchly Sunni Muslim government ruled over a still-frontier territory in which many Greeks and Armenians (and Georgians) remained Christian, many of the Turks were as yet not completely Islamicized, and non-Muslim Mongol power exercised its influence to the east. Rumi tells the tale proper in fourteen lines of Ramal metre verse (*Maṡnavī* 4.3544–74), preceded in the text – as are most of his stories – by a prose heading, summarizing the story along with a somewhat defensive discussion of the genre of its moral (see Appendixes I and II). Rumi's prose heading gives away part of the plot, much of the punch line, and all of the moral, though he nevertheless manages to expand on this moral in verse, making sure that we see the serious spiritual homily (*jidd*) and not just the jest (*hazl*) of this *fabliau*. Towards this end, we are urged to seek the celestial tree that reveals true vision.

"The Parable of that debauched wife [zan-i palīd-kār] who told her husband those illusions [khayālāt] appear to you from the top of the wild pear tree [amrūd-bun]" narrates in four lines (3544–8) how a woman wished to "do it"[10] with her lover in full view of her deluded husband. Towards that specific goal, she pretends to climb a tree to pick fruit for him. At the top of the as-yet unspecified fruit tree, she looks down and, weeping, calls her husband "ma'būn-i radd [a degenerate fag]," saying she sees some lout humping him ("bar tu mīfitad"), and that he is spread-eagled like a woman beneath this fellow, and must therefore be secretly effeminate ("mukhannas"). She thus verbally unmans her husband with this accusation before actually cuckolding him (3547–8).

In lines 3549–55, the husband insists he is all alone and suggests that, because of the height of the tree, the wife's head is spinning. She provides a detailed description of the other man, wearing a cap and really bearing down hard on the husband's back. The husband shouts for her to come down, thinking she has lost her mind. As soon as she gets down from the tree, he clambers up, whereupon she quickly takes her paramour into her intimate embrace. "Who is that, you whore," shouts the husband, "all over you like a monkey!" She retorts, "No, there's no one here but me; you must be dizzy." When he insists upon what he sees, she suggests it is due to the "amrūd-bun," which dictionaries define as a pear tree (*amrūd / armūd* = pear, *bun* = root). An item of foodstuffs specified from the Achaemenid era as **umrūta* in the Persepolis fortification tablets points to a very antique Persian origin for the word *amrūd*, though the precise botanic species intended by the Cuneiform in the fourth century BCE, and by Rumi's usage in thirteenth-century Anatolia, may naturally diverge somewhat.[11] In modern Persian, the word *gulābī* would be expected for pear, but that is not often attested for the earlier period of Persian literature, and seems in any case to be a specific sub-species of *amrūd*, the apparently more comprehensive classificatory term.[12]

In another story from Rumi's *Masnavī* (3.1614ff), a dervish vows not to pick any fruits off the trees, but to wait only for the wind to blow them down, presumably demonstrating his absolute reliance upon God for his sustenance. He lives in a mountain where there are numberless mountain pears ("murūd-i kūhī"),[13] but when the wind blows no pear to the ground for five days straight, he reaches up to pluck the fruit from an *amrūd-bun* branch. This breaking of his vow brings on a divine punishment which "opened his eyes and boxed his ears" (3.1676), perhaps alluding to the association between the pear-root and false perception, and perhaps even to the tree of the forbidden fruit. The dervish is mistakenly arrested with a band of thieves, and his hand is cut off in punishment – a symbolic linking of the plucking of a pear from a pear tree with castration.

Frazer's *Golden Bough* notes a European folklore practice of planting a pear tree with the birth of a girl and an apple tree with a boy.[14] Perhaps, then, the *amrūd-bun* and its fruit have folkloric associations with virility or with aphrodisiacal properties, but in Rumi's episode of the pear tree of deception, the *amrūd*-root has a particular etymological utility and semiotic charge. Boccaccio's punning on the word *pear* and the name *Pirro* constituted an important element of his (and the *Comoedia Lydia*'s) iteration of the pear tree tale. Because *amrūd* phonetically suggests the word *amrad*, meaning catamite (or more precisely a beardless youth, or "ephebe"), we are also in the presence of a pun on the Persian word for pear.[15] The wife claims to see her husband turned into a catamite, an *amrad*, specifically here the object ("maf'ūl") of anal penetration in a male-male sexual encounter.[16] The wife finally explains to him (3556), "You cuckold [qaltabān], I too misperceived [kazh hamī-dīdam] while in the tree," and tells him to come down (3557).

Rumi now cautions the reader (3558–78) not to think of this *fabliau* (*ḥazl* = jesting, often of a lewd nature, a thematic genre label approximately corresponding to the Latin terms *facetiae, ridicula*)[17] as merely funny – it is also instructive. We are not to think of the actual pear tree, but of the pear tree of existence, atop which our ego deceives us, makes us squint and see awry. If we come down from selfishness (*hastī u manī*), we will see straight and speak aright. Rumi proceeds to say that if you are humble, God grants true vision (which even the Prophet Muhammad had to pray for), and then the pear tree will become to you a tree of Moses, transformed by God's creative command "Be" (*amr-i kun* – another phonetic pun on *amrūd-bun*) into a Burning Bush. Now you may see, through divine alchemy, the True tree mentioned in the Qur'an (14.24) as having firm root, its branches in the heavens.

The Arabic Date Tree of Deception

An Arabic version of the tree of deception dating probably to the years between 1170 and 1194, and therefore preceding Rumi's Persian instance of the tale, is attested in the work of ʿAbd al-Raḥmān Ibn al-Jawzī, an author at least some of whose work was well known to Rumi.[18] Ibn al-Jawzī was a Hanbali jurist, Hadith scholar, and historian, who was born in Baghdad about 511 AH/1118 and died in 597 AH/1201, a prolific author credited with anywhere from two hundred to one thousand titles, about two dozen of which have survived. Though the Hanbali school opposed innovations not based upon scripture and the practice of the Prophet, Ibn al-Jawzī nevertheless inclined towards certain aspects of Sufism, as well as belles lettres. Beginning in the early 1160s, he taught as a *madrasa* professor at several institutions, under the patronage of Ibn Hubayra, the Hanbali vizier to the Caliphs al-Muqtafī (r. 530–55 AH /1136–60) and al-Mustanjidd (r. 555–66 AH/1160–70). By the middle of the 1160s, he was authorized to act as a popular preacher (*wāʿiẓ*) in the Caliphal palace, and by the reign of the following Caliph, al-Mustaḍīʾ (r. 566–74 AH/1171–9), when Saladin helped re-establish the Abbasid *khuṭba* in Cairo after the demise of the Fatimids, Ibn al-Jawzī wielded great influence in Baghdad society, his sermons attended by thousands. However, when the vizier Ibn Yūnus was dismissed and arrested, and replaced in office by a Shiʿite vizier, Ibn al-Qaṣṣāb, in 590 AH/1194, Ibn al-Jawzī – who had been active in opposing Shiʿites – suffered house arrest for five years, until shortly before his death.[19]

Ibn al-Jawzī tells a version of the fruit tree of deceit in his *Kitāb al-adhkiyāʾ* (*Book of the Intelligent*), one of a trio of works by him that compile anecdotes illustrating clever and foolish behaviour. The *Book of the Intelligent* recounts anecdotes of a mostly amusing nature structured like religious traditions or Hadith, giving an *isnād*, or chain of transmission.[20] For the particular story that concerns us here, Ibn al-Jawzī seems unable to trace the origin, signalling only that it is not original to him by the phrase "balaghanā" ("it has reached us," or "it has been conveyed to us").[21] This may constitute a literary fiction to establish more antique authority for something created by the imagination of the writer, to distance the author from ribald or theologically suspect material, or simply to maintain a consistent format with other anecdotes in the collection. It may also indicate, on the other hand, that this tale was popularly circulating in the public domain during the time Ibn al-Jawzī recorded it, as a kind of joke for which no particular authorship could be attributed.

Although Ibn al-Jawzī's authorial career seems to have flourished from the 1160s, and his history, *al-Muntaẓam*, covers the caliphate up to the year 574 AH/1179, the date of *Kitāb al-adhkiyā'* has yet to be definitively established. We may simply note that the time frame for the appearance of this Arabic tree of sexual deceit roughly corresponds with the appearance of the *Comoedia Lydia*, thought to have been composed, like the other Latin comedies, in west-central France in the latter half of the twelfth century.

Ibn al-Jawzī's tale, told in a prose paragraph in Arabic, shares the same core features with the others we have discussed, except that the tree in question is a tall date palm ("nakhla"), and the sexual overture comes at the initiative of the lover rather than of the wife (see Appendixes III and IV). The plot develops as follows: a woman has a lover who demands that she devise a stratagem by which "I might swyve you" (to use a Chaucerian word for the equally blunt Arabic term "aṭa'a-ki") in the husband's very presence. Failing to do this, the lover will never speak to the woman again (1–2). She promises to arrange for this to take place at the date palm in their yard (a space of nature enclosed by a wall, like January's garden and presumably also like the garden of Nicostrato, though the location of Rumi's pear tree is not specified in an enclosure). The wife tells her husband that she wants to climb and pick some dates (3), and from the treetop looks down to accuse him of copulating with another woman, in plain view of his own wife (4–5)! The husband swears that he is all alone, but upon coming down from the tree, the wife continues her quarrel with him, until finally the innocent man threatens to divorce her if she will not believe him to have been alone. He has her sit down while he climbs the tree for himself (6–7).

The next scene should be quite predictable: the wife calls her companion, who promptly engages in an act of carnal knowledge with her (8). The husband takes notice ("iṭṭala'a" – perhaps of the noises of love-making, or perhaps of the strange nature of the tree), witnesses the scene below, and immediately forgives the wife for her earlier obstinate assertions about him, realizing that she must also have been deceived by the marvellous view afforded from the tree (8–9). For, he says, "kullu man yaṣ'adu hādhihi al-nakhla yarā mithla mā ra'ayti [whoever climbs this palm tree sees the like of what you saw]" (9–10). This anecdote comes in a chapter entitled "Mention of those who have outsmarted others through their intellect to get what they want."

In Search of the Source of the Pear Tree Episode

In 1888, William Alexander Clouston briefly noted Rumi's pear tree tale as an analogue to the tale of January, May, and Damyan in Chaucer's *Merchant's Tale.* Clouston did not, however, succeed in drawing much attention to this startling analogue, in part because of his marginal inclusion of the example from Rumi, which he mentions only in a supplement ("Additional Notes") to his main treatment of the sources and analogues for this tale, and in part because he was more interested in later Islamicate versions of the tale, which he mistook as direct evidence of its original source.[22] The specific Persian text attracting his attention was the *Bahār-i dānish* (Spring of Knowledge), composed by 'Ināyat Allāh Kanbū of Delhi in 1061 AH/1651.[23] One of the many episodes in this tale does indeed involve a lady who tells a lucky Brahmin that "in the garden of such-and-such a land-owner, there is a palm tree [nakhlī] with exceedingly delicious dates [khurmā], and even more amazing, whoever goes up it sees many wondrous things."[24] The *Bahār-i dānish* version of the tale occurs among the "strange tales and surprising anecdotes in debasement of women, and of the inconstancy of that fickle sex" recounted to the Mughal emperor of India, Sultan Jahāngīr (r. 1605–27) by his courtiers in order to cure him of lovesickness. Not surprisingly, it sets the tale in an Indian locale with a Brahmin in the role of lover, and Clouston (following Edelstand du Méril) supposed India to be the tale's birthplace.[25] However, the Islamicate versions of the story do not first appear in an Indian setting, or with Indian characters, and the *Bahār-i dānish* may itself be contaminated by the Mughal emperor Akbar's (r. 1556–1605) campaign of translation of Persian works to Sanskrit and vice versa, or, as is even more likely, 'Ināyat Allāh Kanbū or his sources may well have been aware of the earlier versions (like Ibn al-Jawzī, he makes it a date tree). However, in the Sanskrit tales told by a parrot, the *Şukasaptatī,* originating in or before the twelfth century (Hemachandra, d. 1172, was aware of them) but not attested in writing until the fifteenth, a different variation of the tree of sexual deception appears. This tale, "The Officious Father-in-Law," does not involve fruit or climbing of the tree, but, as Clouston relates, sexual deception under a tree.[26] The framing premise of the tales presented in the *Şukasaptatī* pivots around a wife wishing to run off with her lover while her husband is away, but who is captivated by a clever parrot's seventy stories until the husband returns. In 730

AH/1330, Nakhshabī prepared a Persian version of these parrot tales, the *Ṭuṭī nāma*, on the basis of the Sanskrit. Here, the tale of the Officious Father-in-Law occurs, vaguely reminiscent of our fruit tree of deception tale, except that no tree is involved at all.[27] This cannot qualify as an analogue for the European "pear tree episodes," but a later Turkish rendition from the History of the Forty Vezirs, a text dedicated to Murād II (r. 1421–51), does present the basic form of the fruit tree of deception tale found in Ibn al-Jawzī and Rumi.[28]

Clouston also mistook a token of this tale type found in the *Arabian Nights* cycle for an earlier version than Rumi's, specifically "Er-Rahwan, the prime minister of King Shah Bakht." We now know that this particular tale was a later addition to the written form of the *Arabian Nights* cycle, of which the earliest surviving manuscript dates to the fourteenth century and does not include the pear tree episode.[29] Clouston relied upon the Habicht-Fleischer edition of the *Arabian Nights*, putatively based upon a late Tunisian manuscript, which must in fact have been an eclectic compilation of various manuscripts and editions, constituting an altogether new and modern recension of the work, which may be infected with translations into Arabic of tales originally composed in Persian or Turkish, or even French.[30]

As for Boccaccio's version of Nicostrato and Lidia,[31] it has been divided by A. Collingwood Lee into two components for purposes of identifying the precursor versions: "the tale of the fetid breath" and "the tale of the pear tree."[32] The former does not concern us here, but Boccaccio's sources for the latter portion of his ninth story of the seventh day may have included a Latin verse fable by Adolphus, composed in 1315, which can be summarized as follows:

> A blind and jealous man has a pretty wife. In a garden one day she asks him to go to a certain pear tree [pyri]. She climbs up to a young man who is hidden in the fork of the tree, and they fulfill their desire. The husband hears the noise they make [audit vir strepitum] because where one sense is lacking, a person's other faculties grow stronger. He accuses his wife of having an adulterer with her, and complains to God, who restores his sight. He now bitterly reproaches his wife [Fallax Femina! … quam fraude mulier mala varia sordet]. She says she had spent much on doctors for him in vain, then in sleep she was bidden [insonuit auribus illa meis] to play with a youth high up a tree [Ludere cum juvene studeas in roboris alto] and her husband would be cured. This she had done and he is whole. He praises her and continues loving her [excolit hanc, adamat vir, alter eam].[33]

As in the Arabic of Ibn al-Jawzī, the element of the husband noticing or hearing the noise of love-play appears here as well. Like Chaucer, Adolphus makes the jealous husband blind.

A version of the tale also appears among the Italian *Novellino*, estimated to have been composed originally between 1281 and 1300.[34] Most of the early manuscripts of the *Novellino*, including the 1525 editio princeps of Gualteruzzi, do not contain the pear tree tale; it does, however, appear in Section II (folios 51–97) of the Panciatichiano-Palatino 32 manuscript, the earliest part of which (folios 1r–50v) dates to the early fourteenth century, presumably about 1320 or earlier, and contains a book entitled *Libro di novelle e di bel parlare gientile* (The book of novel tales and speaking well and courteously). The second part of the manuscript was copied a few years later, probably between 1325 and 1330, and contains, inter alia, further stories, among them the pear tree tale. The stories in this manuscript do not follow the order of the Gualteruzzi edition and differ in many particulars; they were perhaps conceived as a rhetorical manual, or a preacher's guide, not unlike Petrus Alfonsi's *Disciplina clericalis*.[35] The work immediately preceding the *Libro di novelle e di bel parlare gientile* in the Panciatichiano manuscript is *Itinerario ai luoghi Santi* (folios 1r–8v), a pilgrimage journey to the holy land (Oltremare, the Crusader principalities in the Levant), suggesting the possibility that the scribe who penned the manuscript may perhaps have associated the tales with the Orient (and rightly so, as European collections of stories share much in common with Middle Eastern collections of *ḥikāyāt*).

The Panciatichiano version of the pear tree goes as follows: a young man is pining away with love for a woman, but cannot speak to her. She takes pity upon him and makes a long tube out of a cane to put to his ear. She tells him to go to the garden and climb a pear tree laden with beautiful pears ("uno pero che v'àe molto belle pere") and await her. She tells her blind husband that she wishes for pears, and when she insists on getting them herself, he holds onto the tree trunk so that no one can follow her. The love-making that ensues up the pear trunk shakes the tree, dropping pears onto the husband, who asks his wife why so many pears? The wife says that she wants the pears of a certain branch and cannot have any other. Meanwhile, disturbed by this wily infidelity, Saint Peter in heaven asks God to restore the husband's sight in order to stop this deceit, but God says that the woman will nevertheless find an excuse (perhaps God is not without admiration for women's wiles). When the husband looks up and asks what his wife is doing with the man in the tree, she explains that if she had not done this, he would not have regained his sight. The husband seems content with this reply, and so, the moral concludes, you see how unfaithful married women and young girls are, and how quickly they find excuses.[36]

Whether or not Boccaccio knew this Italian example of the tale, he did know a Latin rendition of it, the Latin comedy entitled *Comoedia Lydiae* composed by Arnulf of Orléans in France[37] in the latter half of the twelfth century, approximately 1175.[38] Boccaccio copied this into his miscellany, Codice Laurenziano XXXIII.[39] This 556-line verse (= 228 elegaic distichs) provides not only the basic plot but also (with the exception of the husband, Decius) the names of the principal characters of *Decameron* 7.9: Pyrrhus (Pirro), Lydia (Lidia), and her elderly maidservant, Lusca. It also features several central puns, including many centred on the name Pyrrhus and the pear ("pirus") (e.g., lines 8–9); the opinion that woman is a virus that destroys man ("virum") (36); the inability of Decius, or even ten ("decem") men, to satisfy his lusty wife (102); that Lidia likes play ("ludus") and playing around ("ludere") (147).[40] Here, then, we have the proximate written source of Boccaccio's pear tree episode in the comedy of Lidia, which itself claims to imitate classical models of old (line 3), though the strong suggestion of an "oriental" origin lingers,[41] specifically the connection with Petrus Alfonsi's *Disciplina clericalis* and Spain as "the gateway through which oriental tales entered Europe in this period," mixing Buddhist, Christian, and Muslim apologues in the form of exempla.[42] The pear tree episode, in the form told by Adolphus, also occurs in mid-fifteenth-century European translations of Aesop, such as William Caxton's English edition, *The Book of the Subtyl Hystoryes and Fables of Esope* (1484), and the Spanish *La Vida del Ysopet con sus fabulas hystoriadas* (1489), which tack onto Aesop tales from Petrus Alfonsi, Poggio Bracciolini, and others.[43]

The Analogous Nature of the Fruit Tree of Deception Tales

Chaucer's pear tree episode in the *Merchant's Tale* is classed by Germaine Dempster as an early exemplar of the "Blind Husband and the Fruit Tree" tale, for which she distinguishes two sub-categories, one wherein the blind man is cured spontaneously by two supernatural onlookers (to which Chaucer's version belongs), and other versions in which sight is restored after the man appeals to a deity (to which Adolphus's Latin version corresponds).[44] On the grounds that it does not involve blindness but enchantment ("incantato" in the *Decameron* and "fantasmata" in the Latin of *Comoedia Lydiae*), she rather adamantly distinguishes Chaucer's "Blind Husband and the Fruit Tree" tale-type from the "optical illusion caused by an enchanted tree" tale-type which appears in Boccaccio's *Decameron*. For this reason, she argues that categorizing these tales together as "the pear-tree story" has introduced confusion, and that we know of no oriental version of the blind husband story. Margaret Schlauch had earlier detailed how some of the "western versions" of the pear tree episode follow a blind husband premise (e.g., Adolphus, Chaucer), whereas others follow the premise of illusion or deception, characteristic of the "Oriental versions" and the two "western" instances of the *Comoedia Lydiae* and Boccaccio's *Decameron*.[45] Clouston had made a similar distinction, arguing that because no oriental versions rely upon the husband's blindness, this plot device must be a European invention,[46] though he also speculated that the *Comoedia Lydiae* constituted a common source for both Chaucer and Boccaccio.[47] Dempster believed that Chaucer could not have known the Lidia versions of either Boccaccio or the *Comoedia Lydiae*, and assumed that he was therefore ignorant of the versions of the tale not predicated upon the husband's blindness. This division of blindness and enchantment in parsing the tale into an A- and a B-category is maintained in the more recent article of James Bratcher on the pear tree in the *Enzyklopadie des Marchens*.[48]

The argument has since then been ventured that Chaucer may have seen Boccaccio's version of the pear tree tale while in Italy and adopted elements from it.[49] If true, the two western classes of blindness and misperception/deception cannot be considered as mutually exclusive or unaware of one another. Indeed, Chaucer incorporates components of both the putative "Blind Husband" and "Optical Illusion" tale-types, as January begins the *Merchant's Tale* with his sight, becomes blind in the middle, and then has his sight restored, after which May successfully convinces him that he has not seen what he saw: like a man first waking up, he is bound to be bleary-eyed, his vision unreliable at first. Thus, May places the strong suggestion of an optical illusion in January's mind to deceive him, just as the husbands in Ibn al-Jawzī, Arnulf, Rumi, and Boccaccio are deceived by their wives into believing they have seen an illusion. By contrast, in the *Novellino* version, the husband recovers his sight and understands perfectly well what he saw, and his wife does not attempt to deny it, but explains that it was a regimen prescribed to cure his blindness, an argument that contents the husband ("istette contento"), although the narrator goes on in the final sentence to castigate womankind for her wiliness.[50]

Taking the evidence of the two Islamicate versions into account, the distinction between blindness and illusion cannot clearly and neatly delineate one type of pear tree episode from another. In the Arabic date tree tale, we clearly have an analogue of our Persian pear tree tale. The major differences between these two Middle Eastern versions involve the type of fruit tree and the protagonist instigating the love tryst (in the Arabic, the wife's lover; in the Persian, the wife herself). In both Middle Eastern versions, furthermore, it is the wife who first goes up the tree, and makes a show of looking down upon a scene of love-making. By contrast, the wife's lover/lord's man first looks down from the tree in Boccaccio and the *Comoedia Lydia*, making a pretended protest over the immodest scene of marital merry-making. In all four of these versions, the husband is the second person to climb the tree (ostensibly to see what has caused all the fuss), upon which he is treated to a vision of the real act, taking place below. In Ibn al-Jawzī, the husband entertains no doubt about the illusion-inducing nature of the tree, and immediately forgives his wife for her earlier accusation against him, whereas in Boccaccio and *Lydia* the husband first shouts accusatorily at the wife (who has never set foot in the tree), and only after considerable doubt eventually allows himself to be convinced that what he saw was an illusion. In Rumi, the wife tells her husband that he has seen the same illusion (a man vigorously lying atop the spouse) that she saw from the treetop, and here the dramatic portion of the tale ends, unconcerned with the husband's reaction.[51]

Chaucer, the *Novellino* version, and Adolphus all situate the *flagrante delicto* up in the tree, with both the wife and her lover having climbed up separately. Although in all cases the tree is a pear tree, the versions differ insofar as the husband in Adolphus sees what he sees, but forgives the wife because her dalliance with a youth ("Luder cum juvene studeas in roboris alto / Prisca viro dabitur lux cito, crede mihi," 47–8) was a medicinal regimen vouchsafed to her in a dream after other expensive cures for the husband's blindness had failed.[52] Chaucer has May offer a similar reason for her infoliate indiscretion, but she must still convince January of the illusory nature of what he has seen. Her excuse and her moral conclusion ("he that misconceyveth, he misdemeth," 2410) bears some similarity to Rumi's disquisition on the nature of optical illusions at the end of his pear tree telling. Interestingly, the blind husband of Adolphus suspects infidelity even before his sight returns, because he hears the noise of love-making in the tree above him ("audit vir strepitum," 27), and in the Arabic version of Ibn al-Jawzī, although the husband can see perfectly well, he first "notices" – evidently by hearing – the *swyving* ("fa-waṭa'a-hā fa-ṭṭala'a al-zawj," 8), before looking down to see the deed.

Meanwhile, shared in the versions of Boccaccio and Chaucer is that the cuckolding is perpetrated against the lord of the manor by his own man (Damyan, Pirro), whereas in the Middle Eastern versions, the husband has not previously laid eyes upon the paramour. Ibn al-Jawzī's version, like Chaucer's, locates the origin of sexual desire and unchastity in the person of the wife's lover. But in the Arabic, as in Boccaccio and the *Comoedia Lydiae*, the lover demands that the cuckolding take place in the presence of the husband. In Chaucer, Damyan pines away for May and declares his love to her, but because January never lets her out of his reach, it is she who devises a way to furtively tryst with Damyan. By contrast, Lidia, the wife, initiates the affair in Boccaccio with a loyal and initially suspicious Pirro. Rumi's Persian, meanwhile, posits the wife as the sole instigator of the foliate *flagrante delicto*, while her paramour is merely a prop with no speaking lines.

Rumi may well have known the Arabic version, as he retells other tales by Ibn al-Jawzī.[53] His change from a date tree to a pear tree (*amrūd*) seems to result from its punning relevance to *amrad*. Of course, a desire to localize the tale to the native flora of Anatolia could have spurred a deliberate change, just as the pear tree's association with sexuality and fecundity could have. In the Arabic recitation of this tale, the fruit tree of deception remains standing, and the reader can almost sense the husband's delight in its enchanting powers, as if he might open it to tourism. For Rumi, by contrast, the base-minded may search for the wild pear tree, but those with spiritual insight will look instead to the heavenly tree of true and undistorted perception. Thus, the potential for the tree of deception to produce future mishaps remains open in the Middle Eastern versions, as it does in Chaucer, where May merely leaps down from the pear tree to return to the embrace of January. In contrast, after Lydia/Lidia identifies the pear tree as the source of the unchaste "illusion," it must be felled – in the *Comoedia Lydiae* by the order of the husband (Decius), and in the *Decameron* by the hand of the lord's man/wife's lover (Pirro).

Thus, the common components of the fruit tree tale cannot be so clearly disentangled into clear categories of a blind husband and an optical illusion form of the pear tree tale, as Dempster had argued. If, indeed, the "western" and the "oriental" versions of the pear tree tale had polygenetic origins, the components seem to have cross-pollinated and intertwined by the thirteenth century. Perhaps they even share a common source or sources. The Persian pear tree tale of Rumi in Antaloia (c. 1265–70) antedates that of Adolphus (1315) by forty or fifty years. The Arabic date tree version by Ibn al-Jawzī at Baghdad, and the Latin pear tree of Arnulf's *Comoedia Lydiae* in western France, both stem from the second half of the twelfth century. Arnulf claims to have imitated his Lydia from tales of old ("Ut noua Lidiades ueteres imitata placeret," 3) while Ibn al-Jawzī suggests the tale has reached him second-hand, as well ("balagha-nā"). We may yet hope to discover even earlier examples.

Archetypal Trees: Getting to the Root of the Matter

The pointing of Rumi's version of the pear tree tale with its moral – in selfishness we misperceive, and our ego sees awry – bears a remarkable similarity to the moral drawn by May in the *Merchant's Tale*: "He that misconceyveth, he misdemeth." This concern with epistemology and misperception has been proposed as one of the characteristic features of the *fabliau* genre,[54] and perhaps we can now reconfirm that the seeds of this genre were scattered across the Mediterranean with the increased interchange and international exchange provoked by the Crusades. Yet Rumi is not ultimately concerned with the ribald *fabliau* portion of this tale, but with the transformation of the wild pear tree of deception and misperception into the Mosaic tree of revelation, and the cosmic Qur'anic tree of firm root and over-arching branches (Qur'an 14.24). The association of paradise with a garden reaches back etymologically to the Iranian word *pairidaeza* (walled enclosure), meaning a private garden or park, such as we find in the gardens of Nicostrato and January, as well as in the yard (*dār*) of Ibn al-Jawzī's Arabic version of the fruit tree of deception. The Septuagint rendered the Hebrew word *gan* in Genesis 2.3 as *parádeisos*, thus associating it with the Eden of Adam and Eve. The Qur'an, too (18.107), borrows (whether from Greek or Persian) the Persian word *firdaws* as part of the lexicon of paradise. Rumi specifically describes the transformation we undergo after descending from the pear tree of crooked vision (3563), upon which our selfish ego has made our vision crooked (3562). We now see a fortunate tree with its branches above the seven heavens (3564) through which God grants us straight vision on account of our new-found humility (3566). It is the same pear tree, but it has grown verdant from the divine command (3569), so we can now safely re-climb. It has become like the Mosaic tree (3570), and the fire only makes it green, and its branches cry out, like the mystic Ḥallāj, "Verily, I am God!" (3571).

Within the Islamic topography of paradise, at least three trees might suggest themselves in connection with the transformed tree of true vision. Rumi himself uses the metaphor of the burning bush, but from his description, he may also have in mind the olive tree that is neither of the east nor of the west, and whose oil gives light, though fire does not touch it (Qur'an 24.35). But Rumi's tree of straight vision may rather evoke as its primary Qur'anic association the *Sidrat al-muntahā*, the lote tree beyond which there is no passing. This tree stands near the Garden of abode (53.12–18) where, in the Prophet Muḥammad's ascent into the heavens, he stood within a bow-length of the divine essence, the nearest any being may approach. Here his sight "did not swerve or err" as he witnessed one of the greatest revelations of God. Elsewhere, we learn that the *sidr* trees of paradise are thornless (56.28), and one hadith explains that the cutting down of a *sidr* tree is forbidden by the Prophet, as they offer shadow to man and animal alike. In modern folklore, the leaves of the botanical *sidr* tree were used as an antidote against sorcery – perhaps further indication that the antidote to the pear tree of deception should be the lote tree of prophetic vision, whose leaves may prophylactically guard against sorcery.[55]

Also important in Islamic lore is the tree of Ṭūbā; though not appearing in the Qur'an, it is perhaps the most cosmically significant tree in the Islamic, and especially Shi'ite, tradition. God tells Jesus that God himself planted it. It stands at the foot of God's Throne in paradise. The tree has a trunk that takes a thousand years to cross, yields wonderful fruit, and has roots of pearl, a trunk of rubies, branches of chrysolite, and silk brocade leaves, or other luxurious materials. Its name comes from the question posed to the Prophet about what bliss (*ṭūbā*) is, to which he replied, it is the tree of bliss (*shajarat al-ṭūbā*) in paradise, which has no terrestrial parallel.[56]

In a Christian context, the fruit tree of deception must of course conjure up a memory of the Tree of Knowledge of good and evil (*'eṣ hadda'at ṭov wara'*) and its forbidden fruit in the Hebrew Bible's account of Adam and Eve (Genesis 2.9 and 2.17). Eve, tempted by the serpent, believes the tree good for food, pleasant to the eyes, and hopes it will make one wise. She eats of the fruit and gives it to her husband as well (3.6), whereupon they become ashamed of their nakedness (3.7) and are banished from the garden, apparently to prevent them from also eating of the Tree of Life (3.22–3).[57]

The Qur'an does not give the Tree of Knowledge a particular name, referring to it simply as "hadhihi al-shajara [this tree]" in both Sūrat al-Baqara (2.35–6) and Sūrat al-Aʿrāf (7.19–26). In both accounts, God speaks directly to Adam, telling him to dwell in the Garden with his wife and eat whatever they like, but not to go near "this tree," or they will be of the unjust. Satan tempts them (without the intermediary of a snake) with an evil suggestion, hoping to reveal to them their shame. God does not want you to become immortal angels, Satan says, but I am your sincere adviser. By this deceit, he brings about their fall, for when they taste of the tree, their shame becomes manifest to them, and they began to sew together the leaves of the garden over their bodies. The Lord calls them out for their succumbing to the enemy, Satan, and they admit to the wrong they have done themselves. God sends them down to dwell on earth in enmity for a time (until the resurrection).[58]

The Tree of Knowledge provides a locus of primal disobedience to God, an act of carnal knowledge, a failure in the face of temptation, and the overreaching pride and desire to become angels (a suggestion planted by Iblīs, who has refused to bow to Adam, as he is only a human fashioned of clay, whereas Iblīs is an angel fashioned of light; Qur'an 7.11–18). "This tree" (of knowledge) is thus also a tree of shame that tests Adam and Eve and finds them wanting. In Christian tradition, the fruit of this Tree of Knowledge has of course become associated with the apple, largely because of the homonymic confusion – a primal pun, reminiscent of the paranomasic transference of Pirrus/piro or *amrūd /amrad* – between the Latin for apple (*malum*) and for evil (*malum*). Meanwhile, fruit trees and love are archetypally associated around the world in folklore and mythology, in particular the apple; Hellenistic and Roman depictions of *Venus genetrix* show her holding an apple- or quince-like fruit.[59] In the opening frame tale of the *Arabian Nights*, Shahzamān observes the queen, wife of his brother Shahriyār, walk into the garden with twenty maids, ten white and ten black, who sit down and remove their clothing to reveal ten black men and ten white girls. After the queen calls for her own lover, Masʿūd, to come down from the tree where he has been hiding, he jumps to the ground and mounts the queen, and a veritable orgy ensues in the garden. Masʿūd's tree is not described as a fruit tree, however. In our pear tree tales, the pear may suggest either the male genitalia (specifically the testicles, though by extension also the *membrum virile*) as a symbol of virility, or the female womb as a sign of fecundity.

In Arabic, we have seen the date palm tree as a site of illicit sexual encounter, but the date tree and its fruit can also symbolize fertility. The Qur'an mentions many different types of tree, but perhaps none so frequently as the date palm, which is not surprising, given the flora of the Hijaz. But one particular association of the date palm tree suggests that the date may also function as a fertility symbol. This comes in the scene where Mary suffers in labour all alone after withdrawing from her family "to a place in the East," presumably because of the suspicions surrounding her pregnancy. God sends an angel to her in the form of a man to announce the tidings of the birth of a sanctified son, but she is fearful of the man and incredulous that she can give birth when no man has touched her and she is not unchaste. She withdraws to a distant place where the pangs of childbirth come upon her, and she repairs to a palm tree, where, in her loneliness, she wishes she were dead. A voice then calls to her, pointing out that a stream has been made to flow beneath the tree, and instructing her to shake the trunk of the palm tree towards herself, as this will let fresh ripe dates fall down upon her. In this way she can eat and drink (19.16–26) and the pain of parturition and of loneliness is eased.[60] The scene certainly suggests fertility and divine mercy, but at the same time the shaking of the tree trunk and the raining down of its abundant dates recalls the bountiful pears knocked down on the blind husband by the frolicking lovers in the Latin pear tree tale.

Rumi's pear tree likewise has a Janus-face. It is both a tree of deception and a tree of true vision, depending upon the viewer's spiritual orientation. As such, the fruit tree of sexual deception might plausibly remind us of the Tree of Knowledge, a sacrosanct tree with unspoken virtues, the violation of which leads to the expulsion from paradise. As an inverted image of this tree in paradise, the Qur'an names a fearful tree in hell as the "shajar min zaqqūm [tree of Zaqqūm]" (37.62; 44.43; 56.52), which is elsewhere implicitly intended by the designation "al-shajarata l-malʿūna fī l-Qur'ān [the tree damned in the Qur'an]" (7.60). The Arabic root Z-Q-M suggests hastily swallowing or devouring something. In fact, in pre-Islamic times, Zaqqūm could apparently mean buttered dates, which one would presumably like to gobble up, and which must have quickly slid down the throat. According to Ibn Hishām's life of the Prophet, in fact, Abū Jahl ridiculed Muhammad's depiction of hell, where the Zaqqūm tree grows, by suggesting that the threat of the Zaqqūm tree is nothing but the threat of tasty buttered dates.[61] The Qur'an asserts, however, that it is a bitter punishment swallowed by the unbelievers, washed down with boiling water, that will make them experience the raging thirst of diseased camels (56.22–5). The tree itself appears monstrously grotesque, with its roots in the bottom of hell-fire and fruit stalks like the heads of devils (37.62–8), and what is more, the Qur'an mentions the Tree of Zaqqūm in connection with a fearful vision:

> Surely your Lord encompasses men. And We did not make the vision which We showed you but as a trial for men, and the cursed tree in the Qur'ān, as well. And We cause them to fear, but it only adds to their obstinancy. (17.60)

Can it be that "this tree" in paradise is the same Zaqqūm tree in hell, depending upon the spiritual orientation of the people who approach it? If we view the earthly plane as a mirror, and hell and heaven below and above it, the grotesque image of the Zaqqūm tree inverts the astoundingly rich beauty of the Ṭūbā tree (or perhaps of the Tree of Knowledge, or the Sidrat al-Muntahā). Indeed, in the iconographic tradition, grotesque faces appear on the leaves of the Zaqqūm tree, whereas angelic faces appear on the leaves of the Tree of Knowledge.

Rabbinic material made much of feminine chastity as an index of the community's piety, and gardens and trees (as also in another tale type, "the persecuted empress/chaste wife" motif) also play an important role in one biblical Greek Apocryphon, the Book of Daniel and Susanna, a book perhaps composed initially in Hebrew about 100 BCE. In this book, set in Babylon, Susanna, a very beautiful and very pious woman raised in the law of Moses, marries Joakim, a wealthy man whose house serves as the local court (1–4). Two of the judges, elders in the community, independently lust after her and scheme to find her alone, knowing that she strolls in the garden at noon each day after the people leave court (5–13). The two elder judges discover one another's desire for Susanna, and conspire together to find her alone (14). They hide in her husband's locked garden to spy upon her, and one day she bathes there (in a scene often depicted by painters in the European Renaissance), and sends her maids in waiting to fetch soap. The judges come out of their hiding places and demand that she yield to their desire, or they will falsely charge her with adultery (15–21). She refuses ("I will not do it. It is better to be at your mercy than to sin against the Lord") and is condemned to death for adultery (22–41). During the trial, Susanna, who is normally tightly veiled, is required by the judges to unveil so that "they might feast their eyes on her beauty" (32–3). Susanna prays to God, who sends the young Daniel for her deliverance (42–6). Daniel reopens the trial and exposes the perjury by asking each judge separately under which tree the act took place (46–59). One answers clove, the other yew, but these are English-language translation tricks to preserve a pun in the Greek text, to the effect that each judge will be sawn down – "cloven" in two and "hewn" in half. The Greek Septuagint literally has one judge reply a mastic tree (Ὑπὸ σχῖνον, "hupo schinon") and the other judge, an oak tree (Ὑπὸ πρῖνον, "hupo prinon"), while Daniel urges them to be mindful that an angel stands at the ready to cut (σχίσει, "schisei") the first and pry apart the second (πρίσαι, "prisai"). The false judges are condemned to death instead of Susanna (60–2), and Susanna's parents and her husband give praise for her innocence.[62]

The two judges may just as well have answered with date palm or pear tree, or even "this tree," although they have ended up with the Zaqqūm tree. Whatever the name of the particular tree, the Book of Daniel and Susanna might be a likely ur-seed for the chaste woman tale.[63] Certainly, the Tree of Knowledge is biblical, though our pear/date tree ostensibly performs the opposite function of deceiving, or inducing ignorance and blindness to truth, while in the Book of Daniel we may even have a foreshadowing of the fruit tree of the cuckolded-husband *fabliau*, except that the would-be adulterers are discovered and executed because of the falsehood they attempt to perpetrate with the tree.

Implications for the Study of Boccaccio

It has been argued that the *Decameron* codifies a tradition of medieval prose storytelling, integrating several narrative genres (exemplum, farce, *fabliau*, legend, miracle, *lai*, *vida*, *nova*) into a distinctive model of the *novella* in a way that "will be imitated for centuries," with Boccaccio integrating several narrative genres and setting the model of the *novella* for future epigones. While Boccaccio certainly eclipsed many of his predecessors, we ought not to give him too much credit for inventing the content of his narratives or their particular forms without looking more closely at the sources and analogues – not just from the Latin texts of classical tradition but also from the Islamic world.[64]

Richard Kuhns argues of Boccaccio's storytelling techniques that even seemingly mundane details are invested with meaning and should be understood as constituting a "universe of references" – things like the day of the week, colours, numbers, allusions, saints, etc.[65] Quoting Burckhardt's *Civilization of the Renaissance in Italy*, Kuhns understands Dante and Boccaccio to be living in a time when "wit began to be used as a weapon in theological disputes," and more specifically argues that Boccaccio can be seen thinking through "women's position in trecento society" and intervening sympathetically through the stories he tells in the *Decameron* with an antidote for isolation and lack of intellectual stimulus.[66] Therefore, Boccaccio's stories depicting sexual encounters clamour for metaphorical readings beyond the literal surface meaning or the erotic delectation that at first glance might provide sufficient justification for their inclusion in the *Decameron*. Kuhns thus encourages us to move from the sexual to the serious ideas and principles embedded in such narratives, offering, for example, Boccaccio's familiarity with Arabic numerals, and speculating from this how their shapes may have had sexually suggestive metaphorical value.[67] This seems to me far-fetched, though Rumi would certainly recognize the impulse to move from the bawdy or entertaining to the serious; Rumi will not leave his stories without a homily forcing us to consider exactly this, making sure that we do not miss his purpose or the moral he wants us to draw.

The backstory we have seen for the pear tree tale would suggest neither that Boccaccio is so uniquely original in thinking through the problems embedded in these tales (in the case of the pear tree, a question about the wiles of women and the ability of wives to outsmart husbands, the gender wars being a major concern of the *fabliaux*), nor that we can understand his particular artistry as storyteller, or his eventual intent in telling the tales he selects, without thinking carefully about the pre-history of those same tales.[68] A great many of them were circulating as exempla in entertaining and homiletic collections throughout the Middle East and Europe for two centuries and more before they reached Boccaccio, and they were often tied to particular morals or put to particular purposes, and clustered with other similar tales. To understand how Boccaccio or any other author has shaped this to his or her own purposes requires greater attention to this intertextual condition.

Appendix I: The Deceitful Pear Tree, from Rumi's *Mas̲navī*, Book 4

Transliteration of the Persian Text

Prose heading:

[1] ḥikāyat-i ān zan-i palīd̲-kār kay s̲h̲awhar rā guft: "ān k̲h̲ayālāt az sar-i
[2] amrūd-bun mīnamāyad turā, kay c̲h̲unīn-hā namāyad c̲h̲as̲h̲m-i ādamī rā sar-i ān
[3] amrūd̲-bun. Az sar-i amrūd̲-bun furūd̲ āy tā ān k̲h̲ayāl-hā bi-ravad̲."
[Folio, 4] Va agar kasī gūyad̲ kay ānc̲h̲a ān mard mīdīd k̲h̲ayāl nabūd̲, javāb:
[5] īn mis̲āl-īst, na mis̲l. Dar mis̲āl hamīn qadr bas buvad kay: agar bar sar-i amrūd-
[6] bun na-raftī hargiz ānhā na-dīd̲ī k̲h̲^{w}āh k̲h̲ayāl k̲h̲^{w}āh k̲h̲^{w}āh [sic] ḥaqīqat

[Poetic Text, following Nicholson's line numbers]:

3544 Ān zan-ī mīk̲h̲^{w}āst tā bā mūl-i k̲h̲^{w}ud / bar zanad dar pīs̲h̲-i s̲h̲ū-yi gūl-i k̲h̲^{w}ud
3545 pas bi-s̲h̲awhar guft zan k-ay nīk-bak̲h̲t / man bar āyam mīva c̲h̲īd̲an bar dirak̲h̲t
3546 c̲h̲un bar āmad̲ bar dirak̲h̲t ān zan girīst / c̲h̲un zi bālā sū-yi s̲h̲awhar bi-ngirīst
3547 guft s̲h̲awhar rā ki "ay ma'būn-i rad[d] / kīst ān lūṭī ki bar tu mīfitad?
3548 tu bi-zīr-i ū c̲h̲u zan bug̲h̲nūd̲a'[ī] / ay fulān ~ tu k̲h̲^{w}ud muk̲h̲annas̲ būd̲a'[ī] ?!"
3549 guft s̲h̲awhar, "na, sar-at gū'ī bi-gas̲h̲t / varna īnjā nīst ghayr-i man bi-das̲h̲t."
3550 zan mukarrar kard k-ān bā barṭula / kīst bar pus̲h̲t-at furū k̲h̲ufta? Hila !"
3551 guft "ay zan hīn furūd̲ ā az dirak̲h̲t / ki sar-at gas̲h̲t u k̲h̲irif gas̲h̲tī tu sak̲h̲t"
3552 c̲h̲un furūd āmad̲ bar-āmad̲ s̲h̲awhar-as̲h̲ / zan kis̲h̲īd̲ ān mūl rā andar bar-as̲h̲
3553 guft s̲h̲awhar "kīst ān, ay rūspī / ki bi-bālā-yi tu āmad̲ c̲h̲ūn kapī ?"
3554 guft zan "na, nīst īnjā g̲h̲ayr-i man / hīn sar-at bar gas̲h̲ta s̲h̲ud, harza ma-tan."
3555 ū mukarrar kard bar zan ān suk̲h̲un / guft zan, "īn hast az amrūd̲-bun.

3556 az sar-i amrūd-bun man hamchunān / kazh hamī-dīdam ki tu, ay qaltabān.
3557 hīn furūd ā tā bi-bīnī hīch nīst / īn hama takhayyul az amrū-bun-īst."
3558 hazl ta'līm ast ān rā jid shinaw / tu ma-shaw bar ẓāhir-i hazl-ash giraw
3559 har jidī hazl ast pīsh-i hāzilān / hazl-hā jidd ast pīsh-i 'āqilān
3560 kāhilān amrūd-bun jūyand līk / tā bi-dān amrūd-bun rāhī-st nīk
3561 naql kun z-amrūd-bun k-aknūn bar-ū / gashta'[ī] tu khīra-chashm o khīra-rū
3562 īn manī u hastī-i avval buvad / ki bar ū dīda kazh u aḥval buvad
3563 chun furūd ā'ī az-īn amrūd-bun / kazh na-mānad fikrat u chashm u sukhun
3564 yak dirakht-i bakht bīnī gashta īn / shākh-i ū bar āsimān-i haftumīn
3565 chun furūd ā'ī az-ū gardī judā / mubdal-ash gardānad az raḥmat, khudā
3566 z-īn tavāżu' ki furūd ā'ī, khudā / rāst-bīnī bakhshad ān chashm-i turā
3567 rāst-bīnī gar budī āsān u zab / Muṣṭafā kay kh^{w}āsti ān rā zi rab ?
3568 Guft: "bi-nmā juzv-i juzv az fawq u past / ānchunānka pīsh-i tu ān juzv hast"
3569 ba'd az-ān bar raw bar-ān amrūd-bun / ki mubaddal gasht u sabz az amr-i kun
3570 chun dirakht-i Mūsavī shud īn dirakht / chun sū-yi Mūsā kishānīda tu rakht,
3571 ātash ū rā sabz u khurram mīkunad / shākh-i ū *"innī ana llāh"* mīzanad
3572 zīr-i ẓill-ash jumla ḥājāt-at ravā / īn chunīn bāshad ilāhī-kīmīā
3573 ān manīy u hastī-at bāshad ḥalāl / ki dar-ū bīnī ṣifāt-i Dhu l-Jalāl
3574 shud dirakht-i kazh muqavvim, haq-namā / *"aṣluhu sābit u far'u-hu fī l-samā"*

Appendix II: The Deceitful Pear Tree Tale, Rumi's *Maṯnavī*

Translation from the Persian by Franklin Lewis

[Prose heading, 1] Story of the impure wife who told her husband, "Those illusions appear to you from the top of [2] the wild pear tree, for the top of that wild pear tree reveals such things to the human eye. [3] Come down from the pear tree so that those illusions disappear." [fol. 4v] And the answer, if anyone should say that what that man was seeing from the top of the wild pear tree was not an illusion: [5] This is a parable, not a similitude. As a parable, it is sufficient, for if he had not gone to the top of the wild pear [6] tree, he would never have seen those things, whether they were real or an illusion.

3544 A wife there was who wished to do it with her beau in full view of her deluded husband.
3545 And so she told her husband, "You're in luck, I'll go up the tree to pick some fruit."
3546 When she reached the treetop, the woman wept as she gazed down upon her husband.
3547 She told her husband, "You degenerate fag! Who is that butch who's laying into you!?
3548 You're lying spread out beneath him like a woman – you …! you're a closet fairy!"
3549 "No," said the husband, "your head must be spinning, for there's no one down here on the plain but me!"
3549 The woman repeated, "Who's the guy with the slanted cap who's bearing down so hard on your back!?"
3550 He said, "Woman, get down from that tree! Your head is spinning and you have completely lost your mind."
3551 When she came down, up went her husband. The woman took her beau into her arms.
3552 The husband said, "Who is that, you prostitute, all on top of you like a monkey?!"
3553 The woman said, "No, there's no one here but me. Look, your head is all spun around, don't talk nonsense."
3554 He repeated his words to his wife. The woman said, "It must be from the pear tree.

3555 I too saw all amiss, like you, from the top of the pear tree, you cuckold!
3556 Come on down now, and you'll see it is nothing. All these illusions are from the pear tree."

3557 In jesting is a lesson, give it serious ear – don't tarry on the surface of the joke
3558 To jesters all things serious are jokes; to the wise, all jokes are serious
3559 The lazy seek out this wild pear tree, the other wild pear tree is a good way off.
3560 Tell of the wild pear tree upon which you now are dumbfounded and deceived –
3561 that is, primal egotism and self-assertion, upon which the eye squints and blurs
3562 When you come down from that wild pear tree, your thoughts, sight, and speech are no longer crooked
3563 You'll see it has become a tree of good fortune, its branches touching the highest heaven
3564 When you come down from it and leave it, God in his mercy will transform it
3565 Come down in all humility and God will grant your eyes true vision
3566 If true vision came so easily to us, why then did (Muhammad) the Chosen One beseech the Lord for it?
3567 He said, "Reveal each and every atom from above and below, as they are in Your own sight"
3568 Only then go up that wild pear tree, which has been transformed, made verdant by God's command "Be!"
3569 How does this tree become Mosaic bush? When you draw yourself towards Moses.
3570 The fire makes it green and verdant; its boughs cry out, "Verily, I am God!"
3571 Beneath its shade your every desire is licit – such is the alchemy divine.
3572 Egotism and self-assertion are licit to you, insofar as you see within them the attributes of the All-Majestic
3573 The crooked tree, now straight, reveals the truth: "Its roots firm, it branches in the sky" (Qur'an 14.24)

Appendix III: The Deceitful Palm Tree from Ibn al-Jawzī, *Kitāb al-adhkiyā'*

Transliteration of the Arabic Text

[1] Balaghanā anna 'mra'at^{an} kāna lahā 'ashīq^{un}, fa-ḥalafa 'alay-hā, "in lam taḥtālī ḥattá aṭa'a-ki bi-maḥḍar^{in} **[2]** min zawji-ki, lam ukallim-ki." Fa-wa'adat-hu an taf'ala dhālika, fa-wā'ada-hā yawm^{an}. Wa kāna fī dāri-him nakhlat^{un} **[3]** ṭawīlat^{un} fa-qālat li-zawji-hā, "ashtahī aṣ'ada hādhihi l-nakhlata fa-ajtaniya min ruṭabi-hā bi-yadī." Fa-qāla, **[4]** "if'alī." Fa-lammā ṣārat fī ra'si l-nakhla, ashrafat 'alá zawji-hā wa qālat, "yā fā'il^{un}! Man hādhihi **[5]** l-mar'at^{u} allatī ma'a-ka ?! Waylu-ka ! A-mā tastaḥī tujāmi'u-hā bi-ḥaḍratī!" Wa akhadhat tashtimu-hu wa taṣīḥu, **[6]** wa huwa yaḥlifu anna-hu waḥda-hu wa mā ma'a-hu aḥad. Fa-nazalat fa-ja'alat tukhāṣimu-hu, wa yaḥlifu bi-ṭalāqi-hā anna-hu **[7]** mā kāna illā waḥda-hu. Thumma qāla la-hā, "uq'udī ḥattá aṣ'ada anā." Fa-lammā ṣāra fī ra'si l-nakhla, **[8]** istad'at ṣāḥiba-hā, fa-waṭa'a-hā. Fa 'ṭṭala'a l-zawj^{u} fa-ra'á dhālik fa-qāla la-hā, "ju'iltu fidā-ki ! Lā **[9]** yakūnu fī nafsi-ki shay'^{un} mimmā ramaytī-nī bi-hi, fa-inna kulla man yaṣ'adu hādhihi l-nakhlata yarā mithla mā **[10]** ra'ayti

Appendix IV: The Deceitful Palm Tree from Ibn al-Jawzī, *Kitāb al-adhkiyā'*

Translation from the Arabic by Franklin Lewis

[1] It has come to us that a woman had a lover, who swore the following oath to her: "Unless you devise some stratagem whereby I can swyve you in the presence **[2]** of your husband, I won't speak to you." So she promised him she would do it, and he appointed a day for it.

There was a tall palm tree in their home **[3]** and she said to her husband, "I feel like climbing this palm tree and plucking some of its dates with my own hands."

[4] "Go ahead," he said.

When she reached the top of the palm tree, she looked down upon her husband and said, "You cad![69] Who is that **[5]** woman with you?! You miserable fellow! Aren't you ashamed to swyve her in my presence?!" And she began to revile him and shout.

[6] For his part, he swore he was alone and there was no one with him. She came down and took up quarrelling with him, he swearing, upon pain of divorcing her, that he **[7]** had been all alone. Finally he said, "You sit here while I climb up."

When he had reached the top of the palm tree, **[8]** she called for her companion and he swyved her. Well, the husband took notice and saw it all and said to her, "Bless your heart![70] **[9]** There's nothing wrong with you in all (the accusations) you flung at me, for whoever climbs this palm tree sees the likes of what **[10]** you saw.

NOTES

1 Including, inter alia, *Originals and Analogues of Some of Chaucer's Canterbury Tales*, ed. Frederick James Furnivall, Edmund Brock, and W.A. Clouston (London: Trübner, 1872–87; reprint 1901); *Sources and Analogues of Chaucer's Canterbury Tales*, ed. W.F. Bryan and Germaine Dempster (Chicago: University of Chicago Press, 1941); *Sources and Analogues of the Canterbury Tales*, 2 vols., ed. Robert M. Correale and Mary Hamel (Cambridge: Brewer, 2002–5); Katherine Gittes, *Framing the Canterbury Tales: Chaucer and the Medieval Frame Narrative Tradition* (New York: Greenwood, 1991); and Carol Heffernan, *The Orient in Chaucer and Medieval Romance* (Woodbridge: Brewer, 2003). The early work on Chaucer provided a model for A. Collingwood Lee, *The "Decameron": Its Sources and Analogues* (London: Nutt, 1909; reprint New York: Haskell House, 1996), and for Alessandro D'Ancona, "Del Novellino e delle sue fonti," in *Studi di critica e storia letteraria di Alessandro d'Ancona* (Bologna: Zanichelli, 1880), 217–359. The impressive *Enzyklopädie des Märchens: Handwörterbuch zur historischen vergleichenden Erzählforschung*, ed. Kurt Ranke et al. (Berlin: de Gruyter, 1975–2015) includes coverage of the Middle Eastern background for discrete folklore motifs.

2 Inter alia, René Basset, *Mille et un contes, récits et légendes arabes*, 3 vols. (Paris: Librairie Orientale et Américaine–Maisonneuve Frères, 1926); Hasan M. El-Shamy, *Folk Traditions of the Arab World: A Guide to Motif Classification*, 2 vols. (Bloomington: Indiana University Press, 1995); and Hasan El-Shamy, *Types of the Folktale in the Arab World: A Demographically Oriented Tale-Type Index* (Bloomington: Indiana University Press, 2004). See also several works by Ulrich Marzolph, including his *Typologie des persischen Volksmärchens* (Beirut: Orientinstitut der Deutschen Morgenländischen Gesellschaft, 1984) and *Arabia Ridens: Die humoristische Kurzprosa der frühen adab-Literatur im internationals Traditionsgeflecht*, 2 vols. (Frankfurt am Main: Klostermann, 1992), and his *Ex Orienta Fabula: Beiträge zur narrative Kultur des islamischen Vorderen Orients*, 2 parts (Dortmund: Verlag für Orientkünde, 2005–6); as well as the ongoing "The 'Orient' within 'Us': Narratives from the Muslim World in Western Oral Tradition," a project of the Deutsche Forschungsgemeinschaft.

3 See, for example, James T. Bratcher's entry, "Birnbaum: Der verzauberter B.," in the aforementioned *Enzyklopädie des Märchens*, vol. 2 (1979), 417–21. This is tale-type 1423 according to the Aarne/Thompson classification, per Hans-Jörg Uther, *The Types of International Folktales: A Classification and Bibliography, Based on the System of Antti Aarne and Stith Thompson*, vol. 2

(Helsinki: Suomalainen Tiedeakatemia, Academia Scientiarum Fennica, 2004), 215. See also the new Correale and Hamel *Sources and Analogues of the Canterbury Tales*, vol. 2, 479–81 and 519–34.

4 The current essay is largely based on Franklin Lewis, "One Chaste Muslim Maiden and a Persian in a Pear Tree: Earlier Islamicate Analogues for Two Tales of Chaucer," in *Metaphors and Imagery: Studies in Classical Persian Poetry*, ed. Asghar Seyed-Gohrab (Leiden: Brill, 2011), 137–203. I am grateful to Ulrich Marzolph for his comments on that article. For a longer list of folklore analogues and sources for many of the tales in Rumi's corpus, see Marzolph, "Popular Narratives in Ǧalāloddin Rumi's Masnavi," *The Arabist* 13–14 (1995): 275–87, reprinted in *Ex Oriente Fabula*, pt. 2, 57–68 (the pear tree episode is briefly mentioned at 286 and 67, respectively); and his entry on "Rumi, Ǧalāloddin," in the *Enzyklopädie des Märchens*, vol. 11 (2004), 897–204 (which mentions the pear tree at 900). Carl Brockelmann, "Eine altarabische Version der Geschichte vom Wunderbaum," in *Studien zur vergleichenden Literaturgeschichte*, vol. 8, ed. Max Koch (Berlin: Alexander Duncker, 1908), 237–8, points to an early, vague analogue in al-Jāhiẓ, but with a different shrub (Uscharbaume, which Brockelmann glosses as *Asclepia gigantea*).

5 Giovanni Boccaccio, *Decameron*, ed. Vittore Branca (Milan: Arnoldo Mondadori, 1985), 7.9.1–80 (pp. 612–23). The pear tree comes at 7.9.57–80 (pp. 620–3).

6 Geoffrey Chaucer, *The Canterbury Tales*, in *The Riverside Chaucer*, ed. Larry D. Benson, 3rd ed. (Oxford: Oxford University Press, 1988), with the *Merchant's Tale* on lines 1245–2440 (pp. 154–68). The pear tree comes at lines 2320–2418.

7 Marzolph noted the Arabic and Persian analogues for the pear tree episode in *Arabia ridens*, vol. 2, no. 1185. As to the sources of such narratives, Marzolph would replace Theodor Benfey's assumptions of older Indian origins with a theory about how converts are the likely source of such circulating tales: "The Migration of Didactic Narratives across Religions Boundaries," in *Didaktisches Erzählen: Formen literarischer Belehrung in Orient und Okzident*, ed. Regula Forster and Romy Günthart (Frankfurt am Main: Lang, 2010), 173–88. Marzolph sees the Latin dictum of Horace, *prodesse et delectare*, as a parallel concept to the homiletics of the Arabo-Islamic tradition, as seen in the formulation of *al-jidd wa al-hazl*.

8 Shams al-Dīn al-Aflākī, *Manāqib al-'ārifīn*, ed. Taḥsīn Yāzījī, 2nd ed., vol. 2 (Tehran: Dunyā-yi Kitāb, 1362sh/1983), 742–3.

9 *Masnavī*, 1.2363–4. The numbering of verses from Rumi's *Masnavī* follows that established by R.A. Nicholson, *The Mathnawí of Jalálu'ddín Rúmí*,

E.J.W. Gibb Memorial, n.s., 3 vols. (London: Luzac, 1925–33). A version incorporating all of Nicholson's corrections is provided by Hassan Lahouti, *Ma<u>s</u>navī-yi Ma'navī*, 4 vols. (Tehran: Nashr-i Qaṭra, 1383 sh./2004), citing here from vol. 1, p. 174. The oldest known manuscript, the Konya MS of 677 AH/1278, has been published in facsimile with an introduction by Abdülbâki Gölpınarlı: *Masnavī: Mavlānā Calāl-ad-Dīn Rūmī* (Ankara: T.C. Kültür Bakanlığı [Ministry of Culture], 1993), and it is this latter manuscript that provides the basis for the transliteration and translation I have given in Appendixes I and II.

10 The compound verb *bar zadan* can have a great multiplicity of meanings, including to cheat at cards, to despoil or plunder, to steal, to dock (of a boat at the shore), etc., but the basic meaning involves physical contact (*zadan* = hit) of one thing upon (*bar*) another: to rub up against. It seems clear that, because she wishes to do this with her love (*mul*) in the presence of her deluded husband, it is here an action verb for sexual intercourse.

11 Abdol-Majid Arfaee of the Persepolis-Pasargadae Research Institute confirmed for me the appearance of the word in the Persepolis Fortification Tablets in a lecture he gave for the Persian Circle at the University of Chicago in 2006. See *Umrūta in the meaning "pear" (Middle Persian > *urmōd*, New Persian > *armūd, amrūd*) in Jan Tavernier, *Iranica in the Achaemenid Period (ca. 550–330 B.C.): Linguistic Study of Old Iranian Proper Names and Loanwords, Attested in Non-Iranian Texts* (Dudley: Peeters, 2007), 460, no. 4.4.20.18 (I am grateful to Matthew Stolper for pointing out this reference to me).

12 On the terminology of plants and flowers as they appear in Persian poetry, see *Lughat nāma-yi Dihkhudā* and Bahrām Girāmī, *Gul va giyāh dar hizār sāl-i shi'r-i Fārsī: tashbīhāt va isti'ārāt* (Tehran: Sukhan, 2007), 451.

13 *Ma<u>s</u>navī* 3.1634 and 1373 give the metrically altered form *murūd*, but elsewhere in the story, the form *amrūd* occurs (3.1672). The word does not often occur in the *Dīvān* of Rumi either, but appears as a hapax legomenon in the form *murūd* (ghazal 914 of the Furūzānfar edition). Likewise, I have found no instance of *amrad* in the *Dīvān*, so the pun on *amrūd/amrad* seems unique in Rumi to this tale of the Debauched Wife and the Pear Tree of Illusion.

14 James G. Frazer, *The Golden Bough: A Study in Magic and Religion*, 2nd ed., vol. 3 (London: Macmillan, 1900), 393.

15 Rumi elsewhere uses the word *amrad* in a jocular but scathing critique of the pederastic proclivities of some dervishes (*Ma<u>s</u>navī* 6.3843), contrasting the treatment meted out to two brothers, one who has grown a little chin hair and one who has not.

16 Judith Wilks of Northwestern University (personal communication, 20 February 2004) suggested that the Turkish word *armut* (pear) is used as an insult in some parts of Turkey. Although the insulting connotation was said to arise from its similarity to an ethnic term, *Arnavut* (Albanian), perhaps a relationship between Pers. *amrud*/Turkish *armut* and *amrad* (catamite) has lingered to the present day in Turkey.

17 Marzolph, "The Migration of Didactic Narratives," sees "prodesse et delectare" as the homiletic principle parallel to this.

18 The association was noted in Muḥammad Isti'lāmī's commentary to his edition of *Masnavī-yi Mawlānā Jalāl al-Dīn Balkhī*, rev. ed., vol. 4 (Tehran: Sukhan, 1379 sh/2000), 396. The link between Ibn al-Jawzī's tale, the *Comoedia Lydiae*, and Boccaccio's Lidia was pointed out by Basset, *Mille et un contes*, vol. 2, 150–1.

19 See H. Laoust, *Encyclopaedia of Islam*, 2nd ed., s.v. "Ibn al-Djawzī, 'Abd al-Raḥmān …"

20 He has also composed (577 AH/1181) a collection of *Maqāmāt* in the style of al-Ḥarīrī, though like al-Zamakhsharī, Ibn al-Jawzī does not begin with an *isnād* or mention a transmitter for his picaresque scenarios, but instead narrates in the first person in the name of the character Abū al-Taqwīm. See Devin Stewart, "The Maqāma," in *Arabic Literature in the Post-Classical Period*, ed. Roger Allen and D.S. Richards (Cambridge: Cambridge University Press, 2006), 145–58, esp. 154–6.

21 Ibn al-Jawzī, *Kitāb al-adhkiyā'*, ed. Muḥammad 'Abd al-Karīm Al-Nimrī (Beirut: Muḥammad 'Alī Bayḍūn and Dār al-Kutub al-'Ilmiyya, 2001), 99.

22 Clouston in *Originals and Analogues*, 544, as part of his "Additional Notes" to "The Enchanted Tree," the main discussion of which comes under his "Asiatic Versions and Analogues of Chaucer's Merchant's Tale" (341–64). Clouston notes that in E.H. Whinfield's abridged translation of Rumi's *Masnavi*, the details of "the woman's accusing her husband of pederasty, the unnatural vice to which Persian and Turks, and indeed Asiatics generally are said to be much addicted," is modestly omitted (544).

23 The *Bahār-i dānish* was then quite popular in India and had been much lithographed in the nineteenth century. An English version had been done in Dublin as early as 1769 (*Persian Tales: The Baar danesh; or, Garden of Knowledge* [Dublin: P. and W. Wilson]). Jonathan Scott's translation "from the Persic of Einaiut Oollah" appeared as *Bahar-Danush; or Garden of Knowledge: An Oriental Romance* (Shrewsbury: J. and W. Eddowes, 1799). The Persian text was lithographed in Cawnpore in 1261 AH/1845 and again in 1886, but a more recent printing appeared as *Bahār-i dānish*, ed. Ḥājī Muḥammad Qamar al-Dīn bin Janāb Ḥājī Shaykh Muḥammad Ya'qūb

(Cawnpore: Maṭba'-i Qayyūmī, 1954), which gives the date of composition quoted here (4).

24 *Bahār-i dānish*, 87.

25 Clouston, who reproduces Scott's translation of the tale (*Originals and Analogues*, 344–50), was convinced of its antiquity and thought for certain that it was of "Hindu extraction, and I think it very probable it may be found in the Suka Suptati" (349n1). Clouston's suggestion was taken up both by E. Lackenbacher in his introduction to "Lidia" in *La "Comédie" latine en France au XIIe siècle*, ed. and trans. Gustave Cohen (Paris: Société d'Édition "Les Belles-Lettres," 1931), 218, and by Lee, *The "Decameron": Its Sources and Analogues*, 236–7. Clouston credits Edelstand du Méril with having discovered the analogue (*Originals and Analogues*, 343).

26 Clouston, *Originals and Analogues*, 355–7.

27 Żīyā al-Dīn Nakhshabī, *Ṭūṭī nāma*, ed. Fatḥ Allāh Mujtabā'ī and Ghulām-'Alī Āryā (Tehran: Manūchihrī, 1372 sh/1993), 80–1. This text also contains a version of the chaste wife tale. Nakhshabī, though his *nisba* suggests he is from Nakhshab in the outlying areas of Bukhara, apparently lived in Badâ'on in India.

28 Sheykh-Zāda, *Ḥikāyat arba'īna ṣabāḥin wa masā*, or in its popular Turkish title, *Qirq Vezīrin ve Qirq Khatunin Hikāyetleri*, translated as *History of the Forty Vezirs* by E.J.W. Gibb (London: George Redway, 1886), 303–6. The existence of another Turkish version of this tale (*ḥikāyat*, though it is also transmitted as a joke, or *laṭīfa* in the genre of works in Ottoman Turkish known as *Laṭā'if nāma*) in a manual on sexual intercourse attributed to, or more likely translated by, Kemalpaşazade (d. 1534) has been pointed out to me by Bariş Karacasu of Bilkent University (personal correspondence, 15 December 2007), in a manuscript version of this work entitled *Rücû'ş-Şeyh ilâ Sibâh fi'l-Kuvveti alâ'l-Bâh* (Ankara: Milli Kütüphane, 06 MK. Yz. B514, folios 120a and b). An Arabic work by the same title, *Rujū' al-shaykh ilá ṣibāh fī al-quwwa 'alá al-bāh*, has been published in an edition by Ṭal'at Ḥasan 'Abd al-Qawī (Syria: Dār al-Kitāb al-'Arabī, 2001). Though attributed to Kemalpaşazade (along with his Turkish translation), the Arabic text was perhaps more likely authored by Aḥmad ibn Yūsuf Sharaf al-Dīn al-Tīfāshī, who died in the thirteenth century, possibly before Rumi composed the *Maṡnavī*. This would constitute a potential link between the versions of Ibn al-Jawzī and Rūmī, if the Turkish *Rücû'ş-şeyh* indeed takes this tale from the Arabic work of the same name, *Rujū' al-shaykh* (non vide).

29 This is the Syrian MS of the fourteenth century, held in the BNF, and is the MS from which Antoine Galland began translating *Les mille et une*

nuits into French (1704–17). See the critical text edited by Muḥsin Mahdi, *Kitāb alf layla wa layla: min uṣūlihi al-'arabiyya al-ūlá*, 3 vols. (Leiden: Brill, 1984–94), and also Robert Irwin, *The Arabian Nights: A Companion* (London: Allen Lane, 1994).

30 *Tausend und Eine Nacht Arabisch. Nach einer Handschrift aus Tunis herausgegeben von Dr. Maximilian Habicht* (etc.), *nach seinem Tode fortgesetzt von M. Heinrich Leberecht Fleischer*, 12 vols. (Breslau: J. Max, 1825–43). It also appears in J.B. Macdonald, "Maximilian Habicht and His Recension of the Thousand and One Nights," *Journal of the Royal Asiatic Society* (1909): 685–704; in Ulrich Marzolph and Richard van Leeuwen, *Arabian Nights Encyclopedia*, 2 vols. (Santa Barbara: ABC-CLIO, 2004), s.v. "Habicht," 579–80; and in Irwin, *Arabian Nights: A Companion*, 21–2. Clouston himself was aware of the corrupt nature of Habicht's text (*Originals and Analogues*, 353). Lee, *The "Decameron": Its Sources and Analogues*, follows Clouston in citing the examples of the *Bahār-i dānish* and the Habicht-Fleischer *Tausend und Eine Nacht* edition (236–8).

31 On the textual history of the *Decameron*, see Maurizio Fiorilla, "Decameron," in *Boccaccio autore e copista*, ed. Teresa de Roberti et al. (Florence: Mandragora, 2013), 129–45.

32 Lee, *The "Decameron": Its Sources and Analogues*, 231.

33 This summary translation is mine. The Latin text of the fable is given in Bryan and Dempster, *Sources and Analogues of Chaucer's Canterbury Tales*, 352–3; summary translations also appear there and in Lee, *The "Decameron": Its Sources and Analogues*, 238. It first appeared in print as *Adolphi fabulae* in Polykarp Leyser IV's *Polycarpi Leyseri Historia poetarum et poematum medii Aevi decem* (Halae Magdelburgiae, 1721), 2008–10. It is the first of Adolphus's ten fables ("Caecus erat quidam, cui pulcra virago …) composed in 1315. On this Latin verse telling, and on the prose versions in Latin, French, and English that appeared in the last quarter of the fifteenth century, see Correale and Hamel, *Sources and Analogues of the Canterbury Tales*, vol. 2, 480–1.

34 *The Novellino, or One Hundred Ancient Tales: An Edition and Translation Based on the 1525 Gualteruzzi edition princeps*, ed. and trans. Joseph Consoli (New York: Garland, 1997), xi–xii. On the reasons for this dating, see *Novellino e conti del Duecento*, ed. Sebastiano Lo Nigro (Milan: TEA, 1989), 9n1, following D'Ancona, "Del Novellino e delle sue fonti," in *Studi di critica e storia letteraria*, vol. 2 (Bologna, 1912), 1–163.

35 The *novelle* in the Panciatichiano 32 manuscript of the Biblioteca Nazionale Centrale di Firenze were previously published in *Le novelle antiche dei codici Panciatichiano-Palatino 138 e Laurenziano-Gaddiano 193*, ed. Guido

Biagi (Firenze: Sansoni, 1880), with the pear tree story that concerns us (155) appearing on pp. 199–201. The MS ("the oldest manuscript of the Novellino in the National Library in Florence") has now been published in a new edition with text, transcription, and critical notes by Anna Ciepielewska-Janoschka as *Viaggio d'Oltremare e Libro di novella e di bel parlar gentile: Edizione interpretative* (Berlin: de Gruyter, 2011). The pear tree novella that concerns us here appears on fols. 95r to 96r of the Panciatichiano manuscript (440–3 of the Ciepilewska-Janoschka edition), in which it is the penultimate of 106 stories; in other words, it comes towards the very end of the manuscript. Ciepelewska-Janoschka (3) dates this portion of the manuscript to 1325–30; Correale and Hamel, *Sources and Analogues of the Canterbury Tales*, vol. 2, 518–21, also gives an English translation. Most editions of *Il Novellino* and *Libro di Novelle e di bel parlar gentile* include one hundred tales, but omit the present tale of the pear tree; see, for example, *Il Novellino*, ed. Alberto Conte (Rome: Salerno Editrice, 2001).

36 Apart from the Biagi and the Ciepilewska-Janoschka editions mentioned above, the pear tree novella is also reproduced along with English translation by N.S. Thompson as "Il Novellino," in Correale and Hamel, *Sources and Analogues of the Canterbury Tales*, vol. 2, 518–21; and in Bryan and Dempster, *Sources and Analogues of Chaucer's Canterbury Tales*, 341–3. Both Lee, *The "Decameron": Its Sources and Analogues*, 236–44, and Bryan and Dempster, *Sources and Analogues of Chaucer's Canterbury Tales*, 341–56, list numerous later European tokens of the tale.

37 Matthieu de Vendôme (b. c. 1130) was once thought to be the author, but a consensus is beginning to emerge in favour of the argument first propounded by E. Faral, "Le fabliau latin au Moyen Age," *Romania* 50 (1924): 321–85, that Vendôme was not the composer. Bruno Roy, "Arnulf of Orléans and the Latin 'Comedy,'" *Speculum* 49, no. 2 (1974): 258–66, proposed Arnulf as the author. The Latin text was edited, with French translation, by Lackenbacher as "Lidia" in *La "Comédie" latine*, vol. 1, 211–46. For English translations, see Larry D. Benson and Theodore M. Andersson, "The Comedy of *Lydia*," in *Literary Context of Chaucer's Fabliaux* (Indianapolis: Bobbs-Merrill, 1971), 206–37; and Alison Goddard Elliott, *Seven Medieval Latin Comedies*, Garland Library of Medieval Literature, vol. 20, series B (New York: Garland, 1984), 126–46.

38 The date of 1175 is provided by Elliott (ibid., xlv), following Ferruccio Bertini, "Una novella del Boccaccio e l'Alada di Guglielmo di Blois," *Maia* 29–30 (1977–8): 135–41. Douglas Radcliff-Umstead, "Boccaccio's Adaptation of Some Latin Sources for the Decameron," *Italica* 45,

no. 2 (1968): 186, dates it to 1174 (while still ascribing it to Matthieu de Vendôme).

39 Branca, in Boccaccio, *Decameron*, 861n2 and Correale and Hamel, *Sources and Analogues of the Canterbury Tales*, vol. 2, 480n8. Cf. Elliott, *Seven Medieval Latin Comedies*, who implies the attribution of Boccaccio as scribe is not conclusive (xlvi).

40 Elliott, *Seven Medieval Latin Comedies*, xlvi. Elliott also notes that this is the most cynical and most misogynistic of the Latin comedies. On Boccaccio's rhetorical strategies in adapting material, see Jonathan Usher, "Rhetorical and Narrative Strategies in Boccaccio's Translation of the "Comoedia Lydiae," *Modern Language Review* 84, no. 2 (1989): 337–44, and on the symbolic changes he introduces to his source, see Albert Russell Ascoli, "Pyrrhus' Rules: Playing with Power from Boccaccio to Machiavelli," *Modern Language Notes* 114, no. 1, Italian issue (1999): 14–57. With regard to *ludus/ludere*, recall the more lewdly suggestive *bar zanad* (rub together, or "get it on") of Rumi's pear tree.

41 Correale and Hamel, *Sources and Analogues of the Canterbury Tales*, vol. 2, 479–81, 480n8 and 484. The alternative title, *Comoedia Lidiades*, invokes Ovid's *Heroides*, and several other classical works or scenes are mentioned.

42 Douglas Radcliff-Umstead, "Boccaccio's Adaptation of Some Latin Sources for the *Decameron*," *Italica* 45, no. 2 (1968): 171–94, esp. 177, suggests Alfonsi. Clouston, *Originals and Analogues*, 364, suggests other collections of exempla, such as the *Sermones* of Jacques de Vitry (248 and 260), the *Liber de donis* of Etienne de Bourbon, the *Promptuarium exemplorum* of John Herolt, and the *Summa praedicantium* of John Bromyard, that might contain similar tales. Branca, in Boccaccio, *Decameron*, 861n2, adds the *Speculum* of Vincenzo di Beauvais (III ix 15).

43 Furnivall, Brock, and Clouston, *Originals and Analogues*, 181–2, and Correale and Hamel, *Sources and Analogues of the Canterbury Tales*, vol. 2, 534, give the Caxton version of the tale "of a blynd man and of his wife," from his book of Alfonse, Tale 12. In the Spanish, the pear tree tale of the blind husband comes in Book 8, Story 12. On the history of the text, see *Aesop's Fables*, trans. John Keller and L. Clark Keating (Lexington: University Press of Kentucky, 1993), 3–4, and also 217–18 for the story. The English and Spanish editions follow the Heinrich Steinhöwel edition in German and Latin (Ulm, c. 1482), which attributes the tale to Petrus Alfonsi (Ex Alefonso, xii), although it does not appear in the *Disciplina clericalis*. See *Steinhöwels Äsop*, ed. Hermann Österley, vol. 117 (Tübingen: Litterarischer verein in Stuttgart, 1873), 326–8.

44 Bryan and Dempster, *Sources and Analogues of Chaucer's Canterbury Tales*, 341n1.

45 Margaret Schlauch, "Chaucer's Merchant's Tale and a Russian Legend of King Solomon," *Modern Language Notes* 49, no. 4 (1934): 229–32. Basset, *Mille et un contes*, also makes this distinction between the "L'arbre enchanté" and the blind husband types (151).

46 Clouston, *Originals and Analogues* 364.

47 Clouston (*Originals and Analogues*) attributes the Latin poem, as per then-received opinion, to Matthieu de Vendôme. He also felt that a folk tale version must have existed and circulated prior to that.

48 James Bratcher, "Birnbaum: Der verzauberter B.," *Enzyklopädie des Märchens*, vol. 2 (1979), 417–21.

49 Peter G. Beidler, "Chaucer's Merchant's Tale and the *Decameron*," *Italica* 50, no. 2 (1973): 266–84.

50 Correale and Hamel, *Sources and Analogues of the Canterbury Tales*, vol. 2, 521.

51 Except insofar as Rumi's moral makes the reader identify with the husband, cautioning us that unless we attain a true vision of reality in the spiritual realm we will remain deluded, even cuckolded, in the world.

52 Text as per Bryan and Dempster, *Sources and Analogues of Chaucer's Canterbury Tales*, 353.

53 Rumi's sources for the stories in Book 1 of the *Masnavī* are given in Franklin Lewis, *Rumi: Past and Present, East and West* (Oxford: Oneworld, 2000), 289–91, including one taken from the *Kitāb al-adhkiyā'*. Elsewhere, Rumi borrows from Ibn al-Jawzī's *Talbīs Iblīs*, which has been edited by al-Sayyid al-Jumaylī (Beirut: Dār al-Kitāb al-'Arabī, 1985).

54 Roy J. Pearcy, "Investigations into the Principles of Fabliau Structure," in *Versions of Medieval Comedy*, ed. Paul G. Ruggiers (Norman: University of Oklahoma, 1977), 67–100.

55 See Remke Kruk, "Sidr" in *Encyclopaedia of Islam*, 2nd ed., and David Waines, "Trees" in the *Encyclopaedia of the Qur'ān*, both online (www.brillonline.nl).

56 Nerina Rustomji, *The Garden and the Fire: Heaven and Hell in Islamic Culture* (New York: Columbia University Press, 2009), 67–9, 116–17, 160; and Waines, "Trees."

57 See *A Dictionary of Biblical Tradition in English Literature*, ed. David Lyle Jeffrey (Grand Rapids: Eerdmans, 1992), s.v. "Tree of Knowledge."

58 See Brannon M. Wheeler, *Prophets in the Quran: An Introduction to the Quran and Muslim Exegesis* (London: Continuum, 2002), 15–35, for some of the Islamic traditions about Adam and Eve.

59 Jeffrey, *A Dictionary of Biblical Tradition*, s.v. "Apple."
60 See Wheeler, *Prophets in the Quran*, 299–304, for some of the traditions relating to the pregnancy of Mary and the birth of Jesus.
61 Rustomji, *The Garden and the Fire*, 11–12 and 68–9.
62 Following the New English Bible, with the Apocrypha, Oxford Study Edition (New York: Oxford University Press, 1970). Greek e-text of *Vetus Testamentum graece iuxta LXX interpretes* by J. Gippert at TITUS (based upon the CCAT text [Center for Computer Analysis of Texts at the University of Pennsylvania]), http://titus.fkidg1.uni-frankfurt.de/texte/etcs/grie/sept/sept.htm, Book: Sus.Th. ΣΟΥ6ΑΝΝΑ. For the tree names, see John Rogerson, "Additions to Daniel," in *Eerdman's Commentary on the Bible*, ed. James D.G. Dunn and John W. Rogerson (Grand Rapids: Eerdmans, 2003), 805.
63 See Lewis, "One Chaste Muslim Maiden," 164–80.
64 See, inter alia, Corradina Caporello-Szykman, *The Boccaccian Novella: Creation and Waning of a Genre* (New York: Lang, 1990), 41.
65 Richard Kuhns, *Decameron and the Philosophy of Storytelling: Author as Midwife and Pimp* (New York: Columbia University Press, 2005), 106.
66 Kuhns, *Decameron and the Philosophy of Storytelling*, 107–8. At 112, Kuhns is more explicit about women's status as a central concern of the *Decameron*, and describes the stories of Day Seven as pivoting from the feminine world of words to a more masculine realm of action. F. Regina Psaki, "Voicing Gender in the Decameron," in *The Cambridge Companion to Boccaccio*, ed. Guyda Armstrong, Rhiannon Daniels, and Stephen J. Milner (Cambridge: Cambridge University Press, 2015), 101–17, introduces a caution about over-dichotomizing the gendered worlds of narrative, calling attention to how Boccaccio explores "the specifically gendered dimension of creation" in the *Decameron* through numerous voices, some speaking on behalf of or against women, and that these cannot facilely be equated with the "explicit voice of the Primary Narrator and the implicit voice of the historical author" (102). She argues that the "various levels of gendered voicing" speak to a gendered reception, and an effort by the author to address multiple audiences. See also Marilyn Migiel, *The Ethical Dimension of the Decameron* (Toronto: University of Toronto Press, 2015).
67 Ibid., 108–9 and 114–16. Kuhns leads us, rather unpersuasively I think, in his chapter in *Decameron and the Philosophy of Storytelling* analysing the pear tree story (105–21), which is the sixty-ninth story of the *Decameron*, from the lascivious reputation and implication of the numeral "69" to

Aquinas and Augustine, suggesting the pear tree tale as a commentary on the problems of faith versus reason and original sin.

68 Radcliff-Umstead, "Boccaccio's Adaptation of Some Latin Sources for the Decameron," while pointing out examples of Boccaccio's many borrowings, concludes that Boccaccio always manages to imprint the tales with his own "typically Boccaccian" ethos (188). See also Marco Petoletti, "Boccaccio e i classici latini," in *Boccaccio autore e copista*, 41–9, and "Gli zibaldoni di Giovanni Boccaccio," 291–326, for works with which Boccaccio had clear familiarity.

69 "fā'il" is the agent participle, "doer" in Arabic; grammatically it is both an active participle and a technical term meaning "subject." In legal and medical terminology, however, it means the active partner in sexual relations who penetrates the other party, be it a female or a male orifice. There is thus a double-entendre here. Something like, "You pecker" (who are involved in an act of penetration), and "What are you doing!"

70 "ju'iltu fidā-ki," literally "may I be your sacrifice!"

13 Splitting Pants and Pigs: The *Fabliau* "Barat et Haimet" and Narrative Strategies in *Decameron* 8.5 and 8.6

KATHERINE A. BROWN

Critics have long noted that Giovanni Boccaccio repeats stories in the *Decameron* using the same plot devices in different *novelle*. For example, *Novella* 1.4, which is about a lascivious monk and his hypocritical abbot who both sleep with the same woman in the monk's cell, is effectively rewritten as a gendered inversion with lusty nuns in the second story of Day Nine.[1] Similarly, Marina Brownlee has argued that all of the stories on Day Three form thematic pairs of tales with "both a male and female counterpart," which respond to and undermine each other.[2] Although the repeated themes do not always include gender reversals, they are often associated with tricks. Thematic repetitions appear the most frequently on the days with humorous precepts centred on tricks.[3] The tales of Days Seven and Eight demonstrate such plot similarities, if not exact repetitions, because they deploy the same theme of the *beffa* (trick or practical joke). In many of the tricks of Day Seven, women hide their lovers from their husbands. In particular, *Novella* 7.2 draws on the same source as 5.10, in which a wife hides her young man in a tub.[4] Day Eight also witnesses a number of thematic repetitions and variations, as the topic of the *beffa* continues. Themes such as Florentines outwitting outsiders and groups tricking individuals dominate the tales of Day Eight.[5] In addition to thematic repetition, critics have pointed out structural similarities among the tales of Day Eight, such as the seventh and tenth stories, which both begin with a trick implemented by a woman and end with a retaliatory trick set in motion by a man, or the second tale of Day Eight, which is a retelling of that day's first tale.[6] Although Day Nine lacks a specified theme, many of its *novelle* arguably fit with the two preceding days because of their emphasis on trickery. Certainly the recurring characters in the Calandrino sequence of tales, to be discussed in more detail below, tie the stories of Day Eight, especially the third, sixth, and ninth tales, to the humorous ones of Day Nine, particularly the third and fifth tales.

These examples suggest that the repetition of plot devices correlates strongly with the comic subject matter of the *Decameron*. Indeed, the *beffa* is central to understanding the relationship among repetition, comedy, and artistic creation. For Anna Fontes, the *beffa* serves a social and cultural function as a secular reaction to *Fortuna*, in which worldly intelligence and wit help men manage the vicissitudes of life and its overwhelming uncertainty.[7] Similarly, Olivia Holmes has argued that the *beffe*, particularly on Day Eight, reflect on the stories' ability to teach and ultimately "point towards the reconstruction of an orderly society based on a system of judicial mechanisms."[8] On the other hand, Carla Forno sees the *beffa* as an escape from reality, an ambiguous type of story that lies between play and vengeance, between the tragic and comic.[9] As Michelangelo Picone has noted, there is a meta-literary dimension to the *beffa* in the *Decameron*, especially on Day Eight: "la beffa è qui diventata una creazione personale, quasi un duplicato dell'invenzione letteraria. E il regista della beffa si pone allo stesso livello dei narratori della cornice e dell'autore dell'opera [here, the trick has become a personal creation, almost a duplicate of literary invention. And the director of the trick places himself at the same level as the narrators of the frame and as the author of the work]."[10] The trickster resembles both the storyteller and the author because the creations of each introduce an illusion. Creations of the trickster in the tale mirror the creations of the *brigata* in the frame, which in turn mirror the literary creation that is the *Decameron*. The parallels between trickster and artist – or writer – that the stories of Day Eight help to establish, through what Joy Potter has called frame shifts, suggest that tricks are a type of art, and conversely that art and writing are deceptions.[11] This is not intended to evoke the Neoplatonic notion of the danger of imitation; on the contrary, the *Decameron* as a whole, and Boccaccio's works more generally, seem to point to the utility of art (and literature).[12] For the present discussion, that utility is most evident as a lesson about the nature of composition and reception, about the social implications of the tales.

In addition to the close relationship of the *beffa* with narrative, the repetition of *beffe* in multiple tales underscores the vast possibilities of artistic creation, for the same theme may be crafted in a variety of ways and to different purposes. The repetition of themes reinforces the parallels among the frames and the different levels of creation, as it reveals almost inexhaustible options in the execution of a theme. The storyteller, like the *beffatore*, uses available resources to generate new meanings and creative possibilities. Writers, storytellers, and tricksters are directors of illusion; they use their intellectual and physical resources to impose an order on the world of the audience, even if only temporarily. Tricks, like painting and narrative, draw on available materials – whether texts, paint, or the materials of everyday life – reorganizing and repurposing them. Even tales that repeat themes evidence reorderings, however subtle, of previous material. For this reason, Boccaccio's intertexts on Day Eight are of particular importance because they reveal the ways in which he organized received narrative material.

Though critical discussions have addressed repeated tales, they have in large part left out the relationship to the intertexts that these tales evoke, or rather, the models on which they were most likely based. Although Boccaccio drew from a wide range of sources and traditions, as many of the other essays in this volume show, his model texts on Day Eight imply order at the level of narrative generation. In spite of the link between thematic repetition and humour, specifically in the form of tricks or *beffe*, few studies have pointed out that many of the repeating *novelle* are in large measure indebted to the Old French *fabliau* tradition. The *fabliaux*, which flourished primarily in the northeastern regions of France from the late twelfth through the early fourteenth centuries, serve as one of the main comedic models for the *Decameron*. Moreover, the "favole" that Boccaccio names in the *Proemio* may be considered a reference to the *fabliaux*: "intendo di raccontare cento novelle, o favole o parabole o istorie che dire le vogliamo [I shall narrate a hundred stories or fables [*fabliaux*] or parables or histories, whatever you choose to call them]."[13] Studies devoted to sources of the *Decameron* point out the connections among individual tales and the *fabliaux*, but do not categorically liken them to the *beffa*.[14] In his study of Day Eight, Picone alludes to the *fabliaux* in relation to the fifth and sixth tales, which will be discussed below, but he claims that most of the *beffe* narrated on Day Seven are derived from the Middle Eastern tradition of misogynist literature, specifically from the *Seven Sages of Rome*.[15] He and other critics underestimate the influence of the *fabliau* tradition on the stories of Days Seven and Eight, especially where thematic repetitions are concerned. Indeed, the *fabliaux* must be considered as the bawdy counterpoints to the vast tradition of romance literature, specifically that emanating from northern France, which greatly influenced Boccaccio's work. These parodic and, at times, bourgeois tales in Old French reveal a broad representation of medieval life that is also common to the *Decameron*, a work that, according to Pier Massimo Forni, contains "the totality of human experience in it."[16] I would argue that a part of this experience is represented in, and derived from, the Old French *fabliaux*.[17] The *fabliaux*'s main impact on the *Decameron* involves tales of sexual appetites as much as those that glorify *ingegno* (wit) in producing successful tricks. For this reason, the *fabliaux*'s influence on repeating themes cannot be overstated, because the *fabliaux* also participate in a literary self-consciousness about the nature of artistic creation. Like the *novelle* on Day Eight, the *fabliaux* are stories about telling stories.

The *fabliaux* intertexts furnish another means by which to understand the creative and fruitful narrative potential of a single theme, particularly where the *beffa* is concerned. More to the point, a look at *fabliaux* analogues reveals key narrative strategies in the *Decameron*. One of these strategies is the combination of varied, even opposing, thematic elements, such as the mixture of the sacred and the profane, of religious discourse with the sexual discourse of the *fabliaux*, as in the story of Alibech and Rustico in the last *novella* of Day Three. Forno sees these pairings play out in the diametrically opposed characters of Day Eight – another way these stories serve a meta-literary function.[18] Such combinations of opposites bring divergent narrative material together, creating order from disparity. For Tobias Foster Gittes, the juxtaposition and hybridization of opposing pairs – exemplum and counter-exemplum, virtue and vice – are features of Boccaccio's poetics more generally and serve moral and secular (political) purposes, particularly in the *Decameron*, by allowing readers to select a salubrious choice for what ails them, as the *Proemio* to the *Decameron* illustrates.[19]

While many critics have pointed out the literary combinations and hybridity that mark the *Decameron*, few have focused on the opposite strategy that creates two *novelle* from one (*fabliau*) source.[20] A single Old French *fabliau* is often cited as an analogue, if not a model, for more than one *novella*, frequently for the tales with similar narratives. By way of example, the following pairs of tales all share a narrative nucleus with an Old French *fabliau* antecedent. *Le Vilain de Bailleul* serves as a model for *Novella* 3.8, the story of Ferondo in a pseudo-Purgatory, and for aspects of *Novella* 9.3, in which Calandrino thinks he is pregnant. In all three cases, a stupid husband is convinced of the impossible, either that he is dead or pregnant. Similarly, parts of *Le Prestre qui abevete* are used in some way both for *Novella* 3.4, in which Dom Felice does penance while Friar Puccio entertains his wife, and for the second part of *Novella* 7.9, where Lidia and Pirro cavort in a pear tree in view of her husband.[21] In this group of stories, a husband sees or hears his wife *in flagrante delicto* with another man, but does not believe his senses. As already mentioned, *Novelle* 5.10 and 7.2 both resemble *Le Cuvier*, in which a wife hides her lover either in a tub or a coop when her husband returns home unexpectedly.[22] Finally, *Les Braies li priestre* is arguably one of the shared sources for the aforementioned *Novelle* 1.4 and 9.2 about hypocrisy and sexuality in religious communities. These common analogues reinforce connections among the tales at the thematic and intertextual levels, as they also highlight the potential of the *fabliaux* to be adapted in multiple ways.

Moreover, each retelling of a theme is a new way of ordering the elements of which it is composed, often in combination with new devices and to the exclusion of others. As *novelle* are made up of smaller narrative units, dividing and reassembling the units in different ways achieves new effects, and consequently new meanings. The theory underpinning this view of the *novelle* is that they are composed of separable yet comprehensible components; Boccaccio's rearranging and combining of different narrative elements support this Proppian or narratological approach to the *Decameron*, as Boccaccio's techniques also push the grammar of narrative structure to the limits.[23] The ordering of thematic parts into different stories shows that there are various ways to organize and combine narrative material. Indeed, Picone has argued that the *novelle* of Day Eight inspired new narratives in the form of later rewritings and amplifications in Italian literature, and that they inaugurated the literary traditions of the Renaissance.[24] The tales of Day Eight are especially conducive to rewritings because of their self-conscious awareness as artistic creations, which makes them able to serve in many ways as guides for other artists and storytellers. In effect, the tales of Day Eight may be considered how-to manuals for creating artistic illusions and, as the following discussion will suggest, for writing tales by manipulating previous narrative material for a new purpose. Boccaccio's transformations go beyond mere structural play, implicating rhetoric, reception, indeed all aspects of storytelling. For this reason, the sources and analogues that Boccaccio exposes in the tales of Day Eight are more than just intertextual allusions; they are also examples of how to transform extant narratives.

The previous instances of a single *fabliau* being used as a model for two *novelle* in the *Decameron* demonstrate the repetition of plot devices. In these cases, the reorganization of the narrative material in the tales alters, but still clearly alludes to, the *fabliaux* sources; the connecting themes are evident. The following group will suggest another way in which Boccaccio used the *fabliaux* analogues, and perhaps others. The story "Barat et Haimet" is a *fabliau* whose elements Boccaccio did not repeat but rather bifurcated in order to repurpose the split parts in two divergent narratives: these are Tales 5 and 6 on Day Eight. Although the technique of creating two plots from one story is the opposite of repeating the same narrative in two *novelle*, ultimately both the repetition and the splitting of the *fabliaux* sources serve to underscore the potential of narrative to be adapted in multiple, if not endless, ways. More to the point, Boccaccio's reordering of narrative material, in this case by juxtaposing the *disiecta membra* of the original *fabliau* source, highlights the writer's role in establishing a new order. If, as Gittes has argued, one of Boccaccio's intentions in writing the *Decameron* is to propose a new "myth" and sense of order after the devastation of the Plague, then the poet's role as a "Prometheus" is one that reveals and restores knowledge.[25] Opening the seams of his textual sources to reveal the splitting of the *fabliau* "Barat et Haimet" into two pieces, but situating them side by side so that their split is all the more evident, reveals that for Boccaccio, dismantling established stories must precede reconfiguring and re-creating order – what Nature and Fortune have not undone, the poet may disassemble in service of knowledge. The following analysis will first explain how "Barat et Haimet" is used in each of these *Decameron* stories, and then will draw out the implications for Boccaccio's narrative art.

"Barat et Haimet" was composed by Jean Bodel, the famous *trouvère* from Arras, in the last decade of the twelfth century.[26] The story is divided into two main episodes, which were inspired by different texts of eastern and western origin.[27] It is possible that this internal division furnished the suggestion to Boccaccio to divide his source into two separate narratives. In the *fabliau*, the two parts of the narrative are linked not only by the same characters but also by the notion of theft.[28] Similarly, *Novelle* 8.5 and 8.6 also share theft as a linking theme, but they do not share any characters directly, a point that will be discussed in more detail below.

The first part of the *fabliau* begins with three thieves in the forest, two of whom are brothers. One of the brothers, Haimet – whose name is a derivative of the Old French word *hameçon*, meaning "hook" – decides to prove his prowess in theft by climbing a tree and taking the eggs from the nest of a magpie without attracting the bird's notice.[29] The scene is ironic because the magpie was known in the Middle Ages as a bird that steals objects. Thus the text begins with the trickster-bird being tricked – or, a robber being robbed. This beginning also calls attention to the relationship between animals and theft that will be exploited in the second part of the narrative. After Haimet succeeds in stealing from the bird, his brother Barat, whose name means "trickery" or "guile,"[30] dares him to return the eggs, once again without attracting the bird's notice. Haimet proceeds to climb the tree, unaware that Barat is stealthily following him in order to steal his pants. When Haimet descends from the tree for the second time, having successfully returned the eggs to the nest, his brother Barat mocks him for being unaware that his pants have been stolen and brags that he, Barat, is the best thief. Their friend Travers is so stupefied and discouraged by these feats of skill – they make him realize that he is not as good a thief as the brothers are – that he decides to leave them and return home to his wife to work the land. The name Travers is a bit more ambiguous than the other two, but certainly suggestive of the reasons he will later be tricked. Gary Mole offers the definition *chemin de traverse,* meaning the "back road" or "shortcut," which he connects to the idea of a winding, tortuous path, as though Travers takes an indirect route.[31] The word *travers* can either mean "passage" or "passing," indicating that he was only with the thieves temporarily, or else it can have the meaning of "incorrectly" or "the wrong way," because he chooses to live "incorrectly" by not being a thief, the way of life that is valorized in this tale. All of these explanations seem to validate his being tricked in the second part of the tale. Travers's departure marks the end of the first sequence in the *fabliau.*

This part of the story exhibits clear similarities to *Decameron* 8.5, in which Maso del Saggio and his two friends plot to remove the breeches of the judge from the Marches, Messer Niccola. Picone has already pointed out the broad similarities between "Barat et Haimet" and *Novella* 8.5, having specified details about the victim's nudity in each case.[32] Yet a consideration of some other specifics suggests that Boccaccio did not simply split the parts of the *fabliau* but rather drew from each part of "Barat et Haimet" for Tales 5 and 6 on Day Eight.

The first part of the *fabliau* begins with a bragging game among the thieves, which justifies the theft of the eggs and then the pants, because it establishes theft as a clever and therefore virtuous act. The two thefts effectively constitute a double deception that undermines what the victims believe to be true – the bird is unaware that her eggs are missing, just as Haimet is unaware that his pants are missing. Theft is practically an art in the tale, a skill that must be developed in order to deceive others successfully. In this respect, theft is similar to the *beffa* and to storytelling. *Novella* 8.5 reproduces the ludic intention found at the beginning of the *fabliau* through the introduction of a character, Maso del Saggio, whom the audience already knows to be a trickster from *Novella* 8.3, in which he told Calandrino about the magical properties of the heliotrope. In *Novella* 8.5 as well, stealing the breeches is justified by the character of the victim, for the judge is deemed worthy of being tricked because he is such a ridiculous and unappealing figure. As a non-Florentine who should have no interest in the city, he deserves to be deceived. His low-hanging breeches are yet another physical sign of his being uneducated and unfit as a judge.

In the second part of the *fabliau*, Travers's return to his farm sets him up as a victim for the brothers because he abandoned their lifestyle of theft. That he lives on a farm anticipates Calandrino in 8.6, who not only raised a pig on the farm his wife inherited but also is possibly from the *contado* (countryside) himself. Whereas Ronald Martinez refers to Calandrino as "provincial," Calandrino's simple ways and lack of Florentine savviness have suggested to Carlo Muscetta, Fontes, and Holmes that Calandrino originates from the *contado*.[33] If Calandrino is indeed from the country and not truly Florentine, he may be considered a worthy victim. Regardless of his origins, he finds himself in the country in 8.6, and thus the association of country living with being a deserving dupe seems to hold in both tales. Travers's rejection of theft as a way of life recalls another moment from 8.3, and suggests an even more complex relationship among the intertexts of Day Eight. In *Novella* 8.3, Calandrino is excited about the heliotrope for mercenary reasons. He implicitly deserves punishment from Bruno and Buffalmacco not merely because he is concerned with money over art but also because he rejects painting as a way of life in favour of robbery, whereas Bruno and Buffalmacco are artists and not mere painters.[34] As in the *fabliau*, the victim is punished in 8.3 for his rejection of a superior way of life and for his status as outsider. In all three tales, the victim deserves the trick.

In both the *fabliau* and *Novella* 8.5, the theft of the breeches is part of a *mise-en-abyme* involving theft; in the *fabliau*, the pants are taken while Haimet is in the process of "unstealing" the eggs from the bird's nest; and in the *Decameron*, Maso and his friend Ribi try to distract the judge by holding onto either side of his robe and lodging fake complaints against each other for stealing each other's property, all while their third friend Matteuzzo is under the platform pulling down the judge's breeches. In both instances, the theft of the breeches is intended as humiliation of the victim as much as evidence of skill by the tricksters/thieves, thereby mitigating any moral and legal implications of the theft.[35] The *mise-en-abyme* highlights theft as a performance, a creative act intended to reinforce the superiority of one character over another, as it creates a frame of and for stealing. As such, these performative thefts underscore the definition of the *beffa* of Day Eight as artistic creation and meta-literary construct. Indeed, the opening of the tricks to a broader audience within the tales, whether the courtroom in 8.5 or the town in 8.6, supports the notion of trick as performance and consequently as meta-artistic creation.[36] In terms of order, the tricks impose or restore a certain social hierarchy in the tales based on cleverness, as they also upend the order in which the victims mistakenly believed. Haimet believes he is the best thief, only to be humiliated by his brother once he discovers that Barat removed his, Haimet's, pants as he was climbing. Similarly, the judge considers himself superior by virtue of his profession, while he is being stripped of his pants and publicly humiliated; the result shows that he lacks the respect of the locals and is not a good judge of character, because he could not tell that Maso and Ribi were lying in their complaints. Thus Barat is the best thief and Maso is more worthy of esteem than the judge. In both tales, the hierarchy of social adeptness that the narratives construct in favour of the trickster(s) simultaneously undermines the perceived social status of the victim; the trick overturns the social order and results in disorder for the dupe. The implication is that tricks, like art, create order for some and disorder for others; order and art are relative concepts that need to be interpreted because there are no absolute values in the world of the *Decameron*.[37]

In spite of the similarities between "Barat et Haimet" and *Novella* 8.5, there are some key differences. The *fabliau* begins with Haimet's stealing eggs from a bird's nest, an episode that seemingly has no correspondent in *Novella* 8.5. Yet there is a small moment in the text where Boccaccio seems to acknowledge the bird episode, when Maso first sees the judge, "parendogli che fosse un nuovo uccellone" (8.5.6). G.H. McWilliam has translated this as "he was struck by the man's curious and witless appearance," whereas J.M. Rigg gives the much more fitting translation that Maso "deemed him a fowl of no common feather."[38] Vittore Branca glosses the word *uccellone* as a derivative of the past participle *uccellato*, meaning tricked (from the way a bird is trapped), and this certainly fits with the theme of the *beffa* that dominates the narratives on Day Eight.[39] Another possibility is that the word *uccellone* in conjunction with the *fabliau* intertext is a deliberate, if subtle, reference to the robbed magpie episode of "Barat et Haimet." Like the irony in the *fabliau* of stealing from a magpie – the thief of birds – the *Decameron novella* renders ironic justice by mocking the ill-bred holder of the seat of justice. Moreover, this bird reference furthers the connection to the following tale in which Calandrino is tricked. The name Calandrino is related to the *calandra* (lark) and sets him apart as a dupe par excellence.[40] In this way, all three tales enact theft on inferior, bird-like victims, as they offer new social hierarchies based on secular values such as wit and appropriate justice.

The theft of the breeches in *Novella* 8.5 also draws on other parts of "Barat et Haimet." In the second part of the story, when Barat and his brother Haimet have discovered that Travers has a delicious pig, they go to his house at night and make a hole through which they can get inside: "C'un treu firent desoz la sole / Dont l'en peüst traire une mole [They made a hole beneath the beam through which one could drag a millstone]."[41] This first hole allows the thieves to enter Travers's house undetected. And later, after Travers has stolen back his pig for the final time and decided to cook it, Haimet goes onto the roof and creates another hole, this time over the spot where the pig is cooking, and fashions a sort of fishing pole by which to steal parts of the pig:

> Puis est montez sor le toitel,
> Si le descuevre en cel endroit
> La ou la chaudiere boloit.
> Tant osta de la coverture
> Qu'il vit parmi l'entroverture
> La feme Travers someillier.
>
> [Then he climbed on the roof
> And opened it there in the spot
> Where the cauldron was boiling.
> He lifted enough of the cover
> Until he saw through the opening
> Travers's wife, who was sleeping.][42]

These holes made for stealing are mimicked in *Novella* 8.5, in which the judge sits on a platform that has a break in the plank right by his feet, through which Matteuzzo reaches to pull down his breeches: "e oltre a ciò videro rotta l'asse sopra la quale messer lo giudicio teneva i piedi, tanto che a grande agio vi si poteva mettere la mano e 'l braccio [moreover the plank on which the judge's feet were resting had a large hole in it, through which a hand and an arm could be thrust with the greatest of ease]" (8.5.9). Whereas the theft of the pants in the *fabliau* takes place while the brothers are climbing a tree, Boccaccio seems to borrow the detail of a hole in the floor from the pig-stealing part of "Barat et Haimet." Even the detail of the ample size of this hole is similar to the first hole in the *fabliau*. The reference to a millstone also appears in *Novella* 8.3 as another magical stone that Maso mentions in addition to the heliotrope. Holmes has connected this use of *macigno* (hard sandstone or millstone) to the sexual metaphor *macinare* (to mill or grind) used in *Novella* 8.2.[43] For Martinez, the millstone is ever-present in *Novella* 8.3, in which Calandrino is "dogged" by the millstone; it is even part of the street name where he lives, *Canto alla Macina* (8.3.50).[44] Although the Old French word *mole*, derived from the Latin word *mola*, is semantically related to *macigno* through the process of grinding at a mill, the use of these words in each story is quite different, for *mole* functions in the *fabliau* as a practical, if rustic, reference to describe the relative size of a hole, whereas in the *Decameron*, *macigno* and *macinare* either have magical properties or work as sexual innuendo. That being said, there is a sense in which the second hole in the *fabliau*, the one on the roof right above Travers's sleeping wife, is also sexually suggestive. As with Calandrino, however, the true treasure in Travers's possession is implicitly not his wife, but his pig.

A look at the second part of the *fabliau* and *Novella* 8.6 suggests that the cross-references between the two parts of "Barat et Haimet" are in fact deliberate and more than a mere coincidence or confusion of details as a result of oral transmission. In the second part of "Barat et Haimet," Travers has become such a successful farmer that he has just killed a pig for the winter. While he is out one day, his old friends Barat and Haimet arrive at his house and are greeted cautiously by Travers's wife, Marie. The two thieves spot the pig in the distance, even though Marie thinks she has hidden everything of value from their view. When Travers returns and discovers that two men have visited, he quickly guesses who they are and becomes anxious about losing his pig. As a precaution, he moves the pig before going to bed, but he is still anxious that the brothers will steal it. At night, Barat and Haimet create a hole beneath the pig through which to enter the house and steal the animal, but they do not find it at first. Travers hears their noises and gets up to check on his cow, but Barat outsmarts him and imitates Travers's voice to find out from Marie where the pig has been moved. He then grabs the pig and runs to the forest, with Travers in pursuit. Travers then imitates Haimet and takes the pig from Barat, bringing it back to his house. When the brothers realize they have been tricked, they return to Travers's house, where Barat disguises his appearance and his voice in order to imitate Marie and take charge of the pig from Travers, after performing a fake ritual intended to protect the pig. When Travers realizes he has been tricked, he runs to the forest and scares the brothers by pretending to be a hanged man, which they think is their father's ghost.[45] The brothers then run off and abandon the pig to Travers, who takes it home and decides to let his wife cook it while he sleeps. Barat and Haimet finally arrive and fish for the cooking pork through the roof of Travers's house. Travers wakes up as the pig is being removed and offers to end the affair once and for all by drawing lots to divide the pig; the two brothers leave with their handsome portions and Travers is left with the worst part.

In addition to the basic plot of pig stealing, Boccaccio draws many of the details of *Decameron* 8.6 from this part of the *fabliau*. Boccaccio replaces the nocturnal confusion of the pig's changing hands multiple times with Calandrino's drunkenness and the truth-proving *galle* (sweets) that ultimately implicate Calandrino as the thief of his own pig, even though he cannot enjoy it. In this respect, Calandrino certainly resembles Travers, who actually did steal back his pig several times, only to be deprived of the best part of it. Picone claims that the complex back-and-forth of the pig in the *fabliau* corresponds to the multiplication of *beffe* in the *novella*. He also points out that the magic rite in the *fabliau* that Barat, dressed as Marie, performs on the pig in order to safeguard it has a counterpart in the *novella*: namely, the alleged magical properties of the ginger-aloe pills to reveal the thief and to help Bruno and Buffalmacco retain the pig. Similarly, the details such as the pig's being prepared for Christmas and its being salted and saved for the family are borrowed directly from the *fabliau*.[46]

Although it is possible that the introduction of the magical pills, and even of the priest who is a friend of Bruno and Buffalmacco, are both derived from another story (not necessarily a *fabliau*), Picone's assertion that they have acquired the purpose in the *novella* of functioning as a parallel for the magical-mystical parts of the *fabliau* antecedent seems probable. A couple of other details, however, are most likely remnants of the first part of "Barat et Haimet." When Calandrino first shows the pig to his friends and the priest, it is reminiscent of the bragging gestures at the beginning of "Barat et Haimet," for Calandrino uses the pig to show off his abilities as a farmer: "gli chiamò e disse: 'Voi siate i ben venuti: io voglio che voi veggiate che massaio io sono'; e menatigli in casa, mostrò loro questo porco [he called out to them, saying: 'I bid you a hearty welcome, my friends. Come along inside, and I'll show you what an excellent farmer I am.' And having taken them into the farmhouse, he showed them the pig]" (8.6.6). Just as Haimet offers to show off his skill at stealing by calling attention to the bird's nest, so Calandrino wants attention for his skill in pig raising. In both cases, the man's boasting leads to the loss of his property and to mocking by his friends.

Later in the story, after the pig is stolen, Calandrino asserts for the first time to Bruno and Buffalmacco that he is not the thief. He swears that he is telling the truth, asking if he must hang himself to be believed: "io dico che tu non mi credi, se io no sia impiccato per la gola, che egli m'è stato imbolato! [do I have to hang myself by the neck before I can convince you that it really has been stolen?]" (8.6.23). The reference to hanging is ironic because hanging is the punishment for thieves, and Calandrino will later be implicated as the thief of his own pig. The reference to hanging also recalls two moments in the *fabliau*. In the second part of the *fabliau*, when Travers is trying to recover his pig, he hangs from a tree by his arm, but because of the darkness of night, Barat and Haimet think it is the ghost of their father, who was hanged for theft. This hanging is also foreshadowed in the first part of the *fabliau* when Barat and Haimet are introduced: "S'avoit esté penduz lor pere [their father had been hanged]."[47] The threat of hanging connects the two parts of the *fabliau*, and arguably connects Calandrino's reference to both parts of the *fabliau* as well.

If this is the case, it complicates the idea that Boccaccio merely split the *fabliau* into two discrete parts, for he seems to have borrowed elements from both sections for *Novelle* 8.5 and 8.6. It implies that Boccaccio is using the *fabliau* intertext to further connections among these *novelle*. But these connections are already evident on a thematic level. Not only do 8.5 and 8.6 both involve theft, but at the beginning of 8.6, Filomena draws a parallel to Filostrato, who narrated 8.5, saying, "come Filostrato fu dal nome di Maso tirato a dover dire la novella da lui udita avete, cosí né piú né men son tirata io da quello di Calandrino e de' compagni suoi a dirne un'altra di loro [just as Filostrato was prompted to tell you the previous tale by hearing the name Maso, in precisely the same way I too have been prompted by hearing the names of Calandrino and his companions to tell you another]" (8.6.3). Both *Novella* 8.5 and 8.6 are connected to *Novella* 8.3 through intradiegetic references among the storytellers and through the characters they employ – Maso the trickster in 8.5; Bruno, Buffalmacco, and especially Calandrino in 8.6. For this reason, and because, as already mentioned, these tales deal with theft, a thematic (as well as a character) relationship among all three tales is well established.

The division of characters in 8.3 on the diegetic level into two different narratives, 8.5 and 8.6, is paralleled on the intertextual level by splitting the two main episodes of "Barat et Haimet" into these same stories. As 8.5 and 8.6 are already linked for the audience, why does Boccaccio also connect them by drawing them from the same source, a connection that would most likely not have been perceived by most of his audience?

One reason may be to draw attention to the way he uses sources – at least for the members of his audience aware of such intertexts. Indeed, if we are all either dupes or artists who must generate meaning and order for ourselves, the exposure of how narratives may be effectively reconstructed from various parts is itself instructive and therefore useful knowledge. *Novelle* 8.5 and 8.6 are not isolated as tales with a common source, since Boccaccio deploys the same type of division of a source-story into two tales with another source for Day Eight: the pseudo-Ovidian *De vetula*. Picone argues that the central episode of the *De vetula* was the basis for *Novella* 8.4, whereas the main plot of the whole furnished the model for *Novella* 8.7.[48] Thus Boccaccio split two sources in order to create four *novelle* on Day Eight, framing two tales with a shared source with another set of tales with a shared source. Yet 8.4 also resembles *Le Prestre et Alison*, further implicating the *fabliaux* in the meta-literary message of Day Eight. While such bifurcations allow narrative elements to be married to those of different traditions – whether Islamicate, classical, or local folklore – they also show that fission, just as much as fusion, can generate new forms, new order. Indeed, Boccaccio studies and narrative theory generally tend to privilege hybridization without always exploring fission as a necessary precursor to the dismantling of previous forms.

This sequence of tales, from the fourth to the sixth *novella* of Day Eight, suggests a relationship between order and the *beffa*. As already mentioned, the *beffa* imposes a world order on the victim, one that is at odds with his or her previous perception of order. The *beffa*, however, is mere illusion, a temporary domination of reality.[49] The fragments with which the victim is left are the disordered remnants of the false order imposed by the artist in creating his illusion. The implication for the work as a whole is that writing provides the illusion of order for the audience, but that disorder and chaos ultimately remain. Indeed, the *Decameron* is framed by the disorder of the Plague, from which the members of *brigata* seek escape and to which they return after their storytelling. Although the members of the *brigata*, like the lovesick ladies of the *Proemio*, may be altered by the experience of the storytelling, this experience in itself is not sufficient to diminish chaos. More to the point, there is no order imposed for them on reality, but rather, they must determine order for themselves. Indeed, if the author, like the *beffatore*, offers a new order, he cannot control how it is understood, who believes it, and how long its effects may last. There is a danger in accepting an order provided by an artist, which is that one may be duped. Thus, the duty of creating order must rest with those who are capable of doing so.

Another implication of the splitting and recombining of stories is the relative meaning of narrative parts. Because the theft of a pig or of pants can be moved to any part of a narrative and serve any number of different purposes, there is no absolute meaning in these events. Narrative structure and meaning are derived from the placement of the elements. For this reason, the repetition of narratives also points to the instability or relativity of their meanings. Fontes has argued that all *beffe* are attempts to arrange the future, and that, in 8.6, this process is reversed, for the *beffa* actually uses the future to explain events of the past.[50] The temporal shift exposed by the *beffa* in 8.6 reveals the same relationship to time that Boccaccio has shown through his manipulation of sources: justifying the narrative past by the future is an example of the ways in which dividing and rearranging narrative clusters are devices that alter narrative time and create new order. Perhaps a greater implication of the *beffa*, then, is what it says about time. The ordered succession of events in these stories and their timeliness are essential for creating humour. If the trickster's actions, such as stealing the judge's pants, occurred in the same way at any other moment in the narrative, the result would not necessarily be comic, but rather tragic or meaningless, or possibly funny in a different way. The *beffe*, by rearranging the order of future and past, play with the relationships among events and timeliness; narrative, like time, is fragmentary. The ways in which sources for the *beffe* are reversed, repeated, divided, and reconfigured all suggest that narrative parts and narrative time are not fixed, but may both be relative. In this light, it might also be said that in Boccaccio's art, secular time – earthly time – is not absolute either, or at least human perception of time cannot be absolute.

I began this article by arguing that the splitting of a narrative into two different stories serves the same purpose as repeating a theme: namely to show that narrative has a nearly endless potential for revision and reinterpretation. The rich intertextuality among the tales of Day Eight suggests that the moments of high contrivance are also the ones that reveal the greatest illusion and that most clearly call attention to themselves as art. One distinction is necessary, though. The interconnections on the diegetic level – those created either by repeating a theme or by the redeployment of the same characters, such as Calandrino and Maso – imply limitless narrative possibilities for the composer, as well as interpretive possibilities for the audience. If narrative repetitions underscore variety in creation, they necessarily suggest the multiplicity of personal interpretations. Thus, variations on a theme highlight both creative and interpretive possibilities.

Even in these meta-literary stories, the focus shifts from the author to the work's reception. This distinction is echoed in the unfolding of the plots, for the *beffatori* become secondary to the dupes; scholars even refer to them as Calandrino stories, not as Bruno and Buffalmacco or Maso del Saggio stories. These stories are as much about the stupidity of the dupe as they are about the wit and creation of the trickster. Maso all but disappears from the narrative after humiliating the judge, and the focus is not on the mirth Maso and his friends gain from his trick but rather on the reactions of the victim and society. On the level of the sources – the "writerly" level – lies the inherent potential in narrative for multiple creative possibilities. The manipulation of sources, most likely written sources, is intended for a more specific audience of writers for whom the repurposing of narrative can and must be reimagined.

Like the victim of the *beffatore*'s trick, the inscribed audiences within the *Decameron*, whether the *brigata* or the *donne amorose* whom Boccaccio addresses in the *Proemio*, are offered, and presumably partake in, the temporary diversion that the director's illusion makes accessible. Yet, in this view, artistic creation is not exactly the equivalent of a trick, since the internal and external audiences of the *Decameron* willingly allow themselves to be deceived for the pleasure and solace that it affords them. In contrast to these audiences, many of the victims on Day Eight never even realize they have been tricked, or else feel disappointment at the loss of the world of illusion.

The audience's pleasure or bewilderment at the creation, whether in the form of a narrative or a *beffa*, ultimately hinges on how the illusion is interpreted. Boccaccio points to the question of interpretation in the *Conclusione dell'autore*, suggesting that the meaning of the tales depends at least as much on the response to them as on their creation:

> Niuna corrotta mente intese mai sanamente parola: e cosí come le oneste a quella non giovano, cosí quelle che tanto oneste non sono la ben disposta non posson contaminare, se non come il loto i solari raggi o le terrene brutture le bellezze del cielo. (*Concl. dell'autore*, 11)

> [No word, however pure, was ever wholesomely construed by a mind that was corrupt. And just as seemly language leaves no mark upon a mind that is corrupt, language that is less than seemly cannot contaminate a mind that is well ordered, any more than mud will sully the rays of the sun, or earthly filth the beauties of the heavens.]

If Day Eight, concerning the *beffa,* is a model for how writers can create endlessly by combining and splitting tales, the dupe's tale may also be seen as an exemplum *in malo* for audiences to avoid, for the dupes passively accept the illusion as truth, or else derive no pleasure, but rather dissatisfaction, from the creative movement. It is the responsibility of the members of the audience to discern the truth for themselves, to be dupes or generators of their own order. Thus, the tales on Day Eight initiate the passage of interpretive and creative responsibility from the artist and storyteller to the audience.

NOTES

1 The similarities between these texts have been remarked by Guido Almansi in *The Writer as Liar: Narrative Technique in the "Decameron"* (London: Routledge, 1975), 64–6, and in "Lettura della quarta novella del *Decameron,*" *Strumenti Critici* 13 (1970): 308–17; and by Christopher Kleinhenz in "Stylistic Gravity: Language and Prose Rhythms in *Decameron* I, 4," *Humanities Association Review* 26, no. 4 (1975): 289–99; 289. Pier Massimo Forni also calls attention to the frequency of internal responses, not just rewritings, among tales in the *Decameron* as a commonplace, stating that the purpose of each response varies by context and that it is the job of the critic to articulate the aims of these interconnections within the work; "The *Decameron* and Narrative Form," in *Cambridge Companion to Boccaccio,* ed. Guyda Armstrong, Rhiannon Daniels, and Stephen J. Milner (Cambridge: Cambridge University Press, 2015), 55–64; 56–8. The current essay is more concerned with thematic repetition as a type of internal response, particularly as it is related to the practices of trickery.

2 Marina Scordilis Brownlee, "Wolves and Sheep: Symmetrical Undermining in Day III of the *Decameron,*" *Romance Notes* 24, no. 3 (1984): 262–6; 264.

3 One notable exception, as Donald McGrady has outlined in "Boccaccio Repeats Himself: *Decameron* II, 6 and V, 7," *MLN* 116, no. 1 (2001): 193–7, is the parts of *novelle* 2.6 and 5.7 that repeat each other.

4 For studies of sources for each *novella*, see the notes to individual tales in Giovanni Boccaccio, *Decameron*, ed. Vittore Branca (Turin: Einaudi, 1980, rev. 1992); all references to the *Decameron* are to this edition. See also the entries for each tale in Marcus Landau, *Die Quellen des "Dekameron"* (Stuttgart: J. Scheible, 1884); and A. Collingwood Lee, *The "Decameron": Its Sources and Analogues* (New York: Haskell House, 1972).

5 For a discussion of the tricks of Day Eight that pit Florentines against non-Florentines, see Olivia Holmes, "Trial by *Beffa*: Retributive Justice and In-Group Formation in Day 8," *Annali d'Italianistica* 31 (2013): 355–79; 363–4; and Anna Fontes, "Le thème de la 'beffa' dans le *Décaméron*," in *Formes et signification de la "beffa" dans la littérature italienne de la Renaissance* (Paris: Université de la Sorbonne nouvel, 1972), 11–44, esp. 27–31. For a discussion of groups perpetrating tricks on individuals, see Carla Forno, "L'amaro riso della beffa: VIII giornata," in *Prospettive sul "Decameron"* (Turin: Tirrenia, 1989), 131–47, esp. 134.

6 See Michelangelo Picone, "L'Arte della beffa: L'Ottava giornata," in *Introduzione al "Decameron,"* ed. Michelangelo Picone and Margherita Mesirca (Florence: Cesati, 2004), 203–25; 210–13; Emma Grimaldi, *Il privilegio di Dioneo: l'eccezione e la regola nel sistema del "Decameron"* (Naples: Edizioni scientifiche italiane, 1987), esp. 310–11; Holmes, "Trial by *Beffa*," 365–6, 368n5; and Fontes, "Le thème de la 'beffa,'" esp. 40n47.

7 Ibid., 39.

8 Holmes, "Trial by *Beffa*," 386 and 365.

9 Forno, "L'amaro riso della beffa," 146.

10 Picone, "L'Arte della beffa," 206. All English translations of critical works are my own unless indicated otherwise.

11 For the concept of frame shifts, see Joy Hambuechen Potter, *Five Frames for the "Decameron": Communication and Social Systems in the "Cornice"* (Princeton: Princeton University Press, 1982).

12 For a comprehensive view of Boccaccio's oeuvre and its secular utility, see Tobias Foster Gittes, *Boccaccio's Naked Muse: Eros, Culture, and the Mythopoeic Imagination* (Toronto: University of Toronto Press, 2008).

13 Boccaccio, *Decameron*, *Proemio* 13; *The Decameron*, 2nd ed., trans. G.H. McWilliam (London: Penguin, 1995), 3. All citations of the *Decameron* in English are from this translation. In his edition, Branca points out that the "favole" are in all probability an allusion to the Old French *fabliaux*; see *Decameron*, 9. This point has been much debated, however; for an overview and bibliography of the issue, see Simone Marchesi, *Stratigrafie decameroniane* (Florence: Olschki, 2004), esp. 1–8.

14 See the notes on individual stories in the *Decameron*, ed. Branca; in Landau, *Die Quellen des "Dekameron"*; and in Lee, *The "Decameron": Its Sources and Analogues*.

15 Picone, "L'Arte della beffa," 206. Holmes also alludes to *fabliaux* sources for *novelle* 8.4, 5, and 6, but once again in a non-systematic way, in "Trial by *Beffa*," 373n12 and 375n13. In the previous essay in this volume, Franklin Lewis refers to the Arabic and Persian versions of the pear tree story as *fabliaux*. The dates of composition he gives for these works precede Boccaccio's composition of the *Decameron*, but are mostly concurrent with the production of Old French *fabliaux*. While my essay uses the term "*fabliau*" to refer to a specific type of comic text produced in Old French dialects within a period of a century and a half, the many similarities among Middle Eastern and Western medieval comic and bawdy tales are striking. My point here is not to argue about the historical primacy of Old French over Arabic/Persian sources and comic tales, but rather to explore the direct influence of the Old French *fabliaux* in general on the *Decameron*, and the tale "Barat et Haimet" in particular on two *novelle* in Day Eight. Elsewhere, I have outlined how Boccaccio combines Middle Eastern narratives and framing devices with Old French *fabliaux* themes and Western anthologizing practices; see my *Boccaccio's Fabliaux* (Gainesville: University Press of Florida, 2014), esp. Chapter 3. In this respect, I agree with Lewis that Boccaccio's tales evidence a deliberate hybridity of sources and genres.

16 Forni, "The *Decameron* and Narrative Form," 58.

17 I have argued in *Boccaccio's Fabliaux* that the *fabliau* is itself a hybrid genre that lends itself to combinations with various literary traditions.

18 Forno, "L'amaro riso della beffa," 134.

19 "By uniting Livy's secular utility with a Christian 'sacra utilitas,' Boccaccio has produced a generic hybrid, a secular 'scripture' designed to serve as a panacea for all human ills, physical and spiritual: an eminently practical 'remedy for fortunes fair and foul'" (Gittes, *Boccaccio's Naked Muse*, 227).

20 Numerous critics discuss Boccaccio's combination of sources throughout his career. For recent studies and up-to-date bibliography on the divergent materials Boccaccio combined in his writings, see the essays in *Boccaccio: A Critical Guide to the Complete Works*, ed. Victoria Kirkham, Michael Sherberg, and Janet Levarie Smarr (Chicago: University of Chicago Press, 2013), in particular the essay by Ronald L. Martinez on the *Decameron* and those by David Wallace, Elissa Weaver, and Arielle Saiber for examinations of literary combinations in other of Boccaccio's works. In a slightly different vein, Almansi's chapter on Boccaccio's *ars combinatoria* shows

how Boccaccio exhausted themes such as the bed trick by exploiting every possible combination of sexual partners, for example in *Novella* 9.6 (*The Writer as Liar*, 63–107).

21 For Persian and Arabic analogues for *Dec.* 7.9, see the previous essay in this volume by Franklin Lewis.

22 Although Branca and Lee cite Book 9 of the *Metamorphoses* of Apulieus as the common source for 5.10 and 7.2, both mention *Le Cuvier* as a vague analogue for *Novella* 7.2; see the *Decameron*, ed. Branca, 692 and 798; and Lee, *The "Decameron": Its Sources and Analogues*, 173 and 186–7. The connection between comedy and repetition still holds, as evidenced by the fact that there exists a *fabliau* analogue, even though it is not the common source for the Boccaccian *novelle*. It is possible, however, that the *fabliau* is also based on Apuleius's text.

23 See Vladimir Propp, *Morphology of the Folktale*, trans. Laurence Scott (Austin: University of Texas Press, 1968); on narratology and the *Decameron*, see Tzvetan Todorov, *Grammaire du "Décaméron"* (The Hague: Mouton, 1969).

24 Picone, "L'Arte della beffa," 203–6.

25 Gittes, *Boccaccio's Naked Muse*, esp. 155–80.

26 For an attribution to Jean Bodel and the date of composition, see Charles Foulon, *L'Œuvre de Jehan Bodel* (Paris: Presses universitaires de France, 1958), esp. 21–8; and see the *Nouveau recueil complet des fabliaux* (*NRCF*), vol. 2, ed. Willem Noomen and Nico van den Boogaard (Assen: Van Gorcum, 1984), 29–75; 29–31. All references to "Barat et Haimet" are to this edition and all translations are my own.

27 Gary D. Mole, "Du bacon et de la femme: Pour une relecture de *Barat et Haimet* de Jean Bodel," *Neophilologus* 86, no. 1 (2002): 17–31; 81.

28 Mole provides examples to support his argument about the cohesion of the two parts of the *fabliau*, highlighting linguistic links between the two distinct episodes of theft. He also draws out parallels with Jean Bodel's other works. See ibid., esp. 19.

29 Mole underscores the significance of the characters' names in ibid., 21.

30 Foulon argues that the success of this story led to a strong association between the idea of theft and the names Barat and Haimet for centuries after its composition (*L'Œuvre de Jehan Bodel*, 63).

31 Mole, "Du bacon et de la femme," 21.

32 Picone, "L'Arte della beffa," 212.

33 Ronald Martinez, "Calandrino and the Power of the Stone: Rhetoric, Belief, and the Progress of *Ingegno* in *Decameron* VIII.3," *Heliotropia* 1, no. 1 (2003): 1–32; 3. On Calandrino's origins in the country, see Carlo Muscetta, "Giovanni

Boccaccio e i novellieri," in *Storia della letteratura italiana*, vol. 2 (Milano: Garzanti, 1965), 315–558, esp. 463–4; Holmes, "Trial by *Beffa*," 371 and n11; Fontes, "Le thème de la 'beffa,'" 29–30.

34 Picone, "L'Arte della beffa," 217.

35 The tricks of Day Eight suggest a new kind of justice for Holmes, however ("Trial by *Beffa*," 374).

36 Picone discusses the opening of the tales to an audience on Day Eight as a function of their meta-literary quality, in contrast to the closed love triangles of the *beffe* on Day Seven ("L'Arte della beffa," 208). One might also argue that the tricks are made public on Day Eight in order to underscore the social ramifications of such creations.

37 In this, I agree with Gittes that "Boccaccio negates the possibility of an absolute scale of values" (*Boccaccio's Naked Muse*, 234).

38 Boccaccio, *Decameron*, trans. McWilliam, 576; and the *Decameron*, trans. J.M. Rigg, Decameron Web: Brown University, 8.5.6. http://www.brown.edu/Departments/Italian_Studies/dweb/texts/DecIndex.php?lang=eng (accessed 26 February 2014).

39 *Decameron*, ed. Branca, 929. Holmes also discusses birds as metaphors for fitting victims ("Trial by *Beffa*," 374, 377).

40 For more on the Calandrino/*calandra* derivation, in addition to Holmes, "Trial by *Beffa*," see Picone, "L'Arte della beffa," 215.

41 "Barat et Haimet" (*NRCF*), 211–12.

42 Ibid., 474–9.

43 Holmes, "Trial by *Beffa*," 369 and 370n8.

44 Martinez, "Calandrino and the Power of the Stone," 9.

45 Mole also remarks that Travers hangs from the tree with his pants down, recalling the initial theft of pants in the first part of the *fabliau* ("Du bacon et de la femme," 19).

46 "Sono questi tutti particolari ripresi scrupolosamente nella novella boccacciana: anche Calandrino coltiva un 'poderetto', ammazza il maiale a 'dicembre' e decide di 'farlo salare'" (Picone, "L'Arte della beffa," 212).

47 "Barat et Haimet" (*NRCF*), 10. See also note 30 above.

48 Picone, "L'Arte della beffa," 211.

49 See, for example, Holmes, "Trial by *Beffa*," 365; Fontes, "Le thème de la 'beffa,'" 15–16; and Picone, "L'Arte della beffa," 206: "il beffatore dimostra attraverso la sua azione di saper dominare la realtà circostante, trasformando in evento la quotidianità; fa sentire al beffato di star vivendo un'avventura straordinaria, salvo poi farlo risvegliare con i frammenti del sogno infranto."

50 Fontes, "Le thème de la 'beffa,'" 13.

14 The Tragicomedy of Lament: *La Celestina* and the Elegiac Legacy of Boccaccio's *Fiammetta*

FILIPPO ANDREI

The *novela sentimental* is a distinctive genre of Spanish literature most commonly known for texts written by Diego de San Pedro and Juan de Flores in the final decades of the fifteenth century. Since the time of Marcelino Menendez Pelayo, the honour of giving rise to, and inspiring, the *novela sentimental* has always been attributed to an Italian text: Giovanni Boccaccio's *Elegia di madonna Fiammetta*.[1] In fact, there is an ancient tradition concerning the *Fiammetta*'s fortune in Spain that dates back to the beginning of the fifteenth century, through the end of the same century, before Boccaccio's text was even translated and then printed in Seville in 1496.[2] The definition of the Spanish *novela sentimental*, however, has perplexed many specialists in medieval Spanish studies for over three decades, specifically because the origins of this genre or subgenre of romance are not well defined. More significantly, scholars have always disagreed both on the works to be included in that literary classification and on its peculiar characteristics.

Although many studies on Boccaccio's literary success in Spain have confirmed the importance of the *Fiammetta*, the issue of this work's real influence on Spanish texts remains open for discussion. Menendez Pelayo's thesis on the derivation of the *novela sentimental* as a literary genre from Boccaccio's *Fiammetta* still holds significant currency among scholars,[3] yet it was later reexamined by Carmelo Samonà and Antonio Prieto.[4] Scholars mostly argued over what is both a critical and a philological crux. Fascinated by the charm of classical readings and by the prestige of Italian literature, the authors of sentimental fiction had no scruples about drawing from their authoritative sources – Latin authors in general, Petrarch's or Boccaccio's works in particular – as well as transcribing entire passages word for word from their models. As a consequence, if the *Fiammetta* were really the text that inspired the *novela sentimental* – that is, the text that supposedly gave rise to the genre – it is not clear why these Spanish authors did not imitate it at length, or directly cite it. According to Samonà, a search for quotations of the *Fiammetta* turned out to be in vain, as much in vain as the attempt to see it as a possible direct source of imitation and inspiration. If Samonà's statements are true, the *Fiammetta* would not have had a relevant, textual, or direct influence on the works of the Spanish sentimental fiction, but rather would have influenced them only at the level of style, or at the level of genre.[5] Unable to deny the objective lack of massive imitations of Boccaccio's text in Spanish sentimental romance, Antonio Prieto emphasizes other aspects of the issue without giving much attention to the textual evidence. In his opinion, the *Fiammetta* certainly has the merit of breaching the norms of courtly love in order, on the one hand, to emphasize the various aspects of real life, and, on the other, to represent a tension in feelings of love by means of self-analysis. Overall, Prieto maintains that the *Fiammetta*'s influence on the historical development of the Spanish *novela sentimental* operates on two levels: first, Boccaccio's work provided Spanish sentimental fiction with a lyrical structure with its descriptions of the analytical process of love and its evasions; second, and indirectly, the *Fiammetta* provoked a reaction against its bourgeois character and determined the rise of an introspective phenomenology of love that, through the allusions to *castidad* and the use of allegory, considers the glory of death as a remedy for the pain of love and, as a consequence, a valuable alternative to Fiammetta's final refusal to commit suicide.[6]

If it is difficult to characterize the origins of the *novela sentimental*, to trace the evolution of its distinctive features, and to evaluate the impact of Boccaccio's language in Spanish literature, it is even more difficult to provide an exhaustive definition of the genre of Fernando de Rojas's *La Celestina*, a genre that is only in part linked to the sentimental romance. Many scholars, in fact, have linked the *Celestina* to the Spanish sentimental romance because of some defining characteristics: the painful love story of a noble man for a woman, the analysis of sentiments, the calamitous consequences imposed upon the protagonists, the fierce pragmatism against idealistic love, and the profusion of anguish in connection with a final tragic denouement.[7] More recently, Antonio Cortijo Ocaña also tried to include Fernando de Rojas's *La Celestina* in an expanded sentimental genre that goes beyond the *novela sentimental*. Yet, the *Celestina* unquestionably belongs to the theatrical genre, as its subtitle *Tragicomedia de Calisto y Melibea* already indicates, thus making the definition of its genre more complicated. With regard to the term *tragicomedia*, which essentially indicates a work blending both tragic and comic forms, Aristotle does not provide a specific definition,[8] but among the characteristics that Rojas has assigned to that genre, it is not difficult to single out the combination, and the contrast, of tones and styles. The *Celestina* blends effects of balance and moderation with a tension represented by opposing characters; these effects eventually make the tension culminate in a tragic ending.[9]

Even though critics' taxonomic impulse to catalogue every single aspect of the literary work has given a lot of attention to the *Celestina*, some issues still remain unsolved. Is the *Celestina* a comedy with a tragic ending? Is it a *novela sentimental* in dialogue? Is it a dramatic, philosophical work?[10] In the hope of providing a starting point for criticism that constantly faces the problematic nature of any genre, my contribution will focus on some thematic aspects of Rojas's *Celestina* in comparison with Giovannni Boccaccio's *Fiammetta*, as well as on some textual analogies. The aim is both to emphasize the influence of the *Fiammetta*'s text and to shed some light on the characteristics of the *tragicomedia*. With respect to this latter issue, Stephen Gilman tries to demonstrate how the *Fiammetta* and the *Celestina*, apart from their proximity to the Petrarchan tradition (especially *De remediis utriusque fortunae*), are fundamentally different works in structure and theme.[11] Even if one could agree with such conclusions, considering the originality and uniqueness of the *tragicomedia* genre (after all, Samonà argued along the same lines before Gilman), there are nevertheless imitations of the *Fiammetta*'s text in the *Celestina* that cannot be neglected.[12] Above all, there is an entire analytical description of amorous passions which is unanimously considered to be an essential characteristic of the *novela sentimental*, and which cannot be ignored as a strong link to Boccaccio's work.[13] In fact, even in a superficial reading, the never-ending struggle with inner feelings, as well as the constant weeping of Boccaccio's heroine, is clearly comparable to the laments of Melibea, one of the most important feminine characters of Rojas's *Celestina*.[14] Furthermore, as the impact of Petrarch's works, especially *De remediis utriusque fortunae*, has always overshadowed the importance of other texts for the making of the genre of the *Celestina*, I will look at Rojas's and Boccaccio's texts side by side. In addition to providing textual evidence of Rojas's utilization of Boccaccio's text, my intent is to re-evaluate the effect of the introspective discourse that is abundant in the *Fiammetta*, especially the elegiac style, which will appear to be the most influential feature.[15]

Significantly, on the structural level, one may notice a series of parallelisms between the *Fiammetta* and the *Celestina*. Boccaccio's Fiammetta begins narrating her happy love story and ends recounting her unfortunate experience in which a host of contradictory sentiments drives her to desperation and to an unsuccessful suicide attempt;[16] in Chapter 6, she describes the attempt to kill herself by jumping from the roof of her house.[17] Similarly, the *Celestina* begins as a comedy and ends as a tragedy with the two lovers' deaths, and strikingly with Melibea's actual suicide, jumping from the tower of her house.[18] Furthermore, when considering the author's stated intentions, yet another analogy can be identified on the level of the framework of the two texts. Boccaccio's purpose is to rouse piety in the minds of Fiammetta's female audience, but above all to warn this audience about the vicious ways of men.[19] The book that Fiammetta fictionally sends to her female readers is conceived as an admonishment, or a moral teaching,[20] exactly like that of Rojas, according to his own declared intentions: Rojas's aim, in general, is to teach lovers how to escape from Love's captivity, and, in particular, to warn his unknown friend not to repeat the same mistakes that Rojas committed in childhood.[21]

In order to identify more analogies between the *Celestina* and the *Fiammetta*, it is worth taking a closer look at the texts and analysing the characters' behaviours. Besides being torn by internal discord like Boccaccio's Fiammetta, the protagonists of the *tragicomedia* undergo an evolution throughout the story, a sort of psychological and moral transformation that makes the *Celestina* resemble a mature work of modern literature.[22] From the first to the last act, one can observe a sort of *Bildungsroman* in the manner canonically described and analysed by M.M. Bakhtin.[23] Such an evolution can be seen in the figure of Melibea more than in anybody else. Though initially she is entirely reluctant and inexperienced in love matters, as well as firmly resistant to the amorous offers from Calisto, she finds herself madly in love with him at the end of the story.[24] A similar transformation appears in Fiammetta when she falls in love with Panfilo.[25] Yet, there is a more complex and subtle play in the way Rojas represents his characters' behaviours. By virtue of the author's dramatic ability and the actions of various secondary characters, the meaning of the work – which revolves around moral and philosophical issues, antagonisms and disputes – is revealed.[26] But the nature of the *tragicomedia* genre is also disclosed within the logic of the alternating opposites and is reflected in the protagonists' contrasting sentimental attitudes. Although Melibea experiences a transformation from a reluctant lover to a feminine and passionate person and a devotee of the god Love, the author does not refrain from inserting a few episodes in the text in which the heroine casts doubts on her own transformation. She changes her mind frequently, even retreating to the primal psychological moment of the story when she did not want to have anything to do with Calisto.[27] As a consequence, contrasts between the completely devoted confessions of love and these brief moments of regret are not only caused by Melibea's conflicts in relation to her social duties but also have comic and mimetic implications in the story. In other words, the author seems to conceal an intention to parody the literary tradition when he makes Melibea speak and then rapidly change her attitude towards Calisto within the same line.[28]

When considering the transformation of another character, Calisto, let us focus – among the many examples – on the moment when Sempronio parodies Calisto's discovery of his love passion; here, under the influence of love, Calisto perfectly handles the elegiac style:

> CALISTO. Cierra la ventana y dexa la tiniebla acompañar al *triste* y al desdichado la ceguedad. Mis pensamientos *tristes* no son dignos de luz. !O bienauenturada *muerte* aquella, que desseada a los *afligidos* viene! ¡O si viniéssedes agora, Crato Y Galieno, médicos ! ¿Sentiríades mi mal? (*Celestina* 1.88–9; my emphasis; cf. also 1.91 and 2.132–3)

> [CAL: Close the window: let darkness be company for the unhappy man, and blindness for the unfortunate one. My sad thoughts are not fit for light. Oh, blessed Death, welcomed by sufferers! Oh, if you would come now, Eras and Crato, you physicians, you would recognize my illness!]

Moreover, when Calisto talks to the cordon (ornamental cord or ribbon) that Melibea gave him to heal his physical pain, Celestina reminds him that it is just a cordon and not a human being, and defines his lamentations as "luengas querellas":

> CALISTO. Quanto dixeres, señora, te quiero creer, pues tal joya como esta me truxiste. !O mi gloria y ceñidero de aquella angélica cintura! Yo te veo y no lo creo. !O cordón, cordón! ¿Fuísteme tú enemigo? Dilo cierto. Si lo fuiste, yo te perdono, que de los buenos es propio las culpas perdonar …
>
> CELESTINA. … deues, señor, cessar tu razón, dar fin a tus *luengas querellas*, tratar al cordón como cordón, porque sepas fazer diferencia de fabla, quando con Melibea te veas: no haga tu lengua yguales la persona y el vestido. (*Celestina* 6.187–8; my emphasis)

> [CAL: I can believe whatever you say, my lady, since you brought such a gem as this to me. Oh, my glory, the sash of that angelic waist! I see you, and still I

don't believe it. Oh, cord, cord! Were you my enemy? Tell me the truth if you were, and I will forgive you. It is only proper for good men to forgive faults ...

CEL: ... Stop complaining so much, and treat the cord like a cord, so that you'll be able to know to speak differently when you're with Melibea. Don't let your tongue treat the person and the dress like they were one and the same]

Besides the parody of courtly love,[29] one wonders whether Rojas also wanted to conceal an intention to parody the elegiac tradition. Yet, parody and comedy seem to disappear at the end of the story when the tone changes and parody fades into Calisto's pure elegiac lament and his invocations to the power of the night:

> *O noche* de mi descanso, si fuesses ya tornada! ¡O luziente Febo, date priessa a tu acostumbrado camino! ¡O deleytosas estrellas, apareceos ante de la continua orden! ¡O espacioso relox, avn te vea yo arder en biuo fuego de amor! ... Pero tú, dulce *ymaginación*, tú que puedes, me acorre. Trae a mi fantasía la presencia angélica de aquella ymagen luziente; buelue a mis oydos el suaue son de sus palabras, aquellos desuíos sin gana ... ! Con quánta *pena* salió por su boca! ¡Con quántos desperezos! ¡Con quántas *lágrimas*, que parescían granos de aljófar, que sin sentir se le cayan de aquellos claros y esplandecientes ojos! (*Celestina* 14.292; my emphasis)

> [Oh, night of my respite, if only you were here again now! Oh, bright Phoebus, rush swiftly along your well-traveled road! Oh, pleasant stars, make your appearance before the ordered time! Oh, lumbering clock, I would like to see you burning in the high flames of love! ... But you, sweet imagination, you who are able, come to my aid: bring the angelic presence of that shining image to my fancy. Return to my ears the soft sound of her words: that unwilling modesty ... How sadly it left her mouth, how tremulously! How many tears she shed that were like tiny pearls, and fell senselessly from her clear, shining eyes!]

Parody and comedy also disappear when, after Calisto's accident, both the servant Tristano and Melibea mourn his death:

> TRISTÁN. ¡*Lloro* mi gran mal, *lloro* mis muchos *dolores*! Cayó mi señor Calisto del escala y es muerto. Su cabeça está en tres partes. Sin confessión pereció. Díselo a la *triste* y nueua amiga, que no espere más su *penado* amador. Toma tú, Sosia, dessos pies. Lleuemos el cuerpo de nuestro querido amo donde no padezca su honrra detrimento, avnque sea muerto en

este lugar. Vaya con nosotros *llanto*, acompáñenos soledad, síganos desconsuelo, visítenos *tristeza*, cúbranos *luto y dolorosa xerga*.

MELIBEA. ¡O la más de las *tristes, triste*! ¡Tan tarde alcançado el plazer, tan presto venido el *dolor*! (*Celestina* 19.327–8; my emphasis)

[TRIST: I'm crying for my great catastrophe! I'm crying for all that I am suffering! My master, Calisto, fell from the ladder, and now he's dead. His head lies broken in three parts. He died without confession. Tell his sad new friend that she should no longer await her poor lover. Take hold of his feet, Sosia: although he died here, let's carry our dear master's body to where his honor will not suffer. May our tears go with us, solitude be our company, grief follow us, sorrow visit us, mourning and sackcloth be our cover.

MELIB: Oh, most sorrowful of all sorrows! So late have I found pleasure! So quickly has come pain!]

The need to deepen and render the psychological coherence of the characters as realistically as possible against the backdrop of the mere narration of dramatic action is evident if we compare the development of the action with its internal motivations, especially where a long addition is inserted into the original sixteen-act *La Celestina*.[30] The genesis and motivations of this interpolation can be better understood from the moment one perceives in the comedy a "lack," a need for more coherence in characterization, when one realizes that some aspects of the psychological relations among the characters have not been resolved. As with a symphony, in that very moment, the work manifests the need for "a second movement" in the story: in Act 14, Calisto's temporary forgetfulness of the misfortune of his servants – who have been condemned to death – must be explained and emotionally motivated by a new narrative development, and not left suspended or unfulfilled, as in the original sixteen-act *tragicomedia*. Let us observe this passage in detail. Sosia and Tristano blame Calisto for having forgotten the death of his servants Parmeno and Sempronio.[31] At this point, after the dialogue, Rojas inserts a scene in which Calisto finally recovers his formerly affectionate relationship with his servants. With rhetorically elaborate questions, Calisto laments Parmeno and Sempronio's misfortune in a speech in which he blames the judges for having condemned them:

CALISTO. … ¡Ay, ay, que esto es, esta herida es la que siento agora que se ha resfriado, agora que está elada la sangre que ayer hervía, agora que veo la mengua de mi casa, la falta de mi servicio, la perdición de mi patrimonio, la infamia que a mi persona de la muerte de mis criados se ha seguido!

¿Qué hize? ¿En qué me detove? ¿Cómo me pude çoffrir que nome mostré luego presente como hombre injuriado, vengador sobervio y acelerado de la manifiesta injusticia que me fue hecha? … ¿Por qué no salí a inquerir siquiera la verdad de la secreta causa de mi manifiesta perdición? … O cruel juez, y qué mal pago me as dado del pan que de mi padre comiste. Yo pensava que pudiera con tu favor matar mil hombres sin temor de castigo, iniquo falsario, perseguidor de verdad, hombre de baxo suelo; bien dirán por ti que te hizo alcalde mengua de hombres buenos. (*Celestina* 14.288–9)

[CAL: … Oh, oh! What is happening to me? This is the wound I feel, now that my fever is gone, now that the blood that was boiling yesterday has cooled down. Now that I see the decline of my house: my servants, gone; the loss of my patrimony; the infamy that falls upon me for the death of my servants. What did I do? What did I spend my time on? How could I bear not to appear at once, as a man who has been wronged, vengeful, proud, rushing swiftly at the manifest injustice of what was done to me? … Why did I not even go out to inquire about the hidden cause of my evident perdition? … Oh, cruel judge: how badly you have repaid my father's bread that you did eat! I thought that with your favor, I could kill a thousand men without fear of punishment. Iniquitous liar, persecutor of truth, evil-natured man: how true it will be when they say of you, "You were made a judge for lack of a good man."]

Without the interpolation, the story would have ended with Calisto's accident and left the blame on the protagonist for not having mourned his servants. In sum, the need for a lament appears to be a good reason for adding five acts to the original play, or at least for beginning the inserted episode expressing grief. From this point of view, Severin's theses about the greater coherence and artistic completeness of the primitive *commedia* are completely indefensible.[32] Instead, we can find consistent insight in Gilman's view that, beyond the sixteenth-century additions' frequent diminishing of the stylistic level, the interpolation in the *Celestina* contributes to the general clarity of the text and renders the whole work more coherent and complete in its meaning.[33] Ultimately, however, besides the noteworthy presence of a lament at the beginning of the interpolation, the idea of completing the *Celestina* with five extra acts may have originated from the author's need to develop every aspect of the psychological reality and render it more naturalistic.

As noted above, Melibea's struggle between opposing feelings of sensual love and the desire for chastity (*amor* versus *castidad*) is represented through rapid changes in mood and perspective that comically and powerfullly parody the Petrarchan phenomenology of love. The function of the obstacle between the two lovers, which traditionally was represented by the jealous husband, is performed by the weighty forces of society and the inscrutable actions of Fortune.[34] What is inevitably reflected is the conception of life as universal conflict, which appears to be the theoretical basis of the *Celestina* from the very beginning of the play, a conception drawn from Heraclitus's philosophy, although mediated by Petrarch's *De remediis utriusque fortunae* (see the *Celestina*'s *Prologo*). Besides Petrarch, another more consistent literary model can be found in the elegiac tradition, for which Boccaccio constitutes an authoritative source. When Melibea rebels against her father in Act 16, she compares herself to women from the Bible and classical antiquity. While alluding to Latin elegy, this motif is also present in the *Fiammetta*, where, on several occasions, Boccaccio's heroine compares her misfortunes to those of classical and biblical women in order to demonstrate her great suffering and pain. In the following passages, for instance, a warning against the incestuous fire of love is illustrated by the mention of almost the same famous women from the past. Not coincidentally, while Fiammetta's thoughts are expressed by Venus's voice, Melibea's speech starts by mentioning the Roman goddess of love as an example not to be imitated:[35]

Las quales algunas eran de la gentilidad tenidas por diosas, assí como Venus madre de Eneas y de Cupido, el dios de amor, que siendo casada, corrumpió la prometida fe marital. Y aun otras de *mayores huegos encendidas* cometieron *nefarios y incestuosos yerros*, como *Mira* con su padre, *Semíramis* con su hijo, *Cánasce* con su hermano, y aun aquella forçada Tamar, hija del rey David. Otras aun más cruelmente trespassaron las leyes de natura, como Pasiphe, muger del rey Minos, con el toro. Pues reynas eran y grandes señoras, debaxo de cuyas culpas la razonable mía podrá passar sin denuesto; mi amor fue con justa causa. (*Celestina* 16.304–5, emphasis added)

[Some were considered goddesses by the pagans: like Venus, the mother of Aeneas and of Cupid, the god of love; after marrying, she broke her marital vows. And there were others who, burning with greater flames, committed nefarious and incestuous iniquities. Like Myrrha with her father; Semiramis with her son; Canace with her brother; and that daughter of King David who was raped: Tamar. Other women broke the laws of nature even more cruelly, like Pasiphaë, the wife of King Minos, with the bull. Those were queens and great ladies, and compared to their guilt, what little I have done carries no shame. My love was with just cause.]

Bastiti solamente, o giovine, che di non abominevole fuoco, come Mirra, Semiramìs, Biblìs, Canace e Cleopatra fece, ti molesti. Niuna cosa nuova dal nostro figliuolo verso te sarà operata: egli ha così leggi, come qualunque altro iddio, alle quali seguire tu non se' prima, né d'essere ultima dei avere speranza. (Fiammetta 1.30)	[Be it enough for you, young woman, that he did not molest you with a wicked fire as he did with Myrrha, Semiramis, Byblis, Canace, and Cleopatra. Our son will not do anything new to you; like any other god, he too has rules which you are not the first to follow, nor must you hope to be the last.]

The lament style was the main feature of elegy perceived by the humanistic tradition, and may therefore constitute a first analogy between the *Celestina* and the *Fiammetta*. Calisto's and Pleberio's laments are famous,[36] but more significant for our purposes are the elegiac "melodies" of Melibea,[37] tuned to complaint and mourning:

> Oye, padre viejo, mis últimas palabras, y si como yo spero, las recibes, no culparás mi yerro. Bien ves y oyes este *triste y doloroso sentimiento* que toda la cibdad haze. Bien *oyes* este clamor de campanas, este alarido de gentes, este aullido de canes, este [grande] strépito de armas. De todo esto fue yo [la] causa. Yo cobrí de *luto* y xergas en este día quasi la mayor parte de la cibdadana cavallería; yo dexé [hoy] muchos sirvientes descubiertos de señor, yo quité muchas raciones y limosnas a pobres y envergonçantes. Yo fui ocasión que los muertos toviessen compañía del más acabado hombre que en gracias nació. Yo quité a los vivos el dechado de gentileza, de invenciones galanas, de atavíos y bordaduras, de habla, de andar, de cortesía, de virtud. Yo fui causa que la tierra goze sin tiempo el más noble cuerpo y más fresca juventud que al mundo era en nuestra edad criada. (*Celestina* 20.333; my emphasis)[38]

> [Listen, my aged father, to my last words, and if, as I hope, you will accept them, you will not cast blame on my wrongdoing. You can well see and hear this sad, painful lamentation that comes from the city. You hear well the tolling of bells, the cries of people, the howling of dogs, the great noise of arms. Of all this, I was the cause. On this day I have covered with mourning-clothes and sackcloth nearly all the nobles of the city. Today I have left many servants bereft of their master. I have taken much food and alms away from the poor and from those who beg.

> Because of me, the dead now have as their companion the most perfect man in loveliness ever born. I took from the living the model of grace, of elegant courtly games, of adornments and finery, of speech, of gait, of courtesy, of virtue. It is because of me that the earth enjoys, at an untimely hour, the most noble body, the freshest youth born to the world in our age.]

The invocation of the gods is one of the most typical, rhetorically pathetic features of the elegiac style that we find in the *Fiammetta*.[39] Let us compare it with the *Celestina*:

O Tesifone, infernale furia, o Megera, o Aletto, stimolatrici delle *dolenti anime*, dirizzate li feroci crini, e le *paurose idre* con ira accendete a nuovi *spaventamenti*, e veloci nell'iniqua camera entrate della malvagia donna … O qualunque altro popolo delle nere case di *Dite*, o iddii degl'immortali regni di *Stige*, siate presenti qui, e co' vostri *tristi ramarichii* porgete *paura* ad essi infedeli. O misero gufo, canta sopra l'infelice tetto! E voi, o *Arpie*, date segno di futuro danno! O ombre infernali, o etterno *Caos*, o tenebre d'ogni luce nemiche, occupate l'adultere case, sì che gl'iniqui occhi non godano d'alcuna luce; e li vostri odii, o vendicatrici delle scelerate cose, entrino negli animi acconci a' mutamenti, e *impetuosa guerra* generate fra loro! (*Fiammetta* 6.144; my emphasis; cf. also the invocation to Hell in *Fiammetta* 6.140)

[O Tisiphone, you infernal fury! O Megaera! O Alecto! You who are the tormentors of doleful souls, straighten your fierce manes, inflame the frightening Hydras with rage towards new horrors, swiftly penetrate the wicked bedchamber of the evil woman … O you, whoever you are, dwellers in the dark houses of Dis, and you gods of the immortal kingdom of Styx, come forth and frighten the unfaithful couple with your ugly lamentations! O mournful owl, sing on the unhappy roof! And you, Harpies, give a sign of future harm! O infernal shadows, eternal Chaos, and you, darkness, so inimical to light, invade the adulterous homes so that wicked eyes will enjoy no light, and as avengers of vicious deeds, let your hateful feelings occupy those minds inclined towards fickleness and cause violent strife among them!]

CELESTINA. Conjúrote, *triste Plutón*, señor de la profundidad infernal, emperador de la corte dañada, capitán sobervio de los condenados ángeles, señor de los súlfuros fuegos que los hervientes étnicos montes manan, governador y veedor de los tormentos y atormentadores de las pecadoras ánimas, *regidor de las tres furias, Tesífone, Megera, y Aleto, administrador de todas las cosas negras del regno de Stige y Dite, con todas sus lagunas y sombras infernales y litigioso caos, mantenedor de las bolantes harpías, con toda la otra compañía de espantables y pavorosas ydras.* (*Celestina* 3.147; my emphasis)	[CEL: I conjure you, woeful Pluto, lord of the deep inferno, emperor of the court of the damned, proud captain of the condemned angels; lord of the sulfurous fires that erupt from the seething mountains of Etna; governor and overseer of the torments and tormenters of sinful souls, ruler of the three Furies: Tisiphone, Megaera, and Alecto; administrator of all dark things of the kingdom of Styx and Dis, with all its tears and infernal shades and discordant chaos; keeper of the soaring harpies, with all the other company of the frightful and fearsome hydra.]

But the invocation of the gods, which literally takes on the same tones and expressions as in the *Fiammetta*, turns quickly to witchcraft:

> Yo, Celestina, tu más conoscida cliéntula, te conjuro por la virtud y fuerça destas bermejas letras, por la sangre de aquella noturna ave con que están scritas, por la gravedad de aquestos nombres y signos que en este papel se contienen, por la áspera ponçoña de las bívoras de que este azeyte fue hecho, con el qual unto este hilado; vengas sin tardança a obedeçer mi voluntad y en ello te embolvas … Si no lo hazes con presto movimiento, ternásme por capital enemiga; heriré con luz tus cárceres *tristes y escuras*; acusaré cruelmente tus continuas mentiras; apremiaré con mis ásperas palabras tu *horrible* nombre, y otra y otra vez te conjuro [y], assí confiando en mi mucho poder, me parto para allá con mi hilado, donde creo te llevo ya embuelto. (*Celestina* 3.148; my emphasis)

> [I, Celestina, your most well known patron, do conjure you by the power and force of these bright red letters, by the blood of that nocturnal bird with which they are written, by the gravity of these names and the signs written on this paper, by the bitter poison of vipers of which this oil was made and with which I anoint this thread. Come without delay and obey

> my will, and embed yourself in it … But if you do not do this quickly, you will have me as your greatest enemy. I will strike light into your sad, dark prisons. I will cruelly trumpet your continual lies. I will harass your horrible name with my harsh words. So again and again I conjure you, and thus, trusting in my own great power, I leave to go there with my yarn, where I believe I have you entwined.]

Clearly, the *Celestina* draws on the elegiac tone of the *Fiammetta*.[40] Furthermore, it develops a distinctive Ovidian tone through the use of adjectives like "triste," "escuras," and "horrible," attributed to the infernal divinities (in place of the more simple "misere" of the *Fiammetta*), which are diffusely spread throughout the text[41] and perfectly render a lugubrious and infernal atmosphere.[42]

The fear and anxiousness for the arrival of the lover is another topos of elegy,[43] as Florentino Castro Guisasola points out[44] – a topos that a very attentive reader of the classics like Boccaccio would never have missed, and neither would Rojas, who again uses similar words:

Chi sa se egli, volonteroso più che il dovere di rivedermi e pervenire al posto termine, posposta ogni pietà di padre e lasciato ogni altro affare, si mosse e forse, senza aspettare la pace del turbato mare, credendo a' marinari bugiardi e arrischievoli per voglia di guadagnare, sopra alcuno legno si mise, il quale venuto in ira a' venti e all'onde, in quelle è forse perito? … Ma se pur da questo è campato, forse negli agguati de' ladroni è incappato, e rubato e ritenuto è da loro; o forse nel camino infermato in alcuna parte ora dimora e, ricuperata la sanità, senza fallo qui ne verrà." Ohimè! che qualora *cotali imaginazioni mi teneano*, un freddo sudore m'occupava tutta, e sì di ciò divenia paurosa, che sovente	[I wonder whether he may not have been unduly impatient to see me and to meet the promised deadline so that he put aside all piety for his father and abandoned all other business, leaving perhaps without waiting for the turbulent sea to be calm; and could it be that trusting false and foolhardy seamen eager for gain, he embarked on some vessel that aroused the wrath of wind and waters and perished thereby? … But if he has escaped even this danger, he may have run into an ambush set by robbers; he may have been robbed and is being held by them; or perhaps he was taken ill on his journey and is now staying somewhere and will certainly come back here once he has regained his health.

in prieghi a Dio che ciò cessasse rivolgea il pensiero, né più né meno, come se egli davanti agli occhi in quello pericolo mi fosse presente. E alcuna volta mi ricorda che *io piansi*, quasi come con ferma fede in alcuno de' pensati mali il vedessi. Ma poi fra me diceva: "Ohimè! *che cose sono queste, che i miseri pensieri mi porgono davanti*? *Cessi Iddio che alcuna di queste sia! Innanzi dimori quanto gli piace*, o non torni, che, per contentarmi, a caso si metta che alcuna di queste cose avvenga." (*Fiammetta* 4.72–3; my emphasis)

Alas, whenever I was in the grip of such fantasies, my whole body was covered by cold perspiration, and I became so fearful of them that I often implored God in my thoughts to make them stop, just as if Panfilo were present before my eyes in such dangers. I remember that sometimes I wept as if I were absolutely certain of seeing him in one of the perils I had imagined. But then I said to myself: "Oh, what are these things that my mind is placing before me? May God not allow any of them to be true! He should stay as long as he wishes or not come back at all rather than risk any of these things happening in order to please me."]

MELIBEA. Los ángeles sean en su guarda, su persona esté sin *peligro*; que su tardança, no me *da* pena. Mas cuytada, pienso muchas cosas que desde su casa acá le podrían acaecer. *¿Quién sabe si él con voluntad de venir al prometido plazo* en la forma que los tales mançebos a las tales horas suelen andar, fue topado de los alguaziles nocturnos, y sin le conoçer le han acometido, el qual por se defender los offendió o es dellos offendido? ¿O si por caso los ladradores perros con sus crueles dientes que ninguna differencia saben hazer ni acatamiento de personas, le ayan mordido, o si ha caído en alguna calçada o hoyo donde algún daño le viniesse?

[MELIB: May the angels protect him. May he not be in danger. His being late does not grieve me, but I am worried, and I can imagine many things that could happen to him while coming here from his house. Who knows if, in his desire to come at the promised hour, the way young men are accustomed to going at an hour like this, he might not have run into the night-watch, and without recognizing him, they ran at him? Then, to defend himself, he assaulted them, or they assaulted him? Or perhaps those barking dogs that don't know any difference between the ranks of men, might have bitten him with their cruel teeth? Or he might have

Mas, o mezquina de mí, *¿qué son estos inconvenientes* que *el concebido amor me pone delante* y los *atribulados ymaginamientos* me acarrean? *No plega a Dios que ninguna destas cosas sea, antes esté quanto le plazerá* sin verme. Mas oye, oye, oye, que passos suenan en la calle y aun pareçe que hablan destotra parte del huerto. (*Celestina* 14.283; my emphasis)

fallen on some rocks or into a pit, and hurt himself. But, wretched me, what are these worries that my love places before me and that my tormented imagination brings to me? I pray God that none of these things happen: let him stay without seeing me as long as he likes. But listen: there are footsteps out on the street, and it even sounds as though they are talking on the other side of the garden.]

To this topos, which is also common to dawn lyrics,[45] Rojas simply adds the Ovidian motif of regretting having ever been born; it is also worth considering Pleberio's last words, which are comparable to those of Fiammetta:

Del mundo me quexo porque en sí me crió, porque no me dando vida no engendrara en él a Melibea; no nascida, no amara; no amando, cessara mi quexosa y desconsolada postremería. (*Celestina* 21.343)

[I complain of the world: I was bred in it. If it had not given me life, I would not have begot Melibea in it Had she not been born, she would not have loved. By not loving, my last years would not be filled with mourning and unhappiness.]

Oh maladetto quello giorno, a me più abominevole che alcuno altro, nel quale io nacqui! Oh quanto più felice sarebbe stato se nata non fossi, o se dal tristo parto alla sepultura fossi stata portata, né più lunga età avessi avuta, che i denti seminati da Cadmo, e ad una ora rotte e cominciate avesse Lachesis le sue fila! Nella piccola età si sarebbero rinchiusi gl'infiniti guai, che ora di scrivere trista cagione mi sono. (*Fiammetta* 1.5)

[Cursed be the day I was born, more detestable to me than any other! How much luckier it would have been if I had not been born or if I had not lived longer than the teeth sown by Cadmus and if Lachesis had cut her threads as soon as she had spun them! Innumerable woes, now the sad reason for my writing, would have found a conclusion at a tender age.]

Castro Guisasola emphasizes the extensive use of the metaphor of love as fire in the *Celestina* and observes that such usage appeared frequently in the poets of Latin elegy, such as Ovid and Propertius.[46] Antonio Sanchez Jimenez maintains that this trope is an integral part of the structure, and that it contributes to the moralizing message of *reprobatio amoris* through the association of the fire of love with the famous fires of ancient cities (Troy and Rome). In particular, the trope emphasizes the annihilating power of love and functions as a warning, or a flash-forward, announcing the tragic ending of the two lovers' story.[47] Yet, for an immediate source of the *Celestina*, we should once again turn our attention to the *Fiammetta*. The following passages are remarkable for their elegiac tone and for the topos of love/fire with its illustrious ancient victims. Let us compare the two texts and focus on the striking textual analogies:

Ma se tu forse gli essempli del cielo incredula schifi e cerchi chi del mondo gli abbia sentiti, *tanti sono, che da cui cominciare appena ci occorre*; ma tanto ti diciamo veramente, che tutti sono stati valorosi. Rimirisi primamente al fortissimo figliuolo di Almena [i.e., Hercules], il quale, poste giù le saette e la minaccevole pelle del gran leone, sostenne d'acconciarsi alle dita i verdi smeraldi, e di dar legge alli rozzi capelli, e con quella mano, con la quale poco innanzi portato avea la dura mazza e ucciso il grande Anteo e tirato lo infernale cane, trasse le fila della lana data da Jole dietro al procedente fuso, e gli omeri, sopra li quali l'alto cielo s'era posato mutando spalla Atlante, furono in prima dalle braccia di Jole premuti, e poi coperti, per piacerle, di sottili	[However, if in your diffidence you shun the examples of the heavens and look for someone who may have had such experiences in the world, there are so many that we need only choose where to begin, but we can truly tell you this much: they have all been heroic. Let us first look at the very strong son of Alcmena, who after having set aside the arrows and the frightening skin of the great lion, tolerated having his fingers adorned with green emeralds and his untidy mane groomed and who, with the same hand that had earlier carried the hard club and killed the great Antaeus, dragged out the infernal dog, spun the woolen thread fed by Iole onto the turning spindle; and his shoulders, which had carried the high heavens while Atlas changed sides, were first

vestimenti di porpora. *Che fece Parìs per costui, che Elena, che Clitemestra, e che Egisto, tutto il mondo il conosce*; e similmente di Achille, di Silla, di Adriana, di Leandro, di Didone, *e di più molti, non dico, ché non bisogna. Santo è questo fuoco*, e molto potente, credimi. (*Fiammetta* 1.27; my emphasis)

embraced by Iole's arms and then, to please her, were draped in sheer purple garments. Everyone knows what Paris did because of Love, or Helen, or Clytemnestra, or Aegisthus; and the same is true of Achilles, Scylla, Ariadne, Leander, Dido, and many more I need not mention. It is a holy and very powerful fire, believe me!]

Tu *fuego es ardiente rayo* que jamás haze señal do llega. La leña que gasta tu llama son almas y vidas de humanas criaturas, *las quales son tantas que de quién començar pueda apenas me ocurre*; no sólo de christianos mas de gentiles y judíos y todo en pago de buenos servicios. ¿Qué me dirás de aquel Macías de nuestro tiempo,48 cómo acabó amando, cuyo triste fin tú fuiste la causa? *¿Qué hizo por ti Paris? ¿Qué Helena? ¿Qué hizo Ypermestra? ¿Qué Egisto? Todo el mundo lo sabe.* Pues a Sapho, Ariadna, Leandro ¿qué pago les diste? Hasta David y Salomón no quesiste dexar sin pena. Por tu amistad Sansón pagó lo que meresció por creerse de quien tú le forçaste a darle fe. *Otros muchos que callo porque tengo harto que contar* en mi mal. (*Celestina* 21.342–3; my emphasis)

[Your fire is a lightning bolt that never leaves a mark where it strikes. The pieces of wood that your fire consumes are souls and lives of human creatures. And there are so many of these that I know not where to begin. Not only Christians, but pagans and Jews: and all in payment of their good services. What have you to say to me of that Macias of our own days, the way he met his end: in love. And you were the cause of his sad death. What did Paris do for you? And Helen? What did Hypermnestra do? And Aegisthus? All the world knows. What payment did you make to Sappho, Ariadne, Leander? You did not even want David and Solomon to escape without punishment. Because of your friendship Samson received what he deserved, for believing someone that you forced him to trust. And there were many others about whom I remain silent, for I have enough to recount with my own misery.]

The spirit of elegy also involves the pessimism with which different authors conceive of love.[49] In both the *Fiammetta* and the *Celestina*, a pessimistic attitude eventually annihilates the enjoyment of love. The love experience leads to an unavoidably tragic outcome in which every attempt to conquer the heart of the beloved, or even to enjoy her/his love, is doomed to failure, because of the beloved's final refusal or the development of events beyond the protagonist's control. Fiammetta wants to kill herself when she is persuaded of her lover's betrayal; Calisto is the victim of a fatal accident. In Latin elegy, poets, all addicted to love, conceived of their lives as *servitium*, a form of captivity to a capricious and unfaithful woman.[50] The sentimental relationship is made up of both rare moments of joy and numerous sufferings. The lament style, but also the rhetorical declamation of opposing feelings that derive from the scrutiny of interior phenomenology, over time become distinctive features of the elegiac genre. After all, this style covers a chronologically extended period if we consider its evolution from Ovidian poetry up to Seneca's tragedies, later arriving at Boccaccio and ending up directly (or indirectly) in the work of Rojas. The display of oratorical art, in combination with elegiac motifs, should be considered together with the analysis of interior feelings. Going back to Boccaccio, we must recall the magnificent oratory of Fiammetta's speeches, about which the author cannot refrain from openly confessing: "Ohimè! quanto falsamente argomentava, fatta sofistica contro al vero! [Oh, how falsely I was arguing and quibbling with the truth!]" (*Fiammetta* 3.61). Such oratory could have provided a model for the equally rhetorical speeches of Celestina. The rhetoric of love, which so often takes the style of a philosophical work, seems to be a better match for Calisto's monologues.[51] Samonà's observation on the aspects of the *Fiammetta* that had the greatest fortune among Spanish imitators, namely the taste for rhetoric and oratory, are worth citing here: "Una volta di più si deve registrare, insomma, la parzialità e l'unilateralità del gusto degli imitatori, tesi al persistente dominio della retorica, invischiati nell'equivoco (o nell'illusione) di una elevatezza di stile e di fatica letteraria, che solo il pretesto oratorio, non le sue soluzioni narrative, bastano a garantire e a qualificare."[52]

The view of love as fury may derive directly from Seneca's *Phaedra*. Sánchez Jiménez pointed out that, like Seneca, Rojas uses the trope of love as fire in order to connote Love as a character in the story.[53] However, it seems to me that the theme of madness prevails in the *Celestina*, as the metaphor of love as fire is apparently a common theme in all literary traditions. Interestingly, love as fury also appears in Boccaccio's *Fiammetta* as one of the main themes:[54] "Voi, turba di vaghe giovini, di focosa libidine accese, sospingendovi questa, vi avete trovato *Amore* essere iddio al quale piuttosto giusto titolo sarebbe *furore* … questi, il quale, *per furore, Amore è chiamato*, sempre le dissolute cose appetendo, non altrove s'accosta che alla seconda fortuna [You are all nothing but a mob of senseless young women burning with a fiery lust, and being driven by it you have discovered that Love is a god who should more appropriately be called madness … he who is called Love by reason of his madness is always craving wanton things and goes only where a prosperous fortune is present]" (*Fiammetta* 1.21–2; my emphasis; cf. also 1.6; 1.14; 1.16; 1.75–6; and 1.120). Thus, it is most likely that Rojas imitated Boccaccio rather than Seneca. As mentioned above, in the *Celestina*, the conflict of reason and sentiment appears among the declarations of the *Prologo* concerning the philosophy of life as warfare (see the concept in Petrarch's *De remediis*, or even the description of *polemos* in Heraclitus), but love as *furor* seems to acquire the features of the amorous passion as a simple madness (*locura*) of which we must always be wary. Love is described as *locura* by Pármeno in a dialogue with Sempronio using remarkably sententious words: "Luego locura es amar *y yo soy loco sin seso. Pues si la locura fuesse dolores, en cada casa havría bozes* [Then, is it crazy to be in love? And am I crazy and stupid? Well, if madness was horses, everyone would ride]" (*Celestina* 8.213).[55] Specifically, love is perceived as a disease, the lovesickness as theorized in various medieval and humanistic treaties.[56] For Fiammetta, love as disease leads to madness and takes its origin from the imagination:

> Io alcuna volta *meco medesima fingeva* lui dovere ancora, indietro tornando, venirmi a vedere, e quasi come se venuto fosse, gli occhi all'uscio della mia camera rivolgeva, e rimanendo dal mio consapevole *imaginamento* beffata, così ne rimaneva crucciosa come se con verità fossi stata ingannata. Io più volte per cacciare da me i non utili riguardamenti cominciai molte cose a voler fare; ma vinta da nuove *imaginazioni*, quelle lasciava stare. (*Fiammetta* 3.57–8; my emphasis)

> [At times I pretended to myself that he had returned and was coming to see me again, so I turned my eyes toward the door of my room as if he had really come, and fooled by my conscious fantasy, I was thus left sulking as if I had been deceived with the truth. Several times, to stop these useless

backward glances, I started out wanting to do many things, but I soon let them be, overwhelmed by new fantasies.]

Ohimè! che chiunque è colui li primi riti servante, non è *nella mente infiammato dal cieco furore della non sana Venere*, come io sono né è colui che sé dispose ad abitare ne' colli de' monti, suggetto ad alcuno regno ... (*Fiammetta* 5.120; my emphasis)

[Alas, whoever follows the rites of the ancients does not burn as I do, with the blind fury of the corrupt Venus, nor is the man who chooses to live in some neck of the mountainous woods a subject of any kingdom ...]

Similarly, Calisto expresses his desire for Melibea by invoking the aid of the imagination:[57]

Pero tú, dulce *ymaginación*, tú que puedes, me acorre; trae a mi *fantasía* la presencia angélica de aquella *ymagen* luziente; buelue a mis oydos el suaue son de sus palabras, aquellos desuíos sin gana. (*Celestina* 14.292; my emphasis)

[But you, sweet imagination, you who are able, come to my aid: bring the angelic presence of that shining image to my fancy. Return to my ears the soft sound of her words: that unwilling modesty.]

The fire of love is also a poison that needs an antidote, a medicine, in order to be cured. If Fiammetta foresees her love in a dream in which she is bitten by a snake symbolizing her future lover ("Ma non altramente il tenero piè d'Euridice trafisse il nascoso animale, che me sopra l'erbe distesa, una nascosa serpe vegnente tra quelle ... [But just as the lurking beast pierced the tender foot of Eurydice, a serpent slithered unseen through the grass in which I lay ...]" [*Fiammetta* 1.7]), Melibea laments her love pain, comparing it to the bite of a snake ("Pero ¿cómo lo podré hazer, lastimándome tan cruelmente el ponçoñoso bocado que la vista de su presencia de aquel cavallero me dio? [But how can I do that, after being wounded so cruelly by the poisonous morsel that the sight of that gentleman has given me?]" [*Celestina* 10.238]).[58] Moreover, just as Fiammetta is bitten under her left breast ("parve che sotto la sinistra mammella mi trafiggesse [and seemed to bite me under the left breast]" [*Fiammetta* 1.7]), lovesickness comes from the left breast for Melibea ("Mi mal es de coraçón, la ysquierda teta es su aposentamiento; tiende sus rayos a todas partes [My illness is in my heart. It lies in my left breast and spreads its rays everywhere]" [*Celestina* 10.241]).

The theme of Fortune remains to be considered as strictly related to the calamitous consequences imposed on the protagonists and their love in both the *Celestina* and the *Fiammetta*. This theme is a fundamental element that activates the narration and controls the plot, but it is also a direct interlocutor of the characters when they display their introspective phenomenology. The theme of Fortune pervades the *Fiammetta* (much earlier than the *Decameron*) as well as the *Celestina*; it will eventually reappear in the sentimental romance, and will later on expand its influence. It seems that the theme of Fortune is always associated with the lovers' fates and the impossibility of experiencing their love. In the *Celestina*, Fortune is the wheel that makes the world turn and gives Celestina the opportunity to regret her happy, wealthy past and to complain about her present condition:

> Mundo es, passe, ande su *rueda*, rodee sus alcaduzes, vnos llenos, otros vazíos. La ley es de *fortuna* que ninguna cosa en vn ser mucho tiempo permanesce: su orden es *mudanças*. No puedo dezir sin *lágrimas* la mucha honrra que entonces tenía; avnque por mis pecados y mala dicha poco a poco ha venido en diminución. Como declinauan mis días, assí se diminuya y menguaua mi prouecho. (*Celestina* 9.234; my emphasis)
>
> [But such is this world, it goes on by, it must make its circle, the waterwheel must turn with its buckets, some full, some empty. It's the rule of fate that nothing will remain in its place for a long period of time. Its order is change. I can't tell you, without weeping, about how honored I was back then. Although, for my sins and my bad luck, it has all declined little by little. Just the way my days have declined, my fortune has diminished and become reduced.]

Compare Celestina's words with Fiammetta's, especially in the emphatic usage of the word *mudanças/mutamenti*:

> O *Fortuna*, spaventevole nemica di ciascuno felice, e de piú miseri singulare speranza, tu, *permutatrice de' regni e de' mondani casi adducitrice*, sollevi e avvalli con le tue mani, come il tuo indiscreto giudicio ti porge; e non contenta d'essere tutta d'alcuno, o in uno caso l'essalti e in uno altro il deprimi … Tu, cieca e sorda, *li pianti de' miseri* rifiutando; con gli essaltati ti godi, li quali te ridente e lusingante abbracciando con tutte le forze, con

> inoppinato avvenimento da te si trovano prostrati e allora miseramente te conoscono aver mutato viso … Ohimè! chiunque nelle grandi cose si fida, e potente signoreggia negli alti luoghi, l'animo credulo dando alle cose liete, riguardi me, d'alta donna piccolissima serva tornata, e peggio, che disdegnata sono dal mio signore, e rifiutata. Tu non desti mai, o Fortuna, piú ammaestrevole essemplo di me de' tuoi *mutamenti,* se con sana mente si riguarderà. Io da te, o *Fortuna mutabile,* nel mondo ricevuta fui in copiosa quantità de tuoi beni, se la nobiltà e le ricchezze sono di quelli, sí come io credo; e oltre a ciò in quelle cresciuta fui, né mai ritraesti la mano. Queste cose certo continuamente magnanima possedei, e come *mutabili* le trattai e, oltre alla natura delle femine, liberalissimamente l'ho usate. (*Fiammetta* 5.105–6; my emphasis)
>
> [O Fortune, you are a dreadful enemy of anyone happy and the only hope of those who are very unhappy; you are a barterer of kingdoms and a bestower of human destinies; with your hands you raise and you quash as your rash judgment moves you, and when you are not satisfied to belong entirely to someone, you exalt him in one way or humiliate him in another … Blind and deaf, you ignore the weeping of the miserable and rejoice, smiling and beguiling, with the exalted, who embrace you with all their might but unexpectedly find themselves cast down by you and wretchedly learn that you have changed face … Alas, whoever trusts in great things and is a powerful master in high places and credulously inclined to believe what is pleasing should look at me, who, after having been a great lady, have become the meanest servant, and even worse, since I am scorned and rejected by my lord! If one looks at this with a clear mind, it will be perceived that you, O Fortune, have never given a more instructive example of mutability than me. I was welcomed into the world by you, O fickle Fortune, with a great abundance of your gifts (if, as I believe, nobility and riches are among them), and besides this, I grew up among them, and you never withdrew your generous hand. Of course, always magnanimous, I owned these things and treated them as temporary, and contrary to feminine nature, I used them most liberally.]

Fortune presides over the tragic vicissitudes of love, as is evident from Melibea's final lament:

> Quebrantó con scalas las paredes de tu huerto; quebrantó mi propósito; perdí mi virginidad. *Del qual deleytoso yerro de amor gozamos quasi un mes. Y como esta passada noche viniesse según era acostumbrado,* a la buelta de su

> venida, como de la *fortuna mudable* stoviesse dispuesto y ordenado según su desordenada costumbre ... (*Celestina* 20.334; my emphasis)

> [He overcame the walls of your garden with ladders. He overcame my resistance. I lost my virginity, and we enjoyed the delightful error of love for nearly a month. And he came last night as customary, and when he was about to return home, since ever changing Fortune is disposed and ordered to its own disordered ways ...]

This lament is interestingly comparable to Fiammetta's words:

> *Vivendo adunque contenta, e in festa continua dimorando,* la *fortuna,* sùbita *volvitrice delle cose mondane,* invidiosa de' beni medesimi che essa avea prestati, volendo ritrarre la mano, né sappiendo da qual parte mettere li suoi veleni, con sottile argomento a' miei occhi medesimi fece all'avversità trovare via; e certo niuna altra che quella onde entrò v'era al presente. (*Fiammetta* 1.6–7; my emphasis)

> [While I was living contentedly, and as I was being continually entertained, Fortune, who is quick to overturn human affairs, became envious of the very gifts she had bestowed and wished to retract her favors, but not knowing where to place her venom, with subtle guile she made misfortune find its way through my very own eyes, since at that time there was no other avenue but the one through which she entered.]

> Mentre che io, o carissime donne, in così lieta e graziosa vita, sì come di sopra è descritta, menava i giorni miei, poco alle cose future pensando, la nemica fortuna a me di nascoso temperava li suoi veleni, e me con animosità continua, non conoscendolo io, seguitava. (*Fiammetta* 2.39)

> [As I whiled away my time in the pleasant and delightful life I have just described, dearest ladies, giving little thought to future things, my inimical Fortune was surreptitiously mixing her poisons and pursuing me with relentless animosity, though I was utterly unaware of it.]

In the texts I have examined, in which love is strictly connected to elegy, as well as to philosophical discourse, the theme of consolation emerges clearly in antithesis to that of Fortune. This occurs not only as a reference to the famous, ancient Boethian *Consolation,* or more closely to Petrarch's *De remediis utriusque Fortunae,* but also as an elegiac remedy to suffering. Fiammetta's consolation is not achieved through philosophy, but through other worldly expedients, such as sleep or the amusements that occupy a great part of the narration (see Chapter 5), even if Fiammetta declares herself reluctant to enjoy such pleasures (e.g., in *Fiammetta* 5.147 and 5.150). This theme appears significantly in *Celestina* in Pleberio's famous lament:

> Pues *desconsolado* viejo, ¡qué solo estoy! Yo fui lastimado sin hauer ygual compañero de semejante dolor; avnque más en mi fatigada memoria rebueluo presentes y passados. Que si aquella seueridad y paciencia de Paulo Emilio me viniere a *consolar* con pérdida de dos hijos muertos en siete días, diziendo que su animosidad obró que *consolasse* él al pueblo romano y no el pueblo a él, no me satisfaze, que otros dos le quedauan dados en adobción … Que todo esto bien diferente es a mi mal … ! O incomparable pérdida! ¡O lastimado viejo! Que quanto más busco consuelos, menos razón fallo para me consolar … Pues, mundo halaguero, ¿Qué remedio das a mi fatigada vegez? (*Celestina* 21.339–41; my emphasis)
>
> [Well, miserable old man, how lonely I am! I was wounded and have not the company of anyone with like sorrow, even though I search hard in my weary memory for such persons past and present. For if the severity and patience of Paulus Aemilius should come to console me with the loss of his two sons who died seven days apart, saying that his valor led him to console the Roman people, and not the Romans to console him, that does not content me, for he still had two others who were given to him in adoption … All this is very different from my own affliction … Oh, what an incomparable loss! Oh, wounded old man! The more consolation I seek, the less reason I find to console me … Well, cajoling world, what remedy do you offer to my weary old age?]

The task of consolation seems to be carried out in particular by philosophy, from a consolatory Senecan and Petrarchan perspective.[59]

The normative attributes of Spanish sentimental romance may be identified in its flexibility and capacity to blend heterogeneous categories and, paradoxically, in its ability to have no generic characteristics. The specific legacy of the *Fiammetta* to the genre of the *tragicomedia*, and in particular to the *Celestina*, can be recognized in the skilful and personal usage that Rojas makes of the elegiac tone. This tone is not simply a literary and erudite exercise, but draws on a variety of traditional motifs that were already established and that experimented with both content and rhetorical structure. Such motifs concern both the representation of love as a disturbing and mad passion against which many authors try to warn the lovers, albeit in vain, and the observation of the world, and life, by means of moral and philosophical instruction, with the epistemological power of giving a voice to the conflict between reason and sentiment. Therefore, Rojas's *tragicomedia* can be read as a *Fiammetta*-style elegy, especially if we consider the fact that in the Middle Ages and early modern period this genre was also identified as the "style of the unfortunates." In essence, we can read the *Celestina* as a work with a hybrid style like that of elegy, a style that stands at the crossroads between comic and tragic tones. Boccaccio's elegy is certainly a model of mixed style reflecting mixed content, as well as a model for introspective discourse. Through the imitation of Boccaccio's *Fiammetta,* naturalism and verisimilitude – which were certainly a great part of the ancient elegiac world – begin to take a great aesthetic part also in the *Celestina,* while coming together with many problematic aspects that tie this text to the literary tradition and make literariness emerge in contrast to modernity. In the *Celestina,* the character is always at the centre of the reader's attention as a modern character would be – an individual who speaks with an elegiac voice throughout the text, has a defined personality, and is tormented by powerful inner forces.

Ultimately, the poetics of lament is the element that gives vent to these contrasts. Thus, the elegiac and introspective model operates in the making of the *Celestina,* and it is this elegiac model that we must acknowledge, before emphasizing the direct influence of Boccaccio's work. Furthermore, elegiac elements operate as go-betweens, as elements linking the ancient interior discourse to the modern naturalism of feelings. The elegiac elements by themselves are evidently not enough to create modernity; they still remain cohesive with ancient formal and poetic canons, but they constitute an important bridge towards a modern vision of the interior world. Through the traditional repertoire of themes and motifs, which in this period of Spanish literature was experiencing new developments and creating new poetic structures, Fernando de Rojas showed remarkable literary consciousness and formal rigour, making the *Celestina* an original and innovative literary product, subject to different influences and open to different interpretations according to contemporary genre theory. As far as Boccaccio's elegiac legacy is concerned, perhaps it is not coincidental that, in the epilogue of the *Celestina,* while explaining the reasons that the play has to be called *tragicomedia,* Alonso de Proaza – an editor and possibly a collaborator of Rojas for the frame texts of the *Celestina*[60] – also invites the reader to weep:

> Toca cómo se deuía la obra llamar *Tragicomedia* y no *comedia.*
> *Penados amantes* jamás conseguieron
> dempresa tan alta tan prompta victoria,
> como éstos de quien recuenta la hystoria
> ni sus *grandes penas* tan bien succedieron.
> Mas como firmeza nunca tovieron
> los gozos de aqueste mundo traydor
> supplico que *llores,* discreto lector,
> el trágico fin que todos ovieron.[61]
>
> [It explains why this work should be entitled *Tragicomedy* and not *Comedy.*
> Unfortunate lovers never attained
> such high enterprise, such prompt victory,
> like that of these of whom the story tells,
> nor did their great pains ever happen.
> But, since the joys of this traitor world
> never found attainment,
> I beg, oh discreet reader, that you weep
> at the tragic end that happened to them all.]

NOTES

1 Among the first examples of *novela sentimental,* the *Fiammetta* inspired Juan Rodríguez del Padrón (o de la Cámara) in his *El siervo libre de amor* as well as Diego de San Pedro in his *Cárcel de Amor.* Cf. M. Menéndez y Pelayo, *Orígenes de la novela,* vol. 1 (Madrid: Bailly-Ballière, 1907), 300 and 305 ff.; C.B. Bourland, *Boccaccio and the Decameron in Castilian and Catalan Literature. Extrait de la Revue Hispanique,* vol. 12 (New York: Macon, Protat Frères, 1905), 1–232, in particular 3 and 14. A list of Spanish manuscripts of the *Fiammetta* along with a short description is in ibid., 214–16 (Appendix F); for a list of editions, ibid., 223 ff. Recently, A. Cortijo Ocaña, *La evolución genérica de la ficción sentimental de los siglos XV y XVI: género literario y contexto social* (Woodbridge: Tamesis, 2001) has argued that the genre did not begin in Castile with Juan Rodriguez del Padrón's *Siervo libre de amor* (1445), but with the *Storia de l'amat Frondino e de Brisona,* written in Catalan around 1400. On the *novela sentimental* see Menéndez y Pelayo, *Orígenes*

de la novela, vol. 1, 299–352; C. Samonà, *Studi sul romanzo sentimentale e cortese nella letteratura spagnola del Quattrocento* (Rome: Carucci, 1960); A. Durán, *Estructura y técnicas de la novela sentimental y caballeresca* (Madrid: Gredos, 1973); D. Cvitanovic, *La novela sentimental española* (Madrid: Prensa Española, 1973); A. Prieto, *Morfologia de la novela* (Barcelona: Planeta, 1975); *Studies on the Spanish Sentimental Romance, 1440–1550: Redefining a Genre*, ed. J.J. Gwara and E.M. Gerli (London: Tamesis, 1997); R. Rohland de Langbehn, *La unidad genérica de la novela sentimental española de los siglos XV y XVI* (London: Dept. of Hispanic Studies, Queen Mary and Westfield College, 1999); K. Whinnom, *The Spanish Sentimental Romance, 1440–1550: A Critical Bibliography* (London: Grant and Cutler, 1983); Cortijo Ocaña, *La evolución genérica de la ficción sentimental.*

2 On the longstanding literary success of the *Fiammetta* in Spain, see A. Farinelli, "Note sul Boccaccio in Spagna nell'Età Media," *Archiv für das Studium der neuren Sprachen und Literaturen. Braunschweig* 114 (1905): 397–429; 115 (1905): 368–88; 116 (1906): 67–96; and 117 (1906): 114–41; A. Berenguer Carisomo, "Boccaccio en la literatura española según las observaciones de Menéndez Pelayo," in *Giovanni Boccaccio 1375–1975. Homenaje en el sexto centenario de su muerte*, ed. A.N. Marani (La Plata: Centro de Estudios It., Fac. de Humanidades, Univ. Nac. de La Plata, 1957), 149–83; Bourland, *Boccaccio and the Decameron*; Joaquín Arce, "Boccaccio nella letteratura castigliana: panorama generale e rassegna bibliografico-critica," in *Il Boccaccio nelle culture e letterature nazionali*, ed. F. Mazzoni (Florence: Olschki, 1978), 63–105; C. Alvar Ezquerra, "Boccaccio en Castilla: entre recepción y traducción," *Cuadernos de Filología Italiana* no. extraordinario (2001): 333–50. On Boccaccio's fortune in Iberia and Latin America, see the articles collected in the chapter "Il Boccaccio nella cultura e letteratura iberica e ibero-americana," in *Il Boccaccio nelle culture e letterature nazionali*, 63–259. After the *Corbaccio*, the *Fiammetta* was the most read work of Boccaccio in Spain (cf. Farinelli, "Note sul Boccaccio in Spagna nell'Età Media," 209; Cvitanovic, *La novela sentimental española*, 255–93; Arce, "Boccaccio nella letteratura castigliana," 82–4). There are two fifteenth-century Castilian manuscripts (one of them is incomplete) of the *Fiammetta* held in the Escorial Library, and also a fifteenth-century Catalan version held in the Archivo General de la Corona de Aragón in Barcelona. The first edition of the *Fiammetta* printed in Salamanca dates from 1497; a second print from 1523 in Seville; a third one from 1541 in Lisbon (cf. Bourland, *Boccaccio and the Decameron*, 13; L. Mendi, Vozzo, "L'edizione di una versione: il caso della *Fiammetta* castigliana," in Associazione ispanisti italiani. *Ecdotica e testi ispanici: atti del Convegno nazionale della*

Associazione ispanisti italiani: Verona, 18–19–20 giugno 1981 [Verona: Università degli studi di Padova, Facoltà di economia e commercio, Istituto di lingue e letterature straniere di Verona, 1982], 103–10). A copy of the Seville print is held in Rome, Biblioteca Nazionale di Roma, MS 69.1.C.6.2 (cf. F. Borroni Salvadori, "Edizioni spagnole e catalane delle biblioteche italiane. Contributi ad un census," in *Il Boccaccio nelle culture e letterature nazionali*, 205–8, in particular 205).

3 See Menéndez y Pelayo, *Orígenes de la novela*, vol. 1, 299 ff.; Farinelli, "Note sul Boccaccio in Spagna nell'Età Media," 209; Bourland, *Boccaccio and the Decameron*, 11 and 14. Menéndez Pelayo thinks that the *Fiammetta* left its footprints on the *novelas sentimentales* especially for "la penetración psicológica, que Boccaccio tuvo en alto grado, y aplicó antes que ningún moderno al estudio del alma de la mujer" (*Orígenes de la novela*, vol. 1, 300). Among the scholars who cautiously agree with Menéndez Pelayo's thesis, see E.B. Place, *Manual elemental de novelística española, bosquejo histórico de la novela corta y el cuento durante el siglo de oro* (Madrid: V. Suárez, 1926), 108; Berenguer Carisomo, "Boccaccio en la literatura española según las observaciones de Menéndez Pelayo," 163–4; A. Valbuena Prat, *Historia de la literatura española* (Barcelona: G. Gili, 1968), 278; A. Durán, *Estructura y técnicas de la novela sentimental y caballeresca* (Madrid: Gredos, 1973), 15; D. Cvitanovic, *La novela sentimental española*, 43–54 and 253 ff.; Alvar, "Boccaccio en Castilla: entre recepción y traducción," 346.

4 Samonà, *Studi sul romanzo sentimentale e cortese*, 71–92; Prieto, *Morfologia de la novela*, 272–5. While acknowledging the "enterprising plundering of Ovid and Boccaccio," M.E. Gerli questions the foundations of the romance genre by identifying the source of the *Siervo* in the *Rommant des trois pelerinages* by Guillaume de Deguileville; "The Old French Source of *Siervo libre de amor*," in *Studies on the Spanish Sentimental Romance, 1440–1550*, xvi. Cortijo Ocaña, *La evolución genérica de la ficción sentimental de los siglos XV y XVI*, emphasizes the northern European influences on Iberian romance as a corrective to the traditional dominance of the Italian works.

5 Samonà, *Studi sul romanzo sentimentale e cortese*, 73–5.

6 Prieto, *Morfologia de la novela*, 274–5. Among the most recent collective works on Boccaccio's fortune in Spain, there is no specific study on the influence of the *Fiammetta*. Probably a symptom of a general bias against Boccaccio's literary production, Joaquín Arce does not see any influence of Boccaccio in Spanish literature compared to the deeper impact of Dante and Petrarch as far as language is concerned. If on the one hand Boccaccio was considered a humanist, a moralist, even a philosopher to be imitated from the fifteenth century up to the first half of the sixteenth century, on

the other he was never an example to imitate for his language ("Boccaccio nella letteratura castigliana," 64–5). Given these premises, and considering what Menéndez Pelayo had said about the importance of Boccaccio in Spain (i.e., that Boccaccio had more readers than Dante and Petrarch), it is hard to believe that his language and style never influenced Spanish writers.

7 Rohland de Langbehn, *La unidad genérica de la novela sentimental española*, 22–46. According to Rohland de Langbehn (ibid., 91–6), the works constituting the Spanish sentimental romance actually possess enough formal and discursive characteristics to constitute a separate literary genre.

8 In his *Poetics*, Aristotle describes tragedies with dual endings but does not provide any definition of the tragicomedy. For both Renaissance and modern tragicomedy, cf. V.A. Foster, *The Name and Nature of Tragicomedy* (Aldershot: Ashgate, 2004). G. Evans, "The Minotaur of the Stage: Tragicomedy in Spain," in *Early Modern Tragicomedy*, ed. S. Mukherji and R. Lyne (Woodbridge: Brewer, 2007), 59–75, considers Spanish tragicomedy in the early modern period.

9 The *Celestina* anticipates the genre of the Italian pastoral tale of the sixteenth century and influences subsequent reflections on the nature of this genre. A tangible example is the controversy that was raised on the composition of the *Pastor Fido*, to which Guarini devoted a great deal of energy during the 1580s until the first edition of 1590. Guarini expounded his theories in the *Compendio della poesia tragicomica*, which appeared in 1602 along with the definitive edition of the *Pastor Fido*. Guarini's "mixture" concept is far from the hybridism of genres and styles that we traditionally encounter in baroque art; this "mescolanza" dwells among devices and complications, but, as *Celestina* does, it seeks effects of equilibrium and moderation under a "magnificent" and "polished" style (see G. Ferroni, *Storia della letteratura italiana, Dal Cinquecento al Settecento* [Milan: Mondadori Università, 2012], 269; M. Treherne, "The Difficult Emergence of Pastoral Tragicomedy: Guarini's *Il pastor fido* and Its Critical Reception in Italy, 1586–1601," in *Early Modern Tragicomedy*, 28–42). In many respects, Guarini took his inspiration from the example of the *Celestina* in his search for equilibrium.

10 See Menéndez y Pelayo, *Orígenes de la novela*, vol. 3, 2–3. For *La Celestina* as a humanistic comedy and a *novela sentimental* in dialogue, see A. Deyermond, *A Literary History of Spain*, vol. 1: *The Middle Ages* (London: Ernest Benn, 1971), 169–71; an advocate for the *Celestina* as a dramatic work is M.R. Lida de Malkiel, *La originalidad artística de "La Celestina"* (Buenos Aires: EUDEBA, 1970), 27–8. S. Gilman, *The Art of La Celestina*

(Madison: University of Wisconsin Press, 1956), introduced the concept of "diálogo vívido" to qualify *Celestina*'s genre.

11 Ibid., 181–93.

12 As a first approach to the *Celestina*, see the passages collected by F. Castro Guisasola, *Observaciones sobre las fuentes literarias de "La Celestina"* (Madrid: Jimenez y Molina, 1924), 142–5.

13 Menéndez Pelayo was the first to note this kind of analogy, especially "la retórica sentimental de la obra, en los apóstrofes y exclamaciones patéticas" (*Orígenes de la novela*, vol. 3, 86).

14 On the character of Melibea, see Lida de Malkiel, *La originalidad*, chap. 13, 406–56; E. De Miguel Martínez, "Melibea en amores: vida y literatura. 'Faltándome Calisto, me falte la vida,'" in *El mundo como contienda: estudios sobre La Celestina*, ed. P. Carrasco, and S.M. Nicasio (Málaga: Universidad de Málaga, 2000), 29–66; D.S. Severin, *Tragicomedy and Novelistic Discourse in "Celestina"* (Cambridge: Cambridge University Press, 1989), 95–103; M.E. Lacarra, "La parodia de la ficción sentimental en la *Celestina*," *Celestinesca* 13, no. 1 (1989): 1–29; *Cómo leer La Celestina* (Madrid: Ediciones Júcar, 1990), 66–81; "Las pasiones de Areúsa y Melibea," in *La Celestina 1499–1999: Selected Papers from the International Congress in Commemoration of the Quincentennial Anniversary of "La Celestina." New York 17–19 November 1999*, ed. O. Di Camillo and J. O'Neill (New York: Hispanic Seminary of Medieval Studies, 2005), 75–109, esp. 97–109.

15 All quotations of the Boccaccio text are taken from *Elegia di madonna Fiammetta*, in Giovanni Boccaccio, *Elegia di madonna Fiammetta. Corbaccio*, intro. and notes Francesco Erbani (Milano: Garzanti, 2007); the English translation is taken from G. Boccaccio, *The Elegy of Lady Fiammetta*, ed. and trans. M. Causa-Steindler and T. Mauch (Chicago: University of Chicago Press, 1990). As for Rojas's text, see Fernando de Rojas, *La Celestina*, ed. D.S. Severin (Madrid: Catedra, 2005); the English translation is taken from Fernando de Rojas, *The Celestina*, trans. Robert S. Rudder (Claremont: RSR, 2013). A critical edition of the *Fiammetta* and a complete study of the manuscript tradition do not exist today (a preliminary work on the manuscripts dates from 1957: A. Quaglio, "Per il testo della *Fiammetta*," *Studi di filologia italiana* 15 [1957]: 5–205). As for the Spanish translation, see *Libro de Fiameta*, ed. and intro. Lidia Mendia Vozzo (Pisa: Giardini, 1983). According to Mendia Vozzo (ibid., 57), the Castilian translation of the *Fiammetta* is possibly derived from a contaminated version of the Italian text and is very close, at times *ad verbum*, to the Italian. Given the echo of Boccaccio's *Fiammetta* in Spanish literature and its influence on the *novela sentimental* before the first translations at the end of the fifteenth century,

it is not demonstrated that Rojas read a Spanish translation. For these reasons, but also with the aim of focusing on the influence of Boccaccio's text on the genre of the *Celestina*, I will compare the *Celestina* with the Italian version of the *Fiammetta*.

16 "brievemente allo impromesso mi sforzerò di venire, da' miei amori più felici che stabili cominciando, acciò che da quella felicità allo stato presente argomento prendendo, me più che altra conosciate infelice; e quindi a' casi infelici, onde io con ragione piango, con lagrimevole stilo seguirò come io posso [I shall force myself to come quickly to what I have promised, and I will begin with those feelings of love which were more happy than enduring, so that by comparing that happiness to my present condition, you may know me to be more unhappy than any other woman; therefore, I shall go on, with a tearful pen and to the best of my ability, to those sad events which I lament with good reason]" (*Fiammetta*, prologo, 4).

17 "fra me dicendo: 'Io dell'alte parti della mia casa gittandomi, il corpo rotto in cento parti, per tutte e cento renderà l'infelice anima maculata e rotta a' tristi iddii' [and I said to myself: 'If I throw myself from the highest part of my house, my body, shattering into hundreds of pieces, will release my unhappy, stained, and broken soul through each piece to the fiendish gods']" (*Fiammetta* 6.157).

18 "Argumento del veynteno auto … *Descúbrele* MELIBEA *todo el negocio que avía passado. En fin, déxase caer de la torre abaxo* [Argument of Act Twenty … Melibea reveals to him all the details of what has happened. Finally, she lets herself fall from the tower to the ground]" (*Celestina* 20.329).

19 See: "a te [i.e., to the book] si conviene d'andare rabbuffato con isparte chiome, e macchiato e di squallore pieno, là dove io ti mando, e co' miei infortunii negli animi di quelle che ti leggeranno destare la santa pietà [it is fitting that you go where I am sending you discomposed, with your hair uncombed, stained and full of gloom, to awaken by my misfortunes blessed pity in the minds of those women who will read you]" (*Fiammetta* 9.199–200); and "se savie sono, ne' loro amori savissime ad ovviare agli occulti inganni de' giovini diventino per paura de' nostri mali [so that those ladies who are wise should become most sagacious in matters of love in order to avoid, for fear of our misfortunes, the hidden deceptions of young men]" (*Fiammetta* 9.200).

20 "né questi sono però altri, se non quelli li quali essa [i.e., Fortune] a niuno misero può tòrre, cioè essemplo di sé donare a quelli che sono felici, acciò che essi pongano modo a' loro beni, e fuggano di divenire simili a noi [and they are nothing but those signs which Fortune cannot deprive any miserable person of, namely, the right to make oneself an example to those

who are happy so that these people may set their affairs in order and avoid becoming like us]" (*Fiammetta* 9.200).

21 See: "me venía a la memoria no sólo la necessidad que nuestra común patria tiene de la presente obra por la muchedumbre de galanes y enamorados mancebos que posee, pero aun en particular vuestra mesma persona, cuya juventud de amor ser presa se me representa aver visto y dél cruelmente lastimada, a causa de le faltar defensivas armas para resistir sus fuegos ... y en su processo nuevas sentencias sentía. Vi no sólo ser dulce en su principal ystoria o fición toda junta, pero aun de algunas sus particularidades salían delectables fontezicas de filosophía, de otros agradables donayres, de otros avisos y consejos contra lisongeros y malos sirvientes y falsas mugeres hechizeras [there came to my mind not only the need that our common country has of this present work because of the great numbers of gallants and youths here who are in love, but especially for your own person, whose youth has become captive to love. I have seen this in my mind's eye, and you being cruelly wounded by it because of a lack of defensive arms to resist its fires ... And in this process I noticed new precepts. I saw that it was not only delightful in its main story or narrative in general, but even from some of its particulars there came delightful founts of philosophy and other agreeable pleasantries, other warnings and counsels against fawning, bad servants, and false witches]" (*Celestina* 69); also: "Si bien *queréys ver* mi limpio motivo / ... buscad bien el fin de aquesto que escrivo, / o del principio leed su argumento; / leeldo [y] veréys que, aunque dulce cuento, / amantes, que os muestra salir de cativo [If you indeed wish to discern my clean motive / ... look at the end of what I am writing; / or read the argument at the beginning, / read it and you will see that although a sweet story, / lovers, it shows you how to escape from captivity]" (*Celestina* 72; my emphasis). This translation is from Severin (*Tragicomedy and Novelistic Discourse*, 11–12), who maintains that Rojas changed his stated purpose "in writing the work from an essentially aesthetic and didactic one in the *comedia* to an exclusively didactic one in the *tragicomedia*" (15).

22 Severin reads the *Celestina* according to the Bakhtinian theories of the modern novel and emphasizes its novelistic character (ibid., 2 and 5).

23 M.M. Bakhtin, *Speech Genres and Other Late Essays*, trans. V.W. McGee, ed. C. Emerson and M. Holquist (Austin: University of Texas Press, 1986). As a category of the *Bildungsroman*, the biographical novel shows us the birth of biographical time as a completely real time; the novel of the human emergency (as Bahktin defines the *Bildungsroman*) is strongly linked to the historical emergency and it strongly emphasizes its moments of passage

(ibid., 32). On Melibea's and Parmeno's transformations, see Gilman, *The Art of La Celestina*. J.F. Burke, "Metamorphosis and the Imagery of Alchemy in *La Celestina*," *Revista Canadiense de Estudios Hispánicos* 1, no. 2 (1977): 129–52, talks about a transformation of the characters. Specifically, Burke interprets the *Celestina* in terms of a trajectory of becoming in which its characters undergo a kind of psychological development, but warns that "this movement is a variety perfectly understood by philosophers and thinkers in the late Middle Ages and the Renaissance and is one which bears only a passing resemblance to the type perfected in the modern novel" (130). Moreover, he argues that the metamorphosis which Calisto undergoes can best be understood in terms of imagery associated with and derived from the vast field of alchemical philosophy that flourished in Europe towards the end of the Middle Ages and in the early Renaissance, and suggests that the transformation process of the love of Calisto and Melibea reflects the alchemical movement in which Celestina represents the role of the lower medium (134–5 and 138).

24 See *Celestina* 4.162–63 and 16.303–5.

25 Cf. *Fiammetta* 1.16–17.

26 Not coincidentally, perhaps, Fiammetta's and Melibea's inner struggles have a parallel in Rojas's philosophy of life as warfare – also including a conflict between reason and sentiment – as described in the prologue of the *Celestina*. Cf. *Fiammetta* 6.160: "Poi, gli occhi rivolti per la camera, la quale più mai non sperava vedere, presa da dolore sùbito il cielo perdei, e quasi palpando, e presa da non so che tremito mi volli levare, ma le membra vinte da paura orribile non mi sostennero; anzi ricaddi, e non solo una, ma tre fiate sopra il mio viso, e in me *fierissima battaglia* sentiva tra li paurosi spiriti e l'adirata anima, li quali lei volente fuggire a forza teneano. Ma pure l'anima vincendo, e da me la fredda paura cacciando, tutta di focoso dolore m'accesi, e riebbi le forze (my emphasis) [Then, as I looked around that room which I had no hope of seeing again, I was seized by a sudden pain and I lost my sight; shaken by a mysterious trembling, and feeling my way around, I tried to rise, but my limbs, overcome by terror, did not support me; rather, I fell on my face not once but three times, and I felt a fierce conflict raging inside of me between my irate soul and my frightened spirits, the one forcefully holding back the other that wished to flee. But although my soul won and chased the cold fear away, it made me burn with fiery pain, and I regained my strength]."

27 *Celestina* 14.286–7.

28 One could easily picture Calisto's gesture during Melibea's speech: "MELIBEA. ¿Qué quieres que cante, amor mío? ¿Cómo cantaré, que tu

desseo era el que regía mi son y hazía sonar mi canto? Pues conseguida tu venida, desaparescióse el deseo; destémplase el tono de mi boz. Y pues tú, señor, eres el dechado de cortesía y buena criança, ¿cómo mandas a mi lengua hablar y no a tus manos que estén quedas? … CALISTO. Señora, el que quiere comer el ave, quita primero las plumas [MELIB: What do you wish me to sing, my love? How can I sing? It was my desire for you that governed my voice, and made the music of my song. And now that you are here, the desire has vanished. The tone of my voice is no longer harmonious. And since you, Sir, are the very model of courtesy and good upbringing, how can you order my tongue to speak and not command your hands to be still? … CAL: My lady, one who wished to eat a bird must first pluck its feathers]" (*Celestina* 19.323–4).

29 On the parody of courtly love in the *Celestina*, see J.J. Devlin, *"The Celestina": A Parody of Courtly Love. Toward a Realistic Interpretation of the "Tragicomedia De Calisto Y Meliba"* (Madrid: L.A. Pub. Co., 1971); G. Abbate, "The *Celestina* as a Parody of Courtly Love," *Ariel* 3 (1974): 29–32. According to J.H. Martin, *Love's Fools: Aucassin, Troilus, Calisto and the Parody of the Courtly Lover* (London: Tamesis, 1972), Calisto is a parody of the courtly lover. Severin considers the figure of Calisto a parody of the male character of the *novela sentimental*; more precisely, a parody of Leriano (*Celestina* intro.29).

30 The first edition of *La Celestina* was published in Burgos in 1499 as an anonymous work in sixteen acts under the title of *Comedia de Calisto y Melibea*. The work reached its definitive form as a tragicomedy in 1502 after having been reedited with a new prologue, additions, interpolations, "argumentos," and valedictory stanzas. The final redaction of *La Celestina* consisted of twenty-one acts (the five new acts are interpolated in the middle of act 14). An overview of the textual vicissitudes of the *Celestina* can be found in Severin's edition, 11–15. On the first editions of the *Celestina*, see F.J. Norton, *Printing in Spain, 1501–1520; With a Note on the Early Editions of the "Celestina"* (Cambridge: Cambridge University Press, 1966).

31 "TRISTÁN. Oygo tanto que juzgo a mi amo por el más bienaventurado hombre que nasció; y por mi vida, que aunque soy mochacho, que diesse tan buena cuenta como mi amo. SOSIA. Para con tal joya quienquiera se ternía manos, pero con su pan se la coma, que bien caro le cuesta; dos moços entraron en la salsa destos amores. TRISTÁN. Ya los tiene olvidados. Dexaos morir sirviendo a ruynes, haze locuras en confiança de su defensión; biviendo con el conde, que no matasse *a*l hombre, me dava mi madre por consejo. Veslos a ellos alegres y abraçados, y sus

servidores con harta mengua degollados [TRIST: I can hear so well that I judge my master to be the most fortunate man ever born. And I swear, although I'm just a boy, I could do as good a job as my master is doing. SOS: Who wouldn't like to get his hands on a jewel like that? But let him wallow in it. It's already cost him dearly. He's got two boys in the sauce of this love affair. TRIST: He's already forgotten about them. You'll kill yourself serving scoundrels; you'll do wild things, thinking they'll come to your defense. My mother always told me, 'When you live with a count, don't kill a man' (for the count will die, and you'll be held to account). Look at them, embracing each other, and his servants, in a terrible state, beheaded]" (*Celestina* 14.285–6).

32 Severin, *Tragicomedy and Novelistic Discourse*, 24–6.

33 Gilman, *The Art of La Celestina*, 36.

34 Once again, the sense of honour, and its conflicting relationship with society, may not be a new element, but it is quite a common theme in the elegiac tradition: see, for instance, the inner conflicts in Dido's love for Aeneas in Ovid, *Heroides* 7, and Virgil, *Aeneid* 6.

35 Severin notices the analogies with the *Fiammetta* in this passage, as well as in Pleberio's final words (see below), but does not seem convinced of Boccaccio's influence compared to that of Petrarch (*Tragicomedy and Novelistic Discourse*, 97–8).

36 See B. Wardropper, "Pleberio's Lament for Melibea and the Medieval Elegiac Tradition," *Modern Language Notes* 79 (1964): 140–52. In the genesis of Pleberio's lament, one should mention, as possible sources, the *Reprobación del amor mundano, o Arcipreste de Talavera*, by Alfonso Martínez de Toledo, and the *Cárcel de Amor* (cf. Severin, *Tragicomedy and Novelistic Discourse*, chap. 8).

37 As Paolo Cherchi beautifully explained, the name Melibea may have been chosen by Rojas for its Greek etymology related to "song" or "melody." Yet, strikingly, Cherchi denies any elegiac aspect in the character of Melibea. See "Onomastica nella *Celestina*, tragicomedia del sapere inutile," *Medioevo romanzo* 22, no. 3 (1998): 415–33; 421.

38 Castro Guisasola (*Observaciones sobre las fuentes literarias*, 14–17) claims that this passage shows analogies with *Fiammetta* 6.16–20, yet Lida de Malkiel (*La originalidad*, 11–12) denies the filiations.

39 This passage was noticed by Castro Guisasola (*Observaciones sobre las fuentes literarias*, 143).

40 The invocation of the gods and its relation to witchcraft are famously portrayed in Seneca's *Medea*, but the striking analogies between the texts of the *Celestina* and the *Fiammetta* point to Boccaccio as a direct source.

41 For instance, the word "triste" appears sixty-nine times in the *Celestina*. R. Schevill, *Ovid and the Renaissance in Spain* (Berkeley: University of California Press, 1913), takes the *Fiammetta* and the *Historia de duobus amantibus* as the archetypes of an "Ovidian tale" in Spanish literature and sees these models as much modified by the intrusion of a courtly tradition.

42 Castro Guisasola reports these passages (*Observaciones sobre las fuentes literarias*, 142 ff.).

43 See Ovid, *Heroides* 1.11–12 and 71–4: "Quando ego non timui graviora pericula veris? / res est solliciti plena timoris amor … quid timeam, ignoro – timeo tamen omnia demens, / et patet in curas area lata meas. / quaecumque aequor habet, quaecumque pericula tellus, / tam longae causas suspicor esse morae."

44 Castro Guisasola, *Observaciones sobre las fuentes literarias*, 69, also reports an example of a proverb directly taken from the *Fiammetta*: "Ohimè misera! quanto fu al mio onore nemico sì fatto giorno! Ma che? Le preterite cose mal fatte, si possono molto più agevolmente biasimare che emendare [Alas, miserable me, how hostile was that day to my virtue! But after all, things badly done in the past can be more easily regretted than corrected]" (*Fiammetta* 1.14). He compares this with "Que las malhechas cosas, después de cometidas, más presto se pueden reprehender que emendar [For actions that are ill, after they are committed, may easier be reprehended than amended]" (*Celestina* 14.284).

45 Cf. Ovid, *Amores* 1.13, or for the Spanish tradition, D. Empaytaz de Croome, *Albor: Mediaeval and Renaissance Dawn-Songs in the Iberian Peninsula* (Ann Arbor: Published for Dept. of Spanish and Spanish American Studies, University of London King's College by University Microfilms International, 1980).

46 Castro Guisasola, *Observaciones sobre las fuentes literarias*, 72.

47 A. Sanchez Jimenez, "'Huego de amor': la metáfora amor fuego en la estructura de *Celestina*," *Celestinesca* 29 (2005): 197–209, esp. 205.

48 Medieval Galician poet known for being a great lover and a paragon of virtue. According to a legend, the fearless Macías died from being stabbed with a lance by the husband of his beloved. Curiously, the name Macías appears in the place of Hercules in Boccaccio's text. According to Strabo's *Geography* 8.3.21, the name Maciste is an epithet of Hercules. Can the resemblance between Maciste and Macías have inspired Rojas to replace Hercules with Macías in the *Celestina*?

49 On Rojas's pessimism, see C. Ayllón, *La visión pesimista de La Celestina* (Mexico City: Ediciones de Andrea, 1965).

50 Latin authors in their works, from the *De remedia amoris* on, always tried to warn lovers against this aspect of love. Besides betraying the lover and

making him jealous, the woman will not grant her favours. Thus, another widespread topos of Latin elegy is the *paraklaysithyron*, that of the rejected lover who complains of the cruelty of his beloved in front of her door (cf. Ovid, *Amores* 1.6).

51 According to Farinelli, "Note sul Boccaccio in Spagna nell'Età Media," the interest in Spain in rhetorical discourse can be attributed to the diffusion of Boccaccio's works. Lida de Malkiel (*La originalidad*, 387) notices the analogies between Fiammetta's and Calisto's amorous eloquence.

52 Samonà, *Studi sul romanzo sentimentale e cortese*, 84–5. The use of oratorical art, after all, is also related to Boccaccio's and Rojas's biographies: the former pursued the study of canon law (see Grace Delmolino's essay in this volume); the latter defended his uncle during a trial held by the Inquisition. Apparently, they both took advantage in their works of that same oratory that they also practised. On Boccaccio's biography, see Vittore Branca, *Giovanni Boccaccio: profilo biografico* (Firenze: Sansoni, 1992). On Fernando de Rojas's biography, see S. Gilman, *The Spain of Fernando de Rojas: The Intellectual and Social Landscape of La Celestina* (Princeton: Princeton University Press, 1972).

53 Sanchez Jimenez, "'Huego de amor,'" 199. See also F.A. De Armas, "The Demoniacal in *La Celestina*," *South Atlantic Bulletin* 36, no. 4 (1971): 10–13; M.E. Lacarra, "La ira de Melibea a la luz de la filosofía moral," in *Cinco siglos de Celestina: aportaciones interpretativas*, ed. R. Beltrán Llavador and J.L. Canet Vallés (Valencia: Universitat de València, 1997), 107–20.

54 See M. Serafini, "Le tragedie di Seneca nella *Fiammetta* di Giovanni Boccaccio," *Giornale storico della letteratura italiana* 126, no. 373 (1949): 95–105; and cf. *Fiammetta* 1.49.

55 See also O.H. Green, "La furia de Melibea," *Clavileño* 20, no. 4 (1953): 1–3; G.D. Trotter, "Sobre 'La furia de Melibea' de Otis H. Green," *Clavileño* 25, no. 5 (1954): 55–6.

56 On lovesickness, see M. Peri, *Malato d'amore. La medicina dei poeti e la poesia dei medici* (Soveria Mannelli [Catanzaro]: Rubbettino, 1996); M. Ciavolella, *La malattia d'amore dall'antichità al Medioevo* (Rome: Bulzoni, 1976); M.F. Wack, *Lovesickness in the Middle Ages: The "Viaticum" and Its Commentaries* (Philadelphia: University of Pennsylvania Press, 1990); R. Poma, "Metamorfosi dell'*hereos*. Fonti medievali della psicofisiologia del mal d'amore in età moderna (XVI–XVII)," *Review of Literatures of the European Union* 7 (2007): 39–52; L. Borràs Castanyer, "La maladie amoureuse dans les images et les textes," *Review of Literatures of the European Union* 7 (2007): 295–313; P. Pinotti, "Il *remedium amoris* da Ovidio a Enea Silvio Piccolomini," *Review of Literatures of the European Union* 7 (2007): 275–94. On the relations between the *Celestina* and the medical and philosophical

tradition, see P.M. Cátedra, *Amor y pedagogía en la edad media: estudios de doctrina amorosa y práctica literaria* (Salamanca: Universidad de Salamanca, Secretariado de Publicaciones, 1989), 57–84; G. Illades Aguiar, *La Celestina en el taller salmantino* (Mexico City: Universidad Nacional Autónoma de México, Instituto de Investigaciones Filológicas, 1999); G.A. Shipley, "Concerting through Conceit: Unconventional Uses of Conventional Sickness Images in *La Celestina*," *Modern Language Review* 70, no. 2 (1975): 324–32; D.P. Seniff, "Bernardo de Gordonio's 'Lilio de Medicina': A Possible Source of 'Celestina'?" *Celestinesca* 10 (1986): 13–18. On Melibea's sickness, see M.V. Amasuno, "La enfermedad de Melibea: dos perspectivas médicas de la *ægritudo amoris* en *Celestina*," *Revista de Filología Española* 81, no. 1/2 (2001): 5–47.

57 On love and imagination in Spanish literature, see R. Folger, *Images in Mind: Lovesickness, Spanish Sentimental Fiction and "Don Quijote"* (Chapel Hill: University of North Carolina Press, 2002). A. Linage Conde, "Los caminos de la imaginación medieval: de la *Fiammetta* a la novela sentimental castellana," *Filología Moderna* 55, special issue (Madrid, 1975), 541–61 maintains that the *Siervo* and the *Cárcel* derive from Boccaccio their essential theme – obsessive neurosis – and their analysis of morbid psychology.

58 Lida de Malkiel first noticed this analogy (*La originalidad*, 446n20). The influence of the *Fiammetta*'s text on this image is further confirmed by its same influence on the fourteenth-century allegorical poem *El Sueño*, which describes the same vision with the snake bite. See C.R. Post, *Mediaeval Spanish Allegory* (Westport: Greenwood Press, 1974), 208; Joaquín Arce, "Seis cuestiones sobre el tema Boccaccio en España," *Filología Moderna* 15 (1975): 473–89; and Arce, "Boccaccio nella letteratura castigliana," 76–7. Another instance of the *Fiammetta*'s influence, in terms of the rhetorical and semantic structures mentioned by Arce ("Boccaccio nella letteratura castigliana," 77), is in the poem *Planto que fiço Pantasilea.*

59 For a list of ancient historical characters taken from Petrarch (*De remediis* 2.48), see *Celestina* 21.340, notes 14 and 15. According to Castro Guisasola, the sentence "es alivio a los míseros, como yo, tener compañeros en la pena" (*Celestina* 21.339) recalls one of the *Proverbios de Seneca* by Publilio Siro (*Observaciones sobre las fuentes literarias*, 100).

60 On the figure and works of Alonso de Proaza, see D.W. McPheeters, "The Corrector Alonso de Proaza and *La Celestina*," *Hispanic Review* 25 (1956): 13–25, and *El humanista español Alonso de Proaza* (Valencia: Castalia, 1961).

61 Text: Valencia 1514, in *La Celestina*, ed. Severin, 346n33; my emphasis.

15 Sins, Sex, and Secrets: The Legacy of Confession from the *Decameron* to the *Heptaméron*

NORA MARTIN PETERSON

All the faithful of either sex, after they have reached the age of discernment, should individually confess all their sins in a faithful manner to their own priest at least once a year, and let them take care to do what they can to perform the penance imposed on them. Let them reverently receive the sacrament of the eucharist at least at Easter unless they think, for a good reason and on the advice of their own priest, that they should abstain from receiving it for a time ... Let this salutary decree be frequently published in churches, so that nobody may find the pretence of an excuse in the blindness of ignorance. If any persons wish, for good reasons, to confess their sins to another priest let them first ask and obtain the permission of their own priest; for otherwise the other priest will not have the power to absolve or to bind them. The priest shall be discerning and prudent, so that like a skilled doctor he may pour wine and oil over the wounds of the injured one. Let him carefully inquire about the circumstances of both the sinner and the sin, so that he may prudently discern what sort of advice he ought to give and what remedy to apply, using various means to heal the sick person. Let him take the utmost care, however, not to betray the sinner at all by word or sign or in any other way. If the priest needs wise advice, let him seek it cautiously without any mention of the person concerned.

– *Lateran IV, Canon 21* ("On yearly confession to one's own priest")[1]

The Fourth Lateran Council of 1215 brought about a new age in the history of penance. Now institutionally mandated of all members of the Christian community, the sacrament of confession took front and centre stage as the mechanism through which all sinners had to pass on the road to salvation in the Eucharist. It also served as a regulatory device by which confessors sought to control various sins and tensions between neighbours and, eventually, as a tool with which to tap the secret desires of the individual.[2] This trajectory was not, however, a linear one. Scholars have disagreed about whether or not penance was already an influential practice in pre-Lateran congregations. Some have argued that the full extent of Lateran IV was not widely felt until as late as the fifteenth and sixteenth centuries, shortly before and then during the time of religious reform.[3]

Despite uncertainty, based largely in lack of documentation, about the prevalence of confession and the details surrounding the stringency with which, by whom, and where it was enforced, the deep influence of sacramental confession on fictional literature need not be disputed. The circulation of confessional discourse is widely reflected in non-liturgical texts spanning the period between Lateran IV (1215) and the Council of Trent (1545–63). The *Decameron* (1353) and the *Heptaméron* (1559) are both excellent texts to read together with the development of the sacrament of confession, as each one reflects the changing status of confession as well as its very real presence in their respective cultures. A quick digital search in the *Decameron Web* archive for the term "confess" in Boccaccio's *Decameron* yields seventy-five results.[4] Confession in Boccaccio's text is conspicuously present and, I argue, not coincidental; I believe that roughly one hundred years after the formal induction of the practice of confession, the trope of confession had become a stronghold of the Christian community. In what follows, I will follow the hypotheses put forth by those such as John Bossy and Alexander Murray, who write about confession in the first few centuries before and after Lateran IV as largely public, or, if private, focused on absolution immediately before death.[5] The confessions in the *Decameron* follow the formulaic structure of confession manuals, which were appearing in great numbers during Boccaccio's time. The outcome of successful confession is directed towards the group rather than the individual.[6]

Confession, as both a narrative device and a religious sacrament, is built into both texts. But a few centuries later, the ways in which Marguerite de Navarre uses confession in the *Heptaméron* reflect the changing status in the usage of the sacrament of penance between 1350 and 1550. No longer is the sacrament confined to the conversation between priest and penitent. Confession is seen to be equally effective when made to another member of the community; Marguerite's text explores alternative models of confessional interlocutors (diplomats, women, the author herself). The corruption of the Church and, more particularly, of the sacrament of confession is made amply evident in some of Marguerite's tales, and the increased focus on the narrative of the individual, rather than collectively experienced sins, comes to light in these stories.

If establishing any kind of epistemological history of confession after Lateran IV seems out of reach from today's perspective, readers are nonetheless left with a rich literary archive from which to cull. Because of the explicit link between the *Decameron* and the *Heptaméron*, mapping sacramental confession in both texts can shed new light on the social repercussions of Lateran IV from the time of its enforcement to the religious turbulence of the Reformation and Counter-Reformation.[7] At the same time, I hope that my reading will inspire other explorations of the previously under-studied link between penance as a contentious social rite and its textual manifestations in medieval and early modern literature.

Following the Formula: False Confession in *Decameron* 1.1

The opening *novella* of the *Decameron* features a false confession performed by a wicked man on his deathbed.[8] Readers learn that the protagonist, Ser Ciappelletto, "testimonianze false con sommo diletto diceva [would take great delight in giving false testimony]" (1.1.11). Furthermore, he was a "bestemmiatore di Dio e de' Santi era grandissimo, e per ogni piccola cosa, sí come colui che piú che alcuno altro era iracundo. A chiesa non usava giammai, e i sacramenti di quella tutti come vil cosa con abominevoli parole scherniva [a mighty blasphemer of God and His saints, losing his temper on the tiniest pretext, as if he were the most hot-blooded man alive. He never went to church, and he would use foul language to pour scorn on all of her sacraments, declaring them repugnant]" (1.1.13–14). The narrator makes Ser Ciappelletto's stance on the sacraments very clear, and the final verdict on his character culminates in the exclamation that "egli era il piggiore uomo forse che mai nascesse [he was, perhaps, the worst man ever born]" (1.1.15). As a result, he is often hired to do the dirty work of other men. When he is sent to France on an assignment to collect money on the Franzesi's outstanding loans, he suddenly falls gravely ill and is left in the care of two brothers who are at a loss as to how to handle the precarious situation.

The two men immediately begin to quarrel about whether or not to send for a priest to take Ser Ciappelletto's last confession. On the one hand, they know that by turning him out of the house, they will lose credibility in the eyes of their fellow townspeople. However, they are equally troubled by the prospect of sending for a priest because of the gravity of his sins; convinced that he will refuse to confess, they are concerned that Ser Ciappelletto will be denied absolution and sent to a dishonourable death at their expense (1.1.22–6). Ser Ciappelletto overhears the two men quarrelling and assures them that they should not worry about the status of his mortal soul:

> Io non voglio che voi d'alcuna cosa di me dubitiate né abbiate paura di ricevere per me alcun danno. Io ho inteso ciò che di me ragionato avete e son certissimo che cosí n'averrebbe come voi dite, dove cosí andasse la bisogna come avvisate: ma ella andrà altramenti. Io ho, vivendo, tante ingiurie fatte a Domenedio, che, per farnegli io una ora in su la mia morte, né piú né meno ne farà; e per ciò procacciate di farmi venire un santo e valente frate, il piú che aver potete, se alcun ce n'è; e lasciate fare a me.
>
> [I don't want you to worry in the slightest on my account, nor to fear that I will cause you to suffer any harm. I heard what you were saying about me and I agree entirely that what you predict will actually come to pass, if matters take the course you anticipate; but they will do nothing of the kind. I have done our good Lord so many injuries whilst I lived, that to do Him another now that I am dying will be neither here nor there. So go and bring me the holiest and ablest friar you can find, if there is such a one, and leave everything to me.] (1.1.27–9)

The men decide to send for a holy man who is held in great esteem by the people of the community (1.1.30). When the friar appears to take the sick man's confession, Ser Ciappelletto, showing some knowledge of confessional procedure, responds in line with the deathbed protocol of making a general confession of one's sins before receiving extreme unction at the time of death:

> Al quale ser Ciappelletto, che mai confessato non s'era, rispose: "Padre mio, la mia usanza suole essere di confessarsi ogni settimana almeno una volta, senza che assai sono di quelle che io mi confesso piú; è il vero che poi che io infermai, che son passati da otto dí, io non mi confessai tanta è stata la noia che la infermità m'ha data." Disse allora il frate, "Figliuol mio, bene hai fatto, e cosí si vuol fare per innanzi; e veggio che, poi sí spesso ti confessi, poca fatica avrò d'udire o di dimandare." Disse ser Ciappelletto: "Messo lo frate, non dite cosí: io non mi confessai mai tante volte né

> sí spesso, che io sempre non mi volessi confessare generalmente di tutti i miei peccati che io mi ricordassi dal dí che io nacqui infini a quello che confessato mi sono; e per ciò vi priego, padre mio buono, che cosí puntalmente d'ogni cosa mi domandiate come se mai confessato non mi fossi."
>
> [Ser Ciappelletto, who had never been to confession in his life, replied, "Father, it has always been my custom to go to confession at least once every week, except that there are many weeks in which I go more often. But to tell the truth, since I fell ill, nearly a week ago, my illness has caused me so much discomfort that I haven't been to confession at all." "My son," said the friar, "you have done very well, and you should persevere in this habit of yours. Since you go so often to confession, I can see that there will be very little for me to hear or to ask." "Master friar," said Ser Ciappelleto, "do not speak thus, for however frequently or regularly I confess, it is always my wish that I should make a general confession of all the sins I can remember committing from the day I was born till the day of my confession. I therefore beg you, good father, to question me about everything, just as closely as if I had never been confessed."] (1.1.32–4)

Given that Lateran IV mandated once-yearly confession, and that more frequent usage of the sacrament was not encouraged until several centuries later (in the decades preceding the Council of Trent), the fourteenth-century reader would immediately have been struck by the ridiculous tone of Ser Ciappelletto's imaginary weekly confessions. Despite the priest's rather astonishing willingness to take the false penitent at his word, however, Ser Ciappelletto insists on performing the sacrament true to the form of a last confession, which would indeed have demanded a full narrative of the sins from birth to deathbed. Readers who know the extent of Ser Ciappelletto's wickedness now realize the rules of the game.

When the dying man bids the friar to "question me about everything, just as closely as if I had never been confessed," readers might smile at the irony of the situation, because they know that this will, indeed, be Ser Ciappelletto's first sacramental confession. It is not, however, his first textual confession. In other words, while Ser Ciappelletto has no intention of making his sins known to the priest, and intends to continue them to his death, the text has confessed them on his behalf. The reader is made well aware of Ser Ciappelletto's true nature before he falls ill; if ever one is in doubt about his true character, the narrator ruthlessly underscores that he was the worst man ever to have lived.

Together with the recounting of his many sins (discussed above), there is another layer of confession in play. If the text cannot verbally speak, the storyteller can; thus, although textually bound in his turn, Pamphilo (the narrator of story 1.1), by speaking to an audience, confesses Ser Ciappelletto's sins on his behalf. The text both encompasses the dying man's true identity and also points to the inherently verbal nature of sacramental confession.

Aware of the irony already in play before Ser Ciappelletto begins recounting his "sins," readers are likely amused by the false confession that follows. But they might not be aware that in his examination, the friar follows the formula of confession manuals, which began to appear in increasing numbers following 1215. He goes through a list of mortal and venial sins, following up his inquiries with gentle, probing questions.[9] He begins with carnal knowledge of women (1.1.36), then proceeds to ask about gluttony (1.1.41), avarice (1.1.44), anger (1.1.47), bearing false witness, cheating, and stealing (1.1.53–4).[10]

The friar is dumbfounded by Ser Ciappelletto's over-zealous confession; Ser Ciappelletto "admits to" and condemns sins so trivial and doctrinally insignificant that even the friar admits to having committed them (1.1.57–8). Ser Ciappelletto shows an understanding of which sins would have been condemnable and why, suggesting widespread familiarity not only with the proceedings of the sacrament but also with the explanations that appeared in the confessional manuals for priests. Because the *Decameron* is not a devotional text, the overlap in vocabulary between confession manuals and Ser Ciappelletto's recall of confessional protocol makes it seem likely that priests quoted from manuals word for word or paraphrased the explanations. It also suggests that those performing the sacrament quickly learned the procedure and vocabulary of how to confess. At the same time, confession bears an element of communal education, as presumably everyone confessing to a similar sin would receive the same explanation of why it was wrong.[11]

There are other indicators of the communal orientation of the sacrament. Indeed, despite the community of readers who know better, the fictional community embedded in 1.1 appears to benefit from Ser Ciappelletto's false confession. The friar leaves, convinced that Ciappelletto is the most pious and virtuous man he has ever encountered. He willingly grants the dying man's request to send for the consecrated Body of Christ and performs extreme unction (1.1.76). After his death, Ciappelletto is praised by the friar during a Sunday sermon, the other clergymen in the community pray over his body for days, and a statue is erected in the marketplace to honour his virtuous conduct. As John Bossy writes, "the original bearing of the sacrament was not individual but collective … the effect of the sacrament is to restore a condition of peace between the sinner and the church."[12] Though Ser Ciappelletto is a stranger to the community in which he dies, his penance, however ironic, fulfils the function of reconciling and strengthening the ties between the members of that community and the Church. By contrast, there is no textual evidence to support the theory that confession reconciles the dying Ser Ciappelletto with God, nor was this ever presented as the goal of his confession.

On the other hand, the presence and importance of the community cannot be denied. The fact that the two brothers overhear the false confession makes it much more "real" contextually:

> Li due fratelli, li quali dubitavan forte non ser Ciappelletto gl'ingannasse, s'eran posti appresso a un tavolato, il quale la camera dove ser Ciappelletto giaceva dividea da un'altra, e ascoltando leggiermente udivano e intendevano ciò che ser Ciappelletto al frate diceva; e aveano alcuna volta sí gran voglia di ridere, udendo le cose le quali egli confessava d'aver fatte, che quasi scoppiavano.
>
> [The two brothers, who strongly suspected that Ser Ciappelletto was going to deceive them, had posted themselves behind a wooden partition which separated the room where Ser Ciappelletto was lying from another, and as they stood there listening they could easily follow what Ser Ciappelletto was saying to the friar. When they heard the things he confessed to having done, they were so amused that every so often they nearly exploded with mirth]. (1.1.78)

Their presence here serves more than a comic function. If this confession is not a face-to-face encounter "between two people who would probably have known each other pretty well," as Bossy explains would have been the case in most medieval confessions, it is instead explicitly public, or, as was typically the custom, "in the not-so-remote presence of a large number of neighbours."[13] Gesturing towards confessional privacy, the text upholds a structural separation; the partition separating the sick man from his eavesdroppers loosely resembles attempts at privacy in medieval confession. Though the traditional mandate of confessing in one's own church would have destroyed Ser Ciappelletto's trick, as his own priest would have known his true nature, removing him from his native environment endows the narrative with all the necessary elements of public sacramental confession.[14]

If Ser Ciappelletto's false confession at first reads as nothing more than a very clever trick, the dying man's confession cleverly re-manoeuvres the stakes of penance and absolution. First, the two men who summon the priest are the only people who know the true nature of the deceased scoundrel. The reader might recall that this knowledge is what made them pause before summoning the religious man to begin with:

> Egli è stato sí malvagio uomo, che egli non si vorrà confessare né prendere alcuno sagramento della Chiesa; e, morendo senza confessione, niuna chiesa vorrà il suo corpo ricevere, anzi sarà gittato a' fossi a guisa d'un cane. E, se egli si pur confessa, i peccati suoi son tanti e sí orribili, che il simigliante n'avverrà, per ciò che frate né prete ci sarà che 'l voglia né possa assolvere.
>
> [He has led such a wicked life that he will never be willing to make his confession or receive the sacraments of the Church; and if he dies unconfessed, no church will want to accept his body and he'll be flung into the moat like a dog. But even if he makes his confession, his sins are so many and so appalling that the same thing will happen, because there will be neither friar nor priest who is either willing or able to give him absolution]. (1.1.24–5)

Before the "confession" even begins, the two men know the truth. The reader, too, has learned about Ser Ciappelletto's depravity prior to his illness. Thus, the text has already done the confessing on behalf of its sinning subject. But this kind of confession cannot result in absolution, especially because, in the Catholic community, only an ordained priest could grant absolution; moreover, the confession heard by the friar in this text is a false one. Textual confession leads only to empty absolution, while the penitent's deception results in an absolution by the appropriate party which the reader understands as invalid. The two men listening, too, would have been aware of the prime importance of absolution (as indeed they explain in the passage above); it stands front and centre as the goal of the sacrament of penance.

In *Decameron* 1.1, the friar, his subject, and his narrator all show perfunctory familiarity with the protocols of a properly conducted confession as stipulated by the rules of Lateran IV. However, the friar's interpretive skills do not extend beyond the questions he is bound by protocol to ask. Ser Ciappelletto, on the other hand, slyly outmanoeuvres his confessor, demonstrating his ability to perform the sacrament to perfection. Ser Ciappelletto, known by readers to be a master of verbal manipulation, easily manoeuvres his way through the protocol of confession, anticipating and outwitting the friar at every turn. Ser Ciappelletto fakes his testimony with deceitful words and supplements his performance with the signs of his body: the friar "infers especially intense contrition from the tears and sighing that accompany the confession: he takes them as visible proof of the truth of the speech and believes he can actually see the contrition."[15] Thus, if the friar's questions are based on a codified protocol, Ser Ciappelletto responds with codified performances of his own. He knows that his tears and sighs will be read in a certain manner that corresponds to the false front he is attempting to present as truth. Confession in this tale is ironic, predictable (and therefore performable), and void of all meaning, despite the fact that it fulfils the perfunctory purpose of extracting a deathbed confession. The tone of the *novella* points to an ironic, playful void in the relationship between the sacrament and the person receiving it. Confession, though mandatory, emerges as a rhetorical game between two equal sides, with Ser Ciappelletto gaining the upper hand after his death, despite the ruse of his performance. The outcome of the story underscores the reconciliatory function of public confession and penance that most scholars agree defined the sacrament for the first few centuries following Lateran IV. In this particular *novella*, however, only the reader and other non-religious observers can see the truth.

This textual irony could actually be a reflection of the interpretive limitations and rudimentary enforcement of the new rules surrounding sacramental confession. Ser Ciappelletto's confessions are indeed communally oriented, and the fact that the "real" confession is carried out textually bears the possibility of some kind of textual absolution. Within the narrative, the author shows some familiarity with the religious protocol of the sacrament as it might have occurred in his time. But at the same time, confession in this text bears witness to its own parameters. In the very first tale of his text, Boccaccio demonstrates the dangerous power of falsification, while rhetorically employing it himself. He shows an understanding of the penitential formula but twists it, choosing instead to illuminate its boundaries. Real confession can only take place at one remove from the fictional plot. And real absolution in this story, if indeed it can be granted to the worst man ever to have lived, must be rhetorical also; the only absolution Ser Ciappelletto can receive is the wink of the reader who appreciates the extent to which he is manipulating the penitential formula. Boccaccio endows his own text with the same authority he exhumes from the sacrament of confession.

Raising the Stakes: Confession in the *Heptaméron*

Michel Foucault famously delineated the links between sacramental confession, sexuality, power, and knowledge in the sixteenth and seventeenth centuries. He argues that the heightened insistence upon confession posited by the Counter-Reformation produced an increased interest in the flesh and sexuality, as well as a new emphasis on parsing the innermost desires of the individual, which in turn helped to *create* a culture of individual desires. He writes,

> For a long time, the individual was vouched for by the reference of others … [and] then he was authenticated by the discourse of truth he was able or obliged to pronounce concerning himself. The truthful confession was inscribed at the heart of the procedures of individualization by power … one confesses in public and in private, to one's parents, one's educators, one's doctor, to those one loves; one admits to oneself, in pleasure and in pain, things it would be impossible to tell to anyone else.[16]

Foucault's contention – that confession became the *modus operandi* by which those in power were able to perpetuate their discourse of knowledge, and that individuals became so accustomed to this mode that they internalized it – is a powerful one, with significant implications. He identifies confession as an important component in parsing the network of early modern power, and he uses it to pinpoint a cultural shift during which the individual was simultaneously being confessed and learning the power of internal confession to one's self. While I believe that Foucault's argument is limited to one historical moment and one discourse at a time and, as such, does not account for the uneasy negotiation that often happens outside the text, or even within other contexts, it does provide a useful lens through which to read the evolution of confession since Lateran IV. In what follows, I will use several examples from the frame and stories of the *Heptaméron* to show the extent to which literary documentation of verbal confession has changed in the centuries separating Boccaccio and Marguerite de Navarre. By the sixteenth century, the focus in confession and penance has turned inward, in contrast to the public setting in Boccaccio's text.[17] Marguerite's text reflects new values in the practice of confession, as well as the ways in which the trope of confession was interpreted by clergy and laypeople.

The method by which Marguerite de Navarre sets up her project in the Prologue already bears witness to the different environment in which the tales will be told. If the storytellers of the *Decameron* flee the city in order to escape the Plague, thereby implying physical and moral corruption, Marguerite's *devisants* find themselves stranded as the result of a massive flood. By alluding to the new covenant established after the great flood in Genesis, the *Heptaméron* thus sets a tone of reconciliation. The underlying message is one of resolution and equality; "au jeu," proclaims Hircan, "nous sommes tous égaux [Where games are concerned everybody is equal]" (49; 70).[18] The emphasis on parity need not be taken for granted; following every story, the *devisants* respond heatedly to the issue at hand, creating a narrative complexity that far exceeds the comparatively straightforward approvals given up by Boccaccio's *brigata*. At a time when religious uncertainty and difference would have been on everyone's mind, explicitly setting the record straight for the fictional frame characters allows them to speak freely and without fear. For the reader, it also sends the message that complexity and ambiguity will be the name of the game; if the *devisants* can freely debate their opinions, there will be no clear message as to which actions constitute sins, and no clear agreement about how to judge the characters in each *novella*. Other clues in the Prologue remind the reader of the sacramental setting in which the stories will be told. The *devisants* are stranded at the abbey of Our Lady at Sarrance; this backdrop sets a confessional tone. And lest the reader, or the frame characters, forget the seriousness of their predicament or their great debt to God for having saved them, they begin their day in prayer and then retreat to the abbey for inward reflection and more prayer at the close of each day of storytelling. Finally, Parlamente, one of the two strongest female voices in the frame, insists that the stories they will tell be *true*.[19] The Prologue thus explicitly and deliberately establishes a contrast to the Prologue of Boccaccio's *Decameron*, which makes no such stipulation, and it more explicitly suggests a link between storytelling and confession.[20] The link is strengthened if one considers that on more than one occasion, the resident monks are caught listening to the tales from the bushes. Not only are "real" confessors present, they openly enjoy the stories they hear, suggesting that listening to secrets is pleasurable and takes the listener beyond the call of duty. If listening is pleasurable even for professional confessors, the communal pleasure of the *devisants* and their eavesdropping companions implies that the act of listening to confession is open to anyone. This is an explicitly Reformed idea; Calvinism and other branches of Protestants insist that confession is a communal rite that can be performed to and by any member of the religious community. The frame, then, ensures that the "official" backdrop is textually and metatextually present, and that confession will play a major role in the framework of the stories. Instead of merely pointing to an awareness of confessional protocol, the *Heptaméron* sets up, even beyond the narrative scope, a textual setting that demonstrates acute awareness of confessional elements.

All of this is certainly not to say that the French text does not have its fair share of falsified confession and deceit. In *Novella* 60, an unfaithful wife takes up with one of her husband's cantors while he is away. In order to escape suspicion, she feigns grave illness, and sends for "quelques femmes de bien de la ville pour la venir visiter [some of the honest women of the town to come and visit her]" (429; 471). Having surrounded herself with a community of listeners, she "fit semblant de pleurer et de connaître son péché, en sorte qu'elle faisait pitié à toute la compagnie qui cuidait fermement qu'elle parlât du fond de son coeur [pretended to weep and admit her sins, with the result that all these good ladies, who thought she was speaking from the depths of her heart, were moved to pity]" (429; 471). Having been duped into believing the woman repentant, they immediately send for a religious man to hear her confession (ibid.). He takes her confession, apparently without issue, seeing as there is no mention of it in the body of the text, and he administers extreme unction to the purportedly dying woman. She fakes her death, and after her funeral the cantor digs her up; they go on to live together happily for some years until the truth comes out and she is forced to reconcile with her husband. Two important differences separate this text from *Novella* 1.1 in the *Decameron*. First, while in the Italian text Ser Ciappelletto gets away with his falsified confession, even drawing together the community in the aftermath of his death, this woman is eventually found out. As confession is no longer a formulaic gesture, its representations in sixteenth-century texts insist on digging deeper until things are made right. Oisille, the spiritual leader of the frame narrative, exclaims at the end of the discussion, "Je crois que ce n'est pas pour chercher la confession qu'elles [depraved women like the one in *Novella* 60] cherchent les confesseurs ... elles regardent de s'arrêter au lieu qui leur semble le plus couvert et le plus sûr, que de se soucier d'avoir absolution du mal dont elles ne se repentent point

[I do not think that [they] pursue confessors in order to make their confession. They are … really looking for … the opportunity to sin in secrecy and security rather than the opportunity to seek absolution for sins of which they do not in the least repent]" (431–2; 474). Oisille's stance on the matter acknowledges critical awareness of the abuse of the sacrament in ways Boccaccio's text does not. And despite Marguerite's decidedly female voice in the text, she does not shy away from admonishing those of her own sex who would manipulate a religious sacrament that appears, in her view, to be valuable.

At the same time, the context in which this honest confession should take place appears to be a matter of debate (as indeed was the case in sixteenth-century Reformation Europe). While Marguerite's version does follow the requisite procedures of the sacrament of penance (administering extreme unction after a deathbed confession to a priest), the actual confession *to* the priest is textually omitted. The woman does tell her fake story to a community of honest women – but this is all the readers know. Though one can assume she repeats the same confession to the priest, the role of the religious man in the sacrament of confession is minimal. Whereas in *Decameron* 1.1 the dupery continues over several paragraphs, and is all the more significant because of its adherence to confessional manuals, here readers learn more about the corruption of the Church and its members than they do about the confession itself. And, after all, the woman in question is sleeping with her husband's cantor. In the end, Boccaccio's text reveals a familiarity with the sacrament of penance (despite its formulaic emptiness). Marguerite's, on the other hand, has moved beyond simple acknowledgment of the sacrament; while both authors highlight the corruption of the Church, the stories in which confession appears in the *Heptaméron* highlight the changing nature of the sacrament since Lateran IV and since the time when Boccaccio penned his own collection of tales.

Novella 41 features a singular Christmas Eve confession.[21] Having sent for "un prêcheur suffisant et homme de bien, tant pour prêcher que pour confesser elle et toute sa maison [a competent, honest man who could preach, as well as hear confessions from herself and her whole household]" (340; 377), the Countess of Aiguemeont sends her entire household to confess. The text invokes the tradition of annual confession before receiving the sacrament of communion, usually on major holidays such as Christmas or Easter. The Countess takes the first turn, at which point the text explicitly points out the private setting of her confession: "après s'être confessée en une chapelle bien fermée, afin que la confession fût plus secrète [she made [her confession] in a chapel behind closed doors for the sake of privacy]" (ibid.). Private confessional booths were not commonly used in France until later in the century, but the *novella* marks a shift away from public confessions that take place within earshot of the rest of the community. As a result, the dynamic of what is spoken in confession is explicitly private, with both the sins of the penitent and the reaction of the confessor beyond the reach of public knowledge.

After the Countess makes her confession, she sends her lady of honour, who in turn sends her daughter, to do the same. As readers, we are privy to the conversation that takes place between the girl and her confessor in the *novella*. However, it is worth pointing out that, although we learn that the girl shares seemingly salacious details of a sexual nature about her private life, we do not actually have access to the exact content of her confession. If Ser Ciappelletto shows an acute awareness of the formula of confession in his deathbed trick, the dynamics of confession in this *novella* extend far beyond simple manipulation. Instead of extracting sins with legal or communal consequences, the priest here focuses on private details of a very personal nature. He does not appear to have followed the same handbook as Boccaccio's friar; indeed, there is no indication of a formula at all. Though the details remain securely out of the reader's grasp, the text points to the priest's response as one of sexual excitement.

The text thus maintains control over the secret of the confession.[22] Readers must come to their own conclusions based on the reaction of the preacher, which the text itself proclaims to be "non accoutumée [strange]" (341; 378). He orders the girl to wear his cord against her bare flesh as a penance for her sins. And he insists that he fasten the cord around her with his own hands (341; 377–8). The girl, who is seemingly versed enough in the procedure of the sacrament to be sceptical of the appropriateness of this particular penance, refuses. The preacher accuses her of being a heretic, and refuses absolution. His refusal, as Mary B. McKinley writes, "reflects the early-Reformation polemic on sacramental confession and indicates Marguerite de Navarre's position in that debate."[23] Marguerite intentionally illuminates the manipulative power invested in the sacrament and textually sympathizes with the perspective of Reformers. The innocent, duped girl emerges from the confession "la conscience bien troublée, car elle … avait peur d'avoir failli au refus qu'elle avait fait au père [with a troubled conscience … and afraid lest she had done wrong in refusing the priest]" (341; 378).

The *novella* is resolved when she recounts the details of the failed confession to her mother, who in turn tells the Countess, who has the priest whipped until he admits the truth (342; 378). These two "confessions" that follow the official sacrament comment on the corruption of the office of the Church and imply that, when it comes to extracting a confession in order to achieve justice, laypeople have taken the sacrament into their own hands. The sacrament of the confession, though increasingly personalized and private, holds no legal weight, nor is penance necessarily just, nor does penance, when applied, necessarily result in absolution. The characters in the *novella* reveal a lay population at the mercy of an essentially empty sacrament, on the one hand, and with the power to implement alternative techniques of truth, justice, and absolution, on the other. By displacing resolution from the priest to the Countess, Marguerite offers an alternative to the problem of one-sided confession in which the priest has unequivocal power.

Both elements reappear in *Heptaméron* 72. Here, a young nun is left in the company of a monk at the bed of a dying man. After administering extreme unction and receiving the confession of the man, they both comfort him in his transition to death. Immediately thereafter, the monk rapes the nun. In order to prevent a public scandal, the monk warns the naive girl to "[ne pas] se confesser à autre qu'à lui [not to mention it in her confessions to anyone except himself]" (495; 541). The girl continues to come to the monk for absolution, which leads to an eventual pregnancy. Unable to reveal the corrupt monk's nature, she leaves the convent, hoping that "en confessant son péché aux pieds du pape, recouvrer sa virginité [if she made her confession at the feet of the Pope, she could recover her virginity]" (496; 541). When she gets as far as Lyon, the nun is interrupted at prayer by Marguerite herself, and once the girl learns to whom she is speaking, she confides in her, "[se jetant] à ses pieds ... pleur[ant] et cri[ant] [(throwing) herself at her feet, weeping once more and crying out loud]" (497; 542). After encouraging the girl not to relinquish her repentant spirit, the duchess intervenes on her behalf, "avec lettres à l'évêque du lieu pour donner ordre de faire chasser ce religieux scandaleux [with letters to the bishop of the diocese, instructing him to have the scandalous monk removed]" (497; 543). The author enters the text and takes the role of confessor, granting absolution to the nun in the seventy-second story and removing the clearly corrupted false monk from his position.[24] Not only does confession take place outside the official realm of the sacrament – Marguerite explicitly discourages the nun from seeking confession from the pope, the most high and holy of confessors – but Marguerite's political and personal position of wealth and power allow her to identify and remove the broken link in the confessional chain.

Readers can find more evidence of lay confessions in other tales, and I would point especially to *Heptaméron* 32, in which a German diplomat hears confessions from a man who subjects his unfaithful wife to a macabre and unusual punishment, then convinces the husband to absolve his wife of her sins.[25] The confession trickles down from the husband, who tells the story on his wife's behalf, to the visiting diplomat, who then speaks directly to the guilty wife. She treats their encounter as a confession: "Monsieur, je confesse ma faute être si grande que tous les maux que le seigneur de céans ... me saurait faire ne me sont rien au prix du regret que j'ai de l'avoir offensé [Monsieur, I confess that my sins are so great that all the suffering that is inflicted upon me by the lord of this house ... is as nothing compared with the remorse I feel in having wronged him]" (297; 333). After leaving their household, the diplomat tells her story at court, from whence it makes its way to the fictional storyteller of the frame narrative. The wife's adulterous secret certainly is not held to the same promise of confessional anonymity that at least theoretically existed in the sacrament, but it is just as effective; the diplomat, upon hearing the story, grants the evidently penitent wife absolution and advises the husband to forgive her, if only for the possibility of continuing the family line. His language bears traces of the absolution given after sacramental confession: "vu la grande repentance de votre pauvre femme ... vous devrez user de miséricorde [As your wife's repentance is so deep, it is my belief that you should show some compassion towards her]" (298; 333). Just as Marguerite's presence in *Novella* 72 plays a diplomatic function of standing between the girl's sin and the Catholic Church, here the diplomat negotiates the confessions of husband and wife and offers a path to absolution that occurs explicitly outside the realm of the Church.

Confession, in the context of the *Heptaméron*, only works when it is removed from the sacramental framework in which it was intended to be performed according to the mandates of Lateran IV. While the frame of the text takes care to establish an explicitly confessional setting, the confessions that take place within the tales are much less conventional. If the frame playfully and dialogically vacillates between sacramental and worldly spaces, subverting the spiritual aspects only to re-establish them at the end of each day, the stories themselves bear out a different history. To be sure, the implicit and explicit references to confession throughout the *Heptaméron* bear witness to a continued prevalence of the trope of confession between the fourteenth and sixteenth centuries. Writings such as the *Decameron* and the *Heptaméron* reflect both the prominence and knowledge of the sacrament among layfolk. And both texts point to the challenges of defining the role of confession in the centuries following Lateran IV, particularly as the poles of public and private, and the regulations of each, were under constant negotiation.

Boccaccio's text demonstrates a remarkable familiarity with the conventions of the sacrament of confession. Story 1.1 points to a correlation between the largely communal, legal emphasis of confession in the first few centuries following 1215, and playfully subverts the authority of those performing confession. The *Heptaméron*, on the other hand, reflects the religiously charged time during which it was written, particularly concerning the corruption of the clergy and the need to confess to a designated spiritual leader, as opposed to any other member of the community. Marguerite de Navarre, who was a religious and political leader in her own right, recognized the hermeneutic tension contained within the hotly contested sacrament of confession, and transformed her text into a confessional space where the most pressing religious and social concerns of her time come to light.

Both the *Decameron* and Marguerite de Navarre's *Heptaméron* share a deep interest in documenting and debating the impact of religion in their respective times. Both metaphorically shed light on the corruption of society (the *brigata* is fleeing the Plague; the *deviants*, a catastrophic flood) and in particular, the Church. Religion is written into the frame of both texts, and often cannot be separated from the fabric of storytelling. For example, the *brigata* meet in a church, Santa Maria *Novella* (a name that binds together storytelling and religion). Daily prayer shapes every day of the frame narrative, as it does in the *Heptaméron*. In the later text, the *devisants* are stranded at an abbey, and the monks who host them are implicitly involved, though not explicitly included, in the storytelling. Both texts often insist that the people whose tales they tell are real, a technique that blurs the line between truth and fiction, and one that makes the text itself a site of confession. Because some details are only known to readers, and because the text fulfils or even stands in for the sacrament of confession, these texts, in the very fact of their textuality, participate in reforming confession, even as they both reflect its corruption in practice.

NOTES

1 http://www.ewtn.com/library/councils/lateran4.htm#14.
2 The secondary literature on the history of sacramental confession is vast. For an informative overview of the evolution of the sacrament, see the article "Penitence," by E. Amman and A. Michel, in the *Dictionnaire de théologie catholique*, 1st ed. (Paris: 1909–50), esp. chaps. 4–8. See also Jaroslav Pelikan's *The Christian Tradition: A History of the Development of the Doctrine*, vol. 3, *Reformation of Church and Dogma (1300–1700)* (Chicago: University of Chicago Press, 1984). For a sympathetic but still critical account, see John T. McNeill, *A History of the Cure of Souls* (New York: Harper, 1951). A good collection of primary sources and essays with a primarily socio-historical focus is *A New History of Penance*, ed. Abigail Firey (Leiden: Brill, 2008). For an account of how the sacrament was practised in the Middle Ages, see *Handling Sin: Confession in the Middle Ages*, ed. Peter Biller and A.J. Minnis, *York Studies in Medieval Theology II* (York: York Medieval Press, 1998). Finally, Thomas N. Tentler's study on the evolution and significance of the sacrament is an invaluable resource; see *Sin and Confession on the Eve of the Reformation* (Princeton: Princeton University Press, 1977).
3 See, for example, Merry E. Wiesner-Hanks, *Christianity and Sexuality in the Early Modern World: Regulating Desire, Reforming Practice* (London: Routledge, 2000), 110. David Myers also takes this stance. See *"Poor, Sinning Folk": Confession and Conscience in Counter Reformation Germany* (Ithaca: Cornell University Press, 1996), 33; 45; 56; and 192.
4 My search for the term "confess" rather than "confession" was deliberate; it was meant to include hits of the verb "to confess" as well as the noun.
5 Alexander Murray, "Confession before 1215," *Transactions of the Royal Historical Society*, 6th ser., 3 (1993): 51–81; and John Bossy, "The Social History of Confession in the Age of Reformation," *Transactions of the Royal Historical Society* 25 (1975): 21–38.
6 Though it focuses on a different theme and set of texts, Franklin Lewis's chapter in this volume argues, as I do, that part of Boccaccio's project is to situate a theme (deception) within a larger narrative.
7 Marguerite de Navarre, *Heptaméron*, 1559, ed. Simone de Reyff (Paris: Flammarion, 1982); English translation by P.A. Chilton (New York: Penguin, 1984). Marguerite was familiar with Boccaccio's text, having commissioned a new translation into French. And in the Prologue to the *Heptaméron*, the *devisants* invoke the *Decameron* as a model for their own storytelling project (47–9).

8 Quotations from the *Decameron* are from Giovanni Boccaccio, *Il Decamerone*, 1353, ed. Vittore Branca (*Decameron Web*, 30 August 2013); English translations by G.H. McWilliam, 2nd ed. (New York: Penguin, 1995). The opening *novella* is not the only one in which confession plays a major role (other notable examples include 3.3 and 7.5). Limits of space prevent a more thorough analysis of all three of these stories. I have chosen to focus on this one example because it so explicitly follows certain formulaic conventions and because it very poignantly highlights the prevalence of sacramental confession in a fictional setting.

9 For some examples of confession manuals from Boccaccio's time, see Joseph Goering, "The Internal Forum and the Literature of Penance and Confession," *Traditio* 59 (2004): 175–227; 223–4.

Some later examples include *Short Instructions for Validly Making Sacramental Confession* (Jodocus [morder] Winshemius [Erfurt, 1515]), *Confessionale* (Nuremberg: Engelhardus Kunhofer, 1502), *Penitentiarius* (Nuremberg: Romming, 1522?), and an anonymous *Manual for Parish Priests*. Jean Delumeau examines confession manuals in *L'Aveu et le Pardon: Les difficultés de la confession XIIIe–XVIIIe siècle* (Paris: Fayard, 1990). See also Anne Jacobson Schutte, "Consiglio Spirituale e controlo sociale: Manuali per la Confessione stampati in volgare prima della Controriforma," in *Città Italiane del'500 tra Riforma e Controriforma: Atti del Convegno Internazionale di Studi, Lucca, 13–15 ottobre, 1983* (Lucca: Maria Pacini Fazzi Editore, 1988), 45–59.

10 This particular passage resonates with the index of Tommaso de Vio Cajetan's *Summa caietani: summula de peccatis / reuerendissimi domini Thomae de Vio Caietani s. xisti, sacrae Theologiae professoris celeberrimi, recentissime Summarijs aucta dignissimis ; praeposito sente[n]tiarum specialium repertorio, nunc primum edito ; accedit ite[m] de Noui Testamenti Ientaculis tractatus eiusdem excellentissimus* (1539). Each heading points to the place in the text where one might learn how to question a penitent about a specific sin, for example, under "I," idolatry, impiety, ingratitude, or incest.

11 Though it is a later example of this kind of knowledge, Bertin Bertaut's catechism for confessors (*Le directeur des confesseurs, en forme de catechisme: contenant une methode nouuelle, briéue & facile pour entendre les confessions*, 1662) divides penitents by their professions and status in life, then predicts common sins for each group and explains whether these sins are mortal or not.

12 Bossy, "The Social History of Confession in the Age of Reformation," 22.

13 Ibid., 24.

14 Confessionals with a grill or screen separating the penitent from confessor were not commonplace in the Church until the mid-sixteenth-century.

Until then, confession commonly took place in the pews, or in a small chapel – off to the side but by no means private. See Wiesner-Hanks, *Christianity and Sexuality in the Early Modern World*, 116, and Myers, "*Poor, Sinning Folk*," 134–5.

15 Irene Albers, "The Passions of the Body in Boccaccio's *Decameron*," *MLN* 125, no. 1 (2010): 26–53; 42.

16 Michel Foucault, *The History of Sexuality, Vol. 1: An Introduction*, trans. Robert Hurley (New York: Vintage, 1978), 58–9. See also Wiesner-Hanks's account in *Christianity and Sexuality in the Early Modern World*.

17 Goering, "The Internal Forum," 226.

18 All English citations are from P.A. Chilton's translation (New York: Penguin, 1984). The second page number cited refers to the English edition.

19 One might make a connection between the frame's emphasis on truth and the narrator's insistence in the sixty-second *novella* that her story is true (which is directly followed by a confession of self). I am not implying that the *devisants* are all engaging in confessions; rather, that their emphasis on the veracity of the tales shows their investment in the tales. The emphasis on truth also provides the authoritative justification for telling tales in the first place, and it also qualifies any inappropriate pleasure they might experience.

20 Though Boccaccio's storytellers do insist on various occasions that their tales are true (see *Dec.* 9.5.5), it is not written into the framework of their project in the same way as in Marguerite de Navarre's text.

21 Mary B. McKinley, "Telling Secrets: Sacramental Confession and Narrative Authority in the *Heptameron*," in John Lyons and Mary B. McKinley, *Critical Tales: New Studies of the Heptameron and Early Modern Culture* (Philadelphia: University of Pennsylvania Press, 1993), 146–71. McKinley's chapter provides a rich analysis of sacramental confession in this *novella*, as well as in Tales 22 and 72. Her larger emphasis in the piece is on the female narrative authority placed strategically into confessional spaces, but I draw much of my reading of *Novellas* 41 and 72 from her discussion of the ways in which Marguerite de Navarre's views on absolution and penance coincide with those of many of the early Reformers ostracized in François I's Catholic court. She writes that "penance was a bone of contention in the early Reformation, not only because it implied the efficacy of good works, but because of the passionately contested practice of indulgences … To assign as penance the repetition of the very sin that had brought the penitent to confession would have required a striking perversion of the confessor's role" (161).

22 See ibid., 156.

23 Ibid., 146.

24 See ibid., 159–63. McKinley's reading has inspired mine, particularly in her conviction that "the confessor uses penance as a means of sexual coercion" (160) and in her analysis of how the way Marguerite intervenes in the text corresponds to the Reformers' critique of the corruption to which the sacrament of penance had succumbed (162–3).

25 Other stories in which the *Heptaméron* offers implicit or explicit insight into sacramental confession include Tales 22, 25, and 67.

Index